WHERE IS THE
JUSTICE?
SECOND EDITION

WILLIAM F. HILL

INKS&
BINDINGS

Inks and Bindings
888-290-5218
www.inksandbindings.com
orders@inksandbindings.com

CONTENTS

DEDICATION v

PREFACE...vi

CHAPTER 1 1

CHAPTER 2 17

CHAPTER 3 27

CHAPTER 4 47

CHAPTER 5 72

CHAPTER 6 102

CHAPTER 7 113

CHAPTER 8 121

CHAPTER 9 130

CHAPTER 10 148

CHAPTER 11 159

CHAPTER 12 171

CHAPTER 13 188

CHAPTER 14 203

CHAPTER 15 213

CHAPTER 16 248

CHAPTER 17 263

CHAPTER 18 280

CHAPTER 19 323

CHAPTER 20 342

CHAPTER 21 351

FINAL CHAPTER..389

EPILOGUE 396

ABOUT THE AUTHOR

DEDICATION

I would like to dedicate this book to my family and to the many people who have been very kind to us and helped us through this mess. Also, I would like to dedicate it to the many honest, hardworking people in this country who are struggling to raise their families, get ahead, and make this world a better place to live. I would like for you to make up your own mind, and I would really like to hear from you, the reader, as to your thoughts and your honest opinion about where the justice lies here. You be the jury, which we never had, and we will anxiously await your decision.

PREFACE

I have always felt and thought that here in the United States, we have the greatest country in the world. It has always given me great pleasure to see honest hardworking people and who are willing to take risks to get ahead and succeed. I always felt that this was the way that America got to be great and that we all should be working hard to help improve our own lives and the lives of others by carrying on this great American tradition. As a result of being brought up with this kind of thinking, I have always been more than willing to go out of my way, as many others have, to try to help people succeed and obtain their goals, whether they were already well off or they had nothing but the will to get ahead. To see people succeed in their life's goals and ambitions has always been very gratifying to me and given me a good feeling. Another thing that always gives me a good feeling is to see couples doing things as a family and with their children. To me this is what life is all about and should be about.

It seems that in the last thirty years or so, there have been a number of people who have showed up, especially in high places, who do not share the same philosophy of life that we were raised with. Many of the new thinking people seem to think that their calling in life is to destroy this system and the kind of life that we have known in this country for so many generations. They feel that it is their duty to keep people from reaching their goals. They don't want you and me to use our heads, our ingenuity, and hard work to get ahead. They want us to all to have to share our thoughts and ideas with them so that they can shoot them full of holes and make our life more difficult rather than easier and simpler. They are hell-bent to destroy any success genes that we are born with. Many of this new generation of do-gooders, as they are often called, seem to think that everybody should live on handouts and that anyone who is successful should be cut back down and not allowed to succeed without their input as this is not fair to the less fortunate in this country.

What they do not seem to realize or don't want to realize is that the people who are more successful probably do more to help the less fortunate than all the government and giveaway programs can ever hope to do. A successful person who has obtained his achievements through hard, honest work is usually willing to try to help others reach similar success. A person who is successful usually lives in a little better house. Many now think that this wrong, but that person probably pays several times the property taxes of someone living in a less expensive home. This will benefit everyone as this helps to educate their children and pay for many of the local services that people demand to day. If they hire people to help take care of their homes or properties, they are usually paid for with after tax dollars, and this creates jobs for the people doing the work. Isn't this sharing the wealth? Most successful people help create jobs either by expanding their own business or investing on other business. I think that in order to get people off welfare and off the government rolls, we need all the successful people that we can get in this country. The government has tried to run and control the way that we live and our destinies and look at the mess that they have created.

As someone once said, "As government power grows, our security diminishes." The more power that the government obtains under the disguise of protecting people, the more we should fear the government, and the more the government is going to harass and torment innocent citizens. Most people can endure just about any kind of pain except the pain of injustice, which our own government has imposed on many Americans.

I have always considered myself very lucky in that I have been able to work hard and live the American dream and always felt that I was helping many others to do the same, and I'm grateful to the many people who certainly have helped me. In the past six and a half years, this has all come to a halt. This book is about what has happened to me and my family, about banks and government.

Bill Hill
PO Box 15
Hardwick, Vermont 05843

CHAPTER 1

WHO IS BILL HILL

I was born sixty two years ago, in my parents' house in Hardwick, Vermont, on April 15, 1935. Perhaps being born on April 15 was not the best omen. Both my parents had grown up on farms in the area. My father's family had settled about six miles from here in Greensboro, over two hundred years ago. They had been pioneers, clearing the land, farming, and running sawmills and other small businesses. They suffered many hardships in order to survive in Northern Vermont.

To get here, they journeyed several hundred miles to Greensboro with all their cattle, horses, and belongings, from the mouth of the Connecticut River on Long Island Sound. They had to then clear the land, plant crops, cut hay for their livestock, build a house and barn, build fences, roads, and furniture, build a fireplace, and hunt and fish for their food. They had to cope with severe winters' wild animals, disease, and the threat of Indian visits. There were no stores, doctors, or neighbors nearby, and roads were little more than rough and often muddy paths through deep woods. They later built a sawmill. Other trades that they took up were cobbler, cooper, innkeeper, blacksmith, farmers, carpenters, and operators of a gristmill and a sawmill. One of their mottos was "Do your work so men won't curse you for it after you have gone."

In 1935, the year I was born, my father was getting established in the business of raising potatoes. As soon as I was five or six years old, I started carrying my dinner pail and going to the potato fields with him. While he would work in the potato fields, I would play near the edge of the field, in the woods, and around the toolshed. As I became older, I was able to help more. I always enjoyed being around my dad and working with him. Although we were potato farmers, most of our neighbors were dairy farmers. This was in the early 1940s. Most of the farmers didn't have tractors but did their work with horses and horse- drawn equipment. We, at that time, had a Farmall model F-12 steel-wheel tractor, which we later traded for a Farmall model H. Through July and August, we mostly sprayed the potato plants to protect them from blight, fungus, aphids, and potato bugs. This was the same time that the other farmers were cutting their hay, drying it, and getting it in the barn for winter feed. Anytime that it looked like rain or a storm coming, we would stop spraying as the rain would only wash the spray off the leaves, so it would be wasted. We would put the tractor and sprayer in the shed then look around to see who had hay down that was ready to go in the barn. Whenever it looked like rain, we always went to help any of our neighbors get their hay in before it got rained on. I liked just about everything about farming, so I always looked forward to this, plus I often got to drive the horses. It always made us feel good to know that we had been able to help our neighbors. A number of times, when someone got hurt or was sick, I remember going with my dad to milk their cows and do their chores for them. As I liked farming, I also enjoyed this very much, and it was a great satisfaction to know that you had helped someone.

In the fall of the year, when it came time to dig the potatoes, we would hire forty to fifty people to pick potatoes, and this took about five or six weeks. We would put them in storage in a large building that we called the potato house then spend most of the winter grading them, bagging them, and selling them. Although potato digging was a lot of hard work with long days, I found it very exciting as there were a lot of people around and plenty going on.

Our town had a central school building called Hardwick Academy and Graded School. This one building housed all twelve grades. There were several one-room schools in the rural areas that taught grades one through six or eight. Then if these student wanted to go high school, they had to make their own way to Hardwick Academy. We lived about a mile from the academy school building, so I attended all twelve grades in this one school building. There was no school transportation in those days, so I walked to school in the morning home to dinner and back at noon and then home again at night. This made a little over four miles a day.

My first brother, Steve, was born the fall that I started the first grade. About five years later, my second brother, Jim, was born, and my younger brother, Dan, was born the fall that I started in the ninth grade.

About the time that I started school, my dad took on a second business as a grain distributor for a farmers coop. At that time all the farmers ordered their grain ahead and it came in railroad cars that were parked on the local rail siding. We would notify all the farmers when the grain came in and they would come to the rail siding to pick up their orders. All the grain was in one hundred pound burlap bags. They could also order pastry flour, bread flour gram flour and oat meal in twenty five pound bags. We had three locations where we unloaded, in Hardwick, East Hardwick and Greensboro Bend.

At that time there were several trains a day. There were freight trains mail trains, passenger trains, and a milk train that went through every afternoon picking all the milk cars at all the creameries, which were all located on rail sidings. Each one of these freight yards where we unloaded were very busy places and bustling with activity, as nearly everything came or went by rail in those days. All the engines ran on steam and burned coal. At the Greensboro location there were large coal sheds and a water tower where the engines fueled up. There were creameries at all the locations where all the local farmers brought their milk every morning. The Hardwick area had several granite quarries and stone sheds. Nearly all the granite was loaded on to rail cars for shipment. Also loaded at these sidings were pulp wood, lumber, hay, Christmas trees and anything else that got shipped. Often as soon as we emptied a grain car the Renaud boys or somebody would start loading it with pulp or lumber. Many other supplies came in by rail and were unloaded, new cars, farm machinery, stock for the local merchants, and all the mail.

Not far from the siding in Hardwick was a favorite swimming hole in the Lamoille River. Every afternoon in the summer all the kids in the village would show up there either on foot or with their bicycles to cool off and take a swim.

Around two o'clock, the East Hardwick Creamery, which manufactured powdered milk, and was about three miles upstream, would dump thousands of gallons of skim milk and wash water into the river. This would turn the river white, and when it came down by the swimming hole, most everybody would get out for about twenty minutes while it went by and the water cleared again. Today nobody even swims in the river.

Around 1945 the grain business was going good and had expanded to include fertilizer and other farm supplies. My dad bought a large old building on Wolcott Street from Mrs. Utley where her husband Charles had operated a grain and general store before his death. This building had a rail siding, which was a spur off the St. J. & LC, which was the main line. This spur was part of the old Hardwick Woodbury line that had gone up into Woodbury years earlier to bring the granite from the quarries to the local stone sheds. After that we unloaded most of our grain and farm supplies at this location and the farmers could come and pick up what they wanted anytime. We also delivered a lot or grain. Many of the village people kept a milk cow, chickens, pigs, or horses, so this was very convenient for them.

During the winter months many of the farmers would sit around the wood stove in the office of the feed store to exchange stories and gossip, we always knew what was going on as they all loved to talk about their neighbors as well as themselves. We didn't need a newspaper.

I liked being around the feed store and the potato fields helping out when I wasn't in school. I also worked for several neighbors shoveling snow, helping them with their haying, tending horses and other livestock. We also had a small chicken house where I kept a couple of dozen laying hens and I sold the eggs around the neighborhood.

When I was about eight, I had saved a few dollars so my dad took me with him to Caledonia National Bank in Danville, where he did his banking and I started a savings account. I was really fascinated with the bank. It was a brick building and as you went in the front door to the lobby there was a steel door, on the left, with a small window that had what looked like chicken wire in the glass. Next was the teller's windows, which were covered with bars. The lobby had a very high ceiling so the inside walls did not go clear to the ceiling but instead had several electric wires running along the top to keep anyone from climbing over them. I felt that my money should be safe here. To open an account we had to go into the little room with the glass window but not until the man on the inside pushed a buzzer, which unlocked the door. I learned later that Caledonia Bank had been robbed back in the thirties by a well-known famous bank robber named Eddy Bentz.

When I was a kid, a man was judged by how hard he worked, how well he paid his bills and how well he provided for his family. My father preached those virtues to us many times. Also there was no substitute for honesty; a man's word was his bond. Whenever I got in to a squabble with my brothers, Dad would always bring up the golden rule, which states, "Do unto others as you would have them do unto you." We were also taught to be thrifty. We learned to take care of what we had and not waste anything. We didn't leave the lights on that we were not using. When we worked in the woods, we were taught to be careful not knock down and injure the trees that you weren't cutting. As we were farmers, we were taught how to protect the soil against erosion and it was our job to make the world a better place in which to live I have never forgotten those lessons.

When I was about twelve or thirteen, my dad bought another farm to raise potatoes on. There were about one hundred twenty acres a house a hen house and a cow barn with an upstairs stable. It also had a milk house with a milk cooler and there was a McCormick Deering milking machine. About the only other equipment was a Farmall model F-12 steel-wheel tractor, that you had to hand crank to start and a Sam Daniels horse drawn manure spreader that had been converted over to go behind the tractor.

I was really excited about this as this was the first time that we had actually had a farm with a cow barn and a place to keep chickens. This farm was about three and a half miles from where we lived in the village so I could walk there after school or anytime that I wanted to. I immediately started working extra hard and using my money to buy some dairy calves and chickens. The old steel-wheel tractor wasn't used much in the potato business so I used it around the farm. One thing that I did was team up with John Rowell a neighbor kid whose family had two horse drawn mowing machines. We cut the pole off one of these machines and rigged it to go behind the tractor. We mowed our hay their hay and then we worked out mowing some of the neighbors hay to make a few dollars. We took turns swapping off driving the tractor and riding on the mowing machine. We could mow hay more than twice as fast as the other farmers could with their horses. We also used the tractor to get out some pulp wood, which we sold.

Within a couple of years, I had several heifers ready to calve and start producing milk. My dad saw that I was serious about milking cows although I was still only about fourteen years old. He purchased a few more cows and I took care of them. As we lived about three and a half miles from the farm, he would help me in the mornings. We would get up at four o'clock, eat breakfast and go to the farm do the morning chores then take our milk to the creamery and be back home by seven so that he could go to work and I could go to school. In the afternoon after school I would walk home from school, change my clothes then walk to the farm to do the milking and the rest of the chores then walk back home. Often on the way home it was after dark and was hard to see and follow the road.

We did not use the farmhouse so he had rented it out for twenty dollars a month. One very cold Saturday in January I walked up to do the morning chores. We did not have running water in the cow stable so we had to let the cows out into the barn yard to drink out of a tub that we kept covered to keep from freezing. We had to uncover the water tub and often had to chop the ice with an axe so that the cows could drink. This morning I had let the cows out and cleaned the stable. It was very cold, so I worked fast to try to keep warm and to keep from shivering. I went into the hay barn to pitch down some hay when I noticed that I no longer was cold or shivering, but was starting to get dizzy and everything started to look fuzzy. I staggered back out through the stable and into the barn yard where I fell down. I made my way over to the barn yard fence and pulled myself up. About that time, Dick Pearson the man who rented the house saw me and came over to see what was wrong. He helped me to the house. They had a big round oak wood stove in the living room. I can remember him telling me to go and sit in the chair next to the stove, but by that time I couldn't see either the stove or the chair or anything else. He finally helped me to the chair. The heat felt good and I immediately began to feel better as I warmed up. After a little while, I no longer felt dizzy, I could see all right and I felt fine again. I got up went back to the barn finished my chores, put the cows back in and walked home. It was still very cold but I felt fine. From this experience I realize that freezing to death could be very easy but I don't think it would be very painful.

On my sixteenth birthday I got my driver's license. This made things much handier and a lot easier to get back and forth.

I was not an especially good student as I was much more interest in farming and working than I was in school. Math and science came fairly easy but subjects like English and social studies were not my favorite. At no time in high school did I plan to go on to college so I didn't worry about which courses were necessary to get into college. I took several agriculture and shop classes as this was much more interesting to me. I could not wait to graduate from High school so that I could devote full time to farming. After graduation, I worked hard on the farm hoping to expand and make this my life's work.

My mother wanted me to go to college, which I had no interest in. She brought up the subject several times. I explained to her that I had neither the right courses, credits, nor grades needed to get into college. She was not one to give up easily. She kept insisting that it wouldn't do any harm for me to apply. I knew that this met a lot to her so I applied at the University of Vermont. When the reply came back, it stated that I could not be accepted for all the reasons that I just mentioned, but that if I wanted to I could take an entrance exam that might still let me in if I did well on it. There again wanting to please my mother I agreed to go and take the exam. When the reply came, this time, it stated that I had done very well in the math and science categories but not so well in some the others and to my surprise they had decided to accept me.

By now I knew that it would be very disappointing to her if I didn't go, so I went down and enrolled in the college of agriculture at the University of Vermont. At that time I think that the tuition for Vermont students was $178 per semester but you had to pay for your room and meals. You also had to furnish your own books and supplies but we had to do that in high school back in those days.

Going to college meant that I had to get rid of my cattle and poultry for the time being. When I got into the swing of college, I really liked it and made up my mind that I was going to get the most out of it that I could. Studying was not one of my strong points so I had to really work at it. I came home nearly every weekend and helped with the potatoes and grain business. At the end of my freshman year I was selected as one of two agriculture students from Vermont with a farm background to attend a leadership camp in Michigan. The camp was owned, sponsored and paid for by William Danforth, the founder of the Ralston Purina Company. He had invited two students from each of the fifty states to attend this conference. I felt honored to be one of them.

The rest of the summer months I worked around the potatoes and the grain business plus cutting and putting up the hay on the farm. One year I worked in the woods cutting logs for my father. We cut them with a two man cross cut saw and skidded them out with horses. We then rolled them on to an old ford truck and took them to a local sawmill. A couple of winters on Saturdays I developed a route delivering and selling potatoes to restaurants and ski resorts. One summer I went to Troy Ohio to a welding school at the Hobart welding factory.

While at the college of agriculture I took all the dairy cattle courses that they had. I also got to know many of the top cattlemen around the country. A couple of times I took the job of fitting a string of show cattle for some well-known farms then showing at places like Essex and Rutland Fair, and the Eastern States Exposition in West Springfield Mass.

While in my junior year, another student and I were asked to put on an exhibit to promote Vermont Dairy products at the New England Governors' Conference, which was being held at the Statler Hotel in Boston. We decided to take two cows to Boston and keep them in the lobby of the hotel and to feed and milk them there. We got a clearance from everybody necessary. We pulled into Boston around 11:00 at night and I backed up to the front door of the Statler Hotel with a cattle truck. I think that we must have caused one of the biggest traffic jams in the city in a long time. People were coming from everywhere to see what was going on, and cars and taxi cabs were backed up everywhere. Next thing I knew there were TV cameras all over the place. We kept the cows at the Statler for around three days. We took a canvas tarp and put it on the lobby rug then covered it with shavings and straw then used three steel gates to make a double start leaving the back open so that people could get closer to the cows if they wanted to. It caused a lot of excitement and was a lot of fun. One thing that was especially amusing was to see some salesman who had obviously come from the bar late at night staggering into the lobby and see those cows there. They would rub their eyes, take another look, then rub their eyes and look again in disbelief as to what they were seeing. One man got so startled that he fell down the stairs.

The summer of 1957 between my junior and senior year I took my real estate brokers exam and got a brokers' license. I also went to the Reisch Auction School in Mason City, Iowa. This was a two week course but very intense. The classes started at seven in the morning and went until eleven at night.

About a week before I was to graduate from the university, I started getting calls from insurance agents who wanted to make an appointment to sell me insurance. I'm sure that were contacting all the graduates. They all insisted that the first thing that I was going to need was a good life insurance policy. They were all very persistent and wouldn't take no for an answer. In one of our farm management classes they had warned us about insurance salesmen. Finally instead of trying to discourage them when they called I made an appointment with each one for the next Wednesday at ten o'clock at my apartment, which was down town in an old block upon the third floor and way at the end of the long winding narrow hall. I think that there were either twenty four or twenty six different salesmen that were planning to show up on Wednesday. I moved out on Tuesday and went back home. They must have had an insurance man's convention up in that narrow hall.

This was probably a dirty crick to play on them, but they would not take no for an answer and I couldn't see that this was any worse than making an appointment with each one individually and taking up much more of their time and mine while they each tried to convince me to buy their insurance, which I had no intention of buying and was not interested in.

During my senior year of college, my dad who was only fifty two was not feeling well. He had always been a very honest and conscious hardworking man, but a very poor book keeper although he was good with figures. He kept many things in his head rather than writing them down. When a customer bought a load of potatoes, he would write the amount on the wall in the potato house. At income tax time he would have to rub the dust off the wall and add up his figures. The Hardwick town clerk who did his income taxes for him and always said that he paid more tax than he would if he had a better book keeping system. IRS was starting to pressure him to produce records that he didn't have. This was really bothering him as he felt that they didn't trust him. After college, I was still determined to go back home to farm and to help my dad so as to take some of the pressure off him. I knew that he was getting discouraged. That spring the Town of Hardwick had a steel and concrete bridge over the Lamoille River that they wanted to rebuild. They wanted to break out all the old cement and replace the floor with corrugated steel decking then black top over it. They also wanted to lower one end of the bridge so that it wouldn't be so steep when you drove off the bridge down onto the street. I owned portable welding equipment and a bulldozer, so I decided to bid on the job. I thought that this would be a good way to make some money to help me get started back in farming. I got the job so I hired my brother Steve and a couple of other young fellows and went at it. I worked long hours as I didn't want this job to take any more time than necessary. One noon, when the job was about half done I stopped at the post office to pick up the mail. There was a letter from the government. I opened it, "Congratulations from your friends and neighbors, you have been selected to serve your country in the United States Army." I was to report in ten days for my physical and if I passed that I wouldn't be coming back. I drove up to the potato field and showed the letter to my father. He looked at it but didn't say much except that a lot of other boys have had to go. It now looked like this was going to delay any farming for a couple of more years. The immediate concern was that I had less than ten days to finish the bridge. The thing that bothered me the most was my father's failing health and the fact that he had become very discouraged. I had really planned to help him all that I could and hoped that would take some of the pressure off him and help to get him feeling better again.

We worked hard and fast. We finished the bridge the night before I was to report. I had to be at the bus station in St. Johnsbury, which was about twenty miles away by eleven o'clock the next morning. I still had a lot of things to do including putting my machinery away. I had bought some heifers as I was planning to be back in farming right after the bridge job. I still had to sell and get rid of them. It got to be nearly ten thirty. My mother was waiting in the car to take me to the bus as we drove the last heifers up the tailgate of the cattle truck.

We arrived at the bus stop just in time. There were eight or nine other fellows who had also been called to report. They were all country boys and younger than I was. I don't think that a couple of them had ever been very far from home. The bus took us to the induction center in Manchester New Hampshire, where they put us up in a hotel that night. The next day they tested us for just about everything. Two or three of the fellows were sent back home. They put the rest of us on a train. We rode all night and ended up, the next morning, at Fort Dix New Jersey. The first thing that they did to us was to give us a quick short haircut. The next step I will never forget. We lined up for shots. They had a bunch of medics with large syringes that looked like the kind that the veterinary uses. They would fill them up and each time that they gave a shot would turn a little nut on the plunger stem to allow them to give several shots without refilling. They stood on each side of the line and as we walked by them they jabbed us in the arms from both sides. There didn't seem to worry much about sterilization and they never bothered to change needles. Some of the fellows' arms were covered with blood by the time they got through this line. They then handed us each a card with our name on it and it listed the shots that we had received. They said that it was up to us keep our own shot record and be ready to show them whenever asked. If we lost them, we would need to have all the shots again. They said that very seldom did anyone ever lose his shot record.

I spent ten weeks at Fort Dix in basic training and taking tests. At the end of the ten weeks, we all received our orders. There was some problem in Lebanon at that time and many of the men were sent there.

I was one of the last ones to receive my orders. I was assigned to go for medic training at Brook Army Hospital at Fort Sam Houston in San Antonio Texas. After two or three weeks of this training, several of us received new orders transferring us to the dental course. Upon completion of this course a number of us were assigned to the Dental Detachment at Fort Bliss in Elpaso, Texas. One of the guys had bought an old car. Eight of us piled in with all our duffel bags and belongings and headed for Elpaso. As I think it was around eight hundred miles across Texas, I remember that it was a long, crowded ride with eight of us and all our luggage. We arrived at Fort Bliss the day before Christmas. The base was just about shut down for the Holidays. I was assigned a bed on the second floor of the barracks. This room had about twenty beds. It was the afternoon of Christmas Eve and no one else was around I was sitting on the edge of my bed thinking that this will be the first Christmas away from home and my family. I hadn't been there long when a sergeant who I had not seen before came in and said, "Come on Hill, you are going with me." I followed him not knowing where we were headed. We went into the downstairs barracks and found Mack Carter a Texan who was one of the other fellows that had just rode in from San Antonio with us. He told him to come with us. The sergeant's name was Beiderstat. He took us to his home to spend Christmas Eve and Christmas day with him and his wife and two small children. Things like this really make you appreciate people and make you anxious to help somebody else when you get a chance.

After Christmas, I was assigned to the post dental clinic, which had about thirty-five dentists. I was given the job of working with a fellow named Springer, who was due to get out of the service in a couple of months. He was in charge of the supplies, equipment and maintenance for the clinic. The supply room was about fourteen feet square, with rows of shelves all around the four walls, these stored the supplies. The entrance was a two piece Dutch type door with a shelf on the top of the bottom section. This is where the dentists and dental assistants came to get their supplies. Only Springer and I had keys to this room and no one else was allowed in there. Springer had pretty much been his own boss so he showed me what I needed to know. I ordered most of the supplies from Beaumont Army Hospital, which was just up the road. They would bring them down in an ambulance. For the items that they didn't carry I had a card that allowed me to pick up them from any supply post on the base.

Only two or three of the dentists were career men. The rest were young dentists just out of dental school who were fulfilling their military obligation. Each dentist was assigned eight patients a day, one each hour. Most of the dentists were real nice fellows who took their work very serious. They all talked about opening their own practice as soon as their time was up. There were a couple of dentists, that I soon learned to watch. They were always losing their instruments and asking for replacements or saying that they had never had whatever they were asking for in the first place. I realized that they were taking them home. To me this was stealing and I felt that it was my job to try to prevent this. Whenever I gave them anything that wasn't expendable, I made them sign for it. This made them very unhappy and they grumbled to me about it for a while but it solved the problem.

Fort Bliss was a missile base and there was an outpost called Red Canyon about one hundred and eighty five miles north of the main base. This out post was a bunch of Quonset huts out in the desert. We had a small one chair dental clinic up there. Each Sunday afternoon the army would fly a different dentist up there for the week. Most of them didn't look forward to their turn at Red Canyon. One of the fellows that I took dental training with was in charge of the clinic and stayed up there all the time. One of the dentists who I knew was light fingered and who had complained about having to sign in order to get any more equipment was taking his turn at Red Canyon. Friday afternoon, the day that they came back, I called the kid that was in charge and warned him about this dentist. Around four o'clock he called me back. He was laughing. He said that just before the dentist left, when he wasn't looking he checked his bags. He found one of them was filled with dental equipment. He had removed the equipment and filled the bag with stones. He laughed and said that the dentist had just got onto the helicopter carrying a bag full of stones.

I didn't mind the army, as a matter of fact I kind of enjoyed it. The only things that bothered me were that I felt that I could be putting my time to much better use. I was still anxious to farm and I was worried about my dad.

Soon after I arrived at Fort Bliss I received a letter from my mother saying that part of the feed store had burned. It had caught fire from the wood stove in the office. The stove pipe went through a wall into a back room. This is where the fire started. Dad was having a local carpenter, Joe Lavertu, replace the burned section with a new one- story, clear span building using truss rafters.

In my senior year at the University of Vermont, I met a girl whom I hit it off with real well. We spent a lot of time together, and by the end of the school year, we were talking about getting married. She still had a couple more years of college, so we weren't talking about right off.

Just before leaving for the army I had bought her an engagement ring. Every single day that I had been in the army, I had written to her and she had written to me. I missed her a lot. One Sunday night I got to thinking, what if we were to get married after she got out of school in the spring? That way she could come to Texas and we could rent an off post apartment. She could continue her education at Texas Western College right there in Elpaso. It seemed like a great idea to me so I wrote to her that night and suggested it. I told her that we could experience living in a different part of the country and see and do many things that we might never get another chance to do. Even though we were writing to each other every day, it took about ten days to get a letter up to Vermont and an answer back. It was a long ten days but finally the answer came. She was all excited about the idea but was worried about getting her folks approval. I had to wait a few more days to find out how she handled this. In a few days the answer came, she had convinced her parents, and they had approved. We planned to get married in June. I had to get approved for a leave and find a place to live, which I did.

I flew home and we were married in the Chapel at Norwich University, where her father was a professor. The short time that I was home I found my dad to be very quiet, and he was not himself. This bothered me very much.

Army pay wasn't very great and I realized that I didn't have enough money for both of us to fly back to Texas. I did have an old 1946 Buick that I had given up on a few years earlier. I had parked it out behind the barn. It hadn't run for several years. I got it running and tuned it up the best that I could. The tires were not the greatest, it had one old knobby winter tire on the back. The day after the wedding we packed up and headed for Elpaso. We hadn't gone far when the car started heating up. I think that it had set so long that the engine block was full of rust. I stopped at a garage and got some old two gallon oil cans and filled them with water. About every twenty miles, we would stop, and I would use a rag to take off the radiator cap and add some cool water. We had about three thousand miles to go and less than five days to get there. The weather was very hot and this didn't help very much but I kept adding water we kept going. That knobby tire on back rode rough and made a lot of noise, but we kept going. We were on a straight stretch of road in a rural area of Illinois when there was a big bang and the car bounced all over the road then dropped down onto the rim. That knobby tire had blown out. Before I could get out of the car I noticed that a big circle of paint was rolling up and peeling off the hood. I knew that the engine was on fire. I jumped out and opened the hood then ran to the trunk got one of the cans of water and put the fire out. The jolt from the tire had caused the distributor cap to bounce off causing it to backfire through the carburetor. I clipped the cap back down and started the car. Other than peeling the paint off the hood the fire hadn't done much damage. I added some water to the radiator then started back to change the tire. While I had been running around putting out the fire and getting the car started again I hadn't noticed what Nancy was doing. Thinking that the car was going to burn up she had taken all our belongings and thrown them out in the ditch and over the fence in the pasture. There were clothes, blankets and pots and pans everywhere. I changed the tire replacing it with one that wasn't much better; we gathered up our stuff and were on our way. We made it to Elpaso one day early.

Several of my buddies including Mack Carter had gotten married that spring so we had some good friends to associate with. Nancy enrolled in Texas Western College that fall. The following March on the twenty third our first son, Dean, was born at Beaumont Army hospital. There were fifteen babies born there that day. Dean was the largest. I called Nancy's parents and told them the news then I called my folks. I talked to my mother, then asked to talk to Dad. When I told him about Dean, he said, "Take good care of him." That was about all he had to say. He didn't sound good. Four days later in the afternoon I brought Nancy and Dean home from the hospital to our apartment. We had been home less than an hour when our land lady came rushing in and said that someone from the Red Cross was on the phone and needed to talk to me right away. When I answered the phone, the Red Cross woman said that she was calling to let me know that my father was dead. I was shocked but not surprised, as I had known deep down inside for a long time that something terrible was going to happen to him. I had only about two months left in the service and had hoped to get home and help out before anything did happen.

I called my mother, her sister answered but didn't want to talk about what had happened. My mother came on the phone, she said that Dad had shot himself in his pickup truck in front of the barn. I knew that I had to go home. I went to personal and got an emergency leave. We did not have any money but between a pay advance and a loan from the Red Cross. The three of us were on a plane by eight o'clock that night. We left the old Buick at the airport. When we were changing planes in New York City, we ran into my brother Jim who was flying home from Oregon. We arrived in Burlington Vermont the next morning. My cousin John Hill who lived near the airport picked us up and took us to Hardwick.

CHAPTER 2

AFTER THE ARMY

When we got home, I learned that my father had been real depressed the past few months and that this had really taken a toll on my mother. She had not said anything about this in her letters or on the phone.

My brother, Steve, who had recently gotten married was also in the army. He had just been assigned to a permanent post in Germany. His wife Elaine was planning to join him. He flew home from Germany while she was on her way over there. We had to delay the funeral a day waiting for Steve to get home. Elaine was a couple of weeks getting back.

After I had been home a few days, I received a telegram from the Army telling me not to report back to Fort Bliss as my time left was so short. They said that they would contact me with my separation orders. As soon as I got home, I had started working at the grain store and kept things going. A lot of farmers depended on it for their feed and supplies. Within a week I decided to take the store over and keep it going. I borrowed enough money to operate for about a week then had to plan on the turnover to keep going. There were two delivery men who handled the grain and supplies and delivered to the farmers. This was mostly manual labor. There was a third man, John, who tended the store and the walk in trade. I decided to let two of the men go and kept John on. I figured that if I was going to get ahead and make a real go of it I would have to do most of the work myself.

I think that it pleased my mother to know that I was going to keep things going. She had been under a lot of stress and my father's death had been very hard on her. She was not well, and due to all this she was losing her hair. The IRS man kept coming around and bothering her. Finally he agreed that there had been no real problem with their income taxes and he left her alone. I made up my mind right then that I was going to keep good records and use an accountant to do my income taxes. I knew that I didn't want any problems with the IRS or any other government agency, after seeing how they operated and what it did to my father.

Mother agreed to sell us the farm and finance it for us. Dean, Nancy and I moved into the farmhouse. I worked very hard and when I got a few dollars ahead I would buy one or two head of cattle. Everything that I sold out of the feed store I had to make sure to collect my money so that I could replace it and build my stock up. I soon learned to be a good collector. Some of the accounts that my father had been more lenient with didn't like this at first but they soon accepted the fact. The worst time for people to get behind was around Christmas. Often they would say to me that they had kids and needed to provide them with a good Christmas. I always felt like saying that I also had a family and would like to be able to have a little Christmas too. But I didn't. I usually said nothing and waited until after the holidays to try again to collect from them.

I put in long hours, taking care of the farm, doing the haying, running the feed store, and doing all the delivering. In those days all the grain came in one hundred pound bags. Most farmers didn't have a very handy place to store their grain. Some places I had to lug the bags in from the road especially in the winter time as they were seldom shoveled out. Some stables were upstairs and that was where they wanted their grain. One place I had to put it in through a window then go around inside and lug it the length of the barn and pile it in front of the cows. I usually tried to unload and deliver a carload in a day.

The first winter we burned wood in the farmhouse, both for heat and cooking. We had a wood stove in the living room, the same one that I had sat next to when I nearly froze. The stove pipe went up through the ceiling into an upstairs bedroom then into the chimney. We all slept in this bedroom as it was the only warm room upstairs. One winter night we had put Dean to bed, Nancy and I were working in the kitchen when we heard a loud roaring noise. We rushed into the living room and saw that the wood stove was red hot. The stove pipe was so hot that I could practically see right through it. I ran upstairs where Dean was sleeping. The pipe was just as red hot up there. I had forgotten to close the damper and the fire had gotten away from us. I was able to get it slowed down without any damage. I figured that we were very lucky that we didn't burn the place down or that we hadn't lost Dean. This really scared us. The next morning I went down to Sam Daniels Manufacturing Company, a local furnace manufacture and bought a used furnace that they had taken in trade and had them install it. I didn't know how I was going to pay for it but I ordered it anyway. I worked extra hard and cut all the corners that I could and within a few weeks I managed to pay for it.

That winter we had a lot of snow. One night in February, the roof on the new part of the feed store collapsed and caved in under the snow load. This was a terrible mess as I had just filled the building up with bagged grain. I was lucky. Several local people showed up with shovels and tools to help me. One of them was a young cattle dealer whose name was Noel Lussier. He had a cattle barn just down the road. I called the company in New York who had supplied the rafters when my father had this section of the building built a couple of years before. They said to get hold of Joe Lavertu, the man who had built it and have him there the first thing the next morning. I remember Joe was very nervous as he thought that they were going to try to blame him for the building falling in. Shortly their engineer showed up and asked Joe if he would rebuild it. They said that they could have some new heavier rafters there in two days and that they would pay for everything. I saw a big sigh of relief in Joe's face and I was real pleased with their attitude and willingness to stand behind their rafters and pay for a new building. Several farmers also came to help. One farmer who wasn't even a regular customer of mine went to the bank and borrowed enough money so that he could buy several truckloads of grain to help me out. He didn't even ask for a discount. He only wanted to help.

Within a few days of getting the building back up and in a little less than a year after Dean was born our second child Dianne was born. She had long black hair and was a very pretty baby.

That next summer a lot of farmers were switching over from can milk coolers to bulk tanks to cool and store their milk. For most of them this meant remodeling or building a new milk house. In those days transit mix concrete was not used very much. Most everybody mixed their own concrete using sand, cement and water. This same summer the local power company was rebuilding one of their power dams. I sold and delivered twenty six car loads of cement, handling every bag about four times.

I also hayed several farms that summer, hiring several high school boys to help get the hay in the barns. I needed another tractor. I went to an auction in Irasburg that was being conducted by Noel and Roger Lussier. I bought an older Farmall model M tractor. The next day I had Nancy drop me off to pick it up. As I was driving it home, it started to heat up. I discovered that it had a leak in the radiator. I stopped near a brook to add some water. Noel happened to come by, he stopped and wanted to know what the trouble was. I told him that the radiator leaked and that I was getting some water. He offered to help me then told me to get it fixed and send him the bill. I thought that this more than decent as I had bought it as is and without any guarantee.

By that fall I had enough cattle so that I could start producing milk again. I would get home from the feed store around five or six at night, bundle Dean up and take him to the barn with me. It would take about two hours to do the evening chores. In the morning I was back in the barn by four o'clock so that I could be back in the house by six for breakfast, see the kids and get to the feed store by seven. On the second of October our third child Janet was born. She was very alert and caught on very fast. We all enjoyed her very much.

We were still shipping milk in cans. Often on Sunday morning I would skim two or three quarts of heavy cream off the cans from the Saturday night milking and we would make homemade ice cream. Usually on Sundays we attended the little local Church in East Hardwick.

One very cold day in January I was delivering grain in East Craftsbury. The barn had a high drive with a long steep bridge leading up to the high drive, which is a floor in the very top of the barn. These were designed so that when the hay was brought in it could be rolled off both sides of the wagon in to the bays on each side. This saved all the hard work of having to pitch the hay up from a lower drive. At this farm I had always backed up into the barn to unload the grain. This

20

was actually one of the easier places to deliver. This afternoon I backed up the bridge into the barn as usual. I heard something snap then felt the back of my truck start to drop down a little, then another snap and another drop it kept doing this until my truck was standing straight up and down, hanging in the top of the barn. I kept waiting for it to drop clear down through the barn to the basement as the back of the truck was still two stories above the ground. It just hung there. The back of the body was resting right over the cows down below. I just sat there in the cab. The farmer had heard the commotion and came out to the barn. The cab and front wheels were clear up in the air. The farmer took one look and said, "You might as well shut it off and get out." It took the whole next day to get the truck out, with cables, winches tackle blocks and a big wrecker, furnished by Dona Bessette, a local garage owner. The only damage that it had done to my truck was to bend the drive shaft but it sure had wrecked his barn.

It's funny how things happen, the next day after getting out of there I had a fellow bring me a load of sawdust at the farm. My barn did not have a high drive but had a barn floor that was about ten feet higher than the ground. It had a barn bridge leading up to the barn floor. There were two large swinging barn door that opened to get into the barn. I had a trap door in the barn floor that we dumped the sawdust down through. This was also a cold day and the barn bridge was covered with ice and snow. The sawdust man tried to back up the bridge into the barn but kept spinning. He tried two or three times but couldn't make it. He then pulled way out to the road and really stepped on it, as fast as it would go in reverse. At the top of the bridge was a plank that served as a bottom door jam. When the truck backed over this, it was really traveling. The truck bounced up and when it came down it didn't stop it went right through the barn floor clear to the ground level. All I could see was the bottom of the front of his truck sticking up out through the barn doors. I had to hire the same wrecker and we worked most of the day getting this truck out of my barn. What seemed strange was that I had to pay to get both trucks out and for all the damage to both barns.

For the next several years I worked hard doing pretty much the same things. Once in a while I did an auction or brokered some real estate. In

1965 I was elected to the Hardwick board of selectmen where I served for several years. At that time the selectmen ran the town business with very little interference from the state or the federal government. In big storms we helped the road crew to plow the roads. We took care of anyone who was in need of help or welfare. There were not many of these cases as nearly everybody took the responsibility of looking out for themselves. When anyone was on the town, they were blacklisted, which meant that they couldn't buy any tobacco or alcohol. Once in a while a stranger would show up in town looking for a hand out. If they were not a resident of the town, the town manager would load them in to his pickup truck and take them across the town line to Walden or Greensboro and let them out. There wasn't much welfare in those days.

One winter the water to the farm froze. I had to truck water in milk cans and a gathering tank all the rest of the winter for the farm, the house and all the cattle. This took about four trips a day. I made the first trip about four o'clock in the morning and the last one around eleven at night. This was a cold wet job as the water slopped all over freezing to everything. After a while, I found an old three thousand gallon tank that a fellow let me use. I put it on a four wheel wagon and hitched it behind my Farmall M tractor. I took it to the feed store and used a garden hose to fill it with water. I figured that by drawing one tank a day it would eliminate all the other trips and tugging on milk cans. At that time I had a high school kid, named Delbert, that had been helping me at the farm after school and on weekends. I asked him to stop at the feed store after school and he could drive the tractor with the water up to the farm. He hadn't been gone long when a car drove in the yard with Delbert. He was as white as a ghost. It was very obvious that he had had some kind of a scare. He had started up Slap Hill, a very steep hill, out of Hardwick Village. He had the tractor in fourth gear and was running out of power. He tried to shift down but missed the next lower gear and the tractor started rolling down the hill backward. The brakes wouldn't hold it and he couldn't control it. It hit a house tipping the water tank over onto the porch. It busted the porch up and most of the water had gone into the living room and the cellar. This scared Delbert just about to death. Joe Fisher who owned the house took it real good and said that he was glad that nobody got hurt. I was lucky I had insurance that repaired the damages. It was back to drawing water in milk cans.

In the Hardwick area there were several other feed dealers. We all competed to get each other's customers, but we also had a very good working relationship. I often supplied my competitors with non-brand items such as beet pulp, citrus pulp and barrels of molasses, all of which farmers fed to their cattle. Often when I got in a trailer load of molasses and I didn't have enough empty barrels to hold the whole trailer load I would call a couple of smaller dealers and they would come with their empty barrels and take part of the load. Even though we were in competition we would always go out of our way to help each other.

Eastern States Farmers Exchange, the coop, that I was doing business with would only allow me to sell their feed and supplies within a certain territory that they had designated. I felt that if I was going to grow that I needed to branch out. I decided to take on another brand of feed and fertilizer. The coop was very upset and told me that I couldn't handle two brands. They said it would have to be one or the other. I think that they thought that I would stick with them. I told them if that was the case that I would be dropping them. They tried very hard to take all my customers away from me and I fought hard to keep them. It was a fierce battle but I kept most of them. I then picked up a whole bunch of new accounts.

One reason they thought I wouldn't change was that the grain business was starting to change from bag grain to bulk handling. The Coop had been delivering a few of my customers for me who had already changed over to bulk. It could be expensive for a dealer to convert over to bulk. I was able to rig up my own bulk truck. I bought a new cattle body and a hoist off an old dump truck. I bought a grain blower and we rigged it up. It was not as big and streamlined as the big companies had but it served the purpose.

The first bulk grain that I got in I had shipped in box cars. I then had to shovel it out of the car into an old sawdust conveyer that ran it up into the truck. After a while, I built a conveyer that went under the rail road track. With this I could order grain in fifty ton hopper cars. This saved a lot of work.

In February of 1966 our fourth child, Clay, was born. This gave us two boys and two girls. I was very proud of them all.

At the farm I had up graded my dairy herd. I had acquired and raised quite a few registered Holsteins cows. I had built a new milk house with a bulk tank and a small milking parlor. I had built this with a small apartment upstairs over the milk house and milk parlor. I hired Howard Brown a local fellow. He and his wife lived in the apartment. Howard looked after the cows and did most of the milking. He was very good with the cows. We belonged to the Dairy Herd Improvement Association. They took milk weights and tested the milk once a month for butterfat. There were about two hundred herds in the association that we belonged to. There was a lot of competition among the farmers to see who could develop the highest producing herd. In 1967 we had the highest herd average for the year.

By the winter of 1968 the work and the hours were getting to be almost unbearable, although I liked everything that I was doing. I had to make some changes. I decided that I should sell my cows. I called Roger Lussier, a well-known auctioneer, to help me with the auction. It went very well and the cows brought more than I had anticipated. I was really lost for a while without my cows but was able to devote more time to my other business. I had hired a truck driver to deliver the bulk grain as this business was really growing.

Without my cows and with a truck driver I now had more time to take on some auctions and list some real estate I started buying a few small properties. I bought a seven acre lot on the edge of town overlooking the village. I had planned to build a senior citizens home there. I had the architectural work done and the financing arranged. For some reason Nancy was very much against me putting up this building. When I went into the post office one morning, I bumped into Dona Bessette, a friend of mine, who owned a car and truck dealership. He asked me what I would take for that lot. I mentioned a price. Nothing more was said. On the way home that afternoon I passed by this lot and there was a bulldozer working there. Dona had decided to buy it and build a new house. In those days a person's word was all that you needed.

You could count on it. Another nice thing in those days was that there was no zoning or permits required. If you had an idea or a plan, you could get started right off. You didn't need to ask anybody or tell the whole world your plans.

One day I got a call from the IRS. They wanted to audit my books. Remembering what had happened to my father this made me very nervous, although I couldn't see where they should find any problems. The IRS man came to our house. He kind of indicated that he knew that we had to be doing something wrong and that he was there to find it. His audit took several weeks. At first he was not very friendly but after a while I think that he could see that we had done everything the way that we were supposed to. He became more friendly, and he turned out to be a real nice fellow. He didn't find anything wrong and this was a big relief I have been audited six or seven times since then. Each time it takes several weeks and they usually go through two years of records. Most all the auditors that I have had have been real good to get along with after they have been here a few days. I have never had any serious problems with them. One time the auditor wanted to change my depreciation schedule. I would owe them some more tax hut I would have to pay less tax in future years. Either way it was going to cost me about the same. He said that we could spend a lot of time arguing over this but if I would agree to do it his way they wouldn't charge me any late fees or penalties only the interest and the tax. I agreed to it. After the IRS gets done with an audit, they send a copy to the state tax department. In Vermont the state income tax is a percentage of the federal tax. I received a bill from the state for their share. They had added in late fees, penalties and interest. I sent them a check for the tax and the interest but explained to them that I had agreed with the IRS agent that there would be no late fees or penalties and that as the State tax being based on the federal tax I didn't believe that I owed them any late fees or penalties. A while later I received another bill from them for the penalties and late fees, which had about doubled. I called the tax department and talked to a Ms. Parker. I tried to explain to her what had happened. She didn't listen much. She went up one side of me and down the other, then said that she would get back to me the following week, as it was now late Friday afternoon. I never heard from her, but I did keep getting bills from them each time about double the previous bill. One morning someone from the Vermont tax department called and told Nancy that if I didn't pay this bill by eleven o'clock that morning that they were going to attach everything that we had. This kind of irritated me so I told her to call them right back and tell them to go ahead. About a half an hour later, the tax department called back and said that they had decided that maybe I was right and that they were dropping the charges. Another time when the IRS called to set up an audit, I asked, "How long do you think it will take?" He said about six weeks. I told him that I didn't think that I had that many records. He said that in that case it would probably take six months. It really pays to keep good records and document every cent that you take in or spend.

As I did more auctions and real estate business, I became more acquainted with Noel Lussier. I was thinking of selling the grain business. I had been there ten years and felt that I needed a change. I had taken this business over after my father's death to keep it going. I now felt that it was time to do some of the things that I wanted to do, which included auctions, real estate, and more farming. Noel approached me and said that he would like to have me join him as a partner in the auction, real estate and cattle business. Noel knew a lot of people and had already done a lot of business. This sounded like a good move. I didn't have much trouble finding some buyers for the grain and farm supply business. Noel and I opened an office in a store front on Main Street. I had my farm and he had his farm where he had been conducting his cattle business. With both places this gave us the capacity to handle a lot of cattle. We would buy and gather up large groups of cattle then hold an auction, at the farm. We did a lot of auction and real estate business. Some weeks we would hold several auctions, we pretty much covered Northern Vermont. Noel wasn't an auctioneer so I did all the auctioneering. He was an excellent ring man and got along real well with the crowd and customers. Everybody liked him and always seems to listen to what he said. Noel was a very good partner and I trusted him completely.

CHAPTER 3

THE REAL ESTATE VENTURES

I was born in Hardwick and in my lifetime I could only remember of one new house being built in town. All the rest of them had been built many years ago. There was a twenty acre lot on the top of Slapp Hill just on the edge of the village limits that had once belonged to Cherity Heath. Walter Urie a local surveyor and engineer approached me and said that it was for sale and it would make a good lot for some new houses. I was familiar with this lot as we had played in there when I was a kid. It was mostly wooded with maple trees and overlooked the Village of Hardwick. Walter wanted to do the survey and engineering work if I would buy it. I talked to Noel about it and we agreed to buy it together. We later made my brother Steve who was a carpenter a partner. We divided it into nineteen nice lots. We planned to build two houses, and as soon as we sold one, we would start another as long as they sold. About that time, the State of Vermont had come out with some subdivision regulations that were being administrated by the health department. I called them in Burlington and talked to a Mr. Hood. I told him what we were planning to do and asked him what was required. He asked if I knew Walter Urie. I told him that Walter was doing out engineering work. He said that Walter knew what the requirements were and just have him draw up the plans for the lots and bring them into the health department office. I asked how long it would take to get them approved. He said that if they were complete that they could probably approve them right on the spot.

Walter got the plans done in a short time and I called Mr. Hood and told him that I would be in his office the next morning with them to be approved. When I got to his office, which was about sixty-five miles from Hardwick, the girl behind the counter said that Mr. Hood wasn't in. I told her that I thought I had an appointment with him. She kept looking off to the side and seemed not to be too sure of what to say. It was obvious that she was trying to communicate with someone around the corner without my knowing it. She wasn't a very good faker. There was a swinging gate at the end of the counter. I wanted to see who she was looking at so I pushed the gate open and stepped in. There was Mr. Hood sitting at a desk. I asked him about approving our plans as he had indicated that he could. He said that it couldn't happen quite that fast, it was going to take a few days but to leave them and he would get them right back to us. This was in April. We waited over a month and no approval. I called and was told that it took time but wouldn't be much longer. This happened several times. It got to be August we already had two houses built and sold except for getting this permit. I read in the paper where Dr. Aiken, the head of the health department and Vermont governor Dean Davis were going to be speaking at a meeting in Lyndonville explaining the new health department regulations. I told Noel we better go. We listened to Dr. Aiken explain about what was required and about how quick they would approve all applications that met the requirements. Then governor Davis got up and spoke about how they were not designed to hold up construction or development only to protect the public against health problems relating to water and sewage. They both assured everybody that it was a very short process. There were about two hundred people in attendance. The governor then asked if there were any questions. I jumped up and told him what had happened to us. He became very angry and got right after Dr. Aiken. He told him that was contrary to what he had been telling everybody and ordered him to immediately look into what had happened to our permit. This was about ten o'clock at night. The very next morning when I went to work at seven o'clock there was a man waiting on my office steps with our approved plans.

It seems that every house we built was sold before it was completed so we just kept on building more houses. I think that we sold three or four lots to people to build their own houses and we built the rest. We wanted to give the development a name so we ran and add in the local newspaper offering a new bicycle to the kid who came up with the best name. We had a lot of suggestions. I don't remember who the kid was that won but the name that won was Hide Away Acres. After the project was completed and we figured up everything, we didn't make a cent but felt that it had been good for the town, so I have always felt good about doing it. Noel and Steve and their families moved into a new—in Hide Away Acres. I think that Nancy was kind of envious and would also have liked to have had a new house in Hide Away Acres. I was not interested as the farm was my home and I certainly had no desire to move.

Most of the banks in this area were small and it didn't take long to do business with them. Often when you went in for a loan you could walk out with the money. The bankers knew everybody in the area and there wasn't a lot of paper work. The banks would often finance real estate without a title search, as we know it today. You could get a statement of title from the town clerks for about five dollars and the banks would accept this. This system made sense as the town clerks knew and kept their own records. They should know them better than a lawyer doing a title search. Some town clerks would make out deeds for about two or three dollars. You could get these things done while you waited. It was possible to buy a property in the morning, take a deed to it then sell it in the afternoon and deed it out all in the same day. Today this would take weeks or months.

Noel had three sons and a daughter. I had two sons and two daughters. They all soon learned to help with the auctions. Our wives did the scribing and the book keeping. We didn't have to hire much help. It was nice to have your whole family working with you. Noel and I did a lot of business one year we sold twenty-three farms. Just about all these stayed in farming. We helped quite a few young couples get started in farming.

Noels father had been a director of Caledonia National Bank for years. After Noel and I had been in business for a couple of years, Noel was elected to the board of directors of the Bank. He was very excited about this and wanted to devote much of his time to bank business. We decided to give up our partnership. I moved my office back to the farm. I continued to do auctions and real estate. I kept some cattle and kept farming. My kids were getting big enough to be a lot of help.

In the summer of 1972 Dean went to Auction school in Mason City, Iowa. He went with Larry Lecours, a long-time friend of mine. Larry was a school teacher who had always said that he wanted to be an auctioneer. Dean was eleven years old. When he got back, he was featured on the channel three evening news as being the youngest auctioneer in Vermont.

Dean did quite a bit of auctioneering and did a good job but was not interested in making auctioneering his lifework. I didn't push him. One Saturday soon after they returned from auction school, I had a big consignment sale at the farm. I asked Larry if he would like to help. This was his first auction. It was an all-day event. We had furniture, farm machinery and a lot of cattle to sell. Both Larry and Dean did quite a lot of auctioneering. I had been doing a benefit auction every August since about 1961 for the Woodbury Fire Department. This year it came on the same day as the auction at the farm only it didn't start until six o'clock. We were running a little behind in time so I asked Larry and Dean if they would go to Woodbury and get that auction started. I would be along shortly. I arrived around seven o'clock. Larry was holding up the items and Dean was doing the auctioneering. They were working off a flatbed trailer. I waited a minute, things were going very good except that Larry wasn't saying anything. I went over and climbed up on the trailer to help them. Larry motioned for me to come over near him. He got up real close to me and whispered, with quite a lot of effort, "I've lose my voice, I can't talk." It was a good thing that he had Dean. I have now done the Woodbury auction every August for over thirty years. I had built an auction barn at the farm and for quite a few years we ran a weekly auction, which the whole family helped with.

*Dean Hill, at twelve years old, is the youngest
auctioneer in the state.*

At the same time I was buying a few properties, fixing them up
and reselling them. Several of the banks started contacting me to buy
properties that they had taken in foreclosure. At least three of these banks
set me up with dealer accounts. This allowed me to sell properties and
take back a mortgage then reassign it to the bank. They did not have
to approve each loan. I could approve whoever I wanted to finance.
But if anything went wrong or they didn't make their payments it was

up to me to make sure that the bank got paid. As additional security for these dealer loans, I used my savings account as a reserve account. Usually when I assigned a note to the bank I added some money to this savings account. Often it was my profit. I figured that someday this would be our retirement. I was able to help a lot of people purchase their own homes. I even helped several people to refinance their homes. I remember one family who came and asked me for help. They had been making payments to another bank on their home for quite a number of years. The husband had come down with some crippling disease, which had prevented him from working full- time at his old job. They had gotten behind in their payments and the bank was about to foreclose on them. They had only about four years left on their mortgage buy were about to lose their home. I wrote them a new mortgage stretching the payments out to ten years and cutting them about in half I put it in one of the banks that I had a dealer account with. They never missed a payment and have now paid it in full.

Besides banks I had many people contacting me to purchase their properties. I purchased several large buildings on the main street in Hardwick. Some of these were with owner financing. One of the properties that I was approached to buy was the local post office building. Dave Barcomb had built eight years earlier. He had a lease contract with the government but now wanted to sell. The contract was written for ten years with a clause allowing for four five-year renewals. The rent that the government was paying was very low and did not make it a good investment. I talked to a couple of people from the post office department. They said that the rent was renegotiable at the end of the ten years, which had about two years to go, and that it would be renegotiable at the beginning of each of the five-year renewals. Based on this information I decided to buy it even though it was going to lose money for the next two years. About a year before the ten years was up, I got a call from the post office department saying that they were planning to renew the contract for another five years, which was their option. I inquired about renegotiating the rent. I was informed that the rent was locked in and that it probably wouldn't change until the end of the thirty-year contract. I had been losing money for the past two years and now I was stuck subsidizing the United States Post office for another twenty years. I was not very happy about this. After that whenever they wanted some unnecessary repair or improvement, I would give them a hard time telling them that they were not working for the same salary that they got thirty years ago.

The building was built to government specifications and had a flat roof. These do not work well in Vermont, they most always leak due to the sever changes in the temperature and weather. Each spring and fall I would check the roof and patch the leaks. After doing this for several years, I received a call from a Mr. Cook, a post office official, from the Manchester, New Hampshire, office. He asked to meet me at the post office. He wanted me to tear the roof completely off and replace it with a new flat roof I told him that there was no way that I could do it with the present rent that I was receiving. He said that he could show me a way to do it that wouldn't cost me much. He said that the government wanted some additional improvements that they could pay for and when the government paid for something they usually paid several times the actual cost. He said that I could use this extra money to pay for my share of the new roof. I didn't like the sound of his proposal, it did not sound honest to me.

One of the things that the government would pay for was to install a urethane composite board insulation in the new roof. This would have an insulation R factor of 19. The old roof had no insulation and the government paid for the heat in the building. He had said that the government would pay $7,500 for the insulation and the other improvements that they wanted. I checked into the costs of what they would pay for. They came to more than $7,500. This really bothered me and I thought about it for several days. What he had told me about the cost was untrue and it seemed a shame to replace a flat roof another flat roof, which would probably leak in a short time.

The way that the building was constructed it would be a very simple matter to put up some truss rafters and have a two pitch roof that would not leak. By doing it this way I could blow enough cellulose insulation onto the old roof to bring the R factor up to thirty-eight, twice the insulation of the urethane at R 19. I called Mr. Cook and explained my suggestion. He said that he would get back to me. Within a day he called back and said that they liked the idea. He said to check with an engineer to make sure that the building was able to support the rafters and if it would to go ahead. Due to the low rent I really couldn't afford to do it. I did check with Walter Urie a local engineer who said that there should be no problem with the building supporting the rafters. I went ahead and did the work. It turned out real well. It looked more like the neighboring buildings. It had cost me over $17,000. I sent the government a bill for the $7,500 that they had agreed to pay. Several weeks went by and I heard nothing from them. I sent them a second bill and still no answer. I called Mr. Cook to find out why I hadn't been paid. His answer was that they were not going to pay me as I had changed the plans. I could not believe that the government would do such a thing. I contacted Senator Stafford's office and I kept after them. Finally I believe that I did get a portion of what they had promised.

Another building that I bought on Main Street was the Bemis block. I was sitting next to Waldo Bemis one morning at the counter, in the Village Diner, having coffee when he said that he would like to sell me this building. Waldo was the local fuel oil and coal dealer and was about retirement age. The Bemis block was the largest building on Main Street. It had twenty one apartments and four store fronts. Hardwick had had a history of being kind of a rough town and this building was right in the center of down town. This building had not always had the best reputation. One of the store fronts had been a bar ever since I could remember. It had been the scene of many fights over the years. At first I wasn't too interested but Waldo made me an offer that I couldn't refuse so I agreed to buy it. The building didn't have any insulation. The water pipes for the third floor were in the attic. You could see right out through the cracks in the attic walls but the water apparently never froze as all the heat went up through the attic. There was never any snow on the roof due to the great heat loss. The heating system was a huge old steam boiler in the basement that had been converted from coal to oil. There were two oil tanks and they had to be filled twice a week in the winter time. There was no thermostat in the building to control the heat. It was outside the building and turned the furnace on and off according to the outside temperature. The first thing that I did was to blow insulation in all the side walls and the attic. I covered the pipes in the attic and insulated over them.

I installed an inside thermostat and bought some storm windows. I continued to buy my fuel oil from Waldo. Within a few days he called me and said something was seriously wrong with the heating system. It had only been taking about a quarter the fuel that it ordinarily had taken. I told him what I had done. He said that he couldn't believe that it had made such a difference.

Three of the store fronts were rented. The fourth Waldo had been using to store bagged coal. We cleaned it up, strapped the walls with firing strips and covered them with peg board. The ceiling was real high. I got my brother Steve, who was a good carpentering, to help me and we put a balcony over about two· thirds of the store. This gave us quite a bit of floor space. I bought some close out deals of shoes and clothing and we opened the store. Nancy became very interested in this project and put a lot of time and effort into running it. The kids also cook hold and helped. It did very well and we soon had a large inventory. It was a fun business as we never knew what we were going to buy next, as I got most of our merchandise from auctions and close outs. One time I purchased a lot of ski boots at an auction in Massachusetts. We were selling them for thirty five dollars a pair, which was about a quarter to a third of the regular price. People were coming from Stowe and all the ski areas to buy them. Some fellows, from New Jersey, were up in Stowe skiing when they heard about the boots. They drove up to each get a pair. One of the fellows asked if we took credit cards. At that time we didn't. He said that they had been skiing all week and that he had only enough cash to get back to New Jersey, but he would like to get a pair of boots. I told him to pick out a pair and we would work out something. A few minutes later he came up and put the pair that he wanted on the counter and handed me his credit card. I told him that I couldn't use his credit card. He looked disappointed. I then asked him if he had a checking account back home. He said that he did. I gave him my business card and said, "Here is my name and address. When you get back home, you can send me a check."

He looked at me kind of funny as if he couldn't believe it. He started to write down his name and address.

I said, "I don't need your name and address. You've got mine. Take the boots and just send me a check."

He looked at me in disbelief, and I could hear him mumbling to himself as he went out the door, "Unbelievable. I can't believe it. I have never heard of such a thing."

In about three days, I received his check in the mail.

I had the Bemis block running pretty good, but it still had its problems. I tried to keep good tenants in the apartments and weed out the bad ones. This was hard to do. Another problem was that the front entrance to the apartment area was a large stairway that opened right on to the main street. All the buildings on that side of the main street were build right into a steep bank that was all ledge. There was nothing behind these buildings except vacant land and a short road about second floor level, that went nowhere. There were back doors from the upstairs halls on the second and third floors that opened out to this little road. I often got calls lace at night from the local police who wanted me to come down to take care of something. Often it was a broken window. One Saturday night after midnight I got a call from the local police chief who said that I should come right down as there was a big problem. I got up and went down. When I got there, he and his deputy wanted to know if I had a key to one of the apartments as they needed to get in right away. I asked what the problem was. A young mother from out of town had left her small child with the tenants who lived in this apartment while she had gone out on the town. When she came back to pick up her child, the people were sleeping, and she couldn't wake them so she had called the police. I was kind of disgusted that they had called me down for this. I told them that they probably had the door locked from the inside. I asked them if they had tried banging on the door. I rapped on it several times until I had awakened the woman inside. It was about one o'clock in the morning. She asked who it was I told her it is Bill Hill. She said just a minute and she would open the door. She probably had to get on a bathrobe or something. When she started to open the door, the police officer said to me, "Stand back," and he pulled out his revolver and stuck it right in her face. I don't know what he was thinking of, but imagine answering a knock at your front door at one o'clock in the morning, half a sleep, and have someone shove a gun in your face. I was really disgusted. I couldn't believe it.

Many of my tenants were older people and a real problem that I did have was with young hoodlums going up there and terrorizing them. They would demand food money and cigarettes from them. I tried many times to get the police to do something about it. I think that they were afraid of them. Whenever I would call the police, they would come but they would always blow their siren as they came up the main street just before they got to the building and the young punks would run out the back doors and always be outside. They would just laugh at the police as they knew that they were not going to do anything to them. The police told me that they couldn't do anything about them unless they actually caught them in the building harassing somebody. This happened many times it really irritated me.

On a Wednesday Mr. Ewing who had been very afraid of two of these bums came to me and said that he was really afraid to live there. He kept cigarettes and food to feed them when they picked on him. He also had given them money. The following Saturday I had an auction in Craftsbury. I got back in town around four in the afternoon. In front of my building were three or four state police cars and a big truck that said Crime Lab on the side and the local police car. The street was full of people mulling around. I parked my pickup and proceeded into the building to see what was going on. I went up the front stairs to the second floor. The door to the first apartment to the right was open. That was where Mr. Ewing lived. There was a yellow plastic ribbon strung across the hall about two feet off the floor. I stepped over it and headed toward the open door. Just as I got there the local cop and a state police officer named John Palmer came flying out the door and nailed me up against the wall and started choking me.

Palmer started screaming, "Get out of here! Get out of here, or I will arrest you."

I asked him, "Arrest me for what?" He said, "For trespassing."

I said, "Just a minute. I own this building, and I want to know what is going on." I told him that I would not leave until I found out. He said that somebody had murdered Mr. Ewing. He said that they figured it had happened about five thirty that morning. I said that it should be easy enough to figure out who did it. They didn't want to hear this from me. I immediately went and found the two fellows who

I was sure had killed Mr. Ewing, but the police were not even interested in talking to them, much less arresting them. When I got home that evening, we were discussing it. Dean who had been downtown going to get ready for the auction about six that morning said that he had seen these same two fellows coming down the street from the Bemis Block. We called the Caledonia County state attorney's office and told them what Dean had seen. They said that they would probably want to question him, but they never did. Over fifteen years have gone by and this is still an unsolved murder.

Hardwick's whole down town Main Street business section probably wasn't over a thousand feet long. In years past Hardwick has been a very busy town. On one end of the main street was the town square, which had a dummy in the middle of the street. Facing the square was a good size hotel called Hardwick Inn. On the other end if the business section of Main Street was a big old beautiful hotel called the Eagle Hotel. Both of these hotels had been very busy in the past and right up into the fifties, at which time the Eagle hotel was torn down to make room for a filling station. Maurice Goudreau and his family had owned and operated the Hardwick Inn for several years. Mrs. Goudreau, who was a very hard worker had passed away at a young age. The building needed work and Mr. Goudreau closed the hotel and moved to Barre to seek other employment. The building was empty for several years and had continued to deteriorate. It had a large porch that ran across the front and around the end. The porch roof had fallen down and there was a large hole in the front of the building where a car, which was going too fast, had not made it around the square but instead had driven right into front of the building and ended up in what had been the hotel lobby.

The Lamoille River ran right behind the building and along behind all the buildings on this side of Main Street. A group of local people wanted to tear it down and make the area into a park. They thought that they could get a government grant for this. They started putting articles in the local newspaper about buying this building and demolishing it without making any deal with Mr. Goudreau, the owner. I didn't pay a lot of attention to what was going on until I heard that a bunch of hippies had read in the paper that the hotel might be for sale. They were prepared to buy it and all live there. I certainly didn't want to see the hippies starting a commune on Main Street. I called Maurice Goudreau and asked him what was going on with his building. He said that all he knew was what was in the paper and that he was irritated that they had been condemning his property when they had made no deal to buy it. I asked him if he would sell it to me. He said that he would be in town the next afternoon and to meet him at his son's house. He was anxious to sell it to me. When I got to his son's house, a member of the tear-down committee had been there and Maurice told him that he was selling the building to me. He had become very upset and left in a storm. I gave Maurice a deposit and we signed a purchase and sell agreement. I had no plans for the building except to keep it from becoming a commune, and a bigger eyesore. I called Alfred Lanphere, the town manager and told him that I had bought the building. I told him that if the town had plans for it they could have it for just what I paid for it. I soon got a visit from the people who wanted to tear it down. I explained to them that if I hadn't bought it they probably would not have got it as there were other people were after it. I explained to them that I had only bought it to protect it and that I would be glad to turn it over to them for just what I had paid, and if they wanted it they now had it secured. They were not satisfied with my offer they were still mad that I had bought it.

Time went on and I heard nothing from the committee that wanted the hotel except that they kept putting articles in the paper accusing me of messing up their plans. It began to look to me as if they were not going to get around to do anything so I contacted them and told them that as they had made no offer to buy that I was going to have to do something with it. I was going to start fixing it up. I couldn't just let it set another winter. I told them that they could still have it for just what I had paid or that they could have it at any time in the future at just what I had invested but that what I had invested would going up after I started repairing it up. I still got no positive answers. My sons and I started to work on the old hotel. The back corner next to the river had to be jacked up as much as eighteen inches. We tore out the floor in what had been the bar and grill. We then poured a new cement wall across the building separating this part from the rest of the hotel basement.

This gave us a base to jack up the center of the building. The cellar under the bar and grill we filled with sand and poured a cement floor. We put a new roof on the whole building. Where the porches had been we poured a new cement walk and built a roof over it.

Inflation!

Upstairs on the front of the building there was a door leading out of the onto the porch roof. We built a small balcony up there overlooking the town square. This made a good location for the judges when they held the spring festival parade.

At the time that we were working on the building the local paper was reporting what the committee were saying about us fouling up their plans. They also had several letters to the editor condemning what I was doing. I went in to the barber shop to get a haircut.

The barber said, "Do you realize that you cost this community over thirty-eight thousand dollars?"

I asked him how he figured that. He said that was the figure that the committee was planning to ask the federal government for to tear the hotel down. The editor of the local paper not only reported on what the committee was saying but he kept coming by and asking me what my plans for the building were. I guess that I never gave him much of an answer. The truth was that I didn't have any idea what I was going to do with it. We kept working to fix up the first and the second floors. We did a lot of insulating and lowered many of the ceilings. We installed a new heating system.

We had the building about as far as we could go without knowing what we were going to do with it when luck struck. Robert Richardson who had worked for me years ago in the grain business had developed a very nice garden supply center in Danville about fifteen miles away. He approached me about renting the main part of the hotel to expand his garden supply business to Hardwick. This was great as I knew that he would run a real attractive show place kind of business. We struck a deal and he started to fix up his quarters the way that he wanted them to look. It was beautiful. There was a flower shop across the street that needed larger quarters they came in to the further end of the building. Shirley Moffatt wanted to open a deli so we fixed her a place. Other businesses that came into the building were the Hardwickian, which was the local newspaper, Jeff Jacobson's Craft Shop. The office of Authentic Log Homes, a manufacture of log homes and I located my own Real estate and Auction office in the Hardwick Inn building. After this the old hotel started to get some very good reviews in the newspapers. It was the cover picture on the 1976 Hardwick Town Report.

About the same time that I was fixing up the hotel, I was approached by Robinson Moulton, who I owned a saw mill with and Dan O'Connor a local Insurance man to join with them and purchase another building that had been idle for quite some time. This was the old Sam Daniels Manufacturing Company building. Sam Daniels had manufactured furnaces, milk coolers, milking machines, maple sugar equipment, and manure spreaders. I believe that he also made one of the first chest type freezers ever. Sam Daniels used to brag that he would stand behind everything that he built except his manure spreaders and he would stand beside them. After Sam died, the business had fallen apart until there was nothing but an empty building left. The Daniels family owned the front part of the building and the Town of Hardwick had acquired

41

the back part of the building for taxes. This building was across the Lamoille River from the main street. Years ago Sam had built a swinging foot bridge across the river for his employees and customers, so that they wouldn't have to go way around to get there. The planking had rotted and the bridge had been closed. We decided to buy the building and put it into eight apartments for the elderly. This building was also getting to be quite an eyesore for the down town, so this would be another nice improvement. One problem we had a difficult time dealing with was the back portion of the building that was owned by the town. They had no idea what they were going to do with it and we couldn't find out. It was of little or no value to anyone. We offered to buy it tear it down or do whatever they wanted done with it but they couldn't decide. I think that we finally ended up buying it from them. Nobody was sure who owned the foot bridge us or the town. The local Kiwanis club came to the rescue there. They agreed to fix it up if we would deed any interest that we might have in it to the town and if the town would accept it. Everybody agreed on this and we all helped to put it back in shape to use again.

CENTENNIAL HOUSE ANNUAL REPORT
Town of Hardwick 1976

Robert Richardson who had opened the garden shop in the Hardwick Inn had invested quite a bit of his own money in fixing up his shop and the front of the building. He was interested in buying the hotel building. I felt that he had been more than instrumental in helping me make the Inn a success and he had done a lot to help revitalize Hardwick's downtown. I agreed to sell it to him for just what I had invested in it. I had never got into this project to make a profit only to help save Hardwick's down town. I later bought out Moulton and O'Connor's interest in the Daniels building.

Things continued to go pretty well for us. The kids were growing up and were a lot of help. They had all learned at an early age how to work. Even though we worked hard we always tried to make our work fun. As each of the kids graduated from high school, we through a party at the auction barn for them and their graduating class. We always had a band and invited the whole town. Most of the parents came, and this way they knew where their kids were on graduation night and everybody had a good time.

As our kids got older and started to leave home, Nancy became less and less interested in what I was doing. I don't think that she had ever really liked the farm. She now spent a lot of time at the store but not much time at home. She wanted to take over the store. All of a sudden, she was not interested in doing anything with me. She didn't seem to need me anymore. This bothered me very much and I became quite distressed. I found it hard to concentrate on anything. I didn't book many auctions. I felt that we were at a point in our lives where we could slow down and start doing some fun things together but she didn't see it that way.

Nancy didn't like tenants and wanted me to sell the Bemis block but she wanted to keep the store. I had always thought that this building's income would make us a good retirement. She called a broker and wanted me to list it with him, which I did. He brought us an offer. The buyer didn't want to put much money down.

The former Sam Daniels Manufacturing to Company building, located on the opposite side of the Lamoille River from the village business district, is getting a brand new look. The old structure, which is a historical landmark, is being converted into apartments by Robson Moulton, Dan O'Connor, and William F. Hill who recently purchased it. There will be some eight apartments in the building and the owners believe they will be particularly well suited for older people who want to be conveniently located for shopping, church and services. The facility will include a large community room overlooking the river. This room will before hosting company, social gatherings, and recreation. There will also be laundry facilities.

This he planned to borrow and wanted us to take a second mortgage for the rest. I didn't like this arrangement. He was getting his money from the Merchants Bank who wanted the first mortgage. Instead of a second mortgage I agreed to take back a twenty-year paid-up lease on the store space and one other store. This way he wouldn't have to make any payments to us.

I didn't know it, but the Merchants Bank had agreed to lend him a sizable amount of money to make improvements to the building. At the closing I was surprised that the bank was advancing him all the money before he had done any work. This didn't look like good business to me. I asked Bob Platka, the loan officer, if he couldn't hold back some of the money and advance it to him as he made the prescribed improvements. Platka told me that it was not my business, it was between the bank and the buyer. I didn't like the deal and I was right. The buyer never made any improvements. He removed the laundry equipment that I had installed. He didn't pay the fuel company or anybody else including the bank. He kept the banks money, collected the rents and didn't put anything back. The bank had to foreclose on him. I could have redeemed it but would have had to pay off the Merchants Bank and all the money that they had advanced him, plus restoring the building back to the condition that it was in when we sold it. I would probably feel obligated to pay all the back oil bills. I didn't do it. There went our twenty years paid up lease on the two stores.

I took care of the other properties that I owned and collected the rents and payments but I couldn't make myself look for any new business. One day I was up in Derby collecting rents from some tenants that I had in that area. Many of my tenants were low income people. Many of them had small children. I got to know their children and usually took time to visit with them. One place that I went the mother and the kids were all excited. They said that Sally Lussier was coming to cook with them. Her real name was Charlotte. I asked who was Sally Lussier. They said that she worked for the extension service. That she had been teaching them to cook. As I left, I met Sally coming across the lawn carrying a big bag of cooking stuff. She was all bubbly as she came bouncing along and I could see right away why they liked her. I said hello and went on my way. A couple of hours later, I was at another tenant's house when she showed up there. She asked "Are you following me?" jokingly. I had never seen or heard of her before, but I ran into her twice in the same afternoon. I didn't think much more about her until quite some time later. I got a phone call from her. She said that she heard that I bought mobile homes. She had one for sale and would I be interested in buying it. I hadn't been feeling that good and hadn't been too interested in doing any new business, but said that I would take a look at it. When I got there, I met her and her husband, John. They were living in it. It was a very nice mobile home with a factory built two pitch roof. It was one of the best mobile homes that I had ever seen and it had been well taken care of. There was something about Sally that really had a funny effect on me.

She was like a magnet. Nobody had ever affected me this way before. I didn't want to leave. They told me that they wanted to sell the mobile home and build a house. The price that they were asking was not out of line, so I told them that I would get back to them. Dean had recently gotten married to a very nice girl named Ann. They were living in the apartment up over the milk house. I thought that this mobile home would make them a nice home and would be something that they could afford. I took them to see it and they liked it. I told them that they could put it just down the road from the farmhouse. There was a nice spot there. It was next to the road and electricity. We could dig across the field and run a water pipe over from the farm. They financed it at Caledonia National Bank.

A short while later I received a call from Sally Lussier. She wanted to know if I was interested in buying or selling any more mobile homes and would I be willing to pay her a small commission if she found me some customers. I said that I would as long as there wasn't any land involved as she didn't have a real estate license. She found several customers for mobile homes. She kind of got me interested in doing business again. I started to feel better. I realized that there could still be a future. I spent quite a bit of time working with her. This didn't set very well with Nancy and we just seem to drift further apart. Nancy finally got a lawyer and filed for a divorce. Her lawyer wanted me to get a lawyer. There was no way that I was going to get a lawyer to go against my wife. I sat down with her and told her what we had and that she could pick what she wanted. We agreed on a settlement. She was to have the store, all the furniture the car, the Daniels block and some cash. I wanted to use her good and hoped that she would be happy. I felt that I had failed her.

CHAPTER 4

CHARLOTTE'S STORY AS TOLD TO HER DAUGHTER-IN-LAW BELINDA

My Great-great-grandfather, Peter Aldrich, came from Canada. He was half Indian and half Irish. He met my Great-great grandmother Samantha on an Indian reservation in Swanton. She was full blooded Abenaki Indian. They fell in love, were married, and moved to Belvidere, Vt. They had a son named Chet. Samantha used to go to the woods in her little white apron with her pipe in her pocket. She would gather small twigs, bring them home, and would make fans and wreaths to help trim her home and to give to her friends. She was a funny little character. She wouldn't have her picture taken and kept mainly to herself.

Chet was a lot like his mother. He was tall, lanky, and really ambitious like his mother. He married an Irish lady named Bertha. Bertha wanted to move to the village. Later on they did, and had a big family. One of them was named Katie.

Katie was sure different. She was ornery. Her hair was long, and she wore it in braids. In her older life, she wrapped it around her head. Her husband was a hardworking Englishman named Elijah. At age 19, he had a full head of snow white hair. It was thick, coarse, and really lovely. I can remember it. He worked awful hard. First in the sawmills, and then he went to farming. They had 7 children. One of them was named Bertha; my mother.

She was ambitious too. At a real young age, she went to work in a restaurant and after that, she took a job working for a farmer. That's where she met my dad, Clarence Longley. My dad said what drew my mom to him was that she was so shy. He said they had to clean one of the farmers' houses. They took the horses and sled. He said, "She sat in the back of the sled, and dragged her feet in the snow all the way not saying a word."

My dad came from a real good family. The family came down from Canada, Frank Longley and his three brothers, and bought a whole mountain just out of Montgomery, Vt. The covered bridge leading to the mountain is to this day called Longley Bridge.

Each one of the Longley brothers built a farm and raised their families. They were successful. They had a lot of cattle, nice homes, and cars. The family stuck together. My grandmother was a women who cooked, sewed, and helped on the farm even though she raised 11 children. When she went out in public or had her picture taken, she always dressed up and wore a hat with feathers. This was the way they all were. They had a lot of pride.

As time went on, my dad and mom got married. It wasn't long and they were expecting me. My father worked a lot so my mother was alone quite a bit. As she got closer to her due date, she was afraid to stay alone so she went to stay with my grandmother Longley. Spring came early, so she sent my mother home and had my aunt Eunic go with her. My aunt Eunic said that it was beautiful weather. The water was running down the roads, the birds were chirping, it was really spring. They walked up the road to my mothers' house. They hadn't been home long and the weather changed. There was a terrible snow storm. For three days it snowed. No roads; nothing. What do you think would happen? My mother went into labor. My father hurried to the barn and hitched up the team. He hitched them to the sled from where the manure was drawn. He put hay in it and then wrapped my mother in blankets and put her in. The snow was deep. The horses were sweating. They fell down and my father couldn't get them up. My mother was in pain.

My aunt Eunic was sent ahead to the neighbors' house to call for the doctor, the snowplows, and for my uncles to come and help get my mother down to the main road. My uncles could not get their cars home because there was so much snow. They had to walk five miles through the snow to get to their cars. They said they rushed as fast as they could, got to their cars, shoveled them out, called the snowplow, and called the doctor in Enosburg.

The doctor called for the plows in West Enosburg and Enosburg to get up to where my mother was at the Nickels' farm. The doctor loaded himself and his nurse into his car.

My uncles, by this time, had made it to the Nickels' farm. They helped my father get the horses up, and shoveled a path for the doctor to get to her.

When the doctor arrived, he put my mother in his car and headed for St. Albans. My father stayed behind to help with the horses. He said he thought he was going to lose one of them. You know if you lose a team, there goes your means of transportation, and everything you need to run a farm.

After taking care of the horses, he headed down the road to where my mother was. My mother had not made it to St. Albans. She had made it to Dr. Judd's house, and I was ready to be born. As the sun came up, she had me. Two and a half pounds! I was born on the first day of spring, and the worst snowstorm of the year.

My father arrived and couldn't believe it. I was so tiny. He said he had listened to the radio all the way down and that he was going to call me Charlotte because Charlottetown, North Carolina was all afire. "We will call her Charlotte," he said. "Charlotte Joyce."

For nine days I lived at the doctors' house in a shoe box wrapped up in blankets. In a shoe box on the oven door! I was so tiny that I couldn't nurse a bottle. They had to feed me with a medicine dropper. They could put a tea cup over my head and down over my shoulders. Was I going to make it? I couldn't even nurse a bottle! They said I was determined and the doctor was too. My mother said that she found him up in the middle of the night in the kitchen with a medicine dropper feeding me when it was her turn for feeding. He was bound and determined that I was going to live.

When it came time for my mother to take me home, my aunt Eunic decided she was going to stay with us longer. She ended up staying from March until August. She left when I was big enough for my mother to handle, get the meals, and take care of the house. I grew like a weed.

It seems like I was bound and determined I was going to make it. My mother was taking good care of me.

My father decided to change jobs, and we were going to move closer to town. We moved to the Gibson farm, which really thrilled my mother. She thought that would be better. We were closer to the doctors and everything.

It was a lovely place. The barn was on one side of the road and the house was on the other. It was a nice, big house sitting on a little knoll.

What more could you ask for? We moved in and my mother was petrified. She could hear noises. It sounded like an old man coming down the stairs. My father had his youngest sister Joyce come and stay with us. Aunt Joyce said to me, "Sure enough, that noise would start. I would grab you, put you on my hip, and run out the door with your mother right behind me with a gun in her hand. I often wondered what everyone thought as they went by. Here we were standing on the front lawn, me holding you and your mother with a gun in her hand."

My aunt stayed for a couple of months until they finally realized that it was the water pipes that made the noise.

Winter came and everything was going well. Then on New Year's Eve, we had a tragedy. My parents were awakened in the middle of the night by a man pounding on the door. Our barn was on fire, and so was the house. My father had just enough time to put on his pants and my mother to wrap me in a blanket. Everything burnt to the ground. They had nothing. We had lost everything. They really never knew for sure what started that fire. How lucky we were that a man took the time to come to the house and see if there was anyone in it. We never knew the man's name. My father never saw him again. He was a stranger who had saved our lives.

Time went on. Two years later I had a younger brother named Wayne. Eighteen months later, I had another brother. He was named Wendel.

By this time, I was old enough to remember things. I can remember my father had bought a farm. We had an old car and we would take the calves to Willy Hicks auction. We would load the calves and us kids in the back seat and away we would go. It was dark when we would come home. I would lay my head against the window and watch the moon.

I thought he must love me, that moon, because he would follow me everywhere. I was a funny little kid.

I helped my dad as much as I could. By the time I was 5, I was driving a young pair of colts that my dad had bought from Dale Eastman. He taught me how to drive them and told me if they ever ran away to brace my feet, drop one line, and keep them going in circles until he could get to them. I never thought it would happened but sure enough, one day we were haying and my father had unhooked the hay loader. Those young colts took off up the side hill, onto the flats, and headed for the barn. I can now still remember my father yelling, "Hang on! Hang on!"

I remembered what he had told me to do if they ever took off on me, and spun the horses around and around in a circle until dad caught them. Boy, he never let me drive them again. I guess it really scared him.

I can remember a lot of things on the farm. My father always use to say, "Watch for deer. If you see any, let me know."

One night when he was milking, I can remember running in yelling, "Dad, I just saw a deer cross the field. The big one up in the woods."

He said, "Take the milking machine off the cow and I'll be back shortly."

Sure enough, it wasn't a half hour and my father came down the road hanging onto his pants. He had shot the deer but hadn't killed it. He had taken his belt from his pants, put it around the deer's' neck, and tied it to a tree so it wouldn't run away. He had come back to get a knife or another shell to finish off the deer.

It wasn't long and I had two more brothers. They were named Stewart and Stanley.

My father took another job working in Richford in a factory. We had left the farm and moved into a house we had paid seventy-five for. The well was in the cellar, and the toilet was an outhouse out ack. I had never seen anything like it. We each had two straw filled bags my mother had sewn together that we put upstairs on the floor in a room where the stove pipe came up through. Each of us children had two bags covered with a coat, then used coats as blankets. Those were our beds.

Downstairs there was one bed belonging to my mother and father. We had a television, and a chair that came from the dump that we had made a rope bottom for. I can remember we had a cable, nothing but wooden boxes to sit on, a little oil stove to cook on, and a round oak to keep warm with. It was unreal. Times were hard.

My mother became very sick. So bad that she had to be put in a hospital in Waterbury. This was hard on everyone. The two older boys, Wayne and Wendel, went to stay with our grandmother Longley, and the two younger boys, Stewart and Stanley, went to stay with Grandmother Johnson. I was shuffled around a lot. I would stay with someone for two weeks, and someone else for another two weeks. I was trying to go to school, but every time I moved I was in a different place, in a different book, and needless to say, after going to twenty- four schools in one year, I did not pass.

My father tried hard to keep the family together. He would pick me up every week and we would go to the Waterbury Hospital to see mom. I would sit in the car and wait for my father to come back out. He would cry a lot, but would always cheer up. We would also go around and see my brothers. It was hard on all of us, but my father was very faithful to everyone.

One day my father came to where I was staying. I was staying in Montgomery with the Gambles at that time. I was seven years old. He looked at me and said, "Charlotte, we have a choice to make." He told me the state was after me and wanted to put me in a place called an orphanage in St. Albans. "An orphanage?" I said. "What's that?"

"Oh, it's a big place where kids live when they have no other place to stay. Or we can go to New Hampshire where my brother lives. I can find a job, and we'll stay for a while."

No choice needed to be made. We were going to my uncles. That morning he picked me up and told me to pack my clothes. Pack my clothes? I didn't have much. I had outgrown my shoes. The toes were cut out so they wouldn't rub the ends. I had cardboard in the bottom where the soles had worn out. We had no money for clothing. My sleeves were too long on my shirts. I wore anything anyone would give me.

I can remember arriving at my uncles. I don't think my aunt was really thrilled about having us move in but we did. My father immediately started looking for a job. It didn't take long, less than a week. There was an old bachelor named Mr. Putnam who owned a sawmill in

Hanover. It was back in the boonies. He had a lot of lumber camps. One of them was empty. He took us to it and said we could live there. He was in walking distance where my father would be working in the sawmill. I can remember how pleased my father was, and so was I. We were going to have a home.

I can remember we had a bed, and a stove. I don't remember a refrigerator or a bathroom of our own. There was one outhouse that everybody in that community used. We had to lock the door when we went in. There was an old catalog you would use for toilet paper. I guess we were fortunate, we had that.

My father eventually built on. He added another room. This was going to be a bedroom. He hung my springs from the ceiling with a chain around the beams and put his bed underneath it. He also made another bed just like mine and put another bed underneath that. I asked, "What are we doing dad?"

He replied, "We are going to bring your brothers home. You are big enough now to take care of them."

I was nine. My brother was seven, and the other was six. I was going to be responsible for them? I would do anything to help. I was glad to have them home because then I would have company while dad worked.

I can remember cooking rice and leaving it on the back of the stove and we ate it for days. It was a wonder we didn't get sick. I can remember opening the door and sweeping the dire out. I use to heat the water on the stove and lug it to the back of the house.

One by one we would take a bath. The airport was close, and they would fly by low. We would scoot down in the tub so they wouldn't see us.

We all went to school. One day, the teacher came to me and said, "Your brother Wendel is crying. I don't know what the matter is. Will you come down and talk to him? I can't stop him from crying."

So down the stairs I went to find out what was the matter with my brother. I walked in the room and he was sobbing. I walked over and whispered in his ear, "What's wrong?"

He showed me his dinner pail. I opened up the lard can, for those were our dinner pails, and he had half a can of lard. I had put up the dinners on the broadshelf. We had no cupboards, so the lard can sat there too. He had taken the wrong pail. He had a pail of lard. I told him to stop crying and I gave him my dinner. It seemed like there was always something going on with Wendel who was the youngest. I was always bailing him out one way or another.

We lived way back in the woods, and at night we could hear the bears hooting. We had a little dog hitched to a fence and he would have a fit when the bears would start. My dad said the bears would come so close he believed it would scare the little dog crazy. My father gave all us children a lecture saying, "Stay close to the house. Don't wander off." He told me to watch the boys real close. There was a lot of bears in that area for some reason. But you know how kids can be. We were always doing different things, and getting into a lot of trouble. One night we had decided to play hide and go seek. I was to count and the boys were to hide. I found Wayne without any trouble, but we couldn't find Wendel. We looked, and looked. He was only six years old. I ran to the sawmill remembering what my father had said about the bears. They shut down the sawmill entirely. All the men came to look for my brother. Mr. Putnam said he would call a man with bloodhounds if we couldn't find him. Everyone looked. One hour later, we found him. He was about thirty feet from the camp. While waiting to be found, he had fallen asleep, behind a log.

We lived there for about one year. One day my father came home and said, "Your mother is coming home. We are going to have to move for this place is not big enough for all of us."

We were real pleased my mother was coming home. On the other hand, it was strange. She had been gone so long. She was like a stranger. My mother came home, and we moved to Fairlee, Vt. We didn't stay there but two weeks and moved again. We moved back to Enosburg to that little seventy-five dollars house.

I had grown up a lot since the first time I lived there. I started collecting catalogs with wallpaper in them. I used my fathers' razorblade and cut the paper out, took flour and water and pasted them to the wall, matching them up the best I could. I had found two cans of paint, one red and one blue, at the dump. I painted the cupboards red, and painted the boxes we used as chairs blue. At least they were clean and pretty.

Here we were again in a house with no bathroom. We primed the pump to get water. We had an outhouse, and one acre of land. I don't know why, but my father was always collecting everything. We had a cow, which we hooked to a block of wood. A pig that ran loose. Two ducks, and a turkey who thought he was a duck. He would swim in the brook. There was a dog, a cat, white mice, and all of us kids. We didn't bring Stewart or Stanley. It was more than my mother could handle. She had her hands full with us three.

We walked to school in the cold really not dressed warm enough. I can remember taking biscuits and lard for sandwiches. A quart of milk each week was all we had. Times were hard, but we kept struggling by.

By the time I turned thirteen, I was working outside the home. I would walk five miles to Enosburg where I scrubbed a woman's floors on my hands and knees. She would give me one dollar and I would walk back home. I saved enough money to buy my brother Wayne a nice pair of britches, and some material to make myself a skirt. When school was out, I landed another job in Enosburg. I took care of a lady who was expecting her fifth child. I was taking care of the children, so that when she left for the hospital she had someone she trusted to leave them with. Everything seemed to be going well, then one of the children came down with a high fever. Next thing I knew, the doctor had come to the house and nailed out the sign on the house. None of us could go out. We had Scarlet Fever. We were there for weeks. The children had awful fevers and suffered from dehydration. The doctor came back every couple of days. People brought food and left it on the porch. Everyone in the house had it except me. The doctor couldn't understand it. I was frail. I only weighed 75 pounds. How could I not catch this disease? I explained to the doctor that I never had any childhood illnesses, and very rarely did I have a cold. After the lady had her baby and was back on her feet, I looked for another job.

I was lucky that I found one. There was a lady called Mrs. Jacobs. She was old and people called her grandma Jacobs. She had a dance hall and roller skating rink. She lived there alone. She had two half beds, a stand, rocking chair, telephone, light, and nails on the walls to hang your clothes. We used the public bathrooms and the kitchen where we sold hot dogs and soda pop. She said she would give me five dollars a week if I picked up the beer bottles on Sunday mornings, cleaned the dancehall floor, cook hot dogs, sell tickets, and help line up the skates. It sounded like fun to be around the public. The money I would get I would send home to my dad to buy food for the family.

I also helped dad get a job there too. He became the Saturday night cop. He took his job seriously. Mom would come and sit on the benches with the boys. Dad took his job seriously. Her brother came and got to drinking and showing off. My father wouldn't stand for it. I can remember he picked Uncle Willard up by the seat of his britches and the nap of his neck, pushed open the door and threw him out over the railing. Boy was my mother mad! But my father said, "A job is a job." He was getting paid two dollars, and he did what he had to do.

I enjoyed it there. I learned to skate and to dance. Mrs. Jacobs' granddaughter gave me a couple of nice dresses that fit me perfectly. I gained some weight. We ate good. Mrs. Jacobs was awfully good to me.

When I turned eighteen, I knew I was old enough to earn more money. I left Mrs. Jacobs and went to Jay Peak to work. I was going to be a waitress in the ski lodge. Jay peak was one of the newest and biggest ski lodges around. I got thirteen dollars a week and my room and board. They gave me uniforms to wear. The first three days were the hardest. Mr. Choquette, my boss, did not like the name Charlotte. He named me Sally. After three days of protesting, I finally gave in. I became Sally. I carried that name ever since.

I loved the work. I enjoyed waiting on people, and I liked the tips. I was getting anywhere from $100 to $150 a week in tips.

I saved as much as I could, and one day I went to the Converse Company in Orleans. When I saw the little town, I thought to myself, *What a terrible little town. It sits way down here in the hollow. I wouldn't care to live here.*

I went into the Converse score and bought my mom and dad a brand new kitchenette set, a second hand living room set and a second hand washing machine. I went with the Converse Company to have it delivered up over Jay Peak and down into Enosburg. I can remember my mother couldn't believe it. My father stood there not saying a word. The kitchenette set was pink. The living room set was green. The washing machine really ran. I think it was the first one my mother had. It was an automatic.

I continued working and then started to go out. I went to the fair and met a man named John Aldrich. We went together for over a year and a half, and the next thing I knew, I was pregnant. Lordy, was I scared. He said not to worry, we were going to get married anyway.

We had a big wedding. His mother insisted I have a big, white dress. I was married in a church with candles and all the trimmings. He went to work at Ethan Allen and we lived in a two room apartment in Orleans. Again I had one bed, a tiny fridge, a hot plate with one grill, and a table with two chairs. It was all we had. Time went by fast. In November, I was sitting on the street with my husband & started labor pains. I got to the hospital and had my first son in a half hour. We named him Timothy. That morning, my father arrived. I looked up and he was standing at the foot of my bed crying. He said, "My little girl had a baby."

But how little I knew what lay ahead of me. Fourteen months later, I gave birth to another son. We named him Rodney. He was cute and peachy. This meant moving.

We moved to the upstairs of a house. I can remember my washing machine. It was a wringer type, hue—had no wringers. I had to wring out all the clothes by hand. I can remember running downstairs to hang up the diapers. The water would run down my elbows because I was tiny and not very strong and couldn't wring them very tight.

Fourteen months after my second boy, I had another son named Ronald. I almost died. The doctors said no more. By this time we had moved again into a house we had rented. I had it furnished beautifully. John was gone a lot in the evening. He said he was going to have to go to Massachusetts or Connecticut to find a job and move us down there. I was sad, but I didn't argue with him. I packed his clothes and kissed him goodbye. I knew he would be back shortly after us.

The first week went by and I didn't hear a word. The second week was the same. The third week a lady knocked on my door and said to me, "Would you like to see your husband?"

"Oh yes," I said.

"Go down on Maple Street to your friend Anetas's," she replied.

"He's down there."

I asked her to stay with my children and I walked down to Maple Street. Sure enough, there was a van and a U-Haul trailer. I went up the stairs to her apartment, and there he was taking down the curtains. I asked, "What's going on?" She had on his shirt I had bought him. I walked over and slapped her across the face. I kicked her in the shin and grabbed ahold of the shirt. I ripped the buttons off the front, and pushed her backward. I said to him, "If you want to see your kids, you had better come now or you'll never see them again." I walked out the door.

I would have never done this if I had known she was pregnant with his child. I was devastated. Here I was with three babies, no car, no groceries, no money, no job, and all alone. Completely on my own. I couldn't go home. My mother had two more children, Calvin and Pamela. Pam was only nine months older than my middle son Rodney.

I knew I had to make it. I walked around town looking for a job, but there was nothing. I asked for credit, but no one would give it to me. I finally broke down and called my mother-in-law and asked her to bring us groceries. She said she would if I would give her the two chairs she always liked. Gladly I would give her the chairs.

I couldn't seem to find a job. She suggested that I give her the boys and I go to New York City and start my life over. At that time it sounded good. I called Gassy Souliere and told him I would sell him my furniture. My mother-in-law went to Montgomery Wards and bought me four nice outfits. I had packed up everything and was ready to leave. The furniture was on the truck. My mother-in law was there to pick up the boys. I held one on my hip and the other in my arms. Little Timmy wrapped his arms around my legs and cried. I couldn't give them up. They were my kids. I asked Mr. Souliere, "Please unload my furniture and I'll give you your money back." I told my mother-in-law to get out of there and never come back. The kids and I went back into the house. I knew I had to do something. I had to find a job. We had to eat. I knew I couldn't stay in that place long without money.

I went to see the people that ran the Converse company. They had a daughter just a little younger than I. She was still in high school. They lived across the road from me. I asked them if they would let her babysit my children at night, and I would look for a job. They agreed. Her name was Pam and she was real good with the children.

I found a job at Indian Plywood in Newport. I ran a splicer. I had to carry big sheets of paneling and splice them together from 5:00 p.m. to 2:00 a.m. I paid for a ride home, and went to bed until the boys got up. When they napped, I napped too. I did this for eight or nine months and then got sick. The doctors said I was over exhausted. I weighed only 98 lbs. I worked night and day. The doctor said I had to get out of there, that I wouldn't make it much longer.

I started looking for another job. This also meant another babysitter.

I started looking for someone to watch the boys during the day. I was lucky. The Broom girl couldn't find a job either. She was about 5 years older than I was. I told her I would pay her fifteen dollars a week. She agreed to this.

Now, a job. I found one again in Newport. I was working in a plastic company. I worked there only 6 months and broke out in hives. Back to the doctors I went. He said I was Allergic to fiberglass, and that it would get into my blood system if I didn't leave. I went back with my paper to the job. They fired me. I walked down the road crying. No job. What was I going to do?

I was telling my neighbor what had happened that evening. She said, "Come with me. Rod Montgomery in Hardwick is always looking for someone to sew."

I said, "I can't run a sewing machine." That morning I got up and went to work with them. Rod was real nice. He said, "I'll give you a job only if you wind up your hair so it doesn't get caught in the machines."

I did learn to sew. I was in Hardwick five days a week. I paid five dollars for my ride, fifteen dollars to a babysitter, ten dollars for rent, ten dollars for food, and was left with usually three dollars to my name. I was making ends meet. We worked there all summer. Winter came and the girls decided not to travel. There I was left standing again without a job. I didn't have a car or license. How would I get to work? I had to look for another job.

I looked in the paper and saw an ad. "Wanted: waitress. Apply at the Candelpin Restaurant in Barton." That was close to home. A lot of people went that way. I could find a ride. I got the job working days. The tips were decent. It sure helped. I got home at 4:00 p.m. This meant I could spend time with the boys outside. We lived in a big apartment house. There was six apartments and I was in the middle. We were right on the street so they couldn't go out without me. I was outside a lot with them. I would watch them run and play, and would take them for rides in the carriage.

There was a man who always walked down the street by our house. He was tall, blond, and always said hello. It seemed he went by every night. One night he stopped and talked. His name was John Lussier. Come to find out, he lived at the other end of the street with his parents and had to pass my house on his way to work.

I didn't pay much attention. My world was occupied. I had children. I was always worried the state would come and take them away. I kept a home for them. They had food, and were clean and happy.

When I took the children for a walk one night, he joined me. He told me he was divorced and he had a son. His ex-wife was named Barb. He felt real bad about it. I listened to him and sympathized. I knew what he was going through, except I was lucky. I had my children.

Time went by, and one night he asked me out for supper. He said he would even get me a babysitter. It sounded good. I hadn't been out for years, so I took him up on it. We walked down to the village dinner and had supper. I noticed he drank some, but it didn't mean much. I figured it was Saturday night and thought it was all right. We came back home and he kissed me and left.

We continued going for walks, and he would sit on the porch with me and talk. One night, I told him I had the chance to model for Playboy. "They came in the restaurant today and asked me if I would be interested. The money is good. It could help us," I said.

He looked at me kind of puzzled and said, "What did they tell you?"

I said, "I would sign a contract and they would use my picture for 50 years. They pay real well," I repeated.

"Stop and think about it," he said. "50 years and you have three sons. They could pick up the magazine, and there would be their mother."

That sounded terrible! I wouldn't want my sons to see me that way. The next day when I went back to work, the people came in again. It was a man and a women. I told them I couldn't do it and explained why. They said all right and thanked me. I never saw them again.

I went into work one morning, and like I had done every morning, I walked by the kitchen stove where a double pot of coffee was being perked. It wasn't setting level. As I walked by, the jarring made the pot fall over. It hit my coat and ran down into my boot. I screamed. The cook and the waitress and Stevey Brown, the owner, pulled off my pantyhose and boots. He picked me up and carried me to the car. My leg was bleeding. We went to the hospital in Newport. The doctor packed it in ice and wrapped it up. They kept me for three days. Oh my lord. What was I going to do in the hospital for three days? The sitter took care of my children during the day, and John Lussier took care of them nights. They sent me home after three days. I couldn't walk or do anything. The blisters bubbled up and I went back to the hospital. I had gangrene. They cleared it up and sent me back home. Needless to say, I was having a hard time. This went on for about 6 months. The church brought me a lot of food. I had to sign up for welfare to buy food, pay rent, and pay the babysitter.

My legs wouldn't heal. I had gangrene three times. The doctors said, "We are going to cut off your leg just below your knee."

I replied, "No way. You cut off my leg, and I'll sue you."

They didn't know what to do with me. I was as stubborn as a mule. I was twenty-three years old, and I wasn't going to be left one legged. They decided the only thing they could do was to graft skin from my hips and back onto my leg. The doctors told me that I had burnt all the nerves in my ankle and would never be able to control my leg. I didn't believe him. That was my leg and I wasn't going to be without it. I was going to walk again no matter what.

A couple days later, I went under anesthesia. When I woke up twenty-four hours later, I was lying in a tub of ice with a wash cloth over my face. I can remember Dr. Gage and Dr. Bonvoulior. They were both staring down at my face. Dr. Gage started asking me questions, and I looked up at him and said, "Doctor, you didn't hurt my brain for I didn't have one to start with."

He began to laugh. He said I had had a fever of 104 and had to be packed in ice. They unwrapped my leg three days later and found skin was growing.

John kept taking care of my children. He carried me everywhere. To the bathroom, everywhere. I couldn't walk.

Finally when there was enough skin growth, they allowed me to hobble around on crutches. They still didn't think I would walk.

Eventually, the feeling in my leg and ankle returned. I would walk again. It took a long time.

I was embarrassed to go down street. I figured everyone in town knew I was drawing welfare. I didn't want them to know. I was proud. I had no other choice. I didn't want to lose my sons. I wasn't able to work, because I couldn't stand up long enough.

I began to feel better, and started looking for a job. But John said, "No. Don't work. Stay home and take care of the boys. We'll get married."

Married, again? I didn't want any more children, but he did. I said I wouldn't marry him unless he found a good job and stayed there for 6 months. Then I would consider marrying him.

He was hired at Ethan Allen Furniture Factory. He stayed there 6 months, and we were married. I felt obligated. He had helped me and taken care of my sons. I owed him. There was no one else in my life.

We got married, and two years later, I had my daughter. She was beautiful with coal black hair and long fingers. John said she looked like a witch, but I didn't believe it. She was just a doll.

I did nothing but play with them. I can remember my youngest son Ronald saying, "Mom, let's go out for a walk." I told him we couldn't. Tina was too small, and it was too cold. He said, "Then send her back from where she came from."

I'll never forget that. I knew I had to pay more attention to them all. Ronald was 5, and would be in school next year. I made Tina his baby, which went good.

Four months later, a women knocked on my door. She asked me if I would like to sign up for food stamps.

"No thanks," I said. "We don't need them."

She looked at me oddly and went away. The next day she came back. She came in. She was a big heavy set women. When she found out we lived on forty-two dollars a week, she couldn't believe it. "How do you manage?" she asked.

"Oh, it's not easy, but I do it," I replied.

We had four children. We lived in a downstairs apartment. In the kitchen if you opened up the closet, you could see the outside. There was one living room and two bedrooms. The baby's crib was next to my bed. There was wall to wall mats in the other bedroom. We were happy. We didn't know any different.

She asked me if I was interested in a job. A job? I hadn't thought about going back to work. "What kind of job?" I asked.

"It's called a homemaker. You would get paid every two weeks. You would go into homes, help cook and clean, and run errands." She said I needed a car and a license. I did have a permit and we did have a car, but I never drove.

That night I talked it over with my husband. He said it was up to me.

I called her back and told her I was interested. She said I would have to get my license.

I knew the mailman and his wife. They had a push button car, and I knew if they would let me take it, I could get my license.

I called Mrs. Casavant and asked her if I could borrow her car and the reason why. She agreed. I knew I really couldn't handle the car, and needed to do something to pass. I decided I would make small talk with whomever was the instructor and try to distract them. It worked, and I passed.

The following week I went in for my interview. When I got into the car, I realized it was not push button, but stick shift. It took me a while to get it into reverse. Finally, I headed to Newport, which was only eleven miles away. It took me over an hour. When I arrived in town, I realized I had to park somewhere where I could get out because I couldn't parallel park. I was running late. I hurried up and parked and ran to my interview. I ran through the door and oh Lord, I couldn't believe the people there. I didn't stand a chance. They were all after the same job. I waited and took my turn. They said they would let us know by letter.

That evening, I asked my husband what was wrong with the car. He went out and tried it and said, "You must have driven all the way in low."

Three days later, a letter came. I got the job! I would make ninety-eight dollars every two weeks. This would double our income. It was wonderful! I realized that lady really made it possible for me to get that job.

I worked there one year until the funds ran out. I was automatically changed over to the parent-child center. This job wasn't much different. I was working with families and teaching them how to get along. I did this for about one year and they asked me if I would go to Island Pond to be head of the center and to have seven women working under me. I knew it was a big responsibility but I also needed to job. We got the center working good. I was driving twenty-eight miles one way each day.

The next thing I knew, I was pregnant again. I really didn't want another child. By this time we had moved into a little two bedroom house. I knew we needed something bigger with another child on the way.

Every morning before I went to work, I listened to the Trading Post on the radio. I was always trying to upgrade everything in the house. I had purchased myself a car so my husband could have his own. One morning I heard on the radio a women selling everything she had in the house. It was just two streets up from me. I left early and went to her home. She was a school teacher leaving town. She wanted to sell everything she had. I said, "Look, you have a lot of nice things. If I bring in a lot of people and they buy everything in the house, will you give me your vacuum cleaner and a set of dishes?" She agreed. I told her I would be back Saturday morning.

Saturday morning I had seven carloads of women. They purchased everything in the house. After receiving my free items, she informed me she wanted to sell her house. I asked her what she wanted for it, and she said $12,000. It was the right size. It would be perfect for all of us.

I remembered we had some applications come into the office for low income people for housing. I knew I was going to get this house.

The next morning, I went to John Chater's office. There he sat with his feet on top of his desk. I reached over and picked up one of the applications and stuffed it down my blouse. He said, "What are you doing?"

I replied, "I'm taking one of these and if you try to take it I'll scream.

He smiled at me and told me to take it to my bank. My bank? I didn't have a savings or checking account. I took it home and John filled it out. I took it to the bank. A month later I had the loan. The women hadn't sold the house yet, so we purchased it. My payments were low. Ninety-eight dollars a month. We moved in. I was thrilled. Our first home! We had room for all of us.

I kept working. My belly rubbed on the steering wheel, but I kept going. The women in the center threw me a surprise baby shower. Surprised I was. I had enough for three babies. I couldn't believe they had done this for me.

The doctor ordered me off the road two weeks before my son Paul was born. When he was six weeks old, I went back to work. When he turned one, my husbands' job changed. They put him on the night shift and he hated it. I worked days, and he worked nights. It caused a lot of friction. He kept at me to go to work at the mill. I didn't want to. I loved my job. He insisted I go, so I gave my notice at the parent-child center and went to work at Ethan Allen.

I worked the night shift with John. This meant changing sitters again. The children stayed with a lady at night, and I picked them up at 2:30 a.m. I would bring them home, put them back to bed, get up with them, sent the older ones to school, watched the younger ones, and slept in the afternoon. My husband was happy. I was in seeing distance of him. I hated it. I hated working nights. I hated leaving the children. I hated it all. I missed my old job. I worked there for over a year. One night I came to pick up the children and found a picture of me under my oldest sons' pillow. I realized then that they were as lonely as I was. I didn't see them much. They came home from school at 3:30 and I left at 4:30. I told my husband I was going to give my notice. He was furious but I did it anyway. I knew I needed a job. We had house payments, and car payments. I had put ourselves in the position where we needed two incomes.

I took a job selling Avon. I was everywhere. I was making good money, but I got fired. Too many women were yelling that I was cutting into their business territory.

I came out of the meeting crying. I had no job again. I sat on the street wiping back my tears. A lady came up to me. Her name was Barbara Levens. "What's the matter?" she asked. I told her about losing my job. "Don't worry about that," she said. "I know where there is someone looking for help. Come with me. I'll take you up to the Extension Service."

Up the stairs we walked in this big public building over the post office. I walked into the room and saw a beautiful women. She had long, black hair, a satin blouse, and a plaid, wool skirt that went down to the floor. I looked at her and realized how awful I must have looked compared to her. She smiled at me and said, "I'm Miriam Buckland. I understand you are looking for a job?"

I replied, "Yes, I am."

She continued, "Look, this is a really great job, but it's difficult. I have hired and fired six women. You will have to go for training at UVM in Burlington. Go down there and get your training. I'll give you six weeks trial. If you make it, I'll give you the job. You can leave next week. I'll set up training."

There was only two of us in training. Dot Lyons and myself. We had to learn about nutrition, sanitation, and cooking. The teacher, Alice Right, was wonderful. I went through the six week course holding my breath all the way. No one ever asked me how far I made it in school. I only went through the third grade. The way Alice taught, I could learn. I went on my trial run for six weeks, and then Mrs. Buckland gave me the job. I wanted to be someone. This was my opportunity to make something of myself. This was my chance.

My job went well. I could run classes. I worked well with people. One year came around, and we were all told that everyone needed a high school diploma. I told Alice I didn't have one. Up I went to Newport and I joined the Adult Learning Center. I asked them if I could take one subject per week. "One subject a week?" she asked. "Do you think you'll pass?"

"I need to get my GED or I'll lose my job. I have five children. I have no choice," I said.

I took the books home and made an appointment for the following Monday to take the first test. One by one I took them and passed. In six weeks, I had acquired my GED. She said I was the first person who had done that in Newport. Boy was I proud. That GED was all that mattered. Now I wouldn't lose my job.

Back to work I went, making up my mind that I was going to do a good job. I would do whatever it took to be good. I ran exercise classes, nutrition classes, invited nurses and senators to come. I outgrew my space at St. Paul's and moved to Barton Elementary. I had seventy-three adults in my class. I was interviewed and put in a magazine that ran all over the USA. I was teaching everywhere. I would teach in schools, social welfare and mental health offices, and homes. I went to Washington and Maine for training.

My job was wonderful, but my home life was falling apart. My husband was throwing a fit. He quit his job. He said his back hurt. He went into the hospital. I was driving 73 miles down to Burlington every evening with the children. For three years he didn't work. I maintained the home. He was really angry with me. Why didn't I quit and draw welfare? What was the matter with me? Why didn't I want to stay home? I had the perfect job, babysitter, the older boys were in school, why would I want to quit?

He would have friends in all day long drinking. I would come home at night, and the kitchen bar was covered with dirty dishes. I couldn't understand why he couldn't get his act together. He had really changed. Or was it me?

I had sold the house in Orleans, and we were living in Lowell. He still wasn't happy. We sold that one and moved to Barton. We built a little house next to a golf course. He didn't like that one either. He wanted more land. We sold that one too. He bought ten acres of land out in Irasburg and moved us all into a trailer. By this time, the older boys were gone, so it was only the four of us.

I hated it. I made up my mind that I would get us back into a house. He had gone back to his old job at Ethan Allen. It seemed we were on the right track again. I had heard about another job Saturday mornings and one evening a week cleaning the office for Citizens Utility. I could bring the children with me. It was extra money. It was enough to make a house payment. I worked there 5 years. By this time, Paul and Tina were old enough and didn't need a babysitter. This cut down on my expenses. I began to save money. I had three different savings accounts at three different banks. I saved every dime I could.

I was asked to appear on TV on Across the Fence doing 15 minute segments on nutrition. They gave an award out of Burlington, and to my surprise, I got it. It was for being the best paraprofessional in my line of work in VT. I was proud as I could be. One day I went to work in Derby Line by the Canadian border.

When I got inside, there was a strange man. I knew he wasn't anyone who was going to take a class from me. He was only there for a few minutes. I asked the people who he was and they said his name was William Hill from Hardwick. I finished my class in about 1½ hours then went to Derby. As I was setting up for my next class, there was a knock on the door. The lady let him in. It was him again. "By any chance are you following me?" I asked. His face turned red. Evidently he was collecting rents and he owned these places. There was something about him that I liked. I questioned her as to who he was, and what he did. She told me he sells real estate and that he was their landlord. My brain began to tick. Maybe I could sell him our trailer.

I called Mr. Hill but he was gone to Florida. I got the number and gave him a call. He said when he returned, he would come see it. Boy, I was thrilled.

Mr. Hill returned from Florida and he and another man came to see the trailer. I don't know what it was about him. He fascinated me. He said he wanted to talk to his son. His son was looking for a trailer, and he wanted to help him out. He would let me know. I said okay, and let it go at that. It wasn't much later when he called again and said he wanted to buy the trailer. Yeah! This meant I could build a house.

I sat down with my husband that night and began looking through books. What kind of house would we build? There was only four of us now, it didn't have to be big. Years had gone by and prices had changed. We found the payments very hard and couldn't seem to make it even with the two of us working.

Years went by. We had a hard time. My husband was always complaining that I was always working. We didn't seem to get along. We were drifting apart. We decided to sell the house. I found one in Orleans. It needed a lot of repairs. We worked hard on it and fixed it up. It came out real nice.

One day, my daughter announced she would be getting married. I couldn't believe it. I thought she was too young. She was only 16. He was in the service and they moved to Texas.

My son Paul was a teenager. My family was grown up. My second son had married. My third son was in Kentucky in the army. My first son had his own home and was working at Ethan Allen. Everyone was doing their own thing. But I wasn't happy. I kept working. One day something hit me. What about me? When didn't I count? Why wasn't I happy?

I made up my mind I was going to leave. John and I decided to divorce. I saw more and more of Bill. He and his wife had decided to divorce too. We wanted to be together. It wasn't long and I moved in with him on the farm in Hardwick. I asked Paul to go with me, but he said no. He had friends in graded school and didn't want to leave.

You know me. I had to change everything in the farmhouse. I rewallpapered, revinyled, changed the curtains and carpets, relandscaped the outside, and had the barn and house painted.

Bill and I got married. Paul and two friends of ours were all that attended. It was a very quiet wedding.

I had fixed up a room for my son Paul. I wanted him to move in. He only would come to visit. I tried to understand. His father had remarried. Nancy, Bills' ex, had also remarried.

One night the telephone rang. It was my ex father-in-law Leonard Lussier. He said, "Sally, you need to come to Newport to the hospital. John has been in a fire and is badly burnt. His wife and stepson are dead." Paul had been away that night. He was all right. Bill and I went. John was covered with third degree bums. They didn't know if he would live. I felt so sorry for him. They sent him to Burlington. It took a long time for him to recover. He is now remarried.

Bill began to farm. He bought two hundred head of cattle. This was great. I didn't want to work. I wanted to stay and help on the farm. I raised the calves, did the bookwork, and helped with auctions. I loved it.

It eventually became hard on Bill. He was getting tired. The opportunity came to sell the farm. We sold, and bought a small house down the road and lived there while our new house was being built.

We did a lot of traveling and would get ideas from homes for our house. We always wanted to build a big home up in a field. One night, we set down with a big envelope and drew out on the back what we wanted our house to look like. We wanted a big kitchen, a big family room, an entrance, a nice living room, library, and offices on the first floor. On the second floor we wanted a washroom, two bedrooms with matching baths, and balconies. We thought it would be beautiful.

We called his brother, and began working. I'm sure it wasn't easy for Steve. He had nothing to go by but what we said and a sketch on the piece of paper.

It went along just fine. We sold our little blue house and moved into the cellar. We slept on couches and cooked on a hot place and the grill. We roughed it.

As time went on, we did more improvements on the house. We had a long driveway, and Bill wanted to plane maple trees along the whole drive. We put in a circle drive in front of the house with a water fountain and flower beds. It really looked rich. I had found a set of old wagon wheels that were used to haul granite back when the mine was running. Bill had old light posts from an auction that he put outside around the house. He had the chance to get a pool for doing some work. We got a real good deal. My son Rodney was in the pool business so he came over and helped put it in. We had a pool for everyone to enjoy.

We built patios out by the pool. On the top one, we built a kitchen. It had a small fridge, a sink, stove, fryer, and grill. I use it a lot in the summer when we have family and friends over.

Rodney and Paul built stone steps and a stone wall for a flower bed. Paul and a friend of his dug slate out of the river for a front walkway leading to a big, beautiful front door.

We wanted the house, although new, was starting to look old. We had stone fireplaces, wood floors made from pine boards we got from an auction, and wainscoting. It made the house look old.

I purchased chandeliers from an auction. One I paid only thirty-five dollars for. Some were from a second hand shop. When they were cleaned up, they were beautiful.

We purchased furniture from yard sales and auctions. We would have them refinished and redone. I found an old organ in an old barn that I swapped an air unit for. It cleaned up beautifully. I put it in the best living room. I found old pictures, old mirrors, and antiques. The only thing new was the appliances in the kitchen. We took marble and had a fireplace built in the living room.

Inside it there is an electric log that burns. A year later, I found an old mirror top with pillars and shelves that matched perfectly on the mantle. I had it stained the same color and put old oil lamps and candles on it. It looks beautiful.

We have lived here for 5 or 6 years now. We have family reunions. People come to swim in the summer. My youngest son was married here. Bill was the justice of the peace, and married them. People came from all over. It is really a home. Our family comes every year for holidays. We have 25 grandchildren and enjoy having them come up. We hope to live here the rest of our lives, and be happy.

CHAPTER 5

Nancy had a new man named Harold Stevens. They purchased a house just down the road from the farm. After Nancy moved out of the farmhouse, Charlotte and I moved in and were married by a justice of peace. A short while later Nancy came to see me and said that she and Harold were getting married. I felt good about this as I thought that she would be happy. She said that they were planning a large wedding reception and wanted to know if they could use my auction tent. I was happy to be able to help them. As a matter of fact, a few days later Charlotte and I received an invitation to their wedding reception. Charlotte didn't think that it would be appropriate for us to attend. I said, "Why did they not they invite us?" I think that it really shocked people to see us show up but they had a nice wedding and we had a very nice time. We were both happy for them.

Charlotte continued working for the Extension Service for another two years. She had been there for fourteen years and now wanted to retire. They gave her a nice retirement party. This is what she said.

"I had worked for the Extension service for fourteen years. I loved it! But I was now married to Bill Hill and I loved him, I wanted to be with him. I had worked the first two years of our marriage. I thought it time that I stayed home and made it a home. We had grandchildren coming along and I wanted it to be a real home. We were living on the farm and I loved it. I loved the cattle and being a round Bill. I looked up to him. I had very little education but in my own way I could do things too. I could picture things. I had the house painted then all the barns and even the silos. They now all matched and looked real sharp. I put in flower gardens and a rail fence separating the lawn from the milk house drive. I tore up the kitchen floor and had a new oak floor installed with the money that I had saved.

"I loved having the kids and grandchildren come in for breakfast and lunch. I put on parties for them at Halloween and Easter. One Halloween both my mother and Bill's mother came dressed in Halloween costumes. My sister's husband came dressed in a gorilla suit. This scared some of the smaller grandchildren so he had to take it off. We had a nice family and we did a lot of things."

I didn't know how getting remarried would affect my credit rating, but it didn't seem to hurt. I was still getting calls from the banks asking me to purchase their properties. I continued to do auctions and the real estate business plus I was raising heifers and selling them before they were ready to milk. Charlotte liked the farm and the cattle. I decided to go back into milking. We had a large farm shop that I converted to a milk house and milk parlor. It was large enough to milk fourteen cows at a time, with seven on each side. At first I only used one side until I got up around sixty cows. I kept expanding until we were milking about one hundred and fifty cows.

It was going to take two men besides myself to keep things going smoothly as we were raising most all our own feed except for the grain. I hired three men. Each man would work four days then have two days off. This way there were always two working and one off. The days were long as we started milking at three in the morning and finished the evening milking around six at night. I was usually in the barn by two in the morning to get the cows up and into the holding pen to be milked. Then about ten at night I would go out and mix them up another feed of silage and concentrate. We planted about two hundred acres of silage corn and we chopped haylage all summer to put up for winter feed. These were long days but I really liked it. Charlotte took a real interest in the baby calves and soon took over the job of raising them. I never saw anybody raise calves the way that she did. We kept them in a large pen. When it came time to feed, she would hook each one to the fence with a piece of baler twine. She would call them all by name and they all seemed to relate to her. After she had them all fed, she would turn them loose again then open the gate, and they would all chase her up and down the road and then would follow her right back into the pen. Both she and the calves loved it. She raised about thirty five of them one summer.

Sally and I managed to get away for a little while in the winter. Three different years we went on a trip with the Farm Bureau in January. One year we went to Nashville and Atlanta, the next year we went to California, then the following year, we went to New Orleans. We had an especially good time as we were traveling with other farm people. Charlotte had never hardly been outside of Vermont so she really had a good time. This pleased me.

When we went to New Orleans, we did not fly home with the rest of our group. We rented a car and drove along the gulf coast to Florida. We spent the night at a motel in Homosassa, which is located on the west coast of Florida. We liked the area. The next morning I said to Charlotte, "Let's look at some real estate." We contacted a Broker named Bob Folks at Trotter Real Estate right on US 19. He showed us three houses. I don't think that he thought that we were serious. I made him an offer on two of them. They were both accepted and we bought them. One of them was a bank repossession and was very nice, it had only been neglected a little. The other one belonged to a Canadian and had been completely trashed by the tenants that he had rented to. He was discouraged with it and wanted out.

We still had out plane tickets from New Orleans back to Vermont. It was about the same distance to Atlanta Georgia as it was back to New Orleans so we decided to drive to Atlanta, turn our car in there and fly home. I thought that the cost would be less as it would be a shorter flight. We arrived at the Atlanta airport. I went to turn our car in at the rental office. They charged me three hundred dollars more than it would have been. If we had taken it back to New Orleans. We went to the airline ticket counter thinking that we could get a refund on our airline tickets due to the shorter flight. It didn't work that way, instead it cost us almost five hundred dollars more. We learned an expensive lesson. Later we went back to Florida and fixed up the trashed house. We then sold it a young couple and financed it for them.

The following winter Charlotte and I started going to Florida for a couple of weeks. We still had the other house that we had purchased. Charlotte had furnished it from yard sales and auctions so it was quite comfortable. Each January we attended a real estate conference or seminar while in Florida. In the seminars they talked a lot about the importance of being able to get along with banks and bankers. They always portrayed bankers as being very cold, intimidating, and difficult to get along with. They stressed the importance of getting to know your banker by inviting him out to dinner and etc. I felt that we were very lucky in the part of Vermont where we came from as I knew all my bankers on a personal basis and had never felt intimidated by them. I had been doing many of the things that they were teaching such as buying, fixing up and reselling repossessed properties.

Noel Lussier was now the president of Caledonia National Bank and his brother Roger had been the president of Lyndonville Savings Bank for a number of years. I had been friendly with both the Lussiers and did business with both banks. Neither of the Lussiers had ever been to high school but both their banks were doing a lot of business and growing under their leadership. There was also a lot of competition between the two banks. Both of these banks often called me when they had properties to sell. I usually bought them. The banks had been very good to me. I appreciated this and always worked very hard to make sure to pay them as I agreed. I had a lot of respect for them.

Since giving up my partnership with Noel I had not done much business with him except through the bank. After Noel had been in the bank for a while, he started buying and selling farms again. Besides being president of the bank he was doing a big farm and cattle business. I understand that he was wheeling and dealing in several states. He seemed to be operating big although I never got to talk to him much except occasionally in the bank where he had a part-time office. You couldn't help but have respect for him. One day when I was in his office a fellow came in. He was about to lose his house to a tax sale if he didn't pay his taxes right away. He told Noel that he needed a loan. Noel explained that the bank had not had a very good past experience with him and that there was no way that he could approve another bank loan for him. Noel then pulled out his own check book and wrote him a check for the amount that he needed and told him to pay him back as soon as he could. After the fellow left, Noel turned to me and said, "What would you or I do if we couldn't borrow money when we needed it?" Noel seemed to have a heart of gold. Another time when I was in his office the phone rang. I don't know what the conversation was about except whatever it was that they were talking about Noel told the caller to mail it to the Bank. Noel then told him the name and address of the bank. The caller must have then asked how to spell Caledonia as Noel rummaged around on his desk and found an envelope with the banks return address on it. He then ran his finger along under the letters as he spelled Caledonia for the caller.

While Noel was president of Caledonia National Bank, they merged with two other Vermont banks, Bradford National Bank and First National Bank of Springfield. They put the ownership of all three banks into a holding company called Independent Bank Group and all the stock was converted to Independent Bank Group stock. The banks continued to operate independently of each other. Noel was the Chairman of Independent Bank Group and he became a Director of Bradford National Bank and still maintained the presidency of Caledonia National Bank. This apparently gave him a lot of power. Caledonia National Bank opened two branch offices one in Hardwick and one in St. Johnsbury. Noel hired Bob Platka who had been a vise president at Merchants Bank to come to work for him at Caledonia. He also hired Charlie Bucknam who had once worked for the Howard bank but who the past few years had been involved in a family jewelry business that did not seem to be going to well.

The president of Bradford Bank was Paul Gallerani who had run a slaughter house that had burned prior to his becoming a banker. There was a lot of talk around the country about what a good job Paul was doing and now Bradford Bank had grown under his leadership. I had known Paul when he had the slaughter house as I had sold him cattle on several occasions. I had also done some business with Bradford Bank and built up a good credit rating there.

On the morning November 1 of 1989, I received a call from Noel Lussier who was at Bradford National Bank. He said that he needed to borrow some money. He explained that he had several large farms on hand and was about to buy another farm. He needed to borrow $250,000, but had already borrowed up to his credit limit at Bradford Bank. Paul Gallerani, the Bradford Bank president, told him that if he could put the loan against someone else's credit line he could make Noel the loan. "Call Bill Hill" he said. Noel explained that he had sold some cows sold in Florida and would have no problem paying the loan back as soon as he got paid for the cows. He wanted to know if I would let the bank loan him money against my credit line. I had never known Noel not to do as he agreed or not to repay his debts. I said that it was okay as long as the bank approved. I knew that if Noel didn't pay I would be liable for the debt but I had never known him to not meet his obligations and I didn't question the banks method of doing business. As I explained earlier, I had a dealer credit line, which was set up for just such purposes, the making of third party loans.

Noel's youngest son Matt showed up at our house with two notes both of which had been made out by Paul Gallerani, the bank president. One note was made to Charlotte and me to be signed by Noel, and the other, which was identical except it was made to Bradford Bank for Charlotte and me to sign. After signing the notes, he had another paper, which Paul had made out, which was called a Statement of Purpose. This stated that the purpose of the loan was to purchase a farm, cattle, and machinery for resale. This is what both Noel and Paul had said that the loan was for. I had no problem signing it as the bank had drawn it up. Noel had to renew the loan a couple of times, each time making his own arrangements with the bank. He then paid the note off directly to the bank. The bank sent me back our note marked paid and I gave Noel back the note that he had signed.

When Caledonia Bank opened its branch bank in Hardwick, this made three banks here. Caledonia had bought an old house and converted in to a bank. The other two banks were a branch of Merchants Bank and a branch of Sterling Trust. Awhile later, Merchants Bank bought out Sterling Trust. Sterling had a relatively new building in the shopping center but only leased and didn't own it. Merchants apparently didn't need both locations and so were willing to give up the Sterling location. Noel wanted this building for his Caledonia Branch as it was a much better location than the building that they were presently in. In order to get it he had to purchase the whole shopping center. He kept the bank building and sold the rest of the shopping center to Tony Aiossa, the local attorney.

Caledonia now wanted to sell the building that they were moving out of. Hardwick has its own electric power company. They were interested in buying the building for their offices. Before they could buy it Charlie Bucknam who Noel had hired to be vice president of Caledonia Bank and his Wife Debra, an attorney who had been a partner of Tony Aiossa purchased it. The deed from Caledonia National Bank to the Bucknams was signed by Bob Platka an officer of Caledonia Bank. A few months later the Bucknams sold the building to the Hardwick electric Department.

Noel hired Gary Phillips to run the new branch bank. Gary had been a bank manager in this same bank building a few years earlier when it was owned and operated by Sterling Trust. He had been fired by Sterling for misconduct and making unsafe loans.

After Gary had been manager for a while, he called me and said that the bank wanted to sell a property with a mobile home and small garage on it to Jerry and Edna Clark. The price was $16,000, the Clarks had no down payment and Gary wanted to have me finance it through my dealer account. I thought that this was strange but Jerry Clark had worked for me on the farm, so I agreed to go along. The bank had Tony Aiossa, the local attorney, draw a deed from the bank to the Clarks. They then had him draw a mortgage made out to me and had the Clarks sign it then asked me to endorse over to the bank. I thought that it was odd that the bank wasn't financing their own properties hut instead asked me to. Later we will learn why.

I bought several more properties from both Caledonia and from Lyndonville Savings Bank. Some of these we will talk about later.

I was also involved in the daily operation of the farm still putting in long hours. It was hard to get and keep good help. George Preston had been my neighbor for many years. He had worked on neighboring farms and had held several other jobs. He wanted to come to work for me. George was very good with the cows and the machinery. He really liked farming. It was hard to get him to take a day off. He and his wife purchased a mobile home and set it up on the farm just below where Dean and Ann lived. We had been short of help and George had not been getting any days off. I talked him into taking Sundays off and I would do a double shift. The milking parlor had a pit area where you stood when milking. It was about twenty feet long and five feet wide with the cows on each side. At each end were four steel steps going down into the pit. One Sunday morning when I was milking alone. I ran up the steps to push a cow around in order to get the parlor gate closed. The cement floor was wet and I had on rubber boots and as I went to go back down the steps my feet slipped and I went flying right out over the pit landing with my full weight on the back of my neck and head on the bottom steel step. It kind of knocked me unconscious for a moment and it really hurt. I was able to get up and finish the milking, which probably took a couple of hours. I had to work most of the day as I was alone where there were usually two men. My neck really hurt and it was painful to turn or move my head. It was also hard to remember what I was supposed to be doing. That night I was unable to get into bed so I sat in a chair all night. I worked all week mostly in great pain and spent the nights in a chair.

The following Sunday it was my turn to work alone again. Charlotte came out to help me. Several times I couldn't remember where we were or what I was doing. She insisted that she rake me to the hospital. I reluctantly agreed to go as long as we could get right back as there was a lot of work to do. At the hospital they took some x-rays. The doctor said that I had broken my neck and he wanted to send me right to the Dartmouth Medical Center in Hanover New Hampshire. I told him that Charlotte could take me. He said that I should go immediately. He put one of those big bulky collars or neck braces around my neck and said to leave it on until I got there. When we got back in the car, I told Charlotte that there was no way that I could go to Hanover. I had to get back home and take care of my cattle. She said that she would take me back home but made me agree to go the next morning. On the way home from the hospital Charlotte wanted to stop at Curriers store in Glover to pick up a few groceries. I didn't want anyone to see me wearing that neck brace so I made her park down the road from the store and I slumped down while she was in the store. I had always heard people say when they saw somebody wearing one of those things around their neck. "He's probably trying to get a disability or a large insurance settlement." I didn't want anyone thinking that about me. When we got back to the farm, I worked the rest of the day feeding and milking the cows and all the other chores that go along with it. The next morning George was back Sally and I headed for Hanover. I didn't know it, but she had brought my tooth brush and other things as the doctor had told her that I wouldn't be coming back for a while.

I saw several doctors who gave me various rests and started to prescribe several things that the hospital would have to do to me. It looked like they wanted to keep me for weeks. Then they started to talk about what kind of insurance did I have. I said that I didn't think that I was covered. All of a sudden, all the expensive treatments boiled down to several simple tests and they let me go. I guess that my neck healed okay after a while. It hurt a lot and I had a hard time remembering things. Even today I can't remember everything that happened around that time.

We were raising corn on a neighboring farm and haying and chopping haylage on another rented farm. We were putting in a lot of hours. George was getting very tired and seemed to get worked up and irritated quite easily. One morning he and another hired man were working in the hay field. It was obvious that George was not feeling well. I tried to get him to go home and rest. He refused, he said that there was too much work to do and that he would be all right. Later that afternoon I did talk him into going home and told him that I would do the evening milking for him. Around nine o'clock that night I received a call from George's wife, Evelyn. She wanted to know if I could come right down to their mobile home. I asked what the problem was. She said that "there is something wrong with George. I think that he is dead." I quickly ran down. The rescue squad came and took him to the hospital. Charlotte and I took Evelyn to the hospital in the car. When we got there, the doctor confirmed that George was dead. This upset us very much. The next morning when the other hired man, who had worked with George, came into the barn I told him what had happened. He became very upset and started crying. We all missed George a lot, it was not the same without him.

The Vermont Land Trust bought the farm where we were raising corn. They said that their purpose was to buy up the development rights in agricultural land to make sure that it stayed in farming and would not be developed. They were looking for someone to buy this farm that would farm it. They had put a price on it. I had talked to Theryl Fischer, the land trust director, several times about purchasing it as that was where we raised much of our crops and feed. I wanted to expand and to operate this farm, and was already depending on it to raise much of my corn. I offered her what they were asking and gave her a deposit to show good faith. She kept saying that she was sure that there were some more offers floating around out there. I asked her several times if they had any other offers. She always said not yet but was sure that there would be some. She finally sent me back my deposit and sales agreement, with a letter saying that·they were going to look for another offer. I couldn't understand this. The Land Trust also bought the other farm that joined ours where we were cutting our hay and haylage. This was going to make it impossible for us to farm the way that we had been doing as we would not have enough land to raise our crops. We had three options. Cut our number of cows way down or plan to purchase a big percentage of our feed. Neither of these would leave us with a profitable operation. The third option was to sell.

I was now fifty four years old and still was bothered with my neck. We realized that I wasn't going to be able to keep up with the long hours and hard work for ever. We decided that we would offer the farm for sale. I ran a small ad in the USA Today newspaper. I received a call from a man in Houston, Texas, whose name was Kenneth Assad. He was very much interested in the farm. We made a video tape showing the farm, the land, the cattle, the farmhouse and the milking operation. After he saw this, he called and he and his wife wanted to come up for a real look. I met them at the Burlington Airport. They stayed with us for a couple of days. They were also very interested in the school system here as they had five children. They decided that they wanted to buy the farm, they really liked it. The Assads were citizens of South Africa. They had fled there due to the uncertain and dangerous conditions. They had escaped in a large boat and sailed to Texas with their five children. The Assads were both very well educated. The only problem was that I could see that they didn't have any money. I was not interested in financing the farm. So I introduced them to Noel Lussier the president of the bank and who had probably sold and financed more farms that any other banker in the area. After talking with them, Noel said that he couldn't see any way to get them financing either.

The Assads went back to Houston but didn't give up on their desire to purchase the farm. Ken Assad was calling me or Noel two or three times a day trying to figure out a way. Assad then came up with a Dr. Edwards in Houston who he said was a very good friend of his and had been putting some rather large deals together in the depressed Houston real estate market. Assad said that Edwards had access to foreign money and that perhaps there was a way that he could help to put the farm deal together. When Noel heard about Dr. Edwards and his ability to put large deals together with foreign money, he really perked up and wanted to meet this man.

Noel then brought a John McCormick into the picture. McCormick had appeared in the area a short while before this and represented himself to be a very wealthy man. The banks had set McCormick up in several large deals including two large automobile dealerships, a large manufacturing building in Bradford and a castle to live in, which had been owned by Bradford Bank. Being anxious to get his business the banks had over financed McCormick. Noel told Assad that if Dr. Edwards could arrange a twenty million dollar loan for McCormick, that Assad could have his money for the farm.

Around mid-November Assad and Dr. Edwards flew up to Vermont to meet the challenge. They met with Noel and McCormick. McCormick said that he had a very large trust fund in California called First American Financing Inc. This company purchased hospital receivables at a discount, then waited for the insurance companies to pay them. It was similar to a credit card setup. McCormick said that he could put over twenty million dollars' worth or receivables as security for this twenty million dollar loan. Noel then called a meeting with Assad, Edwards, Paul Gallerani, the Bradford National Bank president, Doug Gilmour, Noels partner and a director of First National Bank, and Tony Aiossa, Noels and the banks attorney. Papers were drawn up for Edwards to arrange the $20,000,000 loan for McCormick. Edwards and Noel were to get a commission of one and three quarters to two and a half percent of the loan amount, and Assad was to get a one million dollar loan at a very favorable rate. This agreement was signed by John McCormick, Kenneth Assad, or. Edwards and Noel Lussier. A second agreement was drawn that stated that if Edwards produced a commitment for the

$20,000,000 loan and McCormick didn't accept it or couldn't come up with the necessary collateral, Noel and the banks would loan Assad the one million dollars. This agreement was signed by Kenneth Assad, Noel Lussier, Caledonia National Bank president Paul Gallerani Bradford National Bank president and Doug Gilmour director of First National Bank, all members of Independent Bank Group.

Assad and Edwards went back to Houston to go to work on putting the $20,000,000 loan together. Shortly after Or. Edwards became ill and his health started failing. He later died. This didn't stop Assad, who continued to work very hard to put together the $20,000,000 loan for McCormick. Assad was on the phone several times a day with Noel, McCormick, Tony Aiossa and the banks. Assad told them that he was close to getting a commitment, but it would be necessary for him to move to Vermont with his family in order to finalize the deal. Noel and the banks arranged for him to move into the Hardwick Village Motel with his family and they ate in the restaurants.

Assad continued to work very hard out of Tony Aiossa's office and John McCormick's office. He finally came up with a loan commitment from an outfit in Englewood, New Jersey, called Leasetek Funding Group, managed by a man named Anthony Rosaro. Rosato furnished the names of six of his credit suppliers. Paul Gallerani said that he checked our all six of those credit institutions and Rosato and that they were all in very good standing.

One day in mid-December I ran into Ken Assad downtown. I asked him how he was making out with the McCormick financing. He said that they were having a meeting that afternoon at the main branch of Caledonia National Bank in Danville to put the finishing touches on the deal. I asked him if he thought that I could attend as I was interested as to whether he was going to buy my farm. He said to meet him before the meeting and he was sure that I would be welcome. Present at the meeting were Assad, McCormick, Lussier, Gallarani, Gilmour, Herb Gray another bank director, Tony Aiossa, and two men from Massachusetts, who were representing an insurance company who was going to insure McCormick's receivables that he was pledging as collateral for this loan. Everything sounded very good and everybody was excited as it looked like the $20,000,000 loan was about ready to close. One of the last things to do was to get a computer printout of McCormick's First American Financing Inc. receivables. This, McCormick said, would take about three days to produce and would be a stack of computer paper about four feet high.

On December 22, I got a call from the bank. It was Lussier who said that everything was in place and that the Assads would like to move out of the motel and into the farmhouse before Christmas. Could we be out? I talked to Charlotte who makes a big thing out of Christmas. The Christmas tree was up and she had the entire house decorated. We were expecting all the kids and grandchildren for Christmas. I had a little house about two miles away that I had bought from Caledonia National Bank. It was empty. We decided that we could move in there and try to hold Christmas there. We said that we would be out. We moved what we could into the little house including the decorated Christmas tree. We had to put most of our belongings in a storage building as this was a very small house as compared to the farmhouse.

I had drawn up a purchase and sale agreement for the sale of the farm plus a lease as we were not going to have the final closing until April 15. That was my birthday and I would be fifty-five, which would allow me to take the once-in-a-lifetime homestead tax deduction on the sale of our home. The price that Assad was paying was $700,000. Six hundred thousand was to go to us and the bank was to get $100,000 for putting the deal together. I was to get $50,000 now and the balance on April 15. Assad was to pay monthly rent in the meantime. We met two days before Christmas. We were out of the house. Present were Ken Assad and his wife Victoria, Charlotte, myself plus Lussier and Gilmour, from the bank. The Assads signed the purchase and sale agreement and the lease. Lussier then presented the Assads a $100,000 note to sign. Assads were to get $50,000 for operating cash and we were to get the other $50,000 for our down payment. Lussier then asked me to endorse the $100,000 note. I refused, as I wasn't going to give them my farm plus be responsible for another $100,000. Lussier explained that this was the only way that the bank could do it as the Assads had not established credit yet and had no collateral until they received title to the farm in April. He said that I did not need to worry as the $100,000 would be added to the real estate mortgage at the final closing. I was not happy with this arrangement so I asked Lussier if he would sign a paper to that effect and that I would be held harmless. He agreed. He signed it and he had Gilmour sign it.

The Assads went out and bought furniture, bicycles and several expensive pets and took over the farm that night. One of the first things that happened after this meeting was that all the Jersey cows that I sold Assads were moved to Lussiers barn. These were some of the best cows.

After Christmas Charlotte and I drove to Florida to spend some time and attend a real estate seminar. Charlotte tells how that worked out:

"Bill and I both liked the real estate seminars. There were classes on real estate and on getting along with banks and how to work with bankers. For some time, my mother had been having trouble with her knee and had gotten to where she could hardly walk. While we were gone she was scheduled to have an operation to replace her knee joint. We called home to see how she had made out. My father said that she didn't go as she was too scared. They had scheduled a new date to try it again. Bill said that we had better fly back home to be with her and see her through the operation. We gave up the seminar, caught a plane back to Vermont and my brother Wendell met us at the airport. Mother would listen to Bill and now agreed to if we would go with her. She had the operation and really looked relieved as soon as it was over. Soon she was walking as good as new. I believe that it was of Bill being there to support her. She looked up to him as I did. He was kind and honest and helped everybody."

A short while after Assads moved onto the farm, Lussier convinced Assad to take over another farm, which the banks were having problems with. This farm was in Randolph, which was over fifty miles away. They immediately transferred some of what had been my cows down there and put new mortgages to the bank on them. This put Assad way in over his head and he was not able to handle it financially or physically. The Randolph farm had been a big loser and was still a big loser. However, Lussier maintained that everything was going well with Assad and that he was going to make it. Assad was working, using his contacts, to put other financial deals together for Lussier. Lussier said that this would bring in extra money for Assad and he would soon be out of debt. The final closing on our farm was to take place on April 15.

85

McCormick's deal never did close. It turned out that McCormick never had any such First American Financing Company and that he had no equity in anything. He had misled the banks with false financial statements and false tax returns. He had apparently done this in Connecticut also before coming to Vermont. McCormick was later sentenced to prison for bank fraud. It was now up to Lussier and the banks to Finance Assad. Tony Aiossa who was supposed to be handling the legal work on the buyer's side kept postponing the closing I was not happy about this and I think that I irritated Tony a little by letting him know that I was not happy with the delay. The closing was finally scheduled for May 4. I thought it strange that it was being held in Aiossa's office rather than the bank. Present were Ken and Victoria Assad, Charlotte and myself. Tony Aiossa and a man named Mannie Cannis from First National Bank. Cannis had brought with him a check for $650,000 from the First National Bank but knew little more than that about what was going on. Aiossa said that the bank wasn't going to accept the $100,000 that it expected to receive right now. They were going to put it in a savings account in my name and have me assign it to the bank. Assad was asked to produce a $1,000,000 life insurance policy with the bank as the beneficiary. Aiossa claimed to have made several mistakes in the paper work and had his secretary type some things over several times even after they had been signed. He was very anxious to get the closing over and he didn't want to bother to prorate the rent that Assad was paying.

The Assads lived a very luxurious life style and everyone thought that they had a lot of money. Every salesman in the country was there to sell him anything or idea that they could. The banks kept lending him money to keep going and Lussier said that he was doing fine. I did not pay much attention to Assads and the farm after the closing. All I knew was that he wasn't running it the way that I ran it.

I had another thirty acre field about a mile from the farm. It was fairly flat and gradually rose up away from the town road. From this higher spot there was a nice view. I took Charlotte up to this spot in the thirty acre field. She liked the location and the view very much. We decided to build another house instead of taking the once in a lifetime tax deduction. That night we drew a diagram of the house that we wanted to build. Charlotte wanted a big kitchen and a big living room due to all the family that we had. I wanted to have some office space as I was now going to again become more active in the real estate and auction business. Within a couple of hours, we had sketched our house pretty much the way that we wanted it. I called my brother Steve, who was a carpenter and asked him if he wanted to build a house. He said that he would as soon as he finished up the jobs that he had going. I got the cellar hole dug and had the foundation poured by the time that Steve was ready. He brought a couple of men with him and I had a couple of men. It didn't take long to frame up the house. It was long with the kitchen on one end and my office space on the other. The living room area was in the center with a large hall and stairway leading up to the two bedrooms and laundry room upstairs. The kitchen and office were only one story. Beyond the kitchen we built a patio with cupboards a sink, stove and restaurant type grill for summer time use.

While we were building the house I heard about a twenty by forty in ground swimming pool in Craftsbury that the owners no longer used and were going to fill in. Rodney one of Charlotte's sons was in the swimming pool business. He came over and we went up and dug this pool up. It was a lot of hard work as we had to break a lot of cement to get it out. We installed it just beyond the patio and put the pump and filters in the cellar. On the other end of the house beyond the office we had a car port.

On our way to Florida and back we had seen several houses with large porches and pillars. We thought that this would look good on our house so we built a big front porch with four pillars and a wooden walk that goes way around the house. Many of the building supplies that we used I had bought at auctions. The offices and the bathroom have wide pine board floors that I got a deal on. The two bathrooms upstairs in the bedrooms each have the old claw foot bath tubs. One of these I got from a fellow who was using it for a cattle water tub out in the pasture. I paid five dollars for it. The other one a cousin of mine was keeping minnows in. I traded him an old stock tank that I had for it. We also bought a lot of odds and ends of tile, which we used in the downstairs bathroom and shower. The colors didn't exactly match but it still looks good. We had enough to do several floors and the halls. We painted the house white and it has a red metal roof. We kept watch and bought old furniture and refinished it to furnish the house with. It took most of the summer to get everything done. Charlotte tells her version:

"We were living in the little blue house that we had moved into after we sold the farm. Bill took me up in a field above the farm that we had kept. He asked me if I would like a home up there I loved it the view was great. That night I helped Bill draw some plans on the back of a big envelope. What I wanted was a big kitchen and a big living room so we could have the family in."

"When we started building, I put in stone walls. My son Paul helped me put in some flower gardens. Bobby, our son-in-law, did all the wiring. Rodney, another son, helped to build stone walls and stone steps. He and Bill dug up a large swimming pool and installed that. We planted some apple trees. Clay, Bill's son built a little elevator in the closet next to the fireplace that brought the wood up from down cellar. This was real neat. Everyone helped to make this our home."

"Bill had a chance to sell the little blue house before our new house was ready. We put an old couch that made into a bed in the cellar of our new house to sleep on. During the day we put a blue tarp over it to keep the dirt and sawdust of it while they were working. We got many of our building supplies from auctions, second hand places and anywhere that we could find them. This home was us, all of us."

I had spent most of the summer working on the house but managed to do a few auctions and real estate deals. Toward the end of August I received a call from Noel Lussier. The bank had a property that they wanted to sell me. It was a large motel in Plymouth New Hampshire. I was really not too interested as it sounded like a big deal, it was too far away and I had no experience in the motel business. He really wanted me to take a look at it. I agreed to take a look. I went with him and Paul Gallariani. The bank had taken it back in the early part of the summer. They had put the motel into a new corporation called BFC, which stood for Bradford Caledonia and First National, the three banks in Independent Bank Group. The motel had one hundred and five guest rooms. There was some large convention rooms with movable walls so that they could be opened up or divided into smaller rooms, depending on the need. There was a large kitchen and a dining room that would seat over two hundred people. There was a good size bar and lounge. Then there was a very large indoor swimming pool.

I was introduced to the motel manager, Rochell Inman who had put together what seemed like a very good marketing plan to gain new business. Paul gave me a copy of an appraisal showing a fair market value of $3,900,000. He said that the BFC Corporation had a Day's Inn franchise that produced a lot of business. He also stated that there was a positive cash flow of forty to fifty thousand per month. I found some projections that the previous owners had made, which didn't substantiate these profits. I asked Paul about this. He said that the White Mountain Motel, which was its previous name, had fifteen owners who were not getting along and who had been skimming the profits from the motel. He said that they came up with these projections to try to get the bank to loan them some more money and lower their payments so that they could skim off some more. That he said is the reason that the Bank had foreclosed on the motel. Paul said that this motel was probably the best money maker that he had ever seen.

Paul and Noel said that as they had already formed the BFC Corporation, which had all the licenses, the Day's Inn franchise, and everything else that the motel needed to operate and make money, it would be an easy transaction and would have no new stand-up costs. They wanted to sell me the corporation so there would be no need to renew any licenses or anything. They made it sound like a good deal but I was not sure that it was for me. Paul said that if he weren't involved in running the bank this motel would be the business that he would want. They wanted $2,600,000 and said that they could finance it one hundred per cent by taking two houses in trade. One was a house in Danville that I had bought from Caledonia National Bank and had fixed up. I had about $125,000 in this house, which the bank was willing to allow me toward the motel. The other house was a house in White River Vermont that they wanted to sell me for $275,000 then take back in trade. They said that Bradford Bank would then take a mortgage on the motel for $2,200,000. I reminded them that I still owed Caledonia National Bank for the Danville house, even though there was no mortgage on it, and that I wasn't in a position to pay for the White River house at the present time. Paul said you don't need to worry about it as the profits from the motel will pay both of them off in a few short months. Paul said that the bank would leave the houses in the names of their present owners until the bank could sell them. I did not make a decision right away. They contacted me several times. I had bought a lot of properties from these banks. They had never misled me that I knew of and I had a lot of respect for both Noel and Paul. Another thing that convinced me that this must be a good deal was the fact that the bank was willing to finance it 100 percent by using the houses. Banks don't usually finance things that can't pay for themselves. I finally told them that I would probably go along with the deal.

About four days later, which was September 12, 1990, I received a call from Noel Lussier saying that Bradford Bank was ready to close on the motel. I had seen nothing in writing about the closing. He said that it had to be done that day. He also said that there might be some things at the closing that I might not like but to go ahead and sign them anyway and that I could straighten them out with Paul later.

I was busy that afternoon so I called Bradford Bank. Paul was not in. I talked to Laurette Sweet, a vice president and loan officer of the bank. She said that the closing had to take place that day and that she would wait at the bank until I could get there no matter what time it was.

I arrived at Bradford Bank about six o'clock that evening. The only people present were Laurette Sweet and Stephen Males, an attorney from Manchester New Hampshire. I had never met or heard of Males. Paul had told me that the bank was planning to take a loss on the two houses of about $150,000. He said that they were taking a big loss on the motel but didn't want to show the whole loss there so were going to show about $150,000 on the two houses. I expected that they would have some sort of agreement at the closing showing that the bank was getting the houses in trade as they were not taking title to them. Instead Males had prepared a $250,000 note for me to sign. This was a non interest bearing note and stated that it would be paid by the sale of the two houses. It was not the way that we had discussed, but I was told by Males that it would serve the same purpose. There was nothing explaining about me paying for the White River house. The $250,000 note was written as if I had already owned it. They had also conveyed the Day's Inn franchise from Bradford Bank to BFC and at the closing they took back a collateral assignment of the franchise. Then there was the big note for $2,200,000, which was secured by the motel. There was a packet of papers about an inch thick that Males had prepared.

As the Danville house was in my name, Paul had asked me to reduce the price with the brokers that I had it listed with down to around $80,000 as they were going to take a loss and get it sold. This I did.

Two days after the closing I went to the motel to meet with Rochell Inman, the manager. No one from the bank had bothered to tell her that I had bought the BFC Corporation that owned the motel.

A few days later I got a call from Noel Lussier saying that Paul Gallarani had called him and said that the $250,000 note, which I had signed at the motel closing had to be paid right off. As a matter of fact, I received several calls, they were in a hurry. This was contrary to what the note said and I couldn't understand this so I went to see Noel at Caledonia Bank in Danville. I met with Noel and Bob Placka who was now the executive officer of Caledonia bank and a director of Bradford Bank. They didn't offer an explanation but said to go to another bank and borrow $80,000 on the Danville house that I owned and send it to Bradford Bank. They said that they would figure out a way to take care of the other $170,000 that was on the White River house. I was uncomfortable about this and I also reminded them that I still owed their bank for the Danville house even though they didn't have a mortgage on it. Placka said that it wasn't the way that they would ordinarily do things but that they needed to keep doing business and that the motel should have no trouble paying it off. I borrowed the $80,000 on the Danville house as they suggested from Lyndonville Savings Bank and sent it to Bradford Bank on September 25, 1990. I gave Lyndonville Savings Bank a first mortgage on the house to secure the loan.

A short while later I received a phone call from Day's Inn of America in Atlanta Georgia. They said that the heard that I had bought the motel. They said that I couldn't continue to operate as a Day's Inn without a franchise. I explained that I had a franchise as I had bought the stock in the BFC Corporation that owned the motel, and who already had a franchise that Bradford Bank had conveyed to BFC. They said that

Bradford Bank owed them about $30,000 but had never had a Day's Inn franchise and neither had BFC. They said that I couldn't use their reservation system or operate as a Day's Inn until I got a franchise. They said that they would send me a new application. It arrived in a few days. In order to apply for a franchise they wanted a $37,000 nonrefundable franchise application fee. A $100 per room fee was also required totaling another $10,500. Then in order to get the franchise they required that I pay the $30,000 that the bank owed them and the past due fees that White Mountain Motel, the former owners of the motel, had never paid them. In all they wanted over $100,000.

I called Steve Males, the attorney that had done the work for the closing. He had charged the Bank over $6,000 and me over $3,500. I didn't think that in this day and age that an attorney could represent both the buyer and the seller. In his bill he had several charges for contacting Day's Inn and for reviewing the franchise. I figured that he had to know that there was never any franchise even though he had prepared documents for the closing that indicated there was one. He did contact Day's Inn but he was not able to do anything to straighten the franchise out. I later learned from Males that he knew that it was necessary for BFC to get a franchise. Males said that he had filed an application with Day's Inn Franchising on behalf of Bradford Bank himself. Males stated that he had been assured by Paul Gallerani that the franchise fees had been paid and that the franchise was all in place. Males further stated that the final terms of the sale and the financing to Hill were faxed to him by Bradford Bank on September 11, 1990 and the bank wanted to close the next day September 12.

Males said that he did not prepare the document entitled "Assignment of Franchise." This he said was something that Gallerani had done on his own. Males went on to say that he had placed in the closing documents language, which said that the "seller makes no warranties or representations of the existence or validity of any franchise agreement with 'Day's Inn.' This was specifically requested by Gallerani to be added to the closing documents." Males said that prior to the closing he questioned the need for this language and was told by Gallerani that Bradford Bank was just acting conservatively. He said that Lorette

Sweet, advised him that Bradford Bank was so conservative that it didn't even know what a condominium was, nor did it want to know.

Males said that he entered this language even though he had prepared the Collateral Assignment of Franchise. He said that he believed that the Franchise was in existence.

Males then said, "I was satisfied with the approval letter and a representation by Gallerani that the documents had been filed and the fee had been paid. I worked with Gallerani for a period of two years with regards to the Day's Inn property in Plymouth, New Hampshire. Over that time I had no information that would lead me to suspect Gallerani of improper dealings or fraudulent behavior. In fact Lorette Sweet had no knowledge of any fraudulent behavior by Gallerani."

By October, only three weeks after I took over the motel, it started to run into cash flow problems. Tom Lauzon, my accountant, Rochell Inman, the motel manager and I spent a lot of time looking for ways to cut costs and to increase business and become more efficient. Tom said that the morel had a fair market value of less than zero from an accounting standpoint, based on past performance. Tom Lauzon and I went to Bradford Bank to explain to Paul Gallarani that the motel was not generating the profits that he had promised. There was no positive cash flow like he has assured me that there would be and that we could see even tougher times for the motel with winter coming on. Paul listened and then he said that his hands were tied and that there was nothing that he could do, "try one of the other banks" he said. I left there kind of discouraged as I felt that Paul had let me down. I then went to see Noel Lussier and told him what had happened. He acted surprised but he called Gary Phillips, the manager of the Hardwick branch of Caledonia Bank and arraigned a $75,000 line of credit for BFC and the motel, to get it on its feet, he said. I did not feel that this was the answer, it was only going to get us in deeper. I did however use the money for operating costs and to make the monthly payments to Bradford Bank.

We did not get on the Day's Inn reservation system for about three months. This did not help business. We were still not on the reservation system in January of 1991 so I went to Atlanta Georgia, to the Day's Inn headquarters and met with Jim Darby, their Vise President. He was very unhappy with the bank for what they had done. I was able to negotiate a new contract for a much smaller fee. I also had it put in the contract that I could transfer the ownership of the motel once without requiring a new franchise fee as long as they approved of the new owner. I figured that this would make it easier for me to resell the motel.

EXTENSION ANNUAL REPORT 1985

Six years ago Jo-Ann Pert lived on the run. Evicted from one broken-down apartment after another, Jo-Ann and her husband not only had no place to call home, but their self-respect was about as low as it could go.

On February 25, 1986, Jo-Ann made the final payment on 14 acres of land, five years after she took out a loan for the land and a mobile home. It is no coincidence that it was also five years ago that Jo-Ann first met Orleans County Extension Nutrition Aide, Sally Hill. The self- respect, courage, and knowledge necessary for taking out the loan were, according to Jo-Ann, a direct result of her classes with Sally.

"It was Sally who helped me get the loan for my house and land," explains Jo-Ann. Hands on her hips, head held back, the same woman who six years ago "paid rent whenever I felt like it," says with a voice full of pride. "Now we've got our own home."

How did EFNEP, the Expanded Food and Nutrition Education Program, evoke such a change? What does Sally Hill teach in her classes?

To be sure the statewide food and nutrition curriculum that has been developed by EFNEP over the past 17 years is a large part of what Sally teaches. With Jo-Ann there were baking lessons, exercises on the four basic food groups, diet programs, and lessons on saving money. Since her home visits ended, Jo-Ann has attended-and organized-several of Sally's group classes: four week sessions on nutrition and budgeting.

For example, at a recent group session Sally packed into an hour and a half a slide show on wise supermarket shopping, a review of the four basic food groups, a baking demonstration of bran muffins for the microwave ("A muffin, a glass of milk, some juice, and there's breakfast for the kids!"), a taste test comparing three brands of vegetables, a cooking demonstration of a cream soup mix, and a group discussion of convenience foods.

What do the women get out of the curriculum? "Before I met Sally, I was always giving my kids candy," confides a member of one of Sally's groups. "Now I give them fruit-they love it-and carrots, that's a real treat for them. They'll eat three pounds of carrots at once if I don't stop them!"

Others agree that their menus are more varied-something their families like a lot. Recipe handouts are a popular part of each class.

And financial savings are enormous, mostly due to increased consumer awareness. Sally's students know how to read labels, know to buy in bulk, and know that there are at least two meals in every chicken. Says Jo Ann, "Six years ago, just with my husband, I was spending sixty to seventy dollars a week on food. Now with three kids I spend less than that, and we're eating better than we ever did."

But along with the recipes and the shopping tips, along with the four basic food groups, come lessons in self-respect, in pride, and in making necessary changes in one's life. "Because," says Sally, "you can't teach them to bake muffins if there are other problems in the way. No one is going to care about what she eats if she doesn't care enough about herself."

So with every visit and group lesson comes a warm, sincere hello, a "My, you're looking good today," and "I can see you've worked hard cleaning this kitchen." The message that Sally cares about her clients is loud and clear.

Also along with every lesson comes the lesson that is inherent in Sally herself: despite having been poor once ("I once lived in a car for a week"), having struggled through many of the same problems her clients face, Sally has motivation, ambition, optimism, and warmth. And this speaks more to her clients, perhaps, then anything else. "Sally has a unique personality for the job," says Judy Boyd Campbell, Extension Home Economist in Orleans County and Sally's supervisor. "It takes that personal touch to make the nutrition information come alive for these families."

Sally estimates she sees 130 different individuals each month, roughly thirty a week. Many of these hear about her by word-of-mouth women whose friends or relatives have had home visits with Sally. Many are referred to her by local agencies such as Orleans/Essex Home Health or Northeast Kingdom Mental Health Services. "The agencies know me very well," says Sally with a laugh. "And because of all our referrals," adds Judy Boyd Campbell, "the agencies speak well of the Extension Service."

"It's the dynamic way she gets involved in the program that makes it so successful," explains Leonard Wellman, district welfare director. "Sally believes in what she's doing. My goal would be to have all 1,200 of our food stamp clients go through her program." Two hundred already have. That's two hundred families who know their four basic food groups, know how to stretch their food dollars, and because they've learned from Sally, know that they have what it takes to own fourteen acres of land, to change their lives.

Says Sally, "The most important thing I can teach these folks is 'Hey, I'm worth something.'"

May 29, 1987

Sally Hill
PO Box 15
29 Elm Street c/o WF Hill
Hardwick, VT
05843

Dear Sally:

I regret that neither I nor Carol Fitzgerald can participate in your farewell party.

The UVM Extension Service wishes you the very best of success as you move to your next career. The Vermont EFNEP program is better today because of your dedication, hard work, enthusiasm, willingness to experiment and try new ways, and your genuine leadership at the local level. You had understanding, empathy and rapport with low income families. You could communicate with them and they could talk to you. You were very effective in helping us tell the EFNEP story to everyone, including influential leaders, community leaders, state senators, and legislators, national policy makers, and others. When you explained it, people listened and became enthused about the concept and its impact.

As associate director in the earlier days and interim director now, I think you have helped me enhance my understanding of the changing needs of low income families. While the morale of Extension faculty and staff vacillated up and down over time, you always, even if funds were to be cut off the next day, maintained an infectious positiveness and optimism.

Thank you for your advice and meritorious service during the past fourteen years. We wish you happiness and success as you move forward. If you are in the Burlington area, be sure to stop in.

Sincerely,
Bob Honnold
Interim Director
BH/c
July 19, 1988

Mr. Pat McKeon
Bank of New England North
61 Merrimack
Lowell, Massachusetts
01853
RE: Market Value Appraisal
Kings Court Inn(105-room motel)
Interstate 93 at Exit 27
(Hw. 3) Plymouth & Campton, New Hampshire

Dear Mr. McKean:

As requested, an inspection and appraisal of the above referenced property has been made. Based upon the data contained in said appraisal report and upon pertinent data available to us as of July 19, 1988, our conclusion as to the estimated fair market value of the subject property, as though converted into a Day's Inn or equal national lodging franchise, was:

$3,910,000
THREE MILLION NINE HUNDRED
TEN THOUSAND DOLLARS

Within the limitations specified herein and hereafter, this appraisal has been made in accordance with the Standards of Professional Ethics of the American Institute of Real Estate Appraisers of the National Association of Realtors and those of the other professional organizations of which the undersigned are members.

The fee for this investigation and appraisal report is in no manner contingent upon the amount of the value estimated herein.

The appraisers have no present or contemplated interest in the property evaluated herein other than that which might properly come before them in their profession as Appraisers-Realtors.

Respectfully submitted,
Reginald-Spencer, MAI, SRPA
Thomas J. Small, Associate

Bill Hill Box 15
Hardwick, Vt. 05843
Dear Bill,

This letter is to affirm that I was present when you and Paul Gallerani visited the property just prior to your purchase.

At that time, I was advised by Paul Gallerani that he would handle the financial discussions and the only input he wanted from me was on the marketing plan.

In my presence, he stated that the hotel could carry itself and would have a positive cash flow immediately. This was definitely contrary to the past history, financial statements and future projections for the property.

I was never asked for my opinion on the matter.

Sincerely,
Rochell R. Inman
General Manager

ASSIGNMENT OF FRANCHISE

FOR VALUABLE CONSIDERATION, Bradford National Bank of PO Box 393, Main Street, Bradford, Vermont 05033, hereby assigns all of its rights, title and interest in and to the Day's Inn Franchise, located in Campton, New Hampshire, including the use of the trade name 'Day's Inn' to BFC INC., a New Hampshire Corporation having its principal place of business at Exit 27 off I-93, Campton, NH.

BRADFORD NATIONAL BANK
By_____
Paul J. Gallerani, witness

CHAPTER 6

Soon after I got the Day's Inn franchise they sent some of their people to inspect the motel for which we received a top rating.

I heard from Donald Coty, a friend of mine, that he had been approached by the same bankers to purchase the motel before I bought it. Coty told me that the banks had offered him a similar deal of taking a house in trade that he owned plus the same White River house that he did not own. He said that the price they were asking him was $2,900,000, which was $300,000 more than they asked me, but they were allowing him $600,000 for the two houses. Coty said that Lussier and Gallerani had just about convinced him to go along with the deal when another bank director walked in to the room. When Gallerani told him that Coty was buying the motel, the other director asked, "What are we getting for it, $2,700,000?" At this point, Coty said that he knew that he was being taken by Lussier and Gallerani. Coty said that he had his son, an accountant, call Fred Deschger, a previous owner of the motel prior to the White Mountain group. Fred said that the motel did not have a positive cash flow as represented by Gallerani Coty had relayed this information back to the bankers. Coty said that a short while later that a bank officer called Fred and told him to keep his mouth shut about the condition of the motel.

In mid-February I received a letter from the New Hampshire Electric company stating that for the motel to be a customer and receive any electricity from them they would need a $20,000 deposit or an irrevocable letter of credit of $20,000 from the bank. This was another shocker that I wasn't prepared for. This was not supposed to happen as I had been assured by Gallerani that the bank had taken care of all these things when they formed the BFC Corporation. We had been paying our monthly bills and were not behind. The Electric company had just found out that I had purchased the BFC Corporation that owned the motel. I sent a copy of their letter to the Bradford Bank to get their reaction. It wasn't long in coming. I receive back a letter from the bank dated March 1, 1991 signed by Laurette Sweet seating that they were not interested in helping me.

I was upset about this so I called Paul Gallerani at the bank. Paul contacted the electric company and got them to delay the deposit or letter of credit until the middle of April. I kept contacting Noel Lussier and Gallerani to try to straighten out the mess with the motel as they had completely misrepresented it and there was no way that it could pay for itself, much less the two houses. They suggested that I try to resell it and get out of it that way. They suggested a few prospects but none of them either had any money or were very interested.

On Tuesday morning April 9, 1991 I read in the Burlington Free Press that Paul Gallerani and Herb Gray, a Bradford Bank director had been fired and expelled from the bank and that Noel Lussier and Doug Gilmour, a First National Bank director had resigned. This was a big shock not only to me but to everybody in Northern Vermont and New Hampshire. This was big news, it was plastered all over the TV and in every newspaper. People couldn't believe it and this was all that people could talk about. They were being accused of bank fraud and mismanagement of the bank business.

I was at a loss as to what to do but I knew that something had to be done about the motel as there was no way that it was going to survive the way that they had set it up and I didn't have the funds to keep it going and make the payments to the bank. I needed to get it across to the bank somehow that this was not working and was not going to work even though we had been slowly improving business. On April 12, I went to Bradford Bank to thy to find out who was now in charge. Also I still needed a letter of credit for the New Hampshire Electric Company. I could not find anybody in the bank that would talk about anything much less make any decisions. Not getting anywhere there I went to see Winston Oaks a Bradford Bank director who owned a large building supply business just down the road a couple of miles from the bank. I told him about the problems with the motel and the electric company. Winston was not happy with the way that the bank had been creating me. He said that he would get right hold of John Zampieri another bank director who was now the acting chairman for Bradford Bank. I didn't hear anything back from them.

The newspaper said that now that Noel Lussier was gone Robert Forguites was the acting chairman of Independent Bank Group, the holding company that owned all three banks. I called Bob on Sunday April 21. I told him about the serious problems that we had with the motel and that I would like to meet with somebody that would be willing to talk about it and that could make some decisions. Bob said that there would be a board meeting the following Tuesday, April 23, at Bradford Bank and that he would make arrangements for me to go in and talk to the whole board. I asked him if they had the power and authority to make decisions so that we could decide what action to take. He assured me that they did.

On Tuesday I drove to Bradford to meet with the board. I told them what the problems were and how the motel had been misrepresented and what had happened with two houses that they had agreed to take in trade. I tried to explain that it was not a problem that was just going to go away and that I would be willing to work with them to reach a solution but that there was no way that I could do it alone. The board listened and asked a few questions. They said that they had never heard of Stephen Males, the lawyer who handled the motel closing. Laurette Sweet explained to them that Paul Gallerani had contacted him. For some reason Paul hadn't wanted to use the banks regular lawyer. The board didn't seem too happy about using Males. I told them about the New Hampshire Electric Company and the need for a letter of credit. They said that they would take care of that right away. Winston Oaks started to talk about the White River house but Laurette Sweet cut in and changed the subject. Nobody wanted to say too much. John Zampieri said that they would get back to me. I did not think that I had heard him right as we had not even tried to discuss any solutions. I told them that I was there to get a decision on what we were going to do. John then said that they could not make any decision because Mike Flipiak, President of First National Bank, wasn't there. John suggested that I go to First National Bank in Springfield and meet with Flipiak. I left the meeting very discouraged. When I got back home, I called Bob Forguites again and told him that John Zampieri said that they couldn't make any deals or decisions because Mike Flipiak wasn't at the meeting. Bob told me that it wasn't necessary for Mike to have been there, that the board had full authority to make any decisions. This was very discouraging.

Back in September, about the time that I bought the motel, Kenneth Assad met with Noel Lussier as he was unable to make his payments to the bank on the farm. Lussier told him that he needed to have an auction and sell his cattle and machinery. Lussier told him that this would get him out of his mess, which he was unable to handle. Assad came to see me told me what Lussier wanted him to do. Assad wanted to know if I would work with Lussier and Doug Gilmour to put on an auction. He said that he would feel better if I was involved. He also felt that I knew more about the farm as I had lived and farmed there for over thirty years. In the short time that Assad had farmed there the machinery had taken an awful beating and become broken and needed a lot of repair. My Son Clay worked sixteen to eighteen hours a day the two weeks before the auction fixing and repairing the machinery and equipment.

Even after the auction there was still not enough money to pay off all of Assad's bills. Lussier and the bank were giving the Assads money to live on.

I decided that I would go to Springfield, which is well over one hundred miles away try to talk to Mike Flipiak, as John Zampiere had suggested. Kenneth Assad, also wanted to talk to Flipiak about the balance of his loan on the farm. We decided to ride down together. I had never met Mike Flipiak. When we got into his office, Mike spent quite a bit of time telling us about how important that he was that he didn't make mistakes and that he documented everything for future reference. He said that he knew everything that went on in his bank, that his bank wasn't like the two other banks. Kenneth Assad told Mike that he had no way to pay off the rest of the loan on the farm and that he would like to deed the farm back to the bank in a friendly foreclosure in exchange for a clean credit rating from the bank. Flipiak listened to him and seem to agree to this. Assad then left the office while I discussed my business with Flipiak. After Assad went out, Flipiak started to question me about the farm deal. He thought that I should be responsible as I had sold it to him. I told him that was not the case nor the agreement when Assad bought the farm. Flipiak said that it was all spelled out in a commitment letter before the closing. I laughed and said what commitment letter, that I had never seen any commitment letter. Flipiak became very frustrated and said that his bank never made any loans without first issuing a commitment letter. I told him that I had never seen one on that deal. He became very angry and started pounding the table and saying, "I will show you the commitment letter I promise that I will show you the commitment letter." I told him that I would like to see it. He had his secretary get the folder that had the paperwork for the farm deal. When he opened the folder, there was only a yellow sheet of paper with a couple of numbers on it. Flipiak became furious. He wanted to know who had closed the deal. I told him that Tony Aiossa closed in his office and that Mattie Canis from the Northfield branch of First National Bank brought the money to the closing. Flipiak went wild. He tried to call Canis but he couldn't dial the phone he was shaking so. He knocked the phone on the floor as he became more wound up.

After that he had his secretary dial it for him. When he got Canis on the phone, he ordered him to fax right down a copy of the commitment letter and the closing papers. He told him that he would give him one minute and that his job was on the line. In about a minute the fax machine rang and out came a copy of that same yellow paper and that was all. This through Flipiak into a terrible tantrum. He started yelling, "I will kill! I will kill!" and swearing. As he ran around the office, he kept leaping up the wall and throwing anything that he could get his hands on. I have never seen anything like it. I left. I did not try to talk to him about the motel.

When I got back home, I called Laurette Sweet at the bank and asked her about Flipiak. She didn't have anything good to say about him. She called him dumb and said that she wouldn't trust him. I then called Winston Oaks and asked him about Flipiak. Winston said that Flipiak had some mental problems an acted this way sometimes. I couldn't imagine how I was going to work out anything with this man. A couple of days later I called Bob Forguites and asked him what kind of a person this Flipiak was and told him what had happened. Bob didn't say much about Flipiak but he did say that there was going to be a holding company meeting that night at Bradford Bank. I called Laurette Sweet at the bank and inquired about the holding company meeting that evening. She said that there was not going to be any meeting and that the bank was going to foreclose on the motel if I couldn't get all the problems corrected in the next thirty days. Being really frustrated I drove to Bradford about sixty miles to see Winston Oaks a Bradford Bank director. Winston said that there was a holding company meeting that evening at Bradford. I told him that I would like to attend to discuss the motel. He said that wouldn't be possible but for me to wait by my phone and that they would call me from the meeting at 7:30 sharp. I waited but no call came. At 8:15 I called Bradford Bank and talked to Laurette Sweet and John Zampieri. They both said that no decision could be reached as only two directors had showed up but that they were going to meet again the following Monday and would have some answers then. Later that evening I called Graham Blake, a director and he told me that there were eight directors at the meeting. I later was able to get a copy of the minutes of the meeting that confirmed this. I had been lied to again. Graham also told me that Jack Howard who worked for Noel Lussier had borrowed $170,000 from Caledonia National bank to pay the rest of the $250,000 note that I had borrowed the $80,000 from Lyndonville Bank for right after the closing.

On Friday April 26, I decided to try Mike Flipiak again so I called him. He said that the banks would take the motel back. He wanted me to come clear back down to Springfield the next Monday and bring a copy of my financial statement with me. I drove all the way to Springfield, over one hundred miles one way, and gave Flipiak my financial statement but got no answers. Flipiak said that he would call me back by Wednesday May 1. He didn't call so I waited until Friday and called him. He still had nothing to offer except he told me not to worry. He said that he wanted to visit the motel and look around. I told him that he was perfectly welcome to. I then called Rochell at the motel and told her to show him whatever he wanted to see.

When I was at the Bradford Bank board meeting, I was told that a letter of credit was being sent to the New Hampshire Electric Company. On May 3, they called from the motel and said that the electric company was there to shut off the electricity even though we were paid up to date, as they had not received any letter from the bank. Stuart Hill who was working in my office took the call and then called Laurette Sweet at the bank. She said that she had phoned it just the night before at 6:00 May 2.

In the next couple of weeks I called Mike Flipiak several times. He always told me that he "was waiting to see what was out there," whatever that meant. Mike had told Rochell at the motel not to worry as the bank would take care of any expense that the motel couldn't cover from its income.

Monday June 10, 1991 I called Mike Flipiak again. Mike said the bank had a new title search done on the motel and the only thing that they found was a lean by Roy's Refrigeration for an unpaid bill I told Mike that this was for some work that the bank had done before I owned the motel but that I had taken care of it and it was no longer in effect. Mike then said that the bank was willing to take back the motel. He said that he was waiting for a new appraisal and that he would call me back Tuesday June 11 with a final proposal. I waited for several days beyond June 11 for Mikes call but it didn't come. I tried to call him several times but I couldn't reach him and he didn't return my calls. When I finally did reach him, he said that the new appraisal came in at $1,450,000. He said that the bank would take the motel back at that figure and not a penny more and that I would be liable for any difference between that and the purchase price, which was $2,600,000. He told me to have my lawyer contact them. I asked Mike to put what he wanted in writing and send it to me. This was unbelievable. Seven months earlier the bank had given me an appraisal that showed the fair market value to be $3,900,000 and now only seven months later it was now $1,450,000 after we had improved it considerably and gained a lot of new business plus obtaining a Day's Inn franchise. I called the bank several times and asked for a copy of the new appraisal. Each time they said that they would send one right out but they never did.

On July 9, the new president of Caledonia National Bank, Charlie Bucknam, put attachments on my home and several other properties that I owned. Other than the motel loans I did not owe Bradford Bank any money. Gallerani and Lussier had not told me that when I financed the motel at Bradford Bank that this would also affect my credit at Caledonia Bank as all three banks were participating in the motel loan. Bradford Bank was the only Bank mentioned or on any of the paper work. I had some unsecured notes at Caledonia such as the note for the Danville house and the $75,000 line of credit that Noel Lussier had set up for the motel. Due to the motel not performing I had not been able to pay them. In their complaint the bank had told the court that they were afraid that I might try to transfer my property into somebody else's name to avoid paying them. This really hurt me as I had always paid them and I had brought a lot of business to that bank, which had made them a lot of money. This was really getting to me I could not sleep nights. I was up pacing around and getting all worked up as I just couldn't believe that this was happening and nobody wanted to work with me to straighten it out. I know that between me and the bankers it was also wearing very hard on Charlotte. I did not talk to the kids or anybody else about it as I couldn't see any need to get them worked up.

While all this was going on I still continued to try to run my regular business and meet my obligations. It was very hard due to the way that the banks were treating us.

Back in 1986 I had held an auction for Vermont Food Industries. This was a large chicken farm that produced eggs. They had a fire and lost their egg processing plant. They had gotten rid of all the thousands of chickens and we sold the rest at auction, which consisted of all the equipment, chicken houses and several parcels of real estate.

There had been one fifteen acre parcel that didn't sell at the auction. This was the one that had the burned out egg processing plant. Still intact were three over four hundred foot long cage layer buildings and a large storage warehouse. Although we couldn't get a good offer for this property at the auction the owners still were anxious to sell it Noel Lussier and Don Coty approached me and wanted me to buy it with them, which I did.

About a year and a half later, I found a customer to sell it to Caledonia National Bank financed the purchase for the customer. Don Coty, Noel and I each signed for the loan with the buyer. We each put $5,000 in a certificate of deposit at the bank and pledged them to as security coward the loan.

The new owners ran a flea market there and did a little other business. After a while, they started to get behind in their payments to the bank. When they did, the bank started to take the payments out of my savings account. They did not bother Cory or Noel, even though Noel was the president of the bank. I made over $17,000 in payments and Cory and Lussier had made none. I wanted to keep my credit good, as I had always done.

The owner had left the area and couldn't be located. He had a son who lived in St. Johnsbury who I went to see several times, but I couldn't get him to tell me where his father was. He said that he thought that he could get power of attorney from his father so that he could sell the chicken farm. I told him that I would give him $500 if he would get the power of attorney and deed the chicken farm to back me. He got the power of attorney and deeded it to me. It turned out that his father was in Florida. There was back taxes and several leans on the property, which I paid off.

I then sold the property to Green Mountain Sanitation, a rubbish collection company. I paid off Caledonia National Bank. I took over an $8,000 loss but it was my obligation to get the bank paid. Don Coty paid me for one third of the loss but I could never get a cent from Noel. I had several other deals that went sour but I managed to get the bank paid on all of them so that the banks didn't lose a cent. When it was my obligation, I always took care of it.

After the bank attached my property, I went to the Hardwick branch and talked with Gary Phillips, the branch manager. He arranged a meeting with him and Charlie Bucknam, the New Caledonia National Bank president on July 30. At the meeting Charlie said that the reason that they had attached my property was on account of the motel deal. He said that they wanted to have the jump on things, as they all knew that I would be headed for trouble with the motel deal. I explained to them all the problems that I was having with the motel and the banks. I told him that I had gotten a lawyer like Mike Flipiak told me to. I showed Charlie a copy of a letter my lawyer, Vincent Illuzzi, had written to John Zampieri, chairman of the Bradford Bank board, and that he had gotten no answer to.

Charlie Bucknam called back later in the week to say that he had arranged a meeting for Tuesday August 6 at 11:00 a.m. at Bradford Bank. I took Vincent Illuzzi, my attorney and Tom Lauzon, my accountant with me. When we arrived at the bank, I told the girl at the desk that we were there to meet with the Bank's board of directors. She said that Mike Flipiak had left the meeting an hour earlier to go to Caledonia National Bank in Danville. I told her that we wanted to meet with the entire board. She called into their meeting but they refused to meet with us. In a few minutes Charlie Bucknam showed up and said that he had only arranged to meet with Mike Flipiak and not the whole board. And now Flipiak was in Danville. Charlie was upset that I had brought my attorney and accountant. I explained that Flipiak had told me to get an attorney. Charlie said that the bank's lawyer had been trying to reach my lawyer Vincent Illuzzi, but we didn't even know who the bank's lawyer was. I was sure that it wasn't Stephen Males. We found out that the banks attorney's name was Paul Mattani, then Vince went to a phone and called him. We set up another meeting at the Bradford Bank office for August 7 at 6:00 p.m. We had wasted another good day.

On Wednesday Vince, Tom and I met at Bradford Bank with Mike Flipiak, Keith Boundy, another First National Bank officer, Charlie Bucknam, Laurette Sweet and their attorney Paul Mattani. We discussed many of the problems including the misrepresentation of the motel and the bank's failure to do anything to correct it. Tom, my accountant, brought up about how the bank had drawn $37,000 out of the Motels account at the time that I purchased it to pay the fire insurance when the bill was only $25,000. He said that the insurance agent had told him that a refund had gone to someone at the bank. Laurette Sweet seem to know quite a bit about this but we didn't get any straight answers. We talked about the White River house that was to be used as part of the down payment. Again Laurette Sweet seemed to think that she knew quite a bit about this but I think that she was confused. The only thing that the bankers and their lawyer seemed to be interested in was getting any damaging information that they could on the fired bank officers. This seemed to be their main objective. They made it very clear that if I could provide them with this that I would get anything that I wanted. Tom and I explained how we had improved the motel's business over the past year and the improvements that we had made to the building. We had even painted the whole outside of the building without hiring any additional help. This was done with the motels workers. They seemed to think that the whole mess was a big joke. They laughed about the $170,000 that Caledonia Bank had provided. Mike kept referring to this as the funny money and then would laugh each time he mentioned it. I felt that we were there to try to settle a very serious matter and that it wasn't a joking matter. I tried to get them to address the fact that they were trying to make me lose over a million dollars, which I didn't have, for the banks mistakes and misrepresentations. I explained that they would be getting back a much improved motel from what they had sold me. I also told them that I felt that I should be due something for all the work that I had done and the harassment that I had been through. They seemed to agree to this. Again they emphasized that I needed to get more damaging information on the former officers. I didn't have any more damaging information about the former officers other than about the way that they had misrepresented the motel and the way that they had set up the down payment. I did however begin to feel that maybe we were getting a little closer to reaching a settlement. Boy was I wrong!

CHAPTER 7

THE FBI GETS INVOLVED

After the Bradford Bank meeting, I presented the Bankers a proposal for straightening out all the problems with the motel, the Danville house and the Caledonia Bank attachments on my home and other property. There were letters and phone calls back and forth between Illuzzie, my lawyer, and the banks lawyer but nothing ever happened to get any closer to a settlement.

A few days later, three men showed up at my house. They were John Hersh from the FBI, Allan Dawson from the Federal Reserve Bank and a third man from the FBI whose name I can't recall. Other than a traffic ticket I had never had anything to do with any law enforcement officers. Hersh did most of the talking. He wanted to know if I would talk to them. He said that they knew all about the motel deal. He said that I was a victim and had been frauded by the banks. Hersh said that they knew that I had been trying hard to get things straightened out but that I wasn't getting any cooperation from the banks. Hersh said that they were there to help me straighten out my problems with the banks if I would talk to them. I really felt good about this and said that I would be glad to talk to them. I could not see any harm in this as I had nothing to hide and they were going to help me get the justice that I felt that I deserved by straightening out the motel mess.

They asked me a lot of questions about the motel, the banks and different people that I knew and some that I didn't know. When they left, they told me not to tell anyone that they had been here. Hersh left me his card and told me to get hold of him if I needed to. I really felt good about their visit as I believed that they were going to bring some pressure on the banks to do the right thing and straighten out this motel mess the way that they should have done in the first place.

I did not hear anymore from the FBI men, but I kept trying to deal with the bankers and reach some agreement. On August 17, I received a letter from Mike Flipiak stating that they would take back the motel and that I would give them all the dirt that I could on their former bank officers. They agreed to release me from the $75,000 loan from Caledonia Bank, but didn't want to give me back my down payment or anything that I had put into it, and they didn't want to release my property that they had the leans on or do any of the other things that they had agreed to do when I bought the motel.

I called Flipiak and made an appointment to see him in his office at First National Bank in Springfield. On September 5, 1991, Charlotte and I drove to the First National Bank in Springfield, over a hundred miles one way to meet with Mike Flipiak. Keith Boundy another bank officer was present at the meeting. By this time both Charlotte and I were getting very upset and depressed over trying to get some results. We were both very tired as we didn't sleep anymore. Charlotte broke down and cried in our meeting and tried to explain to Flipiak and Boundy how this was affecting us. We tried to discuss a settlement with them. Mike did try to call the banks lawyer, Paul Mattaini, who didn't answer. Mike and Boundy said that they had other commitments so we all agreed to meet at the same place the very next day Friday, September 6. Mike said that he would certainly get hold of Mattaini, their lawyer, and would definitely have an answer on how we could settle this mess that we would be happy with. He told us and especially Charlotte not to worry.

Friday Charlotte and I went clear back to Flipiak's office in Springfield to meet again with Flipiak and Keith Boundy. We discussed the Danville house and how the banks had agreed to buy it. They said that made sense and that it wouldn't be any problem for them to buy it as originally agreed. They still didn't want to make any definite commitments as to settling the whole mess. Flipiak said that he had talked to Mattani, and now all that was left to do was to get approval of the banks other officers. He said that there was going to be an all-day meeting the following Tuesday September 10 of all three banks and that they would be sure to reach a decision with a definite answer to my proposal that I had made several months before. Flipiak said to call either him or Keith Boundy on Wednesday September 11 for the final decision.

Wednesday at 11:30 I called the First National Bank as they had said to do. I was told that Flipiak was busy but that he would call right back but he never did. I called several more times but each time I was told that both Flipiak and Boundy were busy and would return my calls but neither of them did. Later that same day I received a call from Vincent Illuzzie, my lawyer. He said that Paul Mattani, the banks lawyer, had called him and told him that Flipiak was not going to make any decisions but that he was going to decide for the banks what steps to take. He then said that he was ready to start foreclosure on the motel.

I did not know what to think as this was all contrary to the discussions that I had been having with the bankers. I tried several times a day to reach Flipiak or Boundy on the phone. Each time I was told that they were both there. The secretary would ask which one I wanted to talk to and who could she say was calling. As soon as I gave her my name, they were both tied up or had just stepped out but would call right back but no calls came. After not being able to get through to Flipiak of Boundy, I called Winston Oaks, a Bradford Bank director, and asked him about the Tuesday all-day meeting. He said that they had met but said that Flipiak hadn't brought up anything about the motel deal, except that the lawyers were working on it. Oaks said that they spent most of the day trying to think up ways to blame the former bank officers for all the banks problems. This was very frustrating as Charlotte and I had been very anxious all weekend to find out what they wanted to do so we could get this settled and go on with our lives.

The next day, Thursday, September 12, I called Charlie Bucknam, the Caledonia Bank president, and asked him if he was at the Tuesday all day meeting. He said that he was and that Flipiak hadn't mentioned anything about the motel deal as he had promised to do. I told Charlie that I had been trying for nearly a year to reach some arrangement with the banks so we all would know where we stood. Charlie said that he would try to reach Flipiak and would call me right back. When he called back, he said that Flipiak had told him that he had only planned to talk to Paul Mattaini, at the meeting, but Paul was not there. Flipiak had told us on Friday that he had already talked to Paul and had only to bring it before the board.

On Monday, September 16, I tried calling the First National Bank again. Each time I was told that Keith Boundy was in, but I could never seem to get through to him. Tuesday, the next morning, I tried calling Boundy at home around 7:30. This time I reached him. He said that he could not remember what happened at the meeting with him and Flipiak the previous Thursday and Friday at the bank. He said that Flipiak hadn't given him any information except that he was leaving any settlement in the hands of their attorney. Boundy then went on to say that there wouldn't be any settlement until I could come up with some information that would be damaging to the former bank officers.

On Tuesday September 11, I called John Zampieri, the chairman of the Bradford Bank board of directors. John said that Bradford had just hired a new bank president whose name was Robert Webber. John said to call Webber and make an appointment to go into the bank and discuss the whole situation with him. John said that Webber would now be handling the negotiation and not Flipiak.

I did as John suggested, I called Bradford Bank several times to make an appointment. Mr. Webber would not come to the phone, would not return calls as the secretary said that he would. She could not get him to set an appointment. I wrote him letters but I never heard anything back from him.

I had been devoting full time trying to get the banks to do something to correct the problem that they had stuck me with. Rochell Inman, the motel manager and her staff had been working very hard to improve business and the operation of the motel. She had picked up a lot of new business. July and August had been the best months that the motel had ever had in its twenty-year history. Still this was not enough to make payments and meet all its obligations although it was getting closer. Still the banks would not negotiate with us to try to do what was best for them as well as for us.

Back at the April meeting with the Bradford Bank board and staff someone suggested that I should talk to Phil Rogers, the chairman of the Caledonia Bank board of directors. I went to see Phil. He said that he had a wife and family that he had to worry about and so would not in any way discuss the motel deal. He acted scared. I don't know why. He said that he didn't want anything to do with Mike Flipiak.

As I said, the motel had run very smoothly, and we had gained a nice increase in business but not enough to carry it. I felt that I had done all anyone could do and that Rochell Inman, the manager and the staff had worked very hard and had made many improvements in the motel and the business that it was doing to try to make it run profitably. Still the bank officers were not willing to make things right. Who would ever think that they would do this to anybody? I could not understand why they were so afraid to talk about it. I do not usually look to blame others for any of my problems, but I began to feel that they had set me up to break me to cover up for their own mistakes.

An article in the May issue of the Time magazine said that the motel business was at an all-time low and that banks were getting stuck with a lot of foreclosed motels. At this same time our motel had the best summer that it ever had in its twenty-year history. You would think that they would want to keep it going rather than see it fail again. The problem wasn't in the management of the motel it was the price and the financing. You would think that the bankers would appreciate this and be anxious to work with us, rather than screw things up.

The Banks Are in Hotel Hell
The next hotel you stay at could be run by a Lender that never really wanted to own one but can't find a way to dump it

By BERNARD BAUMOHL
Time was when the hotel industry mixed glamour and high finance in an intoxicating cocktail that attracted the most flamboyant entrepreneurs of the past century-Conrad Hilton, Richard D'Oyly Carte, Cesar Ricz. But check in today at thousands of US hotel, including Hiltons, Sheratons and Marriott's, and your innkeeper will belong to a far more somber group: Citicorp, Wells Fargo Bank, Travelers insurance and others.

Consultant Lasky's task: revive this money-losing Holiday Inn owned by First National Bank of Maryland.

Lenders are getting stuck with the vast surplus of rooms they helped finance in the '80s.

The jokes are inevitable-it takes a month to get your reservation approved; no room service after 3 p. m. but the banks and insurance companies aren't amused. They are in the hotel business because in the past decade they helped finance a building frenzy that dumped thousands of new rooms on an already glutted market, with disastrous results. Six of every ten hotels in the US aren't able to make a penny in profit, says Bjorn Hanson, an industry expert with the Coopers & Lybrand accounting firm. As losses mount, so do loan defaults, which have forced lenders to foreclose on a record number of ailing properties. More than 3,000 have reverted to lenders in the past three years, and experts expect an additional 7,000 to be repossessed in the next 24 months.

What does a lender do with a foreclosed hotel? With luck he sells it fast and gets his money back; banks and S&Ls have no desire to run these properties. But buyers are hard to find nowadays. "The market to purchase hotels is dead," says Morris Lasky, chief executive of Lodging

Unlimited, a firm based in West Chester, Pennsylvania, that specializes in turning around problem hotels. "Banks are not going to lend to new buyers, and there isn't anybody with cash to buy these things." Among the many anxious sellers is the government's Resolution Trust Corporation, which has 160 hotels in its portfolio of failed S&Ls.

Some of the repossessed properties are landmarks. Bally has effectively agreed to hand over the keys to its Las Vegas and Reno resorts to a group of creditors. The Westin Canal Place in New Orleans was repossessed by Travelers. The Four Seasons hotel in Austin has been foreclosed by Manufacturers Hanover. The Los Angeles Airport Hilton is in the hands of Security Pacific National Bank. "It is unprecedented what has been going on with hotel foreclosures," says David Renton, who heads a hotel investment firm in Stamford, Conn. "This is the worst crisis for the industry since the Great Depression."

Most bank executives realize that hotel management is a job for a professional, and they usually hire new managers to try to revive an ailing property. Says Lasky, who has resuscitated hotels during his thirty-five-year career: "Three years ago, we were getting four or five calls a month from lenders of problem hotels. We're now averaging that many a day." While professional managers can keep operations on crack, every hotel faces decisions that only the owner can make. Does a small roadside hotel really need a Nautilus room? Is it practical to have nightly bed turndowns or a twenty-four-hour doorman?

Bankers aren't equipped to decide, and many are tormented over what to do next. Some refuse to throw more money into a losing business, but experts warn that such a policy can cost more than it saves. "A hotel operation can go quickly into a graveyard spiral if some action isn't taken," says Laurence Geller, who runs a hotel advisory firm in Chicago.

The lenders don't feel any better knowing they have mainly themselves to blame for this fix. Through much of the '80s, they were tripping over one another to offer generous terms for even the unlikeliest projects. "In the madness of that decade, many hotels were over financed and overleveraged," says Bruce Badin, a partner with the consulting firm Pannell Kerr Forster. "A lot of hotels are in trouble because of that."

119

By the time many of the properties were built, corporations were cutting back on business trips to protect profits. The current recession has made things worse. Of the 3.1 million rooms available in the United States, almost half are vacant every night. Since an average hotel needs 65 percent occupancy to break even, that translates into an estimated industry loss of $1.7 billion last year, a record, and this year looks worse. Says Randy Smith, who publishes the authoritative newsletter Lodging Outlook: "I've been doing research on the hotel industry for twenty years, and this first quarter beats anything I have ever seen."

Most lenders are resigned to holding their hotel properties until the market improves, but they'd better be patient. "It is going to be anywhere from five to seven years before the hotel industry gets back to reality," says Lasky. Between now and then demand will increase, but probably not nearly enough to catch up with the huge oversupply of rooms. That means the number of rooms will have to come down. Some hotels will simply be demolished. Others may be converted into condominiums, although there's hardly a shortage of those. Some, depending on design and location, could even be converted into prisons. Don't laugh. At least it's a growth industry.—*Reported by Dan Cray/ Los Angeles and William McWhirter/Chicago*

CHAPTER 8

I KEEP TRYING

A whole year had gone by since I purchased the motel. I had not taken one cent out of the motel. I had worked very hard trying to do what I thought was right with the motel. We kept making improvements and working to gain new business. I had worked very hard for forty years to build up and keep my credit good. I had also made the banks a lot of money and I had taken a lot of properties off their hands. I had been dealing longer with Caledonia National Bank than any of their present directors and officers with the exception of Seldon Houghton. Due to the banks misrepresentation of this motel deal and even worse, their failure and neglect to try to work with me to straighten it out. It seems that I could lose all that I worked a lifetime to gain and this could seriously affect my credit and credibility. In the past Caledonia had sent me a Statement giving me a $750,000 dealer line of credit that I could use to finance other people when I sold them property.

This year they sent me a statement saying that they would give me no credit. In the past, they had always loaned me money to purchase real estate, which I fixed up and resold. Often when I sold it I would take the financing to the bank and they would accept it. This was how I paid them back. Off times I would leave much of the profit in a savings account at the bank. This was the same savings account that I started as a kid when my father took me to the Caledonia National Bank for the first time. I have never taken a cent out of this account, only the bank has taken money out, I have only put money in. This was to be our retirement. I had done this for many years with no real problems. But now they have everything that I own tied up, and they

121

wouldn't take any more dealer financing from me. How would they expect me to pay them anything? I have tried very hard to reason with the bankers but they don't seem to want to listen to reason. I believe that I was much more concerned about the banks losing money than any of the bank officers were. It is no wonder that I have chest pains all the time and can't sleep. It is darn hard to get ahead or just stay even with Bucknam and the banks controlling all your assets and keeping your hands tied tight.

On Thursday, September 26, I went to Caledonia National Bank, in Danville, to try to reason with Charlie Bucknam. The secretary said that he was out but that he would call me the next morning. He never called. I called Winston Oaks, a Bradford Bank director. I told him that he was the only one from the bank who would talk to me. I then told him about trying to reach Robert Webber, the new bank president. Winston was furious and said that he would fax Webber a command to call me immediately and for me to wait right by the phone. No call came. I tried to call Mike Flipiak. The secretary said that Mike was out but that she would have him call me. He didn't call. I tried calling Charlie Bucknam again. I was told that Charlie was unavailable but that he would call right back, but he did not return my call. I went to Caledonia Bank to see Charlie Bucknam. He said that he couldn't see me then but to come back between 1:00 and 2:00 p.m. I returned at 1:20 and was told that he was not available I tried the next day to call Charlie Bucknam and was again told that he would call right back but as usual he didn't.

On Wednesday October 16, 1991 I had faxed then mailed a registered letter to Robert Webber and a copy to Charlie Bucknam stating that I would like to meet with them and inviting them to go with me to see the motel hoping that this would lead to a better relationship and understanding with the bankers. I never received an answer from either one of them.

Rochell Inman, the motel manager, had been complaining that Bradford Bank, where we did the motel banking, wasn't crediting deposits to our checking account for several days after receiving them. On Monday October 8, I received a call from the state of New Hampshire saying that our check for rooms and meals tax for the previous month in the amount of $14,608.49 had been returned by Bradford Bank, for insufficient funds. The caller was not very happy about it. As a consequence, we were served with penalties and lace charges of $2,935.85. According to Rochell we had sufficient funds in the bank to cover the rooms and meals check. Mike Flipiak had assured us not to worry as he would take care of it but he didn't do it.

On Thursday October 31, Vince Illuzzi, my attorney, called me and said that he had talked to the banks attorney, Paul Mattaini who had agreed to devote that day to accepting my proposal that I had made several months before.

On Monday November 4, I talked to Vincent Illuzzi. He had talked to Paul Mattaini who told him not to worry as the bankers were sympathetic to what had happened and that they were going to accept my proposal. The next day Tuesday Vince called to say that the bank board was meeting that evening and would have an answer later that night. I could hardly wait. On Wednesday Vince called again and said that the bank did not bring up anything about the motel and us at the Tuesday night meeting as they had agreed to do. Again they did not do as they had agreed or should have done. This pattern had become very discouraging and frustrating to both Charlotte and me. It seemed almost like a form of torture, but I could not figure out why they kept doing it. Later Vince Illuzzi called and said that he had contacted Mattaini again. Mattani had told him that now some of the bank directors were having second thoughts about meeting my proposal and trying to straighten out this mess. They wouldn't make a decision. Here all the time I thought that they were ready to face the problem. This didn't help to elevate out sleepless nights.

On Monday November 11, I received a call from Rochell, the motel manager, who needed some answers from the bank, about our account, but hadn't been able to get them. It was again time to pay out rooms and meals tax and the Day's Inn franchise fees. She didn't want the bank to return our check as they had done the last month. I called Vince Illuzzi, our attorney, who said that he would call Paul Mattani. He tried several times to reach Mattani but he did not return his calls. Mattani finally got back to Vince and told him that the bank thought that I would be held personally liable if the rooms and meals tax didn't get paid on time, so they weren't going to worry about it. Vince got Mattani to agree to contact the bank again and try to get a more realistic answer as we had a right to know what was happening with our account and whither the bank would cover our checks or not. Mattani agreed to call right back. Vince did not hear back from Mattani and so tried several more times to call him with no luck. Vince called me at 4:30 and said that he had to leave his office and wanted me to keep trying to reach Mattani. Vince was mad as hell and said that he just couldn't understand why they wanted to act the way that they did. I tried several times to reach Mattani but couldn't. I finally faxed him a message saying that I would wait by the phone however late it took for him to call me, but he never called, so we didn't find out anything that day.

I had been talking to some people in Connecticut who were interested in purchasing the motel. They apparently had the money and were willing to pay up to $2,000,000. Mike Flipiak had told me a few months before that the bank had the motel appraised and the fair market value was $1,450,000. I thought that the bank would be excited about this and that we could now work out a deal to sell the motel and everybody could come out all right. I went to Springfield to see Flipiak and told him about the offer. He laughed and didn't seem to be interested at all. He told me that he hadn't had much time lately for banking business as he had been spending all his time with the lawyers and the FBI, trying dig up some more charges that they could bring against the fired bank officers Flipiak said that he was also covering his own tracts and that I should be covering mine. I didn't think that I had any tracks that needed covering. He said that the banks had one law firm in Boston that they were paying $35,000 per week to advise them. He said that he was too busy to talk about selling the motel. That night, which was November 14, 1991, I called John Zamparrie, the chairman of the Bradford Bank board of directors and told him about the offer. He said that he or somebody from the bank would get right back to me the next day. Nobody ever did. However, on November 15, the next day after I talked to Flipiak and Zampieri, I got a call from Vince Illuzzi who said that the banks attorney now told him that the banks three presidents had decided to foreclose on the motel at the Tuesday evening meeting. The three presidents were Charlie Bucknam, Robert Webber and Mike Flipiak. At first they had agreed to accept our proposal to settle the deal at the Tuesday evening meeting. After the meeting, they told us that they hadn't discussed the motel at the Tuesday evening meeting. Now we learn that they decided to foreclose on the motel at the Tuesday evening meeting. Neither Flipiak nor Zampieri had mentioned anything about the Tuesday evening meeting or foreclosure when I talked to them the previous day.

The Connecticut people called me several times about buying the motel. I had to keep stalling them as I couldn't give them any answers as I now had no idea what the bank wanted or was willing to do. I could get no answers from the bank, except that they were going to foreclose. I understand that these people finally bought a motel in New Jersey.

On the morning of November 18, Tom Lauzon, my accountant, and Vincent Illuzzie called me on a conference call. They had talked to Cynthia LaRose, a new lawyer for the bank from Manchester, New Hampshire. She had told them that it was foreclosure and that she couldn't justify keeping the motel open. Tom had tried to explain to her what the losses would be if it were closed.

Vince said that the foreclosure was going to take place in New Hampshire so I would need to get a New Hampshire lawyer to represent me as he was not licensed to practice in New Hampshire. I then called LaRose told her that it would be a big mistake to close the motel. I explained that if the bank wanted it back I thought that we could work out a deal but that I hadn't been able to get even a clue of what the bank wanted up until now. I told her that if the motel was closed that it would probably cost at least a half a million dollars to get it open again. That there would probably be frozen and broken water pipes to say nothing about vandalism. I told her that if the bank tried to sell the empty building at a later date they would be lucky to get $300,000. She didn't seem to care.

On Monday November 18, I talked to Tom Lauzon who had heard from Cynthia LaRose that the bank was now going to release money to the motel to keep it open.

I drove to Bradford to talk to Winston Oaks, a Bradford Bank director. He couldn't believe that the bank was not willing to try to work this out. He said that the bank officers were not keeping the bank directors informed as to what was going on and what they were doing. I pointed out that probably was why they had problems with the previous bank officers, the directors were not informed and didn't bother to find out what they were doing. Winston said that was exactly right. He said that they were having a bank meeting the next day, which was Tuesday. He said that if I would bear with him one more day that he would get to the bottom of it and get back to me and let me know what was going on.

I did not hear back from Winston so Thursday evening I called him at home. He said that he had talked to Cynthia LaRose after the Tuesday meeting and she told him that she was going to foreclose. Winston said that as far as the rest of the bank directors were concerned he felt that they didn't want to get involved. He said that there was no one at the meeting who dared to make a decision, O that Mike Flipiak was supposed to be handling it. All the time they had been telling me that Robert Webber was handling it although I had never been able to communicate with him. I don't know why directors would want to be on the bank board if they couldn't make a decision. Perhaps it was the pay.

The week of November 25, Rochell Innman, the motel manager again needed to find out about what the bank was doing with the motel accounts. She called Tom Lauzon to see if he had found out what was going on. She needed to pay some insurance and other expenses and didn't know if the bank had been crediting our deposits or what they had been doing. Tom told her to call Mike Flipiak at Springfield and ask him. She called Flipiak and he told her Robert Webber was now handling it and that he no longer had anything to do with it so not to call him anymore. Rochell tried to call Webber, but as usual he would not come to the phone. Rochell then called Tom back who told her to call Cynthia LaRose, the banks lawyer. Rochell got hold or LaRose and explained that the withholding tax and the fire insurance had to be paid that day. LaRose told Rochell that she would contact Webber and get right back to her. This was Friday afternoon. LaRose did not call back so at 5:00 p.m. Rochell tried LaRose again and was told that she had left for the week and would not be in all the next week as she was going on vacation.

Previously Tom Lauzon had called Mike Flipiak in Springfield. Flipiak told Tom to call Webber at Bradford Bank. Tom called Bradford and was told that Webber was in Springfield meeting with Flipiak. Tom then called Flipiak back and told him that Webber was supposed to be meeting with him. Flipiak said that he had forgot who he was meeting with. Can you imagine this? The following Monday after Cynthia LaRose didn't call back and had gone on vacation Rochell finally got through to Robert Webber and tried to explain to him what she needed to know concerning the fire insurance and the workers compensation insurance, which were going to be canceled if she didn't pay them. Webber said that he would get right back to her but never did.

Wednesday December 4, 1991, I received five letters from Cynthia LaRose, all stating that the bank was foreclosing on the motel and that the motel was going to be auctioned off on January 6, 1992.

William F. Hill, Associates
Box 15
Hardwick, VT 05843
802-472-6308

Mr. Robert Webber
Bradford National Bank Bradford, VT
05033
Oct. 16, 1991
Dear Mr. Webber:

As you probably know by now, I purchased the stock in BFC Corporation from Independent Bank Group over a year ago. There were some gross misrepresentations made at the time of sale and the motel has not performed as it was supposed to. However, I have been able to increase business considerably from what it was in the past. We have promoted and picked up a lot of new business, we have a great number of reservations already for 1992.

Even at this the motel has not been able to carry its self. I have been trying for the past Eight months to sit down with the bank so that we could work together to map out a solution to this problem as it is not just going to go away. I have written a report of what has happened as I see it. I don't know if you have read this. I'm not happy about it.

I have felt right along that the best solution is to get together and try to work out a plan that is agreeable to both the bank and myself. I know the lawyers are now involved, but that doesn't usually work out to the advantage of anyone. If I could only find out what the bank wants or expects of me, then we could work in that direction.

I would like to pick you up at Bradford in the next few days and drive you to the motel so you can see firsthand what is there and what is happening. It would probably require about three hours, Perhaps Charlie Bucknam from Caledonia Bank would like to accompany us. I anxiously await your answer and look forward to meeting you.

Sincerely,
William E. Hill

Copy: Charlie Bucknam

CHAPTER 9

FORECLOSURE CALLED OFF
AND BANK TAKES OVER

As the motel is located in New Hampshire, it was going to be necessary to get a New Hampshire lawyer. A friend of Vincent Illuzzie's recommended Richard Uchida from the law firm of Raymond P. D'Amante in Concord New Hampshire. I hired Richard and he filed a motion to stop the foreclosure. Richard and I met with the banks lawyers. Cynthia LaRose and David Burns and bank officer. Ed Childs at the Grafton County courthouse on December 31, 1991. The lawyers went into another room for a conference, leaving Ed Childs and me in the courthouse lobby. I had never met Childs as he was new with Bradford Bank. He was tall and wore black and green plaid pants. I tried several times to approach him and talk to him. Each time that I got near him he would scurry to another area in the lobby. Finally he ended up in kind of a corner area where he couldn't get by me very gracefully. I tried to talk to him in a friendly way about the motel and the way that it was misrepresented to me before I purchased it but he seemed very nervous and did not want to talk. I didn't get very far with him.

The banks lawyers agreed to stop the auction for at least sixty days if I would let the bank take over the management of the motel. I was reluctant to do this without a definite settlement. We now had the motel doing the best that it had ever done. We already had over $500,000 worth of advance bookings for 1992. The motel now came closer to paying its way than it ever had. They agreed that within the sixty days that they would reach a settlement with me. I had heard this many times before and was still reluctant to turn it over to them without coming to an agreement first. My new lawyer, Richard Uchida, must have had more faith in them than I did as he advised me to let them run it. He said that we had plenty of leverage to make a favorable settlement with them. I finally gave in against my better judgment. The bank was to take over the management that very day December 31, 1991.

I had some things in Florida that had needed my immediate attention for several months. I had started a meat and seafood delivery business, which had been doing very well until recently. The manager had not been tending to the business and had been siphoning out money to support some bad habits that he had developed. I had not been able to get down there as I had felt that the motel situation was too important to leave and for several months I had felt that we were just days away from trying to agree to something. The next morning January 1, 1992, Charlotte and I headed for Florida I was anxious to check on my business down there and just as important I wanted to get Charlotte away for a while as this bank mess had really done a job on her. Dean my oldest son and his wife Ann followed us down and spent a couple of days with us in Florida at the home we had there. They then went on to Southern Florida to visit their grandparents who were wintering there.

It was already too late to straighten out most of the business problems the meat and seafood business. This was going to be another big loss due to my fooling around with the banks trying to straighten out the motel deal. I spent most of my time working on my properties, painting, fixing roofs and cleaning up some of the messes that some of my tenants had left around. I kept in touch with my new lawyer Richard Uchida, as to what was happening with the banks. Charlotte was a mess and couldn't even enjoy Florida, which she had always loved. I had a very difficult time with her. She was devastated by the way that bankers had been using us and then to see what had happened to our Florida business. On Wednesday Jan 15, Richard Uchida called me. He said that the banks and their lawyers were ready to meet and talk and wanted to do so right away and that I should get back home immediately. He said that they would probably want to meet before I could get there. I canceled everything that I was doing, packed up my car and Charlotte and drove 1600 miles straight back to Vermont. As soon as I got home, I contacted Richard. He said he was waiting to hear from the bank's lawyer, but was sure that we would be meeting in the next day or two. A week went by and we didn't hear anything from them. Again I had messed up my schedule, by coming back home to try to accommodate them.

On Monday January 20, I went to the motel. Business was going fairly well, much better than a year ago as we had built the business up plus we had many advance bookings. However, the moral among the employees was not good. The bank had hired a management company out of New York State to manage the motel. The employees felt that the management company was creating many undue hardships for them. They were still trying to do the best job they could under the circumstances. As people heard about the January 6 auction, even though it had been canceled, and the management company takeover, the motel was getting cancellations of reservations and events that we had worked so hard to get.

By now the banks had spent a tremendous amount of money for lawyers and legal fees to hire an auctioneer and auction advertising then canceling the auction and hiring a management company that they had never even heard of. They had to pay the management company $50,000 to do what I had been doing for nothing. They had neglected to consider a $2,000,000 offer to sell the motel. The bank officers had been spending the banks money like it was water but they didn't seem to care, they and all the lawyers that they had were still getting their salaries. It is hard to say how much over a million dollars this has already cost the banks to say nothing of what it has cost me. There were many stories going around about many other stupid things that the bankers had done and were doing that was costing the bank a lot of money. Many people were saying that the bankers were purposely trying to make the banks fail in order to blame it on the fired officers. It certainly looked that way.

Charlie Bucknam and the bankers had us all tied up and were doing everything that they could to make it impossible for me to conduct my business. It was obvious that they especially Bucknam wanted to break us and make us look as bad as he could. This is one example of what he did. Back when Noel Lussier, Don Coty and I sold the chicken farm property we had each put $5,000 in a certificate of deposit and had pledged them for additional security in case the buyer defaulted. As I explained earlier, he did default and I had worked hard to get the property back and Caledonia Bank paid in full. They didn't lose a cent. The certificate of deposit that I had left in Caledonia Bank matured on Jan 13, 1992. The chicken farm property loan had been paid off back in June of 1991. Therefore, my certificate of deposit was no longer securing the loan. It should be mine to do what I wanted to do with it.

I had two loans at Caledonia Bank that each had a balance of about $4,000. One of these was a balance note and was due. I wanted to pay up both of these loans. The certificate was now worth $7,029.48. It wouldn't quite cover both of these loans but I figured that I would pay off the one that was due and apply the rest on the other one that would bring that balance down to where I could pay that one off co— as soon as I knew what the actual balance was.

I made a photo copy of the maturing Certificate of deposit and typed under it what I wanted to do with the proceeds and sent it to the bank. The whole amount was going to go to the bank, to apply on what I owed them. The bank wrote back that they were rolling my Certificate of deposit over for another thirty six months at an interest rate that was about 3 percent lower than what it had been paying. I contacted Charlie Bucknam and again explained what I wanted to do with my money. He wrote back and said that as long as I had any money in his bank that he could do whatever he wanted with it. He did not apply it to the two loans as I had requested. He decided to do something else with my money. He then reported the loan, which was due and that I wanted to pay off as being delinquent to all the credit reporting agencies. He knew that this would hurt my credit. I later paid the loan off. This is just one of a number of things that Charlie Bucknam did to try to destroy us. I could never could understand why.

On Friday January 31, I drove to Concord New Hampshire, one hundred eighty miles one way, to meet with Richard Uchida and deliver him some papers that he wanted. He said that he had talked with the banks lawyers and that they were sympathetic with our whole situation although they had not scheduled any meeting as they agreed to do even though we have been back in Vermont for over two weeks.

Richard Uchida said that I should hire Jay Hanes, a banking consultant, to put all our bank troubles in perspective. On Thursday February 6, Tom Lauzon and I met at the motel with Jay Hanes. Hanes said that he had seen a lot of banking problems but that he had never seen a bank behave the way these banks were doing. He could not believe what they had done. That's about all I got out of him. His services cost me $2,500 although I can't see where they did me any good. Also I have had some tremendous legal bills plus losing over a year just in frustration trying to get this bank mess settled. I had to sell some of my rental property, that Caledonia had not put a lean, to pay my legal bills and keep going. I sold one house at a $20,000 loss in order to pay my lawyers.

Even though the banks and the management company were running the motel everything was still in my name. On Thursday, February 6, I received a call from Richard Uchida who said that Cynthia LaRose had called him and said that some prospects had showed up for the auction on January 6 even though it was canceled. She wanted me to contact them and see if I could sell it to them. She wanted me to contact Ed Childs at Bradford Bank and work with him on arranging a sale of the motel. I called Childs on the phone as soon as I told him who it was he said that he couldn't talk to me without the permission of all three bank presidents. I thought that this was unbelievable as the banks lawyer had said to contact him. I then called Uchida back and asked him to find out how much I should be trying to get out of the motel and were the banks willing to do any financing. Uchida called back and said that the banks wouldn't give him an answer to either question. Cynthia had sent me a couple of names of prospects that had showed up for the auction. I had contacted them both and made appointments to meet with each of them at the motel on Monday February 17 at different times. Not knowing what to ask I didn't feel that I had too much to go on.

On Saturday February 15, we had some real nasty weather with a lot of snow mixed with freeing rain. I could not get my car into our driveway due to the heavy wet snow, so I left it down next to the road stuck in the snow. About five o'clock Sunday morning, the phone rang. It was our daughter in law, Ann, Dean's wife. She said that Clay another son had been out motor skiing with his wife Pattie and some other friends the evening before. At about eleven o'clock they were headed home on a town road. The viability was not good due to the freezing rain and snow. There was a cow in the road and Clay didn't see it and hit it with his snow mobile. The rescue squad had taken him to the local hospital in Morrisville and they had sent him to the Vermont Medical Center in Burlington.

She said that he was unconscious and that she didn't know how bad he was hurt beyond that.

Charlotte called the hospital and the report that she got was not very good. I went down and shoveled our car out of the snow and Charlotte and I headed for the Burlington hospital, which is about sixty-five miles away, when we arrived we talked to the doctor who didn't give us much encouragement. He said that Clay was unconscious and that he had at least three serious brain injuries. He would not say whether he thought that Clay would ever come to again. He said that if he did survive he would probably never be able to talk due to the location of one of the injuries. Patty, Clay's wife along with her mother, sister and several of our family members were already there. After a while, we got to go in and see Clay. He was all hitched up to wires and rubes. He had what looked like a large spark plug screwed into his head this was connected to a TV monitor and an audio alarm. This was keep tract of the brain pressure due to swelling. Charlotte and I were already devastated by the bank problems and now we were hit with this tragedy. It was almost more than we could take.

They would only let Clay's family in to see him and only for a few minutes at specified times. One of the times was at 4:15 in the morning. The next day Monday I was to show the motel to the two prospects that had showed up at the auction. I hadn't been able to sleep, which was nothing new, and I got up at 2:00 a.m. and headed to the hospital to be there at 4:15 to see Clay. It was very sad to see him lying there not moving a muscle and not knowing what his future held. Clay and Pattie have three of the nicest little daughters that anyone could have. This made it even sadder.

After leaving Clay and the hospital, I headed for the motel in New Hampshire, which was nearly two hundred miles from the hospital. When I arrived at the motel a little after noon, I met with Rochell Inman, who was still the manager, working for the management company and the banks. She was upset as someone from the bank had called and told her not to let Bill Hill show the motel to anyone. She said that they told her that the management company was going to be putting together a brochure and that they were the only ones that they wanted to show it. It was the bank's lawyer, Cynthia LaRose, that had asked me to contact these people and try to sell them the motel. I was dead tired as I hadn't had sleep and all the pressure was just about more than I could stand. I could not believe that these banks could just keep torturing us with their tactics. I tried to call Richard Uchida but there was no answer. I then tried to call Cynthia LaRose and there was no answer there either. I then realized that most people were celebrating Washington's birthday and were not working. I told Rochell that I was going to show the motel and that if the banks didn't like it we could deal with that later. Besides the motel was still in my name.

The people showed up and I showed them the motel and answered all their questions. I didn't feel that either of them were prepared to make any kind of offer that the banks would consider.

Tuesday morning I went back to the hospital, as I did every day to see Clay. There was no change in Clay but I made up my mind and I know that the rest of my family did too that we were not going to give up faith and we were determined to see him recover. I felt that even though Clay was unconscious that he had the same faith and determination. It was very hard for me to go in and visit him, but I was there every day for months. Charlotte could not stand to go, it was just too much for her along with the bank problems.

After getting back home from the hospital, I called Richard Uchida and told him about the bank not wanting me to show the motel. Richard said that was contrary to the last agreement that they had made. Richard called Cynthia LaRose who also knew nothing about not showing the motel and she said to keep looking for offers, then get together with Ed Childs to go over them. Richard said that I should keep trying to sell the motel. I contacted a number of different prospects that I thought might be interested and I was able to get offers from five of them.

On Monday February 4, I called Ed Childs at the bank, and told him that I had some offers on the motel and would like to meet with him to discuss them. Childs said that he would have to contact Cynthia LaRose before that he could meet with me. I explained that LaRose was the one who had told me to get the offers and meet with him. After much hesitation and excuse, making he agreed to see me the next day, Tuesday, February 25, at three o'clock. On Tuesday I went to the Bradford Bank at 3:00 as agreed. Childs office door was open and I could see him in there. He kept me waiting a good half an hour while he just shuffled things and made a couple of phone calls.

While I was standing in the hall waiting to get in to see Childs, Robert Webber, the bank president who I had never been able to meet or talk to, came along. He obviously didn't know who I was. He came up to me and stuck out his hand an announced that he was Robert Webber the Bradford Bank president. I shook his hand and said I'm Bill Hill. He got a very nervous look on his face, turned around, and ran down the hall. That was the first and last that I ever saw of him.

I finally got in to Child's office. He still shuffled things around and didn't say anything for several minutes. He then asked me what I wanted. This seemed strange as I was doing exactly what their lawyer had asked me to do and I had explained to Childs on the phone why I needed to see him. I showed him the written offers that I had gotten. They range from $1,000,000 to $1,500,000. There was one offer for $1,150,000 cash, which I felt was very good. Childs said that the bank was not interest unless I was willing to make up the difference of what they had sold it to me for. This would have been over $1,000,000. He referred to Mike Flipiak's letter of July 3, 1991, stating that I would have to make up the difference. He then went on to say that they wanted me to help them find some more bad information on the former bank officers. I explained that I had been good friends, which Noel Lussier and had done quite a bit of business with him years ago before he got involved with the banks. I told him that I knew nothing about his business in late years, I also pointed out that Lussier had been working with the banks, their officers and directors on a daily basis. If anybody knew what he was doing, it should have been them.

I asked Childs about the misrepresentation of the motel, when I bought it, the $3,900,000 appraisal, the Day's Inn franchise, the $250,000 note that the bank had issued then called, about the White River house that the bank wanted to use in the purchase of the motel, the cash flow claims and the other misrepresentations the bank had made to get me to buy the motel. Childs said that this all took place before he started working for the bank, so it didn't concern him. He was not interested in any of the offers that I had worked hard to get. I left the bank more discouraged than ever and feeling that I had been used and cheated again.

I called Richard Uchida and told him what had happened. Richard said that this was contrary to all his negotiations with Cynthia LaRose and he would call her right then. Richard said that the bank had met earlier that same day and decided that they were going to go through with a foreclosure. Richard said that LaRose sounded like she was getting a little fed up with the bankers. LaRose told Richard that she felt the offers that I had were good ones as she felt that the motel would sell for around $800,000 at a foreclosure auction.

I did not tell Charlotte about this episode as her nerves could not take anymore. I had been having a hard time to keep her calmed down and sat up with her many nights. It was obvious that the bankers were trying to break us and that they were using us to cover up for their own mistakes. I didn't know how much more that I could take either.

On Monday March 2, I took Charlotte to the doctors for the third time in less than a week. This time it was to the University Health Center a branch of the Medical Center Hospital in Burlington, where Clay was. The doctor said her nerves were so bad that it would require a lot rest and no stress if she were to get well again and it could take months. He also said that she would have to continue to have the cortisone shots in her scalp to try to stop her from losing anymore of her hair. I couldn't see how we were going to stop the stress until we could get settled with the banks and they seemed to want to do everything to us that they could except settle.

That afternoon after returning from taking Charlotte to the hospital and seeing Clay I thought that I would try to reason with the bank again as I knew that I had to do something if I was going to save Charlotte's health as well as my own. I called Bradford Bank to again talk to Childs. The girl said that Childs was busy but that she would have him call right back but as usual he didn't. Tuesday morning I got hold of Childs. He said that the bank would take $1,250,000 cash and that they wanted my financial statement. I got hold of the people who had made the $1,150,000 offer. They agreed to come up $50,000 to $1,200,000 and they gave me a deposit of $25,000. I called Childs with the new offer. He was not happy. He said that it had to be $1,250,000 or I would have to kick in the extra $50,000, and get them some bad information on the former bank officers.

I contacted the buyers and told them that the bank said that they had to have $1,250,000. They asked if it would be all right for them to contact Childs at the bank. I told them sure go ahead. They called back and said that Childs told them the he knew that it was a good offer and that the bank would possible take it if I provided whatever else that they wanted. Childs told them that the bank would give an answer within forty eight hours. A whole week went by and I could not get a reply from the bank as to what they wanted to do about the offer. They did not give an answer in forty eight hours as Childs had said that they would. A week or so later the bank's lawyer Cynthia LaRose said that they were going to accept the $1,200,000 cash offer.

Now that the bank had agreed to take the offer I drove to New Hampshire where the buyers lived to try to put the finishing touches on the deal. The buyers and I felt that the deal was all set but there were a couple of things that needed to be agreed on with the bank. We decided that I should try to clear these up with the bank and that I would come back and meet with the buyers the following week on Tuesday March 17. Monday the 16, I met with Richard Uchida, Tom Lauzon and Ed Amidon, another Vermont lawyer that I had hired to handle the bank business that had to be settled in Vermont. I wanted to be sure that when the motel sold that I knew where I stood. Richard Uchida said that he would again try to set up a meeting with Cynthia

LaRose so that we could settle the whole mess at the same time. She refused to meet with us.

Tuesday evening I again drove to New Hampshire to meet with the buyers as we had planned. They were excited about buying the motel. They told me that they had been familiar with this motel ever since it had been built, but that they had never seen it do much business until the time that I owned and that this was what had gotten them interested in buying it. The buyers and I seemed to be in agreement about how the transaction should take place but there were still some questions about the banks position that couldn't be answered. We decided that in order to expedite this transaction it was going to be necessary to have one more meeting and have someone there from the bank who could make decisions.

The next morning I called Richard Uchida and told him we thought it best if we could all meet with the bankers and their lawyers to finalize the agreement. Richard said that he agreed and that he would call Cynthia LaRose and propose the plan to her. Richard called back saying that she told him that they definitely would not meet to discuss the sale. She said that she did not know how to prepare for such a meeting as she did not know what questions might come up. I called the buyers and reported that the bankers and their lawyer would not meet with us. They were furious and wanted to know if it was okay for them to call Ed Childs. I told them to go ahead and give him a call. They called back and said that Childs had agreed to meet with us at 2:00 p.m. Saturday March 21. A few minutes Richard Uchida call confirming the same meeting. Richard said that Childs had agreed to meet in Bradford but had said that he wouldn't meet anywhere else. I planned my schedule for 2:00 p.m. Saturday as did everybody else. I picked up some material from the motel that I thought we might need.

Thursday morning prior to the Saturday meeting I received a call from Richard Uchida who said the Cynthia LaRose had contacted him saying that the bank was not going to take the offer on the motel and instead had decided to go back to the foreclosure route and sell the motel at auction. There would be no meeting on Saturday as planned. Richard said that he would call the buyers and inform them. The buyers were very upset and called Ed Childs who told them that I was the one who had called the meeting off. This was unbelievable.

Charlotte, who was about going crazy decided to call Cynthia LaRose. LaRose didn't want to talk to her. Charlotte told her that she wanted to tell her what she and the banks were doing to her. She told her about the shots that she was getting in her scalp, all Cynthia could say was "Oh my god, oh my god." Charlotte was also going for mental health counseling every week. She felt ashamed and embarrassed going there but realized she needed the help.

There was a lot of talk on the street and among the business community that the present employees of the banks were trying to break the bank. This was hard to believe but it sure looked like that was what they were trying to do along with their well-paid lawyers. Not only was this costly to the bank but I wasted several more weeks plus the expense of running around, paying lawyers, my accountant and to say nothing about all the stress and frustration. I did not need this as I had plenty to do and I couldn't afford it.

I realized that all the bankers and the lawyers were getting well paid. They didn't have a penny invested and that time didn't mean a thing to them. They got paid every week. We were the only ones who were not getting paid and we had everything that we had worked a lifetime for at stake. We were at their mercy and they could care less.

On Wednesday, April 1, I received a call from Richard Uchida, who said that Cynthia LaRose had called him. She stated Charlie Bucknam said that Caledonia National Bank didn't want to be involved in trying to settle the motel deal and said that they hadn't been involved in creating any of the motel problems. This was unbelievable. It was their bank president, Noel Lussier who introduced me to the motel deal and kept pushing to get me to buy it. He was the one who set up the deal using the Danville house and the White River house. It was Caledonia National Bank president Noel Lussier and the Caledonia Bank chief executive Bob Platka who said go to another bank and borrow $80,000 and send it to Bradford Bank and that Caledonia Bank would take care of the other $170,000. If it hadn't been for them, we wouldn't be in this mess.

A number of people were talking about Charlie Bucknam and the way that he was handling the bank business. Many questioned his ability to run a bank. Another thing that was being talked about was when the Hardwick Electric Company was interested in buying the Caledonia National Bank building in Hardwick Bucknam and his wife Debra who is a lawyer purchased it from the bank and sold it to the Electric Company. Some people even suggested that Noel Lussier had been a partner with the Bucknams in this transaction. We decided to check it out. The town of Hardwick records showed that the Bucknams bought the bank building from Caledonia Bank for $75,000. Robert Plaka had signed the deed. A few months later the Bucknams deeded the building to the Hardwick Electric Company for $99,500. This was a profit of $24,500. More strangely the transfer return showed that $10,000 of the profit was derived from the sale of personal property even though the transfer return showed no personal property at the time of purchase. In Vermont there is a land gains tax, which taxes profit on real estate at 30 percent if sold within one year. This allowed the Bucknams to evade the Vermont land gains tax on $10,000 of profit. Stranger still the Hardwick town clerk could not find a copy of the transfer tax return that was filed when the Bucknams sold the property. It was missing from the records. The only people who have access to these records other than the town clerk are the town listers and the lawyers. I had to obtain this information from the Vermont tax department.

You won't believe what happened next.

YOUR CERTIFICATE OF DEPOSIT WILL MATURE
ON THE DATE SHOWN BELOW. THE RATE WILL BE
DETERMINED ON THAT DATE. PLEASE CALL THE
BANK FOR CURRENT BAL.

WILLIAM F. HILL, OR CHARLOTTE HILL
PO BOX 15 HARDWICK, VT
05843-0015
TYPE: 14 TO 56 MONTHS TO ACCOUNT NUMBER:
2802170
BALANCE AT MATURITY: 7,029.48
INTEREST RATE:
MATURITY DATE: 01/13/92

Please use this to pay off note #20026478 and apply the balance
to note #778151. Please send an accounting of the same showing
balance of note 778151

Thank you,
William F. Hill

CERTIFICATE OF DEPOSIT
AUTO RENEWAL NOTICE

YOUR CERTIFICATE OF DEPOSIT HAS BEEN AUTOMATICALLY RENEWED FOR THE ORIGINAL TERM AT THE INTEREST RATE SPECIFIED BELOW.

WILLIAM F. HILL, OR CHARLOTTE HILL
PO BOX 15
HARDWICK, VT
05843-0015
ACCOUNT NUMBER: 2802170
ROLLOVER BALANCE 7,029.48
OLD RATE 8.200
NEW RATE 5.650
DATE RENEWED 01/13/92
NEW MATURITY DATE 02/13/92

William E. Hill, Associates
Box 15
Hardwick, VT 05843
802-472-6308

Mr. Charles W Bucknam
President, Caledonia National Bank
PO Box 195
Danville, VT 05828
Jan. 27, 1992

Dear Charlie:

Thank you for your letter of Jan. 17 explaining where you had credited the proceeds of my CD# 2802170. I can see why you did it this way. However, I had asked that it be used to pay off note# 20026478 and the balance be applied to note # 778151.

This CD was pledged against the property of Wilfred McKenney. I worked two years to get this loan straightened out and the bank paid in full. While I was doing this, the bank deducted over $17,000 from my account although there were two other endorsers on the note. I lost over $8,000 to get the bank whole. I'm not complaining as I realize that this was my obligation.

My point is that it seems that the bank could apply the proceeds as I had requested.

I'm still trying to straighten out the motel deal but, with no cooperation from the bank. They continue to throw away tens of thousands of dollars in legal fees, management co. fees and auction advertising when I still feel that this could have been straightened out by getting together in a joint effort to solve things and salvage all that we could.

I trust that you will apply the proceeds from my CD as I requested.

Thank you,
William F. Hill
January 31, 1992

William F. Hill
William F. Hill, Associates
Box 15
Hardwick, VT 05843

Dear Bill:

We believe we have rights of set-off with respect to any accounts you have here at the bank. The banks set-off rights under the law as, we understand it, allow us to apply your accounts to your indebtedness. Your attempt to direct the payment of that against a specific loan account was, in our opinion, an attempt to override our set-off rights, and would have been, for all intents and purposes, a payment of the account to you, which we were not required to do. While we appreciate the fact that you voluntarily those to have that account apply to your loan accounts, we believe at the same time that our set- off rights allow us to apply that account as we did.

Very truly yours,
Charles W. Bucknarn Jr.
President

Charlie3Feb '91
Account# 20026478 was due in full on Oct. 1 I still insist that the $7,027.48 be credited as I have requested.

Thank you,
Bill Hill

CWB/mc
cc: Valsangiacomo, Detora, McQuesten, Rose & Grearson
Gary McQuesten

CREDIT PROFILE SM

ꞏd CREDIT PROFILE℠   *TRW*

Inquiry Information

IDENTIFICATION NUM

3499953   HILL WILLIAM

03/27/92   04:48:24   BAOS   102   HILL   TVT1   56-446260/4

Subscriber Name / Court Name			Type				Account/Docket Number	Balance / Date	Amount / Past Due		
THE CALEDONIA NAT BK PAID ACCT 10-88 11-87			1196409 ISC	4 11	ORIGI $1500		20013300				
THE CALEDONIA NAT BK DELINQ 120 2-92 9-86			1196409 UNK SCH MONTH PAY	1 36	$22000	14212 126J	20026470 2-19-92 LASTPAY 10-13-9	$4420	C2CCC-C3 CCCCC---C	
THE CALEDONIA NAT BK PAID ACCT 12-88 12-85			1196409 UNK	1 180	$16000		2779066				
THE CALEDONIA NAT BK			1196409	1			2770024				

CHAPTER 10

THE PROBLEMS GET WORSE

I had paid out a tremendous amount of money in legal fees and lawyers in this bank mess. I still needed to pay them some more and I also needed to renew our health insurance, especially with all the problems that Charlotte had developed. Also my Hardwick Town property truces would soon be due. I had three accounts at Bradford National Bank. On April 3, 1992, I went to Bradford and asked the teller to check and see how much I had in each account. She checked and wrote the balances on a paper for me. One savings account had $22,044.92 another had $3,246.98, and the third account had a balance of $2,017.96. That was over $27,000 in all. I told her that I would like to withdraw those accounts from the bank. The teller said that she would have to get Lourette Sweet, a bank officer. Lourette was summoned to the bank lobby. She said that I would have to wait as she had someone in her office that she needed to finish with. I waited quite a while but no one came out of her office until she reappeared and asked me to come in. She said that the bank was not going to release any of my money until the motel deal was settled. I left very frustrated.

The banks were really squeezing me every way that they could and I was trying to decide what to do. I remembered John Hersh from the FBI and the other two men who had visited me the past August had said that I had been frauded by the banks and that they were going to help me straighten things out especially the motel deal. I had never heard from them again, since they were at my house. I decided to give them a call. I called John Hersh I asked him what he had ever done to help as he had agreed that he would. Hersh said that my call was

148

timely and that he would like to have me come to Rutland that very afternoon. He told me where to find him. Rutland is about a hundred miles away but I told him that I would be there.

I went to where Hersh told me to, which was up on the top floor in the back of a three story building. The door was locked and I had to wait to be let in. After I got in, I had to wait quite a while but finally the same three men that had been to my house were all there. They were very friendly and we visited for a while. Hersh asked me a few questions about certain people in my area. Then he told me that I needed to get a lawyer. I told him that I had two lawyers working for me now. He said that I couldn't use my present lawyers, that I needed to get one that he approved of and one that worked with them. I didn't know what he was talking about. I told him that I couldn't afford anymore lawyers. Hersh said that what I had to do would only take about an hour so it wouldn't cost much. I asked what I had to do. He said that when they were at my house the past August that I had agreed to cooperate with them and that everybody who cooperated with them had to plead guilty to something. I remembered that I had told them that I had no problem talking to them, but I didn't remember making any deal of any kind except to answer their questions. I thought that he was kidding. I asked him what I would be pleading guilty to. He said that he didn't know that they would have to come up with something. I became quite upset.

I asked again, "Why can't I use my regular lawyers?"

Hersh said that he didn't even want me to tell my regular lawyers. I asked him why not. He said that way nobody will ever know about it. He said that all I would have to do is go before Judge Billings and plead guilty to some small charge. That I would get a month or two of probation and that nobody would ever know about it. He told me to go see Jimmy Carroll, a Rutland lawyer.

I couldn't believe this; Hersh told me that I was going to have to plead guilty but he didn't know to what. He didn't want me to tell my lawyers. He said that I had to have a lawyer that worked with them and one that he approved of. I had never heard of such a thing, and I couldn't believe it. The next morning I called Jimmy Carroll as Hersh had told me to. Hersh had already contacted him. Carroll wanted me to come to his office in Rutland on May 5. I drove all the way back to Rutland, over a hundred miles one way. I met with Jim Carroll and his partner John Kennelly. I told them that I didn't understand what was going on. Carroll told me not to trust Hersh or anyone from the federal government. He then wanted me to pay him a retainer of $10,000 right then to represent me and he wanted me to agree to plead guilty to any charge that the government might come up with. I think that he could see that I was very upset. To top that off he wanted $10,000 when Hersh had told me that it was only going to take about an hour. Carroll said that if I didn't want to agree to plead guilty that he wanted $30,000 up front to represent me and that I could expect to spend at least $100,000. He told me that there was no way to get away from the Feds once that I had been targeted. I did not hire Jimmy Carroll. I told him that I would let him know.

I had read in the newspapers that the US attorney that was handling the bank problems name was Paul Van De Graff. I called Van De Graff and told him that I wanted to see him. He did not want to talk to me, but I insisted. He finally agreed that he would see me for a few minutes. I drove to the Burlington Federal building to his office. Van De Graff explained that he had recently flipped on a motorcycle. One side of his face was all black and blue. It reminded me of Clay's accident only Van De Graff didn't suffer any brain damage. I told him that he was lucky not to have suffered any head injuries. I tried to discuss some of the bank issues with him but he kept saying that he didn't want to hear them. He kept saying that he was going to charge me with something but he wouldn't or couldn't say what. He told me that if I didn't have the funds to hire a lawyer that one could be assigned to me. He then gave me some forms to fill out if I wanted the court to appoint me a lawyer. The forms were mostly financial information to show that I couldn't afford to hire a lawyer. I didn't dare to fill them out due to the motel deal I didn't know where I stood financially.

I decided to contact some other lawyers. I either called or visited six or seven lawyers. One thing that really upset me was that every one of them told me not to trust any of the feds including the FBI or the US attorney's office. I could not believe that they were telling me not to trust these people. They all also told me that I would stand very little chance of winning against the Feds, if I decided to fight them. They used terms like they got a gun to your head and you might as well give in and cooperate with them. You can't win I was told, the Judge isn't going to listen to you. I was told that the judge is on their side and he is not going to listen to you. This was very frightening. I always thought that their job was to seek the truth and see that justice was done, nor to see how many people that they could get.

Several of the lawyers that I contacted were already involved in some aspect of the bank problems and so could not represent me anyway. I had always heard that Peter Langrock in Middlebury was an excellent lawyer, so I contacted him and made an appointment to see him. Charlotte and I went to his office, which was about one hundred miles away. We liked Peter. He also told me not to trust the Feds. He said that I was like a rowboat setting out there with seventeen torpedo boats pointed at me. It would be hopeless for me to try to fight them unless I had at least $100,000 to spend and even that wouldn't guarantee that I could win. He said that they will keep after you until they get what they want. I couldn't figure what they wanted from me.

Peter said that he would represent me in a guilty plea but was not interested in going against the Feds if I didn't want to plead guilty. He said that a guilty plea wouldn't be so bad as he couldn't see where I had done anything very bad from what I had told him. We still had no idea as to what they were going to charge me with. I decided to use Peter as I had taken a liking to him and I had heard that he was good.

I did not tell Richard Uchida or Ed Amidon about the FBI and the US attorney as Hersh had told me not co. The last report that I had gotten from Richard was that the bank was going ahead with another foreclosure auction on the motel sometime in May. Cynthia LaRose had told him that the federal bank regulators would not allow the bank to make any deal with me to try to solve this mess. LaRose said that the banks had a cease and desist order from the bank regulators forbidding them to do any business with Lyndonville Bank and also from doing any business with any of Noel Lussier's relatives. Roger Lussier, president of Lyndonville Bank is Noel's brother. As I had borrowed the $80,000 from Lyndonville Bank to pay toward the $250,000 note when I purchased the motel, they could not make any settlement or deal with me. Nothing made any sense, the banks were not interested in straightening out a problem, they didn't seem to care how much they spent avoiding it and now they were saying that the federal regulators didn't want it straightened out either. I just couldn't imagine anybody doing business this way.

Earlier in April I had read in the newspaper that Bernie Sanders was going to be speaking at Lyndon College on the evening of April 15.

Bernie is Vermont's only congressman. He is neither a Democrat nor a Republican but a member of the progressive party. I under stood that he was a member of the house banking committee. Bernie is always raving about all the injustices in this country and advocates to always be for the underdog. Lyndon College is only about fifteen miles away. By going over Stannard Mountain. I thought that I would try to talk to Bernie about the bank problems. I called his Burlington office to see if I could arrange to meet briefly with him when he was in Lyndonville. They wanted to know what I wanted to talk to Bernie about. When I said that it was about some bank problems, they said that there was no way that Bernie would see me. I later wrote several letters to his Washington office but he wasn't one bit interested in hearing about any bank problems. I also contacted the offices of our senators, Patrick Leahy and Jim Jeffords. Jeffords wrote me a letter saying that he had contacted the FBI and they had told him that they were handling things and that he shouldn't get involved. Mary Miller in Senator Leahy's office suggested that I contact Tim Hayward, head of the Vermont Bankers Association. I went to see him. He told me that I would not get any help or satisfaction from the senator's or the congressman's office. He said that it was too political. He said that there had been a lot of banking scandals lately and that to many politicians had gotten their fingers burned. He suggested that I write a book. After I left Tim Hayward's office without any encouragement, I decided to go the governor's office. I talked to a lady there who seemed very nice. She said that the governor, who is Howard Dean, certainly would be very concerned and that they would get back to me very soon. I never heard from them. I also tried contacting the Vermont attorney general's office. They sent me a letter saying that they had turned my complaint over to John Hersh of the FBI. I also wrote several letters to the Federal

Reserve, to the FDIC and the Comptroller of Currency. Most of them didn't answer so I tried calling them. They were not interested. I contacted the Vermont Banking and Insurance commissioner several times. They always told me that these were national banks and not state chartered banks and so that they had no control over them. They said that it was the comptroller of currency that I need to contact either in Washington or New York City. I contacted both offices several times but it didn't amount to anything.

Nobody wanted to get involved.

May 11, 1992
Mr. William F. Hill
PO Box 15 Hardwick, VT 05843
Re: UNITED STATES v. HILL, et al.
Dear Mr. Hill:

I am writing to set forth the terms under, which this firm will undertake to represent you in the above referenced matter. These are the terms you, Jim Carroll and I discussed at our meeting at this office last Tuesday.

We will need a retainer of $10,000 to be held, in trust, to cover anticipated costs, expenses and legal services to be rendered in this matter. Our time will be charged and billed on a monthly basis, and you will be sent itemized bills setting forth the time spent, the work performed, and the attorney performing the work. Time will be billed at the following hourly rates:

James P. Carroll $130
John J. Kennelly $110
Thomas A. Zonay $90

We will do everything in our power to keep the costs to a minimum, but we are not in control of these proceedings and the costs are directly correlated to decisions you make, and decisions the government makes. Our representation would include analyzing the various transactions with Lyndonville Savings Bank, and Randolph National Bank. Particularly, we would analyze those transactions in light of the applicable federal criminal law, and any corollary civil statutes. Representation would continue through sentencing, if there is in fact a sentence meted out here.

As we explained at our meeting last week, the initial retainer is based on an assumption that there would be guilty pica to some charge, as suggested by assistant US attorney Van De

Graaf, in return for a promise by the government to move for downward departure for your cooperation.

Such an agreement would entail testifying on the government's behalf The alternative, if there is one, is to not strike any deal with the government and proceed in response to any indictment that may be handed down. In that event, the retainer necessary would be $30,000.

We spoke on the phone this morning and you advised me that you did not have the money for the $10,000 retainer and that you will get back to us. I would like to make clear once again, that we will undertake no representation of you, until the retainer has been received.

It is also important for you to realize that while the government at this point may not be in a rush, there will come a point when they may no longer be willing to pursue any deal with you, for various reasons, including the fact that they may not think a deal is necessary for the successful prosecution of their case against you and all the others they allege to be involved.

In the event you have any questions, please do not hesitate to contact me.

Very truly yours,
John J. Kennelly

JJK/mtb

William F. Hill
Box 15
Hardwick, VT 05843
802-472-6308

June 1, 1992

Mr. Paul Van De Graaf
US Attorney
Federal Building
Burlington, Vt. 05401
Dear Mr. Van De Graaf:

I appreciate you taking the time to see me last week. I hope that your bike injury is coming along good. It looked pretty sore. You are very lucky that you didn't receive a head injury. Every time I go to Burlington to see my son who has been lying there since mid- February from a similar accident I think of you and am thankful that you didn't get seriously hurt.

After leaving your office, I went downstairs, as you suggested, and picked up a form to have an attorney assigned to me. I then contacted several attorneys. They all needed money, lots of money, up front. I have been trying to figure out how to raise it, but can't seem to find a solution. I can't borrow it and wouldn't want to if I could as I now have no way to pay it back.

In talking to different attorneys, one thing really upsets me and scares the hell out of me. With all due respect to you, they all told me not to trust anybody from the Feds. This has been very disturbing. Certainly I want to trust you and get this mess worked out. I got into it by trusting the bankers.

I started to fill out the form that the clerk gave me. It wanted mostly financial information. I always had a financial statement that I felt was very accurate, but right now I don't know where I stand in many areas. The way things have gone, I'm afraid that if I fill it out in order to not have to pay for

156

a lawyer somebody will now or in the future determine that it is not accurate and I will be in trouble for misrepresenting something. Richard Uchida the attorney who represented me from New Hampshire determined my present net worth to be less than a negative $1,000,000 due to the hotel deal and all. I really don't know where I stand in many areas. I really do not know who to trust or who to turn to. I had hoped that I could sit down with you and your people and work out whatever it is that we need to work out.

The bank has recently taken all the money that I had earmarked to pay my property taxes, our health insurance and present lawyers. Ed Amidon had to quit because I couldn't pay him.

I know that you feel that the present bankers are all on the up and up. This is the way that I felt about the old bankers. My wife and I have never been treated so cruelly as we have been by the people who are there now, and they have been less than truthful with us at times. I feel that some of them may be covering their own tracks.

I do not know why some of the bankers can do inside deals and get away with it. I do not wish to get Charlie Bucknam in trouble as I know that he is looking forward to an active and profitable career as president of the new bank, but this is just one example of what I mean.

In the summer of 1987, Caledonia National Bank moved its Hardwick Branch from North Main St to what used to be the Sterling Trust building in the shopping center. The Town of Hardwick was interested in the vacated Bank building for the Hardwick Electric Co. It takes time for municipalities to move on anything and get things done as it had to be voted on. Knowing that the Town and the Electric Co., which is owned by the Town of Hardwick were interested in purchasing the bank building Charlie Bucknam, an officer of CNB, and his wife Debra, a lawyer purchased it for $75,000 and closed on December 18, 1987. The Deed was signed by Bio Platka, an officer of Caledonia National Bank. On August 30, 1988, the Bucknams closed a deal with the Town of Hardwick and Hardwick Electric at a sale price of $99,500, showing a profit of $24,500. More strangely when sold the transfer tax return showed that $10,000 of the sale price was allocated to personal property although, no personal property was shown at the time of purchase. This allowed the Bucknams to evade the VT real estate land gains tax on $10,000 of profit. With a holding period of less than one year, the Vermont land gains tax would be 30 percent of the profit.

Stranger still, the Hardwick Town Clerk could not find a copy of the transfer tax return filed at the time of purchase. It was missing from the records. Outside of the Town Clerk the others who have access to their file are the listers and lawyers. A copy was obtained from the state tax department.

Debra Bucknam is a former law partner of Anthony Aiossia, a Hardwick attorney. Aiossa has been mentioned for improper conduct involving the Independent Bank group although he is still doing work for the Bank. Maybe this is all okay but it looks like the kettle calling the pot black.

As I told John Hersh the two times I met with him, I have nothing to hide and really thought from talking to him that we could work things out. I have tried to answer all his questions. After talking to you, I know that you think that I'm one of the bad guys, which is understandable, but I don't feel that you completely understand how these things happened. I wish that there was some way that we could sit down and iron this all out. I don't understand why we can't but I guess that the law doesn't work this way.

As you can see, I'm really lost as what to do and really scared to fill out that form. I certainly want to trust you and hope that you can tell me what to do.

Sincerely,
William F. Hill

CHAPTER 11

MORE HARASSMENT FOR US AND NEW OWNERS FOR THE MOTEL

On Monday, May 11, our property taxes in the town of Hardwick were going to be due. They were around $14,000 and included the taxes on our house and the post office building. I also needed to pay our health insurance. Around April 20, I went to see Charlie Bucknam. I told him that I would like to use some of my money in Bradford Bank to pay my property taxes. I explained that the taxes were on properties that he had put leans on and that if I didn't pay them on time the tax would only be $1,600 more with the penalty that would be on them the next day. Bucknam said that he would make sure that I could get the money out of my account in Bradford Bank. He said to contact him the day before I needed it. The deadline was on a Monday so I called him on the Friday before. He said there would be no problem but to call him Monday morning, the eleventh, which was the final day. I called him at the bank. He said that everything was all set, they were going to let me have my money, but he wanted me to call him back around noon. When I called him back, he said that the bank wanted to write the checks with my money and wanted me to fax them my tax bills. I didn't think that this was right, as this was my money, but I certainly wanted to pay my taxes so I did as he requested. Time was getting short as the deadline was four o'clock, and it was at least one hour to Bradford each way. Charlotte headed to Bradford to pick up the money. A little while later Bucknam called back and said that I didn't have any money in Bradford Bank.

I asked him, "What do you mean?"

He said, "I'm telling you that you don't have any money in Bradford Bank."

I told him that just a month ago a teller verified that I had over $27,000 in there. Bucknam would only say that I didn't have any money in that bank. After I hung up with Bucknam, I called Gram Gove, a Bradford Bank employee and asked him what was going on. He said that he would try to find out. He looked up my accounts and told me that they had all been drained out on April 20, about the time that I had called Bucknam about using my money. Gove said that he couldn't tell who drew my money out or what they did with it. Gove apologized and said that he knew that whatever had happened didn't look right but that he didn't want to get caught in the middle.

When Charlotte, who had been very upset and even despondent over the way that the banks had been treating us, arrived at the bank to pick up the money, they told her a different story. They said that they couldn't give it to her without my authorization. Not knowing about Bucknam she went to a pay phone and called me and said that they had told her that I needed to call the bank and authorize them to give her the money as the accounts were in my name. I called again and talked to Sara Paul, another bank employee. She said that she would have Ed Childs call me right back, but he never called. By this time it was nearly 3:30, already too late to get to the town clerks by 4:00. At 4:15 I got another call from Charlotte. She said that as she was leaving the bank Charlie Bucknam came in; and when he saw her his face became very red and he slinked into the first office that he came to. She asked if she should go back and see him. I told her to go ahead if she felt like it. When she went back, Bucknam told her that I didn't have any money in that bank and he wouldn't say what had happened to it. She talked to Childs and Bucknam. They gave her a very hard time. At first they would only say that I had no money in that bank. They then told her that our attorney, Richard Uchida knew that I didn't have any money in that bank. Charlotte called again and said they told her that, Richard Uchida, knew that I had no money, in Bradford Bank. When Charlotte told me this, I immediately called Richard. He said that was the first that he had heard about it and that nobody had notified him. He was furious. About a half hour later, Uchida called back and said that he had just received a fax from Cynthia LaRose, the bank's attorney saying that the bank had closed out the $22,093.24 account without any mention of the other two accounts. It was now going to cost us over $1,600 in penalties for not getting our property taxes paid on time. A couple of days later, Charlotte saw the town clerk. He said he wondered if we had forgot to pay our taxes as in the past thirty five years we had never been late before.

This added stress and only made things worse for Charlotte. She was losing her hair and going to several doctors, including the mental health clinic. They are all telling her that if she can't get out from under all this strain and stress that she isn't going to make it. I was starting to have the same kind of headaches that she has had for several months. I had never had headaches before. I didn't realize that anything could hurt so much and they didn't go away. I went to the doctors, and they told me the same thing that they had been telling her; that the only way to get over this was to get out from under the stress and it was going to take several months of rest. Even if I could find a way to get out from under this mess I didn't know how I could rest as I was going to have to work harder than ever to try to pull everything back together.

On Sunday night the day before all this happened Noel Lussier, who had been living on a farm in Florida was in town I went to see him. I told him what a mess that I was in because I had listened to him and the other bankers. He didn't seem to care. He had changed. One thing that I did find out was the reason that Jack Howard's name was on the $170,000 note that I couldn't understand before was that Bradford Bank or Noel had sold him the White River house for $170,000 and Caledonia Bank had financed it. I had paid off the other $80,000 of the $250,000 motel note. That is how Bradford Bank got the motel out of their OREO account. I did not understand it at the time but OREO stands for other real estate owned, by a bank. Banks are not supposed to leave any real estate in their OREO account any longer than they have to. In order to get it out of OREO they are required to get at least a ten percent down payment. I now understood why they set the loan up this way. I later learned that Lussier and not the bank owned the White River house. I could now see that by using this house in the motel sale for $275,000 and the having Jack Howard an employee of his buy it back for $170,000 for him Lussier would stand to make an easy $100,000.

Back on April 21, 1991, when I first met with the bank board at Bradford Bank Winston Oaks mentioned that they had sold the White River house. Laurette Sweet immediately cut him off and changed the subject. I thought that it was funny that no one wanted to talk about this house. I didn't realize that they were covering up anything. Even though this subject has come up several times, especially in talking to Mike Flipiak and Charlie Bucknam neither of them nor anyone from the bank had ever disclosed the truth to me about this house. The bank had even in their suit against the former bankers claimed that Jack Howard had borrowed the money for me and acted on my behalf. I told Richard Uchida about my visit with Lussier. He was unhappy that I went to see him even though I now had the true facts about the White River house. The Bank had now scheduled another auction of the motel for Wednesday May 20. On Tuesday, May 19, the day before the bank was to put the motel on the auction block, I received an urgent call from Richard Uchida. He said that the bank just realized that nobody had shown any interest in the auction. They wanted me to call the buyers that I had for the $1,200,000 cash and again try to sell them the motel. I told him that I wouldn't do it because of the way that the bank had treated them when they were interested in buying it. About 4:30, or five o'clock, Uchida called again and said that the bank's attorney, Cynthia LaRose, had contacted him again and said that they would give me back the $27,000 that they had taken out of my accounts if I could get them to renew their $1,200,000 offer before the auction. This time I did call them. They said that the value of the property had slipped to far back, and that they were not happy with the way that the bank had treated them. They did, however, agree to go to the auction the next day.

Wednesday May 20, the auction was to take place at two o'clock. I certainly wanted to see what happened. I took Stuart Hill, with me to the motel to video the auction. When he walked in with a video camera, Cynthia LaRose and the Auctioneer told him that there would be no pictures. Stuart told LaRose that it was a public auction and that he had a perfect right to take pictures. LaRose called both the local police and the New Hampshire state police who showed up and threatened to arrest him if he didn't put his camera away.

The auction started with about thirty people in attendance, including motel employees, the banks lawyers and several bankers including Ed Childs and Mike Flipiak. Several questions were asked before the auction but LaRose wouldn't give any answers. The only bidder was the customers that I had. They started the bidding at $250,000. The bank immediately bid $300,000. The bidding progressed $50,000 at a time between my customer and the bank until the bank bid $900,000. My customer then bid $925,000 and the bank immediately bid $950,000. My customer didn't bid again. The auctioneer kept teasing him for another bid and kept lowering the bid that he was asking for until he got down to asking them for bid of $951,000. They wouldn't budge. The auctioneer called a recess where he LaRose, Childs and Flipiak went out into the hall. I always thought that the purpose of a recess was for the auctioneer and his staff to work on the bidders to try to get them to bid again. He didn't even speak to them. When they came back in, the auctioneer tried again to get them to raise the bid even by a thousand dollars. I think that this turned them off and they wouldn't bid. This meant that the banks now owned the motel. I thought that the banks were only entitled to one bid. Instead they were by bidding every time my customer bid. I would question the legality of this. I wouldn't let it happen at one of my auctions as it is not very ethical if not illegal.

When LaRose found out that Stuart Hill was with me, she became very nervous about not letting him video the auction. She had made an audio tape of the auction, which she offered to give him. She seemed very nervous about what she had done.

Shortly after the auction Rochell Inman, the manager handed in her resignation and took a job managing the Ramada, a large motel and conference center in Burlington Vermont. After that I did not follow the operation or what was happening at the motel very close. I did however continue to try to reach some agreement with the bank for settling with them. Richard Uchida said that it would now be necessary to file a suit against the banks in order to reach a settlement and get the leans off my properties that they had placed on them. He started to prepare a suit.

Meanwhile I was still trying to negotiate with the banks and their president Charlie Bucknam. Part of my proposal for straightening out the motel mess was that I would deed the North Danville house to the bank for $125,000 as was originally agreed and that they pay off Lyndonville Savings Bank. Mike Flipiak had agreed to this.

In June I sent the bank a deed to this house as Flipiak had agreed. The bank kept the deed but never got it recorded. They never paid off Lyndonville Bank as they agreed to do. I kept getting payment notices from Lyndonville Bank and the taxes were due to the town of Danville. I had several inquiries from people who were interested in buying this house. I did not know what to do as Bucknam's bank was now holding the deed that I had given them. Each time I would call Charlie Bucknam and tell him about the interested buyers and ask him what did he want me to do, try to sell it to them or send them to him. His answer was always the same, he would get back to me, but he never did. I kept getting interest bills from Lyndonville Bank, which I was paying to keep my credit good, and this mess certainly wasn't Lyndonville Bank's fault.

We met twice with Bucknam and their bank's lawyer Gary McQuesten. At the second meeting after much discussion, McQuesten raised his arms and turned to Bucknam and told him that the banks had really harmed the Hill's, which was us. He then told him that he felt that the bank should call in the bonding company and compensate us for all the problems that the bankers had caused us. Bucknam was not interested in hearing this. He didn't want the bonding company looking into all the unethical things that he had been doing. I did not hear anymore from Bucknam.

On August 11, 1992, I took Charlotte to her doctors, and they cut some pieces out of her head to send to a lab to again try to determine if there was anything that they could do to stop her hair loss. The Doctor told her that in her opinion all her hair and nerve problems were caused by the bank business.

Charlotte was really upset and determined to do something to get this mess straightened out. The next day she went to Bradford to again confront Charlie Bucknam about straightening things out, as she couldn't take any more. While she was there he told her that he was advised to take the money out of our accounts at Bradford Bank back on April 20. Yet he had led us to believe that we could use our own money to pay our property taxes right up until the time it was too late to make any other arrangements on May 11, the final day. He told her that he and the bank was out to get everything that we had. She didn't get anywhere with him.

On Sunday, August 9, I called Bucknam at home. He agreed to meet with me at the bank on Wednesday Aug 12. Only this time he didn't want any lawyers present. When we met, Charlie brought up the farm deal with Ken Assad. He was unhappy that when I sold it to Assad that I had reserved water rights, from the well, for Dean and Ann's home and for the other property that did not sell with the farm, which Paul and Belynda had put a home on. I explained that there was plenty of water for everybody. He said that the best offer that they had been able to get on the farm was $150,000. This was not surprising as the bank had made no attempt to clean up around there and only let it go downhill while they had it. He also stated that I was liable for any deficiency on the motel deal. I asked him who had approved the farm loan and supervised the closing with Assads. He didn't want to talk about it. I tried to talk to him about all the misrepresentation of the motel when I bought it and that I had several chances to sell it but the bank couldn't make a decision. He tried to act ignorant about both these deals. I suggested that he read the documents and then we could discuss it. He didn't seem very interested. I also brought up about the lot and mobile home that the bank had sold Jerry Clark and had asked to finance through my dealer account. The bank had sold it to Clarks for $16,000. Even though all the payments had been made the bank was claiming that the balance owed was now over $30,000 and they had a note for that amount from the Clarks with monthly payments of $350 per month that ballooned out at the end of five years at over $35,000. This didn't make any sense. He couldn't explain that either and didn't want to talk about it. I brought up about the trick that he had played on us when we had tried to pay our property taxes. I asked him what he would advise me to do about them. He said that he wanted

165

to meet two days later on Friday and that we could talk about them then. He said that he thought that the bank was going to pay them to protect their liens. I reminded him that they were now $1,600 higher due to not paying them on time. It had been published in the local newspaper that we hadn't paid our property taxes. Our property was being advertised for sale to satisfy our taxes. I asked Bucknam how he would feel to have his property advertised in the newspaper for sale by the tax collector. I asked him if he could walk down the street and hold his head up. He said that he couldn't. I told him that I couldn't either but that didn't seem to bother him. I inquired about the two other accounts that I had in Bradford Bank that had disappeared. They had never acknowledged taking them. He said that he didn't know. Bucknam didn't want to talk about any of these things so he said that we could meet again on Friday August 11 at the Hardwick branch of the bank.

Thursday I took Charlotte back to her doctor to have the stitches removed from her head and get the results of her tests. The doctor said that the lab was having trouble determining the problem and was still running tests.

Again on Friday, August 14, I met with Charlie Bucknam and this time Gary Phillips the Hardwick branch manager was present. I tried to discuss some of the problems that I had been trying to solve with the banks. I had questions about what was happening with some of my dealer notes that I had made payments on. Their usual answers were that they would have to check further. I again brought up about the other two accounts that had disappeared from Bradford Bank Bucknam said that all he could find was sixty nine dollars and that he had no idea what happened to the other $5,500. He acted like it didn't make any difference.

I again inquired about paying our property taxes as the tax sale was coming up on Tuesday of the following week. I had about $80,000 in a savings at Caledonia Bank. I had pledged this for additional security on the dealer notes that I had assigned to the bank. I didn't know how the bank would feel about me taking money from this account. This was the account that I had opened when I was a kid and I had never taken a cent out of it. Bucknam said that the bank would probably pay our taxes to protect their interest on their liens. They had no mortgages on my property. He said that he would get back to me on Monday the day before the tax sale. I reminded him that he had kept telling me that I could use my money in Bradford right up to the last minute and then left us hanging. I said that I hoped that he wasn't still playing the same game.

Monday, August 17, the day before the tax sale, I didn't hear from Bucknam so I called his office at the Danville Bank branch. I was getting very nervous and had been all week end. It was very nerve racking. They said at the bank that Bucknam was in Boston and that they didn't know when he would be back. This really threw me as he had promised to call me and I had been waiting for his call. I called Gary Phillips who had been at the Friday meeting when Bucknam had told me that he would call me on Monday. Phillips said that Bucknam went to Boston on Sunday and he knew at the Friday meeting that he was going and that he wouldn't be back on Monday. Phillips said that he would try to reach him in Boston and get back to me. By 11:00 a.m., I hadn't heard back from Phillips so Charlotte went to the bank to see him. Phillips was tied up so she talked to Judy Nudd, the assistant branch manager. Judy said that she would get an answer for us that day. About noon, Phillips called and said that he hadn't been able to get hold of Bucknam but had left messages in several places in Boston for him to call. At 4:30 Judy called and said that they had tried all day to reach Bucknam without success and that he hadn't returned their calls. She said that she would get hold of Bucknam by seven fifteen am the next morning, and call me. This was the day of the tax sale.

Tuesday morning at eight o'clock I had heard nothing from Judy or the bank so I called Danville looking for Charlie Bucknam. It was now less than two hours until the tax sale. He said that he had been on the phone talking to his lawyer about paying our taxes. He said that he was on the phone half the day Monday talking to attorneys about our taxes. All I knew was that they said was that he was in Boston all day attending a meeting. Bucknam said that he thought that the only thing that the bank could do was to let me take the money out of my savings account. He still didn't give me a definite answer. I told him that I had wasted all day Monday trying to get this straightened out and that his bank employees had wasted a lot of time and phone calls trying to reach him. He said that he would get back to me in half an hour. I was really getting nervous. With about an hour to go I had not heard back from Bucknam. I kept thinking that he was going to do the same thing that he did to us the day that the taxes were due. Just before nine o'clock Bucknam called and said that he had arranged to take the money out of my saving account. He told me to go down to the Hardwick branch and see Judy Nudd the assistant manager. When I arrived, Judy had all the checks made out for my taxes. All I had to do was sign the withdrawal slips to allow them to take the money out of my account. They had also made out a check to pay the taxes on the Jerry Clark property out of my account. This was the property that the bank had sold the Clarks and put against my dealer credit line. They also charged me $194.04 penalty, which Judy said was for early withdrawal. I had never heard of a penalty for early withdrawal from a savings account. Judy said that she could not give me the checks, that the bank was going to deliver them to the tax collector, who was Tony Aiossa.

I needed to send a copy of the paid tax receipt to the Pose Office Department to show that the taxes had been paid on the building that we leased to them. Charlotte took the bill down to get it receipted. The Town Clerk called Tony Aiossa to make sure that the taxes had been paid. Aiossa told him that we hadn't paid our taxes that the bank had to pay them for us. The bank had made out the checks and taken them to Aiossa representing that they were paying our taxes with the banks money when it was our money that they were using. I was upset that they had charged me almost two hundred dollars for early withdrawal. I knew that they could do this with a certificate of deposit but I had never heard of it with a savings account. I called Gary Phillips, the branch manager, and asked him if this was a new practice. Phillips said that there was no such thing as a penalty for early withdrawal from a savings account. When I told him what they had done, he became real disgusted and said that it wasn't right but that he didn't want to get involved.

The following Monday Charlotte had two more doctor's appointments, one with Dr. Hinzman, who had been working with her on her hair loss, and one in the afternoon with Meneal Health Clinic in Newport. She returned home even more discouraged. They had her lab report. They wanted her to go to the hospital that Wednesday for more tests. The doctors had told her that her condition could be affecting other parts of her body. The stress was killing us and still there was no end in sight. It seemed that we had no control over anything.

Charlotte's mother who had been on quite a lot of medicine for a long time was starting to have kidney problems. They had to put her on a kidney dialysis machine three times a week. Charlotte's father had to bring her about fifty miles to the same medical center that Clay was in Clay now had regular visiting hours so we would try to visit him when her mother was there so that we could see them both. It was not fun going to the hospital. It was especially hard for Charlotte.

One thing that did give us a little encouragement was that Clay who had been in the hospital unconscious for the past several months had started to open his eyes a little. After that we could see a little improvement in him each day. Several of the family went to see him just about every day. The hospital staff couldn't get over this. They said that patients with head injuries were often soon neglected by their families, but that was not the case with us. We all had faith and we wanted him better. One day when I went to the hospital to see him he wasn't in his bed. I asked where he was. They told me that I had just walked by him. They had him propped up in a chair. I think that by now he was starting to recognize us. They started giving him therapy. His shoulders and neck seemed to be very stiff and they were trying to limber him up. He had a couple of setbacks. A couple of times his lungs gave out but they got them going again. The second time they had to put a trachea tube in his throat. He still couldn't walk or do much for himself when they decided to transfer him to another unit of the hospital where there was supposed to be more therapy. We had big hopes for this but when he got there it seems that he spent most of his time lying in bed. As he started to get better, he became more restless and they kept him in bed by tying his hands and feet. This really bothered me very much. Whenever I was visiting him, I always untied him. He finally got so that he could walk in an awkward way. We all would spend a lot of time walking up and down the halls with him.

A person recovering from head injuries is apt to get easily irritated. Clay had this problem and they had a dark room with no furniture that they would lock him in. He didn't like this and neither did I. We still did not know if he was going to be able to talk as he had the trachea tube in his throat and it appeared that he had a hard time seeing. These two things really had me worried. Finally came the day when they took the tube out of his throat. He didn't say much at first but did try to talk. I was uncertain what was going to happen. Within a week he was saying a few things that we could understand. Charlotte often made biscuit and sausage gravy for breakfast. This was one of Clay's favorites. As we got ready to leave the hospital, Charlotte asked Clay if there was anything that he wanted. Up until he hadn't said very much. He answered her, "Yep, bring some sausage."

They kept him in this unit for quite a while and he did improve a little but it didn't seem that they were trying hard enough or giving him much therapy.

We heard about a private hospital in Troy New York that specialized in treating people recovering from head injuries. We made a trip down to look at and meet with the staff there. The place was very nice. It was very clean and one thing that impressed me was that hardly nobody was in their rooms. They had them all, even the worst cases out doing something. They had all kinds of therapy and it wasn't only a few minutes a day. It was all day long and they had social programs in the evening. We saw some tough cases there but they had them all trying. In talking to the staff they told us that they didn't have any dark rooms and they would not expect to tie anyone in bed. Also they looked a Clay's medical charts and said that he had been getting way to much medicine to hold him down. They also didn't believe in this. We immediately made arrangements to have him transferred there. This was a wonderful place. It was a lot further to go and see him but it was well worth it. He did real well and kept progressing. I would try to call him on the phone in the evening but could very seldom reach him as he was never in his room. This was good. One night when I called the nurse said that he was down in the activities room calling the bingo game. If only the bank business would turn around.

CHAPTER 12

It was reported that by the end of 1991 the three banks of Independent Bank Group had lost over $13,600,000. Their stock had dropped from eighteen dollars a share to less than two dollars. The Bradford Bank was no longer solvent, so the only way that they could see to save it was to merge it with Caledonia National Bank and First National Bank, the other two banks owned by Independent Bank group. The merger was to take place on July 1, 1992. After the merger, all three banks were to be known as The First National Bank of Vermont. Charlie Bucknam was to be the president of the new combined banks and Mike Flipiak became chairman and chief executive officer. Robert Webber decided to leave the bank and seek employment elsewhere it was reported.

A short while after Noel Lussier and the others were forced out the bank Robert Platka, the chief executive of Caledonia Bank had resigned. The banks had filed a civil suit and Paul Van De Graff the assistant US attorney had brought criminal charges against all five former officers including Platka. Most of the charges had to do with insider loans and improper reporting of these loans. Winston Oaks, a bank director who was not busted from the bank, but was reported to owe the banks $2,300,000, said he and the other directors knew nothing about these loans. Oaks was also reported to be partners in several enterprises, with Paul Gallerani and Herbert Gray, two officers who were ousted. The suit alleged that the former bank officers fraudulently obtained millions of dollars in loans circumventing bank policies and banking regulations that governed how much money they could borrow from their own banks. According to a news article by Dan Billing, a Valley News Staff Writer. Oaks said he and the other remaining directors knew nothing of the alleged in priorities before the federal bank examiners started to unravel the story. The current directors are "as amazed as the public" by the alleged complex frauds detailed in the racketeering suit, Oaks said. Oaks also said it shook his faith to hear the allegations against men he had known for years, and who, in some cases, continue to be his partners in business ventures. "If you can't believe what they call you across the boardroom, you just can't run the institution" Oaks said. "When you take a seat at the [boardroom] table, you assume that the people you talk to—it's a matter of trust. We operate on a basis of trust. We're determined to get this bank straightened out." Oaks went on to say that "the guy that led us through this was Mike Flipiak."

Around the middle of August it was reported in several newspapers that the banks had lost another $2,200,000. It went on to say that stockholders in the company have seen their investment lose 90 percent of its value in two years.

Noel Lussier had an old building, just outside of Hardwick, that had been a calf barn and that he had converted in to an office for his own personal business. This was just down the road from the Hardwick branch of Caledonia National Bank building. Around of July of 1992 the FBI after calling in television cameras and news reporters raided Noel Lussier's office in Hardwick. They removed hundreds of documents including income tax records, computers and disks and even the notes and waste paper in the waste paper baskets. A reporter for the Caledonia Record who showed up and waited for the raid to take place was assaulted by Barbara Lussier, Noel's wife. According to the reporter she had taken several pictures of the building and then went to the front door of the office where she was met by Barbara Lussier. The reporter identified herself and asked what was going on. The reporter stated that Mrs. Lussier told her, "None of your business," and told her to leave the property then hit the reporter with a telephone book. The reporter brought charges against Mrs. Lussier who was ordered to appear in court to answer the charges of simple assault.

The next day after the raid the FBI showed up at Lussier's office again and arrested Noel Lussier, putting him in hand cuffs. Lussier was taken before the US district court in Burlington where he was charged with aiding a drug dealer launder money through his banks for a fee. The Burlington Free Press stated, "Lussier, fifty-five, is charged with aiding a former car dealer who had agreed to help a drug trafficker convert $100,000 cash into a check in 1987." The indictment stated, "Lussier, the president of Independent Bank Group Inc. agreed to for a fee of $10,000 to assist the car dealer in June of 1987 in the money laundering, Lussier agreed not to create a federal currency repon required on transfers of more than $10,000 in cash. Instead Lussier procured a $100,000 loan for the car dealer at Bradford National Bank and allowed him to pay it back with cash payments of less than $10,000. A lot of local people had been standing up for Lussier and telling how much they trusted him until that they heard that he had been involved in laundering drug money. They were really turned off by this.

Later Lussier and the other bankers were charged with many counts of bank fraud including concealing their interests in certain loans. They had conducted Independent Bank Group stock transactions without properly disclosing their own personal interests. According to the Caledonia Record News the grand jury also charged that Lussier Gallerani and a third bank officer participated in falsely inflating Independent Bank Group and its subsidiary bank's profits. They had disguised non-performing loans as performing loans by using new loan funds to pay interest on existing loans.

Also the indictment charged that Lussier and another bank officer had purchased a house in White River in May of 1989 for $220,000. They had the house deeded to Jack Howard an employee of Lussier. Gallerani had approved an unsecured loan to Howard for $215,000, which was used to pay for the house. Lussier had consigned the loan. This was the house that was later used in the motel transaction. It was reported that if Noel Lussier was convicted of all the charges brought against him that he was facing up to four hundred and seventeen years in jail and a nineteen and a half million dollar fine. Gallerani was facing one hundred and fifty five years in jail and a six million, seven hundred and fifty thousand dollar fine.

Robert Platka, the former chief executive officer of Caledonia National Bank and a director of Bradford National bank made a plea agreement with the FEDs and plead guilty to making false entries in bank records and money laundering. By this time Platka had left this area and it was reported that he was living in Nevada. Another banker and several people outside the bank including Anthony Aiossa, the banks and Lussier's attorney and the man who had supplied the money to Lussier for laundering entered into plea agreements with the government agreeing to testify against Lussier, and Gallerani. Noel Lussier's youngest son, who was an accountant and worked for his father was also charged with several counts of bank fraud.

It was in April of 1992 when John Hersh of the FBI had told me that I was going to have to plead guilty to something but that they didn't know what, that they would have to come up with something. It was not until September, five months later, that they came up with a charge for me to plead guilty to. It had to do with the loan back on November 1, 1989, to Noel Lussier from Bradford National bank. That was the loan Lussier and Paul Gallerani had asked if they could put against my credit line. The US attorney wanted me to plead guilty to making a false loan application in order to obtain this loan. I had made no loan application of any kind, so I certainly didn't want to plead guilty. Lussier had applied to Bradford Bank for the loan and the Bradford Bank president, Paul Gallerani, had told him that he could make the loan only if Lussier could put it against somebody else's credit line, call Bill Hill Gallerani told him. I had agreed to it as I certainly had no reason not to trust the bank. They had always been willing to lend me money when I needed it and I only thought it fitting to help them when they asked me to. Then Gallerani prepared the necessary papers.

I talked to Peter Langrock my attorney and several other attorneys and expressed my reluctance to plead guilty to making a false loan application, which I had never made. Even though I explained to them that the bankers had asked if they could use my good credit to make this loan and that I had agreed only because I felt that I was being helpful, every attorney told me that I was no match for the FEDs. Jimmy Carrol, the attorney that Hersh had sent me to told me that there was no sense in trying to fight them. He said that you can't trust them. He had told me that if I was not going to agree to plead guilty to whatever they came up with he would need thirty thousand dollars up front and that I could plan on spending at least one hundred thousand dollars and that I would still have a very slim chance of escaping their charges. I was told that the FEDs have a reckless disregard for the truth.

I was told that if I didn't agree to plead as they wanted all hell would break loose. Other things that I was told were that the government holds all the cards and you can't win; you can't fight the government, they are going to get there way and the judge isn't going to listen to you; the government wields enormous influence over the outcome of court procedures; you need to jump through their hoops if you ever expect to get them off your back, they have got a gun to your head.

This really bothered me. I thought that the Feds job was to seek out the truth and not just target certain people then do everything that they can to get them and ruin their lives regardless of whether they have done anything wrong or not. When John Hersh and the other two men first came to my house, they had told me that they knew about the motel deal and how I had been frauded by the banks. They said that they knew that we had worked hard to try to improve the business and that I had been trying to negotiate with the banks to get a fair deal, but without any cooperation with the bankers. I think that one thing that bothered Hersh was the fact that we were living in a new house that we had built. As I mentioned earlier, it had big pillars in the front and sits on a little rise, which does make it look impressive. Most of our furniture is old but we had refinished it and Charlotte has a real knack for making things look good. Every time I talked to Hersh after they were here. He always mentioned our house and refereed to it as Southport. By this time it was obvious that Hersh nor any of the FEDs had any interest in trying to help us straighten out the motel deal or anything else even though he had assured me that was what they had contacted me for. It now looked more like they were trying to cover up for the motel deal by making me look bad.

I did not tell Richard Uchida or my Vermont attorney anything about the trouble with the FBI and the US attorney as Hersh had instructed me not to mention it to them. Peter Langrock, my new attorney, still insisted that my only choice was to plead guilty to whatever the government wanted me to, which was filing a false loan application, which I had never filed.

Sometime in September Peter Langrock sent me a copy of the charges that the US attorney was planning to bring against me. It charged me of "knowingly making a false statement or report for the purpose of influencing the action of the Bradford National Bank, the accounts which were then and there insured by the Federal Deposit Insurance Corporation, in the application and in advance of a loan in the amount of $250,000, in that Hill signed a statement of purpose listing the purpose of the loan as 'to purchase cattle, farm and machinery for resale,' when in fact Hill knew that the purpose was to re-loan the money to a member of the board of directors of the Bradford National Bank." Along with this was the plea agreement that the US attorney had drawn up and wanted me to sign. It was a six page document. It wanted me to admit that I had made a false statement to Bradford Bank in order to get a loan. This was far from the truth. Bradford Bank had asked me to participate, and they had made all the statements, which I had no reason to doubt. The agreement stated that I would wave all my Fifth Amendment rights against self-incrimination and to wave my sixth amendment right to have an attorney present when I was being questioned by the FEDs, and that I would give up my right to a speedy trial by an impartial jury as guaranteed by the Constitution. It stated that I would agree to testify on behalf of the government at any time or any place. The agreement further stated that the US court could impose on me a sentence of twenty years in jail, five years of probation and a one million dollar fine. It stated that the US attorney could recommend to the court that the sentence be lowered if I could provide enough damaging information about the bankers that were fired. If you don't think that this was intimidating, I don't know what would be. I had rather be looking down the barrel of a cannon. I didn't hurry about signing it and sending it back.

Langrock's office called a couple of times and said that I needed to sign the plea agreement and get it back to them. The more I thought about it, the more disgusted and discouraged I got. Not only did I not want to agree to any such thing I felt that they were asking me to do something that was dishonest by admitting that I had filed a false loan application when I hadn't. I tried to call Peter Langrock and explain to him how I felt. Each time he was out so I decided to write him a letter explaining that I didn't feel that it was the fair and honest thing to do. I was really quite shook over the whole mess. I realized after I sent the letter I had dated it November 16 instead of October 16. Langrock's office called back and wanted me to come to his office in Middlebury. I was planning to go to Troy, New York, on Friday, October 23, to see Clay. My daughter in law Ann and a friend of Clay's were going with me. I figured that we could go by Langrock's office on the way home so I told the secretary that I would be there on the afternoon October 23.

When I got there, it was nearly closing time. Peter was in a hurry. He brought in the plea agreement and placed it on the desk in front of me and said, "Here, sign this."

I asked him, "Do you really want me to sign it?"

He answered, "Yes, I do."

I knew that he was my attorney and probably knew a lot more about this type of thing than I did, so I went ahead and reluctantly signed it and left.

About two weeks later, on November 3, I had to go before Judge Franklin S. Billings Jr. in the United States district court in Rutland Vermont and plead guilty to making a false loan application in advance of a loan. I had not made any such loan application. I sure didn't feel right about pleading guilty. John Hersh had told me that nobody would ever know about this. There were several news reporters in the courtroom writing just as fast as they could. Hersh and the other two men who had been to my house were also there. The judge placed me under $10,000 unsecured appearance bond and restricted my travel to the state of Vermont. I did ask him to let me go to Troy, New York, which is just over the Vermont, New York, border so that I could visit Clay. He agreed to this.

I was then taken into another room by a US marshal and finger printed and they took my picture with me holding a little sign in front of me with a bunch of numbers on it. I could just see it hanging in the local post office. When I came out of there, Peter Langrock was waiting for me . . . but John Hersh came along and said that he needed me to come upstairs with him. I told Langrock that I had to go upstairs with Hersh. "Be good to the SOB," he said. When I got upstairs with Hersh, he fingerprinted me again and then took some more pictures with the numbers sign in front of me. When I finally got ready to leave the courthouse, it was dark. I thought that all the news reporters had left but as I stepped out the front door of the Federal Building I was met by flashing lights as the reporters were waiting there with their cameras. By that evening and the next day it was plastered in all the news media.

I had not told Richard Uchida, my New Hampshire attorney as John Hersh had warned me not to tell him. He read about it in one of the Boston papers. He called me right up and was furious and very upset that I had not told him anything about being charged or agreeing to plead guilty. I had been depending heavily on Richard to help me get the motel deal straightened but this really cooled him off toward me. Richard said that they had done this to me to end any hope that we might have for settling the motel deal. He said that our chances would now be very slim and that he was no longer interested in representing me.

About a month later in the first part of December, Peter Langrock contacted me and said that I would have to go to the Federal Building in Burlington and meet with a woman named Terri Ames. She worked for the probation department of the justice system. Terri was very nice but wanted to know my whole life history and how I had gotten into this mess. I told her all about what had happened. She said that it was a horrible story and that she felt sorry for me. She then gave me some papers to fill out giving my whole financial status. Her forms didn't fit a lot of my financial situation to well so I put all the information on a form that did. I sent it to her and explained that I couldn't get all the information on her form. She sent it back and said that it had to be on the governments form and that I could be held in contempt of court if I didn't put it all on the form provided. I filled out the best that I could and sent it back. I didn't here anymore about it. A week or so later I was summoned to appear before the Grand Jury in Burlington. Although Peter Langrock went with me he was not allowed in the courtroom with me while I was being questioned before the jurors, by Paul Van De Graff, the assistant US attorney. Most of the questions that he asked were about Noel Lussier and the banks.

Afterward, Van De Graff had me go upstairs and talk to an IRS agent. The agent had Roger Lussier, the president of Lyndonville Bank's record books and asked me several questions about what I knew about Rogers's business. I didn't know much. I assumed from this that they must be going after Roger next. The IRS agent then talked about Noel Lussier. He said that he couldn't understand any man dragging all his friends, fellow bankers and even his own sons into the mess that Noel and the banks had created.

Prior to my pleading guilty and all the media publicity, Charlotte's mother had taken a turn for the worse and had started to fail quit rapidly Charlotte, her father, her sister and brothers and I spent her last couple of days and nights at the hospital before she passed away. This only added to our sadness. Charlotte did say that she was glad that her mother never knew about all the mess that we were in.

My mother who was in her mid-eighties and had lived alone for the past thirty three years since my father's death had a hard time dealing with the mess that we were in. She read about it in the newspapers and it was the talk of the town. It reminded her very much of what had happened to my father, due to his problems and stress in dealing with the IRS thirty three years earlier. She had lost her hair and now this was happening to Charlotte. It was almost more than she could take. We tried to spend as much time with her as we could.

Charlotte's youngest son and his wife Belynda who had been married a little over a year were expecting their first baby. Right after Thanksgiving she started to have complications even though the baby wasn't due until around the first of the year. They put Belynda in the hospital in St. Johnsbury then transferred to the Medical Center in Burlington where Clay and Charlotte's mother had been.

There was something wrong with the baby, its heart was racing way to fast. They had to take the baby from her. It was a little boy and they named him Zackary Charlotte and I went to see them. Zackary's little chest was all caved in and his heart was pounding up and down about the speed of a humming bird's wing. They couldn't seem to slow it down. In a few days Belynda came home but they kept Zackary at the hospital I stopped in to check on him a couple of times. I was worried that he wasn't going to make it.

A few days later when I came home for lunch Charlotte and Belynda were in a panic. The hospital had called and said that they were going to fly Zackary to a Boston hospital right off and needed Belynda to sign some consent form so that they could get going. They didn't have a car to get to the hospital. They took my pick up and made it just in time. The Boston hospital with the use of some experimental drug was able to get Zackary's heart slowed down to normal. He came home in a few days. Although they had to keep him on his medication and return to the hospital and the doctor's office quit often for checkups Zackary has come along very well. We are thankful for this and we enjoy him very much. He is our twenty-fourth grandchild.

By now it was Christmas but it was hard to get into the Christmas spirit with all this going on and all the stories in the newspapers. The Burlington Free Press the largest newspaper in the state on at least two occasions stated in their news stories that I had admitted that I had lied to get this loan. This was not true and it really hurt me to think that probably nearly everybody who read it would believe it. Charlotte and I were still able to have Christmas with all our children and grandchildren and Clay was able to come home for the day from the hospital for the first time. I was thankful for this. We also had a Christmas dinner at our house with my mother and my brothers and all their families. But as soon as Christmas was over and the New Year was here, everybody was right back at it.

William F. Hill,
Box 15
Hardwick, VT 05843
802-472-6308

November 16, 1992

Mr. Peter Langrock
Attorney-at-Law
Drawer 351
Middlebury, Vermont 05753
Dear Mr. Langrock:

I tried to call you last week but they said that you would be out all week. I know that we agreed that in order to get out of this mess with the minimum amount of problems with the Feds, I should plead guilty. I have done a lot of thinking and soul searching and there is just know way that I can plead guilty to something that I'm not guilty of. This is not being true to the court, to my family, my friends and not to myself. My conscience will not let me plead to a lie just to try to get the best deal. I know that I don't have the money to fight them, but even if the penalty was only ten dollars and they agreed to leave me alone I couldn't plead guilty.

All the newspapers are calling it a fraud case. I looked up the word fraud in the dictionary.

FRAUD 1-a: deceit; misrepresentation in order to induce another to part with something of value or to surrender a legal right; b: an act of deceiving; trick 2a: imposter b: one who defrauds; theat.

I am fifty-seven years old and have done business with a lot of people in my lifetime and can honestly say that I have never cheated anyone out of a penny.

My family was raised and brought up to live and practice the Golden Rule and I think that I have always done a pretty good job of living that way.

This has devastated my family it has affected my children at their jobs and my grandchildren at school.

According to the definition of fraud, I certainly have been frauded good by the banks, as well as by John Hersh and the feds.

I know that you are working hard to do what is right for me and I have complete faith in you, and appreciate your helping me more than you will ever know. I don't know what we can do and I hope that I'm not letting you down. I do have to be able to live with myself and my conscience.

Sincerely,
William F. Hill

UNITED STATES DISTRICT COURT
FOR THE DISTRICT OF VERMONT
UNITED STATES OF AMERICA V. WILLIAM HILL
MEMORANDUM OF AGREEMENT

The United States attorney for the District of Vermont (hereafter "United States"), in order to pursue the administration of justice, and WILLIAM HILL and his attorney, Peter Langrock, Esq., agree to the following in regard to disposition of pending and potential criminal charges against WILLIAM HILL. The United States enters into this agreement based upon information available that reveals that WILLIAM HILL is in a position to assist law enforcement authorities in identifying and pursuing an investigation of persons with greater relative culpability than that which can be ascribed to WILLIAM HILL.

1. WILLIAM HILL agrees to waive his right to proceed by Indictment and to plead guilty to an Information charging him with one count of false statements to a financial institution, in violation of 18 USC § 1014, arising from the procurement of a nominee loan in the amount of $250,000 from Bradford National Bank in or about November of 1989.

2. WILLIAM HILL understands, agrees and has had explained to him by counsel that the Court may impose the following statutory maximum sentence: (False Statements), twenty years of imprisonment, a five-year period of supervised release, a $1,000,000 fine, and a fifty-dollar special assessment. Full restitution may also be ordered.

3. WILLIAM HILL agrees that he will cooperate completely, candidly and truthfully with all federal, state and local investigators by providing any and all information in his possession relating directly or indirectly to any and all criminal activities or other matters of which he has knowledge. WILLIAM HILL will provide to all federal,

state and local investigators any and all documents, records, writings or tangible objects or materials of any kind in his possession or under his care, custody or control relating directly or indirectly to any criminal activity or related matter. WILLIAM HILL agrees that he will testify under oath completely, candidly, and truthfully before any federal grand jury within the District of Vermont or elsewhere and in any and all trials or other proceedings in the District of Vermont or elsewhere as requested by the United States. WILLIAM HILL understands that this agreement requires that his cooperation may continue even after the time that he has been sentenced by the Court.

4. WILLIAM HILL agrees to waive his Fifth Amendment privilege against self-incrimination and his Sixth Amendment right to the assistance of counsel whenever he is required to provide information to the Government pursuant to this agreement.

5. WILLIAM HILL understands and agrees that he is not to commit any local, state or federal offense. WILLIAM HILL also understands that he is not to have any contact with any defendant or potential defendant in this case without the prior authorization of the United States.

6. WILLIAM HILL agrees to pay the special assessment in the amount of fifty dollars at the time of sentencing.

7. The United States agrees that in the event that WILLIAM HILL fully and completely abides by all conditions of this agreement, the United States will:

   a. Not prosecute WILLIAM HILL in the District of Vermont for any other criminal offenses known to the United States as of the date of the signing of this plea agreement committed by him in the District of Vermont relative to his dealings with Independent Bank Group Inc. or its subsidiary;

   b. Make the nature and extent of the defendant's cooperation known to the Court;

c. Make a motion to allow the Court to depart from the Sentencing Guidelines pursuant to Sentencing Guidelines§ 5K 1.1 if the government, in its sole discretion, determines that the defendant has provided substantial assistance in the investigation or prosecution of another person who has committed an offense;

d. Make whatever sentencing recommendation the Government deems appropriate.

8. The defendant may not withdraw his plea because the Court declines to follow any recommendation, motion or stipulation by the parties to this agreement. No one has promised or guaranteed to the defendant what sentence the Court will impose.

9. WILLIAM HILL agrees and fully understands that in the event that the United States determines that he has failed to comply with any provision of this agreement, made any false statement to investigators or attorneys of the United States or willfully foiled to disclose information pursuant to paragraph 3 of this agreement, made any false statements or committed any perjury before a grand jury or before any trial court, had any unauthorized contact with any potential defendants in this case or since the date of his agreement, committed any other state, local or federal offense or has failed to disclose any crimes he fail to fully comply with any provision of this agreement, the United States will have the right to use the agreement itself against him at any trial, hearing or sentencing. He also understands that the government may use any sworn or unsworn statements given by him and any information, materials, documents or objects provided by him to the United States pursuant to this agreement, including self-incriminating information referred to in paragraph 3 of this agreement, against him. The defendant waives his right to challenge the admissibility of this agreement and

information provided pursuant to this agreement into evidence under Federal Rule of Criminal Procedure 11.

10. It is further understood and agreed by the parties that should the defendant's guilty plea not be accepted by the Court for whatever reason, or later be vacated or withdrawn, this agreement is null and void at the option of the United States and that the defendant may be prosecuted for all offenses listed herein as well as any related offense. In this regard, the defendant, by his signature hereon, waives any defense to the charges he might have under the applicable statute of limitations and/or the Speedy Trial Act. WILLIAM HILL expressly states that he makes this agreement of his own free will, with full knowledge and understanding of the agreement and with the advice and assistance of his counsel, Peter Langrock, Esq. Furthermore, WILLIAM HILL expressly states that he is fully satisfied with the representation provided to him by his attorney, Peter Langrock, Esq., and has had a full opportunity to consult with him concerning this agreement.

11. The defendant's rights under this agreement shall in no way be dependent upon or affected by the outcome of any case in which he may testify.

12. No other agreements have been made by the parties or their counsel other than those contained herein. Dated at Burlington, in the District of Vermont, this_____day of September 1992.

UNITED STATES OF AMERICA
CHARLES A CARUSO
United States Attorney

By:
PAUL J. VAN DEGRAAF
Assistant US Attorney
Fed. Bar ID #000728711

DATEWILLIAM HILL
Defendant
DATEPETER F. LANGROCK, ESQ.
Counsel for Defendant

CHAPTER 13

I neglected to mention in chapter twelve that after pleading guilty and all the news coverage that followed I received a letter from Jean Brown, the executive director of the Vermont Real Estate Commission. She had enclosed a clipping from one of the newspapers that had my picture coming out of the courthouse. She said that the Real Estate Commission would be conducting an investigation due to my guilty plea and a complaint was being referred to the Vermont attorney general's office.

I wrote back to Jean Brown and told her that I would be happy to cooperate in any kind of investigation they wanted to conduct. I thought that I could tell them the truth about what had happened and that they would check it out and that there could be no real problem for me. I explained in my letter that I had contacted Harold Whipple, the real estate investigator over a year before about the banks misrepresenting the motel. He had told me that there was nothing that he could do as there had been no real estate broker involved. I told her that I had talked to Tim Hayward, head of the Vermont Bankers Association. He had stated that this whole thing with the banks was so political that no elected official would look at it. I then told her about going to the attorney general's office where I had talked to a young attorney in the lobby and that she didn't want to talk about it. She hadn't even asked me into her office. I also told her that I had then written to Jeffery Amostoy, the Vermont attorney general, and complained about the banks and the government. I received back a letter stating that they had turned my complaint over to John Hersh from the FBI. A lot of good this did. I explained that I had talked to people in the governor's office who seemed very concerned and said that they would get right back to me but never did. I had contacted the Vermont Banking

Commissioner several times each time being told that these were National Banks so that the Vermont Banking Commission had no control over them. I had contacted the FDIC and was told that the Comptroller of Currency was who I need to get hold of. I had contacted the office of the Comptroller of Currency both in New York and Washington several times both by phone and by mail without any satisfaction or answers. I had contacted our two US senators and our congressman and none of them would agree to see me. Our congressman Bernie Sanders was on the House Banking Committee. Again I told her that I was more than willing for them to conduct an investigation. Somewhere I figured that the truth had to come out and somebody would listen. A few weeks later I received a similar letter from John D. Detore, the Director of the Office of professional Regulation out of the Vermont secretary of state's office. Detore also sent a copy of a different news clipping that showed that I had plead guilty. This time it refereed to my auctioneer's license. I wrote back to him stating that I would welcome an investigation and a hearing so that they could see what had happened. I did not hear back from either the Real Estate Commission or the office of secretary of state right off.

Everybody knew that the three banks, which were now all merged into one, the First National Bank of Vermont had been doing many stupid things, in addition to their handling of the motel deal, which had been losing them a lot of money. Charlie Bucknam and Mike Flipiak had been trying to convince the community and probably the stock holders that they were doing a good job and that the bank was soon going to be strong again.

This was not true. On Friday January 29, 1993, at around six o'clock, just before the banks were to close for the week end, the FDIC moved in with one hundred and sixty of its people, locked the doors keeping the employees in there and took over the First National Bank of Vermont. It was reported that the office of the Comptroller of Currency had appointed the FDIC as receiver of the bank and a notice was posted on the bank door at 6:15. Regulatory officials blamed the bank's problems on poor loan quality and insider abuse and fraud intensified by poor systems, weak controls and lax policies. A press release by the office of the Comptroller of Currency stated, "Despite the efforts of the new management, the condition of the bank has continued to deteriorate."

When the banks reopened Monday morning, it was now the New First National Bank, a care taker bridge bank, with a new president and officers that had been brought in by the government. The newspapers and other news were swamped with stories about the bank closing. They told of many people, as well as churches and schools who had invested a lot of money in the stock of these banks as they had always felt that they were as strong as the rock of Gibraltar. Many people had their entire life savings and retirement in the stock of these banks and now it was all gone.

I had felt that Charlie Bucknam and Mike Flipiak the chief officers had been using their power in the bank to try to break me. I had outlasted the banks but I knew that I couldn't outlast the FDIC and the federal government but now that the FDIC had taken over the banks I thought that I would be able to meet with them and work out the problems that I hadn't been able to work out with the banks. On February 4, I called a Mr. Mel Yarbrough, who worked for the FDIC and was located at the old Bradford National Bank. I told him some of the problems that I had with the banks. He said that he would look into things and would call me back. I did not hear from him so in February I wrote to Mr. Yarbrough confirming our phone call and reminding him that he had agreed to set up a meeting to discuss the bank problems. I wrote to Merrill Sherman, the new bank president that the FDIC had brought in. She wrote back and said that the new bridge bank did not inherit any of the problems of the old bank. She said that the FDIC would be handling that and that I should continue to discuss the matter with Mr. Yarbrough. On March 3, I sent a fax to Mr. Yarbrough to again try to get his attention. A couple of days later I received a letter from Mr. Yarbrough stating that he was in the process of consolidating activities into a field office in Westborough Mass. He said that I would be assigned an Account Officer in Westborough who should be contacting me soon.

About two weeks later, I received a letter from Jyme W. Stoner from the Westborough FDIC office, who said that he would be the account officer that would deal with us. I called Mr. Stoner and asked to set up an appointment with him. He seemed receptive to this and said that he would call me back. On April 2, I wrote to Mr. Stoner to try to explain some of the bank problems to him before we met. On April 21, I met with Mr. Stoner in Westborough. We had what I thought was a good meeting and it sounded like we would be able to work things out. One of the things that we discussed was the Danville house. I told Mr. Stoner what had happened and about Charlie Bucknam and the bank holding the deed but not recording it. He said that would be no problem. He said that the FDIC would find the deed, get the house appraised and put it on the market and that I would get credit for it.

In the meantime Karen Eastman from the FDIC had mailed a letter to Richard Uchida, my former New Hampshire attorney who had filed a suit against Bradford Bank. The letter stated that I would need to file a proof of claim by May 6, 1993, for any claims that I had against the banks or the FDIC. I filed the proof of claim, claiming the accounts that had disappeared from Bradford Bank, the savings account of about $50,000 that I had left at Caledonia National bank and the deficiency and damages on the motel.

On May 6, the very day that the proof of claim was due, Karen Eastman sent me a letter stating that any claim that we had would be disallowed and that if we wanted to contest this disallowance it would be necessary for us to file an action in the US district court in the district of the failed bank or in United States district court in Washington, DC, within sixty days. If I didn't file such an action, it looked like I would lose all my savings and be liable for the losses of the motel. This could wipe us out. I called Karen Eastman and inquired why it wouldn't make more sense and be a lot cheaper for the government and for us if we could just sit down and have a meeting to try to settle this whole mess. She seemed surprised at the idea and said that she didn't believe that the government had any provisions for trying to reach any settlement outside the United States District Court. I showed her letter to Peter Langrock, my attorney that was dealing with the FEDs. He said that it would be necessary to file a suit in the US district court before July 5, 1993, if I wanted to pursue the disallowance of the claim. He said that he was not interested in undertaking the matter. Richard Uchida had already told me that he would not have anything to do with the FDIC.

I talked to a couple of other attorneys about representing me. They all had the same response, they didn't want anything to do with the FDIC. They all said that the government had mountains of money and were impossible to deal with. It looked like that if anybody was going to go up against the FDIC it was going to have to be me alone. I did some research and I filed a suit against the FDIC as the receiver for the failed banks and Independent Bank Group the holding company. I asked for a jury trial. In this suit, I tried to cover all the problems that I had been having with the banks. Most of it hinged on the motel but there were several other things that the banks had done that I felt were improper such as taking over all my dealer accounts, many of which I had a lot equity in. I filed the suit in the US district court in Rutland, Vermont; this was the same judge Franklin S. Billings's court that was handling the criminal matters of the banks. I also filed the suit with the US district court in the District of Columbia and with the US attorney's office. The Government has sixty days to answer a Court complaint, anybody else only has thirty days to answer. In the meantime, I kept trying to talk with Mr. Stoner of the FDIC. I thought that I was getting along pretty good with him when he told me that my case was being transferred to someone else.

I owned two houses in Newport Vermont that Caledonia National Bank had mortgagers on. When Caledonia National Bank stopped giving me credit for my payments, I had stopped making payments to them. Outside of the motel these were the only two mortgages that these banks had. I tried sending my payments to the FDIC and requested that they send me a receipt or at least acknowledge that I was getting credit for these payments and that they were being credited on these mortgages. I never heard from them although they cashed my checks so I didn't send them any more payments.

I learned that the new person at the FDIC who would be handling my case was Enrique Caballero. Caballero had a very Spanish accent and was a little hard to understand however I talked to him several times on the phone. He said that he understood our situation and was very sympathetic to what was happening to us. He made it sound like we should have no trouble settling things with the FDIC but we could never seem to.

Around July I received a call from Paul Van De Graff, the US attorney. He said that he wanted to come to my house and talk to me. I had no idea what he was looking for. When he arrived, he had another FBI man with him named Buddy McGinnis. They wanted to question me about Roger Lussier the Lyndonville Savings Bank President. I had known Roger for a long time and had held some auctions with him. I also had done a lot of business with the Lyndonville Bank and had bought a number of properties from them. A few years earlier I had bought a large building called the Colinade at one of Rogers Auctions. I had taken Arthur Elliott, a Lyndonville Bank Director, in as a partner on this building. We didn't sell this building right off, so Arthur wanted to take Roger in as a third partner, which was fine with me. I had financed the Colinade with the Lyndonville Bank. Van De Graff claimed that Roger had created a conflict of interest by becoming a partner in a property that had been financed by his bank. Roger wasn't a partner when I financed it. I felt that by having Roger as a partner it strengthened the banks position as it would be one more person to make payments, pay expenses and one more person to help to find a buyer for the building. I asked McGinnis and Van De Graff how this affected me. They said that I hadn't done anything wrong, it was Roger who they were after.

Around the first part of September I got a call from Peter Langrock. He said that Roger Lussier had been charged with twenty counts of bank fraud by the US attorney and that Roger was completely innocent of all charges. One of the charges was being a partner in the Colinade. Langrock wanted to represent Roger Lussier but he couldn't while he was representing me. He wanted me to come to his office right away. I went there on September 14. Langrock said that he really wanted to help Roger clear his name and if I would release him so that he could do this he would not charge me for anything that he had done for me. I told him if Roger was innocent as he said and he could help him prove it I certainly didn't want to stand in the way. Langrock said that he could recommend another good attorney to represent me.

He told me about David Gibson an attorney in Brattleboro Vermont that he said was very good. Langrock called Gibson and asked him if he would represent me. He told him that I had was a victim of the bank mess. He then told him that Charlotte was now a basket case and that we needed good representation. Langrock's office is about a hundred miles from home, and Brattleboro must be another eighty miles south of there, so I decided that I would go right then and meet David Gibson. He was a quite man, but he seemed to know what he was talking about. His father had been a former governor of Vermont. I told him about my lawsuit with the FDIC and asked him if he was interested in representing me. He said that the FDIC required a lot of work and patience and that he didn't want to deal with them.

Around the first of November, we had to go before Judge Billings to get permission for Langrock to represent Roger and for me to change over to Gibson. A short while later John Hersh, of the FBI called to ask me some questions. He mentioned something about Peter Langrock. I told him that Langrock was no longer representing me. I told him about David Gibson. He seemed very upset. I asked him if that presented a problem. He said that it sure did, but he didn't say what. A short while later Hersh called back. He wanted me to fire David Gibson and told me that he wanted to get me a lawyer. I didn't fall for it. When I told him that I wasn't interested, he then said that David Gibson was a good lawyer.

I heard from Elizabeth Glenn, a Rutland attorney who had been hired by the FDIC to represent them in the law suit. They had denied all my claims most of them they said for lack of knowledge. She sent me a discovery schedule, which I agreed to. She was quite upset that I was representing myself. She wanted me to hire a lawyer. She suggested several times that I get David Gibson to represent me. He already told me that he wasn't interested and I also knew that I couldn't afford any more lawyers. I then requested a lot of information and material from the records of the banks. She was again upset by this as she said that it was going to take a lot of work on her part to produce it. She did manage to produce about 20 percent of the information that I requested such as copies of the minutes of banks meetings and the new appraisal that the bank had done of the motel showing a fair market value of $1,450,000. I could see why Mike Flipiak didn't want to give me a copy of this appraisal as he had agreed. It stated what good shape that the motel was in, how clean that it was, what good curb appeal that it had and the improvements that had recently been made. These were all things that had happened after I bought it. In August I received a notice that there was going to be a hearing on the twenty-ninth of October 1993 by the attorney general's office and the Real Estate Commission regarding my real estate license. On the morning of October 4, I received a call from Paul Van De Graff. He said that he had heard about the real estate license hearing and he was calling to tell me not to show up.

I said, "They are going to take my real estate license."

He said, "Let them have it. I'm telling you not to go. If you do, I will use it against you at sentencing."

I don't think that he wanted the truth to get out. This kind of upset me, so I called David Gibson and told him what Van De Graff had said. I told him that I really wanted to fight to keep my license. Gibson said that he thought that I should go. He then offered to go with me but I told him that I thought that I could handle it okay and besides it was at least one hundred miles for him each way.

The hearing was held in a hearing room at the secretary of state's office. There was a hearing officer who worked out of the attorney general's office and six or seven members of the Real Estate Commission, none of which I knew. Then there was the assistant attorney general who was representing the state. Her name was Mary Lang. She was very young and quite attractive but she turned out to be very viscous. Ms. Lang opened the hearing by stating, "It is the state's position that Mr. Hill has violated two provisions under our rules for Real Estate Brokers. First, it's the state's position that he is in violation 26vsa 229648 and that he engaged in fraud, fraudulent practices and conspiring to defraud. We also believe that he is in violation of section 22968a8, which states that engaging in any act or conduct which contributes to or demonstrates dishonesty, fraudulent dealings constitutes unprofessional conduct."

She then went on to state that I "was charged by the US attorney, in US district court for the district of Vermont, with not only making a false statement or report for the purpose of influencing the action of a certain bank in the application of an advancement of a loan in the amount of $250,000." She then went on to say, "Mr. Hill pled guilty

195

to that charge." She then told the Real Estate Board the fact that I had pleaded was reason enough to revoke my License.

The hearing officer then asked me if I would like to make an opening statement. I told him that I would like to explain what happened and how this all came about and that I would be happy to answer any questions that anybody had. Mary Lang immediately objected. She didn't want me to do that. I didn't get a chance to talk. She immediately regained the floor. She then introduced a copy of the charges brought by the US attorney and then a copy of the plea agreement. The hearing officer asked me if I had any objection to her introducing these two documents. I said that I didn't, thinking that if I let her say and do what she wanted, she would extend me the same courtesy when and if it came my time. Again the hearing officer said that it was now my opportunity to put on my case.

I explained how that I had done business with these banks for many years and had always had a good banking relationship with them I then went on to explain about the motel and about Lussier and Gallerani calling me from Bradford Bank to ask to put this loan for Lussier against my credit line. Mary Lang again objected. She said, "The state is going to object to any evidence which attempts to contradict the plea of guilty that's been entered into." Some of the board members asked a few questions that I tried to answer, my answers often being objected to by Mary Lang. Her thing was that I had pleaded guilty and that there was no other explanation.

On November 29, I went through the same procedure for my auctioneer's license. The hearing took place in the same room again with Mary Lang representing the state and with a different hearing officer named Sienna Walton. This time there were no board members. Jack Detore, the Director of Professional Regulation sat in for part of the hearing. The hearing went pretty much the same as the first one with the same evidence presented and all the same objections from Mary Lang for anything that I tried to present. On the same day as the auction license hearing a letter was sent to me from the chairman of the Real Estate Commission stating that my license was being revoked immediately. The next day Harold Whipple, the real estate investigator came by and picked it up. In the auctioneer's license hearing, it was

Sienna Walton, the hearing officer who made the recommendation to the secretary of state to revoke my auctioneer's license, which he did. This was going to leave me without a means to make a living.

I decided to appeal the decisions to the Vermont Supreme Court, which I did. I was able to convince the secretary of state, Donald Hooper, to let me keep my auctioneer's license during the appeal process. This aggravated Mary Lang. She wrote him several letters demanding that he immediately revoke my license. When he didn't do it, she demanded that he set up another hearing so that she could protest his action. Although I still had my license I didn't feel comfortable about booking any auctions as I didn't know what Mary Lang and the attorney general's office would do next or if they would succeed at any time to get my license.

One thing that the Supreme Court needed was a transcript of the hearings. The state had recorded them on a tape recorder. I was able to purchase a copy of the tapes from both hearings. My daughter-in-law Belynda agreed to type the transcripts for me. The state had wanted several hundred dollars to do it. When these were presented to the Supreme Court, Mary Lang objected vigorously because I didn't hire somebody from the state to type them up. I filed an answer stating that I couldn't see why they should be any more authentic if the state did them than if I had them done. I suggested that she read the typed transcripts and if she could find any mistakes we could deal with them. The Supreme Court agreed with this. She tried hard to discredit them but all she could find was a couple of misspelled words. Mary Lang and another employ of the attorney general's office filed a number of motions and memorandums with the state all trying to discredit me from getting my licenses back. The Supreme Court said that they had to base their decision on the evidence that was presented and what took place at the two hearings. As all the evidence had been presented by Mary Lang, they decided in favor of the state. I then had to turn in my auctioneer's license. This was around September or October of 1994.

Just prior to this in July of 1994 I was contacted by a good friend of mine, Jim Harvey from Attleboro Massachusetts. Jim had been raised in Hardwick the same town where I lived all my life. A cousin of Jim's had passed away. This was Albert Feeley who had lived all his life, on the same small farm up in West Woodbury, not far from Hardwick. Albert had never been married and the property was still in his folks' name, who had been dead for nearly fifty years. Jim had been named the Administrator of the estate. Jim wanted me to look at the property with him and help him to decide how to dispose of it. The house was very old and almost in tumble down shape. The floor in one of the bedrooms had fallen into the cellar. Albert had never thrown anything away. There was a lot of junk but among it there were many old and interesting items and antiques. When we took one of the beds apart, there was a whole deer between the mattresses. It must have been there for years as it was all dried out and as light as a feather.

I talked Jim into having an auction. Jim not being too familiar with auctions wasn't sure if that was the way to proceed but I convinced him that it was. I told him that we should also plan to sell the real estate at the auction. He got the probate court to agree. The real estate consisted of the old house and a barn that had fallen down and about a hundred and twenty acres of land. We spent quite a bit of time cleaning up around there and getting everything ready. Jim was a little worried about getting a crowd as the property was out on a back road. I told him not to worry as that was my job. I would advertise it well and I had always had a large following for my auctions.

I held the auction on a Tuesday the sixth day of August. I had not had an auction in a while due to the uncertainty of the status of my license. I had my daughters Janet and Dianne to do the scribing and the cashiering. Janet's husband Harold and Sally's son Rodney along with five of our grandsons made up the bulk of the sales crew. We had a crowd that numbered over eight hundred during the course of the day. Needless to say we had a very nice auction. This was the last one that I had.

One thing that I liked about auctions was that I always tried to make them a family affair with everybody helping. My kids grew up doing auctions. It was an excellent way for them to learn about work, earning money and how to get along with people. They learned about salesmanship and selling. There were many interesting lessons to be learned about the merchandise that we sold such as what it was, how it worked, and often some pretty good history lessons learning about some of the antiques and older machinery and tools. We now had at least six grandsons big enough to work at auctions and I really looked forward to spending a lot of time with them. By having my auctioneer's license revoked we could no longer do this. I was really sad as I felt that it was cheating them out some real valuable learning experiences that I had hoped to give them as well as doing things as a family.

I was not getting the cooperation from the FDIC that I thought that I was going to. They had not done anything about the Danville house as Mr. Stoner had said that they would do. More payments were due at Lyndonville Savings Bank so I went to see David Turner who managed the Derby Branch of Lyndonville Bank. Turner was an excellent banker who had done an excellent job of running this branch bank. He knew what the problem was with the Danville house as we had discussed it before. I asked Turner if he had any ideas of how I could straighten it out as I didn't want to try to sell it when I had already given Bucknam's bank a deed to it but I didn't want the loan to become delinquent at Lyndonville Bank.

Turner said that I should have Lyndonville Bank do a foreclosure to clear the title. I didn't like the sound of foreclosure against my name but it did seem like a way to wipe out the deed that I had given to Bucknam's bank.

Turner got Sara Fields the daughter of Andy Fields, who was the bank's attorney to conduct a foreclosure. I cooperated fully to get it done as soon and as inexpensive as possible.

Charlie Bucknam had stayed on with the FDIC when they took over the banks of Independent Bank Group. The FDIC ran these banks while advertising them for sale. Several offers were made and then all three, banks that were now one with thirteen branches, were sold to Merchants, a large Vermont bank.

I did not know what had happened to rest of my savings, which I had in Caledonia National Bank. There should have been about $50,000 still in this account. I later received a statement stating that they had my savings in their bank and assigned it a new account number. I called Merchants thinking that it might be a good idea to get my money out while I still could. I was told that they had my money but that the FDIC had restricted them from giving it to me until we could reach a settlement with them. I did not get any more statements from Merchants after that.

Charlie Bucknam worked for Merchants after they purchased the bank from FDIC when all of a sudden, it was announced that he was to become the Senior Vice President and Loan Officer of Lyndonville Savings Bank. This didn't even make any sense after all three banks of Independent Bank Group had failed under his reign as president.

But what I now thought was that Lyndonville Bank should be able to find out what he had done with the deed to the Danville house, and they could call off the foreclosure and I could get the house sold and Lyndonville bank paid off. At the first directors' meeting that Bucknam attended at Lyndonville he was questioned about the deed. Bucknam told the board that he had given it back to me. This was a lie, he had done no such thing. Bucknam wanted Lyndonville Bank to follow through with the foreclosure so that they instead of me would have control of the house, and he could sell it. I also had a savings account at Lyndonville Bank that Bucknam already had his eye on.

Bill Rockford who had worked for the Vermont Commission of Banking and Insurance had become the president of Lyndonville Savings Bank after Roger Lussier was removed. He didn't stay long and when he quite Charlie Bucknam became the president of Lyndonville Savings Bank. He was now in charge. I wrote to Sara Fields, the attorney handling the foreclosure of the Danville house and the Court to see if they wanted to drop the foreclosure and I would now try to sell the house I advised the Court that it was Bucknam who had caused the foreclosure by holding the deed. If he wanted to take the property, he could but if there was any deficiency when he sold it that I would be looking for him to pay it. The Judge agreed to this. Bucknam soon managed to get rid of most of the longtime employees at Lyndonville Bank, including David Turner, and replaced them with former employees of the failed banks of Independent Bank Group. I had about $80,000 in a savings account in Lyndonville Savings Bank, which I had accumulated over twenty five years of doing business with the Bank Bucknam sold the Danville house for less than $60,000 and deducted $43,505.08 out of my savings account. This was unbelievable, the Town of Danville had the house accessed at $87,100 and town assessments are usually less than the fair market value.

Another deal took the rest of my savings as soon as Bucknam took over. I had a house in Orleans Vt. that I had bought from Lyndonville Bank several years earlier. It was a big house and right next to the Ethan Allen furniture mill, which employed several hundred workers. The house had three stories, so I made it in to two apartments by putting in a new entrance, a new second kitchen, a second heating system, and an outside fire escape. I had done quite a bit of work to this house. It was very easy to rent, being right next to the furniture mill. I had rented it out for several years when I was approached by couple who were interested in buying it.

I sold it to them and financed through my dealer line of credit at Lyndonville Savings Bank. After a couple of years, the buyers had problems making their payments and started to get behind. I told David Turner at the bank that perhaps they would deed it back to me and I would catch up the payments and get it back on schedule. This was the way that I had always handled my dealer accounts. Turner said that he would help me out by drawing up the deed from them back to me. I went and I saw the people in the house. They agreed to deed it back if I would give them thirty days to move. This was okay. I told them to go to the bank and Mr. Turner would have a deed for them to sign. This was just prior to Bucknam's takeover. Turner didn't get to handle the deed Bucknam had the property deeded to the bank and he sold it for $32,000 even though there were two appraisals done on it both over $60,000. One of them was done by the bank, and one by an outside appraiser. Bucknam took $31,448.13 out of my savings to make up the difference of what was owed and what they sold it for. He didn't care as long as he could get the rest out of me.

Another time he took $747.84 out of my savings account. He didn't even send me a notice. I just happened to be looking over my bank statements and noticed that it was gone. I had to contact the bank to find out they had done with it. They claimed that they applied it on somebody else's note. It took me around nine months to get my money back then he wouldn't repay me my lose interest.

Bucknam told me that as long as I had any money in their bank that they could do anything that they wanted to with it. Although I had worked very hard for my money Bucknam called it the banks money.

CHAPTER 14

Going back to December of 1993. Part of my pleading guilty and the plea agreement was that I was supposed to act as a witness in the government's prosecution of the bank officials. The first trial was that of Roger Lussier the Lyndonville Savings Bank President. Roger had pushed for an early trial as he was anxious to clear his name. Prior to any trial the government had moved in on Lussier and taken his pickup truck a farm and a corporation that he owned all valued at over half a million dollars.

The government had a lot of witness lined up to testify in the case. Several days into the trial I received a call from Paul Van De Graff, the US attorney. He wanted me to come to Rutland the afternoon of Wednesday, December 8, and meet with him at the courthouse after the court closed for the day. He then wanted me to get a motel room and stay over to testify the next day. I met with Van De Graff and another US attorney at around five o'clock. They said that they wanted to go over the questions that they were going to ask me on the stand and the answers that I was going to give.

I soon learned that the answers that they expected me to give were not always the truth. I told them that I would answer any questions that they wanted to ask, but that any answers that I gave were going to be the truth. This upset them. We discussed it for quite a while. Van De Graff then told me that if I couldn't give the answers that he wanted that he would use this against me when it came time for my sentencing. I was not happy and neither was he. He again told me that he would expect me to give the answers that he wanted and told me to be at the courthouse the next morning. I went to a little restaurant and had supper then went to my motel room.

I was still quite upset by what Van De Graff wanted me to do and felt that I had been threatened to lie for him. It wasn't long and my phone rang. It was Van De Graff. He and the other attorney had a room in the same motel where I was. He wanted me to come to their room. I went down and met with them. Again Van De Graff tried to convince me to give the answers that he wanted to his questions and still I refused. He again told me that if I couldn't answer the way that he was instructing me to that he could get even with me at my sentencing. I was there for quite a while. I told him that there was no way that I would say anything on the stand but the truth. He was not happy when I left to go back to my room. I did not sleep but there was no way that I was going to cave for him or anybody else.

The next morning I arrived at the courthouse ahead of schedule. I was not allowed in the courtroom. I had to wait in a little room outside until it was my turn to testify. When I was called in, I was sworn in and told to take the witness stand. Van De Graff started by asking about my plea agreement and asked me what I had plead guilty to. I told the court that I had plead guilty to making a false loan application but that I had never made any such loan application. This did not set well with Van De Graff. Judge Billings also raised his eyebrows. Van De Graff then started to ask me questions about the Colonnade building that I had bought at Roger's auction. It seemed like he asked several questions that were designed more to discredit me than Roger. We had not gone over any of these. I did not like his line of questioning but I answered all his questions the best that I could. I didn't lie for him. He asked several questions that I didn't know the answers to. I kept an eye on the jury all the time that I was on the stand trying to figure out how they were reacting to all this. I got the feeling that there were several people on the jury that had probably never done much business or made any great amount of money, so I felt that it would be quite easy to convince them that anybody who had done much better than they had would to have done something crooked.

While I was on the stand some alarm in the federal building went off. I did not know what it was but they cleared the courtroom and all the offices including the post office downstairs. Everybody waited out in the street to see what was going to happen. After a while, they said that someone working in the building had touched off an alarm by getting to close to it with a torch. We all went back inside and took up where we left off. Peter Langrock, my former attorney, who was now representing Roger, asked me a few questions on cross examination. I can't remember what they were but nothing very earth shaking. When I finally got off the stand, I didn't hang around. I headed for home.

A couple of interesting things that I heard about the trial were that one of the witnesses the government had just recently arrested for DWI by the state and John Hersh the FBI officer had offered to take care of the DWI ticket for him in exchange for testifying against Roger Lussier. Also Matt Lussier who was Noel Lussier's youngest son and Rogers nephew was threatened and slammed up against the wall in a small room just outside the courtroom by John Hersh just before going in to testify and told that if he didn't give the answers that the government wanted that he would never see his wife and two and a half-year-old daughter again. I understand that Hersh roughed up others. Many people who attended and followed the trial had said that they felt that Roger would be acquitted on most, if not all, the charges based on the testimony at the trial.

Roger's lawyer, Peter Langrock, had to make known to the government who they planned to call for witnesses. It was reported that each of these witnesses were contacted by the FBI the evening before they were to testify. They said that this made some of them very of nervous about testifying wondering what would happen to them. By this time everybody was afraid of the government.

The jury deliberated for nearly three days. They came back in with guilty verdicts on seventeen of the twenty counts. The newspaper said that Roger was shocked at the guilty verdicts. It also reported that Van De Graff and the prosecution team were surprised at the guilty verdicts. I guess everybody was shocked, I know that I was. One of the guilty verdicts it was reported was for "entering into a secret joint venture in 1988 with Hardwick auctioneer William 'Bill' Hill and fellow Lyndonville Bank director Arthur Elliott to buy the Colonnade Restaurant in Lyndonville at an auction run by Lussier in order to sell it at a profit." As I stated earlier, Roger Lussier was not involved in the purchase of the Colonnade. I hadn't even talked to him or mentioned that I was going to bid on it. I felt that the jury must have been misled as these were not the true facts although Roger did become a partner at a later time. The trial ended just a couple of weeks before Christmas 1993.

February of 1994 began the trial of Herb Gray and Paul Gallerani, two of the fired bank officers of Bradford National Bank. I was also called to testify in this trial because of the motel deal. Van De Graff called me and wanted me to meet him at the Federal Building in Rutland on Monday afternoon, February 21, which was Washington's birthday. When I arrived, the building was locked due to the holiday but there was a note on the door to wait and someone would be down to let me in. We met the same as we had before Roger Lussier's trial, only this time there was not as much pressure from Van De Graff about the answers that he wanted me to give. One thing that I wanted him to do was to bring out the truth surrounding the misrepresentation of the motel at the time that I bought it. I also told him that I would hope that he would also bring out the facts about the loan to Noel Lussier that I had pled guilty to making a false application to. I wanted these facts to be cleared up and the truth brought out. When I mentioned these two things to Van De Graff, he became upset and very angry and told me to mind my own business, he was running the trial and asking the questions. I felt that he didn't want the real truth known.

He told me to be at the courthouse early the next morning to testify. The next morning when I left the motel I turned in my key, stopped at a restraint to eat breakfast and went directly to the courthouse. Again I was not allowed in the courtroom so I had to wait in a little room outside with several other witnesses, some of who were Rochell Inman, who had been the manager of the motel when I owned it. Stephen Males, the lawyer who handled the motel closing, Mike Filipiak the chief executive of the failed banks, and Robert Forguires, the chief executive officer of Independent Bank Group, the bank holding company. They were all called in ahead of me along with several other witnesses. At five o'clock I was still sitting there waiting to be called. I was told that I would have to come back the next day. I went back to the motel but there were no vacancies. I had to look for quite a while to find another room.

The following morning, which was Wednesday, I returned to the courtroom. It was finally my turn to testify, I was sworn in as before and told to rake the stand. Van De Graff started off by asking me several question about my plea agreement with the government. Again I told the court that I had plead guilty to making a false loan application but that I had never made any such application. Van De Graff questioned me more about Noel Lussier than he did Gallerani.

On cross examination Attorney Sartore, who represented Herb Gray, questioned me at length. One of the things that he wanted to know was what exactly had Michael Filipiak proposed to me after Noel Lussier, and Gallerani were ousted from the banks. He wanted to know if Filipiak had tried to make an agreement with me to testify against Gray, Gallerani and the other ousted officers in exchange for forgiveness of the motel note and other obligations related to the motel. Filipiak had done just that and I think that the attorney had a copy of a letter that Filipiak had written to me proposing just such an agreement, but before I got a chance to answer Van De Graff vigorously objected to the question and tried to block any answers on what Filipiak had offered both in letters and in conversation. Judge Billings immediately and strongly upheld Van De Graff's objection. Attorney Sartore tried several times to ask the same question in a different way only to immediately be blocked by Van De Graff and Judge Billings. After three or four attempts by Attorney Sartore, Judge Billings lost his temper and started hollering, shouting and roared like a bull. I did get a chance to explain that I had kept daily records of my activities and conversations with the bankers a copy of which I had supplied the bank, but that neither Flipiak nor the bank hadn't forgiven anything as he had agreed that they would.

Judge Billings declared a recess for noon so I got off the stand. Van De Graff said that he was done with me, but Attorney Sartore asked me to hang around as he wanted to get me back on the stand. I know that the attorneys spent quite a bit of the noon hour in the judges' chambers, probably arguing about putting me back on the stand to answer Attorney Sartore's questions about Mike Filipiak. Judge Billings evidentially blocked his several attempts as I was finally told that I could leave.

According to the newspapers when Mike Filipiak was questioned on the stand he was also confronted by Attorney Sartore about the deal that he had tried to make with me. The Caledonian Record reported that "under cross examination by defense lawyers and additional questioning from Van De Graff, he [Filipiak] explained how after Gray, Lussier and Gallerani were forced off the Bradford Board, the remaining directors talked to Hill about testifying for them. In return, his 2.2-million-dollar loan would be forgiven and the bank would take back the motel." It went on to say, "The overture to Hill by the Bradford board had been characterized Friday as a bribe by John Sartore, who is representing Gray." According to the newspaper report Attorney Sartore was able to get the letter from Filipiak introduced in to evidence this time. It was also brought out that on August 29, 1990, which was just two weeks before the motel closing that Paul Gallerani had fired off a letter to Mike Filipiak emphasizing the need to get rid of the motel as it was losing over $700 per day. Also, Lorett Sweet, the bank officer who handled the motel closing, testified that it was the attorney, Stephen Males, who had decided to draw up the $250,000 note that was supposed to be paid by the sale of the two houses instead of conveying the houses to the bank as the bankers had agreed.

A lot of Gallerani's and Gray's other troubles hinged around some stock deals that they had not properly reported to the bank examiners. Again the newspaper stated that "Gallerani is facing twelve counts and Gray, eleven. If convicted, Gallerani could be sentenced up to 155 years in jail and fined up to $6.75 million. Gray could be sentenced up to thirteen years in jail and fined up to $5.5 million."

As it turned out, both Gray and Gallerani were found guilty of several charges. Matt Lussier Noel's youngest son who was an accountant and worked for his father had been charged with several counts of bank fraud and had been facing two hundred and fifty five years in prison, a twelve and three quarter million fine and a $650 court assessment had made a deal with the government to cooperate with them and testify against the bankers. For this his charges were dropped to one count of aiding and abetting false entries in bank records. I was curious about this so I asked Van De Graff what Matt had actually done. He said that was for bringing the papers from Bradford National Bank to our house for us to sign for the loan that I was charged with making a false loan application. I couldn't believe this. I told Van De Graff that I couldn't believe that it was illegal to take a paper somewhere for a bank to get a signature. Van De Graff replied that it was just like delivering drugs. Van De Graff had also threatened to get even with me at my sentencing for having written to President Clinton complaining about the Feds and Van De Graff. He said that President Clinton was his boss. When all the Whitewater scandals came out, I asked Van De Graff if he had heard from his boss and how was he doing. Van De Graff said, "I think that he is in a lot more trouble than you are."

This whole bank scandal created a lot of talk and interest. It was talked about in this area even more than the O. J. Simpson trial. All the newspapers and the television were carrying stories about what they perceived to be going on. I received a number of calls from different newspaper reporters looking for information that would make a story. At first I talked to them but it seemed that whatever I told them got turned around or taken out of context and very seldom did they report the real truth. After a few times, I refused to talk to any of them anymore.

It really disturbed me to know that people were getting a much distorted picture of the truth. I thought that maybe the thing to do was to invite them in and actually show them some of the information and actual documents so that they could see firsthand that there was other information besides what the US attorney's office and the government had been feeding them.

I decided to call Ross Connelly, the editor and owner of the Hardwick Gazette and offer to open my files so that they take a look at some of the material that the government hadn't made available to them. He seemed very cool about the idea, which surprised me. He did say that he would mention my call to Cassandra Hemenway one of his reporters. She called me and seemed much more excited about my idea. She made an appointment to come to my office. I had never met her. My opinion of her changed as soon as I started to visit with her. It was obvious that she was trying to do a good job and she was very interested in the true facts. After spending over an hour looking over my files and I made her copies of whatever she wanted, she had to leave but, before going, made another appointment to come back.

On the second visit she had me make her more copies of documents, letters and information she wanted. She was real excited and anxious to do a story based on this information. She soon reported back to me Ross Connelly the editor wouldn't allow her to write any story based on my material, although he had been very happy to print whatever the government had been feeding him.

Many business people stopped in to see us. They couldn't believe what was happening to us. I received calls from several bankers who were completely disgusted. I think the most gratifying thing was that a number of people brought us things such as vegetables, potatoes, a chicken wood and a lot of other things. Several of these people were very low income people.

August 15, 1991
Mr. William T. Hill Box 15
Hardwick, VT 05843
Dear Mr. Hill:

I am writing to follow up on our meeting of August 7, 1991. Bradford National Bank (the "Bank") would be willing to consider a proposal relating to the loan by the Bank of BFC, Inc. (the "Borrower") dated September 12, 1990 relating to the Day's Inn in Campton, New Hampshire (the "Loan"), which would include the following elements:

1. The Borrower would (i) deliver a deed in lieu of foreclosure to the Bank granting the Bank unencumbered marketable title to the premises or (ii) at the option of the Bank, transfer title to all outstanding stock of, and other interests in, the Borrower to the Bank;
2. The Bank would release the Borrower and William T. Hill from (i) any liability associated with the Loan and (ii) liability relating to a subsequent advance from Caledonia National Bank ("CNB") in the amount of $75,000. ;
3. William T. Hill would provide the Bank with a statement under oath relating to the circumstances surrounding the origination and administration of the Loan, such statement to be in such forms as the Bank and its counsel may reasonably require. Mr. Hill would also agree to provide subsequent statements and testimony for regulatory filings and/or civil or criminal proceedings relating to the Loan;
4. The Bank shall have received current financial statements of the Borrower and William T. Hill in a form acceptable to the Bank;
5. The Borrower and the Bank and its affiliates would exchange mutual limited releases of all claims relating to the Loan; and

6. The transaction shall be subject to negotiation of an acceptable definitive agreement and the approval of the appropriate Boards of Directors.

We look forward to receiving a proposal consistent with the foregoing. This letter is not to be construed as a waiver of the Bank's cumulative rights and remedies or an admission of any facts by the Bank.

Very truly yours,

Michael H. Filipiak
Director
cc: Paul G. Mattaini, Esq.
Vincent Illuzzi, Esq.

blw
CM; RRR (50MHF)

CHAPTER 15

THE SENTENCES

The sentencing started to take place in the spring of 1994. Noel Lussier who had originally pleaded not gulley later agreed to plead guilty to four charges and the government would drop the other twenty eight charges against him. The four counts that he agreed to plead guilty to were fraud, conspiracy, structuring a currency transaction, and false entries into bank records. This lost charge had to do with the way that he and Gallerani had set up the motel deal.

Noel Lussier was the first to be sentenced. Judge Billings sentenced him to sixty three months in jail plus fines restitution and supervised release.

Although Noel didn't get a trial it is interesting to note that one person responsible for his convictions was a longtime friend and business associate of his, K. Douglas Jolly a New York businessman who was in the business of buying dairy cattle and then leasing them to farmers. Noel had sold Jolly cattle and had been involved in several deals with Jolly as well as lending him money from his banks. Jolly had over the years enlisted many investors to invest in his cattle leasing business. Jolly then started a company that he called Microtech. This company was going to produce and sell computer software to dairy farmers. Jolly also got many people to invest in Microtech but he failed to produce any software. It was reported that Jolly billed his investors out of over eight million dollars.

When the bank problems started to surface and Jolly realized that he was also going to be in hot water, he went to the FBI and US attorney and proceeded to make a deal to have them protect him in exchange for his wearing a tape recorder under his shirt and going around and visiting with Noel Lussier and others that he had done business with trying to get them to say things that would help to incriminate them. Jolly blamed Lussier for all his financial and legal problems. Lussier denied that he had anything to do with Jolly's defrauding his investors but that instead Jolly owed him $400,000.

Many of the people who lost money tried to get the government to prosecute Jolly. "Jolly may be an important witness in one of the more important cases in Vermont criminal history" wrote Robert M. Winn the Washington County, New York, prosecutor. The investors then approached the US attorney's office in Vermont and were told that an agreement with Jolly barred federal prosecutors from filing charges in Vermont. The investors were outraged that the government was coddling Jolly, who had walked off with several million dollars of their money. One investor who claims to have lost over $700,000 with Jolly and who had talked many of his friends into investing with Jolly was Jim Good a former Rochester, New York, area school administrator. Good fought hard to get federal and state prosecutors to file charges against Jolly who he said deceived, retirees and others who put their savings in a computer software marketing scheme as well as earlier cattle deals. Jim Good was incensed that the government wasn't going after Jolly when so many people lost their life savings. "I really think that the cooperation that we have gotten from the US attorney's office is really sad," said Jim Good.

Jim Good and the other investors were finally able to get a New York prosecutor to bring charges against Jolly who was sentenced to thirteen months in jail for mail fraud. Jolly was ordered to pay $810,000 in restitution and received three years of probation. Some of Jim Good's letters appear at the end of this chapter.

Next to be sentenced was Roger Lussier. Judge Billings sentenced Roger to forty six months in jail. Two years supervised release fine of $100,000 and a special assessment of $850.

After Roger Lussier came, Paul Gallerani and Herb Gray. Gallerani was sentenced by Judge Billings to serve thirty seven months in jail and ordered to pay $300,000 in restitution. Gray was sentenced to two years in jail and ordered to pay restitution of $285,000 and a $50,000 fine.

I believe that I was the next one to go before Judge Billings for sentencing. I had asked my attorney, David Gibson. "Don't I ever get a chance to tell my story before the Court." He said that he could ask for a pre-sentence hearing. I told him that I would like to have one. The Court awarded us an hour and a half for this purpose just before I was to be sentenced. It had now been nearly two years since I had pled guilty to making a false loan application, which I had never made. This is a long time to wait especially with the US attorney holding the promise of a twenty-year jail sentence over your head if you don't jump through all his hoops and do all the things that he wants you to do whither they are right or not. This long waiting period had weighed especially heavy on Charlotte as she now had become very unoptimistic about everything. She was sure that they were going to send me to jail. One Sunday night on sixty minutes they showed a jail where they really abused and tortured the prisoners. She was sure that this was what was going to happen to me. It just about drove her insane. I kept trying to convince her that there was no way that I was going to jail as I had done nothing wrong. It had been John Hersh from the FBI who had lied not me. She was and had been a wreck for some time. She wanted to take the stand under oath to try to help bring out the truth and I certainly wanted to take the stand and tell what had happened and be questioned under oath. I had also hoped that we could also get John Hersh on the stand and have Mr. Gibson question him.

A short while before the sentencing hearing I had written to John Hersh and confronted him about the way that he had misled me into thinking that he was going to help me straighten out the motel problem. Then now he told me that I was going to have to plead guilty to some small charge, which nobody would ever know about and the other lies that he had used to get me into this trap. John Hersh did not show up at the hearing.

Just before we were to go into the courtroom Mr. Gibson said to us that there wasn't going to be any presentence hearing. Paul Van De Graff didn't want one, and had convinced my attorney, Mr. Gibson, that he would see that things went better for me if I didn't get on the stand and tell what had actually happened. I am sure he didn't want us to tell the Judge the truth. I did get a chance to make a brief statement.

215

I guess it is customary before being sentenced to stand before the Judge and apologize for whatever it is you have done and say that you are sorry. This is supposed show remorse and to make your sentence more lenient. I certainly wasn't in any mood to apologize for anything but I could see that this was what Judge Billings was looking for. Instead I said that I had learned a lot out of this whole mess. I think that he took this as an apology as he started to nod. What I had learned was not to trust bankers, the FBI and other government employs, of course I didn't say this out loud.

It was then Van De Graff's turn to speak. According to the Plea agreement he was supposed to move for a downward departure for my cooperation. I didn't know how this would work because I had refused to lie for him in the Roger Lussier trial and I had gone to the Real Estate hearing, both of which he had threatened to get even with me at sentencing. Also I had written to President Clinton and this had gotten back to him. He was really upset about this. He told me that President Clinton was his boss and that he would get even with me at my sentencing. Just before we went into the courtroom he had assured David Gibson that if we didn't insist on a presentence hearing that he would be more favorable toward me in his motion for downward departure.

But he really didn't say anything to my credit, only that I had entered into a plea agreement to testify in the other trials in exchange for a downward departure from the sentencing guide lines. He stated that there was a loss to Caledonia National Bank on the Danville house and that I had borrowed $170,000 from Jack Howard, which was not true. He then mentioned the $75,000 loan that Caledonia National Bank had made to keep the motel afloat. He tried to convince Judge Billings that I was an associate of Lussier and Gallerani at the time of the motel purchase. This was absurd. He said that it is why the bankers had not made any deal with me to straighten out the motel mess. He didn't mention why they had put us through all the harassment. He then asked Judge Billings to make it a condition of my sentence that I continue to cooperate with the government.

Judge Billings then immediately started to hand down the sentence. Charlotte was really up tight as she was sure that he was going to send me to prison. I really wasn't too worried about prison as I still felt that I had done nothing wrong and I felt that Judge Billings had to know it by now. He gave me more than I expected though. He sentenced me to two years' probation, a $10,000 fine and one hundred hours community service. Judge Billings then jumped up from his seat and went back into his chambers. Paul Van De Graff and Allen Dawson the Federal Reserve agent who worked with John Hersh came over and shook my hand just like I was being congratulated for something I still don't understand this. There were a couple of news reporters in the room who asked me a few questions.

Charlotte was really happy that I wasn't going to prison and David Gibson said it could have been worse. I really wasn't very happy. There was a US marshal who was always in the courtroom. As soon as I got out into the hall, he came up to me. He was very upset and told me that I had gotten a rotten deal. He seemed to be even more upset than I was. A few minutes later, he came back again and wanted to know if I was all right.

I then had to go and meet with Terri Ames, a probation officer. She was very sympathetic and nice to me she said that she had to read me some things that she knew that I could read myself. It had to do with my probation, I couldn't leave the state of Vermont, couldn't have any firearms and couldn't have any contact with anyone who had a criminal record. After that we were free to leave. I had a couple of rifles and a shot gun. As soon as I got home, I decided to take them down to Deans our son as I could no longer have them and before someone came in and saw them. I couldn't find the Clips and the shells that went with them. Charlotte had hid them. She had been worried that I might do what my father had done due to all the pressure and stress that I was going through I told her that I had no intentions of doing anything of that nature. I wouldn't give the government that satisfaction and we still had a lot of living to do. My brother, Jim, called me several times and said that he was also concerned about what I might do. He really seemed to be worried. I assured him that I had no intentions of doing anything foolish.

Tony Aiossa an attorney who had worked for Noel Lussier and the banks, received his sentence within a short time after I received mine.

According to the records Aiossa had been involved in several nominee loans for Lussier. One loan that Aiossa had taken out for Noel Lussier was for $625,000 from First National Bank. The purpose of the loan was stated to be for the purchase of 400 head of cattle. The loan was approved by a partner of Lussier's who was a director of First National bank. It was reported that Aiossa deposited the money in a couple of different accounts and then wrote a check to Lussier and his partner in exchange for $10,000. It was reported that awhile later, Aiossa concealed from a First National Bank loan officer, during an ongoing examination by federal regulators, the true nature of the $625,000 cow loan. Other loans that Aiossa made for the benefit or Lussier were in 1985, a loan of $100,000 from Caledonia National bank and $45,000 from Bradford Bank. The purpose of the loans was listed as "business investment." Another such loan was for $16,500 taken out by Aiossa for the benefit of Lussier. This is the only nominee loan that Aiossa was charged with.

Aiossa, an attorney, had to know that he was covering up the true purpose of the loans and even got paid $10,000 for laundering the $650,000 loan through several accounts trying to hide the true purpose of where the money was going. I had not done any of that. The loan that I had signed for was not covered up in any way. Gallerani, the bank president knew exactly what the money was for. Lussier had applied for the loan, he didn't ask me to. Gallerani told him that he needed someone with good credit to sign with him. "Call Bill Hill" he told Lussier. I did not apply for anything.

Lussier was the one who had applied for the loan and he was the one who had paid it back directly to the bank.

Van De Graff said at Aiossa's sentencing, "His cooperation was very substantial," noting Aiossa testified at the trial of Roger Lussier. Aiossa had also provided his legal files to the prosecution, which were used as exhibits in the trials. Aiossa had apologized telling Judge Billings, "I do take absolute, total responsibility for what I did, and it's why I am here."

Aiossa received two years' probation for a single conviction of falsifying bank documents, and he also had to perform one hundred hours of community service. He didn't receive any fine. It was said that all the information that Aiossa had given in the Roger Lussier trial was not factual. Perhaps this and being a lawyer is why he got off without any fine, and only probation and community service.

When my attorney, David Gibson, looked into this, he said that I did really get a bad deal. There were several other people who Noel Lussier had used to make nominee loans for him. Some of these people's names and the loans were listed in the newspapers but most were never charged with anything. Noel Lussier was having a tough time but I don't think that anybody knew it at the time. I certainly didn't.

Roger Lussier felt that he didn't get a fair trial. His attorney, Peter Langrock, asked Judge Billings for a new trial but it was denied. After the sentencing, Roger hired F. Lee Bailey to represent him. This was at the same time that Bailey was defending O. J. Simpson. Bailey filed an appeal in the Appeals Court in New York City. One of Bailey's claims was that Peter Langrock had a conflict of interest because he had represent both Roger and me. While they were waiting for the appeal to take place Roger did not have to start serving his prison sentence.

Gallerani's and Gray's lawyers also filed appeals. Herb Gray had reported to prison to start serving his time the same day that the appeal was filed so they let him out after one day to await the answer of the appeal court.

A couple of days after being sentenced I had to report to a probation officer named Mike Wilson. He had an office in the Federal Building in Montpelier, about thirty miles from my home in Hardwick. Mike appeared to be young and was very impressed with his importance and the importance of his job. He really tried to make me feel like the scum of the earth. He lectured me for quite a while about how I was a felon and once a felon I would always be a felon. I was not familiar with the word felon but I assumed that it means crook. He then started to lecture me about drugs. I told him that I had never had any experience with drugs and knew nothing about drugs and had no desire to learn, so he didn't need to talk to me about that. He told me that I could not go into any house or building that might have any firearms. That would include just about everybody that I know including all my kids and relatives. I asked him what if I had a tenant with a leaky Faucet or emergency problem and they had a gun in their house could I go in to fix the problem. He hemmed and hawed and didn't give much of an answer, but didn't say that I couldn't. I felt bad about giving up my rifle as I had always been deer hunting every fall. I used to go with my dad. I took my sons when they were big enough to learn to hunt and now I looked forward each year to going deer hunting with my grandsons.

He said that I could not leave the state of Vermont without his permission. He then told me that if he didn't have any problems with me in the first sixty days that he would release the travel restriction. We talked about community service. I asked him if benefit auctions would count as I did quite a few of them. He said that he would not count them but that he would find something for me to do. He said that I had to pay at least 10 percent of my income each month toward the $10,000 fine. Also I had to keep tract of every cent that I took in each month and report it to him. Also he said that anyone that I did any work for I had to clear it through him first so that he could contact them and tell them that I was a crook.

I told him that I had to take Charlotte to the Dartmouth Hitchcock Medical Center, just across the river in New Hampshire quite often. He said that before I could go that I would need to give him at least a week's notice and that he would let me know if I could take her before it was time to go.

Each month I had to fill out a report that the Court sends me and it goes back to him. It asks such questions as did you talk to any law enforcement officer and if so explain. It has several questions about drugs and substance abuse. That is something that I don't know anything about so I check them all no. It wants to know the make, year and plate number of your car. How much you paid on your fine. Do you have any community service to do and if so how much. Did you come in contact with any other crooks during the month if so who. Did you have any contact with any firearms? Did you go outside of the state of Vermont? Then there is a section where you have to fill in all your income and expenses for the month.

The first month I filled it out the best that I could. My hand writing has never been very good. He called me up and chewed me out for not having better hand writing. I told him that I would try to do better. A few days later Charlotte got a letter from her doctor at the Dartmouth Health Center in Hanover New Hampshire, telling her what day he wanted to see her. The medical center is quite a big place, so they send you a map showing you where to park and what door to use to get to the department that you are going to. The appointment was about two weeks away, so I typed Mr. Wilson a letter explaining that I need to take Charlotte to the doctors, and I included a copy of the doctor's letter stating the time, the place to park, etc. I didn't hear back from Wilson. It was now the day before that we were to go so I called him.

When he answered, I said, "Hello, Mike?"

He snapped back at me, saying, "It is Mr. Wilson, and remember that from now on."

I told him, "I'm sorry about that." I explained that I hadn't heard back from him and I needed to take my wife to the doctors. He started to chew me out. He said that I couldn't fill out the reports that he needed so that he could read them but that when I wanted something I could type up a nice neat letter. He told me not to send him any more letters, that I was to call him if I wanted something. I again asked him about going the next day. He said that he would need some proof that I had been there. He said that he wanted me to purchase something in Hanover and bring back the receipt to show that I had been there. I had sent him a copy of the doctor's letter showing the date and the time along with the map. He said that wasn't good enough he needed proof.

After that I tried not to bother him any more than I had to, and he pretty much left me alone except for the monthly reports. Along in August or September I got a call from him saying that he had come up with the community service that he wanted me to perform. It was doing some repair work for a senior citizens center in Lunenburg Vermont, which was about fifty miles away. He told me who to get hold of which I did. I met with the people in charge of the center. They were all very nice and seemed pleased that I would be doing one hundred hours of repairs for them. I told them that I would like to put in some long days to cut down on the travel. That was fine with them. We left one of the doors unlocked so that I could get into the building early as I usually arrived around six in the morning and I was most always the last one to leave at night. They said that I could eat dinner with them at no cost to me. All the senior citizens were very nice people and I really felt good about helping them to fix up their building.

They had two or three older store buildings that they had fixed up and connected together. One was used for the kitchen and dining room. They had a second hand clothing store and a paper and cloth recycling section. There was an area for other activities. Some of the things that I did was to paint the outside of the, building, patched the roof, painted the floor in the clothing store. I hung some windows and mirrors for them. Part of the basement floor need to be cemented so I mixed and poured concrete there. There was one section of the basement that had caught on fire. I cleaned out this section and sheathed all the walls and ceiling with plywood and painted it. They seemed quite pleased with my work, they thought that I got a lot done in the two weeks that I was there and I felt good about being able to help them.

I now had my community service done and I managed to pay my fine so he could no longer bug me about these. I did ask him to let me go out of the state a couple of times. I didn't have to report to him in person or anything like that. My only other communication with him was on the phone and my monthly reports until the first part of April in 1995. One afternoon I was working in my office, which is in our house, when I heard someone at the door. It was Mr. Wilson but I didn't recognize him as I had only seen him the one time. As soon as he told me who he was, I invited him in. I had no idea what he wanted. We visited a few minutes and he said that he wanted to see my house. I started to take him through until we got to the living room where he was telling me that I would be getting a new probation officer soon. We got to talking about my probation and I forgot that he wanted to see the house. I asked him to sit down. He again reminded me that he wanted to see the house, so I took him all through, the bedrooms, cellar, and everywhere there was to go. I don't know if he was looking for something as every time we went into another room he was really cranking his neck to look all around. When we got back to the living room, we again started discussing my probation. I reminded him that the first time that I had met with him he had told me that he was going to remove the travel restriction at the end of sixty days, but that he had never done as he had agreed. He said that he had changed his mind and that as long as I was on probation he wasn't going to make it too easy for me. He then told me that as I had done everything that I was supposed to do that I could probably get off probation even though I had a year and two months to go. I told him that I didn't realize that and asked him how I would go about it. He said that all I needed to do was write to Judge Billings and tell him that I had paid my fine and completed my community service and ask him to terminate my probation. He said that the Judge would contact him for his recommendation and that if he recommended it he would release me. I was kind of excited about this.

As soon as Mr. Wilson left, I sat down and wrote Judge Billings a letter telling him that Mike Wilson had been here and had recommended that I write to him and ask him to terminate my probation. About two weeks later, I received a letter from Judge Billings. He said that he was contacting the probation department for their impute and an up-to-date report and that as soon as he received it he would get back to me. In about another week I received a second letter from Judge Billings stating that first of all probationers must complete at least one year of probation before being eligible for early release and that my year wouldn't be up for about another seven weeks. He said that he had contacted the Probation Department and that "it appears that it would be appropriate for you to remain on supervision until June 21, 1996." I don't know why Wilson told me to do this if he wasn't going to recommend it.

I believe that about a year and a half passed while Roger Lussier and Gray and Gallerani were waiting to hear from their appeals. When they were finally heard, Roger Lussier's was denied. The Appeals Court over turned Gray's and Gallerani's conviction because of some error that Judge Billings had made when he instructed the Jury about the law covering conspiracy. This meant that they were free, but not for long. Paul Van De Graff, the assistant US attorney immediately announced that he would seek a new trial. Although they got a second chance it would seem that it could be very expensive having to go through the whole thing again. Judges don't have to live by their own rules. They can make mistakes but they don't have to pay fines or restitutions to the defendants or the taxpayers who were going to have to pay for another trial.

About this time, I heard of an Ombudsman. I was told that this was someone who worked for the government that was supposed to see that people dealing with the government got a fair shake. I called and then decided to write to the Ombudsman for the FDIC who was a Ms. Joni Clark. She seemed very nice but told me that I should be contacting the Ombudsman for the FBI who was a Ms. Barbara Duffy. I then wrote to Ms. Duffy explaining what had happened. Not hearing back from her I called her and inquired if she had received my letter. She said that she had and had forwarded it to the proper channels. I asked how long before I would hear from somebody. She said that I would never hear from anybody, that if they decided to take any action no one would know about it. Feeling that I deserved an answer I wrote to Louis Freeh the head of the FBI but never heard back from him either.

William R Hill
PO Box 15
Hardwick, Vermont 05843
802-472-6308 fax 802-472-3389

April 13, 1994

Mr. John Hersh
Federal Bureau of Investigation
PO Box 103
Rutland, Vermont 05702
Dear John:

There are several things that bother me about the recent investigation and charges brought in the bank case. I would like your honest opinion concerning some of these matters. When you, Allen Dawson, and another man came to my house in August of 1991, you told me that I was a victim of the banks wrong doings and that I had been used as a "pawn" by the banks. You stated that you knew about the motel deal, and that I had been trying to straighten it out, but without much cooperation from the banks. You then told me that if I would cooperate with you that you could help me to straighten out this situation. I told you that I had nothing to hide and proceeded to answer all your questions.

I felt good that you were going to help me and that something was finally going to happen. I knew that I had been frauded by the banks and that the law should and must frown on such practices. I believed that you were on my side, as you should have been and that you were going to do what was right to help me correct this problem. You told me not to tell anyone that you were here, which I didn't.

I didn't hear from you or see any progress being made with the banks, as I had expected would happen as a result of your visit.

225

In April of 1992 I called you in Rutland. You wanted me to come right down that same day, which I did. At that time you told me that I had been cooperating with you and that everybody who was cooperating with you would be expected to plead guilty to some charge. In my case you did not or would not say what the charge would be, but only that I would be expected to plead guilty to some charge. You told me that I needed to get a lawyer that would work with you and that I could not use either of the two lawyers that I already had representing me in the bank business. You told me not to even tell my present lawyers anything about pleading guilty.

When I asked why not tell them, you said that nobody would know about it. I then told you that I could not afford another lawyer and you said that what had to be done would only take about an hour so wouldn't cost very much. You told me to contact Jimmy Carroll in Rutland. When I contacted Carroll, he stated that you had already contacted him. He also stated that you told him that I would have to plead guilty to something but that he did not know what. He wanted me to agree right then to plead guilty to some unknown charge. He also wanted $10,000 upfront to represent me in this guilty plea. Needless to say I didn't hire him.

I never discussed this with my present lawyers because you told me not to. I did however contact several other lawyers, who all told me that the only safe way to deal with you was to cooperate in whatever you wanted me to do. I finally and reluctantly pleaded guilty to making a false loan application, which I never made. I believe that you must know as well as I do that I never made any such loan application. I did not even ask the bank to do anything. They asked me to help them make a loan, which I did. I had no reason to mistrust them.

As far as you stating nobody would know about my guilty plea, it was plastered in all the newspapers. The Free Press even reported at least twice that I had admitted to lying to the bank, which was not true. My regular lawyers who I had not told about this read about it in the papers and were very upset with me for not telling them that I had agreed to make a deal with you.

At the trial of Paul Gallerani it would have been very easy for you to question Gallerani, when he was on the stand, about this loan and probably would have gotten the truth. I don't believe that this was done. Also at Gallerani's trial there was an opportunity to bring out all the truth about the motel deal and the way that it was misrepresented to me and to others before me. Also about the handling and later sale of it for $456,000 when the bank had represented to me that it was worth over $3,000,000. I tried to suggest some things that I thought should be brought out to Paul Van De Graff but he didn't want to hear them.

This has gone on since the fall of 1990 and has taken a terrific toll on me and my family as you well know.

I cannot understand how people like Doug Jolly, Charlie Bucknam and Tony Aiossa can get away with some of the things that they did, and I get charged for something that I did not do.

John I trusted you the same as I trusted the bankers. At times I thought that you showed an understanding and a concern for my problems in this mess. You even called my wife and offered to council her for the mental distress that this has caused her. I would like your honest opinion as to whether you think that I have been treated fairly and deserve to go through all this.

Sincerely,
William F. Hill

William F. Hill
PO Box 15 Hardwick, Vermont 05843
802-472-6308 fax 802-472-3389

November 1, 1994
Ms. Joni Clark FDIC
PO Box 5060
Westboro, Mass. 01581
Dear Ms. Clark:

Thank you for talking to me on the phone this morning and giving me the opportunity to discuss my problems with you. I have enclosed a brief summary of what happened to us with the motel deal. I had quite a few dealer notes with Caledonia National Bank and Bradford National Bank. Many of these notes I have made large payments on. In the past the bank always assigned these loans back to the dealer when the bank was paid off so that the dealer could recover any payments that he had made before discharging the loan. These loans have apparently been sold to numerous different investors and I have lost all the payments that I have made.

After the bank stuck me with the motel deal, they shut off all my credit and froze all my accounts as well as putting leans on all our property that they didn't have mortgages on. There were a lot of underhanded things that the banks did, which I won't get into at this time, but I think that you will want to hear about them. I had always worked very hard to keep my credit good and tried to help the banks anytime that I could I could not believe the way that the banks started treating us after they got into trouble. They did everything possible to make it impossible for me to earn any money and take care of my obligation as I had always done in the past and was still working hard to do I was like the worker who was supposed to complete building the house after they had taken all the tools away.

I have run up against many problems in my life, but with a lot of hard work and careful planning been able to overcome them. I have always taken full responsibility for my actions not blamed things on others, but there is a limit to this bank business and the way that the FDIC is handling it.

I have a lot of material and documents to back up and prove all the claims that I have made in the enclosed report. I will be glad to furnish it to you if you are interested. So far I haven't been very successful in finding anybody who can do anything that is interested in the truth or in justice. I have been flooded with calls and visits from people around the country that are outraged at what the banks and the government have done to us. This helps to make us feel good but does very little to correct the situation. If I sold a property and misrepresented the way that the banks did the motel, I would liable for triple damages, as well as consequential and punitive damages. So far I can't even get the FDIC to take a fair look at the situation.

Again I'm not looking to get something for nothing but there is no way that I should be held liable for all the mistakes and fraudulent things that the banks did. In my wife's and my presence, Gary McQuesten, Caledonia National Bank's lawyer, told Charles Bucknam the bank president that the bank should call in their bonding company and compensate us far the unethical things that the bank had done. Bucknam did not want to do this as I feel that he had to many things that he himself was hiding I guess that I have rambled on and am probably taking up your time but I am at the end of my wits as to how survive. I got into all this mess by trying to help the banks and trying to make an honest living, now I'm desperate to find someone who can help us at least a little bit.

I have been talking to an attorney that is trying to encourage me to file for bankruptcy I have always paid my bills and met my obligations and I really don't want to do this. I am sixty years old and have always worked very hard. Again I want to thank you for listening to me. I am anxious to hear what you think.

William F. Hill

Sincerely,
William F. Hill

FDIC
Federal Deposit Insurance Corporation
One Research Drive, Westborough, Massachusetts 01581
(508) 389 5000 Division of Depositor & Asset Services

November 15, 1994
Mr. Williams F. Hill
PO Box 15
Hardwick, Vermont 05843
SUBJECT: 508, Westborough Consolidated Office
4492-First National Bank of Vermont
Ombudsman Inquiry Number:
OMB94-0777-508
Dear Mr. Hill:

Thank you for your letter dated November 1, 1994, which expressed several issues of concern you have as a result of your transactions with former banks which were acquired by the First National Bank of Vermont.

In your letter you referenced several incidences which occurred prior to the failure of the First National Bank of Vermont. As stated in our conversation, these issues should be referred to Ms. Barbara Duffy, Ombudsman for the FBI at

FBI Headquarters
Tenth and Pennsylvania Washington, DC (NW)
20535 (202) 324-2156

In regard to settlement negotiations relating to the loans you currently have with the FDIC as Receiver for the First National Bank of Vermont, we recommend that you contact your Account Officer, Ms. Patti McGuire, at (508) 389-5668.

We appreciate you bringing these matters to our attention, and hope that the above information is helpful. If you feel that your concern was not properly addressed, please do not hesitate to contact this office at (800) 879-4728.

Sincerely,
Joni Clark
Ombudsman Assistant
cc: Barbara Duffy, FBI
Patti McGuire, FDIC

William F. Hill
PO Box 15
Hardwick, Vermont 05843
802-472-6308 fax 802-472-3389

November 8, 1994
Ms. Barbara Duffy
Federal Bureau of Investigation HQ
Room 6640
Ninth and St. Pennsylvania Ave. NW
Washington, DC 20535
Dear Ms. Duffy:

Ms. Joni Clark from the FDIC said that I should contact you concerning some problems with some failed banks and the FBI. I have enclosed a brief report and a few documents to help show that the facts are all there and all true. There is much more documentation that I can supply you if you desire it. John Hersh who called me many times and was at all the hearings that I was required to attend never contacted me again or did he show up at anymore hearings after I confronted him on the phone and wrote him a letter of which a copy is enclosed. He had even called my wife, who was having a very hard time accepting what was happening to us, and wanted her to let him council her. He told her that he was a counselor.

Peter Langrock the attorney who represented me said that I didn't have any choice but to do as Hersh wanted me to do. When I asked Langrock if he really expected me to sign the plea agreement, he said, "Yes I do." I then pleaded guilty as he recommended although I was sick about doing it. I did not believe that it was honest to plead guilty to something that I was not guilty of. Later when Roger Lussier the President of Lyndonville Savings Bank was charged with twenty counts of bank fraud, Langrock called and said that Lussier wanted him to represent him. Lussier had a lot of money, I didn't. Langrock told me that Lussier was completely innocent of all twenty charges and that he wanted to defend him but that would mean that he couldn't continue to represent me. If Lussier was innocent and Langrock could defend him, I certainly didn't want to stand in the way so I agreed. Langrock recommended another lawyer to me who I had never met. His name is David Gibson. A few days later Hersh called me and I told him that Langrock was no longer representing me. This seemed to upset him very much. He did not like it and he liked it even less when I told him who my new lawyer was. A few days later Hersh called back and wanted me to fire Gibson and let him find me a lawyer. I decided to stay with Gibson.

I asked Gibson to try to arrange a presentence hearing so that the true facts could be brought out. The Court agreed to this. This was after I had written Hersh the letter. My wife who had been very ill due to all this mess and I both wanted to testify under oath as to the true faces and Mr. Gibson had it all set up. About five minutes before the hearing, the US attorney convinced Gibson that it wouldn't be a good idea, so we didn't get our chance.

There were other people who were involved with the banks and did a lot of dishonest things who were not charged at all or got off with less than I did.

I feel that Hersh was very dishonest in telling me that he was going to help me straighten out the fraudulent schemes that the banks had pulled on me. If I had sold anything and misrepresented the way that they did, the more I expect that I would be charged with fraud, triple damages, as well as consequential and punitive damages, but it seems when it is the banks, the FDIC, and FBI and the US attorney's office, the whole picture changes.

I am not trying to stir up trouble or looking for revenge just simple justice. I certainly have cooperated with everyone else and will be happy to cooperate with you if you are interested.

I want to thank you for taking the time to listen to me and certainly hope that there is a little bit of help somewhere as this has destroyed everything that my family and I have worked a lifetime to build. Thanks again.

Sincerely,
William E. Hill

William F. Hill
PO Box 15
Hardwick, Vermont 05843
802-472-6308 fax 802-472-3389

December 8, 1994
Mr. Louis J. Freeh
FBI Director
FBI Headquarters Tenth and Pennsylvania
Washington, DC (NW) 20535
Dear Mr. Freeh:

I just recently read an article on the front page of the Investors Daily Called Shuffling the Deck at the FBI. I'm sure that you are familiar with this article. Some people were finding fault with the way you ran your department, but it sounded to me like you were doing an excellent job. More government agencies should follow in your lead.

The reason that I am writing to you is that I feel that I have a real gripe with the way that I was used by one of your FBI personnel. I wrote to Ms. Barbara Duffy in your department about this same thing. When I called her a few days later to see if she had received the information, she said that she had forwarded it to the internal investigation department. I then asked when I would hear from them. She said that I would never hear from them. I feel that I as a lifelong citizen and taxpayer in this country deserve some kind of explanation for the way that I have been used and as to whether the conduct of John Hersh was ethical and acceptable.

I have enclosed several documents and a brief summary of the situation. I have much more information to back up all my claims. I have also enclosed a copy of a letter that I wrote to Hersh who was calling here all the time. After sending this letter, I never heard from him again and he didn't even show up at the Court when I was there after that. It seems that the

FBI should have been on my side as Hersh said that they were when he first visited me rather than using me to cover up for the mistakes and dishonesty of others. I would really like to have an explanation. I hope that I will hear from you. Thanks.

Sincerely,
William E. Hill

PS, I have also enclosed a news clipping from the local paper, which addresses some of the things that Lussier and Gallerani were accused of. It talks about the motel deal. I states that I borrowed money from Jack Howard. That is not true I never even talked to Jack Howard. This was part of the fraudulent scheme that they used to get the motel sold. You will see the names of several other people that Lussier used to borrow money, some he even paid. They were not charged by the FBI or the US attorney. I don't know what the story is with them, but I know that I certainly did not cover up anything. I only did what the bank asked me to do and the bank approved of. I certainly have been used.

March 4, 1996
Honorable Patrick Leahy
United States Senate
Washington, DC 20510
Dear Senator Leahy:
RE: William Hill and Investigation of Vermont FBI Agent
John Hersh Dear Senator Leahy:

You have a Vermont citizen, William F. Hill, who has been wronged by both the civil and criminal courts in Vermont and I would think that an internal investigation on your part would confirm that something must be done to help this resident of your great state.

I have enclosed a copy of the letter Mr. Hill sent you on February 12, 1996 and a letter I am sending today to Michael Shaheen, director of the Office of Professional Responsibility. Both Paul Van De Graaf and John Hersh are corrupt Federal authorities working in your state who must be stopped. I failed in my case against Van De Graaf, but my charges against John Hersh are very serious and I am requesting your support to get involved and ensure that a property investigation is conducted.

I expect to hear from you in a timely manner.

Sincerely,
James E. Good
9076 S. Kings Hill Pl.
Sandy, Utah 84093
801-943-2656

March 4, 1996

Michael E. Shaheen Jr.
Director Office of Professional Responsibility
US Dept. of Justice, Room 4304
Tenth and Constitution Avenue NW
Washington, DC 20530
Re: Investigation of Vermont FBI Agent John Hersh
Dear Mr. Shaheen:

In January 1993 we filed a complaint with your office regarding the actions of a corrupt assistant US attorney in Vermont by the name of Paul Van De Graaf, who granted immunity to K. Douglas Jolly, the biggest scam artist in the history of Washington County, New York on March 5, 1992. You assigned this complaint to Barbara Berman and ultimately Guy Womack who conducted a horrible investigation and concluded there was no wrongdoing despite the fact that Mr. Womack did not interview any of the key witnesses. After our years of pursuing the Jolly scam and fighting the immunity issue, I finally succeeded in getting Jolly to accept a felony plea in the northern district of New York, thanks to assistant US attorney Tom Spina, 518-431-0247. During my investigation I had to deal with another corrupt Vermont Federal Official, FBI agent John Hersh. I am so upset with the actions of Mr. Hersh that I have decided report this misconduct to your office hoping that my past experience with your staff was an exception and not a rule. A brief description of my charges against Mr. Hersh are as follows.

1. January to May 1992: As part of our efforts to determine the status of our original complaint to Washington County district attorney Robert Winn (518-746-2525) regarding K. Douglas Jolly, we were informed that Paul Van De Graaf ((802-951-6725) would be doing the prosecuting

and FBI agent John Hersh, Rutland, Vermont (802-863-6316) was in charge of the investigation. My wife and I were most anxious to have someone to take out testimony regarding the Jolly matter. (At this time everyone was lying to us regarding the fact that Jolly either had been given immunity or was in the process of getting this protection). Consequently, we contacted Hersh on numerous occasions to determine when our statements would be taken. On all occasions Hersh was rude and left the impression that he had no interest in our statements. However, what really upset us was when he threated my wife and myself that if we didn't stop calling calling him or talking to our friends he would have us arrested for trying to influence the investigation.

2. Spring '94: After we finally got Van De Graaf to admit that Jolly was granted immunity, we received a letter from him on March 3, 1993, which indicated that the immunity agreement only binds the Vermont District [which was a damn lie] and was conditioned on Jolly telling the truth and they only agreed not to prosecute him for matters they were aware of at the time of the deal. In June of 1993 we visited Noel Lussier in Hawthorne, Florida to discuss his involvement with Jolly. We not only determined that Jolly had lied about all his dealings with Lussier but we also confirmed that Jolly had given us a copy of a $345,000 note he had with Noel that was a forgery. . We turned this evidence over to the US attorney's office in Vermont and it was assigned to Gregory Waples (802- 951-6725), assistant US attorney, who confirmed that Jolly had lied about the note and the Vermont office determined Jolly had violated his immunity agreement. After Lussier was sentenced in the spring of '94, he confronted Hersh and van De Graaf with the forged note and both individuals admitted they had not seen the document.

3. Spring '95: We traveled to New York in May of94 and 95 to meet with Tom Spina and the FBI agent David Fallon

(518-465-7551), both of who were working to prosecute Jolly for part of his scams. The immunity issue was still a problem (despite what Van De Graaf had indicated) but they were still determined to get Jolly to agree to a plea agreement or indict him for his Microtech crimes.

4. June–August 1995: During this time period Fallon and Spina were close to indicting Jolly but were getting considerable opposition from John Hersh who placed several calls to Fallon advising him to drop the case, indicating that the Jolly immunity was sound. It was also reported that Hersh told Jolly he would testify on his behalf. In addition, Hersh was meeting with Jolly on a regular basis and advising him of how to conduce himself to beat the charges against him. His actions also included taking an unauthorized 302 from Jolly (Which was filled with lies) and calling Fallon on Friday August 25, 1995 informing him that Jolly wanted to meet with Fallon without his attorney on Tuesday August 29, 1995. During this session with Fallon, Jolly admitted he had been counseled by Hersh. Following this session, Hersh made numerous calls to Fallon and continued counseling Jolly. In my opinion, the actions of John Hersh were unethical and definitely designed to influence the outcome of the Jolly investigation.

5. December 18, 1995: By this date I lost my patience with the interference of John Hersh in the Jolly investigation and I called him to discuss the matter. He denied any involvement and slammed down the phone. I immediately, called his superior Nicholas J. Repasky (802-863-6316) and reported the actions of John Hersh to him. He seemed upset and promised to report the matter to appropriate authorities and request an immediate investigation. I have received feedback that both Spina and Fallon have been interviewed regarding this matter by a high level investigator, but nobody has contacted me.

I suppose one could conclude from my above charges that this was an isolated incident and Hersh might be able to convince the powers that be they are blown out of proportion or distorted. However, I have talked to a number of individuals who have shared similar examples where the actions of John Hersh are improper and should be a violation of dept. policy. I would like to share two of these with you:

1. Spring 1994: Matt Lussier (904-481-5207) was scheduled to testify for the prosecution in the Roger Lussier case. Matt had also been implicated in the case against his father Noel and was nervous regarding what was expected of him by the prosecution. As Matt was entering the courtroom to testify, Hersh, grabbed him by the arm and yanked him into aside room in front of a number of witnesses (which I can produce if necessary) and threatened Matt that he would never see his wife or kids again if he didn't support the prosecution's case against Roger Lussier. Matt was frightened and indicated to Hersh in a loud voice that he would not lie for the prosecution. Matt immediately reported this incident to his attorney who advised him not to pursue the matter at that time due to complications with his own case.

2. August 91–April 1992: My research has brought me into contact with a William F. Hill of Hardwick, Vermont (802-472-3389) who had been actively involved in real estate investments for over twenty years. In working with two Independent Bank presidents (Noel Lussier and Paul Gallarini) in August of 1990, he was convinced to purchase a motel in New Hampshire for $2.6 million that turned out to be a very bad investment, primarily due to incorrect information he received from Lussier and Gallarini. He was attempting to get the matter resolved in August 91 when he was approached by John Hersh who agreed he had been defrauded by the banks and asked him to cooperate

with them in their investigation of the IBG banks, Lussier and Gallarini.

You don't have to be a genius to know these are serious charges we are making against Vermont FBI agent John Hersh. Your office would have to be very creative to shove this under the table like you did with our charges against Paul Van De Graaf. We expect you to deal with these charges in a professional manner. For starters, statements should be taken from the victims. In addition, we expect Vermont US senator Patrick Leahy. In support this request and insist on a timely investigation.

In summary, we want Vermont FBI Agent John Hersh stopped from hurting more people and we expect your agency to do a credible job in this investigation and prosecution. I can assure you we will take this matter directly to President Clinton should we see a repent of the Van De Graaf sham.

Sincerely,
James E. Good
9076 S. Kings Hill Pl.
Sandy, Utah 84093
801-943-2656

CC: Senator Leahy
William F. Hill

COMMENTS: Attached is a copy of the letter I received today from inspector Gore in OPR in response to my complaint against Hersh as well as letter I received earlier in the week from Tom Ezell regarding my complaint against Van De Graaf.

I will ask Matt Lussier to supply evidence directly to Gore regarding his encounter with Hersh and will continue follow-up correspondence with Gore and Ezell but I am not optimistic.

I would like to know their definition of serious misconduct. Keep in touch.

July 26, 1996
Mr. James E. Good
9076 South Kings Hill Place Sandy, UT 84093
Dear Mr. Good:

This letter will acknowledge receipt of your letter, dated March 4, 1996, to Mr. Michael E. Shaheen Jr., Office of Professional Responsibility, Department of Justice. Your letter has been referred to the Federal Bureau of Investigation's (FBI) Office of Professional Responsibility (OPR), Inspection Division, for response.

For your information, OPR is the internal affairs entity of the FBI charged with responsibility for investigating allegations of serious misconduct and criminal activity on the part of FBI employees.

OPR reviewed the allegations you made concerning the actions of Special Agent (SA) John Hersh, several of which were brought to our attention in prior correspondence. Most of your recent allegations do not constitute serious misconduct or criminal activity on the pan of SA Hersh or other employees of the FBI, therefore no OPR action will be taken. However, you allege that SA Hersh grabbed Matt Lussier, pulled him aside, and told him "he would never see his wife or kids again if he didn't support the prosecutions [sic] case against Roger Lussier," You provide no information to support this allegation and absent information supporting this allegation, which you are apparently making on behalf on Mr. Lussier, no action will be taken concerning this issue. All of your information will be referred to the Special Agent in Charge of the Albany Division, for his information.

As you are probably aware, K. Douglas Jolly pled guilty on 2/12/96 in United States district court to one count of mail fraud. On 5/2/96, he was sentenced to thirteen (13) months in prison to be followed by three (3) years' probation. He was also ordered to make restitution in the amount of $810,000.

William F. Hill

Thank you for your interest in providing this information.

Sincerely yours,
William D. Gore
Assistant Director
Inspection Division

July 18, 1996
Mr. James E. Good
9076 South Kings Hill Place
Sandy, Utah 84093
Dear Mr. Good:

This will acknowledge receipt of your fax of July 10, 1996. With respect to your request to be advised of the name, address and telephone number of the individual in the FBI's Office of Professional Responsibility who [this Office] turned [your] complaint*** over to," you may contact Mr. David V. Ries, inspector-in-charge, Office of Professional Responsibility, Federal Bureau of Investigation, Washington, DC 20535 (202) 324-2490. You also demanded to be given a status report regarding your complaint against assistant US attorney Van De Graaf. As I advised you in my letter of June 14, the previous case file has been requested and will be reviewed consistent with the priorities established within this Office. Once our review of the file is complete, we will determine if further action is required and we will advise you in writing at that time.

Sincerely,
Michael E. Shaheen Jr.
Counsel

By:

J. Thomas Ezell
Associate Counsel

cc: David V. Ries

CHAPTER 16

In the fall of 1994, I had to turn in my auctioneer's license. Donald Hooper, a Democrat, was the secretary of state at the time. He lost his bid for reelection to Jim Milne a Republican in the November election. I thought that I would approach the new secretary of state Jim Milne to try to get my license back so I wrote to him. His office sent me a list of things that I would have to do. One of them was to get sworn affidavits from at least five other auctioneers. The Secretaries office supplied the forms for this. They then said that I would need some letters from people who could attest to my character.

I had always been happy to do favors for others, but I had never been much of a hand to ask others for favors. I felt kind of awkward about asking people to fill out affidavits and to write letters for me. But I figured that if I was going to get my license back I was going to have to ask some people to help me. Much to my surprise everybody who I approached was way more than willing to do this for me. I even had people, when they heard about it contact me and ask if they could write a letter for me. This really made me feel good. Everybody that I talked to told me that I had gotten a rotten deal from the government.

I had more affidavits than I needed and a lot of letters, which I sent to the secretary. A number of people told me that they had sent letters directly to the Secretaries office. I thought that this would get me my license back as I had more than they had asked for. I also submitted several letters that I had gotten from people over the years thanking and praising me for the good job that I had done. One letter was from Emory Hebard, the former Republican state treasurer, complementing me for an auction that I had done for the State of Vermont.

I then received a copy of a letter that the secretary of state's office sent to the attorney general's office asking for their impute, and it gave them forty five days to answer. This letter was dated February 21, 1995. This kind of disappointed me as I had several people who wanted me to have an auction for them and they were waiting for an answer. Now it could take up to forty five more days and I had learned not to trust the people at the attorney general's office.

On the forty fifth Day, April 7, the attorney general's office responded. I received a copy. It was from an assistant attorney general whose name is Diane Zamos. I had never heard of her and she certainly didn't know me. She was opposed to me getting my license reinstated. She gave five reasons for not giving me back my license. They were:

1. Respondent's petition is untimely.
2. On information and belief, respondent has not been specifically rehabilitated.
3. On information and belief, respondent is unfit to hold an auctioneer's license at this time.
4. Respondent has failed to show that reinstatement will not be detrimental to the integrity of the profession or subversive to the public interest at this time.
5. Respondent has not provided methods of assuring public safety.

WHEREFORE, Respondent's petition for reinstatement as a licensed auctioneer should be DENIED.

Dated this seventh day of April 1995 at Montpelier Vermont.

STATE OF VERMONT
JEFFERY L. AMESTOY
ATTORNEY GENERAL
signed
by Diane E. Zamos
Assistant Attorney General

I was really disappointed, so Charlotte and I went back to Jim Milne's office. He said that he would schedule a hearing for May 2.

He then sent us down the hall to see Sienna Walton who had been the hearing officer when they took my license. She was not happy about having a hearing so quick, but I thought that she worked for Jim Milne so didn't think it was up to her.

I thought that this time that I probably should be represented by an attorney. I talked to David Kelley, a good friend of mine. David had been the Republican candidate for governor in the same election that Jim Milne got elected in. David had not been able to defeat Vermont's Democratic governor Howard Dean, who was probably one of the most popular governors in the country. I then got a letter from Sienna Walton saying that on May 2, there would only be a prehearing conference, which would be conducted by telephone. I couldn't believe it, I had explained to them that I had people waiting for answers as to whether I could do their auction. David called her and said that we would be in her office on the second rather than leaving it to a phone conference call. Diane Zamos was at this conference. She and Sienna wanted to give David a month to come up with a list of witnesses that we would present at the hearing. David told them that we would have it to them within a couple of days. They then set May 23, which was another three weeks away for Diane Zamos to take my deposition. They then set June 2 as the hearing date.

David sent them a list of about thirty witnesses that we would be using at the hearing. About two weeks before the hearing, I started to get some calls from some of our witnesses. The State was sending people around to intimidate our witnesses. One of these intimidators was a fellow named Ron West. He had been a Sheriff or a deputy sheriff in Washington County. He had many problems in this capacity and I believe that he had either been fired or impeached. I understand that he had been arrested for domestic abuse and one person who I asked about him described him as an obnoxious drunk. One of the First people to contact me was John Stevens, a real estate broker, auctioneer and certified appraiser. John had thrown West out of his office and was really worked up that he had been there to try to discredit me. When John had asked West if he knew me, John said that he said he had never met me. They called on several of our witnesses trying to intimidate them and discredit me.

One of the witnesses that I had was our minister Bill Lingelbach. A few days before the hearing Bill discovered that he had to be out of town on June 2. Diane Zamos drove clear to Orleans, about sixty miles to take his testimony.

Finally June 2, the day for the hearing arrived. I had asked that Jim Milne conduce the hearing rather than Sienna Walton and he had agreed to this. Both Jim and Sienna were there, Jim sat next to Sienna but she conducted the hearing. Of course Diane Zamos was there. West and another witness intimidator were there. The first witness that David called was John Stevens. John was still worked up over Wests visit to his office. When he saw West, John became infuriated and let West have it calling him a liar and saying that he never wanted to see him in his office again. David asked all the witnesses about the same line of questioning, such things as: how long that they had known me, what kind of business that they had done with me, did they think that I was honest, would they trust me to hold an auction for them, would they trust me to handle their money. Every witness did a good job and they all agreed that what had happened to me was ridiculous. Diane Zamos cross examined each witness trying to drag something out of them that would make me look bad. She asked several witnesses if they knew anything about my criminal conviction. Jim Harvey said that I had trusted the wrong people. She asked Roger Sanville what the people up in our area were saying about Bill Hill, Roger answered, "They think that he got railroaded." She wanted them to say that they didn't know the circumstances surrounding my conviction but they all knew exactly what had happened. She couldn't get anybody to say anything that could hurt me. After going through several witnesses, she said to David Kelley, "How much more of this have we got to listen to."

We went through twelve or fifteen witnesses then it was my turn, to be questioned. David had told me that what they wanted was for me to admit that I had intentionally done something wrong and that I was sorry and that I was trying to rehabilitate myself. I was going to have to get on my knees and beg them. This was not what happened and I couldn't do it. I answered all their questions but I couldn't say that I had tried to fraud or mislead anyone when I hadn't. Diane Zamos got real disgusted and said, "He hasn't changed his story in four years." She wanted to know what I was doing to rehabilitate myself, she asked if I had been attending any lectures or had I obtained any counseling. I told her that I hadn't had any counseling and that I didn't know of any lecture series in the rural Northeast Kingdom where I lived.

She asked me about my community service. I told her that I felt good about the community service that I had done and that I really enjoyed it as I was helping the senior Citizens and they appreciated what I had done. This answer really seemed to irritate Ms. Zamos. I really don't think that any of those people believe that there should be any satisfaction in trying to help anyone.

When pressured as to whether I had ever committed a crime, I finally said that if trusting people and trying to help people was a crime, then I was guilty. Diane asked me what I had learned from all this I said that I guessed that I was going to have to learn to be less trustful of people and more careful what I signed. It was obvious that this was not the answer that she was looking for. One thing that I had provided David with was a copy of the code of ethics of the National Auctioneers Association. When Jim Milne asked if there was any such thing, David had it right there for him.

Neither Diane Zamos nor the state presented witnesses or testimony against me. David made an offer that if they would reinstate my license that I would be willing to notify the secretary of state's office of all auctions that I conducted, that I would file monthly reports with them and that I would even agree to be supervised by another auctioneer. I needed to be able to make a living. They talked a lot about rehabilitation and honesty with the public. This I could not figure out as in well over one thousand auctions I have not cheated anyone out of one cent. I have not ever had any problems with anyone, and I have always conducted myself with the other person's interest first. I just can't see how anyone can do any more than this, and they have failed to tell me or show me. If there is anything else that I could do, I would like to know what it is.

One thing that I brought up was that I was a Certified Auctioneer. There were only one or two others in the state of Vermont. In order to achieve this designation you had to attend and pass a one week course for three years in Bloomington Indiana, which was sponsored jointly by the National Auctioneer Association and the Indiana State University Business School. Jim Milne then asked if there was a code of ethics that went along with this designation. We didn't have it with us. He wanted to know if I had a copy and if I did would I get to him within a week. I told him that if I had it, it would be in that night's mail and he should have it the next day. Time didn't seem to mean anything to these people. When I got home, I dug out the code of ethics. Article 3 said that "it is the duty of the certified auctioneer to protect the public against fraud, misrepresentation and unethical practices in auction transactions." I knew that they would probably get hung up on that one but I told him that if I had it I would send it to him so I did. Of course they picked up on this as I knew that they would. About ten days later, their decision came back denying me my auctioneer's license.

Charlotte had signed the same note and statement of purpose that the government had used to charge me with and that's why I had lost my license. The government hadn't brought any charges against her for doing the same thing that they had charged me with. As soon as they refused to give me back my license, I sent Charlotte down to the secretary of state's office to get her license. She had never been an auctioneer or done any auctioneering but anybody could get an auctioneer's license just by walking in and paying the price and walk out with the license. That is anybody except me who had had one for thirty five years.

Over the years I have conducted many benefit auctions where I donated my time to help different organizations to raise money.

Some of these organizations are: Woodbury Fire Depart. Greensboro Fire Department, Wolcott Fire Department, Walden Fire Department, Calais Fire Department, Vermont Auctioneers Association, Hardwick Hospital, Kiwanis Club, Knights of Columbus, Hazen Union School, Hardwick United Church, Boy Scouts, The Grange, Greensboro Church of Christ, Greensboro Catholic Church, East Hardwick Church, Masonic Lodge, Booster Club, 4-H Club, and probably many more that I can't even remember. Some of these organizations I had conducted annual auctions for many years.

I had done the Woodbury Fire Departments auction for over thirty years, actually ever since they started the department. They called and wanted to know if I could do it again for them in 1995. I told them that I always looked forward to doing their auction and would be happy to do it again for them if they would contact the secretary of state's office and ask permission from them to let me conduct it as my license had been suspended. I don't think that it even requires an auctioneer's license to conduct a benefit auction but I wanted to be in the clear. The United Church of Hardwick also asked if I was going to be able to do their annual Church auction for them, which I had done for many years. I told them that I would be happy to if they would have the minister call the secretary of state's office and clear it with them. I believe that they both ended up talking to Sienna Walton, the hearing officer. Anyway they were told that I should not be doing their auctions. Can you imagine not even being able to donate your time to help a church or a community fire department to raise money? I did continue to furnish the tent for the United Church auction.

The little church in East Hardwick, which we attended was going to have a community day to get people in the community together and try to raise a little money to make some improvements to the Church. Some people donated things that the church could use to raise money. They thought about raffling these things off but some of the church members were against it as they felt that a raffle was a form of gambling. They talked about giving the things back to the donors. I told Charlotte that would be a good chance for her to do an auction as long as she had a license. She wasn't too sure as she had never done any auctioneering. I told her that I would help her learn and practice. Charlotte had quit a lot of spunk and when she takes on a challenge she puts her whole heart and soul into it. Every evening all week I helped her to learn to chant and call bids. When people heard that she was going to do the church auction, many more donations came in. The Saturday morning of the auction, she was pretty nervous, but she really did a good job and received many complements. People in the church were very happy as the auction did well. I was proud of her.

STATE OF VERMONT
OFFICE OF THE SECRETARY OF STATE

Docket No. AU08-0193
In re William F. Hill Reinstatement Petition
Hearing held at Montpelier, Vermont June 2, 1995
PRESENT: Hon. James F. Milne, Secretary of State
APPEARANCES:
David F. Kelley, Esq. for petitioner
William F. Hill, petitioner
Diane E. Zamos, Assistant Attorney General for respondent

*FINDINGS OF FACT, CONCLUSIONS
OF LAW, OPINION, AND ORDER*

This cause came before the Honorable James F. Milne, secretary of state, on a petition for reinstatement filed by William F. Hill (petitioner). Evidence having been adduced thereon, the secretary of state has determined that the following findings of fact and conclusions of law are supported by the preponderant weight of the evidence.

Findings of Fact

Any proposed findings of fact not adopted below are expressly rejected.

1. Petitioner William F. Hill was formerly licensed as an auctioneer by the secretary of state. He held license number 273.
2. On November 6, I 992, Hill was charged by the United States attorney in the US District Court for the District of Vermont with violating 18 USC §§ 2 and 1014 by knowingly making a false statement or report for the

purpose of influencing the action of a federally-insured bank in the application and advance of a loan.

3. On November 23, 1992, Hill pled guilty to the above-referenced charge of knowingly making a false statement or report for the purpose of influencing the action of a federally-insured bank in the application and advance of a loan. The court accepted Hill's guilty plea.

4. On September 23, 1993, Respondent State of Vermont/Office of the attorney general filed with the secretary of state a specification of charges against Hill.

5. A hearing was held in the matter. In an order entered January 3, 1994, the secretary of state revoked Hill's auctioneer license.

6. Hill requested a stay pending appeal of the secretary's order. His request for a stay was granted.

7. Hill appealed to the Vermont Supreme Court. The Court affirmed the revocation on October 19, 1994. The Court's order dissolved the stay, and Hill's auctioneer license was then revoked.

8. On November 1, 1994, less than two weeks after his auctioneer license had been revoked, Hill wrote to the secretary of state requesting reinstatement. On November 23, 1994, he wrote again to the secretary to request action on his reinstatement request.

9. On December 8, 1994, the director of the Office of Professional Regulation wrote to Hill informing him of the requirements for filing a reinstatement application and enclosing a copy of an application. On February 8, 1995, Hill filed a completed reinstatement application with the secretary of state.

10. On February 21, 1995, the Director of the Office of Professional Regulation forwarded a copy of Hill's reinstatement application to the attorney general's office for review and response. On April 7, 1995, the attorney general's office filed its opposition to Hill's petition for license reinstatement.

11. A prehearing conference was held on May 2, 1995, and the matter was subsequently heard on June 2, 1995. The total amount of time that had elapsed between Hill's license revocation in October 1994 until the hearing on his petition for reinstatement was a little over seven months.

12. A petition for reinstatement following license revocation must show (1) present possession of entry level qualifications, (2) specific rehabilitation, (3) good moral character and fitness, (4) methods of assuring public safety, and (5) that reinstatement will not be detrimental to the integrity of the profession or subversive of the public interest.

13. Regarding entry level qualifications, Hill has been an auctioneer since the 1950's and has conducted over 1,000 auctions during his career. He presently possesses entry level qualifications to practice as an auctioneer.

14. Regarding specific rehabilitation, Hill has not taken meaningful, affirmative steps to change, because he has gained little, if any, real insight into the disciplinary process which he underwent.

15. Throughout the disciplinary process, Hill has maintained that he did not file a loan application, that he was the innocent victim of others, that he did nothing wrong, and that he pled guilty because he received bad advice from his attorney. Only after repeated, pointed questioning did Hill finally and reluctantly admit at the June 2 hearing that his conduce was criminal.

16. Hill continues to blame others for his conviction and subsequent loss of license. As he sees it, he does not need to examine or change his own motives and behavior. Rather, he believes he needs to be more careful when signing documents and needs to be less trusting of others, especially when engaging in financial transactions.

17. Hill's determination to become less trusting and more suspicious of others will not enhance his practice as an

auctioneer. He indicates his continued refusal to accept responsibility for his conduct.

18. Hill has not undertaken any specific rehabilitative seeps such as enrolling in courses, workshops or programs, or engaging in counseling. He has attended church regularly since January 1995 and has done some reading since his license was revoked. His reading has centered on self-improvement books in the business field, including such titles as Everything I Needed to Know about Success I Learned from the Bible, Avoiding Small Business Mistakes, and What You Need to Know about Banks.

19. Regarding good moral character and fitness, Hill presented ten character witnesses at the June 2 hearing and submitted the deposition of an eleventh character witness, William Lingelbach. All of these character witnesses testified that, in their opinion, respondents character was good and that his auctioneer license should be reinstated.

20. The testimony of these character witnesses is not persuasive. Most of them professed to know little if anything about Hill's criminal conviction and the events surrounding it. They based their testimony on events that occurred before Hill was convicted. William Lingelbach's evidence was based upon events occurring after Hill's conviction, but Lingelbach has known Hill for only a few months, since January 1995.

21. At some point in the past, Hill attended a three-week course at Indiana University and became certified by the Certified Auctioneers Institute. Disciplinary Rule 1.2 of the Code of Professional Ethics of the Certified Auctioneers Institute provides that "it is unethical for a member of the Institute to conduct himself in a manner that is dishonest or fraudulent, or involves deceit or misrepresentation."

22. Hill violated the ethical code of his profession by engaging in the conduct which resulted in his criminal conviction. At the June 2 hearing, he presented no evidence to show that his ethics have improved since his license was revoked.

23. Hill has begun to attend church regularly, but only since January 1995. Regular church attendance is some indication of attentiveness to moral precepts but is not definitive proof of moral fitness.

24. Regarding methods of assuring public safety, Hill proposes that, if his license is reinstated, conditions be placed upon it that would provide for (1) notifying the secretary of state's office prior to any auction, (2) filing of monthly financial reports, and (3) working with a supervising auctioneer.

25. These proposed conditions would provide some measure of public protection but would not insure that the type of fraudulent conduct for which Hill was convicted would not recur. Only successful moral and ethical rehabilitation can provide such assurance.

26. Regarding integrity of the profession and protection of the public interest, Hill has not shown that rapid reinstatement of his auctioneer license after a short, seven-month revocation period will not be detrimental to the manner in which the public and other auctioneers view auctioneering.

27. The public must have confidence that the conduct of auctioneers will be impeccable in financial matters. Several of Hill's character witnesses reinforced this concept by stating that auctioneers have a fiduciary duty to the public, because they hold the public's money and make an accounting of it after auctions.

28. The public must also have confidence that auctioneers disciplined for unacceptable conduct will be fully rehabilitated before being reinstated. In the approximately seven months since his auctioneer licensed was revoked, Hill has not achieved the necessary rehabilitation required to protect the public interest.

29. Hill is currently on probation until June 1996. He continues to pay his debt to society for his criminal conduct while his probation is in place. He must continue to work

at his responsibility to rehabilitate himself as an auctioneer while on probation.

30. Hill contends that his livelihood depends upon reinstatement of his auctioneer license. A petitioner's financial status is not relevant to the determination to reinstate a license. Even if it were, Hill is not destitute. He continues to pay his bills with reasonable promptness and derives income from rental properties he owns in Vermont and Florida. He has also started a small business selling plants grown in his greenhouse.

Conclusions of law

Hill's petition for license reinstatement must be denied, because he failed to show specific rehabilitation, good moral character and fitness, methods of assuring public safety, and that reinstatement will not be detrimental to the integrity of the auctioneering or subversive of the public interest.

Opinion

Viloria v. Sobel, 192 AD 2d 969, 597 NYS 2d 218 (1993), is an instructive case on the issues involved in license reinstatement. In Viloria, the licensee failed to gain any insight from his disciplinary proceeding and failed to accept responsibility for engaging in misconduct. While the licensee acknowledged his faulty judgment, he gave no indication that he understood the harm his conduct might have caused others. He also continued to blame others for his problems and failed to take steps to address his problems in his re- education or rehabilitation. Id. at 218–219. Under these circumstances, a New York appellate court upheld the state licensing authority's discretion to deny the licensee's reinstatement request. Id. at 219.

The facts of this case are similar to those of Viloria. Hill has gained little, if any, insight from his auctioneer disciplinary proceeding. He refuses to accept responsibility for the conduct which led to his criminal conviction and views himself as a victim. He does not understand the harmful nature of his misconduct, and rather than making meaningful, positive changes in his behavior, he resolves to be more careful of what he signs and to trust others less. He blames others, including his bankers and his attorney, for the circumstances which resulted in his misconduct, his guilty plea, and his conviction. The only steps he has taken toward reeducation or rehabilitation are to begin attending church regularly and to read some self-help books.

Hill needs more time to work at rehabilitating himself. He must make serious and sustained efforts to learn from what has happened to him and to make positive changes in his behavior. He has not shown that reinstatement of his license at this time would serve the public interest.

It should be noted that, if Hill successfully completes his probation in June 1996, applies for license reinstatement at that time, and is subsequently reinstated, his auctioneer license will, in all probability, have been revoked for a period of time less than the usual two-year auctioneer license renewal period. Such a relatively short period of license revocation does not seem onerous or unjust under the facts of this case. It should also be noted that, with the cooperation of the panics, the hearing on the merits of Hill's reinstatement petition was set very soon after the prehearing conference was held on May 2, 1995. Hill should not automatically expect that any reinstatement petition he files in the future can be heard so quickly.

Order

IT IS HEREBY ORDERED by the secretary of state of the State of Vermont that

1. On the basis of the conclusions of law, the petition of William F. Hill for reinstatement of his auctioneer license is DENIED.

2. Any further petition by Hill for reinstatement of his auctioneer license will not be entertained until he has successfully completed the probation upon which he was placed by the US District Court in US v. Hill, Case No. 92-93-01.
3. This document is a public record under 3 VSA § 131{c} (2){C}.
4. This order takes effect as of the date of entry shown below.

Appeal Rights

This is a final administrative determination. A party may appeal by filing a written notice of appeal with the director of the Office of Professional Regulation, office of the secretary of state, within thirty days of the effective date of this order.

Dated: *June 12, 1995*
SECRETARY OF STATE

_____

James F. Milne
Secretary of State

Date of entry: 6-13-95

CHAPTER 17

When I filed our suit against the FDIC, I had put in the complaint such things as the Jerry Clark deal, the loss or disappearance of my dealer accounts that were in the bank. I had made many payments on these and had at least $40,000 worth of equity that they had taken. I told about what it had done to Charlotte, her nerves and her hair loss.

I had exchanged several letters back and forth with Elizabeth Glynn. Then she filed a motion with Judge Billings asking him dismiss any claims that Charlotte might have for what the bank mess had done to her, we drafted an objection and decided to take it to Rutland. Charlotte thought that she could hand deliver it to Judge Billings and to Elizabeth Glynn, who's office was also in Rutland. She wanted to actually show them both what it had done to her hair. We went to the courthouse first. Judge Billings would not see her, but the clerk took one look at her head and became quite upset at what this had done to her. She said that she would tell Judge Billings about it and be sure that he read our objection before he went home. We then went to Elizabeth Glynn's office but she also refused to see us.

Judge Billings ruled in favor of the FDIC removing any claim that Charlotte might have for emotional distress or hair loss.

About eight or nine months after we filed our complaint with the court, Ms. Glynn filed a counter claim for the FDIC asking Judge Billings to award them around one and a half million dollars for the loss that they were claiming on the motel and the two small houses that I had been trying to make payments on. I filed an objection and explanation of what had happened and why the loss shouldn't be attributed to us. Judge Billings without any hearings or trial ruled in favor of the FDIC and awarded them one and a half million dollars.

Following Judge Billings ruling in favor of the FDIC, David Gibson, an attorney said that we needed to file an appeal in the United States Appeals Court. He said that he would do this for us. He apparently started the process when Independent Bank Group filled bankruptcy. Mr. Gibson didn't follow up on the appeal and it was thrown out for lack of certain documents. Mr. Gibson said that he thought the Independent Bank Group bankruptcy put everything on hold. All I know is that we didn't get to appeal Judge Billings's ruling awarding the FDIC one and a half million dollars.

Shortly after this the FDIC sent someone around to locate all our properties and appraise then to see how much that they could get from us.

I came home one day and a man was trying to get into our house to appraise it he said. Charlotte stood in the doorway with the broom and wouldn't let him in. I apologized to him but also told him that he couldn't go inside. He or someone went around to our tenants and to the people who were buying their homes on a contract and I suppose did an appraisal of these places. At one house that was rented and one of the ones that I owed Caledonia Bank for whoever went there told the people that they would need to move. This upset them and they moved out but not before trashing the place. This left it unrentable.

We realized that we were not going to be able to do anymore auction or real estate business we had to look for another means of making a living, and keeping busy. I had my rental properties and several people were making mortgage payments to us. This just about took care of our expenses but not much more. I didn't know how long that we would have these as the FDIC was going to be right after them.

United States Courthouse
Foley Square
New York 10007

GEORGE LANGE III
Clerk

> DC Initials VTDC
> DC DKT # 93-cv-196
> DC Judge Billings

At a stated term of the United States Court of Appeals for the Second Circuit, held at the United States Courthouse, in the City of New York, on the nineteenth day of September, thousand nine hundred and ninety-four.

Hill
v. Docket No. 94-6227
FDIC

The Civil Appeal Management Plan of this Court Directs that within the (1 0) days after filing a Notice of Appeal, the Appellant shall file and serve a Pre-Argument Statement (FORM C), order a transcript of the proceedings from the court reporter and file and serve a statement concerning same (FORM D), pay docketing fee, and that in the event of default of any of these requirements, the Clerk may dismiss the appeal without further notice.

The appellant herein not having so proceeded, upon consideration thereof, it is ordered that the appeal from the order of July 5, 1994 United States District Court for the VTDC be and it hereby is dismissed.

William F. Hill

GEORGE LANGE III, Clerk

By:

Samuel Mclamore,
Deputy Clerk, USCA
cddflt_frm
frm. dd/dflt/i

Some neighbors had a little business of raising and selling perennial plants, which they wanted to sell. The price wasn't much but it was going to take quite a bit of work to dig it all up and transplant it to relocate it at our home. I was uncertain if we should do this but we decided we would. I plowed up several spots and we carried scones and rocks to build stone walls and drew in dirt and top soil. It took a lot of bark, which I drew by the truck load from a local mill. We dug up all the plants and transplanted them tagging, fertilizing and mulching them. I also put a small greenhouse to start plants in.

There was not much more that we could do with the plants or the greenhouse at this time of year.

At Halloween Charlotte always has a parry for all the grandchildren. She decorates the cellar with pumpkins ghosts, cobwebs and witches. The kids all come in their costumes and play games, bob for apples sing songs and have a good time. It is a lot of fun. This year she didn't feel up to doing it as she was so discouraged. I told her that she should try to do it as all the grandchildren really looked forward to it and would be disappointed if she didn't. She had also always looked forward to doing this and she got a lot of satisfaction out of putting it on for them. I convinced her that she might feel better if she did it. I helped her everybody had a good time and she did feel better for a couple of days.

Toward the end of October, we started cutting balsam brush and making Christmas wreaths. I don't recall how many we made but we didn't have any trouble getting rid of them. In this area a lot of people make Christmas wreaths. The season starts around the last week in October and goes until around the first or second week of December. There is a lot of competition so the profit was small, but we decided to try our hand at it. We made quite a few and that helped to bring in a little extra money.

After the wreath season, it is Christmastime. Charlotte lives all year for Christmas. She decorates the house inside and out. People can't believe the work that she puts into it. She always says that it is because as a kid she never had Christmas. As soon as Christmas is over, she starts shopping for the next year, taking advantage of all the bargains, and she keeps her eyes open all year for a bargain that she thinks that might make a good Christmas present, so by Christmastime, she has enough presents for everybody. We have all our children and grandchildren in usually a few days before Christmas as they now all have their own families to celebrate Christmas with. Charlotte cooks for days and makes fudge, popcorn balls, and Christmas cookies. She always has a big dinner, then we have the tree and everybody has a good time. We also do this with my mother and my brothers and their families. Usually on Christmas day we get together with Charlotte's Dad, brothers and sister and their families. As soon as Christmas is over, Charlotte is already out shopping for bargains and planning for the next Christmas. This really helped her to get her mind off all the bank and government problems for a short while.

After the first of the year, we set up the inside of the greenhouse with benches. We ordered some small planter pots and around the end of February we started to heat the greenhouse and planted several different kinds of flowers and some tomato plants. They grew reasonably well and when it came spring we sold some of them and what we couldn't sell we set out outdoors. I plowed up several acres. I drew some manure from some neighboring farms and from the farm of Janet and Harold our daughter and son-in law. I planted pumpkins, squashes, cucumbers and sweet corn plus we had quite a few tomato's to set out. We had a couple of smaller plots where we raised all the usual garden stuff like beets, carrots, spinach, peas, radishes and etc. I built a couple of little barns and we started raising a few calves. I often worked out helping some farmers with their crops and a few odd jobs.

Many people were surprised to learn that we were in the plant business. Most retail establishments that sold plants had already ordered their spring inventory but said to contact them in the fall to get their orders for another year. Some places even furnish us with copies of what they had bought to give us an idea what they would be ordering another year. Throughout the summer it took quite a bit of work and time to care for the plants that we had growing, they needed weeding, often watering and the insect problems had to be dealt with. After we emptied out the greenhouse, we decided to order some poinsettia cuttings to start for the Christmas trade.

We didn't know it at the time but poinsettias require a lot of care, everything from the kind of water that you have to everything else that they require has to be almost precise. The supplier that we had bought them from called us regularly to keep us advised as to how to care for them. For a while it look like they might not make it but we didn't give up and eventually we had them looking pretty good.

We sold everything that we raised. We didn't make much money, but we figured that it was the first year and another year we could do better. I cleaned up all the old plants and rototilled up several acres to get ready for the following spring. We wanted to put up another greenhouse but were hesitant to do too much. The FDIC was right after us to come up with over two million dollars all because of the banks and the motel deal. They now had a judgement against us and were pushing us to do something about it. We hadn't known for the past five years where we stood and so had not really been able to take any major steps to scare or do anything. We didn't feel comfortable about starting to much not knowing what the future held for us all as a result or our dealing with the banks, and the FDIC breathing down our necks. Charlotte was having a very hard time over all the pressure that the government was putting on us and the not knowing what was going to happen was even worse. She was having a hard time coping. She was going to mental counseling as she had been doing for the past several years.

In order to keep busy and try to make some extra money, this year we thought that we would really work on selling a lot of wreaths and garland for this was very seasonal and would probably be over before the FDIC struck us. We got orders for over seven thousand wreaths and over twenty thousand feet of garland. I sat down and figured out how much we had to turn out each day in order to fill all our orders and have them ready on time. In order to do it, we were going to have to hire quite a bit of help.

Several of the people who we hired were welfare people. Some of them wanted to get paid cash and not have anything reported. I explained to them that we couldn't do that, we were going to deduct withholding tax and social security and report it and pay it to the government. Several of them quite because of this. A couple said that they would call the welfare department to see how it would affect them before starting work. They reported back that the welfare office advised them not to take any job because they would end up losing their welfare benefits.

As they would only be working three or four weeks, you would think that the government would tell them to go ahead and put the money toward their winter fuel, clothing or something that they were going to need. Instead the State and the welfare department were on the news every night whining because the federal government was cutting fuel assistance and talking about welfare reform.

We worked hard for five or six weeks starting about five in the morning and working until ten at night, weekends and all. Often we were out in the freezing rain and snow and it could get pretty cold on your fingers, although most of the help worked in the cellar, where it was much warmer.

We were able to fill all our orders on schedule, but it looked like our expenses were going to be greater than our income. We had to pay the government over $2,500 in taxes and social security. Then the state of Vermont came around and said that we owed them over $700 for unemployment tax. When we got all done, we came out in the hole, but we learned a lot.

By Christmas the FDIC was coming down on us pretty hard. They were demanding that we turn over to them deeds to all our properties title information on our vehicles, which are now seven and eight years old. They wanted a list of everything that we owned or had owned in the past five years. We had spent a tremendous amount of money in legal fees and the banks had taken all our savings. It looked like the end was in sight.

We have always paid our bills and have always planned to always pay our bills and meet our obligations. The FDIC expects us to give up everything that we had worked a lifetime for. They expect us to pay for a motel that was misrepresented to me when I purchased it. Then we improved it and its business, and gave them back a much better motel than they had sold us. They had sold it to me for $2,600,000 and when they got it back they sold it for three or four hundred thousand dollars. They wanted the difference out of us. Their lawyer Elizabeth

Glynn was filing motions with Judge Billings in the US District Court to compel us to turn everything over to them. This made it very hard to think about Christmas and enjoy it the way that we always had hoped to. I kept encouraging Charlotte to forget about the FDIC and the government and work on Christmas as she always had. After all, our family and our grandchildren were the most important thing that we had and meant more to us than anything else. She did work hard decorating the outside of the house as well as the inside. She kind of got into the swing of things and I think that the whole family had a pretty good Christmas after all. But with all the stress this took a lot out of us and especially Charlotte, it really dragged her down. I tried to help her all that I could and I kept trying to deal with the FDIC the Court and Judge Billings.

We had never had a hearing with the FDIC even though we had asked for a jury trial, which I thought was our right according to the seventh amendment to the Constitution. I wrote a letter to Judge Billings asking him to explain how he could make a judgment in favor of the FDIC without any trial or hearing and especially when we had asked and paid for a Jury trial. I told him that I couldn't possibly believe that he had looked at the facts and then ruled as he did. Judge Billings wrote back and said that the information that he based his decisions on were all in the transcript, which I could obtain from the court clerk. I didn't see how there could be any transcript when there had been no hearing or trial.

I wrote to the Court Clerk as Judge Billings suggested. A short while later I received a call from the Court Clerk, Bill Curry, who said that he could find no transcript of the FDIC case as there had been no hearing.

Of course I knew that there had been no hearings but now that Judge Billings was even trying to mislead us with false information I knew that I had to do something if we were going to get any justice at all. I filed a motion with Billings Court, that's what other Judges and the lawyers call it, Billings Court, again asking for a jury trial and a motion for the FDIC to produce the information that I had asked for two years previously. Elizabeth Glynn the FDIC's lawyer immediately filed an answer stating that we were not entitled to any trial or hearing and that she shouldn't have to produce the information requested in the discovery process. We each filed a couple of memorandums with the Court and the Court set up a hearing on February 7, 1996, to dispose of all motions.

I spent considerable time preparing a statement that I could make to Judge Billings and the Court. Ms. Glynn was pressuring Judge Billings to compel me to turn over to her and the FDIC copies of all our deeds, title information on our automobiles, and an inventory of everything that we owned, so that the "FDIC could locate assets on which to execute their judgment," she said.

David Gibson who had been representing me part of the time had assured Ms. Glynn back in October that he would get her the information that she wanted and I had supplied him with the information that he had asked for but I guess that he had never given it to her. David Kelley had been trying to get the FDIC to release a lean on a house that was in my name but belonged to some people who had a contract of deed to purchase it. I had been helping them to buy it. They had been making the payments to me and I had been paying the bank. For about a year they had been approved by a bank to finance the home in their own name and I would no longer be involved. All I needed to do was deed them the house and their new bank was going to pay off the bank where I had been making the payments that they had been paying me. This was the way that it was supposed to work but due to the house being still in my name the FDIC had put a lean on it and were now abusing these people.

We had supplied Ms. Glynn and the FDIC with all kinds of information that they had requested to explain why they needed to release this house for these people but they continued to hold them ransom for the problems that the banks had caused. I guess the best way to explain what took place is to include the motions I filed and my statement to the Court.

WILLIAM E. HILL
PO BOX 15
HARDWICK, VERMONT 05843

Judge Franklin S. Billings Jr.5 December 1995
US District Court
Federal Building
Rutland, Vermont 05701
Dear Judge Billings:

I'm sorry to bother you but I do have some questions that I believe that I deserve answers to. As you may recall, I had a law suit pending in New Hampshire against Bradford National Bank, Noel Lussier and Paul Gallarani for the fraudulent misrepresentation of a motel that the bank had talked me into buying. I did not want to sue the bank as I felt that they would want to work out a reasonable solution that would be fair and that both they and I could live with. They did not chose to do this but instead only gave me a run around and it seemed that they were trying to brake me to cover up for their mistakes. That was the reason for the law suit. I had contacted the FDIC, the OCC and the Federal Reserve and the Comptroller of Currency, both in New York and Washington. None of them seemed to be interested in hearing about the problems with the banks. I understand that some of these regulatory agencies had approved the sale of the motel and that they may have been advising and coaching the banks at the time I was trying to reach an agreement with them. When the FDIC took over the banks, I felt that I then could work things out with them. I made several trips to their office in Westborough Mass to try to talk to them as well as writing them several letters. At first it seemed that we might be able to at least discuss the problems that I had with the banks and how we were going to resolve the problems caused by the misrepresentation of the motel.

I was told that the FDIC had no provision of settling bank matters other than in the courts. Then I received a letter from Karen Eastman of the FDIC saying that it would be necessary for me to file an action in the US district court and that it had to be done within sixty days. I talked to several attorneys, and they all told me that they didn't want anything to do with the FDIC. I felt that I had little choice but to file an action myself. We were talking about a large amount of money and I asked for a jury trial, which I understand is my Constitutional right under the Seventh Amendment to the Constitution of the United States. The FDIC's attorney Elizabeth Glenn then filed a discovery schedule, which I agreed to. When the FDIC failed to provide the information that I requested in discovery, I filed a motion to compel them to supply this information. They objected and you denied my motion.

Certainly the Banks had misrepresented many facts in the sale of the motel and in several other areas that I did not realize until it was too late. Most of these were mentioned in my complaint that I had filed with your Court. About eight months after I filed the initial complaint with your court, the FDIC filed a motion for a judgment against me for nearly two million dollars, which you immediately approved. On a later trip to the FDIC office in Westborough I met with a Pauline Ing, an FDIC lawyer. She told me that the FDIC was not interested in what had happened with the banks, she said that the only thing that they were interested in was what I had and that they were going to have it all.

I cannot believe that you could have looked at the facts in this case, some of which are

1. When the motel was presented to me, that bank showed me an appraisal of $3,900,000 as its fair market value.
2. The bank sold me Day's Inn Franchise when they didn't even have one.

3. The motel had a very negative cash flow as opposed to a positive one that the bank represented that it had.
4. The purchase price for the motel was to be $2,600,000 and the bank agreed to finance it 100 percent.
5. That the bank wanted to use two houses in this same transaction, one of which I owned and the other, which they claimed that they owned and were willing to take a loss on as they wanted to get rid of it, but was later found to be owned by an officer of the bank, and none of this was spelled out at the closing.
6. That in spite of all the misrepresentations made by the bank, I was able to improve the motel and its business considerable, and I approached the banks many times to try work out ways to minimize any losses from the motel.
7. That when the bank's attorney asked me to, I found buyers for the motel that were willing to pay over and above the price of a later appraisal and the bank could not make a decision as whither to take the offers, so no sale was made and as a result there were much greater losses.
8. That the bank decided that they wanted to take over the management of the motel, which led to a big decline in business.
9. That when the FDIC took over the bank they sold the motel for a little of nothing when there were several buyers who were willing and able to pay much more.
10. That even though the attorneys for the FDIC state that none of my claims were backed by any writings, as stated in my complaint and in other documents it is a proven fact that there are documents to prove every single claim.

As to the criminal charge brought against me, I believe that you have to know that I never made any false application as charged. I did plead guilty to this as everyone that I talked to told me that there was no way that I could escape the long arms of the FED's. I was told that the judge isn't going to listen to you and that the FED's control the Courts. I was also told things like the FEDs have got a gun to your head, you're like a rowboat setting in the water with seventeen torpedo boats pointed at you. Before I plead guilty I asked Peter Langrock if I would get a chance to tell my side of the situation. He assured me that a hearing would be scheduled. After Mr. Langrock decided to abandon me so that he could represent Roger Lussier, I asked David Gibson, the attorney that Mr. Langrock introduced me to, to take his place, about a hearing. He said that he would ask for a presentencing hearing. He assured me that we had been allowed an hour and a half for such a hearing. I wanted to take the stand and my wife who has suffered greatly from all this wanted to testify under oath. Also, we wanted to question John Hersh under oath. John Hersh did not show up at the hearing, and just as we were about to go into your courtroom, my attorney, Mr. Gibson, said that the hearing had been canceled and that I would go straight into sentencing. He blamed the cancellation on Paul Van De Graff.

Afterward, Mr. Gibson said that I certainly didn't get a fair shake. I can now see why they wanted me and probably others to plead guilty. By pleading guilty they were holding a twenty-year sentence and a million dollar fine over my head. Prior to both the trials of Roger Lussier and Gallarani & Gray Paul Vander De Grafff told me how he wanted me to answer his questions. On several occasions I told him that I would not give his answers as they were not the truth. His reply was always the same. He told me that if I couldn't give the answers that he wanted he wouldn't be able to use me as a witness and that he would use that against me at sentencing. Several times he threatened me that if I didn't do as he wanted he would use that against me at sentencing. I felt that this was pure blackmail but I refused to lie for him. As a result of pleading guilty, I lost my real estate broker's license and my auctioneer's license, which I depended on to make a living, to pay my bills and support my family. A hearing was scheduled by the Real Estate Commission to take my license.

A few days before the hearing, Paul Van De Graff called me and told me not to show up for this hearing. I told him that they were going to take my license. He said let them have it. He then threatened that if I went to the hearing that he would use it against me at sentencing.

Also, in the Gallarani & Gray trial the attorney for Mr. Gray tried to introduce a letter from Mike Flipiak of the bank in which he felt the bank was blackmailing me. Mr. Van De Graff immediately objected and you upheld his objection. I can see why Van De Graff would object but I cannot see why you wouldn't let it be introduced. As a matter of fact, when the attorney tried a second and a third time to introduce it, you hollered and bellered like a bull and refused to let him even mention it.

It is being talked about that some of the other witnesses that had plead guilty lied on the stand. I don't know if they were persuaded by the US attorney or their memories didn't serve them well, but I do know firsthand that threatening a heavier sentence for not giving the testimony that he wanted was used by US attorney Van De Graff.

I have enclosed an explanation of how I was treated by John Hersh of the FBI and a copy of a letter that I had written him prior to sentencing. I expect that is why he didn't show up at the sentencing and why Mr. Van De Graff found a way to cancel any hearing that might bring out these facts. I believe in justice but I also believe that people who work for the government should be held accountable for their actions.

I certainly would like to have you explain your logic in the motel case and how you could award a one and half million dollar judgment that will take everything that my family and I have worked the past fifty years for without even holding a trial or considering the facts. People talk to me about this every day, and they all believe that it is unconscionable. If you are to take such a drastic action, as to make me pay for the fraudulent mistakes that the banks and the government made, I believe that I am entitled to a detailed explanation of why and in language that I, a nonlawyer, can understand. I do not mean to appear disrespectful but I do believe that if you are going to take everything that I have, including my home, I do deserve a detailed explanation.

Getting back to the suit against Noel Lussier and Paul Gallarani that was filed in New Hampshire, I understand that it was transferred to your court. The attorney that is representing me in that case tells me that it has come up missing or disappeared. He is quite upset about this. I also hope that you can tell us what happened to that. I would like to hear from you soon. I hope that you and your family have a happy Holiday season.

Sincerely,
William F. Hill

December 21, 1995

Mr. William E. Hill
PO Box 15
Hardwick, VT 05843
Dear Mr. Hill:

I am in receipt of your letter of December 5 containing various questions and comments relative to the FDIC case against you and also the criminal case.

The only information that came to my attention in deciding these matters will be contained in the transcript and should be in the respective cases. Therefore, if you desire to obtain that information, you should contact the Clerk of Court to obtain the appropriate transcripts and orders.

I also note that you are not satisfied with the judgments entered. You had the right of appeal of the final judgments within the statutory time limits.

Very truly yours,
Senior US District Judge

FSB/stc

CHAPTER 18

UNITED STATES DISTRICT COURT
DISTRICT OF VERMONT

William F. Hill and Charline J. Hill. Plaintiffs

V

FDIC, Receiver of First National Civil Action No. 15:93-CV-196
Bank of Vermont, Bradford National Bank, Caledonia National
Bank, and Independent Bank Group Inc.
15:93-CV-196

Defendants

PLAINTIFF'S ANSWER TO SANCTIONS/CONTEMPT
Defendants' attorney, Elizabeth Glenn, has repeatedly advised
the Plaintiffs to seek representation of an attorney. Plaintiffs
were unsuccessful in finding any attorney that was willing or
interested in dealing with the FDIC. Out of desperation, the
Plaintiffs have attempted to represent themselves, however not
very successfully.

The Plaintiffs now have two attorneys who are representing
them and Ms. Glenn is not happy or satisfied. The Plaintiffs have
been in contact with both of these attorneys and have supplied
them with most of the information that they have requested.

The Plaintiffs have contacted the office of Elizabeth Glenn
by phone in an attempt to cooperate. Elizabeth Glenn would
not come to the phone and the Plaintiff was told that she would
not discuss anything with him as he was represented by council.

For nearly six years the Plaintiffs have tried to cooperate with the Banks, the FDIC, the FBI, the US attorney and the courts, but we now feel that we have certainly been used by all of them. We now do not feel very comfortable or trusting of any of them, which seems very sad. I can see no need for us to file any further motion with the Court as we know from past experience that it will not be considered. We have suffered tremendously and more that anyone can imagine for the past six years so why doesn't the Government just come in and finish us off as they did in Waco and Ruby Ridge and have it over as we cannot take anymore.

DATED at Hardwick, Vermont this thirtieth day of December 1995.

William F. Hill

William F. Hill

UNITED STATES DISTRICT COURT
DISTRICT OF VERMONT

William E. Hill and Charlotte J. Hill.
Plaintiffs
V
FDIC, Receiver of First National Bank of Vermont, Bradford
National Bank, Caledonia National Bank, and Independent
Bank Group Inc.
Civil Action No. 15:93-CV-l 96

Defendants

PLAINTIFFS WILLIAM E. HILL AND CHARLOTTE J. HILLS MOTION FOR JURY TRIAL AND TO COMPEL DEFENDANTS TO PRODUCE INTEROGOROTORIES AS REQUESTED UNDER DISCOVERY

Plaintiffs William F. Hill and Charlotte J. Hill hereby moves pursuant of the Seventh Amendment of the Constitution of the United States of America that the decision of Judge Billings, Judge in the United States District Court dated July 5, 1995, granting the FDIC a Judgment against the Plaintiffs in the amount of $1,444,807.34, beset aside until a fair and impartial hearing before a Jury can be heard as guaranteed by the Constitution of the United States. Such hearing was requested by the Plaintiffs in the original complaint. Also the Plaintiffs move to have the Defendant FDIC produce interrogatories as requested in Discovery dated November 27, 1993. Plaintiffs William F. Hill and Charlotte J. Hill provides the following memorandum in support of these motions.

MEMORANDUM

Originally the Plaintiffs tried to settle any differences with the failed banks of the Independent Bank Group. This should have been a very simple and inexpensive matter without any great expense to either party. The failed banks could not or would not negotiate in good faith and although several agreements were reached the banks failed to stand by any of these agreements.

When the failed banks were taken over by the FDIC, Plaintiffs again tried to reach an agreeable settlement with the FDIC. Plaintiffs were informed by Karen Eastman of the FDIC that the only avenue for any settlement or agreement would have to be done in the US court. Plaintiffs felt that this was a needless expense of time and money until the parties had at lease attempted to negotiate a reasonable compromise. Plaintiffs contacted several attorneys, all of whom said that they were not interested in dealing with the FDIC.

Plaintiffs then felt that they had no choice but to attempt to reach a settlement in the US court by representing themselves. The Plaintiffs were ill equipped to do this. However, on June 30, 1993, the Plaintiffs filed a Complaint, With the Court, paid the required fee and asked for a Jury trial, which was their Constitutional right. The FDIC's attorney, Elizabeth Glynn, then answered the Complaint and sent the Plaintiffs a Discovery Schedule, which the Plaintiffs agreed to.

On November 27, 1993, the Plaintiffs sent to the FDIC's attorney, Ms. Glynn, their Request to Produce certain information and Documents. After much complaining, by Ms. Glynn, about the work required to produce this information, approximately 20 percent of the information was produced.

Exactly one year after filing the original complaint, the FDIC, through their attorney, filed a counter claim and a motion for summary judgment against the Plaintiffs for nearly one and a half million dollars. Without any hearings or any jury trial, the court immediately ruled in favor of the FDIC and granted them a judgment in the amount of $1,444,807.34, thereby violating the Constitutional Rights of the Plaintiffs to a jury trial.

The Plaintiffs William F. Hill and Charlotte J. Hill requests that the previous motions and decisions in this case beset aside and a jury trial be conducted in accordance with the rights of the Plaintiffs as guaranteed by the Seventh Amendment of the Constitution of the United States of America.

The Plaintiffs further move that the FDIC be required to produce the rest of the information requested under the rules of discovery.

Otherwise, the Plaintiffs would move that the court rule against all claims of both the Plaintiffs and the Defendants as they relate to the failed banks of Independent Bank Group and this Litigation be ended forever.

Dated at Hardwick, Vermont this third day of January 1996.

By_____

William F. Hill
PO Box 15
Hardwick, Vermont 05843

UNITED STATES DISTRICT COURT
FOR THE DISTRICT OF VERMONT

WILLIAM F. HILL and CHARLOTTE J. HILL
CIVIL ACTION NO: 5:93-CV-196
v.
FDIC, RECEIVER OF FIRST NATIONAL BANK
OF VERMONT, BRADFORD NATIONAL BANK,
CALEDONIA NATIONAL BANK and INDEPENDENT
BANK GROUP, INC.
*DEFENDANT FEDERAL DEPOSIT INSURANCE
CORPORATION AS RECEIVER OF FIRST NATIONAL
BANK OF VERMONT'S OBJECTION TO PLAINTIFF
WILLIAM F. HILL AND CHARLOTTE HILL'S MOTION
FOR JURY TRIAL AND TO COMPEL DEFENDANTS TO
PRODUCE INTERROGATORIES AS REQUESTED UNDER
DISCOVERY*

Defendant, Federal Deposit Insurance Corporation as
Receiver of First National Bank of Vermont ("FDIC"), by and
through its attorneys Ryan Smith & Carbine Ltd., objects to
the latest motion by the Plaintiffs William F. Hill and Charlotte
J. Hill, dated January 3, 1996, which is captioned "Motion for
Jury Trial and to Compel Defendants to Produce Interrogatories
as Requested under Discovery." Plaintiffs do have counsel of
record in this matter, Attorney David A. Gibson. Plaintiffs
have chosen instead to file this motion prosee.

Summary Judgment, pursuant to FRCP 56 was granted in
this matter in favor of the FDIC in the amount of $1,444,807.34,
with interest accruing, on July 5, 1994, which is some sixteen
months ago. The Plaintiffs' prosee motion requests that this
Judgment be set aside because the Plaintiffs did not have a jury
trial. FRCP 60 is the rule that governs relief from judgment.
Plaintiff's motion is severely untimely and must be denied.

Plaintiffs have cited no grounds under FRCP 60, which would entitle them to have the Judgment set aside.

Rule 60(a) does not apply as there is no claim of a clerical mistake. Rule 60(b) also does not afford any relief from the Judgment. The Judgment in favor of the FDIC became final on September 6, 1994. Rule 60(b) provides a one-year time limit as to setting aside a judgment for the grounds listed in items 1, 2, and 3 of the Rule. Plaintiffs are far beyond this one-year time period. Further, the Judgment cannot be set aside underground 4 as the Judgment is not void nor can it be set aside under ground 5 as the Judgment has not been satisfied. As to ground 6, there is no reason justifying relief from the operation of this Judgment. As the Defendant FDIC rightfully obtained its Judgment by summary judgment, Plaintiffs were not entitled to a jury trial.

Since July of 1995, the FDIC has been attempting to obtain answers to Post-Judgment Interrogatories and Request to Produce in an effort to locate assets on which to execute on the Judgment. The Hills are resisting these efforts. The FDIC had no choice but to move forward with a Motion for Contempt and Sanctions dated December 29, 1995. In response to that, Plaintiffs filed opposition to the motion, but not the responses to the discovery. Thereafter, the Plaintiffs filed the instant motion seeking to set aside the Judgment. Plaintiffs are resisting all efforts by the FDIC to try and collect on this Judgment. Judgment was entered in this matter over a year and half, and the FDIC has received no payment on the Judgment. The FDIC is entitled to enforce the Judgment and is entitled to the information requested. Plaintiffs are not entitled to the relief they requested.

Dated at Rutland, Vermont this fifth day of January 1996.

FEDERAL DEPOSIT INSURANCE
CORPORATION AS RECEIVER OF FIRST NATIONAL
BANK OF VERMONT

By:_____

Elizabeth A. Glynn, Esq.
Ryan Smith & Carbine Ltd.
PO Box 310
Rutland, Vermont 05702
Federal ID# 000520820

3485/39/63070

UNITED STATES DISTRICT COURT
DISTRICT OF VERMONT

William F. Hill and Charlotte J Hill.
Plaintiffs
V
FDIC, Receiver of First National Bank of Vermont, Bradford
National Bank, Caledonia National Bank, and Independent
Bank Group Inc.

Civil Action No.
15:93-CV-196

Defendants

PLAINTIFFS WILLIAM F. HILL AND CHARLOTTE
J. HILL'S FURTHER PLEADINGS FOR A JURY
TRIAL AND MOTION TO COMPEL TO PRODUCE
INTERROGATORIES AS REQUESTED UNDER
DISCOVERY

The Plaintiffs do not wish to keep bothering the Court
with this case. I am sure that they are as sick of hearing about
it as we are and we feel that it is taking up a lot of valuable time
and expense of everybody involved including the Court. All we
want is to see that Justice is done. We realize that we are not
lawyers and probably don't understand how the law works in
many instances, and we apologize for this.

Ms. Glynn stated in her last correspondence, to the Court,
dated January 5, 1996, that "Plaintiffs were not entitled to a
jury trial." To us this seems unbelievable. Murders, rapist, drug
dealers and even the bombers of the Oklahoma federal building
receive jury trials. According to her logic the Rodney King trial
should never happened. The Court should have watched the

video then convicted and sentenced the police officers involved without any trial. This did not happen.

We realize that this is a civil matter and not a criminal case. However, the sale of the motel, which is the main basis of this action, was fraudulently misrepresented. Paul Gallarani and Noel Lussier who fraudulently and criminally misrepresented the motels values with a fraudulent appraisal, no franchise as represented and conveyed it to us with false performance claims even were afforded a jury trial. You mean that we the victims of such an elaborate scheme of deceit and fraud are not due the same privileges, which is a jury trial in Court.

Gallarani and Lussier were found guilty of bank fraud and much wrongdoing, and now the FDIC and their attorneys are trying to uphold what they did and benefit from their fraudulent acts. Certainly any loses or damages to the banks or the FDIC were not caused by the Plaintiffs in this case. All we are seeking is the same standards of justice that has been afforded to the banks and bankers who are responsible for this mess. Certainly Victims should have rights equal to criminals.

The bankers produced an appraisal of the motel showing a fair market value of $3,900,000. They by using several fraudulent schemes convinced us that it was a good buy at $2,600,000, which is what we agreed to pay.

It has always been said that the true test of fair market value is "what a willing buyer will pay and what a willing seller is willing to take" This is of course with both parties having full knowledge of what they are buying and selling and not subject to fraudulent claims. The FDIC sold this same motel, which was in far better shape than when we bought it for far less than $500,000. If they sold it an arm's length transaction at a fair market price, this would mean the Plaintiffs were frauded out of over $2,000,000. If they did not sell it at a fair market price, it must have been a sweetheart deal and would seem that it should be vigorously investigated as both the United States taxpayers and the Plaintiffs have been seriously frauded.

By not allowing the Plaintiffs to have a jury trial as guaranteed by the Seventh Amendment of the Constitution of the United States justice and several fraudulent acts are being swept under the rug.

Again we, the Plaintiffs pray that the Court, in the interest of Justice, award the Plaintiffs the jury trial that they deserve or that the case be ended and both parties abstain from bothering each other and the Court further. Thank You!

Dated at Hardwick, Vermont, this ninth day of January 1996.

By William F. Hill
PO Box 15
Hardwick, VT 05843

WILLIAM HILL and CHARLOTTE HILL
V.
FDIC, as Receiver for First Nat'l Bank of VT,
Bradford Nat'l Bank, Caledonia Nat'l
Bank, and Independent Bank Group
5:93-cv-196

TAKE NOTICE that the above-entitled case has been
scheduled at 11:00 a.m., on WEDNESDAY, FEBRUARY
7, 1996, at Rutland, Vermont, before Honorable Franklin S.
Billings Jr., Senior US District Judge, for HEARING ON ALL
PENDING MOTIONS.
Room No. Main Courtroom Date mailed: January 9, 1996

RICHARD PAUL WASKO, *Clerk*
By _____
Deputy Clerk

TO:
David Gibson, Esq.
PO Box 1767
Brattleboro, VT 05301-1767
William Hill Charlotte Hill
PO Box 15 Hardwick, VT 05843
Elizabeth Glynn, Esq.
PO Box 310
Rutland, VT 05702-0310

UNITED STATES DISTRICT COURT FOR
THE DISTRICT OF VERMONT

WILLIAM F. Hill and CHARLOTTE J. HILL
CIVIL ACTION NO: 5:93-CV-196

V.

FDIC, RECEIVER OF FIRST NATIONAL BANK
OF VERMONT, BRADFORD NATIONAL BANK,
CALEDONIA NATIONAL BANK and INDEPENDENT
BANK GROUP, INC.

DEFENDANT FEDERAL DEPOSIT INSURANCE
CORPORATION AS RECEIVER FIRST NATIONAL
BANK OF VERMONT'S OBJECTION TO PLAINTIFFS
WILLIAM E. HILL AND CHARLOTTE HILL'S FURTHER
PLEADINGS FOR A JURY TRIAL AND MOTION TO
COMPEL TO PRODUCE INTERROGATORIES AS
REQUESTED UNDER DISCOVERY

Defendant, Federal Deposit Insurance Corporation as Receiver of First National Bank of Vermont ("FDIC"), by and through its attorneys Ryan Smith & Carbine Ltd., again objects to the most recent filing of the Plaintiffs William F. Hill and Charlotte J. Hill, dated January 9, 1996, which is captioned "Plaintiff William F. Hill and Charlotte J. Hill's Further Pleadings for a Jury Trial and Motion to Compel to Produce Interrogatories as Requested under Discovery." Plaintiffs are represented by counsel although their recent filings are filed prosee. Nothing has been received from their counsel of record, Attorney David Gibson. It would seem that Plaintiffs' counsel should be advising them on the appropriateness of summary judgment when the evidence is insufficient and how this negates any right to a jury trial.

The constitutionality of summary judgment is well-settled. In *Fidelity & Deposit Co. v. US, 187 US* 315, 320, 47 L. Ed. 194, 197–98 (1902) the Court explained that a procedure for granting summary judgment does not unconstitutionally deprive a plaintiff of the right to a jury trial. It simply prescribes the means of determining whether there really is an issue of fact for the jury to decide. The purpose of the rule is to protect the court from frivolous claims and defenses. See also *10 C. Wright, A. Miller & M. Kane, Federal Practice & Procedure* (2d) § 2714 at 620–625 (1983).

Plaintiffs, William F. Hill and Charlotte J. Hill, are not entitled to the relief requested. This Court, by Order dated March 9, 1994, granted the FDIC's Motion for Judgment on the Pleadings and Motion for Summary Judgment on the claims of the Hills against the FDIC in their Complaint. After the date of that Order, the Plaintiffs filed an additional reply and the Court, treating this second reply memorandum as a Motion for Reconsideration, filed pursuant to FRCP 59(e), issued an Order dated March 24, 1994, denying the Motion for Reconsideration. By Order and Judgment dated July 5, 1994, this Court granted the FDIC's Motion for Summary Judgment on its Counterclaim and issued judgment in favor of the FDIC in the amount of $1,444,807.34 plus interest from June 9, 1994 to the date of judgment. Such judgment is accruing interest at the legal rate. The final Order of July 5, 1994 was appealed to the Second Circuit and dismissed by the Second Circuit on September 19, 1994. A motion to reinstate the appeal was filed on behalf of the Plaintiffs by their attorney, David Gibson, on February 1, 1995, which was denied on June 7, 1995. On June 16, 1995, FDIC obtained a Writ of Execution from this Court and proceeded to enforce its judgment.

Plaintiffs, in their recent filing, are raising the issues that were set forth in their Complaint on which the FDIC was granted summary judgment in March of 1994. That Order is close to two years old. Plaintiffs are not entitled to have the Judgment set aside under Rule 60(b). The FDIC is entitled to the judgment it received, to execute on the Judgment and is entitled to the responses to the discovery that has been propounded. It is important to note that the most recent filings by the Plaintiffs have only been made in response to the efforts of the FDIC to have the post judgment interrogatories responded to that were served on the Plaintiff July 5, 1995. It appears clear that the Plaintiffs do not want to provide this information to the FDIC. The Plaintiffs' motion should be denied as there is no grounds for the relief requested. The Plaintiffs have had many bites at this apple and it is time to satisfy the Judgment.

Dated at Rutland, Vermont this sixteenth day of January 1996.

FEDERAL DEPOSIT INSURANCE
CORPORATION AS RECEIVER OF FIRST NATIONAL
BANK OF VERMONT

By:
Elizabeth A. Glynn, Esq.
Ryan Smith & Carbine Ltd.
PO Box 310
Rutland, Vermont 05702
Federal ID# 000520820
3485/39/63959

Before going to Court Charlotte had been very nervous and practically out of her head worrying about the outcome and what Judge Billings would do. Neither of us had any objections to paying for anything that we owed and wanted to meet all our obligations but we were being robbed of over two million dollars by the FDIC and the government. This we could not understand nor believe.

This was the first time that we got to meet Ms. Glynn, although this case had been filed with the Court since June of 1993, over two and a half years. This was our first appearance in court with the FDIC. David Gibson showed up at the hearing. I didn't know whether he would or not as I had filed the actions that prompted the hearing. Ms. Glynn made a motion to Judge Billings to issue sanctions against me for not having provided her with all our deeds and other information. David Gibson then addressed the court stating that he had fallen and been injured and was just now recovering and that was the reason that he had not sent the information on to Ms. Glynn. I then asked to make a statement, which the judge allowed. I read my prepared statement and again moved for a jury trial and for the FDIC to produce the information that I had requested and had a right to request back in 1993. I also made another motion that if this wasn't satisfactory that the whole mess be dropped and the whole business.

This was our only appearance in Court with the FDIC.

February 7, 1996

COURT MEMORANDUM

I wish to take this opportunity to thank the Court for allowing us to be here today to present some of the facts in this case, *William F. Hill & Charlotte J. Hill v. FDIC*, receiver for the FNB, BNB, & CNB.

For many years we, the Plaintiff's, did business with CNB and later BNB & FNB. Part of our business had been buying properties from the banks to fix up and resell or lease out. I also had established dealer accounts at these banks, which allowed me to obtain loans for others.

In August of 1990, I was contacted by Noel Lussier, who was the president of CNB & also a director of BNB who wanted to sell me a motel and conference center in Plymouth, New Hampshire. I looked at the motel and conference center with Lussier and Paul Gallarani, the president of BNB.

Gallarani showed me an appraisal of the motel stating it had a fair market value of $3,900,000 and Gallarani said that the motel was at that time showing a daily profit of from $1,300 to $1,600 per day. Gallarani also said that the motel and conference center had a Day's Inn franchise, which produced a lot of business. The banks had formed a corporation called BFC that held title to the motel and conference center and they were operating it.

Gallarani and Lussier said that they would sell me the Motel and conference center for $2,600,000, even though it appraised at $3,900,000. All that had to be done, they said was to transfer the stock in BFC. They said that the bank would finance the purchase 100 percent, due to my good credit and the very positive cash flow of the motel & conference center.

They wanted to use two houses in the transaction and the bank would take them in trade. One of the houses belonged to me and the other I was led to believe already belonged to the bank but they would convey it to me than take it back in trade. Gallarani said they wanted to close the deal this way because they were taking a big loss and that they didn't want to show it all on the motel and conference center.

I questioned about paying for the houses as I still owed for the one that I owned and was going to have to pay for the one that the bank owned. Gallarani said that it would be no problem for me to pay for both houses in a few short months, from the profits from the motel.

A very short while later on September 12, 1990, I received a call from Noel Lussier saying that the bank was ready to close the deal and it had to be done that day.

Neither Lussier nor Gallarani were at the closing. It was handled by Laurette Sweet, a senior bank officer, and Stephen Males, an attorney from Manchester, New Hampshire. They were anxious to get the deal closed as it was after hours and they wanted to go home. Males had set up a noninterest bearing note, which stated it would be paid by the sale of the two houses. This was not what I had discussed with Lussier & Gallarani, but I was told that it would serve the same purpose. I realized after the closing that there had been nothing conveying to me the house that the bank owned or any mention of me paying for it.

Soon after closing the deal and taking over the motel and conference center I discovered that it did not have a positive cash flow, that there was no Day's Inn franchise even though one was conveyed from the BNB to me. There was not an adequate water supply furnishing the property, and there was no way that this motel was going to sustain itself much less make mortgage and principal payments or pay for the two houses as Gallarani had said it would do.

Some of the things that I later learned were that on August 29, 1990, just two weeks before the motel closing Paul Gallarani had sent a letter to Mike Flipiak who was a BNB director and the president of FNB stating the urgent need to get rid of the motel and conference center as it was losing the bank over $700 a day. Gallarani had told me that it had a profit of $1,300 to $1,600 a day.

I soon heard from the Day's Inn people that BNB didn't have any franchise to convey and had never had a franchise. It was going to cost me around $100,000 to get one. Day's Inn had contacted both BNB and their attorney Stephen Males telling them that the motel could not conduct business without a franchise. The most recent letter was on September 7, 1990, just five days before the closing.

According to the minutes of the BNB board of directors meeting on August 28, 1990, the BNB board of directors met with all members present except one and approved the sale of the motel and conference center to me according to the terms previously outlined. CNB approved the sale on August 24. I understand that the sale and closing was approved by the Comptroller of Currency. FNB wanted the note that was supposed to be paid off by the sale of the two houses paid off right away.

Less than a week after the closing I met with Noel Lussier and Robert Platka, the CEO of CNB a director of BNB. They said that the house note had to be paid right away. They told me to borrow $80,000 on the house that I owned and get it to BNB to apply on the house note. They said not to worry about the other house as it wasn't in my name, they would take care of it. I later learned that they sold it to Jack Howard, an employ of Lussier's for $170,000 financed it through CNB and turned the money in on the house note. I later learned, that the house had belonged to Lussier and not BNB as represented and had been in Jack Howard's name all along.

I was informed by some of the employees of the motel that Paul Gallarani had instructed them not to give me any financial information about the operating condition of the motel.

As soon as I realized all these problems, I went to See Paul Gallarani the BNB president, to discuss them with him. He said that his hands were tied and he would not discuss anything. I then went to see Noel Lussier, He gave BFC a $75,000 loan from CNB to get it on its feet he said.

Even though the motel had no way to carry itself and I learned later never had carried it self, we worked very hard to try to improve business and cut costs. I brought an accountant in to try to help us improve the cash flow. He said that I had really been taken and the motel and conference center, from an accounting standpoint had a value of less than zero based on its past performance. I also contacted the bankers ever day or two as I knew that they had frauded me good but I was sure that they would want to straighten out their mistakes and make good on them. I could get no answers from them, only the runaround. Lussier and Gallarani were fired from the banks and a number of charges brought against them for the fraudulent things that they had been doing including the fraudulent handling of the motel. Charlie Bucknam, the new bank president, immediately put liens on our properties including our home. He said that he did this as he knew that we were headed for problems with the motel.

In June of 1991 after we had operated the motel and conference center for nine months the bank had a new appraisal done. I now had a Day's Inn franchise, which I had bought and paid for. The new appraisal stated that the motel looked very good, was very clean, had good curb appeal, and that several recent improvements, which we had made, had helped to increase its value, which they stated was $1,450,000.

In August of 1991 I received a visit from three government employees, John Hersh and another man whose name I can't recall from the FBI and Allan Dawson from the Federal Reserve system. They wanted to talk to me about the motel. They said that they knew all about what had happened and that I had been frauded by the banks and their officers. They said that I had been used as a pawn. They also said that they were aware that I had been trying to improve the motel and its business. They said that they knew that I had been trying to reach some agreement or negotiations with the bank to correct the problems that the banks had caused and that the banks were not cooperating. Hersh told me that if I would cooperate with them and discuss the problems with them they could help me get my problems with the bank straightened out. I really felt good about this as I had been frauded by the banks but I now believed that I had the help that I needed to make things right. Little did I realize at the time that these men were acting in concert with the banks and were out to destroy us to cover up for the banks fraudulent acts instead of helping us as they had promised to do.

Also in August I received a letter from Mike Flipiak, who I had been trying to negotiate with. The letter was dated August 15 1991. Flipiak offered to release me from any liability associated with the motel and the liability relating the CNB loan in the amount of $75,000. This Flipiak said that the bank would do this in exchange for me giving the motel property back to them. Also I must provide the bank with a statement under oath relating to the circumstances surrounding the origination and administration of the loan. I had to agree to provide subsequent statements and testimony for regulatory filings and/or civil or criminal proceedings related to the loan. I also had to provide my financial statement and tax returns.

I did all these. I provided the bank with a ten pages sworn statement relating to the motel purchase. I provided them with financial statements and IRS tax returns and I turned the motel over to them. They never kept their end of the agreement to release me.

I believe that a copy of this Flipiak letter was introduced to this Court at the trial of Paul Gallarani in February of 1994. I also believe that the letter from Paul Gallarani to Mike Flipiak dated August 29, 1990, stating the urgent need for the bank to get rid of the motel due to its $700 per day loss was also introduced to this Court in that same hearing. Lorette Sweet testified that it was Stephen Males, the attorney, who decided to set up the non-interesting bearing note instead of conveying the houses as had been previously proposed by Gallarani &

Lussier. Males claimed that Gallarani had lied to him and had not given him the true facts for the closing.

We also had several meetings with the new bank president, Charlie Bucknam and the bank's attorney, Gary McQueston, to try to arrive at a solution. At the last meeting McQueston attended he turned to Charlie Bucknam, in our presence and told him that the banks have really harmed the Hills and that Bucknam should call in the banks bonding company and compensate us for the damage that the banks had done. Bucknam did not take his attorneys advice as he didn't want the bonding company to find out all the fraudulent and dishonest things that he and the banks had done. After that, when we met with Bucknam, he didn't want McQueston or any lawyers present.

In November of 1991, I had some people who were very interested in purchasing the motel and conference center for a price of $2,000,000. They claimed that they had the cash and were ready to deal. I thought this a very good offer in light of the June appraisal of $1,450,000. I went to Springfield to discuss this with Mike Flipiak. He only laughed and made jokes about the motel and the fired bank officers. He said that he didn't have much time for banking business as he had been spending all his time with the lawyers and the FBI looking for ways to get back at the fired officers and covering his own tracks. Flipiak told me that I should be covering my tracks too. I didn't think that I had any tracks that needed covering.

I contacted John Zampiere the BNB board chairman and told him about the offer. He said that they would get right back to me but never did. Also I talked to Winston Oaks, a BNB director. But I couldn't find anyone in the banks who would even discuss this offer. I understand my customers, finally, went to New Jersey where they bought a motel.

I provided the bank all the statements that they asked for and on December 31, 1991 I turned the motel and conference center over to the bank as they had requested in Mike Flipiak's letter. I also turned over to them over $500,000 of advanced bookings, which we had worked hard to get for 1992. The banks did not release me from the motel obligation as they had agreed but said that they would hold a meeting to try to reach a settlement in the near future. Flipiak told me not to worry.

They left everything in my name and paid some management company $50,000 to do what I had been doing for nothing.

Less than a month and a half after turning the motel over to the banks they contacted me through their lawyer, Cynthia LaRose, asking me to find a buyer for the motel as it was not doing well under their management, but was still in my name. My $2,000,000 customer was gone but I was able to get five more offers from $1,000,000 to $1,500,000. At least one of these offers was for cash. Although they had asked me to find a customer and get it sold the bank kept giving me and the customers the run a round. I tried to arrange a meeting between one of these customers, who had cash, and were ready to close, with the bank but the bank refused to meet with them.

About this time, I needed to pay our property taxes in Hardwick and our health insurance. On April 3, I went to BNB where I had over $28,000 on deposit in three accounts. I talked to a teller and had her write down the amount in each account, all three of, which totaled over $28,000.

The teller told me that in order to withdraw any of my money I would need to talk to Laurette Sweet a senior bank officer. Laurette told me that the bank wasn't going to release any of my money until the motel deal was straightened out.

A couple of weeks later around April 20, I went to see Charlie Bucknam, the bank president. I told Bucknam that I would like to use some of my money to pay our property taxes when they came due on May 10, which was still about three weeks away. Bucknam said that should be no problem and he assured me that he would release my money when the time came. He said to contact him the day before I needed it. I called him as He said to do. He again assured me that there would be no problem. Call him again the next morning, when they were due he said. I called him the next morning. Everything was all set Bucknam said call him again about noon He said. I called him at noon. He told me to fax my tax bills down to BNB and they would have the money already as soon as we could get there, which was about an hour away. I faxed the bills and Charlotte headed for BNB to pick up the money.

When she got there, nobody at the bank knew anything about giving her any money. I then received a call from Bucknam, who was at the Danville bank, telling me that I had no money in BNB. I told him that there had to be a mistake. All he would say is "I'm telling you that you don't have any money in that bank."

I called Gram Gove and BNB employ and asked him to look up my accounts. When he did He said that all three accounts had been closed back on April 20, which was the same time that I had contacted Bucknam Gove, who said that he couldn't figure out who had taken our money or where it went. He said that whatever happened didn't look right but that he really didn't want to get involved. We didn't get our money, so needless to say, our property taxes didn't get paid on time and the next day they were $1,600 more due to the late fee and penalty. All our property including our house was advertised in the paper for tax sale. After bringing much pressure on Bucknam to find out what happened to our money, he admitted that he was the one who had taken it back on April 20, yet he led us to believe that our money was still there and that we could use it to pay our property taxes until it was too late to pay them on time.

I still have not been able to find out what Bucknam did with our money or where it went although I asked many times. Putting us through what Bucknam did cannot be described as anything less than harassment and mental abuse.
This is but one of a number of dirty and expensive tricks that Bucknam has played on us.

Being more frustrated than ever, I decided to call John Hersh the FBI man who said he was going to take care of this bank mess for us. Hersh said that he was glad that I called and wanted me to come to Rutland, that day, which is about 100 miles. I met with Allan Dawson and Hersh who told me that I needed to get a lawyer. When I told them that I already was paying two lawyers, Hersh said that I couldn't use my regular lawyers, that it had to be somebody who worked with the FEDS and that the FEDs approved of When I told them that I could not afford any more lawyers, Hersh said that what I had to do would only take about an hour and so wouldn't cost much. I asked what I had to do. Hersh said that when they came to our house that I had agreed to cooperate with them and that everybody who was cooperating with the government had to plead guilty to something. I thought that he was kidding. I asked what I was going to be pleading guilty co. He said that they didn't know, that they would have to come up with something.

Hersh told me not to worry about it as all I would have to do was to go before Judge Billings and plead guilty to some small charge. That I wouldn't get more than two months' probation and that nobody would ever know about it. He cautioned me about telling anyone about it and told me not to mention it to my regular lawyers.

Hersh then told me to go see Jimmy Carroll, a Rutland lawyer. When I went to see Carroll and his partner, John Kennley, Hersh had already contacted them. Carroll wanted me to give him $10,000 and agree to plead guilty right then and there to anything that Hersh and the government might come up with. I had never heard of such a thing. When I inquired about not pleading guilty, the price that they wanted immediately went up to $30,000 and Carroll told me that I could expect to spend up to $100,000 but that there was no way that I could escape the Feds so I would be foolish to do anything but plead guilty.

About four months later, the government came up with a charge for me to plead guilty to. It was for making a false loan application in advance of a loan. I had never made this loan application. But convinced by several lawyers that pleading guilty was the only real choice that I had and still thinking that Hersh and Dawson were going to help me straighten out the motel mess as they had agreed to do, I reluctantly went ahead and agreed to plead guilty. I did not feel that this was the honest thing to do but I was told that I had no choice. As a result of pleading guilty, I paid a $10,000 fine, did one hundred hours of community service and am presently serving two years' probation. This caused me to lose my real estate broker's license and my auctioneer's license, both of which I have had since 1957, and I probably lost some of my respect—all of which I cherished very much. Along with this went my ability to earn a living.

In the meantime, after asking me to sell the motel for them, the bank did not accept the cash offer that I had, but instead decided to put the motel up to auction. The night before the auction, realizing that there hadn't been any interest in the auction, the banks attorney, Cynthia LaRose contacted me and wanted me to again try to sell the motel to the cash customers that I had for the $1,200,000 that they had offered. I was reluctant to do this because of the shabby way that the bank had treated them. LaRose then said that if I could get them to buy the motel the bank would give me back the $28,000 that Bucknam denied taking out of my accounts at BNB. I contacted the buyers, but they were not interested in giving the $1,200,000 that they had previously offered due to the way the bank had been operating the motel and the fact that they had advertised it for auction. Also they were not happy with the way that the bank had treated them. They did, however, agree to go to the auction the next day. Other than the bank they were the only bidder. They bid up to $925,000 and the bank bid $950,000.

Still not being able to reach any settlement with the bank my New Hampshire attorney, Richard Uchida, filed a court action against the banks in Grafton County, New Hampshire.

But as soon as the FDIC took over the banks and Uchida heard about my pleading guilty he no longer wanted to represent me. He said that neither he nor I were any match for the FDIC and the government. But I now thought and hoped that the FDIC would be anxious to straighten out this mess and would be willing to sit down and try to arrive at a reasonable solution. I contacted them many times and even made at least four trips to Westborough Mass to meet with them Karen Eastman of the FDIC informed me that the only way that they would deal with me was in the US District Court. I talked to Peter Langrock and to David Gibson who both told me that the Government had mountains of money and that the FDIC would probably be impossible to deal with.

They said that I needed to file an action, within sixty days, but that they were not interested in getting involved with the FDIC.

I went ahead and filed an action Prosee and asked for a jury trial. After filing this action, I still stayed in contact with the Westborough office, hoping to arrive at a fair solution.
In May of 1994, we traveled to Westborough again and met with Enrique Caballero, a liquidation specialist and Pauline Ing, an FDIC lawyer. She told us that the FDIC was not interested in what had happened with the banks, that they were only interested in what we had and they were out to get it all.

Caballero told us if we would supply them with all our financial information and tax returns that they would try to reach a settlement with us. I told him that I would do this as long as they would agree not to place anymore leans on our property until we could reach an agreement. He agreed to this and I completed all the forms that they gave me supplying every bit of financial information they asked for and our tax returns.

Within a few days I received a call from Caballero wanting to set up a meeting at our house to try to reach a settlement. Three men drove up to Hardwick from Westborough to meet with us at our home. They wanted us to give them deeds to all our property including our home and at the end of two years they would give them back if we paid them some over half a million dollars. There was no way that we could agree to this as it would be impossible to do under the circumstances. They told us that they would soon get judgments against us as they wielded a lot of power over the Courts.

Getting back to the case in this court, Ms. Glynn filed a discovery schedule, which we agreed to. We asked her to supply certain information and documents that pertained to our business with the banks. To date she has produced only about 20 percent of the material requested.

Several months into the case the FDIC through their attorney filed a counter claim and produced several documents to back up the counter claim. We did not object to these documents but instead tried to explain the circumstances surrounding them.

The Court without any hearings or trial ruled in favor of the FDIC's counter claim based on the doctrine of D'Oench Duhme and Co, vs FDIC, and awarded the FDIC nearly $1,500,000.

As I understand it, the case of *D'Oench Duhme v. FDIC* was a matter that took place back in the 1930s, where a note was given to a bank as an accommodation without consideration. This was apparently done to deceive the creditors or the public examining authority. This note was executed in order to enable the bank to cover up for some past due bonds. This note was given with the understanding that it would not be called for payment. The person who signed this note knew that it was being used so that past due bonds would not appear among the assets of the bank. Therefore it is obvious that the signer of the note knew that its purpose was that of deception.

In the case of *D'Oench Duham v. FDIC*, the signor argued that as the note was not given for consideration it was not an enforceable contract. The FDIC alleged that the note was executed for the purpose of permitting the bank to avoid having its records show any past due accounts. That this constituted a misrepresentation, which was intended to deceive the bank authorities and the FDIC. They argued that the signor participated in misrepresentation not only by reason of his knowledge as to the purpose that the note would serve, which was to appear as a good asset. The maker of the note was party to the theme of deception in the sense that he had full knowledge of the intended use of the note.

Certainly one who gives such a note to a bank with a secret agreement that it will not be forced must be presumed to know that it will conceal the truth from the bank examiners. This signor of this accommodation note knew full well that the whole transaction was aimed at giving the bank an appearance of having assets where there were none.

However, this is not the case with the Plaintiffs in this action. I entered into an enforceable contract for consideration with BNB, who represented all three banks of IBG, to purchase a large motel and conference center for the purchase price of $2,600,000.

I based my decision to enter into this contract upon representations of the officers of BNB. As mentioned earlier, soon after entering into this binding contract, I discovered many of the representations of the bank officers to be false.

It is in this respect that this case bears no resemblance to the case of *D'Oench Duham & Co. v. FDIC*.

This is truly a case of fraud and deception on the pan of the banks and their officers as to the value, to the performance, and the assets of the motel and the way that the loan closing was structured. Again this has no relation to the case of *D'Oench Duham & co. v. FDIC*.

Also the D'Oench Doctrine has been held not to apply to Tort claims. *Vernor v. FDIC 981 F. 2d* (11th cir. 1993) *Astrup v. Midwest Fed Savings 886 F. 2d 1057 1059* (8th cir. 1989).

This case must and can stand on its own merits. It is a very simple case of fraud and deceit by the bank and its officers to get the plaintiff to enter in to a binding contract then the refusal of the bank officers and the FDIC to take honest steps to try to correct the wrongs done by the banks.

The FDIC through their attorneys have alleged that the plaintiffs have not claimed there is any writings that meet all the required elements. This simply is not true. There are more than sufficient writings and documents to prove that fraudulent and false claims were used to persuade the Plaintiffs to enter into a binding contract.

A contract is often referred to private law as opposed to public law and when it meets the criteria of a contract, which is for consideration and not for accommodation it should be upheld by any court. In the case of using fraud and deceit to obtain a contract the agreement should be dissolved by the Court, or a jury when requested, and damages awarded, a right guaranteed by the seventh amendment to the constitution of the USA.

This case goes beyond the realm of breach of a contract in that the Plaintiff even after realizing that they had been frauded and deceived tried to solve all the problems by working hard to steadily improve the motel and its business. The Plaintiff repeatedly tried to meet with the bank officers and the FDIC to work out a plan to minimize any losses to all parties. Neither the banks nor the FDIC were interested in doing the honest thing, which was to try to correct the wrongs that the banks had done.

Instead both the banks and the FDIC chose to act in a manner that undid all the improvements that the plaintiffs achieved. The action of both the banks and the FDIC through their failure to try to solve the problem caused the value to slip even further. These people were very derelict in that they worked against preserving the value of an asset, that could have been preserved if it were not for their actions. It would seem that they should be held accountable for these actions.

When Karen Field of the FDIC informed the Plaintiffs that the only way to settle this was by filing suit in the court, the Plaintiffs were reluctant to do this as it seemed so needless if the FDIC would only try to make an honest attempt to settle the problem.

The Plaintiffs realizing that the FDIC was not going to negotiate and with the threat of having to file an action within sixty days we contacted several attorneys, all of whom said that it was going to be necessary to file an action but none of them was willing to do it for us. They said that the FDIC had mountains of money to spend to get what they wanted and that there was no match for this. They said that the plaintiffs had a good case and that they deserved to win but it was going to be tough dealing with the FDIC.

Given little or no choice the Plaintiffs acting Prosee filed a complaint with this Court requesting a jury trial, which was our constitutional right. The complaint in addition to the motel problems addressed other problems that had arisen from dealing with the banks. These were things that the banks had done that cost the Plaintiffs a lot of additional money. A number of our dealer accounts in which we had thousands of dollars of equity disappeared from our control leaving us with large losses. There was no excuse for this.

The Plaintiffs are not lawyers and do not enjoy this kind of thing but have tried to abide by the rules of the Court and to introduce only important facts that are pertinent or have a direct bearing on the case. We have only exposed the tip of the iceberg as to the awful things that the banks have done.

We did not get into any of this bank mess by doing anything that we felt was wrong. We were only interested in doing what was right, and I had complete faith and trust in the bank officers who frauded and deceived us. Any loss that the banks or the FDIC have incurred can only be blamed on their own actions. Therefore the Plaintiffs cannot be held responsible for any actual loss to the banks or the FDIC. Certainly the Plaintiffs did not intend to inflict any loss on anyone. We are the ones suffering real losses.

We did have equity and net worth as well as very good credit. As a result of dealing with these banks and their officers and, later, the FDIC, we have lost it all. We had around $200,000 in savings accounts, which we worked hard all out lives to accumulate.

My savings accounts at CNB I opened back in the early 1940s. I was a kid, only eight or nine years old when my dad took me to CNB to open this saving account with money that

I had earned from selling newspapers, shoveling driveways, mowing lawns and pedaling around the village. When I was in the army in the 1950s, my pay was around seventy-eight dollars a month. I kept ten dollars for my expenses and sent the other sixty-eight to the bank to be deposited in my savings account and we have worked and struggled ever since to keep adding to our savings.

This was to be out retirement, so that when we got to this age, we could slow down a little and spend some time with our grandchildren and do a few things. Charlie Bucknam, the banks and the FDIC have taken it all. We now have next to nothing. If this case were dropped today and we never heard from the FDIC again, we would still be facing a pack of troubles and problems, all of which were brought on as a result of our dealing with the banks and the government, all of whom we thought to be trustworthy.

Now they want any property we have left including the old automobiles that we are driving and our home, which we designed and built ourselves utilizing family labor, and many of the materials from auctions, yard sales, scrap piles, and junkyards.

The FDIC has also placed liens on the homes of several low income people who I had helped to get their homes by the use of my good credit. We put the homes in my name and financed them through a bank. None of these were financed through IBG banks. I gave them a contract for deed using their payments to pay the bank loan and mortgage with the understanding that I would convey the ownership to them as soon as they could establish credit on their own or that they gained enough equity or good payment record that I could assign them to a bank.

One such home belongs to a couple who have several young kids. It is a cheap older house in need of much repair. These people have worked to improve it and to make their payments. About a year ago, they found a bank that would finance their home in exchange for a first mortgage. This would pay off the present mortgage and I would convey title to them as was our agreement. I would no longer be involved, as they would be on their own.

When it came time to close a last minute, title search discovered that the FDIC had placed a lien on their home as it was still in my name. We have been trying for nearly a year now to clear this title. We have supplied Ms. Glynn and the FDIC, with everything that they asked for such as the original contract for deed, the appraisal that the new bank required a copy of the bank's commitment letter to them, a notice of the close out figure from the bank that now holds the mortgage and an affidavit stating that I wasn't getting a cent out of this.

Still Ms. Glynn and the FDIC have refused to budge but instead continue to abuse and terrorize these people by causing them to believe that they are going to lose their home that they have worked so hard get. I don't understand how anybody can conscientiously do these things to innocent people and be able to live at peace with themselves. These people certainly are not to blame for any of the bank's problems. This is nothing but pure torture of decent innocent people working, hard to achieve the American dream of home ownership.

Ms. Glynn the attorney for the FDIC has alleged that the Plaintiffs are not entitled to a jury trial or any trial at all. In their last memo to the Court she referred to this as a frivolous claim.

As a result of the actions of the bank officers and the FDIC, the Plaintiffs have lost nearly six years of their productive lives trying to do what is right. Not knowing where we stood, we have not been able to start anything new, make any plans or set any goals. We have lost all our savings, as well as our credit and credibility. This has been very damaging to the health of both the Plaintiffs Charlotte and William Hill. Neither of us has been able to get a night's sleep in nearly six years since this mess began. I have terrible chest pains and my heart pounds like a thrashing machine all night. At times I feel like I can't stand it another minute.

Charlotte who had not seen a doctor in years except for an annual checkup, has suffered terribly and has been under the care of doctors for the past four years. She has had well over one hundred appointments with doctors all as a result of the stress caused by the banks.

She has lost a large part of her hair. This will not come back. The surgeons thought three years ago that they might be able to replace some of this hair by a very expensive long and painful procedure of cutting slices out of the side of her head waiting about three weeks and then attempting to sew them back on top, but it wasn't going to do any good to attempt it until the problems causing the stress were removed.

On at least a dozen occasions she has packed the car with her cloths and tried to run away where she can't be found hoping to escape this terrible stress. Each time realizing that there is no place to go and that there is no escape she has returned shortly and unloaded her cloths back into the closet and continued to be very depresses and despondent.

Charlotte was always very hardworking person with a very positive attitude and a bubbly personality always ready and willing to help others. For the past five years she has had a very negative view of life, she has been very despondent and depressed. She has had a very hard time trying to cope with life, this all brought on by the banks and the government.

The only way that we have been able to survive and keep going is from knowing that we have done nothing wrong and that we have worked very hard and tried in every conceivable way to cooperate with the banks, the FDIC, the FBI, and the US attorney to do what is right. For all this we have only received further abuse. We have a strong faith that sooner or later there will be a day or reckoning and we will receive the justice that we deserve. This has been the only thing that has kept us going.

This is not a frivolous case as suggested by Ms. Glynn. We are talking about millions of dollars. This has not just been cup of spilled coffee at McDonalds or somebody making a racial slur. This has been one of the worse forms of torture that one group of human beings could place on another.

This misrepresentation and fraud was done knowingly willfully and intentionally and with the knowledge that it couldn't do anything but harm the Plaintiffs. The refusal of the banks and the FDIC to do anything about it except to try to capitalize on it makes them as guilty as Paul Gallarani and Noel Lussier.

Even Noel Lussier and Paul Gallarani who fraudulently represented the motels values and set up the fraudulent closing have been afforded jury trials. Does the FDIC, their attorney, and this Court believe that we the victims of their fraudulent schemes don't deserve the same privileges?

Paul Gallarani and Noel Lussier were found guilty of bank fraud, Gallarani in a jury trial that devoted much time to the motel deal, and now the FDIC and their attorneys are trying to uphold what they did and benefit from their fraudulent acts at the expense of the victims.

At the time of purchase of the motel the bankers had an appraisal showing a fair market value for the motel & conference center of $3,900,000. By covering up the true facts about the motel they convinced us that it was a good deal at $2,600,000, the purchase price, which we agreed to pay for it.

The FDIC has now sold the same motel, which was in far better shape than when we bought it for less than $500,000. This sale price was even less than the value of the advanced bookings that we turned over to them. This, in itself, indicates that the victims are being frauded out of over two million dollars.

Certainly the Court must uphold the motions of the Plaintiffs to allow them a jury trial as guaranteed by the seventh amendment of the Constitution of the USA and compel the FDIC's attorney to produce the information requested under discovery, or a more practical move as we now have no money and very little energy or courage left would be for the Court to order both parties to abandon all claims and fully release each other from any further action having to do with the banks of IBG Ms. Glynn stated that probably the FDIC would be willing to meet with us and work out something after reviewing all out assets Judge Billings immediately denied all my motions and told me that he would give me to March first 1996, which was about two weeks to come over to the FDIC all our deeds automobile information and a complete inventory of all our belongings. He said that if I didn't do this he would sentence me to jail. He then said that the court was recessed and started to get up out of his chair. Charlotte who had been sitting there crying but hadn't said a word, hopped up, and said, "Your Honor, I would like to ask a question. Judge Billings glared at her as she attempted to ask him to explain something that was bothering her. Judge Billings just glared at her and said this court is recessed ask your lawyer and turned and scooted into his chambers. Ms. Glynn hurried out of the courtroom so we didn't get a chance to talk to her again. It looked like we were at the end of our rope.

Following this two different attorneys, who knew Judge Billings, told me at different times that they felt that Judge Billings was lazy and that he didn't care what he did to people, and by siding with the government he felt safe in the decisions that he handed down.

Another thing that probably didn't help me with Judge Billings was that after the convictions of Herb Gray and Paul Gallarani were over turned because of some screw ups by Judge Billings. I wrote a letter to the editor, which appeared in several newspapers condemning Billings's behavior. It was probably a stupid thing for me to do but I always believed that right was right and wrong was wrong and I couldn't just see how when somebody like Judge Billings fouled up it was perfectly okay no matter how it affected others or what it cost but when a hardworking honest person fouled up the same Judge could ruin his life if he felt like it.

Some friends of ours suggested that I write to Senator Leahy and send him copies to Congressman Sanders and Janet Reno, along with a copy of the statement that I had made in Judge Billings's Court. I sent the letters as they suggested. I received back a letter form Congressman Sanders's office. I believe that it was a form letter, which thanked me for contacting the congressman's office but that they were not able to provide any assistance to us regarding this matter. I have heard nothing from Senator Leahy or Janet Reno's office.

October 20, 1995

Letter to the Editor Dear Editor:

I thought it interesting that the article in Wednesdays Burlington Free Press titled, Court Overturns Ex-bankers Conviction, appeared on the last page of the last section, that had any news on it. I could not find any mention of this news in several newspapers that had devoted much space to this trial and its original outcome, which most of the time had appeared on the front pages.

The article in the Free Press stated that Judge Franklin S. Billings Jr. erred when instructing the Jury about the law covering conspiracy. I would call this very serious as it seriously affected the lives of two men and their families. Perhaps if Judge Billings had not been so anxious to convict and sentence everybody in the bank scandal and had been more interested in the true facts on both sides he wouldn't have made this serious and expensive mistake.

I wonder if Judge Billings will be asked to pay for his mistake as he has made others do for theirs. Will he pay a fine, will he receive probation time, will he have to do community service and will he have to pay restitution for all the thousands of dollars that his mistake has cost the taxpayers and the defendants in this case and for the cost of another trial if there is one. Or will Judge Billings walk away free and continue to receive his big fat pay check from the government and the taxpayers while others pay dearly for their mistakes and his.

Bill Hill
Hardwick, VT

WILLIAM E. HILL
PO BOX 15
HARDWICK, VERMONT 05843
802-472-6308

Honorable Patrick Leahy United States
Senate Washington, DC 20510

February 12, 1996

Dear Senator Leahy:

Over the weekend, I was contacted by some longtime supporters of yours who urged me to contact you by registered mail and to send copies to Congressman Bernie Sanders and Janet Reno. I had contacted your office, several times, back in 1992 about the same problem that I am still facing today. At that time, I talked to Mary Miller. She was very nice but didn't seem to be able to help much.

My problems all stem from being a customer of the banks owned by Independent Bank Group that failed a few years ago. I have enclosed some material to try to explain what happened to us.

I have been contacted by many people including business people, bankers, lawyers and Clergy who all feel that we have been treated very unjustly. Many of these people wanted to help us but said that they were afraid to speak out for fear of what might happen to them.

A short while ago following the Randy Weaver hearings I believe that you made the statement over television that people need to learn to trust their Government. I have certainly trusted them thinking that anyone who worked for the government, especially in the Justice Department had to be especially honest.

Over the years I had bought a number of properties from these banks and other banks. This had worked out good both for the banks and for me. I had developed a very good relationship with these banks and their officers.

I have always worked hard ever since I was a kid. My dad brought us up to enjoy hard work, to live by the golden rule, pay our bills and try to make the world a better place to live for everybody. All my life I have trusted people and I have always lived up to my responsibilities. I have always worked hard, paid my bills and although life has not always been easy it has been good to us. Over the years many people have been very good to us and we have always tried to help others.

My wife, Charlotte, who's nick name is Sally came from a very poor family. About the time that she was old enough to start school, her mother became very ill and could no longer take care of her. She became a homeless kid bouncing from one home to another where people around Franklin County looked out for her. One of the families that she stayed a short time with was Merrill Perley, whom I'm sure you know. She attended over twenty different schools. She was the oldest of seven kids. When she was in the third grade, the state heard about her and her younger brothers and wanted to take them. She didn't want this so her father took them at night to New Hampshire where they lived in a lumber camp and her father worked in a sawmill. She took care of her younger brothers. She was not able to attend school much. Finally her mother got better and they moved back to Franklin County in Vermont where her father worked as a farm laborer for Francis Howrigan. His name is Clarance Longley. Charlotte grew up looking out for her younger brothers and working out scrubbing floors and doing house work for a dollar a day to help her family. She never learned to read and write, but always worked very hard to get ahead and improve herself.

Later in life she got a job with the Extension Service teaching nutrition, budgeting. Home and family management to low income families in Orleans County. I could never understand how she could do this without being able to read and write but she worked hard at it and received much recognition for the work that she did.

Due to her childhood, her biggest fear in life has been that of being homeless. Today this has become a reality and she is having a very hard time coping with it.

As you can see from the material that I have enclosed, we tried very hard to keep the bank from losing any money. We had to file a claim in the US district court as explained. I requested a jury trial as everybody told me that the Judge wasn't going to listen to me. I believed that the Seventh Amendment to the Constitution gave us the right to a jury trial.

Judge Billings ruled in favor of everything that the FDIC lawyers asked for and against every motion that we filed, which several lawyers had told me that he would do. After Judge Billings ruled in favor of the FDIC, awarding them nearly a million and a half dollars, I talked to a lawyer, David Gibson, who had been following what was happening. He told me that I certainly had been used unfairly and that I needed to file an appeal. I asked him how to do this. He said that he would do it for me, which he did. About the same time, Independent Bank Group, the holding company that owned the failed banks, filed for bankruptcy. Mr. Gibson said that this would stop all litigation and so did not follow up on the appeal.

The Appeals Court throughout the appeal because Mr. Gibson did not follow upon it.

The FDIC was right after us to turn over everything that we had to them so that they could collect on Judge Billings's decision. I felt and everybody told me that what was happening to us was legalized steeling on the part of the government who wanted everything, that we had worked hard a lifetime to accumulate, to cover up for their mistakes. They were going to leave us nothing. It just didn't make sense.

I had been misled into buying a motel that was completely misrepresented. I did not destroy it or dispose of any of the assets, but instead worked hard to improve it and obtain over half a million dollars of advanced bookings. They got back a much better motel than they sold me. They then decided to give it away and take everything that we have to cover up for all the fraudulent things that happened to us.

Feeling that this just shouldn't happen I wrote to Judge Billings, I guess you could say that I complained to him about what had happened, and I asked him to explain how he arrived at these decisions to take everything that we had. I did not think this too much to ask seeing that we were losing everything. He wrote back and said that everything that came to his "attention in deciding these maters will be contained in the transcript." Judge Billings went on to say that a copy of the transcript could be obtained from the Court Clerk. I didn't see how there could be any transcript where there had been no hearings or trial. I wrote to the Clerk and inquired about obtaining the transcript. Bill Curry, the Court clerk called me and said that there was no transcript as there had never been a hearing.

I then filed a motion with the Court again requesting a Jury Trial. The Court set a date for the hearing, which was Wednesday, February 7, 1996, just this past week. Judge Billings allowed me to read a statement that I had prepared and I made a motion requesting a Jury Trial. I have enclose a copy of my statement.

Judge Billings denied my motion and told me that he would give me only until March first to turn over to the FDIC all my deeds, all the identifying information on our vehicles and an inventory of everything else that we owned. He then ordered the Court recessed. Charlotte who had been sitting there crying but hadn't said anything said, "Your Honor, I would like to ask a question." Billings who had already jumped up from his seat turned to her and said, "This Court is recessed. Ask your lawyer." He then turned and hustled into his chambers.

I am now told that the only thing that I can do is file bankruptcy and that if we are lucky we could come out with from $15,000 to $30,000 to show for a lifetime of hard work. We started out with nothing and when we got into this mess we had a net worth of close to a million dollars and we worked hard for every cent now the government is going to take it all. I would never believe that this could happen in America. If we owed the money, I would not be complaining but as many have said this is legalized stealing. This is what really makes us sick. Who will be next, could it be some other hardworking citizens? Could it be our or your children or grandchildren?

I'm in my sixties and Charlotte is in her fifties. We have always worked hard and played by the rules thinking that this was the greatest country on earth and wanting to do everything that we could to improve it so that everyone could prosper and enjoy the American dream and this is where we ended up.

As you stated, everybody should learn to trust the government. We did and see what happened.

Sincerely,
William F. Hill

cc: Janet Reno
Congressman Bernie Sanders

CHAPTER 19

We got a call from some friends telling us to watch a television show called Gone in the Night. It was a true story about a young couple whose young daughter had been kidnapped and murdered. The law enforcement officers wanted to come out as heroes for solving this case. They went after the parents and put them through unbelievable hell for several years until they could prove their innocence. When the real killer was found, they wouldn't even go after him as this would make them look real bad for what they had done to the parents. Although their situation was much worse than ours as they lost a daughter and their home the tactics were the same. I'm sure that most people don't realize and can't believe that these things happen, but believe me, they do.

David Kelley had been telling me for quite a while to get out of Judge Billings's Court and file bankruptcy. He kept telling me that this was the place to deal with the FDIC. I had never liked the sound of bankruptcy as I had always paid my bills and never tried or ever wanted to beat anybody out of a cent. But right now we were being beat out of everything that we had worked all our lives for. I talked to David and we decided that if we were going to get away from the FDIC it is going to be necessary to go into bankruptcy court.

While I was getting all my information and financial records ready for the bankruptcy petition I also put together again the information that the FDIC was demanding. I wrote to Elizabeth Glynn telling her that I was giving it to David Gibson and that I was sure that he would have it to her by the March first deadline. I told her that it had been very hard to prepare all the answers that she wanted, as it was like building a scaffolding for your own hanging and it was having a terrible effect on Charlotte. I also told her that she had to know that we had been misled and frauded in the purchase of the motel and that we had worked very hard to try to improve it and keep anybody from losing any money. We had already given the banks and the FDIC much more than they had ever given us and they still wanted everything else that we had. I told her that we could not do to anybody what they had done to us.

After we submitted the information that she wanted, Ms. Glynn filed another motion with Judge Billings to have him fine us $500 and give it to her for not signing our answers to the interrogatories that she had asked for. Nothing had been said about signing them and there was no place on the forms that she has supplied for any signatures. Even if there had been I would be very leery of signing anything for them for fear that they would find some error in what we had done. This is how I got into this mess in the first place by signing what I thought was true and factual.

Ever since the Court hearing Charlotte has been very upset and had a very hard time to do anything. She imagines all sorts of terrible things happening to us. Another thing that is bothering her very much is the fact that she worked very hard to help build and furnish our home to fit her taste. There are many things that we worked very hard to do, which are very special to both of us. Many people who have come here have been fascinated in the way that she has decorated and furnished the whole place with things that she has salvaged from auctions, yard sales, and people's attics. She has always kept it very nice. Several people who have been in and looked around said it must be like living in Heaven. Little did they know that we hadn't been able to enjoy it the way we should have, the past six years had been more like living in hell. There are many things that people have given us, and the kids have worked to help us with. She now feels that she will have to part with all this. It is driving her crazy.

WILLIAM E. HILL
PO BOX 15
HARDWICK, VERMONT 05843
802-472-6308

Ms. Elizabeth A. Glynn
February 24, 1996
PO Box 310
Rutland, Vermont 05702
Dear Ms. Glynn:

I just wanted to let you know that today I have sent to David Gibson all the material that you have been requesting. I wanted to contact you incase Mr. Gibson fails to get it to you on time as he has sometimes in the past been kind of slow.

It has been very hard to prepare this information. It is kind of like trying to build a scaffolding for your own hanging. I hope that we can try to reach some kind of settlement very soon as we have had to live through this terrible nightmare for nearly six years now. It has been very rough and frustrating. Since we were in Court on the seventh Charlotte has had a very difficult time. Nobody can imagine what this can do to a person or how hard it is to live with her and cope with all the problems it has caused her. I don't know if I can pull her through it much longer.

I was pleased to meet you and you seem like a very nice woman. I know that you have probably only been doing your job and that you have been well paid for this. I think that you have to realize that we were misled by the banks and their officers and that I worked very hard to try to keep the banks from losing any money. It was very frustrating to see them continue to destroy the things that I was trying to do to keep both them and us from taking any great loss. I could not understand them except for the fact that they were all getting well paid and didn't have a cent invested and probably didn't care. It was us who was having to pay and had everything that we worked a lifetime to gain that was at stake. I could not do to anybody what they have done to us.

You said that with this information, although I can't see what this has to do with the problem, we would be able to meet with the FDIC and bring this nightmare to an end. I hope that we can do this very soon so that we will know where we stand for the first time in six years.

Sincerely,
William F. Hill

She confessed to me that she had been hiding pictures of our children and grandchildren under the mattress so that the government wouldn't find them and take them. All she can think of is them coming in and taking everything. Another thing that is driving her crazy is that Paul, her youngest son had put a mobile home and built a small barn on a two acre parcel of land that we had kept out from the farm. He and his wife Belynda and their two children had lived there for the past four years. I had put this land in a trust and given them a long term lease to live there. We also had a small maple sugar house and a shop that used to be the auction barn there. She is worried sick about them losing their home. She is up most of the night worrying about it. I tried to explain to her that it was not going to be the end of the world, we are not going to let them have Paul's and Belynda's home, that we have fought as hard as we know how and that we will still fight hard to save their home, but if they take everything perhaps they will leave us alone and we can try to find a way to get ahead and back on our feet. I kept reminding her of the person that she used to be and that she was only hurting herself by worrying all the time. I explained that I could cope with almost anything but her being unhappy. That this was only dragging us both down. I told her that she needed to be strong again and we would make it somehow.

It was obvious that the government wasn't going to leave us alone until they completely break us and make us lose everything that we have. They have now made it clear that they are also planning to take the people's homes that I helped them to get by signing contracts with them. One place that I told you about earlier, where the people were going to get their own financing and pay off the existing mortgage. We had contacted the FDIC's lawyer, Ms. Glynn, to have them release it as I had no equity in it. The house really belonged to the people living there and making the payments, and paying the property taxes. She kept leading us to believe that they were going to release it if I furnished them the information that they requested, which consisted of copies of the contract, the commitment letter from the bank that was going to finance it, the closeout balance of the bank that was now holding the mortgage, a copy of an appraisal and an affidavit from me stating that I wasn't getting a cent out of it. They also wanted the names of the people who were buying it. We furnished them everything that they asked for thinking that they were going to release their lean, which should have never been put there in the first place. Did they release it? No they turned around and had the sheriff serve papers on these innocent people to get their home away from them.

They have already started legal proceedings to force us out our home. They haven't even tried to meet with us as their attorney Elizabeth Glynn had said that they would when we were in court on February 7, if we supplied them the information that they were requesting. It is obvious that you can't trust them and that she doesn't want to do anything to end this action. She has a built in gold mine to keep billing the government.

We were sure by now that we were going to lose our home and everything that we have worked hard for but I plan to fight to help Paul and Belynda and the people who are holding contracts to keep their homes. They don't deserve to be dragged into this terrible mess and I plan to stand up for them even though we have nothing left for ourselves.

Charlotte and I will both miss our home, which we worked very hard to build and put together. We will miss having a place where all the family can get together. I'm going to miss seeing those little granddaughters and grandsons learning to swim in the pool. It is amazing what a good time that they have and how quick that they learn to swim. I will miss growing the crops, the feeding of the ducks that I have attracted to congregate on the pond as well as feeding the fish. Everything that we had saved and planned for our retirement would now be gone.

We knew that when the FDIC takes what we have they will eventually sell it for a few cents on a dollar the same as they did with the motel. They had sent the sheriff around to serve papers on us so that they could take our house based on Judge Billings ruling. I told David Kelley to call the FDIC and tell them that we would give them our house if that would satisfy them and they would leave us alone. David said that Jennifer French at the Franklin, Massachusetts office of the FDIC was now handling our case. He called her and offered her our house. She said that they didn't want our house. Why did they come after it then and what do they want?

We filed for chapter 11 in bankruptcy court around the first of March 1996, hoping that this would get the FDIC to negotiate with us or tell us just what they wanted. Chapter 11 is to give you a chance to reorganize without your creditors bothering you. I felt that this might still give us a chance to negotiate some kind of a settlement with the FDIC. The first meeting of Creditors was held an April tenth. The only one who showed up was John Gravel the attorney who represented Lyndonville Savings Bank. The only questions that he asked where did we have insurance on our house and another property that was mortgaged to Lyndonville Bank. I said that we did and he didn't ask any more questions. The bankruptcy trustee who conducted the meeting told me that I should work very hard to try to negotiate a settlement with the FDIC that we could live with. I got the impression that he wasn't very fond of the FDIC.

One thing that we had to do that I hadn't been told about was to have all our checks labeled "Debtor in Possession." This was very embarrassing every time that you wrote a check, there you were labeled a debtor. Many people asked what this meant on all our checks.

One thing that we had to do was to list all out assets. I did not know what had happened to the $51,000, which was in Merchants Bank. Merchants had found that perhaps they had bitten off more than they could chew when they bought the Independent Bank Group banks. The newspapers were hinting that they might be headed for financial trouble. To avoid this Merchants had sold off some of the branch banks to other banks. I called Merchants to try to find out what had happened with our savings. I was told that Passumpsic Savings Bank had purchased the main branch of Caledonia National bank and that was where my savings had been originally, so that Passumpsic Bank now had my savings. I thought it funny that I hadn't received any statement from them. I called Passumpsic Bank. After searching their files, they said that they had never seen our savings account.

I again called Merchants Bank and reported what I had found out from Passumpsic. Merchants then said that if I would be willing to pay someone in the bank fifteen dollars an hour that they could research their records to try to determine what they had done with our money. I couldn't believe that I should have to pay a bank to find our money, which they couldn't account for, but I agreed to pay them as I didn't just want to lose over $51,000. Several days later they called and said that they had given it to the FDIC. I asked for something in writing they gave me a statement seating that the account had a balance of $51,415.14 on January 10, 1995, but nowhere did it mention anything about giving it to the FDIC.

We had been pushing to get a meeting with someone from the FDIC who could make some decisions. David Kelley assured that now that we were in bankruptcy they would want to meet with us. We tried but we didn't get anywhere. A friend of mine suggested that I contact Congressman Sanders's office and even offered to try to contact him for us. We had contacted Sanders office several times in the past without any success. We then also decided that we would contact Senator Leahy's office again as we had not heard from him. We called him person to person in Washington. He was not in but in about an hour he called back. Senator Leahy at first said that there was nothing that he could do for us. He said that he didn't have a magic wand that would make our troubles go away. I told him that we weren't looking for a magic wand. We only wanted justice and what was fair. I think that he then realized what a predicament that we were in. I asked him if he would try to arrange a meeting between us and somebody from the FDIC who could make some decisions. Both he and Congressman Sanders, who also called us the same day, agreed to try to arrange a meeting for us.

A few days later David Kelley called and said that we had a meeting in Montpelier Vermont with Jennifer French from the FDIC. Charlotte and I got there early and Jennifer showed up a little early before David arrived. Jennifer was very nice, and we discussed with her the problems that we had and how we had gotten into this mess. Charlotte told her about losing her hair and showed her bald spots. When David arrived, he said that he didn't want us discussing anything about what had happened to us. He said that was history and he didn't want us talking about it.

David and Jennifer went over our financial statements and she asked a few questions. She said the FDIC would probably settle for about eighty to 85 percent of what we had instead of insisting on it all. She said that she would meet with her supervisor, Jim Corbitt on Friday and that they would then have to go before a board that met every other Thursday and that they would have a proposal to us in no more than two weeks. Jennifer said that she was leaving the FDIC by the end of the month to go to work for the FBI. I felt that if they left us 15 percent that we could at least save Paul's and Bylinda's home and the other people who should have never been affected in the first place.

More than two weeks went by and we didn't hear anything from Jennifer or the FDIC. I then called Jennifer who said that the FDIC needed more information before reaching a proposal. She said that she would be sending some more papers to David Kelley for us to fill out. When they came, I went to David's office in Orleans to pick them up. There was again a financial statement, which I had already completed for them at least three times. Then there were several pages containing around sixty questions, all of which had been answered before, only this time they were asked in a different way. It looked like they were written to trick us.

There were questions like in the past five years I haven't taken in any money except or I haven't sold anything except. It then stated that if there were any mistakes or false representations that we were "subject under federal law to criminal penalties including up $1,000,000 in fines and thirty years imprisonment."

A few days later, I received a letter from David Weinstein the attorney at Congressman Sanders's office along with a copy of a letter to the congressman from the office of FDIC Legislative Affairs in Washington. This letter stated that we had a meeting with Jennifer French as we had requested and that the FDIC was waiting for us to furnish our financial statement and for us to submit a proposal to the FDIC. This was not what we had agreed on with Jennifer. I called Jennifer at the FDIC. She said that she was leaving to go to work for the FBI and that she was turning out files over to an Arthur Aguirre.

We had answered and sent back the questionnaires but it was our understanding that they were going to make the proposal. I called David Kelley and told him about the letter to the senator's office, but he was sure that they were going to make a proposal to us. After making several calls to the FDIC, David then said that we had to make a proposal to them. I told him to offer them $150,000 and we would try to sell our house to come up with it. David was not happy about our offer, he wanted to offer them a lot more but I felt that was at least $150,000 more than we owed them. He called them. They were not interested in our offer. David said that we would need to file a plan with the bankruptcy court. He drew up a plan with the help of another lawyer. His plan was to give the FDIC just about everything that we owned. He wanted to get rid of this case as it was driving him crazy. He even told me once that he would pay me to get it out of his office. I still wanted to try to negotiate with the FDIC.

Around the first of July I again called Senator Leahy's office and Congressman Sanders's office. I explained what had happened and asked if they would arrange another meeting, with someone in the FDIC who could make some decisions. Ed Pagano an attorney who works for Senator Leahy agreed that we should try to talk to the FDIC. Jim Harvey, a good friend of ours, who lives a short ways from the Franklin, Massachusetts, office of the FDIC went to see Mr. Aguirre to try to talk to him.

After the senator's office got hold of them, the FDIC set up a conference call with David Kelley and myself Art Aguirre did the talking for the FDIC although I believe that there were other people listening in as they were on a speaker phone. I tried to ask Mr. Aguirre a couple of question, such as if he knew what they had sold the motel for and would they negotiate. Aguirre had no idea what the FDIC had sold the motel for. Kelley didn't want me asking any questions. The call lasted about an hour but didn't amount to much in my opinion. Just before we hung up a woman's voice came on the line and said that the senator' office had asked for a meeting, could we consider this phone conference a meeting. I hadn't told Kelley about contacting the senator's office. Kelley said yes we can consider this a meeting.

I was not satisfied as this call hadn't accomplished anything so I called Arthur Aguirre back and told him that I would like to meet with him personally. He was agreeable. We set up a meeting at the Franklin office of the FDIC for the next Tuesday July 9, 1996. Aguirre wanted to know if I was going to bring David Kelley with me. I told him that I didn't feel that I could ask Kelley to tie up a whole day, which was what it was going to take as the round trip would be around five hundred miles.

On Monday the day prior to going to the Franklin office Jim Harvey was in Hardwick. I told him about my appointment. Jim wanted to go with me but said that I should call Aguirre and tell him that Jim was coming with me. I called Aguirre and asked if he would mind if Jim came with me. I guess that Jim must have given Aguirre a very tough time when he visited him as he didn't want Jim coming with me. He even said that he would instruct security not to let Jim in the building. Jim decided not to go after calling Aguirre himself.

Charlotte and I left about five o'clock Tuesday morning and arrived at the Franklin office about ten o'clock. The FDIC occupied a very large office building and we had to go through security to get in. We asked about using the bathrooms. We had to have some accompany us to the bathroom. I asked the security officer how many worked in that office. He said that he wasn't sure, that there had been over seven hundred but he thought that they had now cut back to around four hundred. The lobby was bustling all the time with employees coming and going. They were going outside to smoke, getting coffee and back and forth. I don't know how they got any work done.

We waited about half an hour for Mr. Aguirre to have his coffee. We then met in a small conference room with Mr. Aguirre and his supervisor George Owen. Mr. Aguirre asked me to open the discussion. I asked if I could take a few minutes to tell them how we got into this mess. They both agreed to this. They didn't have a clue what they were after us for except over two million dollars. I started out telling them about the motel deal. Each time that I explained something I handed them a document to back up what I was telling them.

Aguirre was stunned but wasn't too interested in what had happened but his supervisor George Owen was very much interested, and said that we certainly hadn't been used right. When I explained about John Hersh, the FBI, and pleading guilty, George said that he had heard tales about the FDIC using FBI officers to abuse people but that he had not actually ran across it before.

333

I explained about the house that I had sold on contract and that the people had been approved to refinance on their own. Both Aguirre and George said that this should have never happened. When they asked who I had been dealing with, I told them that I had spent over three years trying to get somewhere with Elizabeth Glynn of Smith Ryan and Carbine. They said that they had never heard of them. Can you imagine this? When I told them about Charlie Bucknam taking over $27,000 out of my accounts at Bradford National Bank, George wanted to know if I had ever gotten credit for this. I told them that I hadn't. He then asked if I had ever got an accounting on the motel deal. When I said that I hadn't, George said that this was unbelievable.

I then brought up about the $51,500 that I had in Merchants Bank, which the FDIC was now supposed to have. Mr. Aguirre said that the FDIC had never taken any money of ours from Merchants Bank. I showed them the statement that I had gotten from Merchants. Their mouths really dropped. They said that the FDIC had no record of taking it and that I certainly had never received any credit for it. George said that if the FDIC did have it that it would be credited to any settlement that we made with them.

We talked about Judge Billings's decision. I explained that Judge Billings was an old man and had made a number of mistakes, that he was due to retire and it looked like he just wanted to clean the slate to get out of there. He didn't seem to care about the truth.

George was called out of the room for a while. Aguirre said that the FDIC would sell our house and that they would take 80 percent of the net proceeds and leave us 20 percent. I would have been agreeable to this until he said that they would then sell everything else that we had and leave us 20 percent while they took 80 percent. They would then take 80 percent of anything that we owned in the future. He talked about for the next thirty years. This would make me ninety two. Aguirre said that they would allow us enough to live on. He suggested $300 a month for groceries. This would be ten dollars a day or five dollars apiece a day to eat. He wanted to put all our properties on the market with real estate brokers and sell them for whatever they would bring. I reminded him of what they got for the motel. He would not agree on trying to settle for fixed figure or amount.

George came back into the room. He apologized for having to leave. He said that there had been an emergency in the building. In a later phone conversation George told us that someone had committed suicide in the building while we were there. I tried to explain that the banks had already gotten back the motel in much better condition than when we received it, that they had already gotten much more than they had ever given us. I explained about the $3,900,000 appraisal about them conveying a franchise when they knew that they didn't have one to convey. I told him about the letter from Paul Gallarani to Mike Flipiak seating the urgency to get rid of the motel due to its losing over $700 per day when they had told me that it was making from $1,300 to $1,600 per day. I told them that the bank had gotten $250,000 down, which they kept. I also told them about all the improvements that we had made both to the building and especially to the business. We had painted the entire outside of the building, remodeled several of the rooms replaced the old televisions, new ice machines, had a Day's Inn franchise, plus over $500,000 of advanced bookings. I talked about the $2,000,000 offer. George said that they should have given me credit for the $2,000,000 I showed them the five offers that ranged from $1,000,000 to $1,500,000 and again brought up about the $27,000 from Bradford Bank and the $51,500 from Merchants Bank. I then really put the pressure on Aguirre and told him that we had lost six of what should have been some of the best years of our lives and that we could never get them back and that we were now enough older so that we could never do the things that we should have been doing during those six lost years. We had really been held hostages by the banks and the FDIC.

George said that we had really been abused. Aguirre said that he would write up a proposal and get back to us. He also agreed to look into the house that the people wanted to pay off and take into their own name. Aguirre said that he would get that straightened out right off and that I could tell the people that it would be taken care of within two weeks. I told them that this had been the same kind of meeting that I was having with the banks five and a half years ago where they promised to tell us what they wanted and were just a few days away from a settlement that had never happened. Both George and Aguirre assured us that this wouldn't happen this time.

We left about four thirty very disappointed that we hadn't been able to agree on a dollar figure, but felt that they now had a better idea of where we were coming from.

On July 17, 1996 Paul Gallarani and Herb Gray who had filed appeals received new sentences from a different Judge, Judge J. Garvin Murtha. Gallarani was sentenced to 18 months in prison and fined $5,000. This was down from 37 months in prison and $300,000 restitution that Judge Billings had sentenced him to before the appeal. Gray's sentence was reduced from two years in prison, three years' probation, $285,000 restitution and a $50,000 fine to eleven months in prison and a $10,000 fine. There was no probation or restitution for either of them. The Burlington Free Press said that "the convictions were overturned because of an error made by Judge Billings." I sent clippings of this article to both George Owen and Art Aguirre.

Friday July 19, Art Aguirre called wanted a copy of the letter from Jimmy Carroll's office wanting me to agree to pay him $10,000 and agreeing to plead guilty to any charge that Hersh and Van De Graff might decide to bring. He also wanted copies of the letter from Merchants Bank stating that they had given the FDIC our $51,500, I sent these out priority mail along with several more documents that I felt would help strengthen our position.

About a week went by, and we hadn't heard from the FDIC, so Charlotte called George. He said that we deserved an answer or proposal from them. He said that he would get with Aguirre and come up with something. I really trusted George, but I felt that Aguirre was not too interested in what happened to us. I later learned that he hadn't been there too long, so he was probably bucking for a promotion. Around the twenty-second of July, I called George. He said that he was going to use us good and that we had really been yanked around. He again mentioned that everything that I had told him I had been able to document. Charlotte didn't know that I had called George so she called him the same day. He told her that he wanted to use us right and that anything that had to be sold he would let me sell it. George said that they would have an answer by Friday July 26 with a firm amount that the FDIC would accept from us to clear up this whole mess.

George wanted us to call him back that afternoon. When we called, both Charlotte and I talked to him. George said that the government was so big and inefficient that nobody knew what was going on. He again said that we had gone through a lot of abuse and that he was going to bring this whole thing to a head this week. George said to contact him again Friday, August 2, for a definite answer that we would be pleased with and that he would put it in writing. We really felt good about this.

On Tuesday David Kelley called and said that we needed to complete a plan and get it filed with the bankruptcy court. I had not told him about our meeting with the FDIC. I didn't want him to file any plan with the court, which was going to give the FDIC everything that we had when it looked like we might settle for much less. Kelley wanted me to come to his office that afternoon and work on his plan. He said that he would block out the entire afternoon from one to five to work with me. Again we went over the properties that we owned and the mortgages that I held and on properties I had sold with a contract for deed. We had done this several times previous. David had another lawyer who specializes in bankruptcy help him draw up the plan, which was to give the FDIC practically every property and every mortgage that we owned based on Judge Billings decision. David said that was the way that it had to be or he wanted out. He was really fed up with the whole mess even though he had only been in it for a few months while we had been trying for nearly six years to straighten it out. He even told me that if I would get this case out of his office he would not charge, he even said that he would pay me to get it out of his office. This is how frustrating it was. He said that it was very complicated and that he had enough.

I told David that I would like to hold off a few more days as I thought that the FDIC was going to back off in their demands. David wanted to go full steam ahead with the plan and get the case wrapped up. I talked him into waiting a few more days before filing his plan.

All week we felt that we were going to get a fair proposal from George and the FDIC. I felt that now we were going to know where we stood for the first time in six years. I thought how nice it was going to be able to set some goals and work toward them for the first time since getting into this mess. Nearly every day for several years, I have been talking to and watching other people who were able to go about their business, who were able to get up in the morning after a night's sleep and know what they were going to do that day to reach the goals that they had set for themselves. I had not been able to do this. Many people whom I talked to said to me, "I don't see how you can stand living this way," not knowing we really didn't have any choice but to stand it.

Thursday I got home late. There was a message from David Kelley on my answering machine. He said that Art Aguirre had called him and said that the FDIC was waiting for him to submit his plan. It sounded like something had gone wrong we didn't get any sleep that night.

Friday we called George Owen at the FDIC, Charlotte on one phone and I was on the other. We were anxious to see what was happening and if George had his proposal as he had said he would. They said that George wouldn't be in until the next week. Again this was very disappointing as we had expected George to have an answer for us that day. I asked to talk to Art Aguirre, who George had said was drafting the proposal. Aguirre said that he had talked to the FDIC legal department and that they were not going to make any proposal or deal with us as George had said that they would. We were again very disappointed. I asked Aguirre how we can settle this mess if they won't tell us what they want out of us. Aguirre said that he had talked to David Kelley and Kelley was going to come up with a plan. I asked him how Kelley could draw up a plan when he didn't know what they expected. I couldn't tell him that the plan that Kelley was drawing up was to give them everything that we had, but I got the feeling that he already knew it. This only made us sicker. We were no further along than we had been five and a half years earlier.

A few minutes later David Kelley called and wanted us to come to his office to finalize and sign his plan. I told him that I was too sick to go anywhere. Charlotte called the FDIC several more times that day looking for George hoping that he might show up. His secretary said that she might be able to locate him but never did. David Kelley called me again Saturday morning. He wanted to know if I was feeling any better. He wanted me to meet him on Sunday at his camp to finish up his plan. I have never liked doing business on Sunday. He said that if I wouldn't meet with him so that he could present his plan to the bankruptcy court he was not interested in representing us any longer. We usually go to Church on Sunday but I agreed that we would meet with him Sunday morning. When we met, Kelley said that Judge Billings had really given us a bum deal. He said that it would be possible to file a number of motions to reopen Judge Billings's court decision but that he wasn't going to do it. We went over the same information that we had gone over several times before. I told David not to file anything until I got back to him.

I tried several times on Monday to reach George Owen but he wasn't in. I tried several more times on Tuesday morning and finally reached him around nine o'clock. He said that he was going to have to go along with Art Aguirre. I reminded him that he had promised to give us an answer with a definite dollar amount. George said hang on a minute. I waited on the line for nearly half an hour before George came back on. He said that the FDIC attorneys would not allow him to try to negotiate with us. They wanted David Kelley to file his plan. I convinced George to try again to get them to negotiate with us. I knew that George felt bad for us and was trying to do the right thing. I again told him that we needed a dollar amount. I explained that it would be just another big waste of time for us to present a plan that they wouldn't accept. Of course I didn't tell them that David already had drafted a plan that would give them everything that we had worked a lifetime for. George said that he would try again to get us a number. He said that we had been yanked around enough and that he wanted to help us.

Finally on Friday, August 2, George called and said that he had been working on trying to get us a dollar amount. He said that he felt that he might now be able to get the FDIC to settle for $250,000. We had already given the banks and the FDIC much more than they had given us but $250,000, although it was a lot of money it was a long ways from the courts judgment of over $2,000,000 and David Kelley's plan to give them nearly everything. I asked how much time would the FDIC give us to come up with it. He said that we could get at least one hundred and twenty days and could probably get it extended if we needed to.

I asked him if he would put the $250,000 proposal in writing and fax it to me. He said that it was still subject to approval by other FDIC employees, but he would fax me the proposal, which he did. This was on Friday August 2. George said that he thought that he could get it confirmed by the following Friday, August 9.

David Kelley was getting very nervous and wanted to file his plan. He called again the following Monday and wanted to know what we were going to do as he wanted to file his plan on Tuesday, the next day. I read him George's proposal letter offering to settle for $250,000. I think that he was kind of shocked that we had gotten them to agree to this. Kelley then talked about getting out of bankruptcy. I told him that I wanted to try to patch up the problems that the bankruptcy had caused with some of my other creditors first.

I kept in contact with George at the FDIC office. He said that he was having trouble with Aguirre to get him to agree to the settlement that he had offered. A little while later George called me and said that Aguirre had only been there about a month and that he was no longer there. He said that we would now be dealing with John Quinlan. This would be our sixteenth person from the FDIC that we had tried to deal with. George said that one of the people who were going to have to agree to the settlement was in the hospital with a broken hip. Charlotte told him to take the papers right to the hospital and get them signed. George said that the new man, John Quinlan was one of his best men and that he would be much better than Aguirre to deal with.

I called John Quinlan the new man. John said that everything was going well and he was sure that he could get an approval by Wednesday August 14. On Tuesday I received a call from John saying that he needed a letter from us stating that we would agree to the $250,000 amount and how we planned to pay it. I told him that we would have to sell our house and whatever other property that it took to raise the money. He wanted to know how long it would take. I said that I didn't know but that I would get right on it as soon as I received something in writing. I said that I hated to have to give things away to pay them. He said that he didn't want us to do that. I explained that it was now the second half of August and that the selling season in Vermont was getting short. He wanted to know if six months would be long enough. I agreed to this. I typed him up a letter to that affect. Charlotte and I signed and faxed it to him. John still thought that he could get it approved the next day, which was Wednesday.

Wednesday when I got in there was a message from John saying that he needed to know what properties we had and where they were all located and how much we owed on each one. There was nothing about a signed agreement as we had expected. It was too late to call him back. I was sick about this as I thought that he was doing the same thing that Jennifer French had to us back in May, besides I had given them this several times.

Thursday I called John. He explained that everything was going as planned and he would have our proposal by Friday August 16. He said that he only needed to clarify up a couple of things that he didn't understand about our properties in case the approval committee questioned him about them.

Friday morning John called again. This time he wanted to know if I had provided the FDIC with any copies of my income tax returns. He said that he should also have them. I told him that I had on several occasions provided them to the FDIC. He said that he couldn't find them so I faxed him a copy of my 1995 return. He said that everything was still on track to get everything approved that day.

Just before four o'clock David Kelley called and wanted to know what we were going to do. I told him that I was expecting a final proposal from the FDIC any minute. He wanted me to call the FDIC, which I did. Neither John Quinlan nor George Owen were there. The secretary assured me that she would try to locate them and have them call me before they left for the week end, but no call came. Another week of our lives was gone forever and still no answer. I was saying this same thing over five years ago. This was very nerve wracking and frustrating.

CHAPTER 20

Around the twentieth of August 1996, the letter came from John Quinlan of the FDIC stating that they had agreed to accept $250,000 instead of the $2,000,000 that they had been seeking. We had six months in which to pay it and that if we did this they would completely release us and all our properties from all claims of the FDIC. They were going to provide us with a more formal document, which was going to be drawn up by their legal department. I told David Kelley and he suggested that we get out of our chapter 11 bankruptcy. David filed a motion with the bankruptcy court to dismiss our case, which they did.

When I went into bankruptcy, I was advised not to make any more payments on to Lyndonville Savings Bank as I would only be building equity for the FDIC if we lost. I wasn't even one month behind on my payment when Charlie Bucknam had John Gravel, the banks attorney file a foreclosure action against us. They even filed an action against a Mr. Tailor who I had sold a house co. I kept on making Mr. Tailors payments as there certainly was no reason why he should be drawn into this and they were not behind one day. David Kelley and I were getting nowhere with John Gravel so I decided to write to all six of the Lyndonville Bank directors and ask to meet with them.

I didn't hear back from any of them but David heard from Gravel. Gravel said that no one from the bank would meet with me and it was going to be seeded by litigation, and that I was not to contact anyone to do with Lyndonville Bank but him.

I certainly didn't feel that this was the way to settle anything if the bank wanted to straighten this out which I figured they should want to do. I had met Dan Yates a couple of times. He was fairly new at Lyndonville Bank and was second in command after Bucknam. Several people who had dealt with Mr. Yates had told me that he was honest and fair and did as he agreed. I decided to call him. He agreed to meet with me. We met a couple of times. He agreed that what the bank had done wasn't right and after a couple of meetings he said that the bank would give me back the $31,448.13 that Bucknam had taken from my savings when he sold the Orleans house instead of having it deeded back to me. Mr. Yates said that the North Danville house that I had given the deed to Bucknam while he was still at Caledonia National bank happened before Bucknam came to work for Lyndonville, so he felt that should not be Lyndonville Banks obligation. He agreed to refinance our home if I would put the $31,448.13 toward the balance. I agreed to this. I appreciated what Mr. Yates did and felt that this the way that business should be handled. If the other bankers and the FDIC had operated in the same manner, I think how simple it would have been to avoid all this mess.

Reginal Lussier, an auctioneer and one of Roger Lussier's sons, who had not been very happy with Charlie Bucknam and the directors of Lyndonville bank had heard about the problem that I was having with the bank and the directors not being willing to meet with me. Reg contacted me and said that he was going to give me one share of his stock in Lyndonville Bank and that he wanted me to attend the annual meeting and tell the stock holders what Bucknam and the bank had done to us. Charlie Bucknam had to sign the stock certificate as president of the bank and send it on to me. When he did, he had one of his secretaries type up a letter stating that I could not attend any meeting or participate in any business of the bank due to the problems that I had with the other banks, and the FDIC. Copies of this letter were forwarded to the Vermont Banking Commissioner and the FDIC. I did not try to attend the bank's annual meeting.

Charlotte and I started to promote the sale of our home. I printed up some flyers. Charlotte went to several auctions including a big three day one that Christies had to sell some antique cars and car parts in Orange Vermont. She stood in the road and passed out fliers to everybody hoping to find a buyer for our house.

Both David and the FDIC encouraged us to list out home with a real estate broker. Before losing my license I had been a real estate broker for over thirty five years and I had also bought and sold many properties. I had often had other real estate brokers ask for a listing of properties that I had for sale. I had always been willing to give an open listing to anyone and did this many times. However, I have never had to pay many commissions as I always most always ended up selling my properties myself. I could never figure why the brokers didn't work harder. I never liked exclusive listings and did not take them in all the time that I was in the real estate business. Several times I have seen brokers tie up people's property with an exclusive listing and never get it sold and often not make much effort to sell it but were right there for their commission if the owner or someone else sold it. I never felt that this was right. Numerous times I have sold properties at auction for people who had given a broker an exclusive listing only to be bugged by the broker wanting to know when the closing was going to be so that they could collect their commission for doing nothing. I didn't like this. That is why I never asked people for exclusive listings when I was selling their property. I always wanted to feel that if I couldn't help them I wasn't going to hurt them.

I contacted a local real estate broker who has a dozen or more salespeople in his office. I had hoped to give him an open listing but he insisted that if I would give him an exclusive listing that he would put his whole staff to work on selling our home and that they would conduct a very vigorous advertising campaign. He promised to bring all his salespeople through our house within a couple of days so that they would be familiar with everything. I finally agreed to give him an exclusive agency listing that would still let me sell our home, without being obligated to pay him a commission. He said that he couldn't do that as he needed to get paid for his advertising, but agreed that if I sold it that he would only charge half the regular commission. I didn't like it but also didn't want to see them all work hard as he promised that they would and then have it sold out from under them so I agreed to this arrangement.

After listing it, neither the broker nor any of his salespeople ever returned. Certainly his sales staff couldn't do much of a selling job if they had never seen the inside of the house. I called the broker and went to see him several times but he didn't have anyone who was interested. I advertised it and had a few prospects but by the first of January 1997 there were no buyers and our six months would soon be up. I contacted this broker. He refused to release his exclusive listing although he didn't have any buyers and didn't seem to be very interested in trying to find any. According to his listing we couldn't put the house up to auction and if we knew of any prospects we were supposed to refer them to him. I wouldn't have minded this if he had been willing to work and had our interest at heart as he assured us that he did when he told us that he needed the exclusive listing. I offered to give him a new open listing but he was like a dog in a manger and refused. He had us tied up and our time was just about up and he knew it but he wouldn't budge.

While we are on the subject of real estate brokers, I need to tell you about my brokers and auctioneers' licenses. As you recall, I had applied to get my auctioneer's license back and had a hearing before the secretary of state in June of 1995. I had never tried to get my real estate broker's license back. David Kelley kept telling me that I was going to get my auctioneer's license back in June of 1996 as he had been assured by Diane Zamos from the attorney general's office that if I applied after my probation was completed she wouldn't file any objection as she had done the last time.

On June 22, as soon as I had completed my probation, I wrote to the secretary of state, Jim Milne, to see if I could get my auctioneer's license reinstated and to the Real Estate Commission to get my real estate broker's license back. I did not hear anything back for over two months when I called them to see what was going on. They had done nothing but now they both contacted the attorney general's office as that was the procedure to see if there was any objection from there. Diane Zamos after assuring David Kelley that she would not stand in the way filed objections to both licenses. She sighted the same reason as before, lack of rehabilitation, lack of good moral character and fitness, need to assure public safety, and reinstatement would be detrimental to the integrity of the profession.

It was going to be necessary to conduct two more hearings, one for each license. I talked the office of professional regulation and the hearing officer into doing it in one combined hearing before the Real Estate Commission and the secretary of state. The hearing did not take place until the twenty-first of November 1996, so another selling season was gone by.

This time I didn't ask any witnesses to testify. The last time the state discredited all my witnesses and said that they were not persuasive, although they had no witnesses of their own. I went without a lawyer. Diane Zamos tried to make a big thing out of the fact that I hadn't been rehabilitated. I pointed out that according to the states own definition of rehabilitation one would have to have taken counseling for some substance abuse and I certainly didn't have that problem. It also refereed to restitution to the victim. Again I pointed out that there was no restitution to anyone as nobody had lost anything and that the only victim was me. Nobody had gotten hurt and that there was no personal gain to me except the satisfaction that I had been able to help the bank and their customer. She then asked what I had done to insure the public safety and good moral character. I explained that I had worked very hard all my life to assure public safety with the people that I dealt with and that I felt that I had always maintained good moral character and that I just didn't know how to improve on these.

I presented into evidence the letters that people had written for the previous hearing a year and a half earlier attesting to my character. Diane Zamos tried to say that these letters were stale as they had not been written for this hearing. I pointed out that I was sure that people would be saying the same things now. She kept referring to my knowingly making a false statement on a loan application, which I had never made. I then produced a letter from David Kelley to Diane Zamos questioning her honesty when she assured him that she wasn't going to oppose me again. When I brought this out, Diane came right off her chair and vigorously objected to my reading or to having this letter entered as evidence. The hearing officer over ruled her objection and I was allowed to read David Kelley's letter. Diane's face became very red and she was furious. I then pointed out that she had twisted the facts several times and certainly knowingly made false statements to keep me from making a living.

I was not sure how the Real Estate board members and the secretary of state were taking all this, but I felt that I had gotten my point across and that they had seen through Diane Zamos.

It was several weeks before I heard anything from the hearing but eventually the answers came and I was able to get my auctioneer's license back and could get my real estate broker's license by taking the brokers exam and passing it.

The time for selling our home and paying the FDIC was getting very short and I was getting very nervous about it. If we didn't pay them, they could go back to the $2,000,000 judgment that they had and come after everything that we had. I hadn't tried to borrow any money since I bought the motel, which had been six and a half years. I felt that going to a bank was probably out of the question after being in this mess and all the publicity that it had caused. Besides all the banks that I had done business with had been taken over by someone else. I had talked with a mortgage broker but he said that he couldn't finance our home if it was listed for sale and the broker with the exclusive listing wouldn't budge. This reminded me of the first hearing I had to try to get my auctioneer's license back. One of the reasons that they gave for refusing reinstate my license was that Hill "believes he needs to be more careful when signing documents and needs to be less trusting of others, especially when engaging in financial transactions."

17 "Hill's determination to become less trusting and more suspicious of others will not enhance his practice as an auctioneer. It indicates his continued refusal to accept responsibility for his conduct."

Some of our friends had been asking me what I was going to do. I told them that if I couldn't sell our house right off I didn't know. One good friend who was also in the real estate business and that I had done business within the past told me that perhaps he could help me to raise some money. He found a fellow who I had also known for years to put up a large amount of the money that we needed and only charge us the interest until we could sell our home and pay him back. This was going to put us half way there.

This gave me a lot of encouragement. I called John Quinlan at the FDIC to see if the FDIC had ever given me credit for the $51,000 from the Merchants Bank. John said that he had looked into it but that the FDIC had no record of ever getting it. He said that if I could produce any proof that they had gotten it that I could get credit for it. I told him that I would go back to Merchants Bank and work on it. I called the bank. They said that they now would need twenty dollars an hour to research it. I told them that I needed a copy of the check to the FDIC. I called them several times and then they came up with the check and it had been stamped on the back by the FDIC. This was good news.

I was talking to another longtime friend who had a good business, which he and his family had worked hard to build. He said that he thought that he could borrow against his business and help us out. I told him that I couldn't ask him to do that. He replied, "You didn't ask me. I am offering to do it." These friends have saved much of what it took us a lifetime to accomplish and nobody knows what a relief it is going to be to have the government off our banks and to be able to live like normal people again.

On January 16, 1997, at 2:45 p.m., I faxed a letter to John Quinlan at the FDIC telling him that it looked like we were going to be able to pay them before the dead line of February 18. I outlined in the letter how I proposed to do this, which included the $52,958.44 (actual amount) I told him that I needed something in writing, so that I could assure the people lending me the money that the FDIC would immediately release all their liens that they had on our property. The next morning January 17, I called John Quinlan to ask if he had received my fax from the day before. He said that he had. I then asked him again to confirm in writing that he was in agreement with the fax that I had sent and that they would release all their liens as they had agreed. John said that it should not be necessary to put it in writing again as I already had it in writing in the form of the agreement. I took him at his word and proceeded to get everything in order.

This required title searches to show that after the FDIC released us we still had enough equity to be able to pay off the people lending us the money. There were three lawyers involved one representing each of the lenders and the lawyer that I hired to do the title search.

I had heard of several people who had bought property that the FDIC had liens and even after paying the FDIC had problems getting them to release their liens. Both of the lawyers who represented the lenders had bad experiences with the FDIC and cautioned me to be sure that they did as they agreed. I had sent the FDIC some payments back when they took over the banks and had asked them to credit them to a loan that I had at Caledonia National Bank. The FDIC had cashed my checks but I could never get any receipt or assurance that I was getting credit for these payments.

For this reason, I decided that when I paid them I would go to their office in Franklin, Massachusetts, which would be another five- hundred-mile trip. I wanted to be sure that I got credit and that they released us as they had agreed. I called John Quinlan on Tuesday, February 4, and told him that I would like to make an appointment to come in and pay him on Thursday February 6. John asked why I didn't just put it in the mail. I told him that I would feel better coming in and getting receipts. I didn't expect to get any releases that day as I expected that the FDIC would need a few days for the checks to clear and that they would then issue releases within a week or ten days.

John said that if I was willing to drive way down there he would find the time to meet with me. I also told him about having a copy of the Merchants check.

Charlotte and I left late Wednesday night so that we could be there when the FDIC offices opened Thursday morning, which was February 6. This was the first time that we had met John in person. He took us into the same little conference room where we had met with George Owen and Art Aguirre back in July. We had sold a couple of properties that the FDIC already had the proceeds from. I gave John a copy of the Merchants check with the FDIC endorsement on the back and another check that I had from one of the lawyer's trustee account for $100,000. I then asked John to figure up how much more we now owed him. John calculated for a few minutes and said that the balance that we owed was $79,889. I wrote him a check for this amount and he gave me receipts for both checks. I then told John that I hoped that just as soon as the checks cleared that he could get releases to us as we still would need to sell our home to pay back the money that we had borrowed. I also explained to him as I had several times before that there were several people who should be making payments to us for properties that we had sold them on contract and that these people had been refusing to make any more payments until the FDIC lifted their liens. John assured us that everything would be taken care of and we shook hands and left. This is where I had intended to end the book with the following paragraph.

We were going to still have to work hard to sell our home as soon as we can in order to pay back these good friends who have been good enough to help us. They are all hardworking natives born here, earned their money honestly and lived their lives by the GOLDEN RULE. We do not know where we will live, but that is not the important thing right now. Getting them paid back is.

While we have been trying to straighten out our problems with the banks and the government there have been a lot of people who have been very kind to us, giving us their support and offering to help us. They have been both business people and people with very small incomes. To all these people we will always be grateful. I know that David Kelley sometimes got discouraged and frustrated with our mess and with me for not always doing things the way that he felt that we should but I have got to give David a lot of credit for sticking with us and really having our interest at heart. David worked very hard for us and without him we might not have made it through this mess. We will always be grateful to him. In the end both Senator Leahy's and Congressman Sanders's offices deserve lot of credit for keeping after the FDIC to get them to meet and work with us to get this mess straightened out. We are deeply indebted to the friends who offered to loan us the money so that we could pay off the FDIC and return to a sane life again as soon as we pay them back.

The sad part is that it took over six years and a terrible toll on our lives to say nothing about the expense, eating up our saving, our retirement, losing our home, Charlotte's health, nerves, and losing her hair, which has about devastated her, when it would have been so easy for Charlie Bucknam. Mike Flipiak, the other bankers and the government to have done the honest and responsible thing back six years ago, and neither the banks, the government, nor we would have lost much of anything.

CHAPTER 21

After going to the FDIC office in Franklin, Massachusetts, on February 6, 1997, and paying the FDIC it was nearly four o'clock when we got back home. As soon as we got in the house, the phone rang. It was John Quinlan, who said that after we left, he had discussed the payment from the Merchants Bank with some other FDIC officials and they had told him that as they had received the money prior to our signing the agreement they were not going to give us credit for the $52,958.44. We had explained to them every time that it came up when they had gotten the money. This was all contrary to anything that we had ever discussed and was the very first time that they had even hinted about not giving us credit but instead had assured us all along that if we could prove that they had received it there would certainly be applied toward any settlement agreement that we reached. George Owen had told us that the very first time that it came up.

I was sick, I couldn't believe that they would do this, but I guess that I should have expected them to pull something after all the other sneaky and dirty tricks that the government had pulled on us. Due to borrowing the money, we were now $200,000 deeper in debt and still everything was going to be tied up and that meant that we would still not be able to collect any payments from the people who were supposed to be paying us on contract, all of which we need to make this deal work. We had been tricked again. This really put us into another very difficult position.

As soon as I could think straight, I wrote a letter to John Quinlan and sent a copy to George Owen. I mailed them registered mail, return receipt. They both received them but I have never heard anything from either of them. I sent John Quinlan several faxes but did not hear anything back from him. On March 27, I faxed John another letter pleading with him to straighten things out as they had agreed to do. The next day I did receive a fax from John Quinlan stating the FDIC had not changed their position and that they were not going to give us any credit for the $52,958.44 stating that it had been credited to my account back in January of 1995 the date that they received it. This was contrary to everything that we had discussed with them.

After writing to John Quinlan and George Owen and not receiving any answer, I contacted Senator Leahy's office and Congressman Sanders's office again. David Weinstein, who works in Congressman Sanders called the FDIC a couple of times and was told that the FDIC had given us credit for the $52,958.44. I guess that Sanders office chose to believe them rather than us as they said that there was no more that they could do.

I talked to ED Pagano in Senator Leahy's Washington office a couple of times. He said that they had sent the FDIC a letter that Senator Leahy had signed asking for an answer in writing. We waited quite a while for the answer. Around March 27, the senator's office received a letter from Alice Goodman from the office of Legislative Affairs representing the FDIC. Mr. Pagano faxed me a copy of Ms. Goodman's letter. I could not believe what it said. She said that "in July 1996, Mr. Hill was informed of this fact and was advised that the $52,9958 payment would not be applied to the $250,000 settlement. The August 16, 1996, document that was approved by senior FDIC management to settle the Hills' obligations, specifically accounts for the $52,958 payment under the heading "Collections to Date." She went on to say that "on February 6, 1997, he again inquired as to whether the 1995 payment of $52,958 had been applied to the $250,000 settlement and was advised by telephone on February 7 that it was credited as a loan payment and would not be applied to the August 1996 settlement."

First of all it was in July of 1996 that Art Aguirre and George Owen told us that the FDIC didn't have any of our money. They were shocked when I showed them the paper from Merchants Bank. Then George told us that if we could prove that the FDIC had that money it certainly would have to be part of any settlement that we made. Ms. Goodman also said that we were informed on that same date that the $52,958 would not be part of the $250,000 settlement. At that time nobody had even mentioned or hinted at a $250,000 settlement. This is a deal that we made with George Owen over a month later. She mentions that in August or 1996 that there was a document called "Collections to Date" that specifically accounts for the $52,958. I never saw any such document and how come George Owen and John Quinlan who drew up the proposal didn't know anything about it. If they did, they sure tricked us, which I don't believe was the case. She talks about a February 7 phone call where I was advised that the $52,958 had been credited as a loan payment and was not part of the settlement. This call was actually on February 6 and after we had been to the Franklin office and paid John Quinlan for the FDIC.

Part of our payment to the FDIC had been from a home in Florida that I had sold to a couple from Vermont. These people had spent time in Florida in our home the winter before. The woman was in poor health but felt much better in Florida and couldn't wait to get back there. They paid for the house on September 26, 1996 by sending a check to the title company to close the deal and send the proceeds of the sale to the FDIC who had agreed to release their lien on that one property. This should have taken about two weeks. The Title Company contacted me several times saying that they weren't getting any cooperation from the FDIC. The woman who was buying the property was also contacting me to see what was holding things up as she was real anxious to go to Florida. I kept contacting the FDIC. Each time they had a feeble excuse often trying to put the blame on the title company. The last time that the woman called me she was real stressed that the FDIC, would not release what was supposed to now be their home, which they had paid and their check had been cashed for they couldn't get title, being very frustrated the woman died without ever getting title to her Florida home or getting to live in it. This was very sad and Charlotte and I felt terrible about it.

On April 2, 1997, several months later I received a fax from the Title Company seating that they still didn't have a release from the FDIC even though they had paid the FDIC. I think that these things prove beyond a shadow of a doubt that our government cannot be trusted one bit.

I think that it is very sad that our own government resorts to such tactics. If an individual or private company operated this way, it wouldn't be long before the government would put them out of business and bring criminal charges against them but I guess the government can get away with anything including fraud and extortion.

Senator Leahy's office had been monitoring what was happening and suggested that we meet again with the FDIC to try to straighten the mess out. They said they would contact the FDIC to arrange the meeting.

On April 9, 1997, John Quinlan called and said that the senator's office had requested that they meet with us. John said that he was going to have an attorney present at this meeting and that he was also going to have a stenographer to record the meeting and that way they would have a transcript of the meeting and that we could also have a copy of the transcript. I thought that having a stenographer was an excellent idea. John said the he would also have George Owen and Art Aguirre at the meeting, which was scheduled for ten o'clock on Friday, April 11.

John Quinlan didn't want me to bring Charlotte to this meeting for some reason, but she decided to go anyway. When we arrived, we again met John Quinlan, George Owen and Art Aguirre. John introduced us to Keith Taggart, the attorney, and a young woman who he introduces as the stenographer.

The meeting did not go to well for us as it seemed that every time that I tried to say something I was cut off by one of the three FDIC men. The attorney, Keith Taggart, didn't say a word all through the meeting. Quinlan said that he hadn't understood about the $53,000. Aguirre said that it was in the records all along and that he was aware of it all along and was not part of any agreement. This was not true based on what he had told us at the last meeting and the fact he had made me prove that the FDIC had received the money. When I asked him why he had contacted me to have me prove that they had gotten the $53,000, he got real smart-alecky and offered to give me twenty dollars for my trouble. It was obvious that he was not telling the truth. George Owen said that he remembered telling us that they would give us credit for it but that isn't the way that it turned out and that it would be very difficult to go back to the committee who had approved the

$250,000 settlement and explain to them what had happened. When I again tried to explain how we had been ripped off with the motel, Owen said that was all in the past and that it was the FDIC's job to get all the money that they could for the taxpayers. I guess that they don't realize that we have been two of those taxpayers for forty-some years. They couldn't have had the taxpayers in mind when they sold the motel for only $350,000. Owen said that we weren't the only ones who had been ripped off as the stock holders of the failed banks had also lost money.

It was obvious that they were not going to give us credit for the $53,000 as they had previously agreed. Seeing that I wasn't getting anywhere with the $53,000 I asked if it would be possible to release any of the liens as they must be going to give us credit for the other $197,000 that I had paid them. George Owen spoke up and said they would release all our properties except our house because of the $197,000 that we had paid. They all agreed to this. When I asked how much time that they would give us as we had to sell our house, George Owen said that they would give us six months. When I asked from today, he said yes. I then asked, "Without interest?" George said yes that the FDIC wasn't charging us any interest. George said that they wouldn't need any new signed agreement as they already had the $250,000 agreement. I asked if we could get the releases that day if we were willing to hang around while they prepared them. John Quinlan said that in order to release the liens I would have to tell them what properties were involved. Apparently they didn't know. I told him that I could give him the names of all the towns that they were in. He said that he needed detailed descriptions of each property. I said in that case I would have to go back home and would fax them to him. I asked if I got them to him over the weekend how long it would take to get the releases as I had some people who owed us on several properties and had refused to pay us until they were free and clear of the FDIC. John said that it should take only a couple of days. I had the descriptions to him by the time that he got to work on Monday morning. On Wednesday, April 16, I called John to see how he was coming with the releases. He said that he was looking at them right then. He asked if there was any ones that I needed sooner. I told him about one in Newport Center, that I would like to have just as fast as I could get it. John said that he would try to get that one out that day and that the rest of them should be done by the end of the week.

When I faxed John Quinlan the descriptions, I had also asked him for the transcript of the meeting that he had promised to give me. I did not receive any releases from the FDIC as John had agreed. I then wrote to Keith Taggart, the attorney who had been at the meeting asking him for the releases and the transcript of the meeting. Over a week went by and Keith Taggart called and talked to Charlotte. He told her that the FDIC wasn't going to release any properties until we signed a new agreement with the FDIC guaranteeing to pay the $53,000. At the meeting they had all agreed that it wasn't going to be necessary to sign any new agreement as we already had agreed to pay them the $250,000 and they weren't giving us any credit for the $53,000. About the same time, I received a letter from a Paul Bonin, whom I had never heard of, from the same FDIC office saying that the FDIC was planning to offer to sell our obligation to a private sector entity. I called Mr. Bonin and asked what the balance of our obligation was. He gave me a figure of nearly two million dollars. A couple more days went by and I received a new agreement from John Quinlan, which came by way of Washington, that he wanted us to sign stating that we agreed to pay the FDIC the $53,000 in exchange for them releasing all our property except our house. Signing a new agreement was contrary to what they had told us at the meeting and we had lost another two to three weeks of time. I think by asking for the transcript this made them nervous as there were a number of things in the meeting that they wouldn't want in any transcript and they haven't done any of the things that they agreed to do. We had still not receive any transcript as promised and I had not received any releases as promised, Charlotte and I signed the agreement to again pay them the $53,000, when we sell our home, which we have paid once, but as they still have us in an impossible position that we have no way out of except to do as they say, we added on the bottom under our signatures a statement saying that the reason that we were agreeing to this was that the FDIC had us over a barrel and that we felt that we had no choice, as if they didn't release our properties, there was no way that we were going to exist or be able to pay the people who had lent us the money. This was driving us crazy. This agreement had only given us four months to come up with the $53,000 and not six months as George Owen had promised so we had change this to six months and initialed it. I called George and asked him about the six months that he agreed to. George said that he could not remember agreeing to six months. He then told me to wait while he went and got John Quinlan who also denied that George had agreed to six months.

Keith Taggart, the attorney who had been at the meeting contacted me and said that the FDIC would not accept the new agreement with any changes or anything added on the bottom or the date changed, and that he was sending us a new agreement and he wanted us to just sign it as it was written. I questioned him about the six months that George Owen had agreed to at the meeting. Keith said, "I remember that." He then said that he would have to get back to me. When he did get back to me, he again said that I was right about the six months and that the new agreement that he was sending me would have the date changed from August to October, which it did. We still did not feel good about signing it but did it to try to hold on and meet our commitments and obligations to the other people who we now owed money to. Keith Taggart had told me that he was leaving the FDIC in two weeks and wanted to get this all taken care of before he left. I asked him about the stenographer and the transcript of the meeting. He said that she was only a secretary that took a few notes, He said that he would send me a copy of her notes but never did.

After sending back the new agreement, I called John Quinlan, who had been going to handle the releases to see if he could now do as he had agreed as we were in desperate straits. I was told that John no longer worked for the FDIC. I then called George Owen to find out what was going on. George said that John who had worked under him was gone and that he, George, no longer was involved with our case. I asked about Keith Taggart, as I had not been able to get hold of him. George said that he was sure that Keith had also left the FDIC. I asked who we would now be dealing with. George gave me the names of John McEvily, who I had never heard of and Paul Bonin who had told me that we still owed nearly $2,000,000. George said that he didn't know if our agreement would still be good with the new people. He said that every time an account was transferred to somebody new, things usually got lose and it might be necessary to start all over.

Keith Taggart had told me that he was going to be there until at least Friday, May 23, so I decided to try his number again I got his answering machine so I kept trying. I did not reach him but he called me back. Keith said that it was his last day but he had taken care of everything and all the releases had been sent out, and copies sent to us that if I had any questions I could contact Jean Lauchtte or Bill Jameson, two more FDIC people who I had never heard of. The following Tuesday I received a letter form Keith with what I thought was going to be copies of the releases. All there was three copies of the same release for a property that I had sold in Florida back in September of 1996 and the buyers had paid for in September and the money had gone to the FDIC. They were just getting around to release those. I just could not believe this.

I did not know what to do so I called Jean Lauchtte one of the names that Keith Taggart had given me. She seemed very nice and said that she would take right care of things for us but she did not know what properties that had to be released. I asked if she had seen John Quinlan's files as I had provided him with all the descriptions. She said that she had not seen it but would try to get hold of it. She later called back and said that she now had the file and that she was going to get the Vermont lawyer, who was Elizabeth Glynn and the Florida Title company that I dealt with to draw up the releases. She called me several times to let me know how things were coming. On May 30, the releases for the Vermont properties with the exception of our house were sent out to the various town clerks and Ms. Lauchtte has assured me that the Florida properties were in the process of being released. In dealing with and going through nearly thirty people in the FDIC Ms. Lauchtte is the only one that has done as she agreed to do and the only one who has actually done anything except cost the FDIC and us a lot of money and us a lot of grief. The FDIC still expects us to pay them the $53,000, which they had agreed would be part of this settlement.

When Charlotte went for her mental health counseling last week, they told her that she had now been a patient of theirs for over five years.

Imagine the government doing this to anybody. I thought that only criminals functioned this way and cannot believe our own government would do such things.

At this point it looks like we are still going to have to find a way to pay the FDIC another $53,000 to get them off our backs. Vermont State senator Vincent Illuzzi who has been trying very hard to help us out of this mess wrote several letters to FDIC officials but some of the answers that he got were unbelievable, such as the girl at the meeting was not a stenographer but secretary to the attorney so anything that she took down is covered by attorney client privilege. Another excuse was that a stenographer couldn't be found, so none was present. It is funny that we were told that a stenographer would be present and that she was introduced as a stenographer and then when they didn't do as the agreed and didn't tell the truth in the meeting she is no longer a stenographer. If they couldn't find a stenographer, it seems like they could have said so and a tape recorder could have been used. I have added a few letters that I believe are of interest.

I also learned of a bill concerning the D'Oench Duhme Reform Act that was introduced into the House and Senate Banking committee, but never surface out of the committee. It was this D'Oench Duhme act that the FDIC used in Judge Billings Court to get him to rule in their favor and award the government nearly $2,000,000 in the motel deal. I believe that you will find the testimony of David Hess for the Citizens and Business for D'Oench Duhme Reform Senate Banking claims very similar to what I had been saying and the problems that it caused us. This is included at the end of the book.

I really think that it is time that people started taking a hard look at the way our government uses people and that we all should think about steps that we can take to make them more accountable and honest. I hope that you enjoyed the book and that you never have to go through an experience such as ours.

WILLIAM F. HILL
PO BOX 15
HARDWICK, VERMONT 05843
Tel. 802-472-6308

Mr. Dean Parker August 10, 1996
Director, Lyndonville Savings Bank
Lyndonville, Vermont 05851
Dear Dean:

I'm writing to you as I am having some very serious problems with Lyndonville Bank and I am trying to work them out but without much cooperation on the part of your Bank.

Over the past thirty years I have done business with LSB and I believe that I have made them a lot of money. In the past three years since Charlie Bucknam took over I have brought my direct and indirect accounts from over $700,000 down to less than $250,000. Over the years I have taken many properties off the banks hands and they have been paid for every one of them. Some of these properties were a cheap house on York Street in Lyndonville, the Greensboro Bend Store, Danny Powers house in Waterford, Smith farm in Danville, a cut over lot in Stannard, a cut over one-hundred-acre lot in Lowell, a burnt-out house on Nelson Hill in Derby, a farm in Troy, a house in need of repair in East haven, the Bolen Block in Island Pond, two houses on Tercerault road in Newport, two large commercial buildings on East Main Street in Newport, the Ester brook house in Holland, the Grimes house in Albany, two houses on East Street in Lyndonville, the Barron Bullet property in Bartou, the Roger Murry house on Stannard Mountain, Wheelock Garage, a house in Orleans, to mention only a few.

I got into a mess because I trusted some bankers from the Independent Bank Group. I have been trying for six years to straighten this mess out. One of the biggest obstacles to getting this mess straightened out was Charles Bucknam, who is now president of LSB. On several occasions, he was untruthful with me, he removed funds from my bank account at Bradford Bank and lied about it denying that he had taken them, he misappropriated payments that I made to the bank then reported my accounts delinquent to TRW, the credit reporting agency.

In your bank he has in a very fraudulent and devious way drained all my savings, which totaled around $80,000. This was the profit that I had received from the properties that I purchased from LSB over the years. This was to be our retirement.

Because of the mess that I got into with IBG and then the FDIC I had to file a chapter 11 to try to get it straightened out. Due to the motel that I bought from the IBG banks and the action of the bank officers there including Bucknam the FDIC came after me for over $2,000,000. Due to the dishonest and fraudulent things that Bucknam and the others did to us the FDIC has now lowered the amount that they are asking for by nearly 90 percent.

I have not made any payments to LSB on our home since filing chapter 11 as I was instructed not to by the attorney that was representing me. This is an attorney that Charlie Bucknam contacted to represent me. I did make my other payments as they involved other people such as a Mr. Allan Taylor, whose property Bucknam and his attorney, John Gravel, tried to latch onto even though the payments were up to date. This has been very upsetting to Mr. Taylor, who is an old man. I have another note# 31610899, which I purchased from LSB that I have not been able to collect on as the debtor Karla Rowell believes that her account was not handled correctly by LSB before assigning it to me.

Now that I have made a deal with the FDIC we have put our house and other properties on the market so that we can pay both LSB and the FDIC in the very near future.

I would like to meet with the board of directors of your bank as soon as possible, either with or without Bucknam to try to straighten out our problems in a peaceful manner. I have always had a lot of respect for Lyndonville Savings Bank and cannot see the need for litigation when we want to meet with you and work things out and would hope that you would feel the same. Please let me know what day that I can meet with you.

Sincerely,
Bill Hill

September 12, 1996
VIA TELEFAX
David R Kelley, Esq.
PO Box I
Orleans, VT 05860-0001
Re: William F. Hill Dear Dave:

I am enclosing with this fax a copy of a letter that Mr. Hill sent to Dean Parker, a director of the Lyndonville Savings Bank, on August 10, 1996, and received by Mr. Parker on September 11, 1996. After you read this letter, you will not be surprised to find out that Mr. Bucknam was incensed. Your client has made several imprudent and demeaning comments concerning Mr. Bucknam's character and his abilities as a banker. Mr. Bucknam was inclined to overlook Mr. Hill's previous comments considering their source. However, your client has now chosen to communicate extremely defamatory remarks to the Lyndonville Board of Directors, Mr. Bucknam's employer, and we can no longer overlook his course of conduct.

Your client's letter accuses Mr. Bucknam of lying, misappropriating funds and acting in a fraudulent and devious manner. These statements are libelous per se, and you are hereby advised that unless Mr. Hill immediately ceases all such public comments and directs a letter of apology to each Board member to whom he sent this correspondence, Mr. Bucknam will bring a suit for compensatory damages against Mr. Hill. In short, I find your client's conduct nothing more than outrageous and I sincerely hope that you had nothing to do with the sending of such a letter.

I should also inform you that there will be no meeting between Mr. Hill and the Board of Directors of the Lyndonville Savings Bank. The bank's position is well-stated in my previous correspondence to you, and unless we have an agreement prior to September 23, 1996, I will file the necessary motions for a

Summary Judgment and to shorten the Period of Redemption as soon as the bankruptcy has been dismissed.

I will expect you to contact me as soon as you have received this fax to confirm that you will contact Mr. Hill, and direct him to cease all further communications and that you will direct him to write the appropriate letter of apology forthwith. If your client thought that by sending this letter he would circumvent the legal process, he was severely mistaken.

Please also advise Mr. Hill that all further communications, either from you or from him, that he wishes directed to the bank, must be sent to this office.

Sincerely,
BAUER, ANDERSON & GRAVEL

John C. Gravel, Esq.
JCG/ss

November 25, 1996
William F. Hill
Charlotte Hill
PO Box 15
Hardwick, VT 05843-0015
Dear William and Charlotte Hill:

Enclosed please find Lyndonville Savings Bank and Trust Company stock certificate number 1290. This certificate represents the transfer of ownership of one share of stock from Reginald and Heidi Lussier into your name and that of your wife per Mr. Lussier's instructions.

Section 19 of the Federal Deposit Insurance Act prohibits persons convicted of specified criminal offenses from becoming, or continuing as, an institution-affiliated party and from otherwise participating, directly or indirectly, in the conduct of the affairs of any insured depository institution without the prior written consent of the FDIC. This appears to prohibit voting rights as well as any other direct or indirect participation. I am enclosing a copy of Section 19 referencing the circumstances, prohibitions and penalties for your review.

Thank you.
Sincerely,
Elaine A. Smith
Vice President/Treasurer

cc: Elizabeth Cosde, Commissioner of Banking, Insurance and Securities Patrick Rohan, Regional Director, FDIC

March 25, 1997
Honorable Patrick Leahy
United States Senate
Washington, DC 20510
Dear Senator Leahy:

Thank you for your letter enclosing correspondence from Mr. William F. Hill.

In August 1996, our Franklin, Massachusetts Office reached a settlement agreement with Mr. and Mrs. Hill that specified that they would pay $250,000 as full and final settlement of their obligations. The Federal Deposit Insurance Corporation agreed to release all collateral upon receipt of this payment, and to release the Hills from further liability. The FDIC also agreed to write off the remaining deficiency balance and interest that amounted to $1,830,886 as of August 14, 1996. To settle the obligations in question, Mr. Hill proposed to sell his personal residence and any additional properties necessary to raise the needed funds within six months.

The Franklin Office has reviewed Mr. Hill's loan history and confirmed that the $52,958 payment to which he refers was applied to his obligations when it was received in 1995. In July 1996, Mr. Hill was informed of this fact and was advised that the $52,958 payment would not be applied to the $250,000 settlement. The August 16, 1996 document that was approved by senior FDIC management to settle the Hills' obligations specifically accounts for the $52,958 payment under the heading "Collections to Date." As Mr. Hill states, the agreed- upon settlement amount was $250,000. There was no agreement that previously applied payments on his loans would be deducted from the settlement amount. On February 6, 1997, he again inquired as to whether the 1995 payment of $52,958 had been applied to the $250,000 settlement and was advised by telephone on February 7 that it was credited as a loan payment and would not be applied to the August 1996 settlement.

The FDIC remains willing to release all liens against Mr. Hill's properties upon receipt of the remaining funds in the amount of $53,531.57. If he has further questions, Mr. John Quinlan of the Franklin.

Office will be pleased to continue assisting him to the extent possible at (508) 520-6333.

Your interest in this matter is appreciated, and we regret this response cannot be more favorable. If you have further questions, the Office of Legislative Affairs can be reached at (202) 898-7055.

Sincerely,
Alice C. Goodman
Director
Office of Legislative Affairs

WILLIAM F. HILL
REAL ESTATE BROKER & AUCTIONEER
PO BOX 15
HARDWICK, VERMONT 05843
802-472-6308
Fax 802 472 3389

April 7, 1997
Ms. Alice C. Goodman
Director Office of Legislative Affairs
FDIC
55017th Street
NW Washington, DC 20429
Dear Ms. Goodman:

I am in receipt of a copy of your letter to Senator Patrick Leahy dated March 27, 1997. First I want to thank you for taking the time to look into our problems with the FDIC. We are in our seventh year of trying to straighten out this mess that we got into when we trusted some of the bank officers of the Independent Bank Group in Vermont. The bankers who misled us are now serving time in jail for the misdeeds that they committed.

Although you have the dates in your letter to Senator Leahy correct the facts are not what took place. I did not know what had happened to the $52,958 that is in question. I contacted Merchants Bank who were the last ones that I knew to have it. They didn't know where it was but agreed to research it if I was willing to pay for the time that it took. They finally came back and said that they had given to the FDIC in January of 1995. When I met with George Owen and Art Aguirre on July 9, 1996, I asked them about the $52,958. They both said that the FDIC didn't have it and had never received any money. I showed them the notation that I had received from Merchants Bank saying that they had given our savings to the FDIC. Both Owen and Aguirre could not believe it. They were dumbfounded and said that the FDIC had no record of ever receiving any money. They then went on to tell me that. If I could actually prove that they had received it, that it would have to be part of any settlement agreement that we made with the FDIC.

Also you mention that at the July meeting we were told that the $53,958 would not be part of the $250,000 settlement. This is certainly not true. What I have stated above is what happened and there was no mention of a $250,000 settlement at the July meeting. We were unable to get the FDIC to agree to any settlement at this meeting except that the $52,958 would be credited to any settlement that we made if we could prove that the FDIC had ever received this money. This meeting lasted from about 10:30 in the morning until about 4:30 in the afternoon. We left there very disappointed and frustrated that we couldn't get the FDIC to agree to a dollar amount. I have very good notes and minutes of this meeting.

Several days later I received a call from Aguirre asking me to again give him the date and the amount of the $52,958 as they had looked and could find no record of this money. We negotiated the $250,000 after this, over the phone with George Owen. This was in August.

You mention the August 16, 1996, document approved by senior management of the FDIC, which you state specifically accounts for the $52,958 under the heading "Collections to Date." I have never seen or heard of this document and I'm sure that George Owen nor John Quinlan had never seen it either as they never mentioned but continued to say that they could find no record of any such payment.

In January prior to paying the FDIC I wrote to John Quinlan advising him how I planned to pay the FDIC and asked him to confirm in writing that the FDIC would release all their liens as they had agreed. In this letter to John Quinlan I outlined that the payments would include the $52,958. I then called John to see if he had received my letter again stressed that I would like to have in writing that the FDIC would release us upon our paying as I had proposed. John said that I didn't need it in writing, again as, I already had it in writing but that the FDIC would need proof of receiving the $52,958.

Based on this I was able to borrow the money from some individuals on the assurance of what John had told me and this time I paid the Merchants Bank to again search their records and come up with the check that they had used to pay the FDIC the $52,958.

The lawyers who represented the people who were lending me the money were very leery of any dealings with the FDIC and wanted to be assured that the FDIC would do as they agreed. For this reason I decided that the best thing to do was to drive to the Franklin office of the FDIC and pay John Quinlan personally and get some receipts to prove that I had paid him. I called John on February 4, 1997, and told him that I would like to set up an appointment to meet with him and pay him on the sixth. He asked about the $52,958. I told him that I now had a copy of the check from Merchants Bank with the FDIC's endorsement on the back. He asked why I didn't just send in the payments along with a copy of the Merchants check. It was going to be over five hundred miles round trip but I told him that I would feel better about coming down so that there would be no mix-ups. John said that if I was willing to drive way down that he could find time to meet with us.

We met with John Quinlan on February 6, as agreed, I gave him a copy of the check showing the $52,958, which he said that they still had not been able to find. I gave him another check from a lawyers trust account for $100,000 and we had already given them about $17,000 from a couple of other closings. I asked John to figure up the balance that we owed the FDIC. He calculated for a minute and said that the balance due was $79,889. I wrote him a check for this amount. I told him that I hoped that it wouldn't take very long for them to release everything. He assured me that everything would be taken care of. We shook hands and we left.

It was about four o'clock when we got back home. We had been here only a few minutes when the phone rang. It was John

Quinlan. He said that they had at last been able to locate the $52,958, but that he had talked to some other FDIC employees and they had decided that they were not going to give us credit as they had promised because they had received it prior to us making any agreement. This was very contrary to anything that we had discussed prior to this phone call.

Back in 1994 prior to the Merchants Bank giving this money to the FDIC the FDIC had put a lien against this account but hadn't taken the money at that time we tried to make an agreement with Enrique Caballero, Tom King and Larry L Jones employees of the FDIC. They also assured us that this money would be part of any settlement that we made with the FDIC. At that time we could not reach any agreement with the FDIC that we could possibly live up to. They wanted to hit us for more than the value of all our property by over mortgaging our property. They proposed, and I quote from Larry Jones's proposal: "The cash portion would be satisfied by the $50,000 in our control." Another proposal, which he made, hesitated, "Cash in the amount of $50,000 already in our control and two notes" for a total of $650,000.

I know that this is a lengthy explanation but I think that the facts are very important. This is our seventh year of trying to straighten out this mess. It has taken a terrible toll on our lives. I believe that if you could take a look at all the facts of what the bankers did to us and all the effort that we have gone through the past seven years trying to do the right thing, to make deals with the government and the banks only to have them not honor them you would agree that we should have never owed the FDIC anything in the first place. We only agreed to the $250,000 settlement to get the FDIC off our backs so that we could try to get on with our lives, which have been completely destroyed. Charlotte can't take any more. Her doctor doesn't understand how she has stood this long. She has become a real mental case. If I can't get this straightened out right off, I'm afraid that she will have to be committed to a mental institution for her own good. The doctor said that what we have been through is the worst kind of torture that he has ever witnessed.

I would be willing to drive to the Franklin office of the FDIC to meet again with the FDIC and again try to settle this in a fair way providing that I can do it in the next couple of days. I need to do this before something happens to Charlotte and it is also killing me. Over three years ago, Pauline Ingan, attorney at the Westborough office of the FDIC, warned us that this was the way that the FDIC operated and that they would not leave us alone as long as they thought that we might have anything that they could get. I didn't believe her but I guess that she was right.

PLEASE get back to me with a date that I can again meet with the FDIC. If we can't straighten this out, it leaves me no choice but to go back into bankruptcy and lose another year of our lives. Thank you!

Sincerely,
William F. Hill

April 16, 1997
Mr. William Hill
Ms. Charlotte Hill
PO Box 15
Hardwick, VT 05843
RE: 4562-First National Bank of Vermont
Bradford, VT-Iri Liquidation
Asset Name: William and Charlotte Hill
Asset Number: 4562-004294501 Principal Balance: $1,443,331
Asset Number: 4562-004319021 Principal Balance: $515,770
Dear Mr. & Ms. Hill,

As a result of the meeting that occurred at the FDIC office in Franklin, MA, on 4/11/97, the parties have agreed to the following:

1. The FDIC will release its lien interest on properties owned by Mr. and Ms. Hill located in Vermont and Florida with the exception of their personal residence (located in Hardwick, VT).
2. Mr. and Mrs. Hill will reaffirm the settlement agreement signed on 10/11/96 by the parties stipulating the settling of all debt with the FDIC for the sum of $250,000.
3. Further, Mr. and Ms. Hill have paid $196,468.43 coward this settlement with the remaining $53,531.57 due on or before 8/18/97.

Sincerely,
John F. Quinlan
Credit Specialist

Concur:
William HillDate 26 April 97
Charlotte HillDate 28 April 97

    We agreed to this at the April 11, 1997, meeting in Franklin, not because we owe it but because we could see that the FDIC has all the power and that we had no choice. As I told you that day, when I agree to something, I will not back out. I just wish that the government and the FDIC could do the same. We are working very hard to sell our house and when it is sold we will again pay the $53,000 providing you do as you agree.

May 2, 1997
Mr. William Hill Ms. Charlotte Hill PO Box 15
Hardwick, VT 05843
Re 4562-First National Bank of Vermont
Bradford, VT-In Liquidation
Asset Name: William and Charlotte Hill
Dear Mr. and Ms. Hill:

Enclosed please find a letter dated April 16, 1997, that incorporates the understanding between you and the FDIC with respect to certain issues discussed at our meeting on April 11, 1997.

I was unable to approve the previous letter because of additional language you had typed regarding: (I) a suggestion that you were signing the letter under duress; and (2) a new term concerning the timing of the payment of the $53,000 upon the sale of your home. These were not terms of our understanding and should not appear on the letter. Please, just sign it as it is, if you agree to it. If you do not agree, please contact me.

Sincerely,
Keith Taggart

WILLIAM E. HILL
PO BOX 15
HARDWICK, VERMONT 05843
802-472-6308
Fax 802-472-3389

May 13, 1997
Mr. Keith Taggart
Fax 508-520-2683
Dear Mr. Taggart:

I am pleased that you could remember about the six months statement that George Owen made at the April 11 meeting in your offices. I wish that you could have been at the July 9, 1996, meeting as I'm sure that you would also remember the discussion about the $53,000. We have really been sick about this. As I have told you, we want to do as we agree and always have. It is really upsetting when the banks and the FDIC change their agreements. Back in 1991 we made an agreement with Bradford Bank to give them back the motel and we were going to absorb the down payment and all the time and money that we had expended in the motel and that was it We lived up to this agreement but they never did as they agreed.

In June of 1994 the FDIC proposed an agreement to us that would also give us credit for the $53,000 payment. We could not agree to that proposal as there was no possible way that we could live up to it. I hope that the enclosed material will help to shed some light on where we are coming from and we are really pleased that you are trying and want to be fair with us. This makes us feel a little better and you don't know how much we appreciate this. Thanks!

Sincerely,
William F. Hill

June 9, 1997
Mr. and Mrs. William Hill
Post Office Box 15
Hardwick, Vermont 05843
Dear Mr. and Mrs. Hill:

Your letter to Ms. Alice C. Goodman, Director of the Office of Legislative Affairs of the Federal Deposit Insurance Corporation, has been referred to me for response.

By letter of June 4, 1997 to Vermont State Senator Vincent Illuzzi, Mr. Joseph Minniti, Consolidated Office Director of the Franklin Office, responded to similar concerns that you expressed in a letter to Mr. Keith Taggart, an attorney at the Franklin Office. For your reference, enclosed is a copy of that letter. Additionally, with regard to your request for a copy of a transcript of the meeting held at the Franklin Office on April 11, 1997, I understand that there is no transcript of the meeting since a court reporter/stenographer was not available. Although Attorney Taggert's secretary took notes for him during the meeting, he advises that those notes are subject to attorney-client privilege and therefore are not available.

As noted in Mr. Minniti's letter, the lien releases against your properties in Vermont, with the exception of your personal residence in Hardwick, which remains as collateral for your remaining indebtedness, have been recorded. The Florida releases will be processed upon receipt of the necessary documents from your title company.

If you have further questions, Mr. Paul Bonin of the Franklin Office remains available to assist you to the extent possible at (508) 520- 6347.

Sincerely,
Scan Ivie
Manager
Government/Public Relations

Enclosure

WILLIAM F. HILL
PO BOX 15
HARDWICK, VERMONT 05843
802-472-6308
Fax 802-472-3389

June 16, 1997
Mr. Stan Ivie FDIC
550 Seventeenth Street NW
Washington, DC 20429
Dear Mr. Ive:

Thank you for your letter of June 9 in answer to my fax to Ms. Alice Goodman. First of all I want to say that I believe that we have all our releases with the exception of our house. I do however want to comment on the letter of Mr. Minniti. I cannot believe how your people turn things around and distort the truth. I have never dealt with people like this before.

In Mr. Minniti's third paragraph he states that at the July 9, 1996 meeting we were advised that the $53,000 would not be part of any settlement. This is just not true. At this meeting I told George Owen and Art Aguirre about the $53,000. They said that they had no record of any such payment. Art Aguirre practically called me a liar for telling them about it. George Owen said that if I could prove that the FDIC in dead did have this $53,000 it certainly would be part of any settlement agreement that we made. Following the meeting I received a phone call from Art Aguirre asking for proof that the FDIC had this payment. Mr. Minniti also states that the Hills have been informed on several occasions that all payments received on loans were applied to their loans. This is an out and out lie. We never were informed of any such claim. As a matter of fact, when the FDIC first took over the banks, I sent them several payments and asked them to acknowledge that we were getting credit for them. I never received any response so I quit sending them.

In the next paragraph Mr. Minniti refers to a meeting, which was held in Franklin, Massachusetts, on April 11, 1997. This meeting was arranged by Senator Leahy's office. Prior to the meeting I received a call from John Quinlan of the FDIC on April 9, where he stated that he was going to have an attorney and a stenographer present. That she would provide a transcript of the meeting and that we would be furnished a copy. This conversation with John Quinlan I recorded and I have it on tape. At the meeting John introduced a woman as the stenographer. We were never provided any transcript as promised. This is understandable as there were several misrepresentations made by members of the FDIC at this meeting. When I asked Keith Taggart about the transcript, He said that the girl was not a stenographer but only a secretary that took notes. Keith said that he would send me a copy of her notes but none ever came. I also have this conversation on tape. Keith did not mention anything about attorney-client privilege, but just the opposite, that he would send me a copy of her notes.

In a conversation with Charlotte, which she also recorded, George Owen admits that the $53,000 was supposed to be a part of the settlement but things got screwed up somewhere along the way and that is why it didn't happen.

I do not wish to keep bothering you with these problems but right is right and wrong is wrong and the FDIC has not kept their word on several occasions including the $53,000 and this has put us in an impossible position. We have been trying for seven years to straighten out a mess that was caused by some dishonest bankers who went to jail. Instead of doing what was right the FDIC has upheld the actions of these dishonest bankers and we have paid dearly for it both financially and with our health and our destroyed lives these past seven years.

I already know that you don't plan to do anything about it but I did want to set the record straight.

Sincerely,
William F. Hill

enc.

June 4, 1997

Honorable Vincent Illuzzi
Chair, Senate Institutions Committee
Senate Chamber
State House
Montpelier, Vermont 05602
Dear Senator Illuzzi:

Your letter to Mr. Keith Taggart, on behalf of Mr. and Mrs. William F. Hill of Hardwick, Vermont, has been referred to me for response.

The Federal Deposit Insurance Corporation reached a settlement agreement with Mr. and Mrs. Hill in August of 1996. The agreement specified that they would pay $250,000 as full and final settlement of their obligations. Upon receipt of the funds, the FDIC agreed to release all collateral and the Hills from further liability. The remaining deficiency balance and interest, which amounted to $1,830,886 on August 14, 1996, would be written off by the FDIC.

The $52,958 payment to which Mr. Hill refers was applied to his obligations when it was received in 1995. Mr. Hill was informed of this fact in July 1996 and advised that this payment was not part of the $250,000 settlement. The Hills have been informed on several occasions that all payments received on their loans were applied to their loans. The FDIC never agreed to deduct any previously applied payments on the loans from the settlement amount.

In an effort to clarify questions raised by Mr. Hill with regard to the settlement agreement, a meeting was held at the Franklin Office on April 11, 1997. At the meeting, the Hills agreed to reaffirm the $250,000 settlement agreement and acknowledge that $53,531.57 was still due and payable to the FDIC. The FDIC agreed to extend the time for submission of the funds until October 11, 1997. This reaffirmation was signed by Mr. and Mrs. Hill on May 16, 1997.

The releases for liens in Vermont against the Hills' properties with the exception of their personal residence in Hardwick, Vermont have been recorded. The releases for the Florida properties are still awaiting Mr. Hill's title company's forwarding of same for signature by FDIC legal.

Should Mr. and Mrs. Hill have further questions, Mr. Paul Bonin of the Franklin Office will be pleased to continue assisting them to the extent possible at (508) 520-6347.

Your interest in this matter is appreciated.

Sincerely,
Joseph Minniti
Consolidated Office Director
July 10, 1997

MR JOSEPH MINNITI
CONSOLIDATED OFFICE DIRECTOR FDIC
PO BOX 9104
FRANKLIN MA 02038
Dear Mr. Minniti:

Re: William and Charlotte Hill of Hardwick, Vermont; No. 4562-First National Bank of Vermont, Bradford Vermont; In Liquidation

Thank you for responding to my letter to Keith Taggart, who I understand is no longer with the FDIC.

The first paragraph of your letter is correct in that the FDIC and the Hills did make such an agreement in August of 1996.

The second paragraph is incorrect. At the July 1996 meeting, Mr. Hill informed Arthur Aguirre and George Owen about the $53,000 payment, which had already been made to the FDIC. Neither Owen nor Aguirre were aware that this payment had been received by the FDIC. They claimed that they had seen no record of it, but if Mr. Hill could prove that the FDIC had indeed received this payment, it certainly would be part of any settlement that was to be made.

A while after the meeting, Art Aguirre contacted Mr. Hill by phone and asked him to furnish any proof that this payment had been made to the FDIC.

The Hills had never been informed that any payment had been applied on their loan even once, and certainly not several times as you claim. The Hills had made several other payments to the FDIC when the FDIC took over the First National Bank and the Hills asked for proof or receipts to show that they were getting credit for these payments. The FDIC never responded, and so the Hills stopped sending their payments.

Enrique Caballero, Tom King and Larry Jones of the Westboro Office of the FDIC, who knew about the $53,000, had all assured the Hills that this would be part of any agreement or settlement that was to be made with the FDIC. This was told to them prior to the July 1996 meeting.

In your third paragraph, you state that a meeting to clarify questions was held in Franklin on April 1, 1997. This is true. Prior to this meeting, John Quinlan had called Mr. Hill and informed him that he would have a stenographer at this meeting so that a transcript of the meeting would be available both for the benefit of the FDIC and the Hills. A stenographer was present and sat next to Mrs. Hill. Although Mr. Hill has requested a copy of this transcript several times, none has been forthcoming. Keith Taggart also agreed that he would send the Hills a copy of the notes of the meeting, as he called them, but he never did. Mr. and Mrs. Hill did sign the new agreement, as they were in a very difficult predicament with the FDIC and had no choice.

At the April 11 meeting. John Quinlan had promised that he would have all the releases on the Hill's property, with the exception of their home, out within a week. Quinlan furnished no releases, as he had promised. During the week of June 10, Ms. Jeanne M. Luthette has supplied the Vermont releases and promised that the Florida releases would be forthcoming.

I do not believe the Hills have been treated fairly or honestly by the FDIC. They have entered into several agreements with the banks and the FDIC, where the Hills have lived up to their part of the agreement, only to find out that the FDIC has not lived up to its part. This has been going on for nearly seven years and has practically destroyed their lives.

Again, I am asking you and the committee to reconsider and give the Hills credit for the $53,000, as was previously agreed to by the FDIC. I am enclosing a copy of a report written by Mr. Hill, again explaining what has taken place.

Thank You.

Sincerely,
Senator Vincent Illuzzi
Chair, Senate Institutions Com.
Tel.: 1-800-322-5616
Tel. Pager: 741-9436 (Local Call within Vt.)
E-mail: VILLUZZI@LEG.STATE.VT.US

Vl:djc
Enclosure
cc: William Hill (w/o enclosure)
Sen. Julius Canns (w/o enclosure)
Mary Miller do US Sen. Patrick Leahy, Montpelier Office

July 23, 1997

Honorable Vincent Illuzzi
Chair, Senate Institutions Committee
Senate Chamber
State House
Montpelier, Vermont 05602
Dear Senator Illuzzi:

Thank you for your letter of July 10, 1997, on behalf of Mr. and Mrs. William F. Hill of Hardwick, Vermont.

The Federal Deposit Insurance Corporation has previously responded to the issues raised by the Hills. The Franklin Office personnel agreed to give the Hills credit for the $52,958 payment only if these funds had not previously been applied to their loans. As the Hills are aware, these funds were posted against their outstanding obligations in 1995. The settlement agreement reached with the FDIC in August 1996 and approved by delegated authority was that the Hills would pay $250,000 cash to the FDIC and the remaining deficiency balance and interest of $1,830,886 would be written off. The $250,000 cash settlement was in addition to any other payments made previously on their obligations and the settlement case specifically accounts for the $52,958 payment under the heading "Collections to Date."

Our Westborough personnel did propose in June 1994 three settlement options in the form of cash and notes in the range of $550,000 to $650,000, which took into account the $50,000 Certificate of Deposit. None of the three alternatives were apparently acceptable to Mr. and Mrs. Hill. We can find no evidence that our Westborough personnel agreed to deduct the funds from any future settlement agreement, nor is it conceivable they would or could commit the FDIC to this open ended arrangement given all the unknowns and the Hills' unwillingness to resolve their obligations. The funds in the Certificate of Deposit were released to the FDIC in January 1995 and applied to Mr. Hill's severely delinquent obligations.

With regard to the releases of Mr. Hill's properties, the FDIC had requested Mr. Hill provide the legal descriptions of the properties versus the addresses of the properties. Upon receipt of this information, the FDIC contracted with Vermont outside counsel to prepare the releases on the Vermont properties. The releases were filed on May 30, 1997, and copies were mailed to Mr. Hill on June 3, 1997. The releases for the Florida properties were prepared by Mr. Hill's title company, and received by the FDIC on June 10, 1997, signed, and returned to the title company that same day.

With regard to the issue of a transcript of the April 11, 1997 meeting, unfortunately we were unable to obtain a court reporter to attend the meeting. The notes taken by our attorney's secretary are considered attorney work product and therefore we are asserting that privilege.

We have once again reviewed our files and find no evidence to support the Hills' argument. Mr. and Mrs. Hill agreed in writing to the remaining payment of $53,531.57 due on or before October 11, 1997, and we will abide by the agreement. Should Mr. or Mrs. Hill have further questions, Mr. Paul Bonin of the Franklin Office will be pleased to continue assisting them to the extent possible at (508) 520-5347.

Your interest in this matter is appreciated.

Sincerely,
Joseph Minniti
Consolidated Office Director

July 29, 1997

Honorable Vincent Illuzzi
Chair, Senate Institutions Committee
Senate Chamber
State House
Montpelier, Vermont 05602
Dear Senator Illuzzi:

Thank you for your most recent letter on behalf of Mr. and Mrs. William F. Hill of Hardwick, Vermont.

The settlement agreement with the Hills that was approved by senior management of our Franklin Office in August 1996 specified that the Hills pay $250,000 in cash in full and final settlement of their obligation. The $52,958 payment to which you refer was applied to the Hills' obligation in 1995 and was clearly noted as a prior payment on the case that was approved to settle the Hills' remaining obligation for $250,000. Further, the payment was not part of the settlement agreement executed by the Hills. Through approval of the settlement agreement, the Federal Deposit Insurance Company agreed to forgive over $1.8 million in debt owed by the Hills.

The FDIC has reviewed this matter on numerous occasions and our decision is final. As such, we expect receipt of the remaining funds from the Hills to finalize the settlement no later than October 1 1, 1997.

Sincerely,
Stan Ivie
Manager
Government and Public Relations

FINAL CHAPTER

About the time that we got out of the bank scandal, another situation arose. The government was not done with us yet.

In the late eighties, we had been faring for many years with over three hundred milking cows, on Pumpkin Lane. I was working from two in the morning until after ten at night, seven days a week, and was getting very tired. I had a chance to sell our farm and everything that went with it. We had a large thirty-acre hay field over On Porter Brook with nothing on it. I discussed with Charlotte (who was also known as Sally) building a very nice home there. I had always wanted to provide a good home for Charlotte, a place that all our large family, many of whom don't have very much, could enjoy.

We built a very large, old type farm house, utilizing much family labor. I planted maple trees up both sides of the driveway. At one end of the house, l built a large patio and put in a twenty by forty inground swimming pool, which all the children loved and used often.

Across the field where there was a small brook, I dug a good-sized pond for swimming, fishing, and boating. It was beautiful, and all the family spent time there. Many people were fascinated with what we had done, and we lived there very happily. Charlotte and I always wanted the place to stay in our family, for our family and friends to use and enjoy forever. We planned to leave in very good shape for them.

I also installed a mobile home for our grand-daughter Leigh and her four children. This was very expensive, what with state and local permits, installing a septic tank and sewage system, water, electricity a driveway, and everything else.

Ronald, Charlotte's son, even though he was a good worker, was the only one of our children who didn't own his own home. He usually worked on farms over in Franklin County, and we didn't see him much. He took a job in Massachusetts constructing steel buildings, and somehow hurt his ankle quite badly.

He told us he had a good lawyer, and had received a large settlement. His mother was afraid that he Would soon go through the money and again have nothing. She suggested that he buy our house for a small fee, and we would keep a life lease. Ronald wanted to take over the whole place and continue raising cattle as we were doing. He would eventually build a small home there for us and I would keep on helping with the farming. This was not to be.

Ronald seemed to have plenty of money. We thought it was from his injury settlement. We soon learned that Ronald had another source of money we knew nothing about. It came out in the newspaper that he was being charged with bringing large amounts of drugs in from Canada in grain trucks. We were shocked. The newspaper stated that the government had been watching Ronald bring in these large shipments for over five years. This is unbelievable. Do you think they would watch bank robbery, murder, or any other crime go on for five years without doing anything? By letting him go and keep building up his kingdom, the government had all the more to confiscate and sell. I wonder how many other people got hot from using drugs and getting into the business during those years the government sat back. Seems to me their inaction made the government promoters of drug use.

Soon after that we came home one day to find the yard full of automobiles and about forty FBI and Marshalls or whatever they were in our house, some carrying guns and wearing bulletproof vests. They had smashed in the door and completely trashed the whole place, dumping drawers, files, and everything else.

Charlotte always wanted to have a good Christmas, and she shopped early while the sales were on. She had about one hundred presents gathered and wrapped for next Christmas, and they tore them all open, scattering them around and even breaking some.

Richard M. Carter, their DEA special agent, asked if I had any money around. I told him that I had the money Ronald had paid us. Carter threatened to blow up my safe if I didn't open it immediately. There were eleven packs of twenty-dollar bills. This would have been fifty-five thousand dollars except that I had taken twelve hundred out of one pack, leaving a total of forty-eight thousand dollars. Carter wouldn't count it and said he was taking it to a bank to have them count it. They left.

I later heard from the government that they were taking Ronald's equity in the property. He got twelve years in federal prison. We would be allowed to live out our lifetime lease, but with a lot of stipulations. Several months later, they agreed to give us back the money Carter had taken, but when we got it back it was five thousand, or one bundle, less than what he had taken. I always thought he must have pocketed one bundle, but I never could find out.

The government put our house up for internet auction with a starting bid of seventy thousand. It sold for $129,000. The government refused to tell us who had bought it, but we eventually learned it was Sven Olson, whom we finally met.

When Ronald was in jail, he kept talking about what he was going to do with the place when he got out. I thought this was strange, since I thought Ronald was no longer involved, Olson having bought the place. When Ronald was being released from jail, Olson called and said he wanted to pick Ronald up and bring him here, which also seemed strange, but that's what happened

Ronald moved in with us, bringing some of his family. He started taking over looking after the cattle and nearly everything, as we had agreed on years earlier. He and Olson had several meetings at the house, and Olson said that he was going to transfer the property back to Ronald by issuing him a thirty-year paid-up lease.

One week when some of Ronald's family were there, Olson showed up with his family and put on a very nice meal and party. Ronald and his family refused to take part, staying in the cellar and refusing to have anything to do with Olson and his family. This was very awkward for us. That night, Ronald took off out of town even though he was still under house arrest, which was very upsetting to Charlotte.

Ronald stayed at the house for five or six weeks, and then announced that he had to leave. He said that Olson was in the same business that he had been in, and he wanted out because he didn't want to land back in jail. This really shook Charlotte up, as she could just see the feds coming back and trashing the place again. She didn't want to be around Olson any more. A few days later, when I got back from taking Charlotte to the hospital, Ronald, his family, and all their belongings were gone – leaving us with a few unpaid bills.

The Olson's started coming over quite often, sometimes bringing food and putting on nice meals. I enjoyed these and their company, but Charlotte was very nervous having them in her kitchen after what Ronald had told us. We ate downtown several times in one of the restaurants with them, but this also made Charlotte nervous, and she would find excuses not to go. We went to Holmes' bed and breakfast with them several times, which Charlotte would go along with since she wasn't seen with them in public. I was enjoying their company, even though it bothered Charlotte,

Charlotte began to be a nervous wreck about the Olson's activities on the property. Their boys would play in the cellar very roughly with our grandkids' toys, breaking arms and legs off the little girls' dolls. They broke Charlotte's exercise bicycle, making it unusable. Olson brought and left five or six very large and powerful snow machines and allowed the kids to ride them unsupervised. Several people jumped on Charlotte and told her how dangerous and irresponsible this was. These machines are very powerful. People warned her that not only could a kid get killed on one, but we could then be sued for everything we had. When we weren't there, apparently a kid did hit a wooden fence and knock it down.

One Easter, Olson announced that he was bringing in several families and putting on a large Easter egg hunt. You can imagine what this did to Charlotte's already jangled nerves, all the strangers combing and running through the whole place. Charlotte was suffering badly with cancer. I was taking her to several doctors and hospitals every week, and for all day chemo treatments once a week. All the stress was very bad for her.

Then Olson announced that he was going to have his oldest son move in with us so he could learn farming and establish a Vermont citizenship which would allow him to attend a Vermont college and pay in-state tuition. This really threw Charlotte. She could not stand the thought of anyone living with us at that point.

Olson was showing up often. He wanted to build something and had me dig some test holes, but couldn't find any place that would pass a perk test. I was raising beef cattle as I always did. I had also always raised quite a lot of winter squash and pumpkins. I tried to de an excellent job, and our customers were very happy with everything I raised. I had some very good customers. I was also raising hay for my cattle, and had an excellent com crop every year for my neighbors.

Then Olson came up and asked to use my tractor and plows. He and his boy plowed up quite a bit of the land, including all the corn land. He then informed me that he didn't want any more com grown, and didn't want any chemical fertilizer, herbicide, or manure unless it was organic on the land. The corn field never got planted again. It stayed vacant for a couple of years, and I didn't see how I was going to be able to raise any other crops in the way that he demanded. We had supplied our neighbors the Lagises with hay and corn for many years, and they were upset with us when we told them we could no longer do this. This really upset Charlotte, as we had been long-time friends and neighbors. It also really bothered her that we could no longer provide the pumpkins to the East Side restaurant where the owner is a very good friend. I had an auction on June 14, 2016, and sold all my cattle and farm machinery. I had had to buy hay for the cattle that last year. Our way of life was being destroyed. We could not continue to farm and make a living

We had another big problem with Olson. We had always paid the property taxes and fire insurance on the place. When we filed our tax return, we usually got a very good tax rebate, as the property taxes were too high for our income. The state tax department usually sends the rebate to the town. You are. allowed to use it toward your next property tax bill or any other outstanding government debt. Somehow Olson received the $8,000 rebate from the town and immediately claimed it, although it wasn't his. I don't believe he had ever paid any property taxes to Hardwick on this property or Leigh's mobile home.

I contacted the Vermont tax department. They said the money should have gone to Charlotte and me. They said, "Just have Olson give you a check for the $8000." Olson refused to pay us and said that he was keeping the money to make repairs on the property. This was devastating to Charlotte. She knew how hard we worked, and the money was ours. I continued to pay the property taxes, as part of my lifetime tenancy agreement with the government was that I keep the property taxes up to date, as I always have. I don't understand how this man, who claims to be a legitimate businessman, can act as he does.

Olson also bought the trailer I had put in for our granddaughter, for a small fraction of its worth rented it to six adults for what I heard was a high rent, and forced Leigh and her four children out. She was so upset that she wanted to move out of the area, but had no money. I rented a small home for her in New Hampshire for $800 a month, and have been paying the rent ever since. I couldn't stand to see her and those four beautiful children homeless.

I guess Olson never did the paperwork to show he bought the mobile home. He kept after Charlotte to find Leigh and straighten out his mess with her. Charlotte had nothing to do with him buying it. She knew how much we had spent to put the mobile home there, and how little he paid her. She wanted nothing to do with it, but Olson kept after her. The stress was killing her.

Charlotte's doctors and health providers told me that there was no way she could effectively fight the cancer if she was continually under such heavy stress. I have since learned from attorneys that Olson had no right to be on the property, much less dictate what happened there while we had our life interest, but not knowing that at the time, it seemed that the only way to give her any peace would be to move her away from Olson's presence and influence. I wanted to save her.

I learned of a small house on Dutton Road that was for sale, and I thought moving her over there might help. In order to buy it, I had to sell a nice post office rental property that was paying a good part of our income now that we were not farming. We moved there to try and get a little peace. It was upsetting for Charlotte to leave the home she had helped design and worked so hard to furnish and make beautiful for her family and friends to enjoy with us. She had had many compliments on what she had created there, and took pride in what she had accomplished.

She had hoped it would be in the family for generations to come. I tried everything I could think of to comfort her until she passed away on Tuesday, May 29, 2018, after a courageous five-year battle with cancer.

EPILOGUE

Still having a life estate in the place, I continued going there almost every day after moving Charlotte out, except when I had to work or was taking her to doctors or the hospital.

Olson put Kelly Lacourse in charge of the land and she lived in the house with her friends, renting the land and living space in the house. They asked me to prepare the ground for them, and I did, even furnishing them with seed and trays. They thought they could grow squash, but without any commercial fertilizer or manure they didn't get much of a crop.

I can't believe how they have let the place deteriorate. The farm sign at the end of the driveway is flat on the ground in grass and weeds. The land where they tried to raise crops has never been cleaned -up or reseeded, weeds and plastic mulch still there. A dig section of fence on the left-hand side of the driveway is all smashed down, and the driveway is washing out. The hay fields are all destroyed. There is rubbish all around the house, and window screens have blown off and lie on the ground. The carport is full of debris and trash and has several goats and chickens living in it. The storm drains next to the cellar window that kept water out of the basement is covered with wood and filled with trash; and can't possibly work.

Up back there is some kind of garbage on a trailer and in a building we built up there. The odor is obnoxious. The barnyard fences are all down and dragged around, what a mess. The road that leads by the mobile home is covered with trash, glass, and tin cans, and is not passable. The pond is all grown - up with weeds and brush and impossible to get to. I always kept the grass around the pond mowed with lawn mower, and it looked very nice.

The swimming pool is completely trashed and ruined. When I left, the swimming pool was fine and working. I had chemicals in it and left some for it. The small greenhouse is falling down, has several holes in it, and is full of trash. The deck next to the pool is covered with trash.

I haven't been in the house lately, but know that they have torn out walls and ceilings and moved walls. They have made a mess of it trying to add more bedrooms. The septic permit is for two bedrooms, which is what we had. This was a beautiful home and well cared for. Everyone I know who has seen it can't believe what they have done to the house.

Even sadder than the destruction of a beautiful, well-loved and cared-for home and property is the destruction of the lives of those who lived there so happily. Charlotte's life was made a living hell during the years she was fighting for her life, and needed all the peace she could get. Our four great-grandchildren had not had an easy life before we moved them to the property. Charlotte and I put our whole lives into looking out for all the family, and especially these four small children. We were teaching them to be good citizens who could live honest and productive lives. They started doing quite well in school, and I had two of the girls taking music lessons. Amaya played in the school band, and Promise played in church and concerts and at the farmers Market. I was very proud of them. They had all learned to be good swimmers and had an interest in the cattle and horses, and were learning how to care for animals. They had room to bike, fish, and boat. All that came to end when we were forced out. The only way Charlotte or I could see them was to drive a hundred miles and pick up a couple of them to bring here for a few days. They were always anxious to come. I still have them here as often as I can, but they miss their grandmother terribly, and there is nothing very exciting for them here now, just a few hens.

This whole mess has really destroyed several lives and a family, all due to the selfishness, greed, and lack of integrity of others. I drive by and look at the house and land and other buildings and what was Leigh's mobile home. I am sad as I realize that I worked all my life to have a good home for us and Leigh and her children. I paid for all this with my life's hard work and now have nothing to show for it.

I've gotten to where it is really destroying me. I feel like I can't stand it much longer, but I can't give up, no matter what. Olson needs to at least pay me for my lifetime interest in the property. This is the agreement that we made with the government that he is bound to. He also owes me my $8000 tax refund which he illegally kept. His attorney Kristina Michelson claims he has spent $150,000 fixing up the place, but to me it appears he has done $150,000 damage. I had planned to move back there after Charlotte passed, as I had kept my life estate. After looking the whole place over, I don't see how anyone could ever clean it up and restore it. I want some measure of justice, and will do all in my power to obtain it. Thank you for listening.

Pool with olsa

Olson son

Hill Hom.

This is some of the corn that I had raised for years. Olson asked to borrow my tractor and plows. He plowed up all the corn land and informed me that he didn't want any more corn grown. I thought that he owned the place so I couldn't raise any more corn. The land stayed unplowed for eleven years and only grew up to weeds and brush. this ruined that project.

Green Hous — Hill.

April 2019

Green Hous — olson

Mr. Richard M. CarterMay 15, 2007
U.S. Justice Department
Federal Building
Pearl St.
Burlington, Vt. 05402 Dear Mr. Carter,

It has been over three years since you and many of your
men broke into our house, trashing it, leaving it a mess and
even destroying our children's grandchildren's and great
grandchildren's Christmas presents. You said that you would take
care of repairing the door and door casing which you smashed
to get in. I have never seen any repairs yet. In your complaint
you refer to Ci#1 who said that large loads of marijuana could
have been delivered to the large house in Hardwick. Also Ci#3
who said Aldrich paid $465,000 cash for the residence. Both
of these statements are false. I don't even know what marijuana
looks like and non has ever been here. Also, Ronald has not
even come close to paying us the $200,00 that he agreed to pay.

In number 14 of your complaint you stated "I am aware
that William F. Hill, an auctioneer from Hardwick, Vermont
was prosecuted and convicted in the United Stated District
Court in this district for offense related to large scale bank
fraud scheme in which he participated with Roger Lussier and
other principals of Lyndonville Savings Bank". This is no more
true than the rest of your complaint. I was never charged or
convicted of anything to that I also have a right to know Ci#1
and Ci#3 are that made the false complains.

The other thing which really bothers me is the fact that
when you left here you took with you eleven packets of bills
each containing $5,000 each except one which contained
$3,800. This was a total of $53,800. You refused to count it,
saying that you were going to take it to bank and have them
count it. I did not hear anything for several months. When I
finally did hear it was stated that there was $48,800. This was
exactly $5,000 short or one packet short. I want to know what

you did with the other $5,000 I do not feel that you have been very honest in anything that you have done. This has gone on long enough and I want some answers.

Sincerely,
William F. Hill

August 6, 2007
Second request for Answers

Attorney Joe Perella
December 26, 2007

United States Attorney's Office
Federal BuildingCivil #20 cv-=5

Pearl Street
Burlington Vt. 05402
Dear Mr. Perella:

I am sorry that I haven't gotten back to you sooner. Between looking out for my wife who is having a very hard time, I'm trying to help out granddaughter who has serious cancer and here three small daughters plus taking care of my cattle, there just haven't been enough hours in a day. I do not have the money to hire an attorney to help or advise me in this matter. As you know the government took all the money that we had. However there are several things that really bother me about this whole mess.

First, I have written to Richard Carter three times who broke into our house and trashed it, to find out who Ci-1 and Ci-3 are. If they made accusations against us as he claimed they did I believe that we have the right to know who they are under something called the Jencks Act. I have received no answers from Richard Carter.

We built this house ourselves using mostly family labor and wanted to keep it in the family. Out of our nine children Ronald was the only one who did not own his own home. When we heard about his large settlement from a construction accident. Charlotte, his mother thought that it would be wise for him to invest in our home before he went through all his money. We knew nothing about any of his illegal activities. Even though we build the home ourselves after selling out farm. We had nearly $500,000 in it. The government does not have a penny invested in it. But you tell me that you figured that the government can sell it for at least $700,000 when we are gone. I can't understand why we should lose over $500,00 and the government make $7000,000 when we broke no laws or intended to fool any one. We did not take back a mortgage from Ronald as he was a family member. If we had we could probably foreclose and get the property back keeping the money that Ronald had paid us. That's what banks do all the time.

Part of the deal was that Ronald would take care of the major repairs and would help and look out for us when we got older.

I had no idea that Ronald was going to pay us with any cash. When Richard Carter took the cash from us there was eleven bundles of five thousand each except one which I had taken twelve hundred out of. This would leave $53,800 and you say that there was only $48,800 exactly $5,000 less.

Each time that we discuss a settlement you state that you have to clear it with your superiors. I'm wondering if that could be Mr. VanDegraff or Mr. Gelbert.

You state that the government would give us $48,800 and assume Ronald's interest. Actually Ronald's interest included more than money as I explained. It would seem that you would at least offer the $53,800 which you have had for nearly four years. I always thought that the government paid interest when they held your money. Another thing as I explained to you I don't know how we would make out under Act 60. As it is now we get a sizeable rebate on our property taxes due to our income and all the money that we lost to the government in the bank scandal.

I have never heard how the government settles with Patterson who apparently lived across the road from Ronald and according to the newspaper was found with drugs and not the first time.

Also, the fellow with the garbage trucks, Mark Willey and Mrs. Bergeron. What penalties did they suffer

It was reported in the paper that Ronald sold some kind of illegal drugs to an undercover agent back in 1999. Why didn't they arrest him then instead of watching him for nearly five years. This makes no sense to me except that the government was waiting for him to build up a lot of assets so that they could profit from Ronald's illegal activities. It looks like a set up to me. If they had arrested him when they should we would have known what was going on and certainly would have had no part of it.

I just heard on the radio that Vermont has had eighty drug related deaths this year. This is sickening. I wonder how many of these deaths could have been prevented if the government had stopped Ronald when they first new what he was doing instead of making it possible for him to continue so that the government could haul in a lot of money. Perhaps this the way that some government officials get their promotions. It looks like the worst form of terrorism in this country by our own government. Don't you agree?

Right in this area there are several individuals who don't appear to work, have motorhomes, boats automobiles, good homes, and everybody says that they are selling drugs and have been for years. I have never heard of any arrests. Seems like Richard Carter and his forty or so friends ought be checking them our rather than spending time breaking into our house and trashing it.

As I explained in the beginning we have no money for an attorney and do not really know how to proceed without one. Also we are old tired and worn our and Charlotte's health will not stand much more. I guess that we are at your mercy. I think that you are a very nice guy, it is your superiors that worry me. We will probably wind up doing things your way.

I don't see any alternative for us. We will wait to hear from you. In the mean time we will leave it in God's hands for the right things to happen.

Thank you for your patience.
Sincerely,
William F. Hill

U.S. Department of Justice
Drug Enforcement Administration

Asset Id. 04-DEA-432784
Case Number CF-04-0006 13, April 24

In answer to the seizure of $48,8100.00 in currency Ronald Aldrich is a son of Charlotte J. Hill and a step-some of William F. Hill. Ronald has lived for many years over in Franklin County Vermont which is about sixty miles from Hardwick, where we live. We did not see Ronald very often. He had always worked on farms and had very few assets. We have eight other children, all of who have had good employment and have acquired their own homes. Ronald went to work in Massachusetts on some kind of construction job where he got hurt. Apparently he was unable to work and we were told that he had a good lawyer who had gotten him a very large settlement for his injuries. Charlotte, his mother, was afraid that he would go through the money and soon have nothing. She suggested that he invest in our home which we had built. We would retain a life interest in the home until we both died. They way if Ronald went through all his money he would someday have something and perhaps being older he might be a better manager of his assets.

We agreed to sell him the house for less than half what we had in it but we could always continue to live here: Ronald paid us with quite a bit of cash which he said was from his settlement. We mistrusted nothing. We had not deposited all of the cash as we were planning to use if for spring planting and other things that we need in our farming business this spring.

Had we any idea that Ronald was doing anything illegal we certainly wouldn't have anything to do with him. We are very opposed to drugs or anything to do with them and certainly wouldn't get involved. I had a store down town for many years where they tried to get me to carry cigarettes and I refused no matter how profitable it might be. I wanted nothing to do with anything that might harm peoples health.

I believe that they took more than $48,810.00 when they left here. We certainly did not do anything illegal intentionally and we need our money back as soon as possible so that we can start our springs work. I hope that this the correct way to make our request to you. Thank you.

Sincerely,
William F. Hill
Charlotte J. Hill

At Hardwick this 13th of April 2004 William F. Hill and Charlotte J. Hill, husband and wife, personal appeared and they acknowledged this instrument by them sealed and subscribed to be their free act and deed.

Notary Public

July 6, 2005

Chief Judge William K. Sessions III
United States Court
Pearl St.
Burlington, Vt. 05402

Dear Judge Sessions: Civil #2:04 cv-45

Enclosed are copies of several letters which we have sent to the Justice department and which we have never received any answers to. As explained we did sell an interest to a step-son in our home back in December of 2002. With no idea that he was involved in anything illegal. I did not know that he was going to pay us with any cash.

In February 2004 you authorized Richard Carter and about three dozen other men to break into our home and trash it. We were gone they smashed in the door and destroyed the door casing. When we arrived home, not knowing what was happening, we found them going through everything laughing and having a great time like a bunch of hoodlums. They dumped out drawers, files and just made a royal mess. We have a very large family. Charlotte came from a very poor family and has had to overcome many obstacles in her life. Never having had Christmas as a child she now makes a big thing of Christmas. To save money and be able to have a good Christmas for all our family she does her shopping right after Christmas when all the sales are on and the presents can be bought for much less. She had around a hundred presents all wrapped and tagged with the children's, grand children's and great grand children's names on them. They ripped and tore all the presents open and strewed them all over the place. They even tipped over and strewed the hay for our cattle all around and left much of it lying in the mud which ruined it. I can't imagine what they were looking for. We didn't have anything to hide.

When we arrived home Carter asked me to open my safe or he was going to blow it up. I opened it. There was some cash in there which Ronald had paid us. They took it but refused to count it. There was eleven bundles each containing $5,000 except one bundle which I had taken about $1,200 out of. This would have made about $53,800. When we finally did get an accounting of it several months later they said that there was $48,800. This was exactly $5,000 short. We have complained about this several times but got no answers. Carter or one of his men must have pocketed one of the $5,000 bundles. If this had happened anywhere except by somebody in the government there would have been an investigation and some body would have been held responsible. You know it as well as I do. Perhaps you should authorize a breakin and trashing or their properties as you did with ours. You might be surprised what you might find.

According to the newspapers they claim that they had been watching Ronald and others deal in drugs for over five years. What other crime would they let go on for five years without making an arrest certainly not speeding, continues murders or any other crime they would nab them the first time that they saw them speeding or doing anything illegal except dealing in illegal drugs. Here they wait and watch until they accumulate a lot of wealth which they can nab. In the meantime while this is going on probably a lot of new people have been lured onto drugs and several more dealers gone into business. It looks to me that the government is the one promoting the illegal drug business by watching and using these dealers to do the promoting so that they can take away the large profits that they have accumulated. Had they picked up Ronald the first time that they said they knew that he was dealing in drugs we would not have been able to sell our house to him and probably a lot of people wouldn't been able to obtain drugs It looks like the government is the biggest promoter of illegal drugs.

I believe that illegal drugs are a much bigger threat to this country than terrorism. Look at the precautions that they have taken to burb terrorism. They could do the same thing with illegal drugs if they wanted to.

We sold our house retaining a life lease all legal and certainly not suspecting that there was any problem with Ronald or his money. We have worked very hard all our lives and need our money back and to know where we stand in relation to our home. This has taken a very heavy tole on both of us and especially Charlotte. We cannot do anything about what the government has done to us but you can as you were the one who authorized this whole mess. Please straighten it out for us and also find out what happened to the other $5,000 as we need it and it belongs to us, not the government.

Also a copy of a letter from the tax department to show that we did everything right when we sold our home to Ronald. I am also sending you separately a copy of the book Where is the Justice. I hope that you will read it. We certainly believe in justice as right is right and wrong is wrong but certainly the government doesn't see it that way. We expect to here from you soon and telling us that you are straightening this mess out.

Sincerely,
William F. Hill

When Ronald was in jail he kept talking about what he was going to do with the place when he got out. The Government had already sold it to Sven Olson for $129,000 when they were only asking $70,000 They had put it up on an auction over the internet and Olson would not stop bidding Altho we knew that it was sold the government wouldn't tell; us who bought it. We did find out eventually. Ronald kept talking about coming back home after he got out of jail and talking over. Although we didn't think that he had anything left here When he was to be release Oldson who we had never met called and said that he wanted to pick Ronald up from jail; and bring him here This seemed kind of strange. When Ronald arrived home he moved in here with us and much of his family desended on the place. Charlotte and I continued live here with Ronald and his family… although Ronald was on probation and had some restrictions placed on him he started to become much involved Ronald and Olson had several meetings together and I understand that Olson was going to transfer the property back to Ronald by giving him a thirty year paid up lease Ronald indicated to me that Olson might be in the same business that he was in as Olson seem to have plenty of money and was making trips to Canada in a large mobile home with his family. Ronald told me that he didn't want to get into any more trouble and wind up back in Jail Soon while I was taking Charlotte to the hospital we came home and found Ronald gone leaving us a few unpaid bills.

Olson now has bought Leighs mobile home from her for a little of nothing Charlotte and I have had to move off the place as we could not stand it any longer Olson is now planning to take over and undoing many of the things that we did He expects to make several improvements to the place I have been cooperating with him and trying to help him even though we have nothing left there. I drive by and look at the house the land the other buildings and what was Leighs mobile home. I now realize that I worked all my life To pay for all this and have nothing to show for it.

IF HE ACTUALLY GOT IT. I HAVE THE RIGHT TO
KNOW HOW THE JUDGE CAN ACCEPT SUCH FALSE
STATEMENTS AGANST ME AND NOT TELL ME
WHERE THEY CAME FROM.

ALSO THE COURT HAS ACCEPTED SEVERAL
FALSE STATEMENTS PRESENTED BY OLSONS
LAWYER. YOU SEEM TO BELIEVE ALL HER LIES AS
SHE IS A LAWYER AND REFUSE TO LISTEN TO ANY
OF THE TRUTH .WHICH SHOULD HAVE PLENTY OF
BEARING ON THIS CASE IF THE TRUTH AND YOU
WERE WILLING LOOK IN TO IT

William F./ Hill

PS. You mentioned that I had agreed to pay all the town property taxes plus the .insurance I want you to know that I paid all the taxes as I had agreed to do up until last year even though Olson was living there. I paid the insurance Olson convinced the insurance company that he owned the place, had a deed and was living there. The insurance company canceled the policy that I had paid for and sent me a check for over $600. ..You made it sound like I hadn,t done as I agreed, but I had paid all this even though Olson had taken over. I can,t see where he paid or did any thing. I think that by now you would realize that I aways do as I agree. I wish that I could say that for some other people

William F. Hill
CC Copy to others....

STATE OF VERMONT

SUPERIOR COURT   CIVIL DIVISION
CALEDONIA UNIT   DOCKET NO. 235-10-18 Cacv

WILLIAM HILL

v.

SVEN OLSON and
909 PORTER BROOK ROAD REALTY TRUST

Affidavit Of Leigh Kidder

NOW COMES Leigh Kidder, and being under oath, does hereby depose and says as follows:

1. My name is Leigh Kidder and I live in Berlin, N. H. I am the granddaughter of Bill and Charlotte Hill.

2. I was living on the property in Hardwick in which my grandparents had a life estate to the property.

3. In my opinion, Bill started to develop what appears to be dementia or Alzheimer's disease at about the time that his property was sold to Ronald Aldrich and later purchased by Seven Olson. My grandmother relied on my grandfather, and that allowed Mr. Olson to run roughshod over them regarding his ownership and use of their house and property.

4. Throughout the time that my grandparents lived 909 Porter Brook Road, I will refer to their house and property as the "house" or the "property." Mr. Olson treated the house and property as his own and had no respect whatsoever for the privacy of my grandparents.

5. Based on how he interacted with me, he engaged in conduct which was calculated to cause my grandparents and later me and my children to give up our interest in the property.

6. Ronald Aldrich is Charlotte's son and my uncle.

7. I have four children. At an earlier time, my grandparents purchased a mobile home for me on the property. Bill paid between $7,000 and $9,000 for the mobile home.

He paid around $30,000 to have the septic system designed and built and connected to the mobile home. He paid to have the mobile home moved on to the lot and set up.

8. I used to help my grandparents with household chores and helped my grandmother after she developed cancer, but I had a job elsewhere.

9. The house and property was one of the nicest ones in the town of Hardwick. It was built around 1990 and had a fully finished basement. My grandparents lived in the basement as they built the upper levels of the house.

10. In my conversations with Ronald Aldrich and my grandparents, I learned that he was turned into the police by another person who had been found in possession of a narcotic. In exchange for a deal on his offense, the person gave the police information that led to the arrest of Ronald Aldrich for importing large amounts of marijuana from Canada.

11. Before he was charged, Ronald Aldrich purchased the property from my grandparents and in exchange for a reduced sale price, they retained a life estate in the property.

12. Ronald was sentenced in 2007 to serve 14 years in federal prison. He was convicted of distributing marijuana and money laundering. The federal government forfeited his ownership interest in the property.

13. Mr. Olson purchased Ronald's interest in the property from the federal government.

14. My grandparents remained on the property with their life estate. They were allowed by the U. S. government to keep their life estate.

15. Mr. Olson purchased Ronald's interest in the property in 2012.

16. I was living on the property when Mr. Olson purchased the property.

17. I was living on the property when Ron was released from what I was told was a halfway house in Massachusetts.

18. I wasn't home the moment on the day that Ronald Aldrich arrived at the Hardwick property, but returned within a couple of hours of his arrival on that date.

19. I met Mr. Olson on that day. He arrived with his wife, children, and the girlfriend of one of his children.

20. It was apparent that Mr. Olson and Mr. Aldrich knew each other. They separated from the group and spoke privately for about three hours.

21. Mr. Olson arrived at the Hardwick property in a large recreational vehicle (RV) and he brought four cases of wine and seafood from Massachusetts to throw a "welcome home" party for Ron. He and his wife, Jeannine, and his children, Zack, Olivia who was Zack's girlfriend, Tayt and Oliver stayed in the home of my grandparents, in their RV and at the Kimball House.

22. Ron Aldrich told my grandparents and me that Mr. Olson found out from Ron that the Hardwick property was for sale by the U. S. government.

23. Mr. Olson appeared to have lots of money. He purchased Ron's interest in the property and he offered to purchase a house for me.

24. Ron Aldrich said the reason Olson had an interest in the property is because they had done business in Canada together. The only business which I was aware that Ron did in Canada was to import large amounts of marijuana over a three year period, for which he was eventually charged and convicted. Ron and Mr. Olson never told me Mr. Olson was involved in the farming business, which is why Ron said he would go to Canada.

25. Mr. Olson told me and my grandparents that he purchased the Hardwick property as a way to get it back to Ron. Ron initially wanted the property back. Mr. Olson purchased it from the federal government and the plan was to sell it back to Ron using a 35 year lease.

26. At some point, there was a meeting with Ronald and Mr. Olson at my grandparents' house. The next day, Ron Aldrich and his longtime girlfriend moved out. Ron told my grandparents that Mr. Olson was involved in the same business that he had been and he, Ron, didn't want to go back to jail.

27. After Mr. Olson purchased the Hardwick property, he made it impossible for Bill and Charlotte Hill to enjoy living on the property. He imposed new rules and regulations on Bill and Charlotte on their own property, since they were the "tenants." He imposed restrictions on how they could use the property.

28. Mr. Olson and his family and their guests would randomly visit and stay in the house with my grandparents. The kids would destroy the house. This happened once or twice a month. I recall once every weekend for three months. Then they didn't return for seven months.

29. Mr. Olson had guests stay in my grandparents' home, ranging for two to eight guests at a time, plus their children if they had children.

30. The guests and their children would trash the house. My grandmother used to keep the house very nice and would sometimes need to hire outside help to come and clean the house after they left.

31. He plowed up the fields so the Hills could not raise feed for their animals, shutting down his beef business. Bill depended on the hay to feed the animals and thereby manage to earn a profit.

32. Bill grew vegetables, but Mr. Olson told him he could no longer use pesticides to spray the crops because he wanted the fields to be organic. He then plowed up the fields and Bill could no longer grow vegetables.

33. After Mr. Olson caused my grandparents to move out of their retirement house and off their property, Mr. Olson had guests renting rooms in the house at $100.00 per person. Some of those guests had dogs which peed and pooped in the house, and they destroyed the carpets and damaged the floors.

34. Bill and Charlotte only owned a cat.

35. Mr. Olson brought three snow machines to the property and allowed teenagers, including a six year old, to use or ride on the machines without helmets. The six year old was riding on the machine and was thrown off the back of it.

36. I was present when Bill and Charlotte's friends told them that it was irresponsible to allow the children to ride the machines unsupervised and in a reckless manner around the Hardwick property. This activity placed a lot of stress on my grandmother, which then put a lot of stress on my grandfather.

37. Strangers to my grandparents were in and out of the house. They arrived and left without notice.

38. Mr. Olson would have guests from Canada stay at the house.

39. Charlotte Hill had cancer and wanted to live peacefully in her residence and die there. However, she died in a relatively inexpensive double wide home in another section of town. It appeared to me that my grandparents were under tremendous pressure, based on their comments and appearance. My grandmother cried all of the time.

40. Mr. Olson caused extraordinary pressure on my grandparents. He took advantage of their weakened conditions and advancing age. He made it impossible for them to peacefully live on the property. He effectively forced them to move off their property.

41. Before Mr. Olson purchased the property, the property was in great common. I recall my grandparents telling me it was built around 1990. The greenhouses were in use and the pool was very beautiful. The house was painted. I have photographs of the property on my cell phone.

42. Before Ron was arrested, he helped to maintain the property. He and Bill had the porches painted, a stone wall built, and the fences were up and in good shape. The swimming pool was beautiful. I would say it was a showplace in which my grandparents took a lot of pride.

43. The only problem I saw with the house was in a room in the basement where water would enter in the springtime.

44. After Mr. Olson purchased the property, he began to pay my sister, Kelly Lacourse, and me, in cash and later by check, to remove wallpaper and tear down walls. He wanted to turn the property into a place where he could rent rooms and said wallpaper was not appropriate for a bed and breakfast.

45. The damage to the house was caused by Mr. Olson paying us to remove wallpaper and tear down walls and by his guests and their animals.

46. My sister, Kelly Lacourse, smoked marijuana with Mr. Olson.

47. When Kelly left the property, she was not on good terms with Mr. Olson.

48. However, at about the time of a court hearing was scheduled in this case, on December 10, 2018, my sister contacted me to report that she heard from Mr. Olson and that he wanted to purchase her a vehicle. He ended up purchasing her a Cadillac. The offer came out of nowhere.

49. Kelly lives in the South Royalton/Chelsea area and had not maintained contact with Mr. Olson since after she left the property.

50. He also told me that he wanted to go into the medical marijuana business, in which he could put me and others to work.

51. While Mr. Olson was effectively forcing my grandparents off their property, he started to suggest I move out of my mobile home, which my grandparents had purchased for me, as a way to help my grandparents.

52. Mr. Olson told me that he was going to rent the basement of the house to tenants. However, if I agreed to move into the basement with my children as his guests, and

sell my mobile home, then he could rent my mobile home to tenants. This move would allow me to stay in the basement as a guest for free.

53. To reduce further stress on my grandparents, I agreed.

54. Mr. Olson wanted the trailer sold at auction because he did not want to buy it directly from me. It was auctioned by Wrights Auction Service and I received only $1,100 for it. Mr. Olson began to rent the mobile home to tenants. At one point, he had six people living in it.

55. I moved with my four children into the basement of the house as a favor to my grandparents.

56. Mr. Olson paid me and my sister to remove wallpaper and tear up the carpets. He promised to pay me $1,500, but then only paid me $740. When I requested the balance, he told me to move out of the house with my four children because I was his guest and I was no longer welcome. I had no legal authority to stay because I did not own the property and had no legal recourse.

57. At one point before our falling out, Mr. Oslon wanted to purchase a home for me in the Hardwick area. He said he would purchase and pay for it, and I could pay him back at $200.00 per month for 40 years. After I moved out of my mobile home, that offer was no longer on the table.

LEIGH RIDDER

Subscribed and sworn to before me, this 1st day of MN 2019.

Joseph C Boucher
Notary Public, State of New Hampshire NOTARY PUBLIC
My Commission Expires Feb. 21, 2023

438

WILLIAM F. HILL
PO BOX 15
HARDWICK, VT 05843
802 472 6308

SUPERIOR COURT
CALEDONIA UNIT   DOCKET NO 235 10 18 CACV

1 HILLS ALREADY OWNED THE PROPERTY BY THEIR LIFE
ESTATE AND HAD NO REASON TO MENTION ANY THING ELSE. THE JUDGE
ILLEGALLY TRIED TO DESTROY ANY CLAIM THAT WE LEGALLY HAD ALWAYS
HAD TO THE PROPERTY

2   HILLS FILED NO PLEADINGS ONLY QUESTIONED STATEMENT AND
DIRECTION   THE COURT HAD MADE, HILL ALSO HIRED
AN ATTORNEY AT THE DIRECTION OF THE COURT. THIS ONLY ALLOWED
OLSONS ATTORNEY TO FILE ALL KINDS OF FALSE STATEMENTS THAT THE
JUDGE WAS WILLING TO ACCEPT

3   HILLS DID NOT PLAN TO FILE THE PLAN TO OUST OLSON FROM
THE PROPERTY. THIS WAS ALL INSTIGATED BY ATTORNEY WITH OUT ANY
KNOWLEDGE OF HILL. I DIDN,T KNOW WHAT HE WAS UP TO....THE PROPERTY
WAS ALREADY TO FAR DAMAGED TO WANT IT BACK.. I HAD NO OTHER
BUSINESS WITH THIS OTHER ATTORNEY. I HAD ONLY HIRED HIM AS I WAS
DIRECTED TO DO BY THE COURT I QUESTION IF HE HAD MUCH AUTHORITY

4   THIS IS THE MOST   REDICULAS AND NOTHING BUT SLANDER BY
THE JUDGE AS I STATED I CANT REMEMBER EVERY THING BUT I BELIEVE
THAT I STILL KNOW RIGHT FROM WRONG SHAWN HENIDTY BRENT HUME
ON THE FOX NEWS BOTH DO ADMIT THAT THEY DO HAVE TIMES
REMEMBERING SIMPLE THINGS DUE TO THEIR AGES. THIS IS NORMAL.
WHAT ABOUT YOUR MAN JJOE BIDEN WHO YOU ARE PUSHING TO BE OUR
NEXT PRESIDENT SO THAT HE CAN CONTROL THE WHOLE UNITED STATES
AND RULE THE REST OF THE WORLD ARE YOU GOING TO APPOINT HIM A
GUARDIAN. HOW ABOUT APPOINTING ONE FOF. YOUR SELF YOU STATE THAT
I CAN HIRE COUNSEL. YOU SHOULD BE ABLE TO SEE THAT ALL THE COUNCIL
INVOLVED IN THIS CASE HAVE NOT BEEN VERY RELIABL AND \ NOT VERY
HONEST. ARE THESE THE KIND OF PEOPLE THAT SHOULD BE CONTROLLING
THE COURTS AND YOU WANT THEM CONTROLLING PEOPLES LIVES.

5   I THINK THAT YOU HOULD OF LISTENED TO LEIGHS TEST
AMONEY YOU LISTENED TO TO ALL THE FALSE STATEMENTS OF OLSONS
WITNESSES MOSTLE DRAWN UP AND BY WRITTEN BY OLSONS ATTORNEY

439

6   THIS IS WITH OUT 1 DOUBT THE BIGGEST LIE IN THIS WHOLE CASE. HILLS HAD NO INTENTION OF GIVING UP THEIR HOME THAT THEY HAD BUILT AND WORKED A LIFETIME . FOR YOU AND OLSON BOTH HAD TO BE DISHONEST TO EVEN PROMOTE ANY SUCH LIE. THERE WAS NOTHING SAID ABOUT GIVING UP OUR HOME. THIS WAS THE LAST THING THAT WE WANTED. YOU AND OLSON HAVE NO PROOF OF ANY SUCH IDEA THIS IS ONE OF THE BIGGEST AND MOST DISHONEST THEFTS EVER HEARD OF.

7   YOU DON,T CARE ABOUT ALL THE LIVES OF PEOPLE THAT YOU HAVE DESTROYED. NEITHER YOU OR OSONS LAWYER KNEW ANY OF THEM. YOU HAVE NEVER TRIED TO REACH A FAIR. END AS THERE IS NO WAY FOR A FAIR SETTLEMENT.
I-DON,T KNOW WHY WE HAVE TO DEAL WITH SUCH DISHONEST AND RUTHLESS PEOPLE

HAD RONALD ALDRICH, SPEN OLSON, HIS LAWYER AND JUDGE BENT OF CALEDONIA COUNTY COURT DONE THE HONEST THING INSTEAD OF ALL THE DISHONEST THINGS THEY DID CHARLOTTE HILL, DAN HILL WOULD PROBABLY STILL BEEN ALIVE AND OUR FAMILY COULD STILL BE LIVING IN THE HOME THAT WE WORKED SO HARD TO BUILD WITH OUR FAMILY. OUR GREAT GRAND CHILDREN WOULD BE VERY HAPPY, DOING WELL AND WE WOULD STILL BE GROWING AND MARKETING OUR GOOD BEEF WHICH WAS THE VERY BEST AROUND. I STILL GET CALLS FOR OUR BEEF AND PRODUCE NEARLY EVERY WEEK.
THANKS TO YOU THIS NONE OF THIS NEVER HAPPNED
WILLIM F. HILL

Willim F Hill would

TEL. 802-754-2200
Fax 802-754-2100

VINCENT ILLUZZI
ATTORNEY-AT-LAW
P.O. BOX 226
ORLEANS, VERMONT 05860-0226

LAW OFFICE AT:
38 WATER STREET

July 5, 2019

Bill Hill
P O Box 15
Hardwick, VT 05843

RE: Documents Terminating My Representation
And Notice Of Actions You Must Take In A
Timely Manner

Dear Bill:

The Court has granted my motion and allowed me to withdraw as your attorney from this case. As noted in the documents from the Court that were mailed to you, another copy of which is included with this letter, you need to take certain actions by certain dates to avoid having judgment granted against you.

The Court has sent you information that you need to address within 30 days. That includes a motion for summary judgment (which means if the motion is granted, judgment will be granted to Mr. Olson and you will take nothing from this lawsuit regarding your deeded life estate).

I believe you have a claim against Mr. Olson for the value of your life estate, lost income from the life estate and repayment of the property tax improperly credited to Mr. Olson.

On April 20, 2019, we met at the Village Restaurant in Hardwick and later at your home to review some papers that you could not find, and to work on answers to interrogatories, which you could not fully answer.

I met with you over the Easter Sunday weekend, in person, because you were not able to answer basic questions about your claim. Then, I needed to return, type up the answers, and then follow up again to get them signed in front of a notary.

We have known each other for decades and I have helped you with past legal issues in the past, generally with good result.

I write this letter because of my concerns that you are being exploited and otherwise need some help with day to day activities. I suggest you apply for appointment of a financial guardian through the probate court. It could be your brother or nephew who teaches at the local high school.

In the meantime, I suggest you reach out to family or someone that you can trust to help you manage your finances and your household.

As we discussed on April 20, I reached out to the AAA in St. Johnsbury and it had someone call you. As I understand it, you declined offers of assistance.

Difficulty Organizing And Managing Your Affairs.

You acknowledged receipt of two letters, which contained my answer to the amended counterclaim, discovery requests and draft of my motion to strike the libel claim, but you couldn't find them. They were received by you on Monday, April 15. I resent copies to you.

In looking around your home, it is obvious that you are struggling to keep your papers organized and available as necessary. To this end, I believe that you should work with the Area Agency On Aging for a personal care assistant. Based on your age and income and expenses, I believe that you will qualify. You said **after paying thousands of dollars** to Leigh Kidder every month, and from time to time loaning or giving money to Kelly Lacourse, her sister, you can't afford to put gas in your car. I am glad that you approved me contacting the AAA on your behalf.

The Area Agency on Aging in St. Johnsbury was in touch with you. You declined assistance. You should ask for assistance in helping to manage your day to day financial affairs, including your household.

Recall I tried to get someone to assist you with your computer usage months ago. Only recently, after I again called the vendor did you set up a first meeting. The vendor called me a few months ago and told me he never heard from you and wanted to know what was going on, given your failure to respond.

Financial Exploitation Of A Vulnerable Adult.

Thank you for giving me a copy of your check ledger showing all of the payments to Leigh Kidder. I didn't total it, but it looks like around $20,000, if not more, since August 2018 through April 2019.

You told me that Leigh Kidder told you that child support benefits have been delayed or not paid by the State of New Hampshire and that therefore, in order to support herself and her children, she needed your full financial support.

You wrote her a check in April for $2,000 so she could take a vacation with her children to Colorado, where she will visit her boyfriend who you told me is on federal supervision following a conviction for one or more federal offenses.

You also gave me copies of letters to federal authorities, from the U. S. president on

442

you can't recall very much and are struggling to recall information important to your claims against Sven Olson.

When I have questioned you about the thousands of dollars you are paying Leigh, you become hostile and refuse to acknowledge that the State of New Hampshire, the three or four fathers of her children and she herself are responsible for bringing up those children. She told me that she has a job, but is seasonally unemployed at this time.

New Hampshire Department Of Health & Human Services

As you requested and thought it was a "good idea" on Saturday, I will share with the State of New Hampshire a copy of the check book ledger you gave me to point out that she needs financial assistance and that you can no longer pay out thousands of dollars per month to take care of Leigh and her four children. That's why you gave me the check book ledger.

This should prompt the state of New Hampshire to ensure that benefits are no longer delayed or denied, or both, as Leigh has told you has been happening.

You have told me that you can't afford to buy gas for your car and that you "do nothing" because you have no money because it's all going to Leigh and her children.

The State of New Hampshire provides financial assistance to parents with children. It's easy to apply. Leigh Kidder can do so on line. Here is a section of the website that explains how she can do it:

> The Division of Family Assistance offers online services through NH EASY Gateway to Services, New Hampshire's Electronic Application System. Learn how to apply for assistance, check eligibility, track your application status, and more by visiting the NH EASY Gateway to Services web page.

Non-Payment For Legal Services.

You have an outstanding bill for my legal services. It is now over $9,000.

You said you were selling stocks to pay my bill, but obviously did not do so. It became apparent that you were stringing me along to obtain legal services without compensation.

You have income to pay for my legal services, but you have elected to spend your disposable income on other matters.

You have asked me work on your case, requests dozens of documents, take depositions of your own witnesses, yet you say you won't be able to pay my bill because you are supporting Leigh and her children, paying Leigh Kidder thousands of dollars per month to support her and her four children.

You have repeatedly stated that if we work hard on this case, we can make a lot of money. I signed an hourly fee agreement with you. I need to get paid for my legal work.

I don't want to make "a lot of money" on a contingency fee basis. I was asked by you to reacquire your life estate, and recover your $8,000 in property tax payment received by Mr. Olson.

We signed an hourly fee agreement. I never agreed to a contingency fee agreement. I expected to be paid for my work on an hourly basis.

If you get "rich" as a result of this case, that's great.

Inability To Understand Your Obligations Under The Law And Your Burden In This Lawsuit.

You have been unable to acknowledge your duties under the terms of the deed. I have explained this to you.

You failed to maintain property insurance. The insurance carrier says for "non-payment" of the premium. You say the insurance company didn't want to insure the property because it was in bad condition. You can't prove it and your own insurance agent will testify against your position.

You published a statement in your book which you can't prove is true and which at least on its face is libelous. Although someone else told you that information, the law doesn't allow you to publish it unless you can prove it's true. If you can't prove it's true, then you may be libel for damages for libel.

I don't think there are any "damages" but you need to file a motion with the Court within 60 days of the counterclaim in order to raise the question of damages. I was working on such a motion, but withdrew before I could file it.

You want me to take depositions and make discovery requests that I think are completely largely irrelevant, time consuming and expensive. Your legal theories will not hold up under Vermont law, in my opinion.

We go over the same issues every time you call. "What's going on" is the question you keep asking and which I have answered when you have called. You act as if we haven't communicated for months and that you are in the dark.

Anger Toward Me And Confusion.

When I try to explain your obligations and responsibilities in maintaining this lawsuit, or that information I have received suggesting Leigh is exploiting you, you display anger toward me and are in denial.

William F. Hill
PO Box 15
Hardwick Vt. 05843
802-472-6308

July 2, 2019

Vincent

Ive been reading the report that you sent. There are a few errors in it which I would like to point out.

1. I understand that you have withdrawn from the Olson case I have finnally got a night sleep

2. I remember the night that I met you it was at a Real estate auction that I had at Salem Hights. I have always considered you a friend and you hav helped me many times for whitch I am very greatful

3. I guess that you don't recall that I had my brother Dan helping me he was an accountant who had held several important jobs.

This whole mess was very devastating to him He felt very bad for Sally and all of us... Dan and I were meeting regular trying to get to the   bottom of this mess. I knew that what had happened to Sally and all of us was a lot for him to handle The last day that we were. Too meet   Danwas was comming to. My house at three o'clock. I was waiting for Dan to to show up In a few minutes after three Dean ,my son came in

and said that'   Dan an was on his porch he had just shot his self. I certainly am m0t going to bring any more family into this   mess. Dan was also the   administrator's to Leigh's kids

445

estate The ended that At your suggestion I went to a
lawyer in St   Johnasbury   and had to
start all over with   probate   and. all This was
very expensive

   4. The people from Home Health. Did contact me
They were very nice and willing to be helpful. These were
the same people who helped to take   care of
Sally I di dn,t need any of there services. At this time I
didn,t want take them away from people who could use
them

   5. You complain. that I do have a lot of paper
work Most of is for trying to keep up then you find fast
that I can't find things. You keep   complaining
about helping Leighs. Family You did contact some
agency in New Hampshire trying to help Leigh   All this
did it looks like is   to make. her life more
difficulty; As to hiring somebody to do this it would be
very hard to find anyone who under stood the probem I
have

   I to help Leighs family they are human
beings You help your son and take good care of. Him. I
don't care about. Kelley she has made her life

   but could have made a good witness if you had
contacted her before Olsons lawyer got to her. I. Talk with
the people from Home health they are   very
nice and willing to help if I need them I don't need to take
them from others

   6.   the, first person you told me about lived up
north. I called him. several. Times he was always going to
call back but never did,

REPUBLICAN PRESIDENTIAL TASK TORCE
PO BOX 96206
WASHINGTON DC 20077 7461

DEAR PRESIDENT TRUMP
I WILL BE HAPPY TO SUPPORT YOUR HONOR ROLL

I WILL LIST SOME OF THE THINGS THAT I HAVE DONE TO
SUPPORT THE REPUBLICANS
ONE; A FEW YEARS AGO WHEN GIBSON WAS VERMONTS
GOVERNOR THEY NEEDED SOMEONE TO PROMOTE THE
REPUBLICAN PARTY AND VERMONT AGRICULTURE. I
VOLUNTEERED. I CONTACTED THE STATLER HOTEL IN BOSTON
WHERE THE PROMOTION WAS TO BE HELD THEY AGREED TO LET
ME BRING TWO LARGE COWS IN THEIR LOBBY. I KEPT THEM THERE
THREE OR FOUR DAYS AND CREATED A LOT OF INTEREST. YOU
WOULDN,T BELIVE THE NEWS REPORTERS AND TV CAMERAS
TWO; WHEN RONALD REGAN WAS RUNNING FOR PRESIDENT
THEY HAD A PROMOTION IN BURLINGTON. THE LOCAL
REPUBLICAN COMMITTEE WERE TYING TO SELL TICKETS FOR
ONE HUNDRED DOLLARS. EACH. I SAID THAT I WOULED TAKE SIX.
TICKETS. THEY ALL THOUGHT THAT THEY WERE GOING TO GET
TO GO. BUT INSTEAD I TOOK SIX WELL KNOWN LOCAL
DEMOCRATS. THEY ALL HAD A GOOD TIME AND TALKED ABOUT IT
ALL THE WAY HOME. I DON,T KNOW HOW THEY VOTED.
THREE; WHEN DEAN DAVIS WAS RUNNING FOR VERMONT
GOVERNOR I GOT A CALL ASKING ME IF I WOULD TAKE HIM
AROUND TOWN SOME DAY AND INTRODUCE HIM TO A FEW
PEOPLE. I AGREED I WENT TO SEE THE LADY WHO OWNED THE
LOCAL RESTAURANT AND TOLD HER THAT I WOULD LIKE TO
RENT HER RESTAURANT FOR A COUPLE OF HOURS AND HAVE
HER GIVE OUT FREE COFFEE AND DONUTS, THAT I WOULD PAY
FOR THEM. SHE AGREED AND I ADVERTISED IT. THE PLACE WAS
PACKED WHEN THE GOVERNOR ARRIVED. HE WAS SHOCKED
AND HAD A GREAT TIME POURING COFFEE AND TALKING TO
EVERYBODY. THIS WAS THE SAME RESTAURANT WHERE
BERNNIE SANDERS AND HIS BUDDY LEE ZEMSKYN USE TO SHOW
UP AND DISPLAY ALL THEIR NAKED PICTURES AND

PORONOGRAPHY. PEOPLE DIDN,t LIKE THEM ALSO BERRNIE OWED EVERYBODY. I DON'T BELIVE THAT HE EVER PAID A BILL TO ANYONE

FOUR; I HELPED OUT ON THE LOCAL RESCUE SQUAD FOR A WHILE. IT CAME UP THAT THEY THOUGHT WE WERE GOING TO NEED A NEW AMBULANCE . THEY THOUGHT THAT THEY COULD HIT THE LOCAL TOWNS FOR A FEW HUNDRED DOLLARS EACH YEAR TO PAY FOR IT. I SUGGESTED LETS FORGET THE TOWNS I BELIEVE THAT W E CAN RAISE THE MONEY OURSELVES THEY ALL THOUGHT I WAS CRAZY. BUT WE TRIED PEOPLE WANTED TO HELP AND WE HAD THE MONEY NEEDED IN A VERY SHORT WHILE

FIVE; WHEN RICHARD TARRANT WAS RUNNING AGAINST BERNIE SANDERS FOR THE US SENATE MY WIFE SALLY AND I PUT IN A LOT OF TIME TRYING TO BEAT BERNIE WE PUT ON QUITE A FEW SPAGNETTI SUPPERS.. TARRENT PAID FOR THEM BUT SALLY I AND OUR FRIENDS DID THE WORK WE PUT UP A LOT OF POSTERS BUT EVERY MORNING THEY WERE ALL GONE AS BERNIES PEOPLE TORE THEM DOWN AS FAST AS WE COULD PUT THEM UP.

SIX; FIXED UP REPAIRED AND SAVED SEVERAL OLDER BUILDINGS THAT WERE PART OF THE HISTORY OF OUR TOWN I COULD GO ON BUT THERE IS MUCH MOREIN MY BOOK WHERE IS THE JUSTICE

SEVEN; I HAD A LARGE BARN ON OUR FARM WHERE WE RAN WEEKLEY AUCTIONS. EACH TIME ONE OF MY CHILDREN GRADUATED FROM HIGH SCHOOL I WOULD EMPTY THIS BARN OUT HIRE A LOCAL BAND AN PUT ON A LARGE PARTY FOR ALL THE GRADUATING CLASS. THEN I WOUDL INVITE THE WHOLE TOWN. EVERYBODY CAME AND HAD A GOOD TIME. PARENTS WERE HAPPY AS THEY GOT TO ENJOY THERE CHILDREN - PLUS THEY ALL KNEW WHAT THEY WERE DOING ON GRADUATION NIGHT.

EIGHT; I HELD MANY BENEFIT AUCTIONS FOR FIRE DEPARTMENTS CHURCHES AND MANY WORTH WHILE ASSOCIATIONS. I DID AN AUCTION FOR ONE FIRE DEPARTMENT EACH YEAR FOR FORTY TWO YEARS'

I COULD GO ON ABOUT THE MANY THINGS THAT I AND MY FAMILY DID TO HELP IMPROVE PEOPLES LIVES. YOU CAN READ ABOUT MANY OF THESE THINGS AND THE AWFUL THINGS THAT THE GOVERNMENT DID TO TRY TO DETROY US. THE

GOVERNMENT DIDN,T WANT US TRYING TO HELP PEOPLE. THEY WANTED TO BE THE ONES THAT WERE DESTROYING PEOPLES LIVES, THEY TOLD US THAT POOR PEOPLE SHOULD STAY POOR AND DIDN,T WANT US HELPING THEM. THE GOVERNMENT DID A LOT OF DAMAGE TO ME AND MY FAMILY, YOU CAN AN READ ABOUT A LOT OF THIS IN MY BOOK WHERE IS THE JUSTICE.

JUST NOW MY PHONE RANG. IT WAS SOMEONE WHO SAID THAT THEY WERE RASING MONEY FOR YOU PRESIDENT TRUMP. THEY WERE VERY SARCASTIC AND TOLD ME THAT I NEEDED TO SUPORT THEM WHITCH I HAVE BEEN DOING. THEY WOULDN,T GIVE THEIR NAME OR ADDRESS ONLY IMPLYING THAT I AM A ,CHEAPSKATE THIS DOSENT HELP THE REPUBLICAN CAUSE, SORRY

I WANT TO THANK YOU FOR ALL YOU HAVE DONE I WANT YOU TO KNOW THAT I AM RIGHT BEHIND YOU AND WILL SUPPORT YOU ALL THAT I CAN THANK YOU FOR THINKING OF ME FOR A MEMBER OF YOUR HONOR ROLL
THANK YOU

WILLIAM F [BILL] HILL
PO BOX 15
HARDWICK VT

05843

802-472-6308

WHEN WE CAME HOME AND FOUND RICHARD CARTER AND ALL HIS FORTY SOME MEN IN OUR HOUSE, CARTER AND ALL HIS MEN WERE LAUGHING AND TALKING ABOUT THE BIG SEEN THAT THEH HAD CREATED WHEN THEY WERE ON THEIR WAY HERE AND COMING THROUGH TOWN ALL THE COMMOTION THEY HAD FUN CREATING. DO YOU THINK THAT COULD OF HELPED OUR REPUTATION

ANOTHER THING, NOTHING TO DUE WITH THIS CASE...A FEW YEARS AGO I WAS INVOLVED IN COURT CASE IN THIS SAME COURT IT WAS A REAL ESTATE CASE....THERE WERE TWO WITNESSES THE FIRST WAS A FORMER OWNER OF THE PROPERTY HE HAD ALWAYS BEEN A HARD WORKED AND VERY HONEST BUT HAD ONLY HAD A EIGHTH GRADE EDUCATION. I KNEW THE WHOLE STORY AND HIS TESTIMONY WAS VERY ACTUAL AND TRUFUL THE SECOND WITNESS WAS A GOVERNMENT WORKER THEY BROUGHT IN. I DON,T THINK THAT HE HAD EVER SEEN THE PROPERTY AND HIS STORY WAS VERY UNTRUE FUEL. ALTHOUGH. HE WAS WRONG THE JUDGE SAID WE WILL TAKE HIS STORY OVER THE TRUTH OF THE OTHER WITNESS BECAUSE HE HAS A COLLEGE EDUCATION. IS THIS THE WAY THAT COURTS AND JUDGES MAKE THEIR DECISIONS? YOU NEED TO HAVE A COLLAGE DEGREE OR BE A LAWYER TO BE HEARD

ANOTHER TIME FOR NO REASON EXCEPT A FALSE MOTION BY FDIC GOVERNMENT ATTORNEY WHO WE HAVE HAD A LOT OF TROUBLE WITH JUDGEN BILLINGS AWARDED HER A ONE AND HALF MILLION DOLLAR JUDGMENT AGAINST ME WITH NO HEARING OR ANY WARNING. THIS WAS CERTAINLY VERY DISHONEST ON HIS PART I KNEW THAT JUDGE BILLINGS WAS LIEING AND THAT IS WHY I QUESTIONED HIM. I INQUIRED OF THE COURT CLERK WHO I WAS GETTING TO KNOW. THE CLERK SAID NO QUESTIONS HAD EVER CAME BEFORE THE COURT AS THE JUDGE HAD INDICATED. IT IS VERY SAD HOW THE COURT DID THINGS. THIS IS THE WAY THAT MOST OF JUDGE BILLINGS HANDLED THINGS. MAKE YOU WONDER IF YOU CAN EVER GET A FAIR TRIAL

WILLIAM F, HILL
PO Box 15
Hardwick, Vermont 05843
802-472-6308

I KNEW THAT JUDGE BILLINGS WAS LIEING AND THAT IS WHY I
QUISTONED HIM. I INQUIRED OF THE COURT CLERK WHO I WAS
GETTING TO KNOW. NOₙ OF THESE QUESTIONS HAVE EVER
CAME UP AS THE JUDGE SAID THAT THEY HAD I KNEW THAT HE
WAS COVERING HIS TRACK.S ' THAT IS PRETTY MUCH THE
WHOLE WAY HIS WHOLE COURT WENT VERY SAD THE WAY OUR
LAW IS HANLED;

WILLIAM F. HILL... .

WILLIAM F. HILL

Mr. William E. Hill
PO Box 15
Hardwick, VT 05843

Dear Mr. Hill:

I am in receipt of your letter of December 5 containing various questions and comments relative to the FDIC case against you and also the criminal case.

The only information that came to my attention in deciding these matters will be contained in the transcript and should be in the respective cases. Therefore, if you desire to obtain that information, you should contact the Clerk of Court to obtain the appropriate transcripts and orders.

I also note that you are not satisfied with the judgments entered. You had the right of appeal of the final judgments within the statutory time limits.

Very truly yours,

Senior US District Judge

STATE OF VERMONT

SUPERIOR COURT	CIVIL DIVISION
CALEDONIA UNIT	DOCKET NO: 235-10-18 CACV

WILLIAM HILL   AFFIDAVIT
    Plaintiff,

vs.

SVEN OLSON,
    Defendants

NOW COMES Sven Olson, duly sworn and under oath to state the following:

1. My name is Sven Olson.
2. I reside in Concord, Massachusetts and Hardwick, Vermont.
3. I am the Defendant/Counterclaim Plaintiff in the above-captioned matter.
4. I own and operate the Scale House restaurant in Hardwick, Vermont.
5. I also teach graduate business courses at Northeastern University in Boston.
6. I am married and have five children. My wife is a financial adviser for Merrill Lynch,
7. I purchased the property formerly owned by Bill Hill on Porter Brook Road in Hardwick in 2012.
8. Bill Hill moved out of the premises in 2017.
9. Bill Hill instituted this litigation in or about October 2018 to try to revive the life estate he had prior to moving out of the premises.
10. During the pendency of this litigation and prior to the filing of my counterclaim for defamation, I learned from my attorney that Bill had included a statement about me in his book "Where is the Justice" that suggested I was in the same business as Ronald Aldrich.
11. The book details Ronald Aldrich's history involving federal convictions for drug dealing and drug smuggling. Ronald Aldrich was somewhat infamous in the community for the scale of his crimes and the length of his sentence.
12. I had not read the book, but Bill talked about it often before he moved out and tried to sell it to anyone he could,
13. I was embarrassed when my attorney questioned me about the allegation.
14. I was concerned that even she might have a lesser opinion of me and that it might affect her ability to represent me in this litigation and in other matters she assists me with.

AFFIDAVIT

- 1

15. I own and operate a popular restaurant in downtown Hardwick that caters to local clientele and we hire local workers.
16. I fear that if they have or ever will read what Bill has said that they may stop coming to the restaurant or tell others and that my employees might quit.
17. I am not nor have I ever been a drug dealer or drug smuggler.
18. I had never met Ronald Aldrich prior to meeting him at the Porter Brook Road premises when he got out of prison.
19. Bill Hill had told me that Ronald Aldrich was at a half-way house in Boston just prior to being released from prison. He said the half-way house was near Northeastern University where I teach. I said in passing to Bill that maybe I should pick Ron up and bring him home to Hardwick. I never did and I never did know where the half-way house was exactly.
20. Bill never expressed to me that he or Sally did not want me coming to the house or spending time with them or Leigh and her children.

Dated at __Wellesley__ (town), __MA__ (State) this __22__ day of May 2019.

_____
Sven Olson

Subscribed and sworn to before me this __22__ day of May 2019.

Kristy M Thompson
Notary Public

AFFIDAVIT

453

William F. Hill

.VERMONT

AGENCY OF HUMAN SERVICES

DEPARTMENT OF DISABILITIES, AGING AND INDEPENDENT LIVING
Adult Protective Services
Division of Licensing and Protection
HC 2 South
280 State Drive
Waterbury, VT 05671-2060
http://www.dail.vermont.gov
To Report Adult Abuse: (800) 564-1612
APS Main Phone Line: (802) 241-0512
Fax: (802) 241-0342

December 11, 2018

William Hill
756 Dutton Road
p o box 15
Hardwick, Vermont 05843

Regarding a Report Received by Adult Protective Services (APS)
Reference #: 25152

Dear William Hill:

Adult Protective Services received a report that you may have been maltreated. After reviewing the information provided, we determined an investigation is not warranted at this time.

If you feel that you are being maltreated and would like assistance from Adult Protective Services, please call us at (800) 564-1612 or complete an online report at: www.dlp.vermont.gov.

We often make referrals to service providers or other agencies we believe you may benefit from based on the information in the report. If a referral was made you may be contacted by staff from that agency or service provider. Any referrals we made are indicated below:
    No referral made

If you would like to learn more about programs in your area that could be helpful, we suggest you contact Vermont 2-1-1. They are a confidential resource and referral center that provides free assistance in finding useful benefits and services. You can reach them by dialing 211 from any phone in Vermont at any time.

Adult Protective Services
Division of Licensing and Protection
State of Vermont

William f. Hill
PO box 15
HARDWICK, VT. 05843
802-472-6308

HOW WOULD YOU FEEL TO COME HOME AND FIND YOUR HOME BROKEN INTO AND ALL SMASHED IN AND FULL OF FBI s AND GOVERNMENT MARSHALS WEARING GUNS AND BULETT PROOF VESTS BREAKING UP AND SMASHING EVERYTHING INCLUDING YOUR CHILDS AND GRAND CHILDS CHRISTMAS PRESENTS AND STREWING THEM ALL OVER BROKEN AND RUINED. THEY DESTROYED EVERYTHING THAT THEY COULD. WE WERE UNABLE TO STOP THE ARMED FEDERAL THUGS. THIS REALLY TOOK A TOLL ON MY WIFE SALLY. SHE WAS ALREADY SUFFERING FROM CANCER AND GOVERNMENT ABUSE. THEY STOLE ALL THE MONEY THAT WE HAD ANDS EVEN REFUSED TO COUNT IT

WE HAD ALREADY BEEN WARNED BY SEVERAL ATTORNEYS NEVER STAND UP FOR YOUR RIGHTS AGAINST THE FEDERAL GOVERNMENT. OR THEY WILL REALLY GET YOU.

THE GOVERNNMENT BROUGHT IN AN OUT OF STATER NAMED MR OLSON AND WHO RUINED ALL OUR PROPERTY INCLUDING OUR GOOD FAMILY AND MY WIFS HEALTH. THE GOVERNMENT SOLD OUR LAND TO MR OLSON ON THE BELIEF THAT IT WAS ACTUALLY OWNED BY THE FEDS WHICH IT IS NOT THE JUDGE TOOK MR OLSONS ANDTHE GOVERNMENTS POSITION AND ORDERED ME AND MY WIFE TO STAY OFF OUR OWN PROPERTY

THE STRESS OF ALL OF OLSON,S HATRID AND THE GOVERNMENT ACTION MY WIFE COULDS NOT TAKE THE STRAIN AND ABUSE WHICH WE HAD BEEN TAKING FOR OVER THE TWENTY YEARS FROM THE GOVERNMENT SHE DIED A HORRIBLE DEATH. MY BROTHER DAN HILL COULD NOT TAKE THIS TREATMENT ANY LONGER TOOK HIS OWN LIFE. THIS WHOLE MESS HAS REALLY TAKEN A VERY HARD TOLL ON OUR GRAND DAUGHTER AND HER FOUR CHILDREN. THEYHAVE BEEN DRIVEN OUT OF THEIR HOME AND ARJREALRY SUFFERING FOR IT.

NEVER THOUGHT THAT ANYTHING LIKE WHAT HAS HAPPNED TO US COULD HAPPEN IN THIS COUNTRY. BUT ALONG WIRTH THIS AND A LOT MORE IT HAS DESTROYED OUR LIVES

Pac

I HOPE THAT YOU WILL READ ABOUT THIS IN OUR BOOK WHERE
ISTHE JUSTICE
YOU WONT BELIVE IT THANK YOU BILL HILL

BERNARD SANDERS
VERMONT

COMMITTEES:
BUDGET, RANKING MEMBER
ENERGY AND NATURAL RESOURCES
ENVIRONMENT AND PUBLIC WORKS
HEALTH, EDUCATION, LABOR, AND
PENSIONS
VETERANS' AFFAIRS

United States Senate

WASHINGTON, DC 20510–4504

WASHINGTON, DC 20510
(202) 224-5141

1 CHURCH STREET, 3RD FLOOR
BURLINGTON, VT 05401
(802) 862-0697
1 (800) 339-9834

www.sanders.senate.gov

February 15, 2019

Mr. William Hill
PO Box 15
Hardwick, Vermont 05843

Dear Mr. Hill:

Thank you for contacting Senator Sanders with your concerns regarding the FBI. The purpose of this letter is to provide information that we hope will be helpful to you.

As much as we would like to assist you with this matter, we are limited in what we can do in this situation. As a U.S. Senator, Bernie is a member of the legislative branch of the federal government and has no direct jurisdiction in legal or criminal matters. Furthermore, Senate Ethics Rules prohibit senators from intervening in legal cases.

You may wish to consult with an attorney. If you have not already done so, you may wish to contact Vermont Lawyer Referral Service, which provides a referral service for a 30-minute phone consultation with an attorney familiar with the relevant areas of law for no more than $25. They can be reached by calling 1-800-639-7036 or by emailing info@vtbar.org.

Again, thank you for contacting Senator Sanders. Although it may not be in our power to affect every situation, it is important for our office to hear about the issues Vermonters are facing. In the future, if you believe Bernie may be able to assist you, please do not hesitate to contact our office.

Sincerely,

Greta Hasler
Staff Assistant

457

I

William F. HILL
PO BOX 15
HARDWICK VT.

05843   july 27 2020

802-472-6308

AFTER PETER LANGROCK FORCED ME TO
FALSLEY PLEAD GUILTY TO A CRIME THAT I DIDNT
COMITT HE RESIGNED AS MY LAWYER TO TAKE ON
ANOTHER CLIANT THAT HAD MORE MONEY THAN I
DID. PETER TOLD ME THAT HIS NEW CLIANT WAS
COMPLETELY INNOCENT SO IT WAS VERY
IMPORTANT FOR PETER T0 DEFEND HIM. I DON,T
THINK THAT PETER DID A VERY GOOD JOB FOR HIM
EITHER AS HIS INNOCENT CLIENT GOT SIX YEARS IN
JAIL.

FOLLOWING THIS I HEARD FROM F. LEE BAILEY
WHO WAS BUSY DEFENDING O. J. SMPSON. BAILEY
TOLD NE THAT I NEEDED TO SUE PETER
LANGROCK FOR WHAT HE DID. I DIDN,T DO THIS A
I HAD ALREADY HAD ENOUGH OF LAWYERS AND
LAWSUIT.S.

I LATER HEARD FROM A CARL WATNER- A
PROTECTER OF INDIVIDUAL RIGHTS AND NEO-TEC
CONCERNING   THE FIFTH AMENDMENT
WHICH ESTABLISHES AN INDIVIDUALS   RIGHT NOT
TO TESTIFY AGAINST HIMSELF. INDIVIDUAL RIGHTS
WILL REMAIN   UNOBTAINABLE AS THE STATE AND
GOVERNMENT ARE PERMITTED TO GET AWAY WITH
THAT MANIPULATION.   TODAY AMERICANS ARE

PROTECTED AND BENEFIT EVERY DAY OF THEIR
LIVES BY THE FIFTH AMENDMENT, BY NOT BEING
INFORMED OF THIS IT COST ME TEN THOUSAND
DOLLARS TWO YEARS PROBATION MY
AUCTIONEERS LICENSE MY REAL ESTATE
LICENSE. ALL MY BUSINESS AND AWAY TO MAKE A
LIVING. I GUESS THAT THE LAWYERS THE JUDGE
OR THE COURTS DIDN'T CARE ABOUT THE LAW. I
GET I GET IT FROM EVERY ANGLE

SleighLaw

Protecting individuals against
the powerful since 1983

David C. Sleigh Attorney at Law

Julie Smith Office Manager
Jennifer Cleveland
Case Management Assistant

Email julie@sleighlaw.com
Email jennifer@sleighlaw.com

June 15, 2020

William Hill
P.O. Box 15
Hardwick, VT 05843

Dear William:

Thank you for considering this firm for possible representation with respect to William
Hill v. Sven Olsen, et al, Docket No. 235-10-18 Cacv. However, this firm is unable to
undertake representation of you, because your case falls outside our area of expertise. —

You should not view this declination of representation as any opinion with respect to any
possible merits to a potential claim. If you wish to pursue the matter further, you are
strongly advised to contact other attorneys as soon as possible. The telephone number for
Lawyer Referral is 800-639-7036.

Again, thank you for your consideration of this firm, and we wish you the best of luck in
whatever course of action you wish to pursue.

Sincerely,

David Sleigh

Mailing Address: PO Box 278 | Physical Address: 364 Railroad Street, Suite E | St. Johnsbury, Vermont 05819 | Phone 802 748-5176 | Fax 802 748-6618
www.sleighlaw.com

460

University of Vermont Extension Service
Director's Office
Morrill Hall
Burlington, Vermont 05405-0106

Phone 802-656-2990

May 29, 1987

Sally Hill
P. O. Box 15
29 Elm Street
c/o W.F. Hill
Hardwick, VT
05843

Dear Sally:

I regret that neither I nor Carol Fitzgerald can participate
in your farewell party.

The UVM Extension Service wishes you the very best of success
as you move to your next career. The Vermont EFNEP program is
better today because of your dedication, hard work, enthusiasm,
willingness to experiment and try new ways, and your genuine
leadership at the local level. You had understanding, empathy
and rapport with low income families. You could communicate with
them and they could talk to you. You were very effective in
helping us tell the EFNEP story to everyone, including
influencial leaders, community leaders, State Senators and
Legislators, national policy makers, and others. When you
explained it, people listened and became enthused about the
concept and its impact.

As Associate Director in the earlier days and Interim Director
now, I think you have helped me enhance my understanding of the
changing needs of low income families. While the morale of
Extension faculty and staff vacillated up and down over time, you
always, even if funds were to be cut off the next day, maintained
an infectious positiveness and optimism.

Thank you for your advice and meritorious service during the
past 14 years. We wish you happiness and success as you move
forward. If you are in the Burlington area, be sure to stop in.

Sincerely,

Bob H

Bob Honnold
Interim Director

BH/c

Helping you put knowledge to work.

University of Vermont Extension Service and U.S. Department of Agriculture cooperating, offer education and employment to everyone without regard to race,
color, national origin, sex, religion, age, or handicap

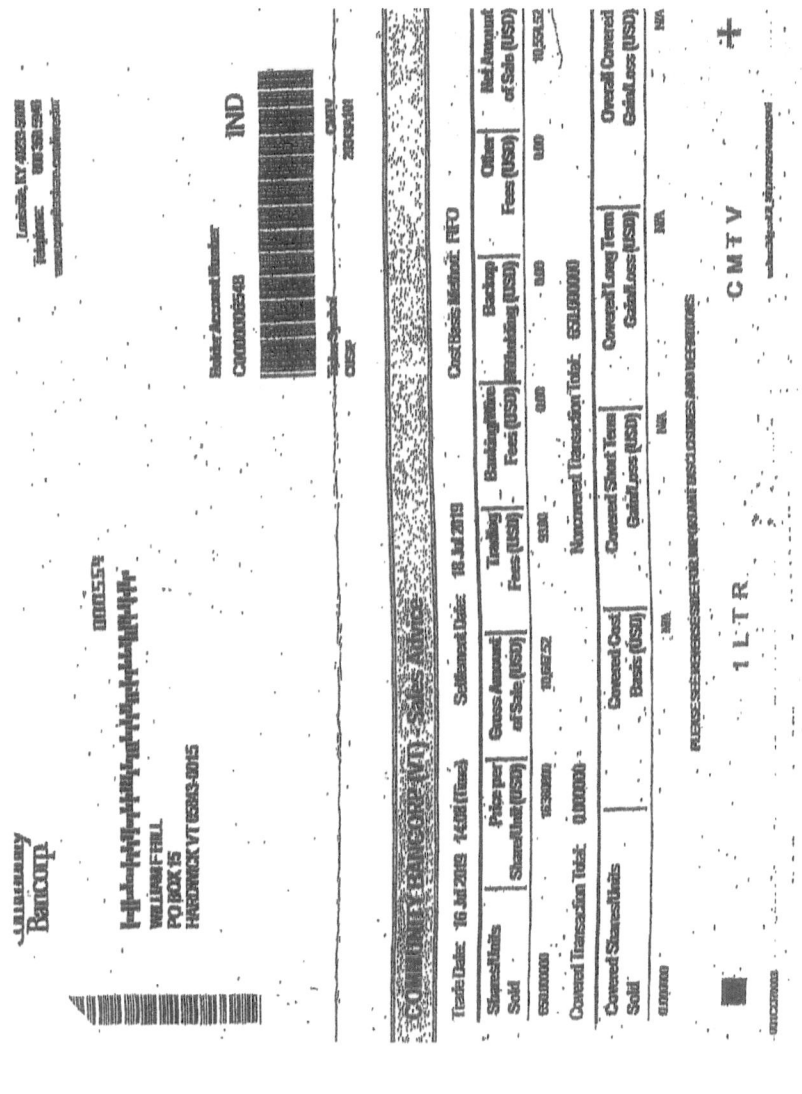

William F. Hill
P.o.BOX 15 Hardwick, Vt. 05843 P.O. Box 15
802-472- 6308.   30 August. 2019

Dear Vince,

Just received another bill from you. When we first started talking about what to do about Olson. You suggested that you could get back my eight thousand dollars. Which Olson had already agreed to pay back seven thousand. You said that you could get back the money that I had paid for the property on Dutton road by selling my Post Office which had been bringing in eight hundred dollars a month. You were going to recover all the rent that Olson had been receiving on my file estate. You were going to recover the money lost from my farming operation.

We agreed on an hourly rate for the work that you were going to do to accomplish all this. I haven't seen any result of any of this. You never have taken any depositions from Kelley, Ronald or any of the other people that we discussed. Instead you have allowed Olsons lawyer to supply all kinds of false testimony. From Ronald, Kelley, Olson and herself none of which was the truth.

You have contacted all kinds of people who really don't have any effect on Olson such as Vermont protective services, Caledonia home health the veterans service New Hampshire health division which only caused more problems. A couple of insurance companies but nothing to do with Olson.

You said that Leigh had given you a good statement which you said would help but then you started to ridicule her and run her down even though she was having a very hard time and trying to cope. You accused me of trying to help them survive I don't think you know what it takes to survive.

You have accused me of not being truthful with you several times which is a big lie. The money from the bank came just the way that I told you it would. Only Im going to use it to help Leigh and her family. Leigh is in a Boston Hospital where she had to have open brain surgery which took for two days and, she has had to been flown back down in an emergency helicopter for more treatment, she now has to have another surgery as the first didn't do the trick. I know that you could care less, but you ought to see what it is doing to her children You were unhappy that I paid for them to go to Colorado, but they brought Aaron back with them who is working six days a week, and really contributing to their needs.

YOU wanted me to deal with two different computer people that you contacted. I kept calling the first one and he kept saying that he would get back to me but never did. The second one even though I had a new computer said that I needed a different kind, the kind that he sold. This cost me over eight hundred dollars. Im taking some lessons on it not from him,I couldn't afford him, I can see that it is going to take a long time to learn, if ever.

You always wanted to meet in restaurants. Where I would have to pay for your meal. I didn't like meeting where all the customers and waitresses were trying to figure out what we were doing, and you said that it made you uncomfortable to come to my place. I can't imagine what you were afraid of.

You advised me to get another Attorney, which tells me that you could have had probably one to the best cases that you ever had. That I should be suing you. I haven't agreed to do this yet as I consider you a good friend and don't like law suites. It was suggested that you retire from trying to practice law, turn in your license, and get some counseling.

As Ever
William Hill
CC others

WILLIAM F. HILL
PO BOX 15
HARDWICK VT 05843
802-472-6308

AS I SAID MY WIFE SALLY AND I DID A LOT   BY HELPIG
RICHARD TARRENT TO TRY TO DEFEAT BERBIE SANDERS
BELOW IS A PICTURE OF   SALLY HOLDING A TARRANT BANNER IN
FRONT OF THE VOTING PLACE ON ELECTION DAY SHE WORKED
VERY HARD AND WAS THE ONLY ONE OUT THERE WE TRIED

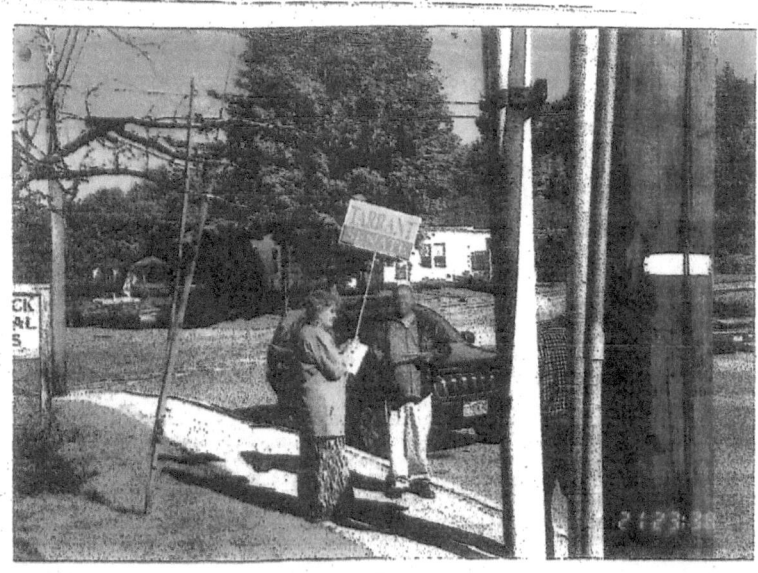

WILLIAM F. HILL

May 15, 2007

Copy

To: Richard M. Carter
U.S. Justice Department
Federal Building
Post St.
Burlington, Vt-05402

Dear Mr. Carter,

It has been over three years since you and many of your men broke
into our house, trashing it, tearing it, and even destroying
our childrens' grandchildrens' and great grandchildrens' Christmas
presents. You said that you would take care of repairing the door
and door casing which you remarked to get in. I have never seen any
repairs you. In your complaint you seize up of Cliff, who said that large
loads of marijuana could have been delivered to the large' house in
Hartford. Also Cliff, who said Aldrich paid $465,000 cash for this
residence. Both of these statements are false. I don't even know what
marijuana looks like and nor has it ever been here. Also, Ronald has
not even come close to paying us the $200.00 that he agreed to pay.

In number 14 of your complaint, you stated, "I am aware that
William F. Hill, in customer front Hartdale, Vermont was prosecuted and convicted in the United States District Court in this district for offenses related to large scale bank fraud schemes in which he
participated with Roger Lussier and other principals of Lyndonville
Savings Bank". This is no space true that that sort of your complaint.
I've never charged or convicted of anything to date I also have a
right to know Cliff and Cliff's are they make the false complaint.

The other thing which really bother me is the fact that when
you told have you took with you clever pickers of bills each containing $5,000 each except one which contained $5,800. This was a total
of $55,800. You refused to count it, saying that you were going to
take it to bank and have them count it. I did not hear anything for
several months. When I finally did hear, it was stated that there was

$46,800. This was nearly $8,000 short or one packet short. I want
to know what you did with that other $8,000. I do not feel that you
have been very fair to me in anything that you have done. This has gone
on long enough and I want some answers.

Sincerely,
William F. Hill

William F. Hill
P.o.BOX 15 Hardwick, Vt. 05843 P.O. Box 15
802-472- 6308.   30 August, 2019

Dear Vince,

Just received another bill from you. When we first started talking about what to do about Olson. You suggested that you could get back my eight thousand dollars. Which Olson had already agreed to pay back seven thousand. You said that you could get back the money that I had paid for the property on Dutton road by selling my Post Office which had been bringing in eight hundred dollars a month. You were going to recover all the rest that Olson had been receiving on my life estate. You were going to recover the money lost from my farming operation.

We agreed on an hourly rate for the work that you were going to do to accomplish all this. I haven't seen any result of any of this. You never have taken any depositions from Kelley, Ronald or any of the other people that we discussed. Instead you have allowed Olsons lawyer to supply all kinds of false testimony. From Ronald, Kelley, Olson and herself none of which was the truth.

You have contacted all kinds of people who really don't have any affect on Olson such as Vermont protective services, Caledonia home health the veterans service New Hampshire health division which only caused more problems. A couple of insurance companies but nothing to do with Olson.

You said that Leigh had given you a good statement which you said would help but then you started to ridicule her and run her down even though she was having a very hard time and trying to cope. You accused me or trying to help them survive I don't think you know what it takes to survive.

You have accused me of not being truthful with you several times which is a big lie. The money from the bank came just the way that I told you it would. Only im going to use it to help Leigh and her family. Leigh is in a Boston Hospital where she had to have open brain surgery which took for two days and, she has had to been flown back down in an emergency helicopter for more treatment, she now has to have another surgery as the first didn't do the trick.

I know that you could care less, but you ought to see what it is doing to her children You were unhappy that I paid for them to go to Colorado, but they brought Aaron back with them who is working six days a week, and really contributing to their needs.

YOU wanted me to deal with two different computer people that you contacted. I kept calling the first one and he kept saying that he would get back to me but never did. The second one even though I had a new computer said that I needed a different kind, the kind that he sold. This cost me over eight hundred dollars. im taking some lessons on it not from him,I couldn't afford him, I can see that it is going to take a long time to learn, if ever.

You always wanted to meet in restaurants. Where I would have to pay for your meal. I didn't like meeting where all the customers and waitresses were trying to figure out what we were doing, and you said that it made you uncomfortable to come to my place. I can't imagine what you were afraid of.

You advised me to get another Attorney, which tells me that you could have had probably one to the best cases that you ever had. That I should be suing you. I haven't agreed to do this yet as I consider you a good friend and don't like her selline. It was suggested that you retire from trying to practice law, turn in your license, and get some counseling.

As Ever
William Hill.
CC others

... renovations in Hardwick. LHP Executive Director Jim Lovinsky is in the background.

Housing Nonprofits 'Celebrate Hardwick'

by Doug McClure

HARDWICK — On Thursday, October 24, the Lamoille Housing Partnership (LHP) and Housing Vermont (HVT) hosted a gathering at the Scale House restaurant to celebrate the nonprofits' latest completed work on three Hardwick Buildings. The Jeudevine Housing renovation project cost $4.45M, according to the LHP's Kevin Lohn. The largest of the three renovation projects was 9 South Main, formerly the Kimball Block and current home to the Clip Joint and seven rental apartments. Included in the restoration was a six-unit, circa 1900 property on Highland Ave. and a five-unit building from the late-1800s/early-1990s on Slapp Hill Road. Along with previously restored housing at Bemis Block, properties on Cherry Street and Maple Street, and the newly-constructed Evergreen Manor, Lamoille Housing now offers more than eighty units of affordable housing in Hardwick.

LHP Board of Trustees Chair David Ford spoke of the LHP's larger goal as "community development," of which the Scale House was also a beneficiary. This past spring, the Preservation Trust of Vermont awarded $65,500 to the restaurant for upgrades through the LHP as a

part of its ongoing renovations to the Bemis Block, where the restaurant is housed. The Bemis Block, which is managed by LHP, has 14 units of residential housing for the elderly and disabled; the Scale House is a commercial tenant in the building. Lohn clarified that for the day's event the Scale House "was a paid venue, paid for by the owners."

Among those speaking were Sen. Jane Kitchel (D-Caledonia) of Danville, who said that Hardwick has undergone "such a transformation" since she first visited the town in 1967. She credited LHP and HVT for the role they have played in the town's evolution. Kitchel, who is chair of the appropriations committee, said "the need is enormous for housing that is safe and affordable," and added that "there is lots more to do."

LHP Executive Director Jim Lovinsky described Hardwick as a "fabulous metropolis," and said LHP has been on the ground since 1993, when a massive fire destroyed two large buildings in the Village. Along with HVT, Lovinsky said LHP brought their resources to bear on the rubble of the Kimball Block, rebuilding it in the 1990s and updating it in the latest round of renovations. Lovinsky said renovators took care to preserve the historical

See HOUSING, 7

Town of Buys Yel

by Alison Low

HARDWICK — The Town of Hardwick has acquired the building that formerly housed the Greensboro Garage on Route 15, commonly referred to as the "Yellow Barn." The site was purchased from the 1781 Group LLC, which acquired it from the previous owners of the Greensboro Garage as part of a plan to develop the site as an agribusiness accelerator and corporate campus. The purchase was made possible by a $250,000 grant from the Northern Border Regional Commission and funds from the town's own Economic Development Revolving Loan Fund. According to a press release from the town, "the Hardwick Yellow Barn Business Accelerator and Corporate Campus will strengthen Vermont's farm- and food-based economy by allowing multiple establishments to grow and expand with other entrepreneurs, develop new products, and improve export to external markets."

The project is a public-private collaboration involving multiple agencies including Hardwick municipal officials, the CAE, Northeastern Vermont Development Association, Vermont Agency of Commerce and Community Development, Northern Forest Center, Vermont Economic Development Authority and a variety of local business leaders. The Yellow Barn Team has also been working with Coe + Coe Architecture on the project.

Testy Board Meeting on Water Tests Puts Gavel To Use

by Will Walters

CABOT — The Oct. 22 select board meeting on municipal water quality test results that showed barely-detectable levels of a contaminant resulted in chair Fred Ducharme's repeated call to order, complete with gavel pounding and ordering a resident to be

are also found in dental floss, pizza boxes, popcorn bags and even "dust in the house," which has tested for 10,000 to 50,000 parts per trillion.

In her role as water superintendent, Goodrich provided copies of test results, information about the tests conducted for the town and links to state websites with

the topic of the test results, but Goodrich did not yet have all the information ready. At the Oct. 22 meeting additional information was provided. Miller said that the information provided was for PFOAs and not for GenX substances. Miller said "there is no analytical analysis standard for

3
14 20-22

WILLIAM F. HILL

PO

BOX 15

HARDWICK, VT 05843

802

472 6308

Dear David Bossie

You are right what has happened the past few years was no exception. The Government has destroyed me and my family. It has caused the death of my wife, my brother and am not sure what is doing to my Grand daughter. They have taken our home my business and everything else that they could get their hands on I would like you to tell me what I did wrong

If you are interested I have enclosed a couple of documents to show what a mess that we have gotten into only by trying to help the Government and others to improve their lives. A few years ago during the bank scandal the government was looking for people that they could try to implicate for anything that they could. I was doing quite a bit of business with people and the local banks trying to help others. Anyway they picked on me but for no reason at all. They have never given up and still find ways to disrupt our lives

    I am not trying to bother you but if you knew what they have done to me and my family you might understand I have plenty   more documents but am not trying to bombard you with all of them   My papers might not make since to you but I am going to try. Thanks for trying to understand

            Sincerely

                  William f. Hill ..

William F. Hill
P O Box 15
Hardwick Vt.05843
802-472-6308

Enclosed material shows some of the tremendous losses that we have taken with Ronald Aldrich and Sven. Olson. We have lost in excess of $300,000. Due to the dishonest tactics of Ronald Aldrich and he could care less. I never thought that he could be that dishonest. Sven Olson has been even more dishonest. As a result of his dishonest dealings I have lost my Wife. my. Grand children. My home that I spent a lifetime; to build and pay for. All my business and. All my money everything that I have worked a. Lifetime to provide for my self and family This has almost driven me insane I had written a book called. WHERE IS THE JUSTICE?. When. I wrote it it was a very good seller.

With all. The new problems I had planed to continue the book. There would be at least a couple more chapters. With all the stress this has cause me I can't seem to. Write any more for the book. So I have enclosed a bunch of notes that I would have used. to continue the book I just can't, seem to do it. There are to many new problems. to. Be able.Finish what. I had started. Im sorry about this but I just can't. Seem. To Do it any more

We do have a lawsuit. Going on against Sven Olson But I don,t feel that my lawyer has the same goal that we should have. He has been fighting to Get the property back. For my life estate Everything that was there is now gone and ruined. I don't want. The place back now that everything is completely destroyed. And there is nothing left certainly not even one good memory. I don't even want to go there It is so sad It has destroyed. Me my Wife and ruined my Great Grand Childrens. Lives What a sad waste of young lives that were finally getting on the. right tract. doing the best that they can do by having to live over in New Hampshire It has. been. My dream and life goal to help them to grow up and have a good life by being good. Hard. Working honest. citizens Ive always wanted a good home for them. And worked night and day to provide IT

I. feel that this should be a legal case due , to. all the dishonest and careless behaveror. Certainly the place should be inspected for any. violations of any kind. Bed and breakfast laws. Fire code. And zoning violations. Illegal. activities When I owned. rental or income property I was checked quite often

I don't want be a trouble maker but that the state should inspect Olsons restaurant on main street in Hardwick. I understands that it may have been temporarily closed for some reason. I believe that when you send some one to check all these places that it would be wise to send more than one person My attorney asked me to go up and check things out. Even though I have a life lease and Olson doesn't even belong there he and a couple of other men through me out and told me not to come back unless brought the police with with me I haven't. Been able to get my attorney to go any where near place. There are some bad things happening in Hardwick I don't belive that any restaurant can survive and pay rent and meet expenses serving only three meals a week. I certainly hope that you will look into this very bad mess very soon. Right is right and wrong is wrong. and don't. See much right here

I. am. Sorry for this. mess and the. Problems that it. Has caused. It is my grand children lives and future that I am sick about. I don't know what. To do

Thank you

WILLIAM F. HILL

WILLIAM F. HILL
PO BOX 15
HARDWICK VT 05843
802 472 6308

OCTOBER 9, 2020

MR THOMAS FITTON
JUDICIAL WATCH
425 THIRD STREET
SUITE 800
WASHINGTON D.C. 20024

THANK YOU FOR YOUR CALENDAR. I READ ALL YOUFR MAIL AND
TRY TO FOLLOW WHAT YOU ARE DOING
    I AM VERY EXCITED ABOUT WHAT YOU ARE DOING.   WE NEED
ALL THE COMMON SENCE VALULE PEOPLE WE CAN GET I HAVE
WORKED VERY HARD ALL MY LIFE FIGHTING FOR THE
CONSERVATIVE CAUSE MY DAD ALWAYS PREACHED THAT, YOU
NEED TO LEAVE THE WORLD A BETTER PLACE AND THINK THAT I
NAVE ALWAYS TRIED TO DO THAT
I HAVE ENCLOSED A FEW OF THE PROBLEMS THAT I HAVE HAD TO
CONTEND WITH. I HAVET LOT RESPECT FOR OUR ,PRESIDENT
DONALD TRUMP. A LOT OF THINGS THAT HE HAS I HAVE DONE I
DID SIMULAR ONLY ON A SMALL SCALE. I HAVE OWNED OVER SIX
HUNDRED PROPERTIES INCLUDING HOMES FARMS AND
BUSINESSES NOW THANKS TO THE GOVERNMENT I HAVE NEXT TO
NOTHING
    WHEN I GOT OUT OF THE ARMY IN 1958 I HAD ALREADY
MADE UP MY MIND THAT I NEEDED TO WORK HARD IF WAS GOING
TO AMOUNT TO SOMETHING. I ALWAYS WORKED VERY HARD AND
HONESTLY AND WANTING TO HELP OTHER PEOPLE TO GET AHEAD
AND HAVE GOOD PRODUCTIVE LIVES. I ALWAYS PREACHED THIS

TO MY CHILDREN AND GRAND CHILDREN AND GREAT GRAND CHILDREN THIS WENT WELL UNTIL THE GOVERNMENT DIDN,T LIKE TO SEE ME TRYING TO HELP SOME LESS FORTUNATE PEOPLE TO GET AHEAD. I WAS TOLD THAT POOR PEOPLE SHOULD STAY POOR... AND THAT I SHOULDN'T BE HELPING THEM I GUESS THAT THIS WAS SO THAT THE LIBERALS COULD CONTROL THEM AND COULD CATER TO THE DISHONEST SUPPORT OF PEOPLE LIKE OLSON AND HIS LAWYER WHO WAS VERY VISCOUS . AND DISHONEST SHE HAS DONE EVERY DISHONEST THING THAT SHE CAN

SALLY, MY WIFE, GOT A GOOD JOB WORKING FOR THE UNIVERSITY OF VERMONT EXTENSION SERVICE TEACHING AND HELPING LOW INCOME PEOPLE. SALLY CAME FROM VERY POOR FAMILY AND NEVER HAD A CHANCE TO GO TO SCHOOL. IN ORDER TO GET THE JOB SHE HAD TO LEARN TO READ. IN A HURREY, SHE IS ALWAYS VERY AMBITIOUS AND WOULD NOT GIVE UP UNTIL SHE LEARNED; SHE REALLY EXCELLED IN HER JOB

IN A FIFTY YEAR PERIOD I CONDUCTED SEVERAL HUNDRED AUCTIONS OF MANY KINDS AND ALWAYS WAS ANXIOUS TO JUMP IN WHERE EVER I SAW AN OPPORTUNITY I HAD SEVERAL BUSINESSES AND WORKED HARD ALL THE TIME

AS I EXPLAINED I GOT IN TROUBLE BY HELPING OTHERS. I THINK I WAS WELL RESPECTED FOR THE THINGS THAT I DID AND WAS ASKED MANY TIMES TO FURNISH A HELPING HAND WHICH I USUALLY DID . I HAVE BEEN WANTING TO WRITE ANOTHER CHAPTER FOR MY BOOK WHERE IS THE JUSTICE. DUE TO ALL MY PROBLEMS WITH THE GOVERNMENT,, A COUNTY JUDGE AND MY AGE I THINK THAT I WILL HAVE TO FORGET ABOUT DOING IT

THANK YOU

BILL HILL

WILLIAM F. HILL
PO BOX 15
HARDWICK, VT. 05843
802-472-6308

CALEDONIA CIVAL COURT
1126 MAIN STREET SUITE 1
ST, JOHNSBURY, VT. 05819

DOCKET # 235-10- CACV

DEAR COURT
     I DON,T UNDERSTAND HOLDING ANOTHER HEARING FOR
THIS CASE. IT ONLY DRAGS THINGS OUT AND ALLOWS OLSONS
LAWYER TO FILE MORE FALSE CLAIMS
I AM ASKING THE COURT AND JUDGE TO HOLD A FINAL TRIAL
PRIOR TO JANUARY 11 2021. THIS CASE HAS TAKEN AND
DESTROYED LIVES, PROPERTY AND WILL ONLY CONTINUE TO DO
SO. THE COURT HAS PLENTY OF INFORMATION TO AWARD
HONEST DECISIONS THAT WILL SETTLE THIS TERRIBLE
SITUATION. IT IS VERY UNFAIR TO CONTINUE TO TAKE PROPERTY
AND TORTUE PEOPLE JUST BECAUSE YOU CAN. I AM LOOSING
MY EYES AND THE USE OF MY FEET AND WILL BE HARD TO GET
TO COURT
     I AM ASKING AND DEMAND THAT THIS COURT AND JUDGE
WHO HAS ALL THE FACTS DO THE HONEST THING AND AWARD
THE PEOPLE THAT IT HAS DESTROYED THEIR DUE JUSTICE.
THERE IS NO WAY TO COMPENSATE THE POOR PEOPLE THAT
YOU HAVE CAUSED TO SUFFER AND LOOSE THEIR LIVES IN THIS
DISHONEST MESS . I WILL BE LOOKING FOR YOUR DECISION TO
DO THE HONEST THING. RIGHT OFF..

     PS OLSON HAS NOW REMOVER LEIGHS MOBILE HOME
FROM THE PROPERTY

WANTING TRUE AND

HONEST JUSTICE

WILLIAM F. HILL

I had been cooperating with them and that every body who cooperated with them had to plead guilty to something   I couldn't believe him I had answered their questions No body had ever said anything about cooperating

Hersh told me to go Jimmy Carrol a Rutland attorney   Carrol told me that I was going to have to do what the government wanted there was no way of excaping them He then told me not to trust John Hersh or any body else that was connected with him   Carrol wanted me to pay him ten thousand dollars and agree to plead guilty to any charge that the government might come up with If I didn't want to plead guilty and fight it he wanted one hundred thousand dollars and told me that there was no way that I could win against the government and Judge Billings   I didn't hire Carrol I contact several other lawyers all didn't want anything to do with the government and they all told me not to trust the government but that I had better cooperate with them I did finally hired Peter Langrock who I understood was very good He had to have ten thousand dollars first Peter seemed to know the government and get along with them to well I thought   He kept telling me that I would have to plead guilty to some thing

After a while the government came up with a charge for me to plead guilty to They wanted me to plead guilty to making a false statement on a loan application Which I had never made   First I had to go before a grand Jury I told Langrock that I couldn't;t possibly plead guilty   to making a false state as this was not true I didn't want to do it but Langrock said that I had no choice I didn't want to do but Langrock took me into the court room where I finally said that I was guilty which I was *not* Hersh had told me not to worry about pleading guilty that nobody would never know about it and I would never get more than three months probation This was a lie as soon as I got off the stand I was taken around and finger printed When I finally got out of the court house The sky lit up there were cammers and news reporters every where The next day all the news papers and and news station had it all plastered from Boston to the Canadian border they kept my name in the news and print everything that the government was feeding them most which was un true   When my

475

WILLIAM F. HILL
PO BOX 15
HARDWICK VT 05843
802-472-6308

HON RPBERT R. BENT
CIVAL DIVISION COURT
DOCKET NO 235 100 18 CAV
SUPERIOR COURT
1126 MAIN STREET SUITE 1
ST. JOHNSBURY VT. 05819\

DEAR JUDGE BENT

I M SENDING YOU A FEW ODD NOTES THAT THAT I HAVE
COLLECTED AND PLANNED TO USE IN WRITING ANOTHER CHAPTER
TO MY BOOK WHERE IS THE JUSTICE. I KNOW THAT YOU WILL
NOT LOOK AT THEM AS I AM NOT A LAWYER.. AS YOU MUST KNOW
MY FAMILY HAS BEEN .COMPLETLY DESTROYED MY WIFE IS
DEAD MY BROTHER ;DAN HILL; HAS LOST HIS LIFE. YOU HAVE
DRIVEN US ALL FROM OUR HOME AND WAY OF LIFE WHICH WE ALL
WORKED HARD TO PRESERVE AND HELP OTHERS. MY GRAND
DAUGHTER AND ALL OF US WERE DRIVEN OUT OUR HOMES BY
YOU' AND OLSON WHEN THEY GOT TO NEW HAMPSHIRE THEY
ALL WORKED HARD AND TRIED TO MAKE SOME NEW FRIENDS.
THEY GOT INTO TROUBLE WITH SOME OF THE WRONG PEOPLE.
WHO HAVE BEEN ABLE TO DESTOY THERE ALREADY UNHAPPY
LIVES. NOW I AM HAVING TO TRY TO HELP THEM AND PAY FOR
COUNCLING AND DRUG TREATMENTS FOR THEM THANK YOU A
LOT I CAN,T BELIVE THIS
I CANT BELIEVE THAT YOU KNEW OR HAVE EVER MET ANY
OF THESE PEOPLE THE ONES WHOSE LIVES THAT YOU HAVE
TRIED TO CONTROL OR HAVE DESTROYED HOW COULD YOU DO
THIS. YOU LISTNED TO OLSONS LAWYER WHO DIDN;T KNOW
THEM EITHER
I HOPE THAT YOU ARE VERY HAPPY WITH THE DECISIONS
THAT YOU HAVE MADE . I N YOUR DECISION YOU STATE THAT WE

ARE STILL TO BE COMPENSATED FOR OUR SHARE OF WHAT WE LOST, THE PROPERTY THAT YOU GAVE TO OLSON AND HIS LAWYER. I HAVENT SEEN YOU DOING ANY THING TO BRING THIS ABOUT I EXPECT THAT IT WILL BE EASIER TO WAIT UNTIL I AM DEAD AND THEN YOU CAN SWEEP IT ALL UNDER THE RUG

HOW DO YOU PUT A VALUE ON THE LIFE OF MY WIFE CHARLOTTE MY BROTHER DAN HILL, THESE WERE VERY HONEST HARD WORKING PEOPLE WITH FAMILIES THE DESTRUCTION OF MY GRAND DAUGHTER AN HER BEAUTIFUL CHILDREN AND WHAT YOU HAVE DONE TO THEM. LOOK WHAT HAS HAPNED ME AND MY MANY LONG YEARS OF HARD WORK AND ALL THE PEOPLE THAT I HAVE HELPED PLUS THE PROPERTY THAT YOU AND OLSON HAVE DESTROYED

JUST AS AN EXAMPLE OF JUST ONE OF THE SAD THINGS THAT JUST HAPNED. WHEN WE ALL LIVED HERE THE GIRLS WERE RASING ANIMALS AND PLANNING TO HAVE A VERY GOOD LIFE BY ALWAYS BEING VALUE PRODUCERS AND NOT VALUE DESTROYERS' THEY NOW HAVE SOME DUCKS, BUT NO PLACE TO KEEP AND RAISE THEM....THEY HAVE BEEN TRYING TO KEEP THEM IN A SHED. DUCKS NEED WATER TO SURVIVE AND DO WELL. WHEN WE LIVED ON OUR OWN PLACE WE HAD A BEAUTIFUL POND WHICH I HAD BUILT AND WAS PERFECT FOR DUCKS WE ALWAYS HAD ENJOYED HAVING DUCKSS NOW UNABLE TO SEE THE DUCKS WHOSE IS BEING DESTROYED THEY HAVE HAD TO GET RID OF THEM RATHER THAN SEE THEM BEING ABUSED BY HAVING TO DESTROY THEIR LIFESTYLE VERY UNHAPPY CHILDREN. DO THEY DESERVE THIS!? I GUESS THAT THIS DOSE,NT MATTER TO YOU

I KNOW THAT I DON;T HAVE MUCH LIFE..LEFT AND I AM REALLY CONCERNED ABOUT THE YOUNGER MEMBERS OF MY LIFE WHICH I HAVE TRIED HELP AND INFLUENCE TO BE GOOD CITIZENS AND CONTRIBUTE TO OUR WAY OF LIFE

THE ONLY REASON THAT I HIRED VINCE ILLUZZI WAS I WAS TRYING TO WORK OUT A DEAL WITH OLSON WE WERE TRYIG TO AGREE ON SOMETHING. OLSON TOLD ME THAT HIS LAWYER WOULD GET BACK TO ME IN TWO DAYS. SHE DID AND TOLD ME THAT SHE COULD NOT TALK TO ME OR MAKE AY DEAL UNLESS I WAS REPRESENTED BY A LAWYER. AS YOU KNOW LAWYERS

LOOK OUT FOR LAWYERS AND THEIR POCKET BOOKS I TOLD
ILLUZZI ABOUT THIS AND ASKED HIM FOR HIS HELP. LLUZZI TOOK
RIGHT OVER AND CONTACTED ALL KINDS OF PEOPLE WHO I DON;T
THINK HAD ANY THING TO DO WITH THE SITUATION I COULDN,T
FIGURE OUT WHAT HE WAS TRYING TO DO EXCEPT CONTACTING
VARIOUS PEOPLE AND RUNNING UP A LARGE BILL. I DON,T THINK
THAT HE WAS ALL THERE. HE GOT EVERY THING WRONG AND
KEPT ACCUSING ME OF LIEING TO HIM WHICH I DIDN,T...THEN HE
QUITE AND I WAS NOT UNHAPPY

    AT THE DIRECTION OF THE COURT I HAD TO HIRE ANOTHER
LAWYER   WHICH I DON,T UNDERSTAND WHAT HE IS GOING TO DO
WHICH HE ALWAYS WANTS MONEY FOR

    A FEW YEARS AGO I PURCHASED A GRAVE LOT NEAR MY
FOLKS AND PLANED TO PUT A STONE ON IT.   I STLL HAVE THE LOT
BUT WILL NEVER PUT A STONE MARKER ON IT, I DON;T WANT ANY
ONE TO LOOK BACK REMEMBER THE LIFE THAT I HAVE LIVED FOR
ME AND MY FAMILY

    THANKS TO YOU RONALD, OLSON ,HIS LAWYER AND SATEN
YOU SHOULD ALL BE HAPPY

DECEMBER 24 0019

Hon Robert R. Bent
Civil Division Court
Docket No235 10 18 Cav
Caledonia
Superior Court
1126 Main Street Suite 1
St. Johnsbury Vt 05819

Dear Judge Bent

I cannot beleive the information that you just sent me I have sent you most of the information on what has taken place. certainly you didn,t look at the facts which I supplied. Every fact is the actual truth. You can,t say that about Olsons and his attorney of which there is very little truth. Bill Hill has paid all the property traxes up until this year at least two years after Olson took over and claimed owner ship. Hill paid all the property and fire insurnce until Olson convinced the insurance that Hill had nothing to do with the the insurance as he held title and was living there You state that I gave Olson the keys to the property when I had to move my wife out I did give him the keys not so that he could move in and take over but so that he could get his computer and his stuff out which didn,t belong in my house not for him to move in. Olson understood this. Instead He moved Kelley Lacourse in with him who had been homeless for quite a while. - she had abandon her Children and was staying in a horse trailer filled with hay and was heavy into drugs. Olson had Kelley doing all his dirty work for him plus charging her rent and he rented her a used car which as not inspected for 80 dollars a week. He made her work hard getting in wood and cleaning up after everybody and all their animals He really made a slave out of her . I thought there was a law against slavery in Vermont. Kelley finally found a way to excape from Olson and couldn,t leave fast enough. She wanted to write a complaint against Olson but due to all the problems and drugs she

479

didn,t dare to do it and hadn,t done it When Olson found about this he and his lawyer got right hold of her to change her mind How do you think that she got that Cadillac car I don,t think that Kelley wrote the complaint...looks more like Olsons lawyer did it and there isn,t a word or truth in it

I know that you were wiling to listen to all Olsons stories but disregarded what I reported as I didn,t have a lawyer I am 85 years old and have done business with thousands of people and I will chalange you to find one dishonest thing that I have ever done or any person that I have ever been untrueful with. This is the way that we were raised. I would like to here from you The way that you have got it is certainly not fair or true I hope that you will look at the real truth and get the facts straight I thought that was what Courts and Judges were supposed to do. I am looking for a truefull and fair solution to this horable mess which has cost me everything All for trying to help Ronald Aldrich, My wifes son, to improve his life and help all the family to benefit forever from my hard work I hope that you will be honest and we can settle this right the way it should be As I said Im no lawyer but I do beleave that I do know wrong from right

William F. Hill

What happened to Roger Stone is very tragic. And shows how careless and heartless our government can be. I know because what they did to him. They did to my wife and me much worse. The government had made it very plain that they didn't approve of the way that we were doing business by trying to make a living and helping others at the same time to get ahead. My wife came from very poor family and only learned to read and write after giving a job working for the Extension Service. She taught low income people to cook and take care of them she has received much praise for the work that she did. I had several businesses that I had started. One was buying foreclosed properties mostly from banks and fixing them up and improving them. I was selling these improved properties to people who couldn't get their own homes. I had very good credit and so was able to help them to get financing for their own home. And improving their lives.

The government didn't like us doing this. They didn't want us helping others the government told me that POOR PEOPLE SHOULD STAY POOR. The U.S. attorney and the FBI. Brought false charges against me and said that I had made a false statement on a bank loan at a local bank. I had never made such a false statement or even a loan application At any local bank

A few years. Ago got a call from Paul Gallimie president of Bradford Bank He said that Noel Lussier President of Caledonia. Bank and a large dealer in farms and farm property. Was at Bradford Bank to get a $250,000 loan but he was already up to his credit limit in Bradford Bank Paul said that the only way that he could make the loan was for Noel to put it against somebody else credit line Call Bill Hill Paul told him. They called me from the bank and cleared it with me and as I knew both of these men and. I knew that Lussier would soon pay back Bradford. I didn't go to the bank they brought a note to my house for me to sign and Lussier handled his own business soon paying the bank back as he had agreed Although I had done nothing wrong. And they all knew it I was charged with making false statement to get a bank loan. They took my real estate license and my auctioneers license. I had pay a ten thousand dollar fine and do one hundred hours of community service and made me a felon. I was later told by several other bankers that there was nothing wrong with this loan. It is what the cal a nomine. loan and is perfectly legal. I also heard of several other people using these same two bankers. To get nominie. Loans. several larger than the one that I was inolved in. Some of them were even paid for their participation. I received nothing non. Of them were even charged with anything

A while later we came back from having breakfast with a couple of friends to find our driveway filled with over thirty cars. We couldn't what was going on. Our front door was all smashed in and. There were over forty FBIs and marshalls. Our what ever they were in our house trashing everything Some with guns and wearing bullet proof vests. They were dumping all my files and anything else. That they could get their hands on My wife had come from Avery poor family and had never had much of a Christmas. Until we got on our feet. She now went Christmas shoping after Christmas to save money. She had over one-hundred presents all wrapped and tagged for all the Children, Grandchildren and Great Grandchildren. They had opened all the presents breaking many and strewing them all over. This really got on Sallys nerves to see them all destroyed. It didn't bother them. They could have carried less. Richard Carter the DEA agent in charge said that if I didn't openly my safe. That he was prepared to blow it up. When I opened it there. Were eleven packs of tgamty dollar bills. This would have made fifty five thousand dollars except I had taken twelve hundred dollar out ion one pack leavinG fifty three thousand eight hundred dollars total. Carter would not count it but said that he would take it to a bank and have them count it. They did not charge us for anything after doing all this damage as there was nothing to charge us with.

THE government decided to take over Ronalds equity in the place but leaving Sally and me our life estate and later said that they would give us back the money that CKarter had stolen from my safe. When we got the money back it was five thousand dollars less than what they had taken. I tried to find out where the other five thousand went but Carter or the nobody from. The government would talk about or give any answers. This is the way that the government works

C

WILLIAM F. HILL
PO BOX 15
HARDWICK VERMONT 05843
802 472 6308

February 13 2019

Law
Office of Kristina Michelsen
26 South Main Street
P.O Box 1304
Hardwick Vermont 5843

Dear Ms Michelsen

IM very sad to see what has happened to all the property of Our life estate There was no need for any of it The big green house which just fell in was in excusable I tried to help Olson from time to time but when he ordered me off the property and told me not to come back unless I brought the cops with me I stayed away even thought I still had a life estate there There was no need to loose this beautiful green house He should have known that it wouldn't stand the snow load I was afraid this would collapse and fall in if he didn't get the snow off If I had gone up there I could have saved it in about twenty minutes as I have done many times over the years All that you had to do was to turn on a switch that I had installed in the green house and it would take about twenty minute for all the snow to slide off

I can;t believe the damage and destruction since Olson has been running the place None of this ever happened when we were there

I have always tried to help the Olsons and I can;t believe that he can think of any time that I haven't tried to be helpful

I have lost my wife my home all my business and all the things that Sally and I have worked for and what it has done to our family I trusted Olson until I learned how dishonest and greedy that he could be and his involvement with Ronald

William F. Hill

WILLIAM F. HILL
PO BOX 15
HARDWICK VT 05843
802 472 6308

FBURARY 13 20

22
SUPERIOR COURT
DIVISION
CALEDONIA UNIT
235-10-18-Cacv

CIVIL

Docket No

Im probably waisting my time. I am not a very emotional person but I wanted to say something when I was in Court on the forth but I couldnt. When I walk into the
Court house the first thing that I see on the wall is a picture of my Wife and a picture of my Brother Dan Hill I am happy to have there but they have both lost there lives due to this mess I already know that I am licked. I have

already been told that any thing that I say will be discarded be cause I am not a lawyer But any thing that Olsons Lawyer presents is ok. I am assuming that woman there was Olsons Lawyer in the Court room although I had never met her and she dusted out so fast that never got a chance to speak to her. But she can feed the Court all kinds of false information and make up false statements for others and the Court laps it right up. because she is a Lawyer

I am enclosing another statement about Roger Stone and what happened to us which is much worse for us than Roger as he must have done something wrong and we never did. But being an insider his actions are being defended by President Trump and the United States Attorney. This Court and its false attorneys will for sure try to destroy us which you have aleeasy done a very good job of it

when I was there you gave me another paper frpm the Court and told me that I needed to get another Lawyer for what.? I did as you said and went to see a lawyer He said that he would take care of it for $500. All you care about is Lawyers and your aurhoriry I can;t take anymroe of it SORRY
t

Sincerely

Page 1 of 2

484

Charlotte J. "Sally" Hill, 77, of Hardwick died at home Tuesday, May 29, 2018 after a courageous five year battle with cancer. She was born April 20, 1941 the eldest of Clarence and Bertha (Johnson) Longley's seven children. Educated largely by life experience, Sally's motivation, ambition, optimism and warmth along with her unique personality served her well as a teacher for UVM Extension's Expanded Food and Nutrition Education Program. Sally's teaching of recipes, shopping tips, and the four basic food groups was coupled with lessons in self-respect, pride, and in making necessary changes in one's life. UVM recognized her abilities both at her retirement after 14 years and in their book, "100 Years of UVM Extension". Sally was well known for her extraordinary gift of caring for people in all walks of life

In 1984 Sally married William F. Hill in Orleans. Their life together included church, travel, and work whether on the farm, at auctions, in the greenhouse, in real estate, or selling beef at Farmers' Markets. Realizing a dream in 1990 they built a new house where they graciously welcomed family and friends into their home. Bill and Sally share 9 children, 26 grandchildren, 23 great-grandchildren and a wide circle of family and friends.

Always generous Sally has donated her body to the University of Vermont Medical Center for education. Students call this gift "The Greatest Teacher".

A CELEBRATION OF LIFE is planned for Friday, June 22, 2018 at 11:00 AM at the United Church of Hardwick, 216 S. Main Street / Rt. 14, Hardwick, VT. After the remembrance, lunch will be served in the church dining hall. (handicap accessible from outside)

In lieu of flowers, contributions in memory of Charlotte "Sally" Hill may be sent to the Lamoille Area Cancer Network, 198 Farr Ave., Morrisville, Vt 05661.

> When tomorrow starts without me
> Don't think we're far apart
> For every time you think of me
> I'm right here – inside your heart.

Lost 8

Gwy

The last couple of months she couldn't eat and keep anything down she was starving but I kept trying to fix anything that she would be able to eat The Doctors couldn't seem to help especially with her bloating all the time I guess that you would really say that she starved to death It was very sad

She was very upset about leaving her home which she had worked so hard to help design and worked hard to furnish it This she had done for all of us her family friends and took great pride in what she had accomplished She wanted this to stay in the family for generations to come, and Ronald had agreed to do it Sadley this didn't happen,. She couldn't stand it when she saw Olson tearing down all the walls ceiling and destroying all that she had worked so hard for and received many great and beautiful comments for This was the last straw She continually went down hill after this I tried everything that I could think of to try to comfort her right up till the night that she passed away

She didn't want a funeral but a memorial service She wanted the University of Vermont to have her body for research and study

Several of her very good friends. put on an excellent service and a very good meal for her at the United Church in Hardwick attended by around two hundred friends and family.

I couldn't believe that we did not hear a thing from Olson and his family: no calls no cards they didn't even show up at the Memorial service Very sad after what they have done to her

STATE OF VERMONT

SUPERIOR COURT
Caledonia Unit

CIVIL DIVISION
Docket No. 235-10-18 Cacv

William Hill,
    Plaintiff

v.

Sven Olson,
    Defendant

ENTRY ORDER

FILED
OCT 26 2020
VERMONT SUPERIOR COURT
CALEDONIA UNIT

In this case the court has previously ruled in favor of Defendant, Sven Olsen, granting summary judgment against William Hill on the issue of whether Hill's life estate in property owned in fee by Olsen had been extinguished. Hill did not file responsive documents to the motion.

Following that decision which issued December 16, 2019, Hill filed various pleadings which the court interpreted as a motion to reconsider. Because of the nature of the proceeding by which judgment had been granted, ie: summary judgment, the court allowed more time for response and recommended Hill consider hiring counsel.

Hill had initially been represented by counsel when he commenced the action seeking to oust Olsen from his occupancy in the property at issue. At about the time the motion for summary judgment was filed his attorney withdrew. The court subsequently heard from another non-admitted attorney who represented he was representing Mr. Hill in other matters. The court invited his participation in a status conference with assistance from local counsel. At that Status conference no local counsel was available thus the court did not hear from out of state counsel.

The court had learned of some concerns raised by others for Mr. Hill's competence. In conversation with him during the status conference the court's concerns were sufficiently dispelled so as to proceed with the litigation process without a guardian being appointed for Mr. Hill or other protective steps being put in place. Mr. Hill appears able to hire counsel, but has chosen not to.

The court also requested Defendant's counsel to address the potential impact of one document filed by Mr. Hill, among a plethora of other documents, an affidavit of one Leigh Kidder. That document appeared to have been one Mr. Hill's prior counsel had developed and addressed in part the theory espoused by Hill in his complaint, that Olsen had forced Hill out.

The court declines to consider, in this context, the affidavit as establishing facts sufficient to either allow reconsideration of the grant of summary judgment. Simply put, the affidavit without accompanying argument and other evidence not in the record is insufficient for the court to hold other than it has held, that Hill and his wife, permanently moved from the property at issue and even if they had another intent, are estopped from asserting otherwise.

We. Can't take this any longer. Probably due to all the stress which has killed my wife Sally my Brother Dan and about finished the rest of us Leigh's has now developed some serious brain problems probably due to the over bearing stress caused by Seven Olson Now she has been flown by emergency. Helicopters to Boston where. She has. Had; brain surgery each time. We can't. stand Any more. This whole mess has destroyed us. all and you can;t believe what it is doing to her family

Thank You William F. Hill

WILLIAM F. HILL
P.O.BOX 15
HARDWICK, VERMONT 05843
802-472-6308

Sally Hill has always been a very active person liking all people and doing many things to bring them happiness Five years ago she started gaining weight and did not feel as good as usual She went to Hanover to the Dartmouth Hitchcock hospital where she was diagnosed with cancer One week later she underwent a major operation to try to remove the cancer Doctor Demers said that she felt that they removed most of the cancer cells and she felt that kemo would take care of the rest After several all-day kemo treatments her cancer count went down to almost nothing The problem seem to be that she was under a lot of stress and the cancer count shot back up to higher than it was before

She had to go back on kemo nearly every week Since then I have probably taken her to at least forty all day kemo treatments at the Dartmouth Hitchcock Norris Cotton Cancer Center I have had to take her to the Copley emergency room where they they spent several hours trying to help her but couldn't help her so sent her to Dartmouth Hitchcock in an ambulance in the middle of the night where she stayed for a while After getting her back home I had to continually take her to several hospitals for treatment I had to make several trips to St Johnsbury Hospital and to the North Haveral New Hampshire Hospital where they had to keep drawing fluid from her adman. One time I had to take her all the way to Hanover. There they told me that it was good that I got her there when I did as they said that she would not have lasted another day because she would have suffocated

You can't imagine what we went through to try to keep her alive and she really wanted to live for her family and all else She has already got all this years Christmas presents ready and wrapped and planed to have Christmas This July as she was sure that she would not make to another December Her present are all here and she didn't get the chance to give them out

William F. Hill

ANSWER TO SEVIN OLSON COMPLAINT. 22 June. 2019

11

8.Bill Hill dd not leave the place for good I needed to care of my wife Im sure that Olson would have done the. Same if it was his wife or family member and we would have stood behind him all the way trying to help

9. This litigation was instituted by Bill Hills attorney who thought that he should get the life lease back he filed a motion in Court last winter to get the lease back. and have Olson elicited from the property The Judge rulledled against it

10. Bill Hill only quoted only what was said by Ronald Aldrich

11 Ronald along with his brother Paul Lussier was involved in the illegal drug business. According acordingtoI the goverment

12. Not true I was not selling the book at this time

13. Not my fault

15I understand that this restaurant has been closed for the last several weeks

18. False Seven Olson told me that he knew where Ronald Aldrich was and wanted to be the one to pick him up and bring him hear. whitch he did. I don't see any thing wrong with this

19. Seven Olson told me that he knew where to pick up Ronald Aldrich. I didn't have any idea as to where he was I had heard somewhere in Massachuties

20. Sally and I liked Seven and his family and tried to make them welcome at any time. At times their kids were a little rowdy by that was only being kids

]]

William F. Hill

ANSWER TO RONALD ALDRICH COMPLAINT   22 Jan 20019

5. Agreed

6. Not before going to prison

7. Ronald was brought home from prision by Seven Olson who had told me that he knew   where Ronald was stationed and wanted to be the one to g0 and bring Ronald back here
I didn't think. thar Ronald had anything left here I thought the government had taken his interest
and sold it to SevenOlson
8. It was obvious as that Ronald and Olson were   aquainted Ronald;s family knew about   Olson. I don't know how they knew or what they knew

9. Not true Ronald came home with Olson

11 All I knolw is the statement that Ronald made concerning getting involved with Olson

12. See # Seven told me that he was planning to sell the property back to Ronald by setting up a thirty-five paid up lease
I never accused OLson of having anything do with drugs. His lawyer keeps bringing this up don't know wjhatshew knows

13. Ronald and Donna moved into the cellar and lived there for several weeks Ronalds family   often came. With his children and stayed Paul Lussier Ronalds brother was there every night meeting with.   Ronald   until late

14. Ronald or Donna never complained about the condition of the walls or property

15. Not true the house was eighteen years,old bur not rotted or peeling

16 The pool had not been cared for by Olson or Kelley PoOls require a lot of upkeep and maintenance. They had   neglected   to take care of the pool . still very usableThe pool was second hand when we put it in eighteen years ago
it was the same as it was when Olson bought it only they hadn't,t taken care of it

!7. The car port had settled a little in the center due to being eighteen years old. It was very usable we had used it every day m   m

18 The fences were built and installed by Ronald and his crew. Before he went to

491

prison. I was not in favor of   him   building them   as they don't last forever and soon rot out plus taking up a lot of land

19. The burner was a Jet Air very expensive and came Wirth four burners Sally only. wanted two   When Donna was living here with Ronald she   installed the other two   whitcx we had

20.He is right

21 Ronald had agreed to put up a small; home for his mother and me in exchange for giving him our home lands   business   It didn't look like Ronald was coming back to stay so we set up a place for LEIGH and her four children
Ronald and his brother Pauls family were very mean. To Leigh and her Children We had GIVEN Ronald a nice   home our I   land equipment and business. The government said   that just the real estate had a value of over   seven hundred thousand dollars. We had A. Life lease and had the rightto do with the place what we wanted I. gave.
Paul and Belinda their land and sugar place and put in there septic
system for them and charged   them nothing Think of the greed who did they think that they were not even a thank you

24. Leigh.s children were quite well behavd. They had had a very hard life and desearved a chance in as did   Ronald and PAUL. I never got as much as a thank you from either Paul or RonaldI guess that Paul and Ronald through
that they were privileged and Leighs Children weren't   I never gave thew combination to my safe to anyone

25 Ronaldis right we did lose a lot of money but it. Was not with Promise as he accuses. Never gave any one the   combination to my safe Sally had. Hid the combination but it was later determined that a girl that Kelley

brought here that we didn't.t know   found it. And was able to get into the safe. It had nothing to do with Promise or any
y of Leighs I don't understand   why they want to start stories and blame the. kids

26. Ronald had no business telling Leigh that they were not welcome at our house. Who did he think that he was

27 We were very unhappy to think that he would treat these children this way

28. Both Ronald and Paul refused to help Leigh and her children although I

asked them to help out. I sure helped   Paul and Ronald

29 We liked. Olson and his family but were surprised when Ronald announce
that he was picking Ronald   and. Bringing him here which he did   We did ntt even
know where Ronald was getting out of prison from

30. Seven came and went as he pleased and we had no problem with this

31. Olson. And his family did put on several big meals I whitch were very nice.
The. Only problem was that Ronalds   family family would have nothing to do
with Olson and his family, They would stay down cellar and not   associate in any
way   This made it very awkward. For Sally and me

32. Sally was very upset about Olson bringing in a unch of strangers   she was
under a lot of stress already I   believe that Ronalds talked Olson into not doing this.
Sally was pleased that Ronald did this for her

r33. Olson did bring in five or six big snow machines. He didn't,t tell 0r asked
me if it was ok His kids mostly rode them
        I didn't like this but had nothing   to do with this. Sally was a very upset as
people were telling her all   the problems
        that these snow machines could cause

34. Sally didn't,t know that we were moving at the time. With the rebate that we
were getting every year the taxes   were no higher than they are here on the
house where we live now

Sally was still getting up stairs ok and didnt want to stay down stairs. We moved
a bed down into the office at   suggestion of the home health nurse Sally wasn't
happy with this and had it moved back upstairs as soon as the   nurse was gone.
Sally was able to get upstairs and insisted. on being up there and I spent every night
with her

37 Olson didn't.take down the farm   sign. I did. But Olson told me
that hje would like keep it up there   so I put it back Since then he has. L et the
sign fall down or was knocked down and is still on the ground

38. Ronald didn't,t show. Up as he had agreed\

39. I told Ronald that I didn see where he could get into any trouble I told him to
answer all questions trufeully but he ran to the lawyer and lied about everything. He is
a lot more trouble by lying than he would be if he "+. *l* *-/, *) * *H*
41. Ronald knows that his mother his not a whiiner and does not complainae.
about anybody
   40. This is completely false
42. Sally was never left alone I slept with her every single day that she wasn't in
the hospital even the day that she   died. I was with her Ronald or Paul didn't do

42. Sally was never left alone I slept with her every single day that she wasn't in the hospital even the day that she   died. I was with her Ronald or Paul didn't do anything to help her not even to help her move

I think that part off that family problem is that Sallys first two husbands were not family orientated. and did not show the affection that kids need this made it very hard for Sally. She loved her kids and wanted them to have good lives She   always kept after me. To do anything that I could do to help them I felt the same way and always tried to make good   family out of all of them. Why do you think that I was anxious to take Ronald in to my farm business and give him to   a chance in life and make something of him self and his family I also gave Paul and Belinda there place so that they   could have a good life. There are several other members of that family that I have worked just as hard-too help.

I don,,t feel bad for helping them but I wish that they would appreciate it and been better too their mother

All I know is what

William F. Hill
P.o. Box i5
Hardwick, Vt 05843
802-472-6308-

MY Wife is dead My Brother is dead I dont know if my Grand Daughter is going to make it

MY Great Grand Children and all of us have been forced out of our homes and our lives destroyed. Some body should pay for this. Nothing will ever bring it back. Where do we go from here Lives have been destroyed, Our lives work and our family have been destroyed beyond repair and think of the lives that have been totally destroyed and the lifetime of hard work all destroyed by the dishonest greed of these people What is the court going to do WHERE IS THE JUSTICE. I am prayiING for some JUSTICE to prevail but we all know that nothing can ever overturn this mess

I am asking the Court to arrive at some type of deadline although they cant reverse what has happened Buy please bring this to a deadline even it can never recover or restore the damage that has been caused TIME IS OF ESSENCE What else can I say

William F. HILL
One of the few whose life has been destroyed

WILLIAM F. HILL

Bill Hill's book, Where Is The Justice?, was one of the most compelling books that I have ever read.

Reading this book gives you the feeling that you are sitting with Bill and Sally Hill and they are personally telling you their stories. It is written by them with true "Vermonter" flare.

Since reading the book I have had the opportunity to meet both Bill and Sally Hill. I can't help but wonder what God had in mind when he designed Sally Hill's life. She has overcome more obstacles in her life than any of us could even imagine. Regardless, she meets you at her door with an infectious smile that leaves you feeling warm and welcome.

When meeting Bill for the first time, the first question that I asked him was, "How did you manage to write this book without showing any bitterness?" His reply was that he wasn't bitter about what had happened to him, that wasn't why he had written the book, he just wants to make everyone in this country aware of what our own government is capable of doing to us.

I probably read 200 books a year. The only style of books that I don't care for are horror stories. Much to my amazement, at the conclusion of this book, I realized that I had just read one. This was probably one of the scariest books I have ever put my hands on. To think that our own government was capable of doing this to one of it's own. It would be easy to think this must be science fiction if it were not for all the documentation of the actions of the feds, lawyers and bankers.

The affect that this book had on my husband was incredible. I don't believe that he had read a book for more than 20 years. This is the first book I have ever seen him read. He could not put it down.

He went out and purchased copies for his parents as well as neighbors.

This is a must read book for everyone. We recommend everyone read this book!

God Help Us All!

Terri Gamble .
Former Federal Credit Union Employee

Terri M. Gamble

Garry Gamble
Independent Contractor

Garry Gamble

Walden VT

802 - 274 - 4601
802 - 563 - 2346

The person who purchased the subject property at substantially below its appraised value from the USA was Mr. Olson, who at that time was friends or acquainted with Mr. Aldrich. The property sold at below FMV because the Hills retained the life estate.

Mrs. Hill is in the final stages of cancer. She has been under a lot of stress for the past 20 years. First, Bill Hill was convicted in the 1990s of making a false statement on a bank loan application. As collateral consequences, Mr. Hill, at age 63, lost his real estate and auctioneer licenses, effectively putting him out of business. The Hills survived on Mr. Hill's previously accumulated savings and property and from farming the subject property.

Second, the Hills claim that Mr. Olson took steps to effectively force them off the property and stop them from farming. Mr. Olson would not allow them to raise crops on the property and he started remodeling the home on the subject property while they were living in it, claiming that the Hills were not maintaining the property.

The Hills claim that some personal property was stolen and other property vandalized. The Hardwick Police Department has not taken any action on Mr. Hill's complaints because he is a convicted felon and because they claim the personal property was "probably sold" by the USA to Mr. Olson.

The Hills around March 2017 purchased a relatively modest home in another section of Hardwick and moved out of the subject property.

Mr. Hill recalls you telling him that if he and his wife ever wanted to sell their life estate in the subject property, they should contact you. Thus, he asked me to write you this letter.

Mr. Hill is now 83 years old and his wife is not expected to live beyond the end of 2018.

Please let me know if the USA is interested in purchasing their life estate.

Thank you.

Sincerely,

Vincent Illuzzi

Enclosures

497

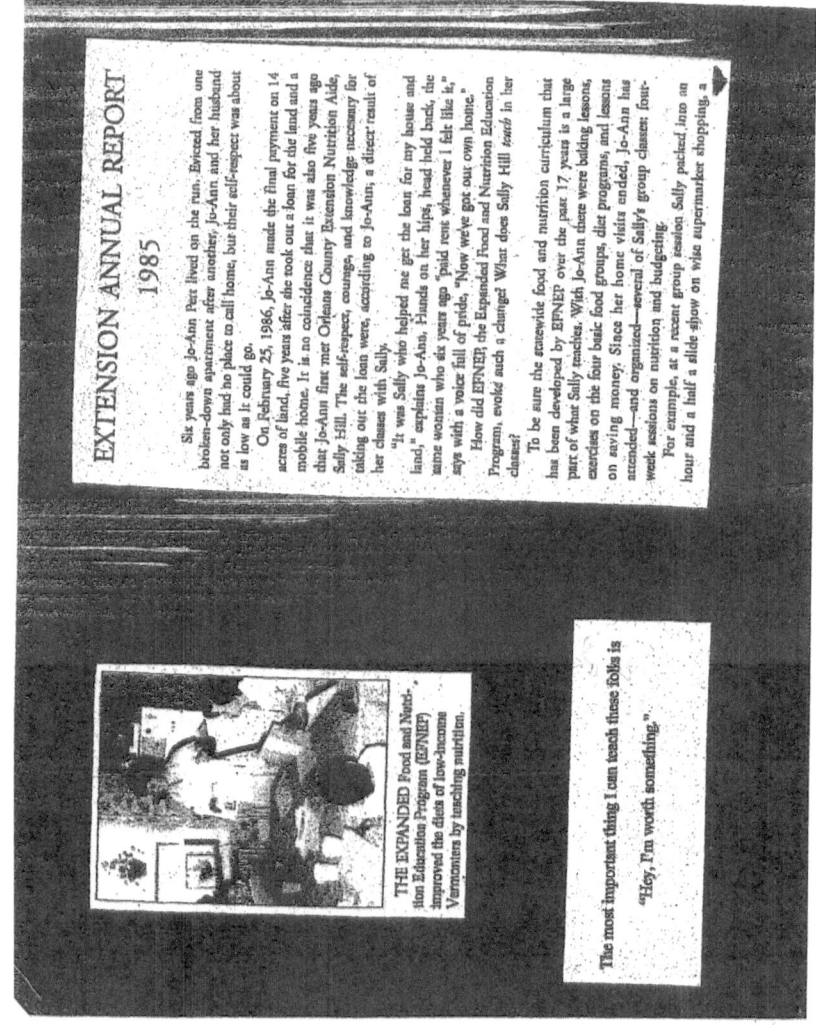

EXTENSION ANNUAL REPORT
1985

Six years ago Jo-Ann Perr lived on the run. Evicted from one broken-down apartment after another, Jo-Ann and her husband not only had no place to call home, but their self-respect was about as low as it could go.

On February 25, 1986, Jo-Ann made the final payment on 14 acres of land, five years after she took out a loan for the land and a mobile home. It is no coincidence that it was also five years ago that Jo-Ann first met Orleans County Extension Nutrition Aide, Sally Hill. The self-respect, courage, and knowledge necessary for taking out the loan were, according to Jo-Ann, a direct result of her classes with Sally.

"It was Sally who helped me get the loan for my house and land," explains Jo-Ann. Hands on her hips, head held back, the same woman who six years ago "paid rent whenever I felt like it," says with a voice full of pride, "Now we've got our own home."

How did EFNEP, the Expanded Food and Nutrition Education Program, evoke such a change? What does Sally Hill *teach* in her classes?

To be sure the statewide food and nutrition curriculum that has been developed by EFNEP over the past 17 years is a large part of what Sally teaches. With Jo-Ann there were balding lessons, exercises on the four basic food groups, diet programs, and lessons on saving money. Since her home visits ended, Jo-Ann has attended—and organized—several of Sally's group classes: four-week sessions on nutrition and budgeting.

For example, at a recent group session Sally packed into an hour and a half a slide show on wise supermarket shopping, a

THE EXPANDED Food and Nutrition Education Program (EFNEP) improved the diets of low-income Vermonters by teaching nutrition.

The most important thing I can teach these folks is "Hey, I'm worth something."

3/21/94

To whom it may concern,

With hope that someone who reads my letter will be be able to help Sally Hill.

On April 23,1992 I enrolled Sally as a student who wanted to upgrade her academic skills,especially to improve her reading. She was a vibrant enthusiastic person who wanted to study everything we were offering at Adult Basic Education. She studied hard and improved her reading skills to a higher level,five levels higher. Then,about the time the trouble with banks started,Sally slowly began to lose her ability to function as a viable student. She would forget which day I was coming to her home,and forget her homework. Then, last fall, I noticed how pre-occupied she became with her hair loss, which became noticable, especially to her. As hard as she tries Sally is not able to do her studies at this time because of the stress she is suffering because of the continuing bombardment of ills that never seem to stop. Every week that passes their is more.

Sally is doing everything that she can to keep herself together. She will continue to get my support. I hope there is someone out there who can legally help this person who has suffered enough. If not, I will suggest to her to go public. What else if there?

Sincerely
Polly Bisson
Polly Bisson

End of Chanpter 11

High Street
P.O. Box 535
Hardwick
Vermont 05843

(802) 472-3300

HARDWICK HEALTH CENTER

March 29, 1994

RE: Charlotte Hill
DOB: 3/20/41

To whom it may concern:

    I have had the pleasure of seeing Charlotte over the last few years and around October 1991 she had made mention to me the fact that she had noted she was losing some hair. I had suggested she consider seeing Dr. Janet Hinzman for an evaluation and Dr. Hinzman had diagnosed alopecia areatum and had suggested inter-lesional injections. There is no mention of her previously having any history of hair loss prior to October of 1991. She was experiencing significant stress around this time. It had also been suggested that she consider seeing Mental Health for support.

    In reviewing the record dating back to 12/29/86, there is no evidence of her ever having had alopecia areatum or any documentation of a stress disorder.

    Thank you for taking the time to review her case. If I may be of any further assistance please feel free to contact me.

Respectfully submitted,

Charles G. Butterick, PA-C

CGB/rmf

A UNIT OF
NORTHERN
COUNTIES HEALTH
CARE, INC.
P.O. BOX 388
ST. JOHNSBURY
VERMONT 05819

501

STATE OF VERMONT

SUPERIOR COURT
CALEDONIA UNIT

CIVIL DIVISION
DOCKET NO: 235-10-18 CACV

WILLIAM HILL
      Plaintiff,

vs.

SVEN OLSON,
      Defendants

AFFIDAVIT

Missing #17,18

NOW COMES Ronald Aldrich, duly sworn and under oath to state the following:

1. My name is Ronald Aldrich.
2. I reside at 512 Jay Road in Richford, Vermont.
3. I am the son of Charlotte (Sally) Hill and stepson of William F. Hill (Bill).
4. Bill and Sally sold me their home on Porter Brook Road in or about December 5, 2002. They retained a life estate.
5. I paid them $200,000 for the house.
6. I did not live at the premises after I bought the house.
7. I moved into the house when I was released from prison and on house arrest on or about February, 2015.
8. I had never met nor spoken to Sven Olson prior to being released from prison.
9. The first time I ever met or heard of Sven Olson was when I met him at the house after I had been released from prison when I was on house arrest.
10. I never had any relationship, business, or otherwise, with Sven Olson.
11. I have no information from any source that would indicate that Sven Olson is in any way involved with illegal drugs.
12. I have never indicated or suggested to Bill Hill that Sven Olson was in any way involved in business with me or was in any way involved with illegal drugs.
13. When I moved into the premises after being released from prison, the house and grounds were in terrible condition.
14. Bill had not been performing basic acts of maintenance. For example, there was a huge buildup of mold in the basement that had travelled up the walls and into the main floor walls and ceilings. Bill had taken no steps to address the mold.
15. The paint on the exterior clapboards was peeling and the wood was rotting.
16. The concrete of the pool was cracked in many places causing the walls of the pool to be weak. The liner was torn and leaky. The pool fence was broken. The pool was not usable in these conditions.

AFFIDAVIT

- 1

... property were rotten and falling down.

19. Only two of the burners on the kitchen cook stove functioned. Once of the ovens did not work.

20. Prior to my going to prison, I hired workers to maintain the premises, and they were in pristine condition. The place was beautiful.

21. While I was in prison, Bill told my significant other, Donna Hislop, who had my power of attorney, that she needed to sign some documents at the Town Clerk's office so that he could have some work done on the sewer at the premises. It turns out that what she signed was a permit application for placing a mobile on the property. She did not know that at the time and neither she nor I would have consented to putting a mobile home on the property because the place was so beautiful.

22. I learned that they had put the trailer on the property when I called my mother, Sally. She told me that they put the trailer there for Leigh, Sally's granddaughter, to live with her children. She told me that they would be gone when I came home.

23. Leigh and her family were still living in the trailer when I moved back home.

24. Leigh's children were ill-behaved, but beloved by Bill and could do no wrong in his eyes to the point that Bill gave the combination to the lock on his safe to Promise, who was 9 years old at the time.

25. Subsequently, money would come up missing from the safe and Promise was the only person he had given the combination to.

26. I told Leigh that her kids could not come over to the house any more.

27. This caused bad feelings with Bill and Sally.

28. The trailer always had trash all around it and at times it reached up the sides of the trailer. Bill called and asked me to help move the trash. I declined.

29. I was home about a week before I met Sven and his family. Up until then, Bill and Sally told me only good things about him.

30. When I lived there Sven and his family visited maybe three times that I remember.

31. My recollection is that they came to the house, Sven's wife went running, and Sven cooked a big dinner. They had some of their own kids and their friends with them. He was very polite about coming again. He did not want to be intrusive or be a bother. Bill made it very obvious that he wanted him to come over. They stayed overnight in the camper.

32. I told Sven at some point that a big Easter celebration would be too much for Sally. He was fine with that.

33. Then Sven brought some snow machines up to the house. I told Bill he shouldn't let the kids ride them because it was dangerous and they were unsupervised. Bill had no concern. He wanted Sven to be comfortable. Sven also was really nice to Leigh and her children, which Bill really liked.

34. Sally called me to tell me they were moving and they were really excited to be moving and that they should have done it years before. She said that the taxes were too high and she was having a hard time getting up and down the stairs.

AFFIDAVIT

- 2

35. Sally did not mention Sven Olson as one of the reasons she wanted to move.
36. Sally never told me that Sven acted in any manner that upset her. If she had I would have had a conversation with Sven.
37. Bill never told me that he had a problem with Sven until he called me after Sven took down the sign at the end of the driveway, which was well after Bill had already moved out.
38. Approximately 10 days ago, Bill called me and said "We need to get together to get our stories straight and get on the same page." He wanted me to go over questions related to his court case with Sven Olson.
39. I asked Bill why my name was in the papers. Bill said there is no way you can get in any trouble. He told me to answer all the questions.
40. After I moved out, I called Sally about once a week. I didn't visit the house because Sally told me Bill gave her a hard time about me because he didn't want to see me.
41. I spoke to her regularly and she never confided in me that Sven Olson was upsetting her or causing her to want to move out of the house.
42. She told me she wanted to move out because she was scared when she had to stay on the first floor because it had become too hard to get up and down the stairs because of arthritis in her feet. She was relieved and happy to be moving out.

Dated at Hardwick this 8th day of April 2019.

_____
Ronald Aldrich

Subscribed and sworn to before me this 8th day of April 2019.

_____
Notary Public

KRISTINA L. MICHELSEN
Notary Public, State of Vermont
Commission No. 0003405
My Commission Expires 1/31/21

AFFIDAVIT

– 3

NKMHS

Caledonia, Essex and Orleans Counties

NORTHEAST KINGDOM MENTAL HEALTH SERVICE, INC.

EXECUTIVE DIRECTOR

George Coulter

60 Broadview Avenue
P.O. Box 724
Newport, Vt. 05855-0724
Phone 802-334-6744

141 Railroad St.
P.O. Box 365
St. Johnsbury, Vt. 05819-0368
Phone 802-748-3181

March 25, 1994

Re: Charlotte Hill

To Whom It May Concern:

This woman sought services at our Community Mental Health Center in April 1992 and she has been seen at one or two week intervals since that time for individual counseling. She reports a long history of well respected employment for the Extension Service that ended with her planned departure in 1987. Ms. Hill was actively involved in teaching people in the community about nutrition and budgeting. She also participated in recordkeeping for auctions that her husband conducted. Additionally she was involved in her husband's real estate business and she actively pursued rehabilitating homes for eventual sale.

Approximately a year prior to her seeking our services she became distraught and overwhelmed by the significant financial problems she and her husband were experiencing. The burden of the legal and financial problems were such that Ms. Hill could no longer function at her previous level. She has had trouble with her short term memory, significant sleep disturbance, crying episodes, anxiety, worry and hair loss. As a result of these stressful circumstances Ms. Hill experiences a burning sensation on her scalp and she is gradually developing bald spots from the resulting hair loss. She is very distressed about these events. She applied for and was granted Social Security Disability benefits and she is disabled as a result of this stress and unable to be gainfully employed.

I am in hopes that this information will be of assistance to you in appreciating the impact that the legal and financial problems have had for Ms. Hill.

Sincerely,

Maureen McGuire, BSN
Psychiatric Nurse Practitioner

MM/all

Community Mental Health & Mental Retardation Services

505

William F. Hill

University of Vermont Extension Service
Human Nutrition and Foods Department
College of Agriculture and Life Sciences
Terrill Hall
Burlington, Vermont   05405-0148
Phone 802-656-3374

June 1, 1987

Dear Sally:

Thank you for your dedicated and valuable work in EFNEP over the past fourteen years. Your enthusiasm and excellent teaching have helped countless homemakers and families to manage better in all aspects of food and nutrition. Your examples and encouragement have helped many improve their lives.

Your ability to cooperate with other agencies has been of the highest quality and has spread and enhanced the reputation of the University of Vermont Extension Service.

I will personally miss your support and enthusiasm. You were, always ready to take on any new project, whatever it might entail. This is indeed a valuable attribute and is the ingredient needed to get things done! I appreciated it greatly.

My very best wishes go with you in whatever new endeavors you undertake. If I can be of any help, please ask.

On a personal note, our friendship, has been, and will continue to be, very important to me.

Very Sincerely,

Alice M. Wright
EFNEP Coordinator

W .F.HILL
P O BOX 15
HARDWICK VT. 05843
 802=472= 6308

    ENCLOSED WHAT I HAD WANTED TO DO.   HAVE OLSON
EVICTED FROM OUR HOME WHEE HE DIDN;T BELONG AND WAS
KILLING SALLY WHITCH SHE COULD;NT TAKE ANY MORE.   YOU CAN
SEE. WHAT. HAPNED NOTHING NEW. TAKE A LOOK

Thanks   Bill

b

In the late eighties we had been farming for many years with over three hundred milking cows, on Pumpkin Lane. I was working from two in the morning until after ten at night, seven days a week, and was getting very tired. I had a chance to sell our farm and everything that went with it. We had a large thirty acre hay field over on Porter Brook with nothing on it . I discussed with Charlotte (who was also known as Sally) building a very nice home there. I had always wanted to provide a good home for Charlotte, a place that all our large family, many of whom don't have very much, could enjoy.

We built a very large, old type farm house, utilizing much family labor. I planted maple trees up both sides of the driveway. At one end of the house I built a large patio and put in a twenty by forty inground swimming pool, which all the children loved and used often.

Across the field where there was a small brook, I dug a good-sized pond for swimming, fishing, and boating. It was beautiful, and all the family spent time there. Many people were fascinated with what we had done, and we lived there very happily. Charlotte and I always wanted the place to stay in our family, for our family and friends to use and enjoy forever. We planned to leave it in very good shape for them.

I also installed a mobile home for grand-daughter Leigh and her four children. This was very expensive, what with state and local permits, installing a septic tank and sewage system , water, electricity a driveway, and everything else.

Ronald, Charlotte's son, even though he was a good worker, was the only one of our children who didn't own his own home. He usually worked on farms over in Franklin County, and we didn't see him much. He took a job in Massachusetts constructing steel buildings, and somehow hurt his ankle quite badly.

He told us he had a good lawyer, and had received a large settlement. His mother was afraid that he would soon go through the money and again have nothing. She suggested that he buy our house for a small fee, and we would keep a life lease. Ronald wanted to take over the whole place and continue raising cattle as we were doing. He would eventually build a small home there for us and I would keep on helping with the farming. This was not to be.

Ronald seemed to have plenty of money. We thought it was from his injury settlement. We soon learned that Ronald had another source of money we knew nothing about. It came out in the newspaper that he was being charged with bringing large amounts of drugs in from Canada in grain trucks. We were shocked. The newspaper stated that the government had been watching Ronald bring in these large shipments for over five years. This is unbelievable. Do you think they would watch bank robbery, murder, or any other crime go on for five years without doing anything? By letting him go and keep building up his kingdom, the government had all the more to confiscate and sell. I wonder how many other people got hurt from using drugs and getting into the business during those years the government sat back. Seems to me their inaction made the government promoters of drug use.

Soon after that we came home one day to find find the yard full of automobiles and about forty FBI and Marshalls or whatever they were, in our house, some carrying guns and wearing bulletproof vests. They had smashed in the door and completely trashed the whole place, dumping drawers, files, and everything else.

Charlotte always wanted to have a good Christmas, and she shopped early while the sales were on. She had about one hundred presents gathered and wrapped for next Christmas, and they tore them all

William F. Hill
PO BOX15
HADWICK, VT. 05843
802-472-6308

CIVIL DIVISION
DOCKETNO.235-10 18 CACV
TO. HARDWICK POLICE. DEPARTMENT. AND NEVER HEARD OF
AGENCY OF HUMAN SERVICES. AS WELL AS THE DCF

EVERY BODY KNOWS THAT THE HILLS ARE ENTITLED TO TO
THEIR OWN PROPERTY WHITCH. THEY WORKED A LIFE TIME TO
PRODUCE FOR THEM. SELVES. AND. THEIR FAMILY. THE ONLY
EXCEPTION SHOULD BE ABOUT THE. ONE FOURTH WHICH WAS
DEEDED TO RONALD ALDRICH BEFORE WE HAD ANY KNOWLEDGE
OR. I DEAR THAT RONAD AND OLSON WERE DESTROYING SALLYS.
AND OUR LIFE. YOU. HAVE BEEN READING ABOUT AND DOING
MANY THINGS. TO. MAKE SALLY FEEL VERY UNSECURED. AND
DAILY DESTROYING HER CANCER. WHITCH THEY. DIDN;T SEEM TO
CARE ABOUT OLSON AND HIS FAMILY. DID MORE THINGS. TO MAKE
OUR LIVES VERY DESTRUCTIVE ON US AND SALLY. AND. HER
CANCER
IT WAS BECOMING VERY. UNBEARABLE HAVING OLSON AND
HIS FAMILY. AROUND ALL THE TIME.. THEY HAD NO. REAL RIGHT TO
BE HEAR. WE NEVER KNEW THEM OLSON WAS BROUGHT HERE BY
RONALD ALDICH. AND THE GOVERNMENT. WE DIDN;T KNOW HIM. I
FELT THAT I. HAD NO REASON FOR NOT FILING A MOTION TO HAVE
OLSON REMOVED. AROUND AS . HE WAS DESTROYING SALLY AND
US. OLSONS LAWYER IMMEDIATELY. OBJECT AGAINST MY MOTION.
JUDGE. BENT JUST WENT RIGHT. AHEAD. WITH NO REASON EXCEPT
HE WAS A VERY. DISHONEST LAWYER WHO JUDGE BENT ALWAYS
SIDEED WITH OLSON AND HIS LAWYER. AND I WAS NOT A LAWYER
SO I DIDN;T ACCOUNT FOR ANY THING IN HIS MIND. JUDGE BENT
AND. OLSONS LAWYER . WHO REALLY HAD NO LEGAL REASON TO
BE A. ROUND SALLY ANY OF US OR. ON OUR PROPERTY. MADE A

RULING AGAINST SALLY ME AND ALL OF US. WHO WERE LIVING IN OUR HOME WHICH WE HAD BUILT AND PAID FOR. JUDGE. BENT RULED THAT WE NEEDED TO MOVE OUT AS OLSON WANTED THE PLACE FOR HIS VACATION HOME. JUDGE BENT RULLED THAT. SALLY AND ALL OF THIS RULED THAT SALLY AND ALL OF OUR FAMILY NEEDED TO LEAVE OUR HOME FOR OLSONS. USE. AND HIS VACATION AND THAT. SALLY AND I WOULD NO LONGER BE ALLOWED TO EVEN. ENTER OR VISIT OUR OWN HOME WHERE WE HAD BUILT AND PAID. FOR. US AND OUR GREAT GRAND CHILDREN

I THINK THAT EVERY ONE KNOWS WHAT HAS TAKEN PLACE . SINCE OLSON HAS COMPLETELY RUINED AND DESTROYED THE. PLACE. AS WELL AS BRINGING IN QUITE AFEW BOARDERS AS WELL AS KELLEY. LaCOURSE. AND MANY YOUNG GIRLS A. FINAL DETERMINATION. HAS BEEN MADE. ADDING KELLEY LaCOURSE. NAME TO THE ADULT ABUSE REGISTRY. AND DONE MANY. THINGS TO DESTROY ALL OUR LIVES. LOOK THIS ALL UP FOR YOUR SELVES

STATE OF VERMONT

SUPERIOR COURT
Caledonia Unit

CIVIL DIVISION
Docket No. 235-10-18 Cacv

William Hill
    Plaintiff

v.

Sven Olson,
    Defendant

FILED
DEC 16 2019
CALEDONIACOURTS

DECISION ON DEFENDANT'S MOTION FOR SUMMARY JUDGMENT

In this case, Defendant Sven Olson has moved for summary judgment on Plaintiff William Hill's claim that he still holds a life estate in real property located in Hardwick, Vermont. Sven Olson is represented by Attorney Kristina Michelsen. William Hill was represented in prior proceedings, but counsel withdrew just as this motion ripened. Plaintiff Hill proceeds pro se.

Procedural Background

Plaintiff Hill filed this case in October 26, 2018, seeking a preliminary injunction and declaratory judgment on the grounds that Defendant Olson wrongfully interfered with his tenancy on the Porter Brook Road property, and that his life estate should be restored and/or that he is entitled to compensation for the value of the life estate. In response, Defendant Olson denied allegations of interference and Hill's continuing interest in the property and filed a counterclaim.

Defendant moved for summary judgment on July 1, 2019, supporting his request and assertions of fact with a number of affidavits and other documents properly presented under V.R.C.P. Rule 56. Plaintiff, who now is a self-represented litigant, filed many pages in opposition to Defendant's motion but the court cannot consider the bulk of them in its decision because they were not presented in a manner that could allow the court to do so. It is clear Mr. Hill opposes the motion for summary judgment, however, being without counsel, he has not properly provided factual support for his opposition.

Uncontested Facts

The property at issue in this case is located at 909 Porter Brook Road (sometimes referred to as 500 or 601 Porter Brook Road) in Hardwick, Vermont. William Hill was a licensed real estate agent for about 50 years. He and his now deceased wife, Charlotte Hill, built a nice home on the property. The property is rural and agricultural. Charlotte was diagnosed with cancer in 2013 and died in 2018.

1

ecember 5, 2002. The deed executed on that date conveyed the ~~~~~
Ronald but reserved a life estate for Mr. and Ms. Hill. Ronald did not live at the property.

In June 2007, the U.S. District Court of Vermont sentenced Ronald to prison on charges related to drug smuggling and money laundering, and ordered him to forfeit his interest in multiple properties, including the Porter Brook Road property. William and Charlotte Hill objected to the forfeiture of their interest in the property and as a result, entered into a stipulation with the federal government which redefined their interest in the property. The agreement preserved their life estate as detailed in the December 5, 2002 deed but changed the terms of its expiration. The following terms were included in the settlement agreement that both Charlotte and William signed, unrepresented, on February 20, 2008:

15. Subject to the terms of this agreement, the Hills each agree to the entry of a final order of forfeiture in the criminal proceeding that orders the forfeiture of the remainder interest in the Real Property (formerly held by Ronald Aldrich) to the United States. Subject to the terms of this agreement, the Government agrees that the Hills retain their estate interest in the Real Property as reflected in the deed executed on December 5, 2002 and recorded in the Town of Hardwick at Volume 114, Page 150 of the Hardwick Land Records.

16. The Hills each agree that they will not transfer, or otherwise convey their life estate interest to a third party.

17. The Hills each agree that their life estate in the Real Property expires upon the earliest of the following two events:
    (1) The Hills both become deceased, or
    (2) The Hills permanently vacate the Real Property.
Upon the occurrence of either of the above events, the Hills, and/or their heirs, have 30 days to remove all personal property from the Real Property. After that time, all personal property will be presumed to be abandoned and may be liquidated or destroyed by the U.S. Marshals Service or its assigns without any accounting of the proceeds to the Hills or their heirs.

18. The Hills, jointly and severally, agree to timely pay all property taxes currently due and owing and to timely pay all future property taxes that come due throughout the duration of their life estate. The Hills, jointly and severally, also agree to maintain sufficient property (homeowners) insurance on the Real Property. . . .

19. The Hills, jointly and severally, agree to exercise ordinary care to maintain the Real Property and make such repairs as necessary to preserve the Real Property in the condition it is in at the time of signing this settlement agreement.

20. In the event that the Hills: (1) fail to pay the property taxes on the Real Property within 120 days of the date such taxes are due; (2) fail to maintain sufficient real property (homeowners) insurance on the Real Property for any time period during their life estate;

2

(3) *permanently vacate* the Real Property; or (4) fail to maintain the Real Property in its present condition, the Hills agree that their interest in the Real Property is subject to sale by the U.S. Marshals Service or its assigns. From the proceeds of such sale, the Hills agree they would be entitled to only the fair market value of their life estate interest less any property taxes owed and/or the cost of necessary repairs; the U.S. Marshals Service or its assigns would be entitled to the remainder of the proceeds . . . .

27. If the Hills abandon or permanently vacate the Real Property, they shall notify the U.S. Marshals Service immediately and the Real Property shall thereupon become wholly the property of the United States . . . .

United States v. Ronald Aldrich, Criminal No. 2:03-CR-147-01 (D. Vt. Mar. 6, 2008) (emphasis added).

On August 3, 2012, Defendant Sven Olson purchased the property from the United States through the 909 Porter Brook Road Realty Trust. Defendant Olson purchased the property as a vacation home. The Hills were living on the property as their primary residence at the time and the deed for that sale recognizes their life estate.

The Hills held an auction selling their cattle and machinery on June 14, 2016. On June 1, 2017, they purchased real property on Dutton Road in Hardwick, VT, and subsequently moved into that property.[1]

The Hills held a second auction at the Porter Brook Road property in July 2017 for their personal property. At this auction, Mr. Hill handed the keys to the property to Mr. Olson, the principal of the trust which had purchased the property. Mr. Olson had no knowledge of any intent on the part of the Hills to return to the residence at Porter Brook Road. In this respect, Mr. Hill did not advise Mr. Olson that he had any intention to return. Nor did Mr. Hill tell anyone he

---

[1] The court is aware of Plaintiff Hill's assertions that Sven Olson and his family unreasonably entered the property in contravention to the life estate he and his wife held, and that he and his wife were so upset that they felt they had to leave and "establish another primary residence." Defendant Olson has introduced substantial evidence through affidavits from Kelly Lacourse and Ronald Aldrich as witnesses, and narratives from the Hardwick Police, which distinctly paint a different picture as to the source of Mr. and Ms. Hill's unhappiness. The exhibits submitted by Defendant Olson describe Leigh Kidder's presence on the property as a source of conflict, but not Defendant Olson or his family. Plaintiff Hill's contentions as to any inappropriate conduct by Defendant Olson have not been adequately presented to the court and thus the court does not consider them. V.R.C.P. 56(c) (among other things, requiring a party asserting that a fact is genuinely disputed to support the assertion by filing a separate and concise statement of undisputed or disputed material facts in accordance with subdivision c and referencing specific materials in the records, or showing that materials cited do not establish the absence of a genuine dispute).

3

..ned to return to the premises to live out his life estate, rather he had no plans at that time
..er than to care for his wife who was very ill with cancer.[2]

After being given the keys at the June 2017 auction, Mr. Olson started staying in the
Porter Brook Road residence, making renovations to the property as well as commencing a
business in the Hardwick community.

Mr. Olson purchased, at auction, a trailer which had been occupied by one of Charlotte
Hill's granddaughters, Leigh Kidder.

Analysis

A court will grant a motion for summary judgment if the "movant shows that there is no
genuine dispute as to any material fact and the movant is entitled to judgment as a matter of
law." V.R.C.P. Rule 56(a); *Gauthier v. Keurig Green Mountain, Inc.*, 2015 VT 108, ¶ 13, 200
Vt. 125, 133. It is up to the movant to prove the absence of any genuine issue, and "the
nonmoving party receives the benefit of all reasonable doubts and inferences." *Robertson v.
Mylan Labs., Inc.*, 2004 VT 15, ¶ 15, 176 Vt. 356, 363. However, a party opposing a summary
judgment motion "cannot simply rely on mere allegations in the pleadings to rebut credible
documentary evidence or affidavits . . . but must respond with specific facts that would justify
submitting her claims to a factfinder." *Id.* "If a party fails to properly support an assertion of
fact or fails to properly address another party's assertion of fact as required by Rule 56(c), the
court may . . . consider the fact undisputed for purposes of the motion." V.R.C.P. Rule 56(e).

Because the Hills agreed in the February 2008 settlement agreement that the Porter Brook
Road property would be subject to sale in the event that they "permanently vacate[d] the Real
Estate," the critical question is whether Mr. Hill and Ms. Hill, in fact, permanently vacated the
property when they left the residence.[3] The court concludes that they did. In this case, the Hills
had an initial auction in June 2016, at which they sold their cattle and machinery, property
associated with the use of the real estate. Subsequently, the Hills purchased and moved into a
new residence on Dutton Road. In July 2017, the Hills held still another auction for the sale of
their personal property at Porter Brook Road. At the same time, the Hills gave Defendant Olson
the keys to the property without any mention of an intent to return. Plaintiff Hill has admitted
that his only plan was to care for his ailing wife. Further, the record is devoid of any admissible
evidence from which the court could conclude that Defendant Olson forced the Hills to vacate

---

[2] These uncontested facts are derived from Plaintiff's responses to requests to admit. See
V.R.C.P. 36(b).

[3] "No party has indicated that any of the other events triggering the sale clause of provision 20 of
the settlement agreement—failure to pay the property taxes, failure to maintain property
insurance, and failure to maintain the condition of the property—arose before the federal
government sold the property to Defendant Olson."

4

rmer residence.[4]. Under these circumstances, the court finds that ~~~
~m to or remain on the subject property.

In sum, Plaintiff Hill has not provided evidence to contradict Olson's assertions of fact in
manner that could show that there is a genuine issue of material fact. Plaintiff Hill's own
allegations are the sole support for his claims that Defendant Olson interfered with his life estate
and that he did not intend to permanently vacate the Porter Brook Road property when he moved
out. Such conclusory allegations do not suffice to defend against a motion for summary
judgment. *Mello v. Cohen*, 168 Vt. 639, 641 (1998) ("[T]o defend against a summary judgment
motion, a plaintiff cannot rely on conclusory allegations or mere conjecture."). Accordingly, the
court concludes that summary judgment is warranted as a matter of law.

Defendant Olson has also raised an equitable estoppel argument in his motion for
summary judgment. The doctrine of equitable estoppel is an affirmative defense. V.R.C.P. Rule
8(c); *Mellin v. Flood Brook Union Sch. Dist.*, 173 Vt. 202, 221 (2001). Grounded in public
policy, "equitable estoppel works to prevent one party from asserting rights which may have
existed against another party who in good faith has changed his or her position in reliance upon
earlier representations." *Fisher v. Poole*, 142 Vt. 162, 168 (1982). "All of the circumstances of
the case must be evaluated in determining whether the doctrine applies, but generally it 'will not
be invoked in favor of one whose own omissions or inadvertences contributed to the
problem.'" *Beecher v. Stratton Corp.*, 170 Vt. 137, 140 (1999) (quoting *Fisher*, 142 Vt. at 169).
The burden is on the party claiming estoppel to establish four elements:

> first, the party to be estopped must know the facts; second, the party being estopped must
> intend that his conduct shall be acted upon or the acts must be such that the party
> asserting the estoppel has a right to believe it is so intended; third, the latter must be
> ignorant of the true facts; and finally, the party asserting the estoppel must rely on the
> conduct of the party to be estopped to his detriment.

Fisher, 142 Vt. at 168; *In re Langlois/Novicki Variance Denial*, 2017 VT 76, ¶ 12, 205 Vt. 340,
346 (2017) (also relying on these elements).

Here, the first element is met because Plaintiff Hill knew of his own intentions when he
and Charlotte left the Porter Brook Road property. Second, Plaintiff Hill's conduct in holding
two auctions, purchasing a new home, and then giving Defendant Olson the keys to the Porter
Brook Road property, would have reasonably led Olson to believe that Plaintiff Hill intended for
him to take possession. Third, Defendant Olson did not know that Hill intended to return to the
property. Finally, Defendant Olson relied on Plaintiff Hill's conduct to his detriment by
investing financial resources into renovations on the property and opening a business in the
community.

---

[4] Notably, even if the conduct of Mr. Olson prompted the Hills to depart the subject property,
such reason for their departure would not, in itself, evince an intent to vacate the residence only
temporarily.

5

at it would be inequitable to now allow Plaintiff Hill's change of heart with regard to having left the life estate to impede Defendant Olson's established rights. Having permanently vacated the property, Plaintiff no longer has a life estate on the Porter Brook Road property, and he is estopped from asserting one.

Order

For the foregoing reasons, Defendant's motion for summary judgment is granted.

While not addressed in the pleadings, even though Mr. Hill no longer has a life estate which supports occupancy, having permanently vacated the property, it appears that he is entitled to have his life estate valued and receive compensation. The court does not see the District Court's order as one which creates a forfeiture for the Hills when they move out. Although the language of the agreement leaves a number of questions, it does appear to contemplate compensation upon vacating the property. The court will thus schedule the matter for further status conference to hear from the parties on how this case should proceed.

In any event, Mr. Hill has no right to re-enter the property. A reasonable reading of the agreement would not allow him to change his mind after permanently vacating the property.

Judgment for Olson on the motion for summary judgment.

12/16/19

Hon. Robert R. Bent
Hon. Robert R. Bent

4 JANUARY 2022

DEAR JUDGE BENT

    I STILL CAN;T BELIEVE THE DECISION THAT YOU MADE IN FAVOR OF SVEN OLSON SALLY WAS VERY ILL AND COULD NOT TAKE THE PRESSURE FROM OLSON AND HIS FAMILY. THE PRESSURE THAT THEY CAUSED WAS JUST UNBEARABLE AND SHE COULDN;T TAKE IT ANY MORE I HAD TO GET HER AWAY FROM ALL OF OLSONS PRESSURE. YOU HAVE COPIES OF MANY OF THE THINGS THAT WERE BOTHERING HER IF YOU LOOKED AT THEM. THE DOCTORS SAID IF SHE WAS GOING TO MAKE IT SHE HAD TO GET AWAY FROM THERE. I HAD TWO CHOICES EITHER MOVE HER INTO A NURSING HOME OR FIND A PLACE WHERE I COULD LOOK OUT FOR HER. EVEN THOUGH THAT SHE HAD CANCER THAT WAS KILLING HER SHE WAS STILL ABLE TO DO SOME THINGS MY ONLY THOUGHT WAS TO TRY TO MOVE HER SOME PLACE WHERE I COULD TRY TO CARE FOR HER. THAT IS WHY I PURCHASED THE SMALL HOUSE ON DUTTON ROAD. THE PLACE NEEDED A LOT OF WORK BUT WE WERE ABLE TO DO IT. WHEN I MARRIED HER I TOOK AN OATH TO LOOK OUT FOR HER UNTIL DEATH DO US PART... I HAVE NEVER BACKED OUT ON MY WORD AND

CERTAINLY COULDN;T THINK OF DOING IT NOW. I
LOOKED OUT FOR HER EVERY DAY OF HER LIFE
FOR THE MANY YEARS THAT WE WERE MARRIED
AND WAS RIGHT THERE BE SIDE THE BED HOLDING
HER HAND WHEN SHE TOOK HER LAST BREATH.
PRETTY SAD WOULD;T YOU AGREE

MOVING INTO THE DUTTON HOUSE WAS NO
DIFFERENT THAN GOING TO A HOSPITAL OR A
NURSING HOME..ONLY IT GAVE OLSON A CHANCE TO
MOVE IN AND TAKE OVER . OLSONS LAWYER TALKS
ABOUT US HAVING AN AUCTION AND SELLING OUR
STUFF... I HAVE BEEN AN AUCTIONEER FOR
OVER FIFTY YEARS AND HAD HUNDREDS OF
AUCTIONS I DID NOT WANT TO HAVE THIS ONE BUT
SALLY INSISTED AS SHE COULDN;T STAND TO
LEAVE AND HAVE OLSON TAKING OVER ALL OUR
STUFF AND DESTROYING IT THE SAME WAY THAT
HE HAD DONE WITH EVERYTHING ELSE. SHE
WANTED TO GET RID OF IT A COUPLE OF YEARS
AGO WE HAD OUR HOUSE HOLD PROPERTY
APPRAISED BY AN APPRAISER, RICHARD LEMAY OF
HYDE PARK,,,HE CAME UP WITH A VALUE IN EXCESS
OF EIGHTY THOUSAND DOLLARS. FROM THE
AUCTION THAT SHE WANTED IT BROUGHT US TEN
THOUSAND DOLLARS BUT TO ME IT WAS LOOKING
OUT FOR HER AND NOTHING ELSE MATTERED

OLSONS LAWYER CLAIMS THAT HE SPENT ONE
HUNDRED AND FIFTY THOUSAND MAKING NEEDED
REPAIRS. I WOULD CHALLENGE HER TO SHOW ME
WHERE THEY MADE FIFTEEN CENTS OF NEEDED

REPAIRS INSTEAD HE HAS CONTINUALLY
DESTROYED WHAT WAS A BEAUTIFUL PLACE. I
HAVE FURNISHED THE COURT SOME PICTURES OF
THE DESTRUCTION THAT HE HAS CAUSED. I WISH
THAT YOU WOUD COME AND SEE THEM YOU
WOULD BE FLABBERGASTED.

WHEN RONALD GOT INTO TROUBLE FOR WHAT
HE DID SALLY AND I WERE PRETTY DISGUSTED
WITH WHAT HE DID BUT REALIZED THAT WE HAD
TO GO ON WITH OUR LIVES WE WERE NOT HAPPY
WITH RONALDS BEHAVIOR. WHEN RONALD GOT
OUT OF JAIL HE BROUGHT OLSON INTO THE
PROBLEM THE GOVERNMENT GOT INVOLVED AND
DECIDED TO SEIZE THE PROPERTY AND AUCTION
IT OFF ON TV. OLSON AND RONALD WERE IN THIS
TOGETHER. THE GOVERNMENT REFUSED TO TELL
US WHO BOUGHT IT, PROBABLY FOR A GOOD
REASON EVEN THOUGH WE INQUIRED OF THEM
SEVERAL TIMES THEY WOULDN;T TELL US. WE
LATER LEARNED THAT IT WAS SPEN OLSON. RIGHT
AFTER THIS RONALD CAME BACK IN THE PICTURE
AND SAID THAT HE WAS PLANNING TO RUN THE
PLACE ALONG WITH SALLY AND ME. OLSON
CONFIRMED THIS BY SAYING THAT HE WAS
PLANNING TO CONVEY HIS INTEREST TO RONALD
WITH A THIRTY YEAR PAID UP LEASE. OLSON
WENT AND PICKED UP RONALD FROM JAIL AND
BROUGHT HIM BACK HERE WHERE HE MOVED IN

THE BIG HOUSE WITH SALLY AND ME. HE
IMMEDIATELY STARTED HELPING WITH THE
CHORES AND SEEM TO BE VERY HAPPY. THEN ALL
OF A SUDEN AFTER SEVERAL WEEKS RONALD
ANNOUNCED THAT HE MUST LEAVE RIGHT AWAY
AS HE AND OLSON WERE IN THE SAME BUSINESS
AND HE DIDN;T WANT TO WIND UP BACK IN JAIL. I
DO NOT KNOW WHO PAID THE $129,000 TO THE
GOVERNMENT RONALD KEPT LARGE AMOUNTS OF
MONEY AT PAUL LUSSIERS HOUSE AND WAS ABLE
TO GO AND GET ANY AMOUNT OF MONEY WHEN
EVER HE NEEDED....I THINK THAT IT IS UP TO THE
COURT AND THE GOVERNMENT TO FIGURE THIS
ALL OUT AND TAKE WHAT EVER ACTION TO FIND
OUT MORE ABOUT OLSON. THIS DISGUSTING AND
VERY SAD SITUATION HAVE BEEN GOING ON FOR
TO LONG AND TO MANY LIVES DESTROYED BUT
NOBODY SEEMS TO CARE ABOUT HARD WORKING
HONEST PEOPLE REALLY THIS IS UNBELIEVABLE. I
KNOW AND REALIZE THAT THERE IN NO WAY TO
REVERSE THIS OR TO RETURN ANYTHING TO ITS
ORIGINAL GOOD NORMAL AND HAPPY SITUATION
I HOPE AND PRAY THAT YOU WILL DO THE BEST
THING POSSIBLE

                                        THANK
YOU

WILLIAM F. HILL

STATE OF VERMONT

SUPERIOR COURT   CIVIL DIVISION
CALEDONIA UNIT   DOCKET NO: 235-10-18 CACV

WILLIAM HILL   AFFIDAVIT
          Plaintiff

vs.

SVEN OLSON
          Defendants

NOW COMES Kelly Lacourse duly sworn and under oath to state the following:

1. My name is Kelly Lacourse.

2. I reside in Chelsea, Vermont.

3. I am the granddaughter of Charlotte Hill and step-granddaughter of Bill Hill.

4. During the later part of my grandmother's illness, I lived in the house and helped care for my grandmother who was sick with cancer and had been for many years.

5. I lived at the mansion from March 2017 until November 2018. During the time that I lived at the mansion I was responsible for cleaning and general maintenance. There was a lot that I did not do and that my grandfather did not do that led to the deterioration of the siding and the pool and other items that my grandfather did not take care of. He did have me clean the mold every year in the basement because he did not want to pay to have the leak fixed.

6. I was at the mansion when Sven Olson bought the property and began to visit with his family.

7. The Olson's did not stay in the mansion. They may have stayed on the premises in their camper once or twice, but they usually stayed at the Kimball House Bed and Breakfast.

8. When the Olson's came, they brought food and wine and prepared meals for all of us and cleaned up after the meals.

9. The Olson's were particulary nice to my sister Leigh's children. They lived in the trailer on the property. The Olson's brought them clothes and took them on trips. My grandparents loved that the Olson's were so nice to Leigh and her children.

10. I did not get the sense that Sven knew Ron before meeting at the house.

11. Never did I hear from anyone, Leigh or Bill or Charlotte or Ron or Sven that Sven had any prior relationship with Ron of any kind and definitely I never heard or was led to believe that Sven was in any way involved in the sale or distribution of illegal drugs.

12. Bill on occasion would gripe about Sven having so much money and would wonder aloud

3628 about where he got it, but I got the sense that it was jealousy because Sven wasn't frugal
3629 with his money and as long as everyone around Sven was happy and having fun, Sven did
3630 not care how much it cost. Making people happy is what Sven likes to do.
3631
3632 13. My grandmother often said that caring for Leigh's kids constantly was going to kill her
3633 because she couldn't care for herself.
3634
3635 14. For a long time my grandmother would say she wanted to live in a smaller place where
3636 Leigh would have to call before bringing the kids over and also a home that she could clean
3637 and take care of so she would feel in control again.
3638
3639 15. She also could not get up the stairs anymore. My grandfather would not sleep with her
3640 downstairs and she did not want to sleep there by herself. One time she tried to drag herself
3641 upstairs and couldn't make it.
3642
3643 16. I told Sven about the auction of the property.
3644
3645 17. I had a conversation with Bill and Sven about me staying on the property after Bill and
3646 Charlotte moved out to help out and Sven was good with that so long as I still went to
3647 Dutton Road to help care for my grandmother.
3648
3649 18. My grandparents did not complain about Sven or his family before they moved out of the
3650 house.
3651
3652 19. My grandfather only starting griping about Sven when Sven did ot pay him the state tax
3653 payment right away.
3654
3655 20. Sven hired me and my sister, Leigh, to do work at the house after my grandparents moved
3656 out. Any work we did removing wall paper or making renovations happened after my
3657 grandparents moved out of the house.
3658
3659 21. Sven did not buy me a Cadillac, my husband did.
3660
3661 22. Since this lawsuit had been going on, Bill has been contacting me trying to get me to come
3662 to his lawyers office to sign a paper saying that Sven caused my grandmother so much stress
3663 that she died. I have refused to do this because it is not true.
3664
3665 23. Last Wednesday night or Thursday morning Bill left a voicemail message on my phone
3666 saying that his lawyer said that if I don't come to sign the paper, I'm going to get wrapped
3667 up in the criminal charges against Sven and go to jail. He said his lawyer said that I would
3668 be considered an accessory to Olson's criminal activity. I have the recording.
3669
3670 24. My grandparents have been supporting Leigh and her children for as long as I can
3671 remember. They bought her the trailer on the property. They bought her the house she now
3672 lives in in Berlin. Leigh would not do anything to put that support at risk. That is why I
3673 believe she is saying the untrue things about Sven.
3674
3675

William F. Hill

3676   Dated at Chelsea this 22 day of May 2019
3677
3678
3679   Kelly Lacourse
3680
3681
3682   Subscribed and sworn to before me this 22 day of May 2019
3683
3684
3685   Notary Public
3686   Bonnie Straut
3687

3688 William F. Hill
3689
3690 PO BOX 15
3691 Hardwick Vt. 05843
3692
3693 802-472-6308
3694
3695   Answers to Kelley Lacourse Complaints. June 30 20019
3696
3697   4. Kelley stayed in the house after moving out of my horse trailer which she packs with hay to
3698 keep warm and used plenty of electricity from my greenhouse. And Leigh's mobile home. She later
3699 stayed in the house and entertained several boy friends. When ever she did anything for me or her
3700 Grandmother. She always presented a bill. Often for more time than she actually put in. Her
3701 Grandmother had not been sick with cancer for many years
3702   Kelley could be a very good worker when. She wanted to be. But always presented a bill for
3703 money. There were several things that I had asked her to do that she didn't do When we had the
3704 equipment auction She had agreed to take [picture of all the machinery. As it was a sold She never
3705 came up with a single picture even though she was around all day. I really felt bad was I had around
3706 fifteen classic tractors. And allot of unique equipment. I was very sad that she hadn't, done as she had
3707 agreed to do.
3708   5 She had a variety of friends hanging around. I even had to kick some of them out to all the
3709 troubles they caused One of them dumped a gallon of house paint into the engine of my. nearly. New
3710 riding lawnmower. Another time on a Sunday morning I had to go down town with my pickup
3711   I had one of the. Kids with me and it started to handle funny. I discovered that some one had
3712 taken two of the lug nuts off one front wheel and loosened up the others Was lucky that Bear happed.
3713 To be at his garage and helped to get it fixed. We could have been killed. Another time I had my pick
3714 up down at the garage 'Vermonters. Helping Vermonters. When somebody broke out two of the
3715 windows and one of his trucks. Kelley and her friends knew. Who. it was. Another fellow. Kelley
3716 Howard who she was or still is married took many things Sally and I were riding by their house when
3717 Sally spotted one of our dinning room sets in they are where they lived. We went and got it Just a
3718 couple of weeks ago Kelley was on the news for some trouble that he had caused The news Sid that
3719 they had to close route sixteen for six hours
3720   6 Probably. Was. But not involved
3721   7. Agreed
3722   8. They did. We all cleaned up
3723   9. Back then the Olsons were good to all the children and did take Leigh's children with them
3724 on vacations with them I thought that this was great I felt that they would; go places and see things
3725 that. They might Never see again and I felt that a family setting for them was great
3726   10. I don't recall kelley being around Ronald or Olson when they were together Ronald didn't
3727 like Kelley and wanted nothing to do with her
3728   11. Im sure that none of us ever discussed this with Kelley
3729   12. Certainly not true why would; I be upset about how much money that the Olsons had
3730   13. That is not true Sally loved having these children around right up to the last
3731   14. She did like to keep things very clean. Sally never knew. Anything about a small house until
3732 after I purchased the Dutton Home and told her that I had purchased it I showed to her and asked if
3733 she would lie to live there
3734   15. This is an out and out lie Sally always went. Up stairs and. We never. Slept apart right up until
3735 the day that she. Died

WILLIAM F. HLL
PO BOX15
HARDWICK, VT. 05843
802-472-6308

`SURPRIOR COURT   CIVIL. DIVISION
                                  DOCKET # 235-10-18 CACV\

William F. Hill. PLAINTIFF

VS

SVEN OLSEN. DEFENDANTS

   WILLIAM HILL ONLY WANTS. OLSONS LAWYER TO CORRECT. THE FALSES
STATEMENTS SHE. HAS USED IN DRAFTING ; KELLEY LACOURSES, RONALD
ALDRICHES. AND SPEN OLSONS   DEPOSITIONS.. PLUS HER OWN FALSE
STATMENTS. LEIGH KIDDERS DEPOSITION SEEMS TO PRETTY. MUCH FOLLOW
THE. TRUTH. SHE DID. THIS WITH OUT THE HELP OF A LAWYER
   . . . YOU ARE NOW NOW WHINING ABOUT THE. FACT THAT THIS IS COSTING OLSON
MONEY. WHO DOES SHE THINK THAT. SHE HAS CAUSED. A LOT OF MONEY AND. GRIEF
FOR. BY FILING FALSE STATEMENTS. IN. OLSONS. NAME. KELLEY LACOURSE. AND RONALD
ALDRICH   NAME AS WELLAS HER OWN TEST A MONEY. YOU AND OSON ARE. THE ONES
DOING. THIS. HATFUL MASSACRE WHO ELSE? P[LEASE ANSWER ME. PD Q.
YOU. HAVE CAUSED AT LEAST TWO PEOPLE TO LOOSE THEIR. LIVES. DUE TO ALL. THE
STRESS THAT. YOU CAUSED. WHAT ABOUT THE INNOCENT PEOPLE AND SMALL CHILDREN
WHO YOU OLSON, AND OLSONS. LAWYER. WHOES LIVES YOU HAVE CRULEY
DESTROYED. BY DRIVING THEM OUT OF THEIR HOMES AND. DESTROYED THEIR LIVES
BEYOND REPAIR NOT EVEN KNOWING THEM AND. KNOWING THAT. NONE OF THEM HAD
EVER DONE. ANYTHING WRONG OR EVER HURT. ANY ONE. THIS HATE HAS. GONE ON FOR
YEARS.   SALLY HILL. HAS BEEN DEAD FOUR YEARS. PLUS HER SEVERAL YEARS OF
SUFFERING DUE TO THE TERRIBLE HATE ON YOUR PART. HOW ABOUT ALL THE CROPS
HARD WORK. LAND AND BUILDINGS THAT YOU HAVE. UNBELIEVABLE DESTROYED. I
HOPE THAT YOU WILL COME TO AND REALIZE. WHAT YOU . HAVE DONE.
I STILL CANT BELIEVE THAT   YOU A JUDGE,,, OR COURT CAN BE SO RUTHLESS. AND
AND JUST. TRY . TO WALK. AWAY KNOWING HOW BAD YOU HAVE DESTROYED. EVERY
THING BY USING FALSE. STATEMENTS TO TRY TO DESTOY SEVERAL INNOCENT LIVES
YOU HAVE DESTROYED MANY LIVES AND AWAY OF LIFE. WHAT ELSE WOULD YOU LIKE

                 THANK .YOU. BILL HILL

William F. Hill

 .VERMONT

AGENCY OF HUMAN SERVICES

DEPARTMENT OF DISABILITIES, AGING AND INDEPENDENT LIVING

Adult Protective Services
Division of Licensing and Protection
HC 2 South
280 State Drive
Waterbury, VT 05671-2060
https://dlp.vermont.gov/aps
To Report Adult Abuse: (800) 564-1612

January 10, 2022

William Hill
756 Dutton Road
Hardwick, Vermont 05843

FINAL DETERMINATION
APS Investigation Number: 10848

Dear William Hill:

A final determination has been made to substantiate the allegation that Kelly LaCourse maltreated you. As a result, their name has been added to the Adult Abuse Registry.

State of Vermont Adult Protective Services
Division of Licensing and Protection

```
```

William F. Hill

PO B0x 15

Hardwick Vt. 05843

802-472-6308

Answers to Kelley

Lacers. Complaints. June 30 20019

4. Kelley stayed in the house after moving out of my horse trailer which she packs with hay to keep warm and used plenty of electricity from   my greenhouse. And Leigh's mobile home. She later stayed in the house and entertained several boy friends. Whenever she did anything for me or   her Grandmother. She always presented a bill. Often for more time than she actually put in. Her Grandmother had not been sick with cancer for many   years

Kelley could be a very good worker when. She wanted to be. But always presented a bill for money. There were several things that I had asked her to   do that she didn,t do   When we had the equipment auction She had agreed to take [picture of all the machinery. As it was a sold   She. never came up r with a single picture even though she was around all day. I really felt bad was I had around fifteen classic tractors. And allot of unique

527

equipment. I was very sad that she hadn't, done as she had agreed to do.

5 She had a variety of friends hanging around. I even had to kick some of them out use to all the troubles they caused One of them dumped a   gallon of house paint into the engine of my. nearly. New riding lawnmower. Another time on a Sunday morning I had to go down town with my pickup

I had one of the. Kids with me and it started to handle funny . I discovered that some one had taken two of the lug nuts off one front wheel and loosened   up the others Was lucky that Bear happed. To be at his garage and helped to get it fixed. We could have been killed. Another time I had my pick up   down at the garage 'Vermonters. Helping Vermonters. When somebody broke out two of the windows and one of his trucks. Kelley and her friends   knew. Who. it was. Another fellow. Kelley Howard who she was or still is married took many things Sally and I were riding by their house when Sally spotted one of our dinning room sets in they are where they lived. We went and got it Just a couple of weeks ago Kelley was on the news for some   trouble that he had caused The news Sid that they had to close route sixteen for six hours   *S my*

6 Probably. Was. But not involved

7. Agreed

8. They did. We all cleaned up

9. Back then the Olsons were good to all the children

and did take Leigh's children with them on vacations with them I thought that this was great I felt that they would; go places and see things that. They might. Never see again andl felt that a family setting for them was great

10. I don't recall kelley being around Ronald or Olson when they were together Ronald didn't like Kelley and wanted nothing to do with her

11. Im sure that none of us ever discussed this with Kelley

12. Certainly not true why would; I be upset about how much money that the Olsons had

13. That is not true Sally loved having these children around right up to the last

14. She didl like to keep things very clean. Sally never knew. Any thing about a small house until after I purchased the Dutton Home and told her that I had purchased it I showed to her and asked if she would lie to live there

15. This is an out and out lie Sally always went. Up stairs and. We never. Slept apart right up until the day that she. Died

16. Every body knew. About the auction

17. I had nothing to do with Kelley moving in with Olson I certainly didn't, approve it

18. I think that she is right

19. Olson did owe us the money that the. State. Refunded. But this was none of Kelleys business

20. Im sure that Olson hired them but they sure destroyed a beautiful house

21. Ive. Got no idea

22 I don't believe that Kelley and Olson parted on very good terms and she had been wanting to get back at him for some time

We hadn't, seen. Kelley; for quirt some time after her Grand mother died Kelley and brother started coming here several weekends. I was surprised Both Kelley and /Branson started talking and. Complaining about Olson. And all the terrible things he had done to hurt them They both wanted. To write. Up stories about what they talking about. They wanted to bring their Kids here the following week end and I agreed to put on feed for them and try to give them a good time. Kelley borrowed some money from me and said that she would pay it back the next. week end when they came. they never came again nor did I see any of my money. This is not unusual for Kelley

23. I did call Kelley after a dozen tries and asked about her statement that she was going to produce. I remember that there are a number off things that you and Olson were involved in I told her to always tell the truth even if it wasn't good but don't lie about. Any thing

24. Kelley has been very Jealous of Leigh as Leigh hasn't abandoned her kids Kelley talks about Leigh and her kids having a home that I helped them

get. Who does she think bought and paid for the home where her kids are living. In Glover. Where would they be without it. I have tried to help Kelley many times. When her second child was born I stood behind them. I made several trips to. the hospital to check. On them and if there was anything that I could do He was in the

Dartmouth hospital Kelley said he wasn't, doing very well and was quite worried about him. I called the Shriners in Boston. I feel that they did quite a lot to save his life and he is hear today

Sally always wanted to do for all the kids She had bought gifts for all of them and had them wrapped with their names on them after sally died I saw that they all got them at Christmas time I tried to get Kelley to pick the presents for her kids. She couldn't, be bothered and they never received

received theirs

We have always tried to help Kelley. But with a lot of problems. She and a boyfriend named Lussier lived in one of my houses down town. They wouldn't, even pick up the garbage that they dumped on the lawn. The garbage man who I was paying complained I went down to see Kelley and ask her to please keep it picked up and in the container. She called the Hardwick policed said that I was harassing. Her . Lussier the man that she was living with told me that he didn't feel that they should be getting welfare and food stamps. That he should be working and supporting them, I. Couldn't, agree more. He said that he had a good job up in Sheffield but needed a way to get there. We had good van and even though we were still using it in our business. I agreed to sell it to them for fifty dollars a month so that he could get to work and support them. Lussier and Kelley took the van and sold it the next day. They never worked and I did not get one cent

Lussier. Soon. disappeared. I believe that he is the father of one of her children. Kelley soon found another man. Kelley and one of her friends could see how we were growing and selling vegetables Kelley wanted to get

involved She started taking. some off the vegetable and apples to the farmers market where. We were sent up. Although she sold some we   never saw any money

We had good stores where we delivered vegetables and meat. Kelley started servicing some of them for us she delivered some vegetables to   big store in Newport. When she came back she said that. They hadn't, paid her that she was going to have to collect later ,I Was going to Newport   and knew these peOple well so I said that I would stop and pick up the money. They already had paid Kelley and had some receipts for over two hundred dollars that they. paid Kelley. Kelley had kept the money and even signed the receipts Several times we have had. checks taken and our   check book

names forged   and used in local stores The Hardwick police know about all-out these As. Far as the stories about all the mold by   Ronald and. Kelley.

That room never leaked and I doubt that it does now. That room was so packed with stuff that it was impossible to get into until   after the auction. After

that Kelley said that all of Olsons tenants kept there dogs and animals in there and it was always a mess one-off Kelleys complaints was   that Olsion made her clean. up after them

Kelley had started to write up a complaint against Olson about what he made her do, the old car that he sold her that wasn't even inspected for eighty dollars a week. She didn't, even dare to drive its or. go any where with it One of the things that bothered her was that she wanted to tell everything but was afraid to talk about all the drugs. That was used up there. I have never clamed anything about Olson and drugs even though I have heard several stories Kelley came to our place several times high on something. She hollered and yelled stated that somebody Owed her fifty thousand dollars. That she was flagrant she did not say by who. The whole thing is very sad

Many of the complaints are very false. Expect that Olson and his attorney had much to bo with the contents of them. Olsons attorney is not interested in talking about what happened. Or the truth I thought that this case was to arive at the truth and reach a reasonable solution not to see. How much Damage one side can do to the other The only way to solve a problem is to talk about it and. arrive at a reasonable solution. Winston Churchill wonce said that the only way to solve problem was to jaw about it not to go to war

Both Kelley and her brorther Branon had planed to write up statements. About their activitys. With Olson. Kelley felt that Olson controlled her often against her wishes. He made her clean up after all his tenants their dogs and animals. Which was very bad. Olson had some big parties involving. Many people. Which she had to clean up after Some guests came with big expensive cars and there was plenty of booze and other refreshments He made her work late at night to get in the wood for the two wood stoves. She claimed that he kept her supplied with drugs and we saw her pretty high several times. Her life was becoming more of a mess than it had been. Kelley and Branon were really both against Olson for several things that they said weren't right. I have never accused Olson of buying selling or distrubting drugs as I have never seen it but have heard of many stories

I don't know what changed Kelleys and Branons mind about making statements. They both claimed that Olson still owed them money Although they were coming around and wanting to do it I don't know what happened I haven't seen them since. It looks like Oslons attorney fabricate some ofee Kelleys complaints

He manipulated your granddaughte
Kelly who he knew ~~had~~ ^{was} mentally handicap
and had just gotten out of the mental
hospital a few month earlier. He got her
to rip the wall paper off, an tear down
walls, he even got her to do or say
what he wanted so it looked as if we
(my wife & I) were in the wrong.

Grandaughters name:

    Kelly L LaCourse

    written by Kelly

William F. HILL
PO Box 15
HARDWICK, VT. 05843
802-472-6308

DIVISION OF LICENSING AND PROECTION
HC 2 SOUTH 280 STATE DRIVE
WATERBURY, VT. 05671. 2060

REFERENCE # 25257

DEAR ADULT. SERICES

    I AM ENCLOSING A LETTER THAT I RECEIVED FROM. YOU A WHILE AGO. I AM NOT SURE WHO SENT IT TO YOU. MY FAMILY AND I HAVE ALWAYS WORKED HARD PAID OUR BILLS AND SPENT OUR. LIVES TRYING TO HELP OTHER PEOPLE.. AS A RESULT IT. HAS COST ME ABOUT EVERY THING. I LOST MY WIFE, MY BROTHER. MY HOME AND ALL. MY BUSINESS AND MY FAMILY HAS BEEN DESTROYED...MOSTLY DUE TO GREED AND DISHONEST ACTIONS OF OTHERS. I WAS TOLD BY THE GOVERNMENT. THAT. WE SHOULDNT, BE TRYING TO HELP OTHERS TO TRY TO GET. A HEAD, THAT. POOR PEOPLE WERE SUPPOSED TO STAY POOR.

    AS A RESULT I AM SENDING YOU A FEW PAPERS EXPLAINING THIS THERE ARE PLENTY MORE WHERE THESE CAME FROM. I HOPE THAT YOU CAN TAKE A LOOK AND HOPE THAT. YOU WILL SHARE THIS INFORMATION. WITH VERMONTS ATTORNEY GENERAL AND OTHERS, I DON,T KNOW. HOW. A WHILE AGO I DID WRITE A BOOK WHERE IS THE JUSTICE. IT SOLD GOOD AROUND HERE.

    THANK YOU. FOR HELPING . AND I HOPE. THAT SOME GOOD RESULTS. WILL COME OF IT.
I. WANT TO THANK YOU

        SINCERELY

           WILLIAM F. HILL

4130   About the Author
4131   Bill Hill was born on April 15, 1935, on North Main Street in Hardwick, Vermont. His father was a
4132   large potato farmer in this area. Bill grew up helping in the potato fields. He attended Hardwick Grade
4133   School and Academy, where he graduated in 1953. All the time that he attended school, he raised his
4134   own chickens and cattle, shipping milk to the Hood Creamery in Hardwick from his own cows at the
4135   age of thirteen. He has always felt that he needed to produce food for people to eat. Bill then attended
4136   the University of Vermont, where he graduated with a degree in agriculture. He also took a one-year
4137   graduate course at Saint Johnsbury Trade School, where he majored in auto mechanics. While
4138   attending the University of Vermont, Bill was selected to attend a two-week camp in Northern
4139   Michigan, owned and operated by William Danforth, the founder and owner of Ralston Purina
4140   Company. Mr. Danforth was a very interesting man, and spending two weeks with him was very
4141   inspirational.
4142   After college, Bill served two years in the army. Following the army, he purchased Hills Feed Store
4143   from his father's estate, now Poulin Lumber. Here he not only supplied local farmers with feed,
4144   fertilizer equipment, farm building supplies, silos, and bar cleaners, he, along with the Beacon Feed
4145   Specialist, set feed programs for many dairymen, helping them to improve their production
4146   profitability. In his own dairy herd he achieved the highest production average in in the local DHIA
4147   association with over two hundred herds competing. Bill sprayed many fields for weeds sand with
4148   fertilizer all over Northern Vermont.
4149   Bill was also active in many other fields mostly to do with agriculture and farming. He graduated from
4150   Reisch American School of Auctioneering in Mason City, Iowa, also the Certified Auction Institute at
4151   the Indiana Business University in Bloomington, Indiana, as well as Graham Cattle School of Scientific
4152   Breeding, Hobart School of Welding in Troy, Ohio, Dale Carnegie Course, and the Dale Carnegie
4153   Sales School.
4154   Bill was also a Hardwick Selectman for several years. He was on the local rescue squad. He served on
4155   the local zoning board for a while and was a bank director at Sterling Trust in Johnson, Vermont. He
4156   was one of two Holstein Sire Selectors from Vermont, which involved locating and purchasing
4157   Holstein bulls for the New England Selective Artificial Breeders Association headquartered in
4158   Woodbridge, Connecticut. Bill was also a director and past president of the Northeast Kingdom
4159   Holstein Club. He belonged to the Vermont Auctioneers Association and the National Auctioneers.
4160   Bill conducted a couple thousand of auctions of all types over a fifty-year period. He also brokered a
4161   lot of real estate for others.
4162   Bill was also chairman of Hardwick Development, a corporation of twenty-six members selected from
4163   the town and village of Hardwick. Some of their accomplishments were building a large poultry
4164   eggplant where All Metals Recycling is today and the log yard behind Lamoille Valley Ford. Bill had
4165   an airplane, which he landed on the farm and used for his business and gave many rides to his family
4166   and local people.
4167   Bill owned several properties and other business in the area, some of which were a welding shop
4168   building truck bodies and trailers, which was later taken over by his son, Clay. He owned Authentic
4169   Log Homes and Saw Mill; half interest in Morrisville Commission Sales, which was the largest weekly
4170   dairy sale in New England; the Bemis Block & Trading Center and the Centennial House & Daniels
4171   Block, both of which were headed for demolition, which he restored; and he also owned the Hardwick
4172   Post Office. Bill also owned a meat and seafood business in Florida called Hardwick Farms with
4173   fourteen trucks and twenty-six salesman on the road. Bill bought and sold a number of properties in
4174   Florida where he still owns a post office. He has purchased several homes and farms throughout
4175   Northern Vermont, which he sold mostly to local people and was able to help get them financed. Bill
4176   and his crew weatherized many homes and businesses with blown-in insulation. He developed the
4177   streets and lots and built several homes, taking on two partners in Hideaway Acres in Hardwick,

4178   Vermont. Bill's children worked hard and helped while they were growing up with auctions, the
4179   farming, the insulation business, real estate, and everything else.
4180   Bill and his wife, Sally, have nine children between them, twenty-six grandchildren, and twenty-three
4181   great-grandchildren. After selling their farm, they built their house in 1990, where they now live. They
4182   had much family help, including Bill's brother, Steve; son in-law Bob; and sons Clay, Rodney, and
4183   Paul. They all had a hand in it.
4184   Bill also served twenty-five years as a member and past President of Hardwick Kiwanis Club and is a
4185   fifty-year member of the Free and Accepted Masons Caspian Lake Lodge No. 87.
4186   Bill wrote a book called *Where Is the Justice*, which was a very good seller, telling about his and others'
4187   troubles with the federal and state government along with some local bankers.
4188   When Bill sold his farm in 1990, which he had run for many years; he was milking over 250 cows in a
4189   double seven milking parlor. For several years, along with his wife and family, they made a lot of
4190   wreaths and garland, hiring around thirty people during the wreath season.
4191   Bill has dealt with a lot of people and tried to help the many people who have been very helpful to
4192   him and his family. Bill likes to see people do well and be the best that they can be.
4193   Bill always worked seventy-five to eighty hours a week but still found time for family and usually
4194   attended church on Sunday.
4195   Today, Bill raises vegetables and steer beef, which is in demand from a large area of customers and
4196   sold at several farmer's markets and local restaurants. He also has several mules, which he works and
4197   drives, and he spends many hours with his friends, family, and grandchildren.
4198
4199
4200   Blurb
4201   I have always felt that we have greatest country in the world. It has always given me great pleasure to
4202   see honest, hardworking people and who are willing to take risks to get ahead and succeed. I always
4203   felt that this was that America got to be great and that we all should be working hard to help
4204   improve our own lives and the lives of others by carrying on this great American tradition. As a
4205   result of being brought up with this thinking, I am more than willing to go out of my way to try to
4206   help people succeed and obtain their goals. To see people succeed in their life's goals and ambitions
4207   has always been very gratifying to me and given me a good feeling.
4208   Another thing that always gives me a good feeling is to see couples doing things as a family and with
4209   their children. To me this is what life is all about and should be about. Many of this new generations
4210   of do-gooders, as they are often called, seem to think that everybody should live on handouts and
4211   that anyone who is successful should be cut back down and not allowed to succeed without their
4212   input as this is not fair to the less fortunate in this country.
4213   What they do not seem to realize or don't want to realize is that the people who are more successful
4214   probably do more to help the less fortunate than all the government and giveaway programs can
4215   ever hope to do. A successful person who has obtained his achievements through hard, honest work
4216   is usually willing to try to help others reach similar success. A person who is successful usually lives
4217   in a little better house. Many now think that this wrong, but that person probably pays several times
4218   the property taxes of someone living in a less expensive home. This will benefit everyone as this
4219   helps to educate their children and pay for many of the local services that people demand today. If
4220   they hire people to help take care of their homes or properties, they are usually paid for with after
4221   tax dollars, and this creates jobs for the people doing the work. Isn't this sharing the wealth? Most
4222   successful people help create jobs either by expanding their own business or investing on other
4223   business. I think that in order to get people off welfare and off the government rolls, we need all the
4224   successful people that we can get in this country.
4225

WHEN IN COURT ON MONDAY YOU ASKED ME HOW MUCH THAT I THOUGHT THAT THE COURT SHOULD AWARD THOSE WHO THEY HAVE HURT. I TOLD YOU THAT I WASANT SHURE HOW MUCH IS MY WIFES LIFE WORTH OR MY BROTHER, DAN HILLS LIFE WORTH. WHAT ABOUT WHAT JUDGE BENT DID TO MY GRAND DAUGHTER LEIGH WHO IS STILL HAVING BRAIN SURGERY IN BOSTON AND UNABLE TO WORK TO HELP CARE FOR HER FAMILY; WHAT ABOUT THE PROPERTY THAT JUDGE GAVE TO OLSONS AND I GOT NOTHING FOR THE GOVERNMENT CLAIMED THAT IT SHOULD BE WORTH SEVEN HUNDRD THOUSAND DOLLARS. YOU CANT IMAGINE HOW MUCH MONEY WE HAVE SPENT TO KEEP THEM IN NEW HAMPSHIRE

William F. Hill

William F. Hll
P O BOX 15
Hardwick Vt 05843
802 472 6308

DECEMBER 27 0019

Hon Robert R. Bent
Civil Division Court
Docket No235 10 18 Cav
Caledonia
Superior Court B
1126 Main Street Suite 1
St. Johnsbury Vt 05819

Dear Judge Bent

    I JUST WANT TO POINT OUT SOME THINGS IN THIS CASE.
1 YOU STATED I N YOUR ORIGINAL DECISION THAT HILLS GAVE
OLSON THE KEYS TO THEIR PROPERTY SO THAT HE COULD MOVE
IN AND TAKE OVER YOU KNOW THIS NOT TRUE. HILLS HAD NO
REASON TO GIVEUP THEIR PROPERTY TO OLSON

2   YOU STATE THAT HILLS AND OLSON WILL HAVE THE RIGHT
TO HAVE THE PROPERTY APPRAISED TO ARRIVE AT A FAIR
SETTLEMENT FOR DIVIDING THE PROPERTY. THIS SHOULD HAVE
NEVER BEEN AS THE HILLS STILL OWNED THE BIGGEST SHARE OF
THE PROPERTY AND YOU HAD CONFISCATED RONALDS SHARE
EVEN THOUGH THIS WASANT RIGHT WHEN HILL ASKED TO HAVE
THIS DONE AND HAD FOUND AN APPRAISER WHO COULD DO IT
YOU AND OLSON BOTH REFUSED TO HAVE THIS DONE

3   YOU ORDERD HILL TO GET ANOTHER . LAWYER,   .HILL DID
THIS TO TRY TO PLEASE YOU. HILL WAS TOLD THAT THIS LAWYER
WAS WELL QUALIFIED . YOU STATED THAT THE ONLY REASON
THAT HILL HIRED HIM WAS BECAUSE THAT HE WAS ALREADY
REPRESENTING HILL IN OTHER MATTERS. THIS WAS NOT TRUE.
HILL DID NOT KNOW THIS LAWYER AND NEVER HAD ANY OTHER
BUSINESS WITH HIM. THIS WAS ANOTHER FALSE STATEMENT

BUY YOU

4   YOU DID NOT KNOW ANY OF THE PEOPLE WHOS LIVES THAT YOU HAVE TAKEN OR ANY OF THE OTHER CHILDREN WHOS LIVES THAT YOU HAVE DESTROYED. NONE OF THESE WERE KNOWN BY OLSONS LAWYER WHO TOOK GREAT PRIDE IN DESTROYING . THEM.

5   YOU ACUSED ME OF NOT PAYING THE PROPERTY TAXES OR ANY INSURANCE. AS YOU KNOW I PAID ALL THE TAXES AND PROPERTY INSURANCE AS I HAD AGREED AND I STILL OWNED THE PROPERTY EVEN THOUGH YOU HAD GIVEN IT DISHONESTLY TO OLSON

6   I NOW UNDERSTAND FROM THE COURT THAT YOU HAVE NOW ABANDONED THIS CASE AFTER STRINGING EVERYBODY ALONG FOR NO GOOD REASON. YOU HAD TO KNOW THE CASE FROM BEGINNING TO END AS YOU WERE RUNNING THE WHOLE SHOW HOW COULD YOU DO THIS/

7   I CAN NOT BELIVE THAT AFTER DESTROYING EVERY BODYES LIVES AND ANY FUTURE THAT THEY SHOULD EVER HAVE. AS YOU KNEW NONE OF THEM HAVE NOT DONE ANY THING WRONG DISHONEST OR ILLEGAL . HOW COULD YOU DO THESE DISHONEST AND DREADFUL THINGS TO PERFECTLY INNOCENT PEOPLE AND CHILDREN AND DESTROY THEIR LIVES

8   YOU HAVE BEEN TRYING TO FIND A WAY TO DESTROY ME THE SAME AS YOU DID TO MY WIFE AND BROTHER. YOU ALMOST DID IT. I HAVE GONE THROUGH SOME VERY TENSE AND HORRIBLE TIMES AS A RESULT OF YOURS AND OLSONS BEHAVIOR AS A RESULT I DO NOW HAVE SOME SERIOUS HEART PROB YOULEMS THAT I NEVER HAD BEFORE. I AM BEING TREATED FOR THIS BY THE VETERANS ASSOCIATION IN WHITE RIVER I DON,T PLAN TO GIVE UP.

9   I KNOW THAT YOU HAVE BEEN LOOKING FOR A WAY TO DISPOSE OF THIS CASE. YOU HAVE MADE SEVERAL STATEMENTS LOOKING FOR AWAY OUT.

10   AFTER ALL YOU HAVE DONE TO THESE INNOCENT PEOPLE
HOW CAN YOU JUST TURN THIS OVER TO A NEW JUDGE AN JUST
WALK AWAY. KNOWING WHAT YOU HAVE DONE TO EVERYBODY. I
HAVE DONE BUSINESS WITH THOUSANDS OF PEOPLE IN MY   LIFE
BUT YOU HAVE GOT TO BE THE MOST DISHONEST AND THE
BIGGEST COWARD THERE IS, I THINK THAT THE LORD WILL
SETTLE WITH YOU SOON.

1 1 WE WILL GET THIS   HORRIBLE SITUATION SETTLED SOON

        AS EVER

                        WILLIAM F. HILL

William F. Hill
PO Box 15
HARDWICK, VT. 05843
802-472-6306. 802-472-3631

OCTOBER 18, 2021

BILL DAVIES
PO Box 303
BARTON, VT 05822

DEAR ATTORNEY DAVIES,

I AM SENDING YOU A COPY OF YOUR LETTER "TAX COLLECTORS REPORT OF SALE'. THIS IS THE FIRST CORRESPONDENCE THAT I HAVE RECEIVED FROM YOU ABOUT THE TAX SALE.
I KNEW NOTHING ABOUT THE SALE UNTIL A FEW DAYS AGO. SOMEBODY TOLD ME THAT OLSONS PROPERTY WAS COMING UP FOR TAX SALE. THIS WAS THE FIRST THAT I HAD HEARD ABOUT IT. I WENT RIGHT TO THE HARDWICK TOWN CLERKS OFFICE AND INQUIRED IF THERE WAS A TAX SALE COMING UP SOON. I WAS TOLD THAT THERE WOULD BE ONE IN A FEW DAYS AND THAT MY PROPERTY WAS THE FIRST ONE ON THE. LIST... I DID CONTACT THE CALEDONIA COURT AND LET THEM KNOW, BUT AS USUAL I HEARD NOTHING BACK FROM THEM.
I DO RECEIVE THE NEWS AND CITIZEN NEWSPAPER, BUT DIDN'T HAPPEN TO SEE IT ADVERTISED IN THE PAPER, I WASN'T LOOKING FOR IT. YOU MENTION THAT YOU AND THE TOWN CLERK SENT ME NOTICES WHICH I HAD TO SIGN FOR, I HAVE SEEN NO NOTICES. UNTIL I JUST GOT YOUR LETTER FOLLOWING THE SALE . AS I HAVE EXPLAINED, I HAD RECEIVED NO MENTION OF ANY SALE. EVEN THOUGH I HAVE GOT A LIFE LEASE AND HAVE PAID ALL THE TAXES THAT HAVE EVER BEEN PAID ON THAT PROPERTY. I STILL HAVE THE RIGHT ISSUED BY THE COURT TO HAVE THE PROPERTY APPRAISED AND BE COMPENSATED FOR MY SHARE. I HAVE TRIED TO GET THIS DONE BUT HAVE HAD NO CORPORATION FROM THE COURT OR OLSON'S LAWYER.
PLEASE HELP ME TO STRAIGHTEN THIS OUT AS IT IS NOT RIGHT AS IT IS.

SINCERELY,

William F. Hill

543

366 wasn't his. I don't believe he had ever paid any property taxes to Hardwick on this property or Leigh's
367 mobile home.
368
369 I contacted the Vermont Tax Department. They said the money should have gone to Charlotte and
370 They said "Just have Olson give you a check for the $8000." Olson refused to pay us and said that he
371 was keeping the money to make repairs on the property. This was devastating to Charlotte. She knew
372 how hard we worked, and the money was ours. I continued to pay the property taxes, as part of the
373 lifetime tenancy agreement with the government was that I keep the property taxes up to date, as I
374 always have, I don't understand how this man, who claims to be a legitimate businessman, can act as
375 he does.
376
377 Olson also bought the trailer I had put in for our granddaughter, for a small fraction of its worth,
378 rented it to six adults for what I heard was a high rent and forced Leigh and her four children out. She
379 was so upset that she wanted to move out of the area, but had no money. I rented a small house for
380 her in New Hampshire for $800 a month, and have been paying the rent ever since. I couldn't stand
381 to see her and those four beautiful children homeless.
382
383 I guess Olson never did the paperwork to show he bought the mobile home. He kept after Charlotte
384 to find Leigh and straighten out his mess with her. Charlotte had nothing to do with him buying it.
385 She knew how much we had to spend to put the mobile home there, and how little he paid her. She
386 wanted nothing to do with it, but Olson kept after her. The stress was killing her.
387
388 Charlotte's doctors and health providers told me that there was no way she could effectively fight the
389 cancer if she was continually under such heavy stress. I have since learned from attorneys that Olson
390 had no right to be on the property, much less dictate what happened there while we had our life interest,
391 but not knowing that at the time, it seemed that the only way to give her any peace would be to move
392 her away from Olson's presence and influence. I wanted to save her.
393
394 I learned of a small house on Dutton Road that was for sale, and I thought moving her over there
395 might help. In order to buy it, I had to sell a nice post office rental property that was paying a good
396 part of our income now that we were not farming. We moved there to try and get a little peace. It was
397 upsetting for Charlotte to leave the home she had helped design and worked so hard to furnish and
398 make beautiful for her family and friends to enjoy with us. She had many compliments on what she
399 had created there, and took pride in what she had accomplished. She had hoped it would be in the
400 family for generations to come. I tried everything I could think of to comfort her until she passed
401 away on Tuesday, May 29, 2018, after a courageous five year battle with cancer.
402
403 Epilogue
404
405 Still having a life estate in place, I continued going there almost every day after moving Charlotte out,
406 except when I had to work or was taking her to doctors or hospital.
407
408 Olson put Kelly Lacourse in charge of the land and she lived in the house with her friends, renting
409 the land and living space in the house. They asked me to prepare the ground for them, and I did, even
410 furnishings them with seeds and trays. They thought they could grow squash, but without any
411 commercial fertilizer or manure they didn't get much of a crop.
412
413 I can't believe how they have let the place deteriorate. The farm sign at the end of the driveway is flat

414 on the ground in grass and weeds. The land where they tried to raise crops had never been cleaned up
415 or reseeded, weeds and plastic mulch still there. A big section of fence on the left hand side of the
416 driveway is all smashed down, and the driveway is washing out. The hay fields are all destroyed. There
417 is rubbish all around the house, and window screens have blown off and lie on the ground. The carport
418 is full of debris and trash and has several goats and chickens living in it. The storm drain next to the
419 cellar window that kept water out of the basement is covered with wood and filled with trash, and
420 can't possible work.
421
422 Up back there is some kind of garbage on a trailer and in a building we built up there. The odor is
423 obnoxious. The barnyard fences are all down and dragged around, what a mess. The road that leads
424 by the mobile home is covered with trash, grass, and tin cans, and is not passable. The pond is all
425 grown up with weeds and brush and impossible to get to. I always kept the grass around the pond
426 mowed with a lawn mower, and it looked very nice.
427
428 The swimming pool is completely trashed and ruined. When I left, the swimming pool was fine and
429 working. I had chemicals in it and left some of it. The small greenhouse is falling down, has several
430 holes in it, and is full of trash. The deck next to the pool is covered with trash.
431
432 I haven't been in the house lately, but know that they have torn out walls and ceilings and moved
433 walls. They have made a mess of it trying to add more bedrooms. The septic permit is for two
434 bedrooms, which is what we had. This was a beautiful home and well cared for. Everyone I know who
435 has seen it can't believe what they have done to the house.
436
437 Even sadder than the destruction of a beautiful, well-loved and cared for home and property is the
438 destruction of the lives of those who lived there so happily. Charlotte's life was made a living hell
439 during the years she was fighting for her life, and needed all the peace she could get. Our four great
440 grandchildren had not had an easy life before we moved them to the property. Charlotte and I put our
441 whole lives into looking out for all the family, and especially these four small children. We were
442 teaching them to be good citizens who could live honest and productive lives. They started doing
443 quite well in school, and I had two of the girl taking music lessons. Amaya played in the school band,
444 and Promise played in church and concerts and at the farmers market. I was a very proud of them.
445 They had all learned to be good swimmers and had an interest in the cattle and horses, and were
446 learning how to care for animals. They had room to bike, fish, and boat. All that came to an end when
447 we were forced out. The only way Charlotte or I could see them was to drive a hundred miles and
448 pick up a couple of them to bring here for a few days. They were always anxious to come. I still have
449 them here as often as I can, but they miss their grandmother terrible, and there is nothing very exciting
450 for them here now, just a few hens.
451
452 This whole mess has really destroyed several lives and a family, all due to selfishness, greed, and lack
453 of integrity of others. I drive by and look at the house and land and other buildings and what was
454 Leigh's mobile home. I am sad and I realize that I worked all my live to have a good home for us and
455 Leigh and her children. I paid for all this with my life's hard work and now have nothing to show for
456 it.
457
458 I've gotten to where it is really destroying me. I feel like I can't stand it much longer, but I can't give
459 up, no matter what. Olson needs to at least pay me for my lifetime interest in the property. This is the
460 agreement that we made with the government that he is bound to. He also owes me my $8000 tax
461 refund which he illegally kept. His attorney Kristina Michelson claims he has spent $150,000 fixing up

Show me when he spend 15 cents

William F. Hill
PO BOX 15
HARDWICK VT. 05843
802-472-6308

HI. PROMISE

I. WAS GLAD TO HEAR FROM YOU. YESTERDAY I CAN UNDERSTAND THAT YOU ARE NOT VERY HAPPY. I. WENT THROUGH A LOT AFTER WE. WENT DOWN. TO. SOUTHERN. NEW. HAMPSHIRE. YOU WONT BELIEVE. WHAT THEY PUT ME THROUGH. BUT NOW I AM GETTING BACK ON MY FEET. AND DON;T PLAN TO LET IT KEEP ME DOWN. I HOPE THAT YOU CAN DO THE SAME THING. I PRAY TO GOD EVERY DAY FOR YOU AND ME. GOD HAS BEEN GOOD TO ME. AND I THINK HE WILL BE GOOD TO YOU AND HELP YOU TO GET BACK ON YOUR FEET.

YOU USED TO. BELIVE IN GOD AND JEASUS. REMEMBER/ YOU USED TO CONDUCT. CHURCH AND. SUNDAY. CLASSES IN OUR LIVING ROOM. AT THAT TIME EVERY THING WAS GOING. MUCH BETTER AND WE. ALL. SEAM TO BE HAPPY. YOU. NEED TO GET GOD BACK IN YOUR LIFE. GOD HAS BEEN HELPING ME A LOT. AND HE WILL HELP YOUR LIFE IF YOU LET HIM. THINGS ARE GOING TO GET BETTER. YOU JUST NEED TO HANG ON AND WE ARE GOING TO HAVE A GOOD. LIFE. WE CANT LET THINGS. GET US DOWN. YOU WERE ALWAYS STRONG AND WAS ABLE TO DEAL. WITH MANY. PROBLEMS AND LOOK A HEAD. WE ALL GO THROUGH SOME ROUGH TIMES. BUT LEARN. TO. GET AROUND THINGS....YOU CAN. TOO. I HOPE THAT WE CAN GET BACK TOGETHER. SOON. GOOD THINGS CAN TAKE A LITTLE. TIME SO. WE HAE GOT TO TRY TO MAKE THINGS BETTER. IF ONLY A LITTLE. AT A TIME. WE. ARE GONG TO MAKE IT. IF THINGS IN THE PAST ARE BOTHERING YOU. TRY TO GET THEM OUT OF YOUR MIND. AND I. WILL ALWAYS. LOVE YOU AND BE ON YOUR SIDE. LOOK WHAT WE HAVE BEEN THROUGH. AND GOOD THINGS. WILL. HAPPEN AGAIN. I HOPE THAT YOU WILL CALL ME WHENEVER. YOU CAN. WE ARE GOING TO GET TO. GATHER SOON AND I CANT. WATE. CALL WHEN. YOU CAN. I WILL BE WATING. I LOVE YOU

GRAMP

BILL HILL

William F. Hill
PO Box 15
HARDWICK VT.05843
802-472-6308

SUPERIOR COURT

DOCKET. NO 235-10-18-CACV

CALEDONIA UNIT

WILLIAM F, HILL.   PLAINTIFF

VS
SVEN OLSON. DEFENDANT

RESPONSE TO KRISTINA . ATTORNEY FOR SPEN OLSON

KRISTINA LIKES TO BELITTLE ME AS I AM NOT A LAWYER.   I ADMIT
THAT I HAVE NEVER BEEN TO LAW SCHOOL SO DON.T KNOW ALL THE LINGO
THAT. AWYERS AND. JUDGES. USE TO BELITTLE US. I HAVE DONE A LOT OF
BUSINESS WITH HUNDREDS OF PEOPLE. MOSTLY NOT. EDUCATED. LAWYERS
     I THINK A LOT OF HER REASONING SHOWS. HER LACK OF TRUTH.
HAVE HIRED SEVERAL LAWYES AND CONTACTED SEVERAL MORE. OF
WHITCH ARE. NOT INTERESTED IN. DEALING WITH THIS LAWYER AND
COURT I HAVE CONTACTED SEVERAL OTHER LAWYERS THATI ONLY GAVE
VERBAL ANSWERS I THINK THAT YOU SHOULD UNDERSTAND

     RONALD COULD GO DOWN TO PAUL AND BELIDA LUSSIER. HOME AND
PICK UP ANY. AMOUNT OF MONEY WHERE HE HAD I T STORED.

547

THAT HAD BEEN. AROUND WERE HER TWO BOY-FRIENDS. MY AIR
TANK WAS. GONE. THE COPS KNEW WHERE IT WAS. BUT AS
USUAL. THE. POLICE. LIKE ALWAYS SAID THAT THERE. WAS
NOTHING THAT THEY COULD DO SO I AM OUT MY STUFF

WE. HAVE SINSE CHECKED OUR GARAGE AND FOUND. A NUMBER OF
TOOLS MISSING. THERE. WERE A NUMBER OF TOOLS LINED UP AGAINST THE
OUT. SIDE DOORS AS. THOUGH THEW WERE READY TO. DISAPPEAR. AN
number OF THINGS WERE GONE BUT. IS HARD O TELL WHAT THE LOCAL
COPS HAD ME SIGN A PAPER GIVING THEM A RIGHT. TO CHECK ON THE
PLACE. AND KEEP TRACT OF ANY. VANDALISM. DON,T KNOW WHAT THEY
HAVE DONE. I HAVE NOT HEARD FROM THEM. THERE WAS A. NEW 25 FOOT
SET OF. JUNPER CABLES. Cabler

William F. Hill
PO BOX 15
HRDWICK. VT 05843

HARDWICK TOWN POLICE,

    THERE. ARE MANY MORE THNGS GONE INCLUDING. HAND TOOLS
TWO NICE CHAIN SAWS A STEEL and A HYSKSVARNA. SOME WELDING SUPPLIES. I SIGNED. A PA
PER. FOR YOU THAT YOU PRODUCED STATING THAT YOU . WOULD WATCH AND LOOK OUT FOR T
HE STUFF IN OUR BARN. BUT NOW QUITE A FEW THINGS ARE MISSING. WE HAVE NOT. EVEN SEEN
THE NICE AIR TANK THATYOU SAY YOU KNOW. WHERE IT. IS AT.
    HOW COME WE HERE ABOUT. ALL THE BREAK INS AND STUFF. THAT THEY
ARE TRYING TO RECOVER UP NORTH. DOES HARDWICK POLICE GO OUT
LOOKING FOR ALL THE STUFF THAT HAS. BEEN STOLEN IN THIS AREA. I FEEL THAT. IT WOULD HAVE
BEEN A VERY SIMPLE MATTER TO FIND OUR. COMPUTER
IT IS TO BAD AS WE HAD. A LOT OF USEFUL INFORMATION. STORED O IT THAT WE WILL PROBABLY
NOT BE ABLE TO RECOVER
    IT IS VERY SAD THAT WE. ALL PAY BIG MONEY FOR THIS PROTECTION
AND. NEVER TO GET TO USE IT.

WILLIAM F. HILL
PO Box 15
HARDWICK VT. 05843
802-472-6908

SALLY HILL. ALSO TAUGHT SUNDAY SCHOOL AT. HOPE COMMUNITY CHURCH
IN. WALDEN EVERY SUNDAY. THE STUDENTS REALLY LIKED I HER AND SEEM TO
GET A LOT OUT OF IT. SHE WAS REALLY. RESPECTED FOR. IT. I HELPED HER TO
PREPARE HER CLASSES. AT HOME DURING THE WEEK.

IF. EVERY BODY HAD MINDED THER OWN BUSINESS AND NOT BEEN SO
ANXOIS TO CAUSE TROUBLE FOR THESE HONEST PEOPLE AND DESTROYING
THEIR LIVES. WE WOULD ALL BE LIVING IN OUR HOME HAPPY AND PEACEFUL THE
CHILDREN WOULD BE DOING VERY WELL AND LIVING A VERY PRODUCTIVE LIFE.
WE WOULD PROBABLY BE RAISING OUR CATTLE AND THE GREAT GRAND
CHILDREN WOULD. BE WELL CARED FOR. I REALLY HOPE THAT ALL THE PEOPLE
WHO HAVE CAUSED THIS. VERY SAD PROBLEM. REALLY SOMEDAY REALIZE WHAT
THEY HAVE DONE TO. ALL. THESE INNOCENT PEOPLE. SEEMS LIKE THE COURT
WOULD BRING THIS TO A HEAD ALTHOUGH I DON,T KNOW. WHAT GOOD IT WILL DO.
THERE ARE STILL TWO SMALL CHILDREN WHOES LIVES ARE BEING DESTROYED.
HOW CAN YOU JUST SIT I DAILLY BY AND WATCH THIS GO ON
I DON,T KNOW WHAT. TO DO. THIS HAS. GOT TO BE THE MOST CRULE THING
THAT THIS COURT COULD DO FOR NO REASON. I DON,T UNDERSTAND. HOW YOU
PEOPLE CAN BE SO RUTHLESS AND CRULE AND AGANST THESE. INNOCENT
CHILDREN. YOU HAVE ALREADY DESTROYED THE ADULTS. THIS KIND OF THING
MUST MAKE MAKE YOU HAPPY. I DON,T SEE HOW YOU CAN CALL YOUR SELVES
HUMAN. I DON,T SEE HOW. ANYTHING CAN BE ANYMORE. CRULE OR SAD. I GUESS
I AM STILL WASTING MY TIME AND LIFE. WHY CAN,T YOU DO SOMETHING
SINCERLY. BILL HILL

William F. Hill

William F. Hill
PO BOX 15
HRDWICK. VT 05843

HARDWICK TOWN POLICE

. IT MAKES ME QUITE DEPRESSED TO SEE THE SWINNGING BRIDGE DOWN AND. CLOSED. SEVERAL YEARS AGO THE BRIDGE WAS DOWN AND CLOSED LIKE IT IS NOW. I PURCHSDED THE BRIDGE FROM THE DANIELS. FAMILY. I WORKED NIGHTS FURNISHING THE LUMBER AND CUTTING OUT. THE FLOORING FOR THE BRIDGE. IT NEEDED OTHER SUPPLIES WHICH I FURNISHED. ALFRED LANPHERE AND. SOME MEMBERS OT THE HARDWICK KIWANIS CLUB HELPED ME TO RESTORE THE BRIDGE LIKE NEW. AFTER WE GOT IT FIXED I GAVE THE BRIDGE TO THE TOWN FORTHE USE OF. EVERBODY. MANY PEOPLE WERE. VERY GLAD TO GET IT BACK. I KNOW THE TOWN THINKS THAT THEY CAN,T FIX IT WITHOUT A GOVERNMENT GRANT. I CAN,T BELEIVE THIS. OVER THEYEARS. I HAVE DONE A LOT OF THINGS. TO HELP HARDWICK. I HAVE NEVER HAD A HANDOUT OR GRANT FROM FOR ANYTHING.

WITH OUY HAVING TO LOOK OUT FOR GREENSBORO. NOW PERHAPS. HARDWICK EXTRA POLICEL COULD FIND TIME TO REPRARE THE SWING ING BRIDGE FOR THE PEOPLE OF HARDWICK

OVER THE YEARS ANY TIME THAT I HAVE CALLED ON THE HARDWICK POLICE FOR HELP THEY HAVE ALWAYS HAD THE SAME STOCK ANSWER; THERE IS NOTHING THAT WE CA N DO AND THAT. IS ALL YOU DO.

YOU DON,T PROBABLY RECALL WHO WAS RESPONSIBLE FOR CLOSING DOWN AND AND DEFUNDING THE HARDWICK. VILLAGE POLICE DEPARTMEN. THEN GOING AHEAD AND ESTABLI SHING ORGANIZING AND SETTING UP THE. PRESENT HARDWICK POLICE DEPARTMENT. WITH OUT THIS YOU MIGHT NOT HAVE A JOB. THINK ABOUT IT.

ANOTHER THING PERHAPS YOU. SHOULD RESEARCH WHO HAS PROBABLY BEEN ONE OF T HE HIGHEST PROPERTY TAX PAYERS. IN HARDWICK OVER THE YEARS. MUCH OF THIS TAX MONEY HAS GONE TO SUPPORT THE HARDWICK POLICE DEPARTMENT. PERHAPS YOU SHOULD. TAKE TIME TO THINK ABOUT THIS

550

To All Concerned,

It is unbelievable what the Federal Government can do in this country to honest, hardworking people. They did all that they could do to take everything we had worked our whole lives to build.

The Federal Government never liked that I did business with local banks by purchasing delinquent properties that had been foreclosed on, fixing them up, and re-selling them. I gave hundreds of people the opportunity to purchase their own, home while government officials said "poor people should stay poor".

We were successful Vermont dairy farmers for over 50 years. When we sold our farm and business we built a big brand new home, which so upset the government that they falsely accused me of making a statement on a loan application I had not made. I hadn't even been near a bank.

An executive at Bradford Bank where I had excellent credit, called me and said that he needed to make a loan to the president of another bank who was up to his credit limit, but would soon be caught up. I had done previous business both these men and had plenty of respect for them. Bradford bank made the loan direct and I only had to sign on the note which the bank brought to me. The note was soon paid off directly to the bank from the creditor.

I received nothing for my help. Later when I checked with other banks and several attorneys, they all said that this was what is called a "nominee loan," and was perfectly legal, yet the government charged me with making a "false statement" on a loan application which I never made. They called me a felon, which caused me to lose my credibility and my respect. I also lost my real estate licenses and auctioneers license. They threatened to use this against me at sentencing if I refused to lie for them at anothers trial. Because I would not lie for them, they fined me $10,000 and 100 hours of community service, haven't left me alone since.

You need to read my book, "Where Is The Justice", to really understand how they did to us what they did to us, and especially to my now deceased wife, Sally, so that it won't happen to you.

In the mid eighties we kept a good home for us and our family. When our son Ronald got into trouble, we knew nothing about the illegal things that he was doing until it came out in the newspaper.

The Federal Government ended up taking our home and sold it for only $190 thousand. We designed and built the house ourselves, investing over $500 thousand. The Federal Government got the sale money and we were got nothing.

We are, and have always been, simple, honest, hard working people, with no intention of ever doing anything wrong. We certainly would not have been working with Ronald if we had any idea that he was doing anything illegal.

The Federal Government claimed that they knew for at least five years about Ronald's activities, yet they kept quiet and let us fall into their trap so that they could reap more and more from the sale of everything that we worked all our lives to attain. Where Is The Justice?

WILLIAM F. HILL
PO Box I5
HARDWICK, VT.

05843   13 JAN 202

802-472 - 6308

SORRY TO BOTHER YOU   BUT YOU ALWAYS
SEEM TO DO A. G00D JOB. I HAVE BEEN
WATCHING YOU FOR. A LONG TIME
I HAVE. ENCLOSED A FEW PAPERS. OF WHICH I
HAVE. MANY. MORE.   I. AND MY. FAMILY HAVE BEEN
THROUGH A VERY HARD TIME FOR THE PAST
FORTY. YEARS. I DON;T MEAN TO BOTHER YOU.
BUT IF I CAN;T   TELL SOMEBODY. WE ARN;T GOING
TO MAKE IT I DON;T KNOW WHAT I HAVE DONE
WRONG. I AM. NOW EIGHTY SEVEN YEARS OLD
AND IF I CANT REACH SOME RESOLUTION FOR
THEM   I DON;T SEE ANY FUURE FOR MY GREAT
GRAND CHILDREN. THEY ARE VERY GOOD
CHILDREN BUT CAN STAND SOME GUIDANCE
SOON IF THEY ARE GOING TO MAKE IT

THANKS AGAIN

BILL

HILL`

WILLIAM F. HILL
P.O.BOX 15
HARDWICK, VERMONT 05843
802-472-6308

Sally Hill has always been a very active person liking all people and doing many things to bring them happiness Five years ago she started gaining weight and did not feel as good as usual She went to Hanover to the Dartmouth Hitchcock hospital where she was diagnosed with cancer One week later she underwent a major operation to try to remove the cancer Doctor Demers said that she felt that they removed most of the cancer cells and she felt that kemo would take care of the rest After several all-day kemo treatments her cancer count went down to almost nothing The problem seem to be that she was under a lot of stress and the cancer count shot back up to higher than it was before

She had to go back on kemo nearly every week Since then I have probably taken her to at least forty all day kemo treatments at the Dartmouth Hitchcock Norris Cotton Cancer Center I have had to take her to the Copley emergency room where they they spent several hours trying to help her but couldn't help her so sent her to Dartmouth Hitchcock in an ambulance in the middle of the night where she stayed for a while After getting her back home I had to continually take her to several hospitals for treatment I had to make several trips to St Johnsbury Hospital and to the North Haveral New Hampshire Hospital where they had to keep drawing fluid from her adman. One time I had to take her all the way to Hanover. There they told me that it was good that I got her there when I did as they said that she would not have lasted another day because she would have suffocated

You can't imagine what we went through to try to keep her alive and she really wanted to live for her family and all else She has already got all this years Christmas presents ready and wrapped and planed to have Christmas This July as she was sure that she would not make to another December Her present are all here and she didn't get the chance to give them out

William F. Hill

March 25, 1994

Re: Charlotte Hill

To Whom It May Concern:

This woman sought services at our Community Mental Health Center in April 1992 and she has been seen at one or two week intervals since that time for individual counseling. She reports a long history of well respected employment for the Extension Service that ended with her planned departure in 1987. Ms. Hill was actively involved in teaching people in the community about nutrition and budgeting. She also participated in recordkeeping for auctions that her husband conducted. Additionally she was involved in her husband's real estate business and she actively pursued rehabilitating homes for eventual sale.

Approximately a year prior to her seeking our services she became distraught and overwhelmed by the significant financial problems she and her husband were experiencing. The burden of the legal and financial problems were such that Ms. Hill could no longer function at her previous level. She has had trouble with her short term memory, significant sleep disturbance, crying episodes, anxiety, worry and hair loss. As a result of these stressful circumstances Ms. Hill experiences a burning sensation on her scalp and she is gradually developing bald spots from the resulting hair loss. She is very distressed about these events. She applied for and was granted Social Security Disability benefits and she is disabled as a result of this stress and unable to be gainfully employed.

I am in hopes that this information will be of assistance to you in appreciating the impact that the legal and financial problems have had for Ms. Hill.

Sincerely,

Maureen McGuire, BSN
Psychiatric Nurse Practitioner

MM/all

March 25, 1994

Re: Charlotte "Sally" Hill

To Whom It May Concern:

    This woman sought services at our Community Mental Health Center in April 1992 and she has been seen at one or two week intervals since that time for individual counseling. She reports a long history of well respected employment for the Extension Service that ended with her planned departure in 1987. Ms. Hill was actively involved in teaching people in the community about nutrition and budgeting. She also participated in recordkeeping for auctions that her husband conducted. Additionally she was involved in her husband's real estate business and she actively pursued rehabilitating homes for eventual sale.

    Approximately a year prior to her seeking our services she became distraught and overwhelmed by the significant financial problems she and her husband were experiencing. The burden of the legal and financial problems were such that Ms. Hill could no longer function at her previous level. She has had trouble with her short term memory, significant sleep disturbance, crying episodes, anxiety, worry and hair loss. As a result of these stressful circumstances Ms. Hill experiences a burning sensation on her scalp and- she is gradually developing bald spots from the resulting hair loss. She is very distressed about these events. She applied for and was granted Social Security Disability benefits and she is disabled as a result of this stress and unable to be gainfully employed.

    I am in hopes that this information will be of assistance to you in appreciating the impact that the legal and financial problems have had for Ms. Hill.

Sincerely,

Maureen McGuire, BSN
Psychiatric Nurse Practitioner

MM/all

2347	Sally Hill	March 26, 1987
2348	P.O.Box 15	
2349	29 Elm Street	
2350	c/o W.F. Hill	
2351	Hardwick, VT 05843	
2352		
2353	Dear Sally,	
2354		

2355 It is with regret that we accept your resignation as Nutrition Aide in Orleans County. No one in the
2356 Extension Service (faculty or staff) over the years showed more dedication, enthusiasm, and genuine
2357 drive than you did. Your pursuit of excellence in working with low income or limited resource people
2358 to achieve improved nutrition for their families set and example which will be matched by few who
2359 follow.
2360
2361 It was always a pleasure to work with you. Again, thank you for a job well done. Sally, you did make a
2362 difference in the lives of others. You were "Mrs. EFNEP" in your county and state.
2363
2364 If you ever change your mind on coming back or need a recommendation, please let me know. Feel
2365 free to stop in when you are in Burlington.
2366 Sincerely,
2367 Bob Honnold
2368 Interim Director
2369

May 29, 1987

Sally Hill
P. O. Box 15
29 Elm Street
c/o W. F. Hill
Hardwick, VT
05843

Dear Sally:

I regret that neither I nor Carol Fitzgerald can participate in your farewell party.

The UVM Extension Service wishes you the very best of success as you move to your next career. The Vermont EFNEP program is better today because of your dedication, hard work, enthusiasm, willingness to experiment and try new ways, and your genuine leadership at the local level. You had understanding, empathy and rapport with low income families. You could communicate with them and they could talk to you. You were very effective in helping us tell the EFNEP story to everyone, including influencial leaders, community leaders, State Senators and Legislators, national policy makers, and others. When you explained it, people listened and became enthused about the concept and its impact.

As Associate Director in the earlier days and Interim Director now, I think you have helped me enhance my understanding of the changing needs of low income families. While the morale of Extension faculty and staff vacillated up and down over time, you always, even if funds were to be cut off the next day, maintained an infectious positiveness and optimism.

Thank you for your advice and meritorious service during the past 14 years. We wish you happiness and success as you move forward. If you are in the Burlington area, be sure to stop in.

Sincerely,

Bob Honnold
Interim Director

BH/c

June 1, 1987

Dear Sally:

    Thank you for your dedicated and valuable work in EFNEP over the past fourteen years. Your enthusiasm and excellent teaching have helped countless homemakers and families to manage better in all aspects of food and nutrition. Your examples and encouragement have helped many improve their lives.

    Your ability to cooperate with other agencies has been of the highest quality and has spread and enhanced the reputation of the University of Vermont Extension Service.

    I will personally miss your support and enthusiasm. You were, always ready to take on any new project, whatever it might entail. This is indeed a valuable attribute and is the ingredient needed to get things done! I appreciated it greatly.

    My very best wishes go with you in whatever new endeavors you undertake. If I can be of any help, please ask.

    On a personal note, our friendship, has been, and will continue to be, very important to me.

                        Very Sincerely,

                        Alice M. Wright
                        EFNEP Coordinator

Sally Hill   March 26, 1987
P.O.Box 15
29 Elm Street
c/o W.F. Hill
Hardwick, VT 05843

Dear Sally,

It is with regret that we accept your resignation as
Nutrition Aide in Orleans County. No one in the Extension
Service (faculty or staff) over the years showed more
dedication, enthusiasm, and genuine drive than you did.
Your pursuit of excellence in working with low income or
limited resource people to achieve improved nutrition for
their families set and example which will be matched by
few who follow.

It was always a pleasure to work with you. Again,thank
you for a job well done. Sally, you did make a difference in
the lives of others. You were "Mrs. EFNEP" in your county
and state.

If you ever change your mind on coming back or need a
recommendation, please let me know. Feel free to stop in
when you are in Burlington.
Sincerely,
Bob Honnold
Interim Director

191211 MEH WORKING DRAFT WILLIAM HILL COMPLAINT
UNITED STATES DISTRICT COURT
Working Draft for Litigation Funding

Working Draft for Litigation Funding ·

****

WILLIAM HILL,

    Plaintiff,

v.

                                       No.

UNITED STATES OF AMERICA,
SVEN OLSON,
AND
VINCENT ILLUZZI,
      Defendants   .

****

COMPLAINT
Introduction

- This is a complaint for injunctive relief and damages N stemming from the federal government's convicting William Hill's stepson, Ronald Aldrich, of drug trafficking, and then seizing the family farm he (Aldrich) bought from his mother and stepfather (William Hill) who reserved to themselves a life estate ("Life Estate")—which was ignored by defendant Sven Olson when the U.S.A. sold the farm as having been purchased with drug money to him (Olson), and which Vincent Illuzzi – Mr. Hill's lawyer – did nothing about but take Mr. Hill's money. As a result Olson was able, _de facto_, to evict Mr. Hill and his now-dead wife from the home he (Mr. Hill) personally built.

PARTIES

- William Hill is Breault ("Mr. Breault") is an individual who at all relevant times herein was and is a resident of Hardwick, Vermont.
- The United States of America came into existence following the Revolutionary War and exists pursuant to the Constitution of the United States of America.
- Sven Olson is an in individual residing illegally in Mr. Hill's home in Hardwick, Vermont.
- Vincent Illuzzi is an individual attorney living and practicing law at all relevant times herein in Orleans County in northern Vermont. Illuzzi

"represented" (malpracticed with respect to) Mr. Hill in
connection with his (Illuzzi's) failed attempt to restore
Mr. Hill to his life estate and stop Sven Olson from
continuing to exclude him (Hill) from the home he built in
Hardwick.

JURISDICTION AND VENUE

- Federal Question. Jurisdiction lies in this Court based
on 28 U.S.C. §1331, inasmuch as plaintiffs seek relief in
the nature of civil damages and injunctive relief under
RICO, 18 U.S.C. § 1964. This Court may exercise
jurisdiction over plaintiffs' state law claims under
principles of pendent jurisdiction.

- Venue is proper within the Southern District of New York
because the United States of America is present there.

FACTS COMMON TO ALL COUNTS

- Mr. Hill built his home -- the "Mansion" - in Hardwick,
Vermont, on land he owned, many years ago.

- Mr. Hill's wife at all relevant times herein had a son, Mr.
Hill's stepson, Ronald Aldrich, who bought The Mansion from
his mother and stepfather with them reserving to themselves
the Life Estate.

- Thereafter Aldrich was convicted of drug trafficking.

- Ultimately the defendant USA seized The Mansion as having
been purchased with drug money and, in that connection,
Aldrich went to federal prison for a fourteen-year (14
year) term.

- Ultimately the U.S. Marshals auctioned The Mansion to the
defendant Sven Olson.

- The United States is of record admitting—in writing—that
Mr. Hill and his wife owned the Life Estate in The Mansion
and were entitled to live there.

- Defendant Olson ignored the Life Estate and harassed Mr.
Hill and his wife into leaving The Mansion.

- Mr. Hill's wife died, as a proximate result of the
incompetence of the U.S. Marshalls and the harassment of
the Defendant Olson, who constructively evicted Mr. Hill
and his wife by his continual harassment. Mr. Hill's
brother also died—by suicide—as a proximate result of the
same incompetence and harassment.

- Mr. Hill hired defendant Vincent Illuzzi to enforce his
(Mr. Hill's) rights in the Life Estate in The Mansion.
Illuzzi took over $2000.00 (two thousand and no/100
dollars) from Mr. Hill but did nothing save demand more
money (for work not performed) and, when Mr. Hill declined
to give Illuzzi additional money, Illuzzi withdrew from
further representation having effectively done nothing
whatever for the over $2000.00 (two thousand and no/100

dollars) Mr. Hill had paid him.
- This litigation followed.

COUNT ONE - R.I.C.O.
(Mail Fraud/Wire Fraud/Fraud)

- Paragraphs one through 17 are incorporated by reference.

- activity (mail and wire fraud/scheme to defraud) which did, in fact, defraud Mr. Hill of the life estate he reserved to himself and his wife when he and his wife sold their farm to Ronald Aldrich.
- EACH MAILING RELATED TO THE SALE TO SVEN OLSON IS A SEPARATE COUNT OF MAIL AND WIRE FRAUD COLLECTIVELY COMPRISING A PATTERN OF RACKETEERING ACTIVITY ACTIONABLE UNDER 18 U.S.C. §1964(C) (CIVIL RICO)
- The conduct alleged constitutes multiple violations of Federal criminal laws barring mail and wire fraud AND FRAUD, 18 U.S.C §§1341, 1343, All these acts, viewed in their entirety, constitute a pattern of racketeering activity in violation of 18 U.S.C. §1962.
- Mr. Hill is entitled to judgment against Defendants, jointly and severally, pursuant to 18 U.S.C. §1964 in an amount of threefold the damages ha has sustained as a result of the fraudulent activity alleged in this Complaint as may be proven at trial, together with the cost of this suit, including a reasonable attorney's fee.

COUNT TWO
(negligent/intentional infliction of emotional distress/
elder abuse)

- Paragraphs one through 22 are incorporated by reference.
- Mr. Hill has been all-but-devastated by the defendants and their fraudulent conduct. He has lost his home, his wife, his brother, his money, his dignity, his pride...everything except the vain hope that this lawsuit will generate a "little bit" (his words) of money to leave to his grandchildren.
- Mr. Hill is entitled to damages for negligent infliction of emotional distress, intentional infliction of emotional distress, and, additionally against Defendant Illuzzi, a) return of the money Mr. Hill paid Illuzzi to represent him, and b) damages for malpractice against Defendant Illuzzi.

WHEREFORE, Plaintiff demands tha this Court enter judgment
    A. For a preliminary and permanent injunction ordering Defendants to return The Mansion to Mr. Hill to him pursuant to the terms of the Life Estate;
- B. For such damages as Mr. Hill may prove at trial, trebled; and

C. For such other and further relief as may appear to this honorable Court to be just and proper.

respectfully submitted,

WILLIAM HILL

By his attorneys,

Miles E. Hoisington
attorney at law

Law Office of Miles E. Hoisington

57 W. 57th Street
New York, N.Y. 10019
tel 929.302.3643
lawofcmilesehoisington
@gmail.com

Richard Schoenstein, Esq
Tarter Krinsky Drogen LLP
1350 Broadway
New York, NY 10018
ph 212.216.1120

rschoenstein@tarterkrinsky.com

#30#

William F. Hill

WILLIAM F. HILL
PO BOE 15
HARDWICK VERMONT 05843
802 472 6308

Vincent Iliuzzi
PO Box 226
Orleans VT 05860

Dear Vince.

Have we ever heard any answers to our interrogator questions from Olson and his lawyer

I would like to request an explanation of Olson to question No 17

17 What were the dates that you took Great Grand Daughters Promise age 12 and Mersadies 13 on this last vacation . Where did you go
Who went with you Were your Wife and children on the this vacation

Why did you drop these girls off at the Days Inn in Champion New Hampshire and ask Bill Hill to pick them up there rather than bringing them back home where you had got them Why was your Wife not with you when you dropped them off Had she been with you

After dropping them off Mersadies cried and said that she would never go with you again and never wanted to see you again Promise has had several violent spells and been very depressed at times since returning from this trip

What happened on this vacation to turn these young girls this way

564

Vt. 62, 65–66 (1983) ("Had the court been in doubt about appellant's condition, it could have required a showing sufficient to enable it to make a judicial determination as to whether appellant was competent to proceed without the appointment of a guardian ad litem").

The court will take Mr. Hoisington up on his suggestion that a status conference be held. The conference will take place as soon as the current emergency orders by the Vermont Supreme Court allow. Mr. Hoisington should make arrangements to have local counsel assist. If he does not participate, the court will still hold a hearing regarding the question of Mr. Hill's ability to act on his own behalf. Obviously if Mr. Hill is actually withdrawing his request for restoration of the property, then the court will not need to act further on the motion.

Set this matter for status. Copy Attorney Hoisington on this entry as well as parties.

Electronically signed on April 16, 2020 at 11:54 AM pursuant to V.R.E.F. 7(d).

Robert R. Bent,
Judge

William F. Hill

William F. Hill
P0 BOX 15
HARDWICK VT. 05843
802-472-6308

HI. PROMISE

   I. WAS GLAD TO HEAR FROM YOU. YESTERDAY I CAN UNDERSTAND THAT YOU ARE NOT VERY HAPPY. I. WENT THROUGH A LOT AFTER WE. WENT DOWN. TO. SOUTHERN. NEW. HAMPSHIRE. YOU WONT BELIEVE. WHAT THEY PUT ME THROUGH. BUT NOW I AM GETTING BACK ON MY FEET. AND DON;T PLAN TO LET IT KEEP ME DOWN. I HOPE THAT YOU CAN DO THE SAME THING. I PRAY TO GOD EVERY DAY FOR YOU AND ME. GOD HAS BEEN GOOD TO ME. AND I THINK HE WILL BE GOOD TO YOU AND HELP YOU TO GET BACK ON YOUR FEET.
   YOU USED TO. BELIVE IN GOD AND JEASUS. REMEMBER/ YOU USED TO CONDUCT. CHURCH AND. SUNDAY. CLASSES IN OUR LIVING ROOM. AT THAT TIME EVERY THING WAS GOING. MUCH BETTER AND WE. ALL. SEAM TO BE HAPPY. YOU. NEED TO GET GOD BACK IN YOUR LIFE. GOD HAS BEEN HELPING ME A LOT. AND HE WILL HELP YOUR LIFE IF YOU LET HIM. THINGS ARE GOING TO GET BETTER. YOU JUST NEED TO HANG ON AND WE ARE GOING TO HAVE A GOOD. LIFE. WE CANT LET THINGS. GET US DOWN. YOU WERE ALWAYS STRONG AND WAS ABLE TO DEAL. WITH MANY. PROBLEMS AND LOOK A HEAD. WE ALL GO THROUGH SOME ROUGH TIMES. BUT LEARN. TO. GET AROUND THINGS....YOU CAN. TOO.   I HOPE THAT WE CAN GET BACK TOGETHER. SOON. GOOD THINGS CAN TAKE A LITTLE. TIME SO. WE HAE GOT TO TRY TO MAKE THINGS BETTER. IF ONLY A LITTLE. AT A TIME. WE. ARE GONG TO MAKE IT. IF THINGS IN THE PAST ARE BOTHERING YOU. TRY TO GET THEM OUT OF YOUR MIND. AND I. WILL ALWAYS. LOVE YOU AND BE ON YOUR SIDE. LOOK WHAT WE HAVE BEEN THROUGH. AND GOOD THINGS. WILL. HAPPEN AGAIN. I HOPE THAT YOU WILL CALL ME WHENEVER. YOU CAN. WE ARE GOING TO GET TO. GATHER SOON AND I CANT. WATE. CALL WHEN. YOU CAN. I WILL BE WATING. I LOVE YOU

        GRAMP

        BILL HILL

566

WILLIAM. F. HILL
PO Box 15
HARDWICK VT. 05843
802-472-6308

SALLY HILL. ALSO TAUGHT SUNDAY SCHOOL AT. HOPE COMMUNITY CHURCH
IN. WALDEN EVERY SUNDAY. THE STUDENTS REALLY LIKED I HER AND SEEM TO
GET A LOT OUT OF IT. SHE WAS REALLY. RESPECTED FOR. IT. I HELPED HER. TO
PREPARE HER CLASSES. AT HOME DURING THE WEEK.

IF. EVERY BODY HAD MINDED THER OWN BUSINESS AND NOT BEEN SO
ANXOIS TO CAUSE TROUBLE FOR THESE HONEST PEOPLE AND DESTROYING
THEIR LIVES. WE WOULD ALL BE LIVING IN OUR HOME HAPPY AND PEACEFUL. THE
CHILDREN WOULD BE DOING VERY WELL AND LIVING A VERY PRODUCTIVE LIVES.
WE WOULD PROBABLY BE RAISING OUR CATTLE AND THE GREAT GRAND
CHILDREN WOULD. BE WELL CARED FOR. I REALLY HOPE THAT ALL THE PEOPLE
WHO HAVE CAUSED THIS. VERY SAD PROBLEM. REALLY SOMEDAY REALIZE WHAT
THEY HAVE DONE TO. ALL THESE INNOCENT PEOPLE. SEEMS LIKE THE COURT
WOULD BRING THIS TO A HEAD ALTHOUGH I DON,T KNOW. WHAT GOOD IT WILL DO.
THERE ARE STILL TWO SMALL CHILDREN WHOES LIVES ARE BEING DESTROYED.
HOW CAN YOU JUST SIT I DAILLY BY AND WATCH THIS GO ON
I DON,T KNOW WHAT. TO DO. THIS HAS. GOT TO BE THE MOST CRULE THING
THAT THIS COURT COULD DO FOR NO REASON. I DON,T UNDERSTAND. HOW YOU
PEOPLE CAN BE SO RUTHLESS AND CRULE AND AGANST THESE. INNOCENT
CHILDREN. YOU HAVE ALREADY DESTROYED THE ADULTS. THIS KIND OF THING
MUST MAKE MAKE YOU HAPPY. I DON,T SEE HOW YOU CAN CALL YOUR SELVES
HUMAN. I DON,T SEE HOW. ANYTHING CAN BE ANYMORE. CRULE OR SAD. I GUESS
I AM STILL WASTING MY TIME AND LIFE. WHY CAN,T YOU DO SOMETHING
SINCERLY. BILLHILL

William F. Hill

WILLIAM. F. HIL
PO Box 15
HARDWICK, VT..05843
802-472-8308

DEAR PROMISE

I DON;T HEAR MUCH FROM YOU LATLEY. I HOPE THINGS ARE GOING ALRIGHT. I REALLY MISS. YOU. PLEASE. TRY TO GET HOLD OF ME. AND LET ME KNOW WHAT IS GOING ON. IF YOU CAN. I DON;T BELIEVE THAT THINGS ARE GOING WELL. FOR. YOU. I NEED. TO HEAR. FROM YOU. YOU AND WE HAVE ALWAYS BEEN VERY CLOSE. AS YOU KNOW YOU ARE THE MOST IMPORTANT PERSON IN MY LIFE AND I NEED YOU.

YOU WERE. TAKING YOUR GED TESTS TO IMPROVE YOUR LIFE. THEN. YOU WERE PLANNING TO TAKE A COURSE WHERE YOU COULD GET A DIPLOMA, THIS PLEASED ME I AM VERY PROUD OF YOU. I HOPE THAT YOU CAN STILL DO THESE THINGS. YOU ARE GOING TO BE SOMEBODY. AND I PRAY FOR YOU EVERY DAY. PLEASE TELL ME WHAT I CAN DO TO HELP. YOU HAVE GOT A LOT OF POTENTIAL. AND SHOULD NEVER LOOSE. IT. AS YOU KNOW. I WANT TO HELP YOU. ANY. WAY THAT I CAN, YOU ARE THE MOST IMPORTANT PERSON. IN MY LIFE. IT. WOULD. BE NICE IF WE. COULD GET TOGETHER SOON. SO. BE GOOD AND. DON;T. RUN AWAY. I HOPE.THAT YOU ARE STILL DOING YOUR HOME WORK. THAT IS VERY IMPORTANT WE WILL WORK THIS ALL OUT SOON AND. YOU. ARE GOING TO HAVE A. GOOD LIFE. WHICH. YOU. HAVE. EARNED....A LITTLE TIME AND IT. IS ALWAYS GOING TO WORK. OUT AND. BY NOT GIVING UP WE. WILL MAKE IT.....IF YOU CAN CONTACT ME PLEASE DO. YOU ARE WHAT I LIVE FOR. AND WE ARE GOING TO MAKE IT
I WILL. ALWAYS LOVE. YOU

AS ALWAYS

GRAMP. BILL HILL

William F. Hill
PO Box 15
HARDWICK, VT. 05843
802-472-6308

SUPERIOR COURT
CALEDONIA UNIT
JUDGE ROBERT R. BENT
NEW JUDGE OR WHAT EVER JUDGE IS THERE

HARDWICK. POLICE DEPARTMENT. 24 SEPT.   . 20=21

AS YOU KNOW THAT OVER THE YEARS I HAVE. HAD A LOT OF PROPERTY STOLEN FROM ME AND A LOT OF. VANDERLISIM ALL OF. WHITH YOU HAVE NEVER CARED ABOUT. YOUR ANSWER IS ALWAYS. THE SAME./. THERE. IS NOTHING THAT WE CAN DO ABOUT IT. I CAN;T FIGURE WHY WE EVEN HAVE. A HARDWICK POLICE FORCE AND CONTINUE TO PAY YOU

AS YOU KNOW THEY EVEN HAD MY PICKUP LOADED . WITH MY TOOLS AND STUFF.   THEY TOOK IT AND WRECKED IT THEN TOOK IT. TO GATES JUNK YARD. AND. SOLD IT AND GOT PAID FOR IT. I HAVED TRIED TO DISCUSS THIS. WITH YOU BUT WITH LITTLE RESULTS. WHAT HAVE YOU. DONE TO BRING JUSTICE

A SHORT WHILE AGO MY HOUSE AND BARN WERE ROBED . I LOST MANY TOOLS THEY TOOK MY NEARLY NEW COMPUTER WHITCH HAD A LOT OF IMPORTANT INFORMATION ON IT. I THOUGHT IT WOULD BE VERY EASY TO FIND OUT WHO. HAD IT AND GET IT BACK,   YOU COULDN.T CARE ABOUT. THIS'. LATER ON WHEN. I. WAS TALKING TO ONE OF YOUR OFFICERS. I WAS TOLD THAT MY COMPUTER AND OTHER STUFF WAS UP TO ROCKWELL AUTO GARAGE. IN. NORTH WOLCOT. WHERE. IT HAD BEEN THERE EVERY IT. SINCE THAT IT WAS STOLEN.   I WENT UP THERE . AND GOT MY AIR TANK WHICH I KNEW THAT KELLEY LACOURSE . HAD STOLEN. I DIDN;T. KNOW THAT MY. OTHER. TOOLS WERE UP THERE

I THOUGHT THAT I SAW THAT SMALL CAR THAT HAD. BEEN PARKED AT MY HOUSE. EARLER   I COULD NOT FIGURE WHAT. WAS DOING. THERE. I THOUGHT IT HAD BEEN STOLEN AND WAS THE ONE. THAT THEY HAD WRITTEN THE $1600 CHECK. ON MY ACOUNT FOR.

IT IS OBVIOUS THAT OLSONS GROUP AND THE HARDWICK POLICE PLUS OLSONS LAWYERS AND JUDGE BENT ARE IN THIS TO SEE. HOW SOON THAT THEY CAN DESTROY HARDWICK. AND THE. GOOD INNOCENT PEOPLE   THAT LIVE HERE. WHILE. THIS. WAS. GOING ON AND. MY. DAUGHTERS. HAD TRIED TO TAKE OVER. SOMEONE. HAD. SHOT THROUGH. THROUGH MY. HOUSE AND LEFT A BULLET HOLE THROUGH THE OUT SIDE WALL

DEAR COURT YOU HAVE MOST OF THE INFOWMATION ON THIS CASE IF YOU HAVE TAKEN THE TIME TO. LOOK AT IT'. I HAVE ALWAYS PAID THE TOWN PROPERTY TAXES. EVEN THOUGH   YOU HAVE TRIED TO GIVE OUR PROPERTY TO SPEN OLSON.   I DON;T BELIEVE THAT OLSON HAS PAID ANY. TAXES TO THE

Town of Har

YOU STATE THAT OLSON IMEDIATLY   TOOK POSSESSION OFTHE PROPERTY AS SOON AS THE HILLS
WERE OUT YOU SAID TO PRESERVE THE PROPERTY. WOULD YOU CLAIM THAT OLSON DID ANYTHI
NG THAT HELPED TO PRESERVE
, THE PLACE WHEN ALL HE DID WAS TO COMPLELY DESTROY EVERY THING. . THIS IS WHY SALLY W
ANTED ALL HER POPERTY AUCTIONED OF
OFF BRFORE OLSON GOT HOLD OF IT AND RUINED EVERYTHING.. AS I SAID I WASAN,T IN FAVOR O
F THE AUCTION WHICH RON WRIGHT DID. FOR LEIGH AT THE INSISTANCE OF SPEN OLSON. SHE DI
D TAKE A BIG LOSS AS OLSON WAS THE ONLY ONE. TO BID ON IT AND LEIGH RECIEVED ONLY ABOU
T ONE
THOUSAND DOLLARS FOR HER. EIGHTY. THOUSAND. DOLLAR OROPERTY
GO UP AND VISIT. THE PLACE. YOU DON,T. NEED TO BE A LAWYER TO SEE
WHAT OLSON AND JUDGE BENT HAVE DONE TO   THE PLACE. HILL DID NOT TERMINATE THE LEA
SE ,OLSON DID LIEING ABOUT ME GIVING HIM
THE KEY. AS HE KNOWS HE IS LIEING AS THIS IS NOT WHAT HAPPNED.
      YOU BRING UP ABOUT ME NOT PAYING THE INURANCE AND PROPERTY
TAXES'. AS YOU KNOW I PAID THEM ALL FOR TWO YEARS AFTER OLSON WAS ILLEGUALLY LIVING IN
MY HOUSE. I. DID NOT ABANDON THE PROPERTY AND.
WAS UP THERE NEARLY EVERY DAY UNTIL OLSON AND TWO OTHER MEN, WHO I DIDN;T KNOW T
HROUGH
ME OUT AND TOLD ME NOT TO COME BACK. UNLESS I BROUGHT THE COPS WITH. ME
      THAT PARAGRAPH ON PAGE FIVE OF YOUR COMPLAINT IS ALMOST
LAUGHABLE. AS IT IS COMPELTLY WRITTEN TO GIVE A FALSE INFORMATION
      I AM READING A PARAGRAPH OF YOUR COMLAINT ARE YOU NOW A JUDGE.
IN. DICTATING PARA GRAPH
ON PAGE SEVEN LOOKS LIKE YOU ARE. IMPERSNATING A JUDGE. AS RONALD WAS THE ONE WHO M
ADE THE
STATEMENT ABOUT OLSON AND DRUGS YOU. SHOULD BE ABLE. TO GO AFTER RONALD FOR SAYIN
G IT
IT WAS HIM AND NOT ME WHO SAID IT AND HIS LAWER KEPT BRINGING IT UP SHE NOW THINKS TH
AT SHE \IS THE JUDGE
1 THE LIFE ESTATE HAS NEVER BEEN TERMINATED BY ANY ONE. OLSONS LAWAWYER NOW THINKS
THAT SHE IS THEJUDGE
      PARAGRAPH TWO STATES THAT THE HILLS   ARE   PERMITED TO KEEP
THEIR LIFE ESTATE
#4. IT STATES THAT. THE LIFE. ESTATE ENDS WHEN EVER THE HILLS. DIE OR PERMALEY VACATE THE
P ROPERTS
NONE OFTHESE HAVE EVER HAPPNED.   ONLY THING THAT. HAS HAPPNED. IS THAT OLSON LIED TO
THE JUDGE WHO SHOULD HAVE KNOWN BETTER, I DID NOT GIVE OLSON THE KEYS SO THAT HE C
OULD MOVE IN AND TRASH THE PLACE.
      THERE. IS NO MENTION OF THE. FACT THAT OLSON WAS BUYING THE
 PROPRETY FOR RONALD AND WAS BRINGING RONALD BACK TO TAKE OVER. WHY NOT LOOK AT T
HE TRUE FACTS AND BE TRUFUL RATHER THAN DESTROY AND. RUIN HELPLESS INOCENT LIVES,
      I HAVE ENCLOSED THE STATEMENTS. OF OLSON, KELLEY LACOURSE, AND RONALD., AS. WELL
AS A STATEMENT OF. LEIGH LACOURSE. YOU BETTER READ THESE AND REALIZE WHERE. THEY ARE
COMMING FROM
      YOUR LIFE MIGHT BE MUCH BETTER IF YOU DID STICK TO THE TRUTH

William F. Hill
HARDWICK, VT. 05843
PO. BOX. 15
802-472-5308

I HAVE. SEEN. THE PAST. EIGHT YEARS.
WAISTED AND DESTROYED. SINCE JUDGE BENT
KILLED MY WIFE AND MY BROTHER,   THEN THE SO
CALLED AMERICAN SYSTEM HAS COMPLETELY.
RUINED SEVERAL VERY GOOD LIVES BY PLACING
MY GREAT GRAND CHILDREN   IN ISOLATION AND
AND RUINING THEIR VERY. PRECIOUS LIVES.
THESE ARE VERY INTELLIGENT CHLDREN. WHO
HAVE ALWAYS TRIED TO IMPROVE THEIR LIVES AS
WELL AS THOSE. AROUND THEM   THE SAME AS. I
HAVE. THIS HAS BEEN OUR LIFE.   JUDGE BENT
AND SPEN OLSON HAD NO. REGRETS ABOUT.
DESTROYING   GOOD LIVES

AS A RESULT. ALL OUR LIVES HAE BEEN
DESTROYED. YHE PAST SEVERAL YEARS. OUR
PLAN WAS TO ALL RETIRE AND LOOK OUT FOR
EACH OTHER.   AS YOU CAN SEE. THE
GOVERNMENT HAS GONE ALL OUT TO DESTROY US
ALL.   I. WORKED VERY HARD ALL MY LIFE AND
FELT. THAT I HAD PLENTY OF EXPERRIANCE   TO
HELP THEM BECOME VERY GOOD. CITIZENS, BUT
AS YOU CAN SEE. DCF AND SOME DISCOURANG
POWER OF THESE ORGANIZATIONS   HAVE USED.
THEIR. POWER TO. DESTROY. PLENTY OF LIVES.
THEY. HAVE FORCED ME. TO LIVE A VERY SAD
LONLEY AND . DIC OURAGING   LIFE. IS THIS THEY
THS COUNTRY. WAS. MADE. I WORKED VERY HARD

THS COUNTRY. WAS. MADE. I WORKED VERY HARD
ALL. MY LIFE TO. TRY. TO. IMPROVE LIVES FOR.
EVERYBODY. I GUESS THAT IS NOT THE WAY THAT
THS COUNTRY NOW. OPERATES. I AM. REALLY
DOWN AND FEEL NEEDLESS DESTROYED . FOR...
OVER EIGHTY YEARS OF HARD WORK, I AM NOW.
EIGHTY. SVEN YEARS. OLD. AND PLAN TO LIVE.
LONG ENOUGH TO SAVE MY. GREAT GRAND
CHILDREN AND SEE THEM MAKE. IT. AND HAVE
GOOD PRODUCTIVE LIVES

AFTER. THEY SENT ME DOWN TO. CANTERBERY
INN TO GET RID OF ME. THE HARDWICK. POLICE
ALONG. WITH MY TWO DAUGHTERS. DIANNE AND
JANET WHO HAD THE KEYS TO MY HOUSE GIVEN
TO THEM BY THE WOMAN FROM. DCF. WENT IN AND
RANSACKED. IT ALONG WITH THE HARDWICK
POLICE . LEAVING. ALMOST. NOTHING, YET WHEN I
CALLED THE HARDWICK POLICE DEPARTMENT. AND
TALKED TO. I FELT WAS THE CHIEF. I WAS TOLD
THAT HE WAS TO BUSY TO TALK ABOUT IT BUT
THAT THEY WOULD. HAVE A MEETING TO DISCUSS
IT AND. GET BACK TO ME. I HAVE HEARD NOTHING.
FROM THEM. I DON,T. KNOW WHAT GOOD TO. MY
FAMILY THAT. THIS WILL DO. THE HARDWICK
POLICE WILL FIND ANY WAY TO PREVENT ME
FROM CONTACTING ANY ONE. INCLUDING. MY
FAMILY I NOW HAVE NO CONTACT. WITH ANY
BODY, OR MY HARDWICK PHONE BOOKS. OTHER
THAN THAT I AM ISOLATED FROM THE REST OF
THE WORLD'. AND I DON;T KNOW WHAT TO DO.
THEY. EVEN TOOK. ALL MY MAIL, EVEN. MY. GRAND

KNOW THAT YOU HAVE GOT. TO   UNDERSTAND
     I WORKED HARD ALL MY LIFE. ONLY TAKING
TIME OUT TO TRY TO HELP AND MAKE THE LIVES
OF MY GREAT GRAND CHILDREN BETTER. I HAD
WORKED VERY HARD AND PLANED TO SPEND MY
RETIREMENT LIFE LOOKING OUT. FOR THESE. LESS
THAN FORTUNATE GREAT GRAND CHILDREN.
FOR FIVE YEARS NOW I HAVE BEEN LIVING ALL
ALONE BY MYSELF. OFTEN SPENDING TIME BY
MYSELF. HOPEING TO MAKE OUR DREAM. COME
TRUE.   THIS HAS NEVER HAPPENED   DUE TO THE
RUTHLESS ACTIONS OF THE GOVERNMENT AND
THE DCF WHO ARE THE MOST RUTHLESS. PEOPLE
THAT. I HAVE COME UP AGAINEST   I DON;T KNOW
WHERE THEY GREW UP

  THANK S. BILL HILL

On January 2 Mr. Hill filed pleadings the court took to be a motion for reconsideration. On February 3, 2020 the court gave Mr. Hill an additional opportunity to properly support his response to the summary judgment motion. In its decision on reconsideration, the court advised Mr. Hill to seek counsel because of the complexity of the case.

On March 9, the court received an objection from Mr. Olson's attorney to a pleading which had not been filed with the court. On request, that pleading was provided by Olson's attorney. The document was an email purportedly addressed to the court and copied to Olsen's attorney. It was from Attorney Miles Hoisington who practices in North Conway, NH.

In the document, Attorney Hoisington acknowledged that he was not licensed to practice in Vermont but was trying to help Mr. Hill out and was requesting, with appropriate pro hac vice assistance, a status conference. He asserted he was representing Mr. Hill in a suit in New York seeking compensation under the terms of the federal settlement and that Mr. Hill was electing to not return to the property, making the need for further litigation on the life estate moot.

The objection to the filing was primarily because it came from an unlicensed attorney who had not entered an appearance in this matter.

Mr. Hill subsequently filed pleadings which included three affidavits and some other documents seemingly in furtherance of his argument against the motion for summary judgment. One of the affidavits is a complete copy of the affidavit of Leigh Kidder, a partial copy of which was filed in his initial response to the summary judgment motion. The other two affidavits are copies of those filed by Mr. Olsen's attorney in connection with the motion for summary judgment. No cogent argument was made by Mr. Hill regarding how these various filings helped his case was made. Mr. Hill has since filed several other letters with the court. One such letter acknowledged that he hired New Hampshire counsel, Attorney Hoisington, to help him as suggested by the court, and inquiring whether the court had heard from that attorney. By that letter it does appear there is an attorney client relationship between Hill and Hoisington.

Of all the filings, the complete affidavit of Leigh Kidder may be of consequence to the court's consideration of the motion for summary judgment.

Before considering whether Leigh Kidder's affidavit serves to create factual issues which could preclude the grant of summary judgment, the court notes that the affidavit includes the proposition that Mr. Hill has been suffering from some form of dementia. The court cannot discern the truth of this claim, but it raises the question of how well Mr. Hill is comprehending his circumstances and obligations in this case.

Since representing himself Mr. Hill has filed a number of letters with the court which state his view of the case and explain what he sees as his plight. He has also included a number of political letters in praise of President Trump and asserting sympathy for Roger Stone. While the court has no quarrel with Mr. Hill's right to his political beliefs, it questions his thought process in including them with his correspondence with the court. Considering the circumstances, the nature of the filings the court has received including that from Ms. Kidder questioning his mental competence, it is worth taking the time to look further into the issue. V.R.C.P. Rule 17(b) (giving the court the authority to "appoint a guardian ad litem for an infant or incompetent person not otherwise represented in an action or . . . make such other order as it deems proper for the protection of the infant or incompetent person"); Guardianship of H.L., 143

Vt. 62, 65–66 (1983) ("Had the court been in doubt about appellant's condition, it could have required a showing sufficient to enable it to make a judicial determination as to whether appellant was competent to proceed without the appointment of a guardian ad litem").

The court will take Mr. Hoisington up on his suggestion that a status conference be held. The conference will take place as soon as the current emergency orders by the Vermont Supreme Court allow. Mr. Hoisington should make arrangements to have local counsel assist. If he does not participate, the court will still hold a hearing regarding the question of Mr. Hill's ability to act on his own behalf. Obviously if Mr. Hill is actually withdrawing his request for restoration of the property, then the court will not need to act further on the motion.

Set this matter for status. Copy Attorney Hoisington on this entry as well as parties.

Electronically signed on April 16, 2020 at 11:54 AM pursuant to V.R.E.F. 7(d).

Robert R. Bent,
Judge

William F. Hill

SUPERIOR COURT.
CALEDONIA A UNIT
CACV

CIVIL DIVISION
DOCKET NO. 235- 10-18

WILLIAM F. HILL

Plaintiff

OPPISITION TO OLSONS

MOTION

Vs

SEVEN OLSON

Defendants

In opposition to Seven Olsons attorney to deny William HILLS opposition to statement about Ronald Aldrich and Seven Olson. I only repeated what Ronald had said about his relationship
With Seven Olson. Ronald. repeated this several times not only to me but to his Grandmother and others Can there be anything wrong with quoating what Ronald had said not once but several times After staying with Olson and us for several weeks Ronald did move out without telling anybody There is no accusation about or mention of any drugs mentioned Olsons Lawyer seems to have a thing about drugs I wonder what she knows

Bill Hill and has family have lost every thing Including his wife his brother all his property his business his home and family as well as his life This all happned from trying to help Ronald Aldrich. Make a new life for him self and family. Bill; Hill had no part of getting involved with Seven Olson. But always tried to accommodate him in any way. Certainly Bill Hill has lost everything and Olson has only been enriched buy this mess The government said that the Realestate should be Easley worth $7oo,ooo dollars and I got nothing for all the work and sweat of building the place plus everything else that I lost

I don't feel; the either lawyer Vincent Illuzzi Or Kristna Michelsen did one thing to try to solve this problem. They only looked for more ways to fatten their own pockets. and have not been very trueful

I am asking. the Court to establish a fair settlement between the Hills and Olson as soon as. possible I don't have any more money And cant stand any more pressure. Please arrive at a fair solution as soon as possible. I can.r stand any more and want out

I don,t know if I have done this right but I hope that the Court will understand and close this case as soon. As possible. PLeaSE DON,T FOOL AROUND.

THANK YOU. WILLIAM F HILL

PS Since all this mess Leighr has developed some serious brain problems and is in

The government was upset with the big house the we built after selling our farm. I helped a number of people purchase homes, and property for themselves. The government didn't like this. They told me that "poor people should stay poor".

To get even with me, they accused me of making a false statement on a loan application. I had made no such loan application. I hadn't even been near a bank. Bradford bank, where I had excellent credit, called me and said that they needed to make a loan to another customer who was the president of another bank and was up to his credit limit with them, that he would soon be caught up.

I knew both these men and had plenty of respect for both of them. Bradford bank made all the arrangements and made the loan direct. I did have to sign on the note which the bank brought to me. The note was soon paid off directly to the bank.

As agreed, I had nothing to do with any part of this and received nothing for my help. I later checked with other banks and several attorneys. They all said that this was what is called a "nominee loan," and was perfectly legal.

For this, the government charged me with making a false statement on a loan application which I never made. They called me a felon, which caused me to lose my credibility and my respect. I also lost my real estate licenses and auctioneers license. They threatened to use this against me at sentencing if I refused to lie for them at another's trial. I would not lie for them and they haven't left me alone since.

You need to read my book, "Where is the justice", to really see what they did to us, especially my wife Sally.

In the mid eighties when our son Ronald got into trouble, who we had only tried to help him and keep good home for us and our family. We knew nothing about the illegal things that he was doing until it was too late.

The government took all our property and sold it for only $129 thousand. We had nearly $500 thousand invested. The government was getting the sale money and we were getting nothing.

We had done nothing wrong intentionally or never tried to be dishonest. We certainly would not have been working with Ronald if we had any idea that he was doing anything illegal.

The government claimed that they knew for at least five years about Ronald, yet they kept quiet and let us fall into this trap so that they could reap a big profit from us while we lost nearly everything that we worked for all our lives very hard. They smashed our doors down and about forty of them trashed our home. Where Is The Justice?

It is very sad what has happened to Sally and her family. We always worked very hard and tried to help others get ahead and experience a good life.

Although we worked very hard and devoted our lives to helping others, the government, and the Olson's, have no conscience about destroying our lives. Sally is now gone and this is very sad. I hope that these people will someday realize what they have done and how tragic it was.

Bill Hill

UTILITY FLATBED BODY
FOR PICKUPS & ¾ TON TRUCKS

FLATBED WITH
1 FT. SIDES

FLATBED WITH
STAKE HOLES

All steel construction: Replaces regular half or three-quarter ton pickup body. The deck is 3/16 diamond plate steel and measures 80 inches wide by eight feet long. The underframe is rugged three inch channel and angle iron. Expanded metal mesh covers and protects the rear window. Three inch angle iron frame extends above cab to serve as rolbar and can be used as support when hauling long objects that extend out over cab.

This body will mount right on frame of your half or three quarter ton and will give added strength when bolted, gripped or welded to it. Flatbed bodies come with three stake holes on each side as well as across the back.

This body can also be equipped with a trap door and a recessed trailer ball for hauling gooseneck trailers. Also, an electric hoist can be mounted under body for easy dumping.

MANUFACTURED AND SOLD BY:

William F. Hill
Hardwick, Vermont 05843
802·472·6308

579

WILLIAM F. HILL

Questions for Steven olscer +

Attorney

All Answers must be truthful +

Sworn to

these Ya

Under F Li

REQUEST TO ADMIT

1. WHEN YOU AND KELLEY TOOK OVER THE SWIMMING POOL WAS WORKING AND BEING USED

2. WHAT HAPPNED TO THE SWIMMING POOL HOW DID IT GET ALL SMASHED UP AND DUMPED ON THE BACK LAWN

3. WHAT WERE THE DATES THAT YOU TOOK YOUR LAST VACATION AND YOU TOOK MY GREAT GRAND DAUGHTERS PROMISE AGE TWELVE AND MERSADIES, AGE THIRTEEN WITH YOU. WHERE DID YOU GO AND HOW MANY DAYS

4. WAS YOUR WIFE WITH YOU?

5. WHY DID YOU NOT BRING THEM BACK HOME BUT DROPPED THEM OFF AT DAYS INN IN ACAMPION NEW HAMPSHIRE. OVER ONE HUNDRED MILES AWAY AND WHERE WAS YOUR WIFE SHE WAS NOT WITH YOU. BILL HILL HAD TO PICK THEM UP

,6 AFTER DROPPING THEM OFF MERSADIES CRIED AND SAID THAT SHE NEVER WANTED TO GO WITH YOU AGAIN AND NEVER WANTED TO SEE YOU AGAIN SHE HAD A VERY HARD TIME AND CRIED; PROMISE ALSO WAS VERY UP SET OVER WHAT HAPPNED PLEASE TELL US WHAT HAPPNED TO THESE SMALL GIRLS TO UPSET THE THEM THIS WAY

7. SEVERAL TIMES WE SOLD YOU A BEEF ALL CUT AND WRAPPED. TO TAKE BACK HOME WITH YOU. YOU SAID THAT YOU WANTED TO RETAIL OUR BEEF. EACH TIME IT WAS VERY HARD FOR YOU TO PAY US. I HAD TO FOLLOW YOU ALL THE WAY TO WOODSTOCK TO GET PAID

8. IF YOU HAD A HARD TIME TO PAY FOR TWO BEEF HOW DID YOU COME UP WITH ONE HUNDRED AND TWENTY THOUSAND TO PAY THE GOVERNMENT

9. YOU SAID SEVERAL TIMES THAT YOU WERE BUYING THE PROPERTY BACK FOR RONALD ALDRICH AND WAS GOING TO CONVEY IT BACK TO RONLD BY GIVING HIM A THIRTY YEAR PAID UP LEASE. HOW DID THIS WORK

10. DID ANY OF THE MONEY COME FROM PAUL LUSSIERS HOUSE

11. YOU TOLD JUDGE BENT THAT I

YOU OBTAIN THIS KNOWLEDGE

17. AFTER TAKING THE KEYS TO
OUR HOUSE AND MOVING IN YOU KNEW THAT SALLY WAS FAILING
FAST,.,WHAT DID YOU DO IF ANY THING TO TRY TO
COMFORT OR HELP HER ALL SALLY HAS
DONE FOR YOU AND YOUR FAMILY? YOU HAD LIVED IN OUR
HOMES AND MADE YOUR SELF
WELCOME TO EVERYTHING . WE DID NOT HEAR A THING FROM
ANY OF YOU ; NO CALL NO CARD NO ANYTHING OR OFFER ANY
HELP AND   YOU DIDN;T EVEN
ATTEND HER MEMORIAL SERVICE PLEASE EXPLAIN THIS.

18, WHEN I STOPPED UP TO SEE
YOU, YOU WERE LIVING IN MY HOUSE YOU AND TWO OTHER
FELLOWS THROUGH ME OUT AND TOLD ME NEVER
TO   COME BACK AGAIN UNLES I BROUGHT
THE POLICE WITH ME. WHO WERE THESE OTHER TWO MEN, AND
WHAT DID THEY HAVE TO DO
WITH   THE PLACE

19 DID KELLEY LACOURSE LIVE
WITH YOU IN THE BIG HOUSE AFTER YOU TOOK OVER. HOW DID
YOU PAY HER? WHAT TYPE OF THINGS DID YOU
SUPPLY HER WITH?

20   WHERE DID KELLEY SLEEP?
21   WHAT DID KELLEY DO FOR
WORK FOR YOU?

22 WAS KELLEY RENTING OUT
ROOMS IN THE BIG HOUSE?

23 HOW DID YOU   CONVINCE
LEIGH TO PUT HER MOBILE HOME UP FOR SALE BY RON RIGHTS
AUCTION-SERVICE26, WERE YOU THE
ONLEY PERSON BIDDING ON IT ? IS THAT WHY SHE
ONLY GOT A LITTLE OVER ONE THOUSAND DOLLARS FOR IT?
YOU HAD LEIGH AND HER

FAMILY LEAVE SO THAT YOU COULD RENT THE MOBIL HOME TO OTHERS FOR BIG MONEY IS THIS RIGHT?

24 YOU RENTED LEIGH OUR BIG HOME WHICH WAS NOT YOURS AND HIRED HER TO TEAR OUT SOME WALLS THEN REFUSED TO PAY HER

25i I HAVE NEVER ACCUSED YOU OFF BEING IN THE DRUG BUSINESS BUT HAVE HEARD MANY STORIES. YOUR LAWYER SEEMS TO KNOW QUITE A BIT LIKE WHAT?

26 ALL THE GREEN HOUSES WHICH WE TOOK GOOD CARE OF AND USED THEM IN OUR BUSINESS ARE ALL NOW WRECKED AND DESTROYED.
THIS IS A TERRIBLE SHAME

27 WHEN THE TOWN SENT US A REBATE FOR OUR PROPERTY TAXES YOU GRABBED THE CHECK AND REFUSED TO GIVE IT BACK, EVEN THOUGH THE
TAX DEPARTMENT SAID TO GIVE IT TO US, ITS RIGHTFUL OWNERS BUT YOU REFUSED

28 WHEN YOU FOCED LEIGH AND HER FAMILY OUT THEY HAD TO HAVE A PLACE TO LIVE. DO YOU KNOW HOW THIS HAS DESTROYED THERE
LIVES AND HOW EXPENSIVE THIS HAS BEEN, DO YOU EVEN CARE.?

29 AFTER YOU TROUGH LEIGH OUT OF HER MOBILE HOME DID YOU EVER GET A TITLE TO IT AND DO YOU HAVE IT NOW?

30. WHAT HAS HAPPNED TO THE MOBILE HOME?. I UNDERSTAND THAT IT IS NO LONGER ON THE PROPERTY

State of Vermont
APS Investigative Summary

Investigation Number 10848

    h. AV's Written Statement
    i. Copy of Two Checks Written on Peoples United Bank Account # 0024522156, belonging to AV.
    j. Check # 2681 dated 05/13/2021, written out to AP for $1600.00. Memo states "Honda Civic Hybrid 07."
    k. Check # 2682, dated 05/17/2021, written out to AP for $1700.00. Memo states, "Property Maintenance."
2) Caledonia Unit Case Summary for Docket No. 21-CR-04949.
3) Vermont Judiciary Public Portal record for LaCourse and AP.
4) Vermont Crime Information Center Record Request for LaCourse and AP.
5) Copy of surveillance video from North Country Federal Credit Union.
6) Copy of the White River Junction VA Hospital Discharge Summary for AV dated 08/11/2021 to 08/23/2021.

Part 5: Investigation Description

---

1) A records check was completed on both the AV and the AP's. Vermont Judiciary Public Portal showed the arrest of AP, associated with this incident in Caledonia County Superior Court. Nothing relevant to this investigation was found on LaCourse.

2) A check of the Wellsky Reporting system showed no associated investigations and two associated intakes.

3) On June 14, 2021, I met with Officer Scott Gagnon of the Hardwick Police Department. Officer Gagnon provided me with a copy of Detective Corporal Kevin Lehoe's criminal case report on AP. Said report indicated that two checks written on AV's Peoples United Bank, Account # 0024522156 and been fraudulently cashed at the North Country Federal Credit Union in Newport, Vermont. The first check # 2681, dated 05/13/2021, was made out to AP for $1600.00. In the memo for section was written, "Honda Civic Hybrid 07." The second check # 2682, dated 05/17/2021, was made out to AP for $1700.00. In the memo for section was written "Property Maintenance." According to Officer Gagnon, AV had written a sworn statement attesting that he did not write or authorize these checks to be written. AV expressed that the signatures on the checks were not his. Officer Gagnon advised that Detective Lehoe was in the process of applying for an arrest warrant for AP as he has been unable to locate him.

4) On June 15, 2021, I spoke over the phone with AV. During our phone conversation AV provided the following information:

    a) Some personal property had been stolen from his property during the time his granddaughter, LaCourse and another male were staying with AV.
    b) A male had cashed two checks belonging to AV totaling $3200.00.
    c) Said male had been arrested by the Hardwick Police Department.

State of Vermont
APS Investigative Summary

Investigation Number 10848

Part I: Investigation Participants and Investigation Conclusion	
Investigator	Donald A. Demar
Alleged Victim (AV) Hereafter referred to as AV	William Hill
Alleged Perpetrator (AP) Hereafter referred to as AP	Paul Laviolette
Investigation Conclusion	Recommendation of Substantiation

Part 2: Allegations Summary

A) On May 28, 2021, APS received a report with the following allegations:
   a. AP had stolen items and checks from AV
   b. That AP had cashed some of the checks leading to his arrest.

B) The report was assigned to Investigator Donald A. Demar 06/04/2021.

Part 3: Investigative Sources – Interviews

A) AV
B) AP
C) Officer Scott Gagnon, Hardwick Police Department
D) Kelly LaCourse, granddaughter of AV, was mailed a letter to contact this investigator.
E) Detective Kevin Lehoe, Hardwick Police Department.
F) Deputy States Attorney, Maria Byford.

Part 4: Investigative Sources – All Other Evidence

1) Hardwick Police Department Incident Number 21HW000782, Laviolette's Arrest Report. Includes:
   a. Arrest Summary Report
   b. Valcour Record
   c. AP's Criminal History Report
   d. Hardwick Police Department Evidence List
   e. AP's Banking Records from North Country Federal Credit Union between 05/13/2021 to 05/15/2021.
   f. Copies of Inquest Subpoena(s) requesting above bank records and video surveillance.
   g. Affidavit of Detective Corporal Kevin Lehoe

585

William F. Hill

    d) AV told me that AV was safe and in no need for services.

5) On July 8, 2021, I spoke over the phone with AV. At that time, we scheduled to meet at AV's residence on July 9, 2021.

6) On July 9, 2021, I met with AV at his residence located at 756 Dutton Road in the Town of Hardwick. AV provided the following information:

    a) AV has resided at the current address since March of 2017. AV currently resides alone, performs all his IADLS, drives, and does his own shopping.

    b) On March 6, 2021, AV's granddaughter, Kelly LaCourse had asked AV if she could stay a few days with AV. LaCourse was accompanied by an unknown young male.

    c) LaCourse acted like she "owned" the residence.

    d) AV did not approve of LaCourse and this male having relations in his home and AV subsequently asked them to leave.

    e) AV believed they were at AV's residence for less than two weeks.

    f) During the time LaCourse and the unknown male stayed with him they stole AV's computer, assorted tools, and checks from AV's check book.

    g) After LaCourse and the unknown male left, AV has not seen the unknown male again, but LaCourse was back at the residence on May 14, 2021, when AV was not home.

    h) LaCourse was told by AV to leave the residence.

    i) On May 18, 2021, AV was contacted by Peoples Bank and advised of the fraudulent activity with his checking account.

    j) AV contacted the Hardwick Police Department and reported the criminal activity.

7) During our conversation, I found AV to be polite and articulate. AV was lucid when answering my questions. AV presented with infirmities of aging in cognitive memory. That is, AV could recall some issues, but could not recall simple things, like the names of his grandchildren.

8) A warrant was issued for AP on June 23, 2021, for the charge of False Pretense.

9) AP was arrested on July 6, 2021, and arraigned on July 7, 2021. AP presented to the court an address of 29 Caswell Ave. Apt. 1, Derby Line, Vermont.

10) On July 9, 2021, I went to 29 Caswell Ave. Apt. 1, Derby Line, Vermont to speak with AP. I was advised by the current tenant in apartment 1 that there was no AP residing there, nor do they know anyone by that name.

11) On July 12, 2021, I emailed Caledonia County Deputy States Attorney, Maria Byford regarding AP's fictitious address. DSA Byford emailed me back advising that AP's next court appearance was scheduled for July 19, 2021, at 0900 hours.

State of Vermont
APS Investigative Summary

Investigation Number 10848

12) On July 12, 2021, I called the LaCourse 802-525-3933 and left a message asking her to call me back. LaCourse never returned my phone call.

13) On July 19, 2021, I called LaCourse again but now the phone had been disconnected.

14) On July 22, 2021, I went to the LaCourse's listed address of 9 Bartlett Road in Greensboro Bend, Vermont, only to learn that there is no such address.

15) On July 22, 2021, I met with Detective Lehoe. During our conversation, Detective Lehoe explained to me the circumstances surrounding his investigation of AP and his request for an arrest warrant. Detective Lehoe relayed that AV had not reported any items stolen and only found out about the missing checks after being notified by Peoples United Bank. Detective Lehoe went on to say that he had obtained a surveillance video of AP cashing the check.

16) On July 22, 2021, I visited AV and dropped off some paperwork.

17) On July 22, 2021, I went to 417 Sunset Acres, Newport, Vermont to speak with AP. Upon my arrival, AP was located outside the residence. During our conversation AP provided the following information:

    a) Knows AV and has had dinner with AV. Did some work for AV.

    b) LaCourse asked AP to cash the checks for her because AP had a banking account and LaCourse did not.

    c) LaCourse told AP the checks were "legit." LaCourse alleged that she had done some work for AV, and "that was money owed to her. "

    d) The checks were made out to AP. When questioned about this AP reported that was because LaCourse had AV write them out to AP. I asked about why the check memo indicated that it was for the purchase of car. AP did not recall that on the checks.

    e) AP maintained that AP did not fill out or sign the checks, "I didn't sign nothing."

    f) AP Only signed the back of the check to cash them.

    g) AP expressed that if AP knew the checks were not legal, why would AP use his account to cash them.

    h) Bank notified AP that the checks were bad.

    i) AP did not receive any compensation for cashing them. "I didn't get anything out of it." AP gave the money to LaCourse.

    j) When LaCourse was staying at AV's residence he would stop by and help.

    k) AP advised that AP was not staying with AV, another male by the name of Ryan Thatcher was.

    l) Last time he had heard from LaCourse was two weeks ago. AP believed LaCourse was staying in the St.Johnsbury area.

    m) LaCourse had told AP that the address in Greensboro was fictitious.

    n) LaCourse's parents live in Glover, Vermont. LaCourses's kids live with them.

Page 4

Confidential Report – Not Subject to Public Disclosure

State of Vermont
APS Investigative Summary   Investigation Number | 10848

- o) AP Cashed two checks each for $1700.00.
- p) I asked AP what LaCourse would say when I spoke with her and AP said, "Don't know what she'll say." "I wouldn't lie to you about it; I have no reason to."
- q) AP talked about the DSA adding two counts of Possession of Stolen Property.
- r) AP stated that he didn't go in the home and "I didn't take them, it was all LaCourse."
- s) AP has not spoken with Hardwick Police Department but is planning to.

18) All attempts to locate LaCourse have been unsuccessful. Therefore, on August 10, 2021, I mailed LaCourse a letter to her parents addresses of 8 Mary White Road in the Town of Chelsea, Vermont. Said letter advised LaCourse of the investigation and offered AP a chance to participate in the investigation.

19) On 08/12/2021, subsequent information was obtained that AV had self-admitted himself to the White River VA Hospital. At that time, AV presented with a UTI, mild cognitive impairment, mild Parkinson's disease, and possible paranoia. A Saint Louis University Mental Status (SLUMS) examination was performed on AV in which he scored 18 out of 30 consistent with mild dementia. (See WRJVA Discharge Summary for more information)

20) On 10/05/2021 I contacted VA Social Worker Susan Rounds. During our conversation, she relayed that AV had left the Canterbury Inn and most likely went home. Ms. Rounds agreed to send me the AV's Discharge Summary from the VA Hospital. See attached.

21) On 10/05/2021 I contacted the Hardwick Police Department and spoke with Officer Scott Gagnon. During our conversation, Officer Gagnon told me that the AV's daughter, Diane Lacasse had reported to the Hardwick Police Department the uttering of multiple checks belonging to the AV. Officer Gagnon advised that on 09/12/2021 three checks had been forged one for $875.00, one for $865.00, and one for $230.00. On 09/16/2021 one check had been cashed for $650.00. One 09/21/2021 another check had been cashed for $475.00. Officer Gagnon subsequently emailed me a copy of the above checks. See attached.

22) On 10/06/2021 I was contacted by Dianne Hill, AV's biological daughter. Ms. Hill relayed that when her father was in the VA Hospital and then the Canterbury Inn in St.Johnsbury, person(s) had entered AV's residence and removed numerous personal checks and proceeded to cash same. It was Ms. Hill's position that Promise LaCourse had stolen the checks. A report had been made to the Hardwick Police Department.

23) During continued conversation, Ms. Hill reported that two weeks earlier, AV had left the Canterbury Inn. According to Ms. Hill, AV had a friend pick him up for lunch and AV never returned. Ms. Hill expressed that AV is not receptive to help. AV has accused her of stealing money from AV as she is the financial guardian. Ms. Hill relayed that she is at the point of "wiping my hands of the situation."

State of Vermont
APS Investigative Summary

Investigation Number | 10848

Part 6: Alleged Victim Determination of Vulnerable Status

Definition of a Vulnerable Adult found at 33 V.S.A. §6902
****

(14) "Vulnerable adult" means any person 18 years of age or older who:

(A) is a resident of a facility required to be licensed under chapter 71 of this title;

(B) is a resident of a psychiatric hospital or a psychiatric unit of a hospital;

(C) has been receiving personal care services for more than one month from a home health agency certified by the Vermont Department of Health or from a person or organization that offers, provides, or arranges for personal care; or

(D) regardless of residence or whether any type of service is received, is impaired due to brain damage, infirmities of aging, mental condition, or physical, psychiatric, or developmental disability:

> (i) that results in some impairment of the individual's ability to provide for his or her own care without assistance, including the provision of food, shelter, clothing, health care, supervision, or management of finances; or

> (ii) because of the disability or infirmity, the individual has an impaired ability to protect himself or herself from abuse, neglect, or exploitation.

1) The preponderance of evidence establishes the AV meets the statutory definition of a vulnerable adult due to the AV having cognitive infirmities of aging that impair the AV's ability to protect the AV from financial exploitation.

Part 7: Investigation Recommendation – Abuse

Definition of Abuse found at 33 V.S.A. §6902
****

(1) "Abuse" means:

(A) Any treatment of a vulnerable adult which places life, health, or welfare in jeopardy or which is likely to result in impairment of health.

(B) Any conduct committed with an intent or reckless disregard that such conduct is likely to cause unnecessary harm, unnecessary pain, or unnecessary suffering to a vulnerable adult.

(C) Unnecessary or unlawful confinement or unnecessary or unlawful restraint of a vulnerable adult.

(D) Any sexual activity with a vulnerable adult by a caregiver who volunteers for or is paid by a caregiving facility or program. This definition shall not apply to a consensual relationship between a vulnerable adult and a spouse, nor to a consensual relationship between a vulnerable adult and a caregiver hired, supervised, and directed by the vulnerable adult.

(E) Intentionally subjecting a vulnerable adult to behavior which should reasonably be expected to result in intimidation, fear, humiliation, degradation, agitation, disorientation, or other forms of serious emotional distress.

(F) Administration, or threatened administration, of a drug, substance, or preparation to a vulnerable adult for a purpose other than legitimate and lawful medical or therapeutic treatment.

1) There was no report of abuse made, nor was any discovered during this investigation.

2) I do not recommend substantiation for abuse.

State of Vermont
APS Investigative Summary   Investigation Number | 10848

Part 8: Investigation Recommendation – Neglect

Definition of Neglect and Caregiver found at 33 V.S.A. §6902
****

(7)(A) "Neglect" means purposeful or reckless failure or omission by a caregiver to:

    (i) provide care or arrange for goods or services necessary to maintain the health or safety of a vulnerable adult, including food, clothing, medicine, shelter, supervision, and medical services, unless the caregiver is acting pursuant to the wishes of the vulnerable adult or his or her representative, or an advance directive, as defined in 18 V.S.A. § 9701;

    (ii) make a reasonable effort, in accordance with the authority granted the caregiver, to protect a vulnerable adult from abuse, neglect, or exploitation by others;

    (iii) carry out a plan of care for a vulnerable adult when such failure results in or could reasonably be expected to result in physical or psychological harm or a substantial risk of death to the vulnerable adult, unless the caregiver is acting pursuant to the wishes of the vulnerable adult or his or her representative, or advance directive, as defined in 18 V.S.A. § 9701; or

    (iv) report significant changes in the health status of a vulnerable adult to a physician, nurse, or immediate supervisor, when the caregiver is employed by an organization that offers, provides or arranges for personal care.
****

(2) "Caregiver" means a person, agency, facility, or other organization with responsibility for providing subsistence or medical or other care to an adult who is an elder or has a disability, who has assumed the responsibility voluntarily, by contract, or by an order of the Court; or a person providing care, including medical care, custodial care, personal care, mental health services, rehabilitative services, or any other kind of care provided which is required because of another's age or disability.

1) There was no report of neglect made, nor was any discovered during this investigation.

2) I do not recommend substantiation for neglect.

Part 9: Investigation Recommendation – Exploitation

Definition of Exploitation found at 33 V.S.A. §6902
****

(6) "Exploitation" means:

(A) willfully using, withholding, transferring, or disposing of funds or property of a vulnerable adult without or in excess of legal authority for the wrongful profit or advantage of another;

(B) acquiring possession or control of or an interest in funds or property of a vulnerable adult through the use of undue influence, harassment, duress, or fraud;

(C) the act of forcing or compelling a vulnerable adult against his or her will to perform services for the profit or advantage of another;

(D) any sexual activity with a vulnerable adult when the vulnerable adult does not consent or when the actor knows or should know that the vulnerable adult is incapable of resisting or

Where Is The Justice?

declining consent to the sexual activity due to age or disability or due to fear of retribution or hardship, whether or not the actor has actual knowledge of vulnerable status.

1) The preponderance of evidence supports the AP (A) willfully used, withheld, transferred, or disposed of funds or property of a vulnerable adult without or in excess of legal authority for the wrongful profit or advantage of another; by:

   a) Cashing AV's personal checks without his knowledge or permission.

2) I recommend substantiation for exploitation.

Part 10: Investigator and Reviewer Signatures

I certify that I conducted this APS investigation and am the sole author of this document.

Donald A. Demar		November 8, 2021
Printed Name of Investigator	Signature of Investigator	Date

591

William F. Hill

A Farmer's Creed

I believe a man's greatest possession is his dignity and that no calling bestows this more abundantly than farming.

I believe hard work and honest sweat are the building blocks of a person's character.

I believe that farming, despite its hardships and disappointments, is the most honest and honorable way a man can spend his days on this earth.

I believe farming nurtures the close family ties that make life rich in ways money can't buy.

I believe my children are learning values that will last a lifetime and can be learned in no other way.

I believe farming provides education for life and that no other occupation teaches so much about birth, growth and maturity in such a variety of ways.

I believe many of the best things in life are indeed free: the splendor of a sunrise, the rapture of wide open spaces, the exhilarating sight of your land greening each spring.

I believe true happiness comes from watching your crops ripen in the field, your children grow tall in the sun, your whole family feel the pride that springs from their shared experience.

I believe that by my toil I am giving more to the world than I am taking from it, an honor that does not come to all men.

I believe my life will be measured ultimately by what I have done for my fellowman, and by this standard I fear no judgment.

I believe when a man grows old and sums up his days, he should be able to stand tall and feel pride in the life he's lived.

I believe in farming because it makes all this possible.

PROMISE KEMPTON

Promise, life with you was never boring.You kept us all on our toes
with your playfulness and sense of humor.
Always so friendly to others, helping others without being asked.
Each day you became more excited about learning,
and learned a lot about solving problems with friends.
Everyone enjoyed your energy and enthusiasm!
Keep reading and writing, and making others smile.

Circle of Courage™

2014 SUMMER SESSION

Back Pack Program

Laraway School

Certificate

of

Recognition

This certificate is awarded to

PROMISE

In recognition for

HARD WORK ALL SUMMER AND AWESOME SENSE OF HUMOR! ☺ GREAT JOB! ☺

Signature _____ Date 8/5/14

Signature _____ Date 8/5/14

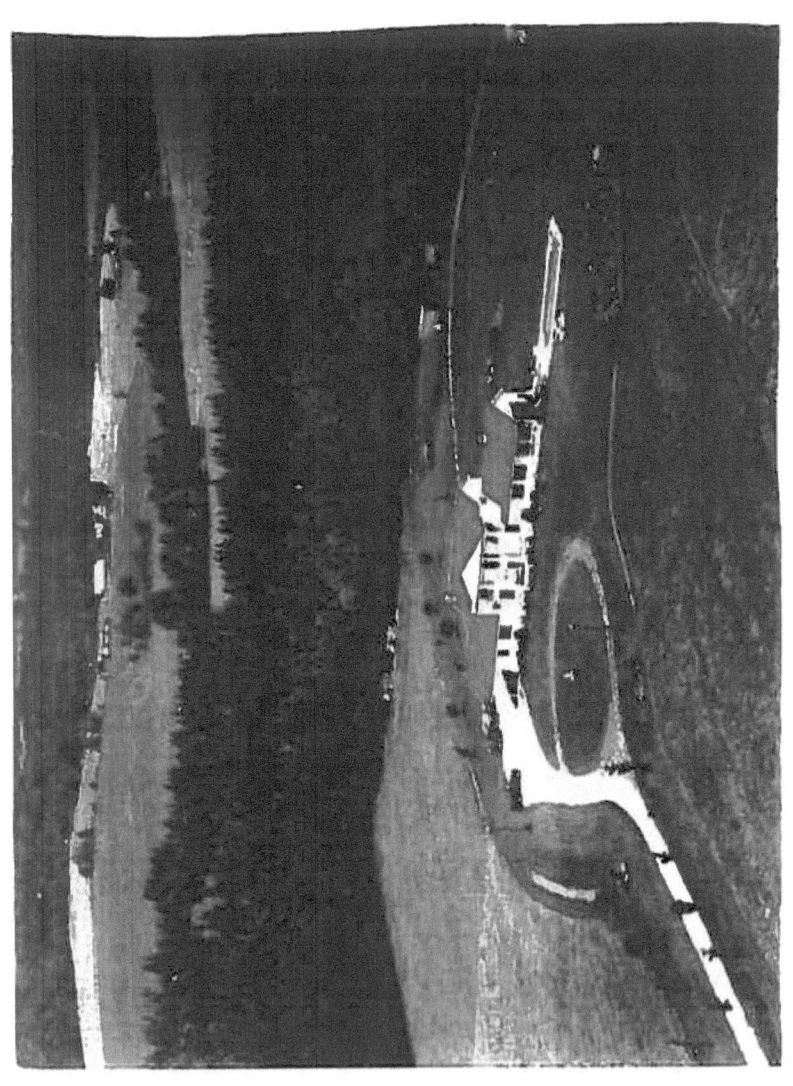

Bill Hill

by Tena Starr

Bill Hill is convinced that the secret to the quality of his beef is his unique feeding program. The beef is lean, it's very tender, and it's flavorful.

"We've had really good success," he said. "Everybody raves about it, and that makes us feel pretty good."

Unique Feeding Program

Stacks of vegetable boxes wait to be packed with tons of winter squash.

Leads to Tenderlean Meat

Bill and his wife, Sally, raise beef and winter squash - about 50 tons of it - in Hardwick, VT. The 80 steers they currently have on the farm are fed no roughage at all - no hay, no grass. They eat white shell corn and a protein supplement, which the Hills get mixed locally. The supplement gives the cattle the nutrients the corn doesn't provide.

The feeding program was developed in the 1960s in New York State, Bill said, and he knows of no one else who's using it. The animals are housed in pens, each with a shelter. They have plenty of room to move around, and both the pens and the cattle are immaculate.

The meat is unusually tender, and the cattle grow rapidly, he said. The Hills call their product "tenderlean" beef.

The Hills went into the beef business eight or nine years ago, although Bill, who is in his 70s, said he's had cows most of his life. As a kid, he brought milk from the farm to the local creamery, and he had chickens. He sold a lot of eggs in those days.

Until a couple of months ago the Hills had 40 whiteface cows, but they sold those. Now they have the 80 steers, and about three a week get butchered. "It's not a real big operation," Bill said. "We're not getting rich, but it gives us something to do."

The meat costs about $3 a pound for hamburger, $5 for steak, he said, but that price is low, and he'll probably increase it soon. He'd also like the operation to get a little bigger. At the moment it's "nip and tuck," he said, meaning that

breeds. "We prefer Jerseys," he said. For one thing, Holstein calves are expensive at the moment; for another, Jerseys seem to provide tastier meat, he said.

The cows are butchered by Moore Beef in St. Johnsbury, VT. The meat is vacuum packed and frozen. There's an inspector on site constantly, so the meat is USDA inspected and approved before it comes back to the Hills' farm.

They sell some to restaurants, but most customers are individuals who buy anything from a whole cow to a pound of hamburger. There are freezers in the front room of the Hills' home, and customers can drop in and buy what they want.

"We have a lot of people who buy a half beef," Bill said. "Some who buy a whole. Some people come in every week."

They're licensed by the Vermont Agriculture Department to sell the meat, Sally said. "We have three licenses."

She fetched some frozen hamburger to demonstrate the packaging. The vacuum pack keeps it from getting freezer burn, she noted.

They advertise their product on the radio, but the best advertisement has been word of mouth, Sally said. People are always showing up saying, "I had some of

Bill and Sally Hill figure they have close to 50 tons of winter squash for sale this year. They grow both Butternut and Buttercup, which store well and can be sold from now until Thanksgiving.

supply is just barely keeping up with demand.

Most of the animals he raises are dairy breeds rather than the traditional meat

your meat," she said. Maybe someone took a roast to a church supper, or a customer tasted it in a restaurant.

17

William F. Hill

WILLIAM F. HILL
P.O. BOX 15
HARDWICK, VT 05843
802-472-6308

JULY 5, 2022

SUPERIOR COURT
CIVIL DIVISION
ATTENTION: JUDGE BENT
ST JOHNSBURY VT

DEAR JUDGE BENT,

I AM WRITING TO HELP YOU TO GET YOUR FACTS STRAIGHT. I
REALLY DON'T HAVE ANY TIME FOR THIS. YOU AWAYS GO WITH
OLSON AND HIS LYING ATTORNEY.   WHERE DID YOU GET THE IDEA
THAT I HAVE HAD A CHANGE OF HEART? I HAVE NOT CHANGED MY
MIND ABOUT ANYTHING. WHY DID YOU HAVE TO GET THIS
WRONG? YOU HAVE USED FALSE INFORMATION TO KICK ME AND
MY FAMILY OUT OF OUR HOME WIHCH WE WORKED VERY HARD TO
HAVE. I HAVE NOT PREMATURELY VACATED OUR HOME. YOU
HAVE DISHONESTLY RUINED THE LIVES OF ME AND MY FAMILY. I
SUPPOSE THAT BY BEING A WELL PAID JUDGE THAT YOU FIGURE
THAT YOU CAN GET AWAY WITH ANYTHING. EVEN WHEN IT IS NOT
THE TRUTH.

I DON'T KNOW WHAT YOU PLAN TO DO ABOUT THIS. BUT IF YOU
DON'T I'M GOING TO.

THANK YOU FOR ANY ASSISTANCE IN THIS MATTER.

William F. Hill

CC COPIES TO OTHERS

William F. Hill
PO BOX 15
HARDWICK, VT

05843
802-472-6308

TO ALL WHO WANT JUSTICE. THIS I HOPE
MEANS YOU

ENCLOSED ARE A BUNCH OF PAPERS TELLING
ABOUT OUR PROBLEMS. WE HAVE GOT TO GET
PROMISE KEMPTON OUT OF THIS MESS IT IS
DESTROYING HER. SHE AND HER OLDER SISTER
MERSADIES ARE PERFECTLY CAPBLE OF MAKING IT
ON THEIR OWN THEY HAVE DONE IT FOR YEARS.
THEY HAVE ALWAYS KEPT THIS PLACE IN VERY
GOOD SHAPE AND IT WILL ALWAYS BE THEIRS.
THEY WILL ALWAYS BE BETTER OFF THAN THEY
HAVE BEEN IN YEARS AND I WILL BE THERE TO
HELP.
THIS PLACE HAS ALL THE EXTRAS, TWO
BEDROOMS WITH GOOD BATHS AND SHOWERS AND
ALL THE APPLIANCES. THERE IS A NICE HOUSE
WITH SEVEN ACRES, OF GOOD LAND TWO
CHICKEN HOUSES, A SHOP PLENTY OF ROOM TO
GROW CROPS. THESE GIRLS KNOW HOW TO DO
ALL THESE THINGS. THEY LEARNED A LOT WHEN
WE ALL LIVED TOGETHER. IT IS THE PERFECT
SETUP FOR THEM. AND THEIR MOTHER IS
ALWAYS TRYING TO GET THEM INTO TERRIBLE
SITUATIONS. ` TRYING TO GET THEM HOOKED UP
WITH SOME OF HER TERRIBLE FRIENDS. SOME

601

GIRL ON TELEVISION IS BEING ARRESTED FOR DOING THIS. WITH YOUNGER GIRLS AND PROBABLY GOING TO JAIL, WE DON'T NEED THIS AND CAN'T STAND IT. THESE GIRLS HAVE BEEN RIGHT AFTER ME TO GET THEM A HOUSE OF THEIR OWN.

THEY CANNOT STAND TO LIVE THIS WAY AND DO ANYTHING THAT LEIGH AND HER MALE FRIENDS FORCE THEM TO DO. RIGHT NOW I UNDERSTAND THAT ALL THE FOUR CHILDREN HAVE BEEN CONFISCATED BY DCF AND ARE VERY UNHAPPY. PROMISE HAD BEEN SAYING THINGS LIKE I HOPE THAT DCF WILL COME AND TAKE US OUT OF HERE. WHY CAN'T I BE A HILL. SHE CAN BE A HILL. I WANT TO ADOPT THEM ALL. I HAVE ALWAYS WANTED TO BE THEIR FATHER, BECAUSE ONLY TO BE DEFEATED BY THERE MOTHER AND DCF. THEY ALREADY HAVE A HOUSE OF THEIR OWN, SALLY AND I HAVE PLANNED FOR YEARS FOR THEM TO HAVE THIS PLACE FOR THEIR OWN. WE HAVE DEEDED IT TO PROMISE, BY PROBATING IT THROUGH A FAMILY MEMBER, ARRON HILL WHO IS THE ADMINISTRATOR OF HER ESTATE SO THAT THE DEED WILL PASS ON TO PROMISE. AS SOON AS SHE IS LEGALLY OLD ENOUGH TO OWN ON IT ON HER OWN. I THINK THAT WE HAVE THIS ALL WORKED OUT LEGALLY.

I HAVE BEEN WORKING FOR THIS MOST OF MY LIFE AND CAN'T. WAITE TO SEE IT HAPPEN ALL WE NEED IS YOUR HELP TO MAKE IT WORK. THERE IS INCLUDED A GOOD CAR. LETS DO IT SOON. TODAY WILL NOT BE TO SOON. WE ARE

READY. IF ANYTHING HAPPENS TO ME THEY WILL
BE ALL SET TO GO ON WITH THERE LIVES.

THERE ARE TWO YOUNGER CHILDREN, NICK
AND AMAYA. I UNDERSTAND THAT THEY HAVE
BEEN DROPED OFF AT THE
GRANDPARENTS IN GLOVER BY DCF. THIS IS
WHERE LEIGH AND KELLEY WERE RAISED. AND
KELLEYS KIDS STILL LIVE.   IS THIS THE PERFECT
PLACE FOR THESE TWO VERY INTELLIGENT KIDS.
THEY BOTH HAVE GOT A LOT OF SPUNK AND DRIVE
TO GET A HEAD AND LOVE TO WORK. AND I CAN'T
WAIT TO HELP THEM AND SPEND TIME WITH THEM.

RIGHT NOW THEY HAVE SEPARATED. PROMISE
AND MERSADIES PUTTING MERSADIES IN A SMALL
APARTMENT   WHICH THEY HAVE MADE ME PAY
FTFTEEN HUDRED. DOLLARS FOR WITH THE BABY
THEY HAVE TAKEN PROMISE DOWN TO LEIGHS
PARENTS IN GLOVER AND SEPERATED. PROMISE
FROM. HER SISTER AND THE BABY I DON,T KNOW
THEY CAN BE SO MEAN AND RUTHLESS. THIS HAS
GOT. TO BE THW WORST TORTURE ALMOST
POSSIBLE   WHAT CAN WE DO. PLEASE HELP

THANK YOU

BIIL HILL

William F. HILL
PO Box 15
HARDWICK,

VT.05843

802-472-6308

VERMONT SUPERIOR COURT
1126 Main Street SUITE ONE
ST. JOHNSBURY, VT 05819

DEAR COURT,

I AM VERY SORRY TO HERE THAT JUDGE MARY
TEACHOUT IS NOT FEELING WELL. I HAVE HAD A
VERY HARD TIME WITH MY LEFT SIDE OF MY JAW.
SINCE THIS MESS WITH OLSONS AND THEIR
ATTORNEY, MY BLOOD PRESSURE HAS GONE RIGHT
THROUGH THE ROOF. I NEVER HAD HIGH BLOOD
PRESSURE BEFORE. ALSO I HAVE BEEN HAVING A
LOT OF PAIN IN MY LEFT EAR AND THAT SIDE OF MY
FACE.
   I SPENT MOST OF THE. NIGHT LAST
WEDNESDAY IN THE. EMERGENCY ROOM AT
COPLEY HOSPIAL I WANTED TO. TRY TO. FEEL A
LITTLE BETTER SO THAT I COULD VISIT WITH
EVERYBODY AT THE HEARING ON 'FRIDAY THE
TWENTY FORTH.   I WAS UP. MOST OF THE NIGHT ON
THURSDAY.
   FRIDAY I DIDN;T FEEL ANY BETTER. COPLEY
SAID THAT I SHOULD GO TO THE VA HOSPITAL IN
New Hampshire. THEY SAID THAT THAT THERE WAS
NOTHING THAT THEY COULD DO FOR ME,M TRY ST

THAT A LOT OF THERE PROBLEMS STEM BACK TO
THE WAY THAT THEY WERE RAISED. THEIR
PARENTS WERE OFTEN VERY CRUEL TO THEM
AND THEY GOT AWAY FROM THERE (PARENTS)
AND RAN AWAY OUT OF STATE RUBBED OFF TO MY
DAUGHTERS. NANCY, THOUGH SHE DIDN'T WANT
ME SHE FOUND ANOTHER MAN AND I THOUGHT
THAT SHE WOULD BE HAPPY. WHEN SHE DECIDED
TO MARRY. HAROLD STEVENS NANCY CALLED ME
AND. ASKED ME TO SET UP MY. AUCTION TENT FOR.
HER WEDDING. I. WAS GLAD TO DO IT AND HOPED
THAT SHE WAS GOING TO BE VERY HAPPY. Uy
GO AS SHE HAD ASKED US. I THINKT THIS.
SURPRISED EVERY BODY BUT THINK THAT THEY
ALL HAD A VERY GOOD TIME, AFTER THIS I
MARRED SALLY AND. HAVE BEEN VERY HAPPY.
UNTIL SHE. WAS KILLED BY. SPEN OLSON JUDJE
BENT PASSED AWAY FIVE YEARS. AGO. SEVEN.
OLSON, HIS

SVEN OLSON AND HIS LAWYER JUDGE BENT;
AND OLSONS. LAWYER HAVE DONE MUCH MORE
THAN ANYBODY TO DESTROY US ALL. AND ARE
STILL TRYING TO DO THE SAME THING
KILLING SALLY WIFE AND MY BROTHER DAN AND
DESTROYING THE LIVES OF MUCH OF MY FAMILY. I
HOPE THAT YOU DON'T. FEEL THAT I AM BITTER. I
HAVE ALWAYS TRIED TO TAKE THIS ALL IN STRIDE, I
THINK THAT IS THE ONLY REASON THAT I AM STILL
HERE.

PS. YOU HAVE GOT TO HELP ME GET MY
FAMILY BACK TO GATHER, NON OF US CAN TAKE
THIS ANY LONGER WE ALL NEED THIS AND CAN;T

William F. Hill

William F. Hill
PO Box. I5
HARDWICK, VT.

05843

802-472-6308

DECEMBER 8, 2021
STATE OF VERMONT, AGENCY OF HUMAN
SERVICES, DEPT OF DISABILITIES, AGING &
INDEPENDENT LIVING, HC 2 SOUTH, 280 STATE
DRIVE, WATERBURY, VT 05671

APS INVESTIGATIVE SUMMARY.
INVESTIGATION NUMBER. 10848

DEAR COMMITTEE,

WE TALK ABOUT MANY OF THE PROBLEMS IN
THIS. WORLD. IT WOULD BE EASY TO NAME AND
POINT SOME OF THEM OUT, ONE OF THE THE
WORST IS. DCF .OR DCYF. WE DIDN;T HAVE ANY
OF THESE A FEW YEARS AGO. NOW THEY HAVE
TAKEN OVER AND DESTROYED MANY LIVES, HOMES
FAMILIES AND DON,T CARE. THIS IS TERRIBLE AND
IS TOLERATED. BY MANY WHO DON;T SEEM TO
UNDERSTAND WHAT DAMAGE IT IS DOING TO THE
WHOLE COUNTRY, AND EVERY BODYS LIVES.
PLUS OUR ANOTHER TERRIBLE THING IS PLANED.
PARENTHOOD,   WHAT ABOUT ALL THE
PROMOTIONS OF. MERIWANNA AND MANY OTHER

DRUGS. THAT ARE. BEING PROMOTED BY OUR.
ELECTED OFFICIALS. FEW. PEOPLE WANT TO
WORK AND THERE IS SO MUCH GREED. I CAN,T
FIGURE ANY BODY BEING AS HORABLE

A FEW YEARS AGO OUR SCHOOLS TAUGHT
SUCH THINGS AS HOMECK, COOKING. WOOD
WORKING ELECTRICAL COURSES. BOOK KEEPING.
AND. MUCH MORE THERE WERE MANY PLANS
SUCH AS 4-H,,FUTURE FARMERS WHERE MAY
STUDENTS LEARNED TO TAKE CARE OF ANIMALS
CROPS. AND LOOK OUT FOR THEM. YOUNG
PEOPLE BELONGED TO CHURCH GROUPS. AND
PLACES OF WORSHIP. PEOPLE GOT TOGETHER
AND KNEW EACH OTHER ALWAYS READY TO STEP
IN AND LEAND A HELPING HAND WHEN NEADED.
HOW MANY DO THAT TODAY.

JUDGE BENT. WHO TURNED OUT TO BE VERY
DISHONEST AND CROOKED IS THE ONE WHO
STOLD OUR HOME FROM ME AND AWARDED TO.
OLSON. I DON;T KNOW WHAT HE GOT OUT OF IT
BUT MUST OF GOT SOMETHING

I AM PLEASED THAT YOU ARE LOOKING INTO THIS
LONG GOING SERIOUS PROBLEM. I HAVE
ENCLOSED SEVERAL PAPERS THAT WILL SHOW
SOME OF THE PROBLEMS THAT I HAVE HAD. THEY
ARE A MESS. I THINK THAT I HAVE AWAYS TRIED TO
DO THE RIGHT THINGS AND WANTED TO SEE
EVERYBODY HAVE A GOOD HAPPY AND
PRODUCTIVE LIFE. ESPECIALLY MY. FAMILY.
KELLEY AND LEIGH HAVE ALWAYS FOUND WAYS TO
FOULE UP THEIR OWN LIVES, A LOT OF IT I BELIEVE.

ABUSING SALLY UNTIL THEY KILLED HER. THEY
HAVE SUCCEED   IN DESTROYING OUR FAMILY
GREAT GRAND CHILDREN   OUR BUSINESS.AND
EVERY THING ELSE, WE DIDN;T. KNOW THE
OLSONS BUT. WE WERE VERY GOOD TO THEM THE
SAME AS WE WERE TO ANY FAMILY MEMBER'. I
DIDN;T. REALZE HOW MUCH THAT. THEY HAD
TAKEN OVER AND HOW CRULE THAT THEY WERE
TO SALLY. WHO WAS TRYING TO HELP. THEM ALL
THE TIME. OR. WHAT HE WAS DOING TO OUR
BUSINESS.   SINCE THEN THE COURT. HAS
ORDERED ALL OF US OUT OF. OUT HOME WHICH WE
BUILT AND PAID FOR THEN GAVE IT TO OLSON WHO
REALLY DIDN,T BELONG HERE. SINCE THEN
OLSONS HAVE COMPLEATLY. RUINED AND
DESTROYED EVERY THING. WE HAVE PAID DEARLY
FOR THIS.   OLSON STOLD MY GRAND DAUGHTER.
MOBILE. HOME WHICH WE HAD PURCHASED FOR
HER.   YOU HAVE SEEN ALL THE PAPERS THAT ARE
IN THE COURT. NOW YOU ARE GOING TO HAVE A
TRILE AND LET THEM. DO SOME MORE DAMAGE
  I KNOW THAT IT WONT MATTER. I WOULED.
LIKE TO MAKE A MOTION TO THE COURT TO STOP
THIS TRILE AND. PLEASE. LEAVE US ALONE,
HAVEN'T THEY DONE ENOUGH DAMMAGE WITH
OUT EVEN BELONGING HERE SORRY FOR ALL THIS
AND I HOPE THAT YOU FEEL BETTER'

SINCERLY
William F. Hill

AND FAMILY, WHATS. LEFT OF IT

THERE (PARENTS)   AND RAN AWAY WHEN THEY
WERE VERY YOUNG.   I BELIEF THAT KELLEYS.
KIDS ARE STILL THERE I FEEL THAT I HAVE ALWAYS
TRIED TO DO THINGS TO IMPROVE THEIR LIVES.   IT
HAS NOT BEEN EASY.   I STILL WOULD LIKE TO SEE
THEM STRAIGHTEN OUT.   PROBABLY IF   IT IS NOT
TO LATE BUT I HAVEN'T GIVEN UP. IF THERE IS ANY
THING THAT WILL HELP I SURE WOULD LIKE TO
HEAR ABOUT IT. DCF AND SOME OF THOSE
ORGANIZATIONS I FEEL HAVE NOT DONE THINGS
THAT HAVE HELPED THE SITUATION.

    DCF. IF THERE IS ANY ADVICE IF IT IS
PROBABLY NOT TO LATE I STILL WANT TO HELP.
ESPECIALLY WITH THOSE GREAT GRANDCHILDREN.
THEY ARE ABOVE AVERAGE INTELLIGENCE AND
ARE VERY ANXIOUS TO IMPROVE THEIR LIVES.
THAT IS WHAT I ALWAYS WANTED FOR THEM. WHAT
BOTHERS ME IS THAT I AM GETTING TO OLD. I
HOPE THAT I AM NOT BOTHERING Y0U. THANKS
FOR ANYTHING THAT YOU CAN DO.   AND LET ME
KNOW WHERE I HAVE GONE WRONG. THANK YOU.

    MY FAMILY DOESN'T COME AROUND ANYMORE
EXCEPT FOR CLAY, MY YOUNGEST SON. HE HAS
BEEN VERY GOOD TO ME.   I CAN'T FIGURE WHAT
HAS HAPPENED WITH THE THREE OLDER ONES. I
ALWAYS FELT THAT I WAS VERY GOOD TO THEM
AND DID A LOT FOR THEM. I DON'T KNOW IF I HAVE
DONE SOMETHING TO OFFEND THEM.   THERE
MOTHER WHO I FELT THAT I WAS VERY GOOD TO
HER, NEVER REALLY LIKED ME. HAS NEVER LIKED
ME AND I BELIEVE THAT HAS RUBBED OFF TO MY
DAUGHTERS. NANCY, THOUGH SHE DIDN'T WANT

ME SHE FOUND ANOTHER MAN AND I THOUGHT
THAT SHE WOULD BE HAPPY. WHEN SHE DECIDED
TO MARRY. HAROLD STEVENS NANCY CALLED ME
AND. ASKED ME TO SET UP MY. AUCTION TENT FOR.
HER WEDDING. I. WAS GLAD TO DO IT AND HOPED
THAT SHE WAS GOING TO BE HAPPY. NANCY.
THEN SENT SALLY AND. ME AN INVITATION TO
THEIR WEDDING. I TOLD SALLY THAT WE SHOULD.
GO AS SHE HAD ASKED US. I THINK THAT THIS.
SURPRISED EVERY BODY BUT THINK THAT THEY
ALL HAD AVERY GOOD TIME
    SVEN OLSON AND HIS LAWYER HAVE DONE
MUCH MORE THAN ANYBODY TO DESTROY US ALL.
KILLING MY WIFE AND MY BROTHER AND
DESTROYING THE LIVES OF MUCH OF MY FAMILY. I
HOPE THAT YOU DON'T. FEEL THAT I AM BITTER. I
HAVE ALWAYS TRIED TO TAKE THIS ALL IN STRIDE, I
THINK THAT IS THE ONLY REASON THAT I AM STILL
HERE.

THANK YOU. SORRY FOR ALL THIS,

BILL HILL

WILLIAM F, HILL

PO BO 15 .   10 10848
HARDWICK, VT. O5843
802-472-6308

.,SUPERIOR C0URT
CALDONIA UNIT

I HAVE SPENT THE. BETTER LAST PART OF. MY LIFE, OVER FIFTEEN YEARS HEAR TRYING TO LOOK. OUT FOR MY FAMILY. THEY HAVE GONE THROUGH THE WORST TIMES THAT YOU CAN. THINK OF. THEIR MOTHER HAS BEEN VERY UNMOTHER. LIKE AND VERY HARD ON THEM, THIS. IS VERY SAD RIGHT NOW I BELIVE. THAT THESE CHILDREN HAVE. BEEN TAKEN. OVER BY DCF,.. PROMISE HAS. MANAGED TO. REACH ME. ONCE BY PHONE, SHE DOES NOT SOUND VERY. HAPPY; SHE DOES NOT DESERVE. THIS,   SHE HAS BEEN THROUGH A LOT I DON;T. UNDERSTAND HOW SHE HAS SURVIVED THIS AND STAYED SANE

THE OLDER SISTER NINETEEN . MERSADIES. KEMPTON NOW. HAS A BABY AND. NEEDS. A GOOD HOME. WE HAVE THAT HERE AND SHE IS. WELCOME. PROMISE HAS. LIVED BY HERSELF. FOR THE PAST EIGHT MONTHS. AND PAID HER OWN RENT. WHEN HER MOTHER. GOT. HER BACK AND. SHE HAS BEEN VERY UNHAPPY EVERY SENCE

MY. FORMER WIFE WHO HAS NOW DECEASED. AND I HAVE ALREADY DEEDED OUR HOME TO PROMISE SHE. IS ONLY SEVENTEEN SO WE HAVE DEEDED THROUGH A FAMILY MEMBER UNTIL. SHE OLD ENOUGH. TO TAKE   POSSESSION . IN HER OWN NAME. THERE ARE TWO FULL SIZE BEDROOMS. WITH. NICE. BATHS AND VERY LIVABLE.   I. WILL PLAN TO LIVE IN. THE LIVING ROOM WHERE. I HAVE BEEN LIVING RIGHT A LONG.   I WOULD LIKE TO LEGALLY ADOPT BOTH THESE GIRLS AND MRSADIES.BABY AND IT WILL ALL BELONG TO THEM, IT WILL MAKE THEM A VERY NICE HOME AND WILL BE THERES. FOR EVER OR. AS LONG. AS THEY WANT. TO KEEP IT. I WANT TO GET THIS DONE AS LONG AS I AM STILL ALIVE. AND THEY ARE. VERV NICE. CHILDREN. AND. DESEVE. THIS AFTER ALL THEY. HAVE BEEN THROUGH.   THIS NOT A NEW IDEA, IT HAS BEEN OUR PLAN FOR SEVERAL. YEARS

SINCERELY. WILIAM F. HILL

PS WE HAVE EVERYTHING THAT THEY WILL NEED AND BY ADOPTING THEM THEY. WILL BE IN LINE FOR MUCH OTHER PROPERTY. BEFORE. ANY BODY. ELSE CAN GRAB IT. I JUST PRAY THAT YOU CAN HELP ME. MAKE THIS. WORK VERY SOON. I. HAVE EVERY CONFIDENCE THEY ARE VERY CAPABLE OF MAKING THIS. WORK, I THINK THAT THIS CAN BE MADE TO WORK. LAMOILE. SCHOOL HAS A VARIETY PROGRAMS. JUST FOR KIDS. LIKE PROMISE AND MERSADIES. THE SCHOOL BUS GOES RIGHT BY OUR HOUSE EVERY MORNING AND RETURNS IN THE AFTERNON PLEASE MAKE THIS WORK. AS SOON AS POSSIBLE. ALL. I CAN SAY IS PLEASE AND THANK YOU

I AM STILL. EXCITED ABOUT. WHAT YOU ARE DOING ABOUT KELLEY. LACOURSE, BUT I FEEL. THAT THIS MUCH MORE IMPORTANT. THANK YOU. WFH

ABOUT THE AUTHOR

Bill Hill was born on April 15, 1935, on North Main Street in Hardwick, Vermont. His father was a large potato farmer in this area. Bill grew up helping in the potato fields. He attended Hardwick Grade School and Academy, where he graduated in 1953. All the time that he attended school, he raised his own chickens and cattle, shipping milk to the Hood Creamery in Hardwick from his own cows at the age of thirteen. He has always felt that he needed to produce food for people to eat. Bill then attended the University of Vermont, where he graduated with a degree in agriculture. He also took a one-year graduate course at Saint Johnsbury Trade School, where he majored in auto mechanics. While attending the University of Vermont, Bill was selected to attend a two-week camp in Northern Michigan, owned and operated by William Danforth, the founder and owner of Ralston Purina Company. Mr. Danforth was a very interesting man, and spending two weeks with him was very inspirational.

After college, Bill served two years in the army. Following the army, he purchased Hills Feed Store from his father's estate, now Poulin Lumber. Here he not only supplied local farmers with feed, fertilizer equipment, farm building supplies, silos, and bar cleaners, he, along with the Beacon Feed Specialist, set feed programs for many dairymen, helping them to improve their production profitability. In his own dairy herd he achieved the highest production average in in the local DHIA association with over two hundred herds competing. Bill sprayed many fields for weeds sand with fertilizer all over Northern Vermont.

Bill was also active in many other fields mostly to do with agriculture and farming. He graduated from Reisch American School of Auctioneering in Mason City, Iowa, also the Certified Auction Institute at the Indiana Business University in Bloomington, Indiana, as well as Graham Cattle School of Scientific Breeding, Hobart School of Welding in Troy, Ohio, Dale Carnegie Course, and the Dale Carnegie Sales School.

Bill was also a Hardwick Selectman for several years. He was on the local rescue squad. He served on the local zoning board for a while and was a bank director at Sterling Trust in Johnson, Vermont. He was one of two Holstein Sire Selectors from Vermont, which involved locating and purchasing Holstein bulls for the New England Selective Artificial Breeders Association headquartered in Woodbridge, Connecticut. Bill was also a director and past president of the Northeast Kingdom Holstein Club. He belonged to the Vermont Auctioneers Association and the National Auctioneers. Bill conducted a couple thousand of auctions of all types over a fifty-year period. He also brokered a lot of real estate for others.

Bill was also chairman of Hardwick Development, a corporation of twenty-six members selected from the town and village of Hardwick. Some of their accomplishments were building a large poultry eggplant where All Metals Recycling is today and the log yard behind Lamoille Valley Ford. Bill had an airplane, which he landed on the farm and used for his business and gave many rides to his family and local people.

Bill owned several properties and other business in the area, some of which were a welding shop building truck bodies and trailers, which was later taken over by his son, Clay. He owned Authentic Log Homes and Saw Mill; half interest in Morrisville Commission Sales, which was the largest weekly dairy sale in New England; the Bemis Block & Trading Center and the Centennial House & Daniels Block, both of which were headed for demolition, which he restored; and he also owned the Hardwick Post Office. Bill also owned a meat and seafood business in Florida called Hardwick Farms with fourteen trucks and twenty-six salesman on the road. Bill bought and sold a number of properties in Florida where he still owns a post office. He has purchased several homes and farms throughout Northern Vermont, which he sold mostly to local people and was able to help get them financed. Bill and his crew weatherized many homes and businesses with blown-in insulation. He developed the streets and lots and built several homes, taking on two partners in Hideaway Acres in Hardwick, Vermont.

Bill's children worked hard and helped while they were growing up with auctions, the farming, the insulation business, real estate, and everything else.

Bill and his wife, Sally, have nine children between them, twenty-six grandchildren, and twenty-three great-grandchildren. After selling their farm, they built their house in 1990, where they now live. They had much family help, including Bill's brother, Steve; son in-law Bob; and sons Clay, Rodney, and Paul. They all had a hand in it.

Bill also served twenty-five years as a member and past President of Hardwick Kiwanis Club and is a fifty-year member of the Free and Accepted Masons Caspian Lake Lodge No. 87.

Bill wrote a book called Where Is the Justice, which was a very good seller, telling about his and others' troubles with the federal and state government along with some local bankers.

When Bill sold his farm in 1990, which he had run for many years; he was milking over 250 cows in a double seven milking parlor. For several years, along with his wife and family, they made a lot of wreaths and garland, hiring around thirty people during the wreath season.

Bill has dealt with a lot of people and tried to help the many people who have been very helpful to him and his family. Bill likes to see people do well and be the best that they can be.

Bill always worked seventy-five to eighty hours a week but still found time for family and usually attended church on Sunday.

Today, Bill raises vegetables and steer beef, which is in demand from a large area of customers and sold at several farmer's markets and local restaurants. He also has several mules, which he works and drives, and he spends many hours with his friends, family, and grandchildren.

www.ingramcontent.com/pod-product-compliance
Lightning Source LLC
Chambersburg PA
CBHW020426130626
46549CB00001B/9